The Life and Times of
Lynette Alice Fromme

Squeaky

Jess Bravin

FRONT ENDPAPER: Her fellow performers recognized Lynette's talent. Here, on a visit to a military
base, the Lariats hoist Lynette (*right*) and her friend Nora Lynn Stevens above the crowd.
(Credit: Courtesy J. Tillman Hall)

BACK ENDPAPER: Secret Service agents and Sacramento city police officers arrest Lynette "Squeaky"
Fromme in Capitol Park, September 5, 1975, moments after she tried to shoot President Gerald Ford as
he walked through the park to the state capitol building. (Credit: Dick Schmidt, *Sacramento Bee*)

Design by Brian Mulligan

Library of Congress Cataloging-in-Publication Data

Bravin, Jess.
    Squeaky : the life and times of Lynette Alice Fromme / Jess Bravin.
        p.   cm.
    Includes bibliographical references.
    ISBN 0-312-15663-4
    1. Fromme, Lynette Alice, 1948–   . 2. Ford, Gerald R., 1913–
—Assassination attempt, 1975 (September 5) 3. Assassins—United
States—Biography. 4. Manson, Charles, 1934–   —Friends and
associates—Biography. 5. Fromme, Lynnette Alice, 1948–   —Trials,
litigation, etc. I. Title.
E866.3.B73   1997
973.925'092—dc21   96-54514
                                                           CIP

First Buzz Book Edition: June 1997

10   9   8   7   6   5   4   3   2   1

For Ben and Sjon,
my parents

The mind is its own place, and in itself
Can make a Heav'n of Hell, a Hell of Heav'n.

—John Milton, *Paradise Lost*

Author's Note

Events and conversations in this book were reconstructed based on news reports and other published sources, trial transcripts, police, school and other official records, private letters and papers, and interviews conducted by the author.

Contents

Part 3 — Blue

Squeaky

Prologue

Oh, What a Beautiful Day

Gerald Rudolph Ford, Jr., the thirty-eighth President of the United States, had no intention of visiting Mr. Morgan's sixth-grade class at Riverside Elementary School. That, however, did not dampen the children's excitement about the once-in-a-decade event, a presidential visit to Sacramento.

He had been in office barely a year, yet President Ford had captured the children's imagination. They vested the president with powers approaching omnipotence, yet saw him not only as the leader of the world but a potential friend as well.

"He looks kind of nice and all smiley and smart," eleven-and-a-half-year-old Caroline Bernard told the *Sacramento Union.*

"I wish he would come to my house," said Jodi Green, age twelve, but she knew he probably wouldn't. And Anna Liza Ivazian, though only ten years old, might well have been speaking for many Americans in September of 1975. She didn't quite know much about President Ford, except that, all things considered, "He's sure better than Nixon."

But why was the president coming to Sacramento in the first place? None of the sixth graders was quite sure, though Samra Mitchell had a theory: "To get drunk and get his mind off all the problems?"

Similar questions were being pondered throughout the state capital of California, which, despite a permanent population of bureaucrats and a transient class of politicians, rarely lured national figures away from the far larger media markets of San Francisco and Los Angeles. California in 1975 was America's most populous state, the birthplace of its recently resigned president, Richard M. Nixon, and the home of increasingly visible, if hardly consistent, governors: incumbent Jerry Brown and his immediate predecessor, Ronald Reagan. Still, as one journalist who had covered both the White House and the Statehouse put it, Sacramento was "less a little Washington than a big Carson City." It might share a sweltering summer climate with the federal capital, but Sacramento still was a place better known for a brand of tomato juice than for its presence on the national stage.

Surrounded by a tidy little park and several blocks of government buildings, the state Capitol loomed over a seedy, low-rise downtown of failing retail stores, over a residential district of peeling Victorians and cheap stucco apartment houses. Once the rollicking center of Gold Rush California, historic Sacramento had fallen into decay. It was as if the city had taken to heart the nickname bestowed by sneering San Franciscans—"Excremento"—and, ashamed, given up trying to emulate the cosmopolitan verve of its rival on the Bay.

Instead, Sacramento had sought the comfort offered by the suburban dream of postwar America, expanding outward as century-old agricultural fields gave way to new subdivisions, and new interstates. Its economy underpinned by agriculture, military bases, and a growing collection of processing centers for banks and utilities, Sacramento might as well have been Akron without the snow or Spokane without the rain. By 1975, Sacramento was a place so average that Procter & Gamble went there to test-market new brands of detergent. It was a place where, for all its legislators and lobbyists, presidents just didn't go.

So when the White House announced that Ford would spend, if not quite a day, fifteen hours and fifty-five minutes in Sacramento, the city prepared. The fading, fifty-one-year-old Senator Hotel, where the president would stay, gussied itself up, shampooing its aged red carpet, polishing tarnished brass doorknobs, even importing two cases of Coors; the Colorado beer, then not sold in California, was known to be the president's favorite. Sacramento's newspapers and television stations, which generally offered a mix of crime stories, agricultural reports, and mild features on suburban living, covered preparations for the visit as if it were a summit meeting with Mao and Brezhnev. Each facet of the upcoming event emerged in detail; Sacramentans, it was reported, might be treated to a glimpse not only of the president but of the presidential limousine, a twenty-two-foot-long, specially built armored version of the 1972 Lincoln Continental, carpeted in medium gray nylon, and certified as meeting federal emissions standards.

"Sacramento is honored by President Ford's visit and bids the affable chief executive a cordial welcome," began the *Sacramento Bee*'s lead editorial of September 4, 1975. Commensurately, those who failed to share in the fervor were chastised. The *Sacramento Union*, which had filled most of its Friday paper with features on Ford's impending arrival, published a ten-paragraph story about a television repairman who *hadn't* heard of the presidential visit.

For those who weren't oblivious, the papers published Ford's itinerary in to-the-minute detail. After returning from a 7:25 A.M. speech to the annual Sacramento Host Breakfast, the president was to go back to the Senator Hotel, and, at 9:55 A.M., "walk across the street to the Capitol for a thirty-minute meeting with Brown." He then would confer privately with Republican politicians, deliver an address to the state legislature, and sit for an interview with a television reporter from Los Angeles, before returning to Washington.

The itinerary made clear that the president would use his armored limousine for almost all his travels in Sacramento. The general public would only be able to see Ford in the flesh for the briefest period, during his walk from the Senator Hotel across J Street, through Capitol Park, and into the Statehouse. At a leisurely pace, the walk would take perhaps two minutes.

Despite all the security precautions, there were premonitions that the president's visit might not go as well as planned. Before Ford arrived, Secret Service agents in Sacramento visited a woman who had called with disturbing information about Air Force One.

"I had a vision of the president's aircraft with the word *trouble* written across it," she told the agents. "Then I saw the aircraft crash to the ground!" It was a warning from heaven, she said, a warning of trouble she wanted to see averted.

Don't take this lightly, the woman cautioned. Her visions often came true, such as the one she had on November 22, 1963, about the assassination of President Kennedy.

Lyn dressed as she usually did: simply. She put on a collarless, scoopneck flower-print dress, kind of an old-fashioned look, low-cut, with its hem falling below the knee. But what to do with the gun?

The .45 would not fit in Lyn's purse, overstuffed as it was with her sunglasses, hairbrush, wallet, prayer beads, envelopes, notebooks, and a small crucifix on a silver chain. She had a leather holster for the gun, so she could strap it on. But if she wore it around her waist, Wyatt Earp style, it would show through the dress.

She got an elastic belt, threaded it through the holster's belt loop, and wrapped it around her left calf. She had to wrap it three times, until it was tight enough not to leave too much of the belt dangling. The gun weighed almost three pounds, though, and it swayed when she walked. To stop that, she got another belt and ran it through the holster's bottom loop.

But while the gun didn't bulge, it still peeked out under her dress; long as her hemline was, the gun barrel, at eighteen inches, was longer. Luckily, it wouldn't show under Lyn's robe, which she had intended to wear anyway. She had sewn the red ceremonial gown, to wear when she went about her work cleaning the earth. That's what she was on today, a cleaning mission. A red bandanna around her head would complete the look.

Lyn took out the gun and held it. She admired it, really; it was a clean, even elegant piece of machinery, as impressive this morning as the day it was made more than sixty years ago. Slammed into the grip was the magazine, with five cartridges taken from a small box of ammunition she kept in the bathroom. She held the hammer back with her thumb, a technique that made arming the weapon easier, because it relieved some of the spring tension on the slide. She gripped the slide and pulled it back, with all the force of her slender arm. As she pulled the slide back over the grip, the magazine spring forced the top cartridge into line. Still holding the slide, she let the recoil spring pull it back into position; as it did, the front breechblock face of the bolt stripped the cartridge from between the magazine lips and chambered it.

The weapon was armed. Pull the trigger and a bullet would fly out at 810 feet per second, putting out about 380 foot pounds in force. At point-blank range, it wouldn't just kill someone, but blow him to bits. Turn a head into a smashed pumpkin, burst a belly, or blow off a limb. President Ford wouldn't be president anymore, or even alive.

She looked at the gun, oiled and gleaming, marked with the rearing Colt logo on the barrel.

"Well," Lyn asked herself, "are you going to use it?"

She ejected the bullet she just had chambered, and watched as it fell to the floor.

And then she answered herself. "I don't know. Let's just go and check it out."

But before she left, she went to the bathroom and took a Contac cold capsule.

As Lyn walked over from P Street, smiling as she passed a neighbor, she realized that a last-minute change of plans might deprive her of the chance to see her president.

When she got to Capitol Park, though, it seemed likely that Ford's route would be as planned. There was still maybe an hour before he was to emerge from the Senator Hotel, but police, reporters, and spectators already were taking their positions. Just to be sure, Lyn asked a postman when Ford was to arrive.

"I don't know," the postman said.

So Lyn waited, until she got nervous that Ford might be coming from another direction. She went for a walk down L Street, drawing occasional glances for her bright red attire, until she got too far to tell if Ford was following his original route after all. She spun around and headed back.

Capitol Park, the ten-square-block expanse surrounding the Statehouse, had been designed as a living monument to California's bounty, planted throughout with flora from each of the state's fifty-eight counties. Elms and oaks, palms from Southern California and redwoods from the north towered over the park's well-kept lawns, flower beds, and historical statues. Like the state it symbolized, Capitol Park had a split personality. By day, office workers on breaks would flood the park, unbuttoning their collars in the heat, picking up their sandwich wrappers before heading back to the grind.

At night, the park served as a flophouse of last resort. Young drifters, kids who had lost their roots in the sixties and never found them, often crashed there while heading through Sacramento. They shared the space uneasily with the older, more traditional homeless men—hobos, really—who viewed the park as their turf. It wasn't a place to venture after dark. Muggings and robberies, though not as prevalent as they loomed in the suburban imagination, were common enough to dissuade most folks from taking an evening stroll through the park. Today, though, the police presence seemed ample.

As Lyn walked along L Street, she saw a Sacramento police car pull over on Fourteenth, and two patrolmen emerge. Officers Michael Houghton and Guadalupe Rangel had completed their morning shift, guarding the press room during Ford's appearance at the Earl Warren Community Convention Center. For the rest of the presidential trip, they were to patrol the area between the Senator Hotel and the convention center.

Lyn approached them in her polite and deferential tone.

"Excuse me, officer, but do you know where the President is?"

"He's back in his hotel," said Houghton.

"He's at the hotel, or over at the Capitol with the governor," Rangel added. The officers were used to inquiries from interested Sacramentans.

"Oh, that's right," Lyn said. "He has a meeting."

If Ford had a meeting at the Capitol, and he was going to walk there from his hotel, he assuredly would come along the path. Lyn headed back into the park.

She continued toward the growing crowd of spectators, jostling her way to the front of the line. Most, even the older folks, tried to act as though they didn't find her appearance distracting, and when she bumped into Lee Christy, a bartender at the Elks Lodge, he politely moved aside to let her through. Discreetly, he then checked his pocket to make sure his wallet was still there.

Lyn turned to the person next to her, twenty-four-year-old Stephanie Malaspina.

"Has he come out yet?" Lyn asked, without a trace of excitement. By her tone of voice, she could have been waiting to see the dentist.

"No," said Malaspina and the woman ahead of her, simultaneously. Malaspina thought it odd that the questioner, who seemed to be in her thirties, was so detached about the president's visit. She eyed Lyn carefully, especially when she noticed another hippie type, a shaggy-haired male, standing a few feet away by a garbage can. Troublemakers?

To Lyn, it seemed awfully crowded on the east edge of the path, especially since no one was standing on the opposite side. She crossed over the line and stood by some hedges. The hundreds of spectators, waiting in the midmorning for something to look at, focused on Lyn.

"What a pretty young girl in the gypsy bandanna," thought Nancy Bain, who had worked at the Senator Hotel until her retirement. Mrs. Bain couldn't quite see Lyn's face—it was in silhouette—but could tell she wore a wistful smile.

"Not very good-looking," thought Jim Damir, a government major at Sacramento State University. He nodded to his brother, Steve, who had joined him for an 8:30 A.M. bicycle ride to Capitol Park. The girl standing in the restricted area had an awfully old-looking face for someone in her twenties, Jim thought.

A motorcycle officer had also noticed Lyn's movement across the path and approached her at once.

"Oh, I can't stand here?" the crowd heard her say. Obediently, she crossed back to the east side and took a place in the front row, beneath a tall elm. She turned to a girl in a denim jacket.

"Is he going to speak to the Assembly?" Lyn asked. The girl just shrugged her shoulders: "Don't know."

Janette Vine, who was nineteen years old, overheard. She knew that Ford was to address the legislature, but that the general public was not invited. She said as much to her friend, Sue Folsom. Lyn spun around.

"Have you seen him yet?" she asked.

In fact, Vine had. She and Folsom had gotten to Capitol Park just when the presidential motorcade was returning from the Host Breakfast.

Lyn acknowledged the information and turned away. But she was back when Vine pointed out a guard atop the Capitol's roof. His human form was incongruous amid the white marble statuary that adorned the building's pediment. Folsom waved at him.

"Do you know him?" Lyn's voice interrupted.

"No," Folsom said.

"Did he see you?"

"I don't know."

"Do either of you work in the Capitol building?"

Both were students. "No," they said.

"Do you work somewhere in Capitol area?"

"No." While not particularly friendly, Vine thought, this red-dress girl wa persistent.

But Lyn gave up on the two teenagers. She gazed at the Senator Hotel and clenched her big red purse close to her, under her arm.

"He is not a public servant," she said quietly. The .45, strapped to her leg, had been making its presence felt all morning. "I'm a public servant, and I'm doing what I'm supposed to do," she reassured herself.

Behind her came Karen Skelton, a freshman from C. K. McClatchy High School, dressed in a young teen's uniform: buttoned-up blouse, slacks, and brown loafers. Karen's parents, both newspaper reporters, had told her about the schedule in Capitol Park, and Karen had ditched class to see the president. After hopping off the bus, she had made her way through the crowd, unthinkingly drawn by the red cloak in the front row.

Lyn turned to her. "Oh, what a beautiful day," she said. Karen nodded. "Yes, you're right." It *was* a beautiful day. She looked at Lyn. To Karen, awkward at fourteen, excited to be in the crowd, Lyn seemed so calm, so confident, like it was no big deal, like she saw the president every day. She seemed much taller, older, *wiser* than Karen. Lyn, with her long hair, free of makeup, looked so down-to-earth, like the kind of woman who could bake her own bread or sew her own dresses. Probably not from Sacramento, Karen thought, but one of the smaller towns nearby, California bluegrass country.

"Probably," Karen thought, "Folsom."

Suddenly, a commotion began by the park's entrance. The president, fronted by a phalanx of aides, guards, and photographers, was on his way.

In an instant, he was upon them, his blue coat unbuttoned, lodging himself in their midst. Twenty-three-year-old Richard Cady, a mail-room worker in the state consumer affairs department, reached out for Ford's hand, but managed only to touch a patch of presidential flesh. Professor Oscar Reyes, a tourist from Honduras, got a photo of his wife shaking hands with the president, a souvenir even better than his snapshots of Disneyland and the Black Hills. But Cissy Anderson was surprised by the terse, businesslike demeanor of the man who grabbed her hand and instantly moved ahead; on television, Ford had seemed so much more friendly and jovial.

On and on the president moved, acknowledging face after face he didn't recognize and would never see again. Suddenly, by a tree, something caught Ford's eye: in the sea of wide-collared, fair-haired well-wishers, a tiny elf in a flowing headdress, a bloodred gown amid the waves of earth-toned casualwear, floated toward him.

He knew at once she wanted to reach out to him, to shake hands or even speak with him. Though he already had passed her by and was grasping someone else's hand, he paused and turned back toward her. In an instant she was there, and Ford registered the oddest face he ever had seen, weathered, to his eyes, and aged.

They were a strange pair in the split second they faced each other: Jerry Ford, the football player, whose height and broad shoulders seemed to further diminish the Lilliputian creature so eager to encounter him. Up came her right arm, like so many before it, and, as he stopped 127 feet into Capitol Park, Ford prepared to return the gesture.

At that instant, Ford's face transmogrified from the rosy, athletic glow retained from a Heartland youth to a zombie's pallor, a ghostly white betraying a sensation Americans never see in the face of their presidents: Fear.

As Ford flashed on fear, the sensation passed to Irene Morrison, on Lyn's right; it was Morrison's hand Ford had been shaking, and she had hoped the president was about to say something to her. Instead, as his color drained and his features contorted, Ford sucked up air and reflexively jerked back, yanking the twenty-eight-year-old secretary along with him. His right hand flew up to cover his face, his left hand down over his groin, toward which a red-sleeved arm was angling.

The kaleidoscope of faces and hands surrounding Ford vanished, replaced with one image: that of a weapon so large it dwarfed the hand that wielded it.

Others fixed on the gun. At Lyn's left, Linda Worlow, twenty-seven, had seen the ripple of fabric as the arm twisted within the gown's folds, emerging with the crimson-draped pistol. Worlow saw the grip, she saw the trigger, and she dived forward, hitting the ground flat.

Secret Service Agent Larry Buendorf saw it, too. "Forty-five!" he shouted as he grabbed the weapon with his right hand, cutting the web between his thumb and forefinger. From the pistol's heft and weight, he knew instantly it was the real thing, so real that, as camera shutters snapped all around, it seemed to go *click!* as he struggled to break it from her grip. With a grunt, he forced the weapon down and seized her free arm with his left hand, swung her around and marched her forward, through the crowd, away from the president.

She fought as he twisted her, and she began to scream. All Buendorf could hear as he yanked her arm hard behind her was, "It didn't go off, it didn't go off!" Some would describe her tone as disappointment, others as wonderment, still others as if she were trying to offer a reason for the agents to release her. "Can you believe it? It didn't go off."

Men rushed to assist Buendorf—Agents Gerald Kluber and Tom McCarter, and Jerry Fox, a part-time stonemason who happened to be standing where the struggle began. Fox grabbed her left arm as they pushed her to the ground, flat on her back.

"Who are you?" McCarter kept asking Fox, a bearded twenty-three-year-old, but Buendorf stayed focused on the weapon, wrestling with the woman as she lay on the ground until, it seemed, she just gave up. "Don't batter me, I don't have anything else!" she said, grimacing. Buendorf got the weapon away from her and brought it up alongside his thigh, holding it close to his stomach; she might, Buendorf knew, have accomplices in the crowd who could try to snatch it.

"I'll take the gun!" said a voice, but Buendorf, his adrenaline pumping, wouldn't release it. It was Kluber. When Buendorf didn't respond, Kluber grabbed her right arm.

Buendorf now drew her up, crouching over her, forcing her to kneel beneath him as he anchored her left arm and shoulder between his legs. Again, he was asked for the gun—it was McCarter now, and Buendorf, beginning to come down, looked at him, recognized the face, and handed it over.

"I've got the gun!" McCarter then yelled, his remark aimed at the other agents but heard by everyone. McCarter looked at the pistol: the hammer was down, no round in the firing chamber. The weapon, he knew, was no danger, and he turned his attention to the developing scene.

A Sacramento police officer, Gaylen Peterson, had rushed over, too, knocking down a woman bystander as he ran, reaching Buendorf in time to proffer his handcuffs. He immediately put them to use.

"Easy, boys, take it easy, I'm still," she said as Buendorf slapped on the bracelets, yanked her up, and thrust her to a magnolia tree. Peterson, his baton drawn, called other officers over to form a protective ring around Buendorf and his quarry, as bystanders gaped, reporters scribbled, and television cameramen grinded away. The NBC News correspondent, Tom Brokaw, immediately recognized the suspect. He yelled her a question, just to be sure: "What's your name?"

But though she kept talking all the way through, she wasn't answering questions. Instead, amid other utterings, she chided Buendorf: "You shouldn't be protecting him, he's not a public servant." She repeated the remark to those at large, as if it were an explanation: "He's not a public servant." Her face seemed a bit flushed, but to Kluber, she looked awfully unruffled about the whole affair, far more composed than the officers. Agent Jim Gavin, noticing that Lyn's purse was dangling uncomfortably between her handcuffed wrists, unbuckled the strap and removed it. He held the purse in his right hand, while his left kept hold of Lyn.

Moments later, a Sacramento squad car pulled up on the pathway. Buendorf, his hand bleeding from the fight, ran to the Capitol to catch up with the president. Gavin and McCarter put the prisoner in the car, locked the doors, and drove away.

Others also had seen the pistol and reacted as quickly as Buendorf. While Buendorf was tackling the woman, Secret Service Agent Ron Pontius had yelled, "Gun—forty-five! Move! Run! Straight to the Capitol!"

Agents Skip Williams and Ernie Luzania had grabbed Ford, throwing their arms around him and thrusting him to his knees—sacrificing presidential dignity in order to obscure him as a target. Each taking an arm, they hustled Ford toward the Capitol, behind a flying wedge formed by the detail. "Let's go!" Luzania cried. Reporters later described it as a special code agents used when they had to remove the president from imminent danger.

Presidential aides Eric Rosenberger and Frank Ursomarso, just ahead, began hurling photographers out of Ford's way, so roughly that Ursomarso cut his left hand, he thought, on a sharp camera edge.

"Straight to the holding room! To the Capitol! Right across the grass!" Williams shouted. The agents bolted forward, knocking down photographers and bystanders caught in their path—a coordinated motion that onlookers likened to a professional football play.

"Okay, okay, I'll go wherever you want," muttered the stunned Ford, carried forth on the wings of his sunglassed rescuers. Winded and ashen-faced, he pleaded, "I'm okay, let's slow down."

Decelerating to a brisk jog, the agents moved Ford to the Statehouse, some two hundred yards away, past the now-prone Rosenberger—in the commotion, he had sprained his ankle and fallen in the grass near the side door. They soon were followed by press secretary Ron Nessen, tugging on a fellow aide's shoulders to get him inside quickly. Nessen had been an NBC News reporter in Vietnam, and feared shots might be fired at any moment.

Steve Bell, an ABC News correspondent, shouted: "Mr. President, are you all right?"

"Sure," Ford replied, too faintly for Bell to hear.

The agents brought the president up the stairs, into the relative safety of the California Capitol, past a sign no one had time to read:

> WARNING! THE CALIFORNIA STATE ARCHITECT ADVISES
> THAT THIS BUILDING IS STRUCTURALLY UNSAFE.
> ENTER AT YOUR OWN RISK.

Lyn had talked and talked as first she struggled, and then surrendered to the men who tackled her. Reporters and investigators, gathering the same information for different purposes, stopped every witness they could find to ask what had happened.

In the chaos of the moment, *Sacramento Bee* reporter Nancy Skelton found her daughter, Karen.

"I was standing next to that woman, Mom!" Karen excitedly said.

Instantly, the journalist grabbed her daughter and dragged her across the street to a pay phone.

"This is Nancy Skelton, calling from the scene. The President of the United States was confronted by a red-garbed woman who apparently pointed a gun at him," she began to dictate, careful to use the qualifiers that journalists employ to tell a story without committing to it.

Then she turned to her daughter. "Say *exactly* what it was she said to you," she began, interviewing Karen at the pay phone. After extracting the details, Skelton left to gather the rest of her story, and Karen wandered inside the Capitol to see what else was going on.

She saw her father there, George Skelton of the *Los Angeles Times*' Sacramento bureau, along with the men she thought of as the "boy reporters," the clubby set of male correspondents who had covered the Capitol for years. They were jostling for pay phones, their notebooks flipped open and ties loosened. It was a scene from a Charles MacArthur play.

"What happened?" "Where's the President?" "Who is she?"—the red woman—"*Who is she?*"

"Hey, Dad," Karen said to her father, then standing next to Carl Ingram, UPI's Sacramento bureau chief.

"I'm sort of busy," Skelton rasped, suggesting that Karen stay out of his way.

"I was standing right next to her," Karen said. Instantly, Skelton's expression changed.

"Get over here!" he yelled, then hustled her away from Ingram and other prying ears, wedging her against the wall beside a display case celebrating the produce of California's counties. Skelton quickly got the story from his daughter, and grinned as he contemplated a scoop. He had just one more question.

"You haven't told anyone else yet, have you?"

"No," Karen said. "Except Mom."

Skelton rolled his eyes. There was no one worse his daughter could have told.

Ingram, meanwhile, had his own scoop. He had been standing behind Ford when the Secret Service tackled him. That positioning helped UPI beat its arch-rival, the Associated Press, by a full eight minutes in getting the story out on the wire. The victory over AP would be celebrated by a midnight revel at Frank Fat's, the downtown Sacramento restaurant favored by the Capitol crowd.

Tom Brokaw was not so lucky. At a pay phone in the Senator Hotel, he frantically dialed the NBC News desk in New York and reported, "We've got an assassination attempt. I want to talk to someone." He paused. "So they went to lunch! That's terrific!" he added sarcastically.

While reporters flooded their editors with quickly gathered—and sometimes inaccurate—accounts of the morning's event, Sacramento police, Secret Service agents, and FBI men culled statements from all the witnesses they could find.

Many said they had heard Lyn exclaim, "It didn't go off," or some variation. It was, "Don't worry, it didn't go off," to Roy Miller. Bruce Rogers, a junior college student, heard it as "Shit, it didn't go off."

Irene Morrison, who worked for the Assembly Republican Caucus, thought she heard Lyn say, "This country is going to pot," and "He's not your public servant," over and over.

Cissy Anderson recalled it as "It didn't go off.... This country is a mess! He's not a public servant, a public servant would try to clean up the mess."

And William L. Perkins, the director of the California Tourism Council, remembered it as "Easy fellows, it didn't go off, the damn thing didn't go off.... He's not your president, he's not serving you."

Jim Damir, the Sacramento State student who had found Lyn so unattractive, thought he had heard something slightly different. At 11:25 A.M., less than ninety minutes after the incident, he gave his account to Officer Paul Boettin of the Sacramento Police Department.

Damir hadn't heard a *click.* He had heard her say, "He is not a public servant, anyway." And, Damir recalled, she had added one more thing moments later.

"It's not loaded anyway, it's not loaded anyway," he remembered Lyn saying.

Part One

Red

Chapter 1

Houses

with

Doors

"We all came from houses with doors," Lyn wrote in the early 1970s, when she was trying to make her life seem comprehensible to strangers. "Doors that were to be closed when there were things going on that we weren't supposed to see, and when our pants were down.

"We girls had bras strapped on us and learned to 'grow up.' By painting our lips, and crossing our legs, and mowing down the soft hairs that grow on us that are not 'lady-like,' and finding out that the worst possible thing a girl could do was get pregnant! . . .

"We learned early that devotion and open love was laughably foolish. And little by little, action by action, we learned not to believe . . . in anything. . . . In essence, we learned all the guilt, the heavy guilt, that makes bad out of feeling good."

Lyn made it seem that she and her friends in what became the Manson Family had sprung from a caricature of 1950s America, all sexual repression and social conformity, a scene replicated in suburban households across the country. But there were some details that she left out.

April 8, 1942

It was a brisk spring day in New York City when twenty-one-year-old William Millar Fromme walked into the Armed Forces induction center at 39 Whitehall Street and declared he was ready to serve. Barely four months had passed since the infamous day the Japanese bombed Pearl Harbor, and all across America, young men by the tens of thousands were putting aside career aspirations and romantic pursuits to take part in the war against tyranny.

An induction officer called Fromme's name. More likely than not, the Brooklyn-born Fromme corrected him.

"Frum-me." The interview began.

"Occupation?"

"Student." Six weeks earlier, Fromme had received his bachelor of science degree from New York University's School of Education. The credential qualified him to teach science in junior or senior high school, but Fromme had notions of continuing his education. Besides, to say "unemployed" might be a ticket to the infantry.

"Firearms experience?"

"Never fired."

"Horsemanship?"

"Never mounted." Brooklyn was not known for its equestrian traditions. Not much use for the cavalry in a mechanized war anyway. Fromme had a science background and was interested in aviation. So William Fromme, to his satisfaction, received a plum assignment: the San Antonio Aviation Cadet Center at Randolph Field in Texas.

Randolph Field's facilities included the Army Air Forces Basic Flying School, which trained the men who fought the air war, the legendary aces who flew P-51 Mustangs over Hitler's Fortress Europe. Fromme found himself in the 114th Cadet Squadron, a unit of about 125 men and two dozen officers that posed the first hurdle for those who yearned to be pilots.

Fromme faced six weeks of basic training, then ground school, primary instruction in light and small aircraft, flight school, and, to finish up the course in elementary airmanship, cross-country flight training. After graduation, the cadets were divided into single- or multi-engine aircraft sections, completed their specialized training, and headed off to war.

But not all would earn the glory of being an Army pilot. At each step of the training regimen, the cadet corps was winnowed down, with poorer performers sent to bombardier or navigator schools, retained as ground crews, or, for the truly unlucky, transferred to regular infantry units.

Cadet Fromme neither was graduated nor sent to a less selective assignment. Instead, on October 9, 1942, after six months and two days of service, he received an honorable discharge, typical only for those who were severely injured or disfigured in training. Major Charles H. Ray, who signed Fromme's separation papers, was brief in reporting the details—"Commendations: None. Physical Condition when Discharged: Poor."

Unqualified to fly airplanes, Fromme determined instead to build them. In 1943, during some of the war's darkest days, Fromme sought a place on the home front. He headed to Southern California, where a burgeoning industry was building aircraft round the clock, constantly restocking the arsenal of democracy.

In the 1940s, Douglas, Lockheed, and Northrop loomed as large over Los Angeles as Fox, Warners, and MGM. Together with hundreds of smaller firms and machine shops, the aircraft factories were desperate for labor, especially for skilled young men. Fromme's teaching credential wasn't enough to land him the kind of job he wanted, however, so he enrolled in the University of Southern California to obtain a second bachelor's degree, in engineering.

Like many newcomers to Los Angeles, Fromme first lived in the Hollywood flats, the working-class section of the movie capital where small bungalows and nondescript soundstages stretched for miles, baking in the endless summer sun. Fromme's Marathon Street apartment was just a few blocks east of Paramount Studios' ornate gates and the sanctified grounds of Hollywood Cemetery, landmarks of what passed for Old Los Angeles.

The industry that would come to be called aerospace was centered on the coast, however, in an arc of suburbs stretching from Santa Monica to Long Beach. So, in August 1948, after receiving his USC degree and securing an engineering job, Fromme moved to a house less than two miles from the beach, at 2101 Virginia Avenue in Santa Monica. In those days, even a young engineer could afford to live near the ocean.

He was now married to the former Gertrude Helen Benzinger, two and a half years his junior and the product of rural Minnesota. Plain and small—"mousy," many would say—Helen Fromme was the sixth child of an Otter Tail County farmer, the second-born of a pair of twins. Unlike her own birth in 1922, where the only attendant was her father, Archie, Helen Fromme delivered her child in the modern surroundings of Santa Monica Hospital, under a physician's care. Lynette Alice Fromme was born at 5:37 A.M. on October 22, 1948. According to the attending physician, there were no apparent complications.

A son, William Curtis, followed in January 1950, and by the following year the growing family had settled in Westchester, a new Los Angeles subdivision six miles south of Santa Monica. They would live at 6511 West Eighty-second Street for more than a decade, seeing the birth of a third child, Julie, in September 1956.

Unlike Santa Monica, which was founded in 1875 and had a reputation for corrupt police and seedy bayside enterprises, Westchester was a model postwar development. Carved from a Pacific Ocean bluff that previously housed bean fields and pig farms, Westchester's tract homes ranged from cozy to spacious, offering veterans of all incomes a chance to share the dream of two-car garages and culs-de-sac. With its business district safely out of walking distance, Westchester's wide streets, barbecue-ready backyards, and homogenous population of young families made it, as often was said, a perfect place to raise kids. About the only arguable drawback was its proximity to the rapidly expanding Los Angeles International Airport. Since many Westchester residents worked in the aircraft industry, however, the facility's presence underscored the progress they were helping to build.

In her early years in Westchester, Lynette—Lynny, she was called—became a neighborhood darling. She seemed to reach out to the flowers and the animals around her, even more than other children did. Decades later, one of Lynny's childhood playmates would recall the way Lynny opened her senses to the natural world. Cuddling her friend's pet beagle, Lynny would gaze into the dog's face and swoon. "Oh, those eyes! Look at those eyes!" she would say, captivated, as if trying to touch the animal's soul. The friend, Nora Lynn Stevens, recalled her mother's response: "Well, look at Lynette's eyes." Forty years later, Nora remembered those eyes as "deep," part of a "spiritual self" that set Lynny Fromme apart from other children.

Lynny shared her enthusiasm for animals with her little sister, Julie.

"I love aaa-nee-mules!" Julie would say, and Lynny smiled proudly. Even in a neighborhood bursting with kids, the Fromme children, particularly the little girls, charmed all they met. They exemplified the generation poised to redeem America's abundant promise, children who would grow up free of Depression and war, ready to reach for the stars.

What the neighbors did not know, until years later, was that something had happened in the Fromme household that would alter the children's fates. Something had turned William Fromme, the once-promising aviation cadet, into a bitter, cruel, nearly impossible man who wreaked venom on his young wife and family. Despite the home, car, and job that formed the material foundation of the American dream, the Eighty-second Street house would incubate not merely one who rejected conventional society, but one who would seek to destroy it.

The Lariats

The Baby Boom hit Westchester hard, and the community responded by building new schools and playing fields, by organizing Scout troops, athletic leagues, and after-school activities for all manner of youngsters. The Frommes' neighbors, J. Tillman and Louise Hall, had come from Big Sandy, Tennessee, in the 1930s; among the first to move to the new subdivision, they now were local fixtures. In 1950, they started holding Friday afternoon dance classes at Cowan Avenue and Kentwood Avenue elementary schools, and local parents hustled to get their children in. The Frommes rarely appeared at community gatherings, but their next-door neighbor, Alice Downs, had a daughter in Hall's group. One day, Mrs. Downs brought redheaded Lynny Fromme along with her daughter to dance class. Lynny loved it.

Hall, a professor of physical education at USC, had organized his better dancers into a performing troupe, the Westchester Lariats. Practicing afternoons and weekends, the Lariats began with—and took their name from—square dances Hall had brought from Tennessee. Soon, though, their shows expanded to include all manner of folk dances—traditional numbers from other lands, along with a few American standards, contemporary pieces, and specially choreographed works.

Some residents seemed skeptical of the troupe's value, especially for boys. Hall defended his project in law and order terms. They were "teaching the dances as our contribution to avoiding juvenile delinquency." In building character, he liked to say, "we heartily believe a dance project of this nature is as effective as scouting."

The Lariats, seventy or so strong, ranged from second graders to some of Hall's college students. They constituted a world of their own, apart from family, school, or the kids on the block. On Friday afternoons from five to seven, and for another three or four hours on Saturday mornings, the Lariats practiced at the Westchester Women's Club, at Airport Junior High School, or in other recently erected community buildings, preparing for performances and trying out new steps.

Though she was one of the youngest members, Lynny soon became a favorite both of the Halls and of the older kids. She loved to do the Highland fling, the whirling Italian tarantella, and the *tinikling*, a Filipino dance inspired by a long-legged marsh bird that roamed amid bamboo poles. Lynny, Hall soon realized, was a natural performer. He gave her prominence among the tiny trio of girls—brunette Nora Lynn, blonde Larrine, and redheaded Lynny—who made up the youngest dance team. To many audiences, Lynny personified the Lariats. Hall would feature her on the troupe's promotional posters, posing cheerfully in a kilt or a frilly dress, an infectious smile splashed across her freckled face.

Hall discovered that Lynny sang as brightly as she danced. She didn't just vocalize the show tunes and folk ditties, she performed them as if they were prize roles, blossoming in the spotlight. In her solo, "Doin' What Comes Naturally" from *Annie Get Your Gun*, the spunky California girl adopted a hillbilly accent straight out of *Li'l Abner*. With parents who encouraged her, Hall thought, Lynny could have been a star. But while Lynny's mother occasionally sewed costumes for the dance shows, Hall found the Frommes surprisingly uninterested in their daughter's progress as a performer.

The bigger kids weren't put off by Lynny's talent; they found her a delight to have around, and let her tag along to Tiny Naylor's coffee shop, at Manchester Avenue and Sepulveda Boulevard, after their Saturday evening shows. For obvious reasons, they liked to call her Red.

Lynny, however, was not so popular with the members her own age, particularly other girls, most of whom were relegated to chorus or supporting roles in the troupe. They teased Dr. Hall's favored trio, jealous of their prominence within the group and their popularity with audiences. Nora Lynn Stevens, Lynny's best friend, would fight back with an assertive, and not altogether ladylike, "Forget you!" But Lynny took to heart the relentless teasing, which seized on her shiny red hair, the forest of freckles covering her face, her pale complexion in a community of beachgoers. Unsure what she had done to so displease her peers, Lynny would strive to make them like her—if only she could be extra nice to them, maybe they'd be nice to her back.

But by revealing how vulnerable her feelings were, Lynny just seemed to increase the hostility of her rivals in the competitive world of the dance troupe. And when they weren't picking on her, they ostracized her. So Lynny focused on the few friends she had, on charming the adults and older kids, and, most of all, on her dancing. When she danced, everyone paid attention.

The Fromme house on Eighty-second Street was modest but tidy, furnished in the latest style, Danish Modern. Not unexpectedly, Lynny shared a room with her younger sister, Julie.

Lynny's friends who came over to play were struck, though, by the parents' bedroom, which seemed almost apart from the rest of the house, as if it had been enlarged or added on to the small frame. Not only was the parents' room large, it was dominated by an oversize bed, outfitted with what seemed odd to others in the neighborhood: satin sheets.

Lynny's relationship with her mother also seemed strange to her friends. Mrs. Fromme was polite and pleasant, but unusually quiet compared to the energetic suburban moms of Westchester. To Nora Lynn, it often seemed that Lynny's personality far outweighed that of her mother. Mrs. Fromme would put food on the table, but when they spoke, which was less often than might have been expected, it was Lynny who dominated the conversations. Mrs. Fromme seemed cowed, even beaten, by her world.

The figure in the household who provoked the greatest reaction was Lynny's father, William Fromme. Rarely seen by Lynny's friends, the occasions when he was present often were difficult, and sometimes frightening. When he walked into a room, Fromme's wife and children would tense up. Activity ceased.

With steel blue eyes and sandy brown hair in a military-style crew cut, William Fromme's square jaw betrayed a man rigid even for his conservative times. The neighborhood children called him "scary."

He wasn't tall, but especially to children he seemed stocky, well built—"strong like a bull," one recalled, an image underscored by his domineering behavior. Loud and pushy to those he considered his inferiors, he seemed particularly hostile and dismissive to Lynny, as if dealing with a hated stepchild; while the rest of the family ate in the dining room, often Lynny would have her meals alone, in the kitchen. Fromme's treatment of his daughter was so cruel, on occasion, that neighbors speculated whether Lynny might even be a stepchild.

On one occasion, the Frommes took their children and a couple of their playmates to Anaheim, for a day of fun with their friends. At a skating rink, William Fromme seemed to go out of control, taking over the space, skating against traffic, commanding the children to follow his example. His exaggerated, wild gestures upset Lynny's friends, springing as they did from no apparent source. In his frightening, ineffectual way, Fromme seemed to be trying to communicate that he was having fun—but people discreetly moved away from the loud, argumentative man whose own children obeyed in silence.

Nora Lynn, whose parents adored Lynny but only reluctantly let their own daughter spend time at the Frommes, promised herself: "I'm staying clear of Mr. Fromme."

Adults drew a different impression. To some neighbors and colleagues, the bespectacled William Fromme could seem diffident, uncomfortable in social situations, a Caspar Milquetoast with a slide rule. His unassuming presence in adult circles contrasted sharply with the rumors circulating about troubles in the Fromme household, but there were rare moments that seemed to hint at the two sides of the man.

One Saturday afternoon, Lynny, then about eleven years old, had gone to practice with the Lariats in the Halls' backyard. Unannounced, William Fromme pulled up to the house in his gray two-seat convertible, a sporty import that stood out in a neighborhood full of lumbering Chevrolet Bel-Airs and Ford Fairlanes. Even though Lynny had been in the Lariats for years, it was the first time her father ever had met the Halls, much less come to a rehearsal or performance.

Politely, Fromme asked Louise Hall if Lynette was there. Thinking he just wanted a word with the girl, Mrs. Hall went to fetch her.

When Lynny saw her father, her demeanor changed at once. The bouncy, playful girl instantly transformed, Mrs. Hall thought, into "a little zombie." Mrs. Hall was well aware of the rumors about William Fromme; she watched uncomfortably as Lynny somberly marched to the car, her father following right behind, bellowing instructions. Later, Lynny told Mrs. Hall that she had been prohibited from leaving the house that day, but didn't think her father would get home early enough to find out. Mrs. Hall didn't ask what punishment Lynette might have suffered as a result of her disobedience.

The Lariats soon figured among Southern California's most prominent 1950s dance troupes, thanks to the children's lively performances—and the Halls' extensive connections. Mrs. Hall managed a community center for the Los Angeles Recreation and Parks Department, and could easily book the troupe into city auditoriums. Her husband, meanwhile, had risen to chair USC's Physical Education Department, a position of great influence at the sports-crazed college—and with the many Trojan alumni who held important positions throughout Southern California. (Curiously, Hall never ran across William Fromme, who would attend USC periodically from 1944 through 1966, earning, in addition to his B.Sc., master's degrees in engineering and business.)

As an authority on physical education, he had contacts at schools and colleges across the country. More impressive, Hall had a direct line to the top names in music and dance; he had been Gene Kelly's drill instructor in the Navy, and their mutual interests led to a lifelong friendship. The legendary dancer enjoyed the Lariat shows and occasionally even stopped backstage to greet the dancers.

The Lariats performed at Los Angeles' most famous venues. They regularly appeared at the Shrine Auditorium's annual International Folk Dance Festival. At the Hollywood Bowl in 1959 they were featured performers in a song and dance extravaganza staged by Meredith Willson, author of *The Music Man*.

Lynny, Nora Lynn, and Larrine had practiced a new number for the show, "The Three Blind Mice," choreographed by one of Hall's graduate students. Donning black leotards with pink bows, tights, and wiry tails, they took the stage in the 18,000-seat Hollywood Bowl.

The number began as might have been expected, the girls dancing in tightly controlled steps as they sang: *Three blind mice, Three blind mice, See how they run, See how they run.* Almost imperceptibly, however, the tempo changed as one of the mice—Lynny—separated herself from the others and began to move in a wilder, impressionistic way.

The other two mice reacted, at first, with shock: *She ran away! She ran away!* they intoned. Then they marched out and confronted Lynny. *You must satisfy your ego within the group!* they instructed.

In the group? Lynny asked, pleading for her independence. When she wouldn't conform, Nora Lynn and Larrine dragged her back and forced her to follow their rhythm, lock-step; *You must satisfy your ego within the group!* they commanded. The third blind mouse would not be permitted to go her own way.

"The Three Blind Mice" seemed a radical departure from the Lariats' repertoire. Lynny, Nora Lynn, and Larrine, who had gone all the way to a dance studio in Redondo Beach to learn the number, were fascinated by it. They knew it wasn't just a folk dance, although they weren't quite sure what it meant.

Some adults, however, felt certain of what they were seeing. They grumbled that "The Three Blind Mice" bordered on the subversive, instilling "socialism" into the children. Hall refused to drop the dance from the Lariats' program. "I don't know what you're talking about," the plainspoken Tennessean told critics. "That dance is just something this gal"—Hall's graduate student, a candidate for an MFA in dance—"put together."

The Lariats, though, were wholesome enough for television, and Lynny and her friends performed on the nationally broadcast programs of Lawrence Welk, Dinah Shore, and Art Linkletter. (A decade later, Linkletter would write the foreword to one of the first books on the Manson Family, *Witness to Evil.*) The troupe starred in Disneyland's annual Christmas festivals—in a pageant promoting international brotherhood, the Lariats represented the United States—and became a favorite of Walt Disney himself. Lynny smiled as Disney kissed Nora Lynn on the cheek, after he presented her with a trophy for the troupe's performance.

The Lariats were invited to a party at Disney's ranch north of Los Angeles, where Annette Funicello and the other guests were treated not only to a performance but to square dance lessons. The only act that managed to upstage the Westchester dancers was a heavily besotted Ray Bolger. Beloved to the children as the Scarecrow in *The Wizard of Oz*, Bolger paddled a canoe into Disney's private lake, stood up to sing a song—and promptly tumbled into the water.

Some members of the Lariats stood out because of their skills and personalities. The Nolan kids were renowned as Irish dancers, and Pat Nolan would grow up to be one of the most prominent Lariat alumni—and like Lynny, end up in federal prison. (In 1994, Nolan, then a California assemblyman, pleaded guilty to corruption charges.) Others, like Chuck Lynch, a fireman's son, prized the camaraderie above the dancing. A few years older than Lynny, he took her under his wing and looked out for her when the troupe went on the road.

And it was on those extended bus trips, which started in 1957, that Lynny first experienced the bond that can develop among fellow travelers. Hall, working with some of the parents, arranged six-week itineraries in which the Lariats would visit colleges, fairs, and military posts, putting on shows in exchange for room and board. Crossing the continent by bus, four dozen kids would sleep on gym floors and rise at five o'clock when Hall banged on a pan. They performed at the Seattle World's Fair and danced at Alaska's isolated Fort Richardson, where grateful servicemen presented the Lariats with the antlers of a just-bagged moose. Hall mounted the antlers at the front of the Lariat bus.

While on the road, Hall would strum his guitar and sing old tunes from Tennessee. The man from Big Sandy constantly lectured his charges, on subjects ranging from USC's superiority to all other universities—it had won so many national championships—to the imminent fall of the United States, which Hall likened to the last days of the Roman Empire.

Other adults who traveled with the group also made an impression. Noel Schutt, who, like Hall, held a doctorate in education, would tell the children his theories of mind over matter. He proved to Lynny and the others that he could "think" himself cold: as the Lariat bus crossed Texas in the scorching summer sun, Schutt would hold his arm out the window, then draw it back in covered with goosebumps.

Sometimes covering four hundred miles in a day, Lynny and her friends saw everything from rural Saskatchewan to cosmopolitan New York. They received special tours of Strategic Air Command bases and got the run of the grounds at exclusive lodges and resorts. On trips to Washington, D.C., they visited the Smithsonian Institution and performed at the unusual Watergate Theater—where the stage jutted out into the Potomac River, and the audience watched the performance from land. The theater later was replaced by the Watergate complex, made famous by a 1972 political scandal.

On two occasions, they visited the White House as special guests. On their first trip there, the Lariats thrilled when they learned that Vice President Nixon planned to welcome them personally. He never did show up—the children were told that Mr. Nixon had been called away on important business—but the group was treated to a private tour of the portraits of the First Ladies. Lynny, wearing a kerchief, smiled coyly for the souvenir photo taken on the White House steps.

The weeks away from home were wondrous times for Lynny. Despite occasional conflicts within the group, the people she met on the road showered her with affection. On a trip to Sacramento to perform at the state college, Lynny forgot her purse in a restaurant. By the time she noticed it was missing, the troupe had already moved on to its next engagement, at the Fallon, Nevada, high school. But Lynny got her purse back after all; its finder had mailed it, with every penny intact, back to Lynny's parents.

Adults who hosted Lynny would often press dollar bills into her hand when she left, as spending money for the road. And they would write her parents to say how much they adored the girl.

"She was such a dear that my husband and I said, If we had any children, we wished them to be exactly like...Lynette," wrote Francelle Buckminster of Oak Ridge, Tennessee, who played host to Lynny and Nora Lynn during the 1959 Lariat tour. "Thank you for letting us share the pleasure of your sweet daughter."

Lynny came to feel more comfortable on the road than back home, because as she grew from a bright child into a young adolescent—now calling herself as Lynne—her life at the Eighty-second Street house turned increasingly difficult.

The Utopians

In an era of conspicuous consumption, and in a conventional middle-class neighborhood where status and displayed wealth were synonymous, the Fromme residence ranked among the more humble of homes. With a small living room centered around a fireplace, and an even smaller dining room and kitchen, the sparsely furnished tract house now was barely large enough to contain the five Frommes. Lynne's friends sensed that the place was always gray and gloomy—although, years later, they couldn't say whether that impression sprung from the color scheme, the lighting, or the general sense of foreboding they felt.

For now, Lynne's pals understood that they weren't quite welcome at the Fromme home, a home that never seemed to entertain guests or host dinner parties, a household that always appeared, in overheard snatches of grown-up conversations, short of money. Never prominent, Helen Fromme now seemed all but invisible in the neighborhood; she, along with young Billy and Julie, faded away like dingy furniture beside the stern presence of Mr. Fromme.

William Fromme was a staff engineer at Northrop Corporation's Aircraft Division, which designed supersonic fighter planes such as the T-38 Talon and the F-5 series, whose sales to some three dozen foreign air forces brought in a huge share of the company's profits. But despite his well-paying job, William Fromme seemed to grow obsessed with controlling his money and property—and to number his wife and young children among these possessions. When going out of town on business, he was known to confiscate the car keys and the household cash, forcing his wife to scrub neighbors' floors to raise enough money to buy groceries. Fromme scrupulously noted the odometer readings of the family car, making sure his wife didn't drive farther than he had authorized. He erupted in fury over minor transgressions, such as failing to meet him precisely on time when his flight arrived at the airport. The neighborhood buzzed with stories of what went on when Mrs. Fromme displeased her husband.

In later years, it would be reported, in carefully chosen words, that William Fromme was "disappointed" with his wife's lack of a college education, that he treated her as an inferior, and that the marriage was, at best, "not a happy one." It also would be claimed that when Lynette was little, her father loved her and favored her, taking her hunting with him, regularly overruling his wife to give Lynny her way.

But while trouble in the Fromme family was clear to Lynne's friends and neighbors, there was little evidence of her father's love. To avoid running into Mr. Fromme, Lynne's friends of driving age would drop her off at the corner and let her walk to her house alone. Then whispered rumors mushroomed into gothic scenes. Not much would have surprised the neighbors, for it was well known that Fromme regularly locked Lynette in her room and denied her supper. No one was quite sure why; when Lynette was asked about her treatment at home, she said she didn't know the reasons her father punished her so often, and so harshly. She simply seemed to accept it. Random, severe punishments were just a fact of life.

In tidy, staid Westchester, the neighbors began to discuss the idea of removing Lynne from her father's control. After she learned to escape her house—locked into her room, she sometimes managed to get out through the window—Lynne made her way to homes she thought might be sympathetic, those of friends and kindly adults, sometimes getting as far as Nora Lynn's home in Playa del Rey, nearly four miles away.

One night, she appeared at the Halls' door and begged them to adopt her. "I don't know what's wrong," she wept. "My dad won't speak to me. He won't let me eat with the rest of them." Other families also considered taking her in, but no one knew how to begin such an effort. In the suburbia of the 1950s, no one meddled in another man's affairs. "How," one neighbor said many years later, "do you tell a man you want to adopt his child?"

William Fromme responded by trying to keep his daughter away from those he felt were interfering with his business. In earlier years, it had been Helen Fromme who sometimes voiced concern over Lynette going on the long Lariat trips, only to be overruled by her husband. But as Lynette entered junior high school, her father began raising objections, that the trips weren't appropriate, that they cost too much—even though the charge was about $25 for a six-week trip. Other parents clashed with Fromme over his daughter's participation, even offering to pay if it was money that stood in the way of her presence on tour.

And Lynne, learning to be as headstrong as her father when conflicts arose, did get to go on every Lariat trip until she was thirteen.

In aerospace-proud Westchester, the junior high school was, inevitably, named after Orville Wright. When Lynne entered the school in the fall of 1960, the grown-ups' political debate had trickled down to the seventh grade, evidenced by the large number of Nixon stickers on student notebooks, along with a smaller contingent favoring Kennedy. Invariably, the children supported whomever their parents did, and Westchester was Republican territory.

For a junior high school, Orville Wright would manage to connect with more than its share of celebrities. Sex symbols Tony Curtis and Rock Hudson granted interviews to the school newspaper, while television star Soupy Sales came down to Orville Wright to entertain at the after-school festival, Sportsnight.

Many of the Lariats who matriculated to Orville Wright plunged into drill teams and pep clubs, boosting school spirit. In her first year, Lynne worked in the physical education office, was initiated into the Athenian Honor Society, and joined the modern dance team of the Girls' Athletic Club. But she soon began to grow disaffected from formal groups. Lynne started associating with the more eccentric, creative circles at the school—the kids who would have listened to Bob Dylan instead of Connie Stevens. Her new friends included Phil Hartman, a surfer who quickly established himself as one of the school's most clever and versatile actors. Decades later, Hartman's comic skills would win him roles on television's *Saturday Night Live* and *News Radio*.

In junior high school, Hartman took drama with Lynne, putting on scenes in class from Shakespeare and Molière. She had, by then, taken to wearing black cardigan sweaters and her red hair in a bob. "Very sweet—and very shy," Hartman summed her up. Though they were friendly, Lynne was not the kind of girl he would ask out. Anyway, it seemed to some of her friends, Lynne was quietly dating older boys. For there had been something of a change that took place when Lynne was thirteen or fourteen; her girlfriends sensed a sophistication, a difference that set her apart. They wondered: Had she made it with a boy?

Lynne also seemed to grow more spiritual, an outgrowth, perhaps, of her early affinity for the natural world. As a younger girl, Lynne had sometimes attended Catholic services with her mother. Sitting in the back and fidgeting, she never felt at home in church. Traditional religion didn't seem to answer Lynne's growing existential quandary, and she began to explore its alternatives.

Among her friends, Lynne's early explorations took the form of entertainment. As a Lariat, she had often performed some of the spookier material, including the Halloween song that went: "It's the night when the goblins prowl here and there / Off the shelf come tiny elves, better beware!"

Now she transfixed her friends with the scariest, creepiest tales—the ghost stories where an unsuspecting couple might find themselves tormented by a possessed spirit, or pestered by a persistent severed hand. On one occasion at Nora Lynn's home, Lynne ushered everyone into the bathroom and proceeded to conduct a séance. Using a Ouija board, Lynne somehow managed to conjure a spirit, its astral fingers moving the planchette, the redheaded channeler conveying an inscrutable message. The episode disturbed Nora Lynn, whose religious parents had taught her that Ouija boards were nothing less than deviltry, an introduction to the occult used to snare young minds.

Most members of Orville Wright Junior High's Class of 1963 took their future for granted, looking forward to an adulthood guaranteed by the institutions and beliefs that had served their parents well. In the third year of John F. Kennedy's presidency, the senior class voted to call themselves the "Utopians."

To the surprise of many, Lynne's sweet, shy, yet apparently deep character had made an impression among her peers—as did her willingness to do almost anything for her friends. When the Utopians selected their class favorites, they voted Nora Lynn Stevens as Cutest Girl, Phil Hartman as Happy-Go-Lucky Boy—and Lynette Fromme as Personality Plus.

For the first time since she was a little girl, Lynne would not go on the Westchester Lariats' summer tour. On the eve of the troupe's departure, Chuck Lynch, who also was staying home for the first time in many years, picked up Lynne in his father's 1951 Buick, and they drove over to bid their friends goodbye. It was a sad farewell, but those who stayed behind found other ways to spend the summer.

Chuck and Lynne had been close for years; he always had gone out of his way to include her, bringing her along to get-togethers with friends his age. The kids would talk, sip purloined liquor, and play records: Fabian, Elvis Presley, and when they felt like something on the wild side, Ray Charles. When other boys brought dates, Chuck, himself a little shy, would bring Lynne.

Now that they were teenagers, their feelings toward each other became more complicated. After a double date at the drive-in, Chuck drove Lynne home to Eighty-second Street. Boldly, he parked in Mr. Fromme's driveway. Then he leaned over and kissed her.

Lynne, who was fourteen, didn't resist.

But then she said: "I don't want it to be like this. I want us to be friends like we've always been."

Chuck, who was sixteen, stopped.

"Chuck," Lynne said in her determined tone, "I think of you like a brother. An older brother."

Chuck nodded. After some awkward good nights, Lynne hopped out of the car and entered the house through the back door. At least there would be no conflict here tonight. William Fromme wasn't home.

Lynne entered Westchester High School in September 1963. With an enrollment reaching three thousand, Westchester was a young school, its low-rise, modern campus of bungalows and covered walkways just seven years old. Bursting with activities, the school boasted legions of honor students, championship teams in varsity football, baseball, basketball, and gymnastics, and a sister-school relationship with Kikuzato High of Nagoya, Japan. That agreement, by which Westchester and Kikuzato would each send a student to study at the other's campus, was signed on November 22, 1963. The same day, classroom loudspeakers announced the assassination of President Kennedy. School was closed and the students were sent home, to watch the aftermath of the Dallas shooting unfold on television.

Lynne joined some of her friends from the Lariats in the Roncherees, a girls' service group affiliated with the YMCA. In their uniform pink sweatshirts, the Roncherees visited girls from troubled homes who had been placed in county facilities, and took fun trips to places like Crestline in the San Bernardino Mountains and the Big Bear ski resort.

Chuck Lynch was a prominent senior during Lynne's freshman year, a student body officer who could introduce her to the school's popular kids. Chuck and his friends Mark Volman and Howard Kaplan sang in Westchester High's a capella choir, and the latter two often performed at school dances. A few years later, Volman and Kaplan would form the Turtles, who produced one of the 1960s' biggest pop hits, the mellow "Happy Together."

Throughout her years in the Westchester schools, Lynne's grades had hovered between a B+ and an A− average. She had Miss Guegel for English in tenth grade, and read such classics as Shakespeare's *Julius Caesar*, Victor Hugo's *Les Misérables*, and Charles Dickens's *A Tale of Two Cities*. Sandy Guegel considered Lynne a good, though quiet, student, much as she had Patricia Krenwinkel, who took the course the year before and then moved out of state.

Lynne also left Westchester at the end of the academic year, for William Fromme had decided the family would move farther south along the coast. The Frommes' new home was in Redondo Beach at 1314 Amethyst Street, on a cul-de-sac by Dominguez Park.

Lynne sadly told Dr. and Mrs. Hall she could no longer continue in the Lariats. Her father owned two cars, a station wagon as well as the convertible, but he forbade Helen Fromme to drive Lynne the six miles back to Westchester. With no car of her own, Lynne said, "I just can't get back and forth." The Halls wished Lynne well in her new town.

Fortunepropheteller

Redondo Beach's name was a romantic reference to the slight curve of its coastline. Politically, it was conservative; the signs at the Redondo Union High School athletic fields announced meetings of the local John Birch Society. And like Westchester, Redondo Beach was dominated by the defense industry. Its connections to aerospace reached back decades, to the days when young Charles Lindbergh attended Redondo High, Lynne's new school. Redondo High was proud of more recent alumni, too, having produced the Smothers Brothers, one of the country's top young comedy acts.

But the move did not offer Lynne a fresh start at home. She felt distant from her younger siblings; rather than supporting her, they were "in competition with me," she would later tell a probation officer. "We never found the time or space to run and play, or sit loving each other's company." Indeed, it was known that though Bill and Julie hardly were pampered at home, they seemed to escape the harsh treatment meted out to the eldest child. William Fromme was fixated on controlling his firstborn, and she looked for any place to be but under his power.

As Lynne began to seek other places of refuge—other friends, other young people whose disaffection fed a nascent counterculture—conflicts with her father grew. Helen Fromme, facing a difficult marriage, sympathized with her daughter perhaps, but sided with her husband. Lynne had little respect for her, saying much later: "I wanted my mother to come my way, to be the child and to let me be the parent. She didn't understand me, she didn't want to accept my way, so I left her"—emotionally as well physically. Throughout her teen years, Lynne would leave home for days or even months at a time, staying with friends, taking on jobs—as a waitress, or in a pet store—fending for herself.

She was drinking now, sometimes a great deal. When she got too wasted to make her way home safely, she often called her old friend Chuck Lynch. Dutifully, he would drop everything and head out to parties, held at homes when the parents were out, where he might find Lynne, gigglingly drunk with other girls. Chuck was concerned; he knew what could happen to girls who didn't watch their liquor at parties. He also felt left out; how come Lynne never invited him to these get-togethers? Lynne tired of his judgmental presence, and eventually dropped him.

Despite the problems at home and attendance that grew increasingly erratic, Lynne soon stood out at her new school. She was shy at first, and no longer bothered to correct people when they pronounced her surname with a silent "e." She never spoke of her family, of her days in Westchester or in the Lariats. Her dress—gray sweaters with matching hats and ribbons, hair in short curls or a pageboy—struck some as conservative, others as a hip disregard for fashion. It didn't occur to the affluent Redondo kids that perhaps Lynne couldn't afford newer clothes, or to have her hair regularly permed; instead, they admired her resistance to peer pressure. She didn't seem really close to anyone, but she impressed them in ways that seemed quirky, even Beat.

One day, skipping up—and no one in high school still skipped—to classmate Christy Curtis in the cafeteria, Lynne somewhat formally made an offering.

"Here," she said sincerely, "I want you to have this." In her outstretched arms was an ordinary, unpeeled orange—but Lynne acted as if this were a precious gift from the bottom of her heart.

Christy understood the moment as one of great significance. A popular, attractive teen who had transferred from the preparatory Marlborough School for Girls, Christy was an unlikely peer for Lynne. But they got along in class, and Christy admired what she saw as a free spirit. She pondered the orange incident for many weeks. Even thirty years later the gesture stood out as a strangely solemn moment. How odd that Lynne would find so much significance in such an ordinary thing!

As she had in the Lariats, Lynne made a particular impression as a performer. Able to recite lines convincingly and quickly switch accents, inflections, and characters, she excelled in the Theatre Arts Club, often playing prim supporting roles in school productions. In the student-written varsity show, which told of an airplane crash in Shangri-La, Lynne, typically, played the stewardess, while her friend Marjorie Arnold was cast as the starlet.

Lynne tried, however, to make the most of her parts. Given the small role of shy, fourteen-year-old Bessie Watty in a class reading of *The Corn Is Green*, Lynne stole the hour by performing her lines in a rollicking Cockney accent. The others had merely recited, their lazy Southern California vowels not quite bringing to life the nineteenth-century Welsh and English characters of Emlyn Williams's play.

And to the surprise of many, Lynne soon was dating one of the most popular boys in school, varsity swimmer Bill Siddons.

A senior who also had just transferred to Redondo, Bill was handsome and outgoing. Though the quiet Lynne had more bookish traits—despite living in sunny Redondo, she preferred to stay indoors writing poetry—Bill sensed her venturesome spirit. They would go for walks, and sometimes Bill even coaxed Lynne into the water, getting her to don a print bikini and splash around in a pool. And they'd hang around with Bill's friends, cool guys like Joe Sandino, a mean guitar player and a distant relative of the Nicaraguan revolutionary Cesar Augusto Sandino.

Mainly, though, they did what all Southern California teenagers did: they went cruising. Driving through the hilly coastal region that Angelenos called the South Bay—Redondo Beach and its neighboring suburbs of Manhattan Beach, Hermosa Beach, and Torrance—they passed through small-town business districts hanging on from a prewar past, and newer strip malls with acres of parking lots. They drove around the endless residential sections, newly developed tracts with ranch-style homes built in the 1950s, or boxy, small apartment houses of the 1960s, often landscaped with palms and given names like The Tiki-ti or The Nomar.

Wherever Lynne and Bill drove, they came upon more signs of progress. Giant generating plants dotted the South Bay, with rows of billowing smokestacks behind barbed-wire fences. In a gully off Prospect Avenue—between the Fromme house and Redondo High—a column of huge electrical towers cut the east side of the town off from the coast, their ceaseless buzz droning through the misty sea air and into the sunny summer days. There were armaments makers, too, and across the city limit in more downscale Torrance, chemical plants and oil refineries stretched for acres, their sulfur odors often wafting far beyond the factory gates.

Bill Siddons had a sympathetic air about him, and he knew something about family problems. His parents were divorced, still uncommon in the mid-1960s, and he had been shuttled around three Los Angeles–area schools in as many years. Lynne began to confide in him.

She had had a fight with her father and he hadn't spoken to her since, Lynne said. It really bothered her.

These things usually cleared up, Bill assured her. But Lynne wasn't assured. The fight, she said, had taken place three years ago. When she was thirteen. It had ended, Lynne said, with a pronouncement from her father: "You're not part of this family anymore."

Bill couldn't quite comprehend it. The idea of living in the same house with someone who never spoke to you seemed impossible.

"What about your mom?" Bill asked.

"I can't talk to her, either. She has to side with Dad," Lynne said.

Bill didn't press the subject; he didn't quite know what to say. His own mother, who rarely interfered in his life, cautioned him. "Be real careful with her, she's *disturbed.*" The word hinted at problems that respectable people didn't explore. Bill took his mother's advice and drew away from Lynne. The romance ended after about three months. Bill moved on to other girls and finished out his senior year. Later, Bill's friends heard about the job he got in Hollywood: manager of a new rock group, the Doors.

For Lynne, it was another frustrating relationship, the promise of something that never panned out. She took on odd jobs, working for a while at a hamburger stand, and at a storefront canvas factory. Her mother occasionally gave her money, but increasingly Lynne had to support herself. Her attendance at school was inconsistent, at best. She threw herself, however, into her new passion— poetry—after finding a masterful teacher in her senior year.

Jim Van Wagoner taught Redondo High's honors English class and had directed Tommy and Dick Smothers in the school shows where they developed their act. A published poet himself, Van Wagoner also had co-written episodes of televi- sion's *Bonanza*, one of which was directed by a young Robert Altman. Film scholars later interpreted the themes of Van Wagoner's episode—"The Dream

Riders," in which Hoss, played by Dan Blocker, flies over the Ponderosa in a balloon—as a forerunner of Altman's later work on *Brewster McCloud*, the story of a man who builds an ill-fated flying machine. *Bonanza*, one of the last successful westerns on television, was shot in part at the San Fernando Valley's Spahn Movie Ranch.

If Jim Van Wagoner could influence Robert Altman, he mesmerized his high school charges, several of whom grew up to be poets and literary scholars. With his demanding workload, his rapturous recitations, and almost intimate interest in each student, the dashing, curly-haired teacher particularly impressed his female pupils; unspoken crushes were legion in Van Wagoner's Room 306. He gave plenty of assignments, but Van Wagoner showed his students he would work at least as hard as they: if they were required to produce a sonnet or a poem in a fixed meter, he might write his remarks in the same format.

Van Wagoner's reading list surveyed twentieth-century poets, including Kipling, Yeats, Robert Frost, Thomas Hardy, Wallace Stevens, W. H. Auden, e.e. cummings, and Edna St. Vincent Millay—whose great-great-granddaughter, coincidentally, played the female lead in "The Dream Riders" episode. But Van Wagoner centered the class on Dylan Thomas.

"You think you guys know what's wild," he challenged his students. "Well, let me tell you about Dylan Thomas. We're talking wild, man, wild." The class, perhaps already curious about Dylan Thomas because of Bob Dylan's eponymous homage, dived into the works of the late Welsh poet.

Van Wagoner had the school's best students, whose top grades and scores got them into the class. But he also took a few with more modest records, if something about them hinted at special talent. Lynne was one of those students, and if Van Wagoner had a teacher's pet in the 1965–66 school year, it was she.

Lynne had perhaps the worst attendance of any of his students—Van Wagoner had heard that she had problems at home, with her father—and yet when she did show up, she might present five poems when the assignment called for only one. If Van Wagoner criticized her work, she preferred to write three new poems than to rewrite an old one. And more than any of Van Wagoner's students, she was inspired by the deeply personal focus and the virtuosic wordplay of Dylan Thomas.

Written in her formal, elegant cursive, Lynne's poems seemed at times to come from beyond the adolescent experience. In a poem entitled "An Autobiographical Fantasy in the Checkered Pajamas (subsufficient subtitle)," a stanza of sorts read:

Down the space caged me there!
The succulent Red I could not touch.
But up? Jump—flop—grasp the air!
Pull myself out of dry stale grey?

Other students marveled at Lynne's verbal dexterity. She wasn't one to raise her hand, but when called on could expound at length whatever the subject, and cleverly, occasionally with sarcasm. Lynne not only kept up with Van Wagoner, her classmate Tamara Simon thought, she often put him to shame. "She's almost *too* brilliant," the Berkeley-bound honor student said to herself, too brilliant for the shy Tamara to try to make friends with.

Jeanine Gardner, a cheerleader who sat in front of Lynne, considered her the most cynical student in class: "quiet, but always pissed off about conventionality, school, society, everything. We were all kind of that way," Jeanine later recalled, "but we were just experimenting with it. She was for real."

Jeanine sensed that Lynne was somehow judging her—and finding her wanting. Though Lynne spoke to Jeanine and nominally considered her a friend, "I felt she thought I was kind of stupid."

And yet other students saw Lynne as too shy herself to make friends. Tammy Simon's sister, Maurya, was two years younger, but found it difficult to converse with Lynne because she seemed so uncomfortable talking. "She kept her chin tilted down, she spoke very softly. It seemed so painful for her to communicate," Maurya recalled.

Although her frequent absences precluded her from serving as an editor of Redondo High's annual poetry journal, the *Compass*, two of Lynne's poems were included and she was appointed to help judge the submissions. The student editors dedicated the 1966 volume to Dylan Thomas—titling it *Do Not Go Gentle*—and in a preface compared "Lynne's success" to "our collective dry run" at understanding the Welsh bard:

> Only one of us (Lynne Fromme, page 6) was able to capture him at all, and she was not a member of the regular "working" staff which strove all year long to somehow *talk* Dylan Thomas into existence or *listen* him to comprehension from his recordings or *shape* the substance of the man from the dismembered fragments of his poetry.

The editors honored Lynne by placing her poem, "Dylan," first. It went, in part:

> Why would he ever try to hide his curly beauty
>   under a raw, runny nose,
> Or escape into the now of a strange
>   woman's rose
> (some blooming, some withering)
> Was he undiscerning—worm-slithering
> Across an apathetic age of only himself?

The work crowned Lynne's reputation as the school's finest poet, emulating Thomas's style to encapsulate his life, and comment, playfully, on his alcoholic death. Lynne wrote that a "fortunepropheteller" or any who paid attention to the "superficials of poet-picaros" could have foretold Thomas's end by his initials, D.T. With a thinly veiled sexual reference and an intimation of Lynne's emerging concept of "Now," it revealed a sophistication far beyond that of students struggling to fit into meter their observations of ships, starlight, or adolescent posing. Lynne liked her classmates, but she longed for the "fortunepropheteller," the "poet-picaro" who could match her visions.

It wasn't, for all her efforts, Jim Van Wagoner. He indulged her tales of woe—about the difficulty of retaining a job, of the problems finding a place to stay—but insisted that he needed her to continue in his class. He seemed like such a clever, concerned man, such a father figure.

In the middle of the night, drunk, she called him on the phone.

"Hello, Mr. Van Wagoner? This is Lynne Fromme."

"Lynne?" The teacher, sleepy, was surprised.

"I just wanted you to know that I'm out here. In a phone booth." She paused. "Alone."

"My goodness, Lynne, do you have a way home?"

"Uh-huh."

"Promise me that when you hang up, you'll go straight home?"

Lynne sighed. "Okay," she said. "Yeah, okay."

"Now, hang up, and go home!"

She hung up. Van Wagoner went back to sleep, and was pleased when he saw her later that week in class. "She's going to make it," he told himself.

But Van Wagoner didn't see the bruises and black eyes that Lynne sometimes wore to school; she had become adept at covering them. Some of her classmates noticed, but Lynne didn't care to speak of the damage. None felt it appropriate to press the topic. But they didn't know that, after confrontations with her father, Lynne would at one point overdose on barbiturates, at another try to slit her wrists. She didn't come to school on those days.

The Class of '66

Lynne was now past the homely pubescent years, and her features had grown delicate, even pretty, framed by waves of dark red hair. In her senior year, her dress had become less gray and more black, her manner still friendly, often shy but somehow more intense. Among the more arty circles at Redondo High, she seemed a person of great mystery, even, as one put it, of "great power." Males and females alike gravitated to her, adolescents looking for clues to whatever special awareness she had.

Randy Hammonds, whose parents owned the canvas factory where he and Lynne worked, wasn't one of the English Department types—a transfer from

Sylmar High in the San Fernando Valley, he was good at math and shop, destined to become a carpenter. Nevertheless, he and Lynne, who shared both an outward shyness and a wry humor, became pals during their last two years of high school.

Though he considered her attractive, Randy didn't view Lynne as a potential girlfriend: he was dating Christy Curtis, and Lynne seemed the only girl in school he could talk to without a subtext of sexual tension. They would hang out at Joe Sandino's place, where Joe would play flamenco guitar and, if Joe's mother wasn't around, down a few beers. They talked about the day's issues—Lynne strongly favored the civil rights movement—and about the sometimes stifling conformity of Redondo's student life.

Once, Randy persuaded Lynne to tag along with him to see a special student film screening in Long Beach, as an extra credit assignment for government class. The government teacher, one of Redondo's most conservative old instructors, considered himself the last voice of decency the students would encounter before heading to the decadent wilds of college. So Randy and Lynne were amused—if not wholly surprised—when the film turned out to be an evangelical story, produced by Billy Graham's organization.

Sitting in the back of the auditorium, Lynne and Randy giggled as the protagonist—Johnny Crawford, who had played Chuck Connors's son on television's *The Rifleman*—got a girl pregnant, contracted venereal disease, and suffered a host of other plagues as a result of his unchecked sinfulness. After the picture, several students in the audience went up to the podium to get saved by the attending pastor. Lynne and Randy found it entertaining.

Another canvas factory regular was Craig South, a surfer, a water polo player and a swimmer, a yell leader, and a member of the Ivy Chain. He too found himself drawn to the decidedly unathletic Lynne Fromme.

"She was thoughtful in the strictest sense of the word—she *thought* a lot," he remembered. "I was—I won't say *afraid* of her, but I certainly approached her humbly. I wanted to learn something from her."

Craig, who had been introduced to Lynne by Christy Curtis, asked her out. "I wasn't dating for the sake of dating. It was more trying to figure out, What's going on here? What do you know that I don't know?" To Lynne, Craig was another pleasant if bland boy with whom to pass a few hours. They might catch an occasional movie, like *The Endless Summer*.

Most of their time together was spent at the canvas factory, where Lynne worked as many as twenty hours a week. Canvas stretching took place on the bottom floor, while next door Randy's mother, Mabel, ran an art gallery and painted her own works.

Lynne usually acted upbeat and cheerful, and the teenagers would listen to the radio and talk as they worked, rolling the canvas off spools and onto the frames, stretching the fabric taut and affixing it with a staple gun.

Lynne liked Randy's family, getting along equally well with his parents and three brothers, but particularly nine-year-old Mark. Unlike Randy's other friends,

Lynne treated Mark as an equal, sharing penny candy with him and discussing the meaning of popular songs. Mark loved Lynne's "Dylan" poem, especially because he understood its sly reference to delirium tremens. She inscribed a copy of the *Compass* for him: "To a child with an especially adult mind." She became Mark's idol.

Lynne formed a special bond with Randy and Mark's mother, Mabel. An artist who had been part of Los Angeles' Beat scene in the 1950s, Mabel Hammonds was dying of cancer in 1966, and she and Lynne spent hours in deep conversation. Lynne gave her an autographed *Compass* as well; she annotated "Dylan," writing, by the stanza "Why would he vilify the very sky," the question, "Why would he look to the sky, with open fly?" She signed it: "Thank you, Mabel, for your concern."

But much as they liked Lynne, her friends had difficulty understanding her. As senior year progressed, she grew more and more depressed. On some days at the shop, she would brood silently, or enter what seemed to be trances. Several times, Randy came across Lynne burning herself with lighted cigarettes, holding them against her flesh without flinching, scarring herself again and again.

On another occasion, Randy and Craig watched as Lynne took a staple gun and methodically shot staples into her left forearm, from her elbow to her wrist, at precise three-inch intervals. She stapled herself with the same care and attention she applied to the canvas and wooden frames.

Everyone who worked at the canvas factory had, by accident, stapled his finger, or even worse, his thumbnail. The pain could be excruciating, even for big guys like Craig and Randy. But Lynne—petite and freckled, a redhead with delicate, fair skin—said nothing. She resumed her work, continuing to stretch canvas for another hour with the staples still in her arm. The boys bowed their heads and continued their tasks; if she was testing anyone, it wasn't them. Besides, they told themselves, there wasn't any visible blood. The staples plugged the punctures. Randy mentioned the incident to his mother, but didn't discuss it with anyone else. "Someone has that kind of a problem, she doesn't need to be judged by a whole lot of people," he told himself.

Lynne missed school for much of that week. When she did show up, it was outside Room 306—Mr. Van Wagoner's classroom. She rapped on the window, interrupting his lecture. The teacher walked outside to talk to her.

"Lynne, what are you up to now?" he said. "Why weren't you in class?"

"Look what happened," she replied, indicating her arm. Clumsy me, she seemed to say. "I had a little accident."

"My class is in session, Lynne, what do you want me to do?"

She smiled weakly. He left his classroom and took her to the school nurse. The nurse brought Lynne to the hospital, and after class, Van Wagoner visited her there. She felt better. But when the teacher saw she was all right, he went home and she disappeared. Van Wagoner didn't know where she went.

No one else at school was quite sure where she went, either. Because no one ever heard mention of Mrs. Fromme, the rumors went that her parents had separated and Lynne was living with her father. Others thought Lynne was on her own, or that she moved in and out of her house so frequently no one could be sure where she lived. Years later, with little elaboration, the Frommes would tell federal agents that they had placed their daughter under psychiatric care in 1966.

Sometimes, Lynne's friends would walk with her after school—they to their homes, she to her job at the hamburger stand, where she had to wear a goofy costume and paper hat. Toward the end of senior year, Tamara Simon and Jeanine Gardner tried to broach the mysterious subject of Lynne's out-of-school life.

Would Lynne be going back to her parents' place after work? Jeanine wanted to know.

No, Lynne said, she wasn't living there anyway. Her father had moved from Amethyst Street to an apartment complex in Torrance, outside of Redondo High's attendance district.

So where was she living? Lynne confided her secret: With a guy, down by the beach. Tammy and Jeanine were stunned—*living with a man?* Like other members of the Class of 1966, the two girls had resolved that they were going to make a difference with their lives—to become political activists, maybe fight for civil rights. But, Jeanine thought, "Lynne's already doing it. She's *living* it." She and Tammy drank in the implications of Lynne's revelation: how sophisticated, how exciting! But they didn't query her further; it might reveal to Lynne how uncool they were.

As the year wound to a close, Lynne was less and less a presence at school. In her absence, her reputation grew. Many were pleased when she returned to sign their annuals, even though she had missed school the day yearbook photos were taken. Her inscriptions stood out among the spate of entreaties to "have a great summer" or "stay in touch."

To Tammy Simon, whom she described as a "most sensitive *good* person," she wrote: " 'Success' or contentment . . . in any of your pursuits from the most inane, wild dream to down, ground, around-the-corner realities."

To Margie Arnold—the student actress who later would appear on *Room 222* and *Marcus Welby*—she was more blunt: "Success in the Big cold world." The capital B in "Big" was drawn so that it looked, at first glance, more like the letter "P."

It wasn't the last Margie saw of her. When walking home one day near the end of school, she came across Lynne—normally so reserved—weeping.

"What's wrong, Lynne?" Margie asked.

Her father, Lynne explained, had kicked her out of the house. Again. She didn't understand why he always was so angry with her, why he always rejected her. Besides, Lynne told Margie, she had nowhere now to go.

Margie was touched. Her own mother had died the year before, and like Lynne, she was one for whom high school was not all parties and games. She asked her father if Lynne might stay with them for the summer. He said no. Years later, when he saw what became of Lynne's life, he told Margie how much he regretted that decision.

Lynne eventually did find a place to spend the summer, house-sitting for a friend who was traveling with her family through Australia. Lynne decided to shelter other friends in the house as well, including Joe Sandino. Joe's family had moved to Pasadena, some twenty-four miles inland, but he preferred to remain in Redondo with his sixteen-year-old girlfriend, Rachel Hickerson.

Rachel was a slender, wide-eyed blonde who had come from New Orleans after, in her parents' eyes, edging too close to delinquency. After a year of shoplifting, drinking beer, and joyriding with older boys, Rachel's marks had fallen from A's in eighth grade to D's in ninth. The Hickersons decided their daughter needed a change. Rachel's father, education scholar Nathaniel Hickerson, obtained a faculty appointment at the University of Southern California, and in August 1965, the family relocated to Redondo Beach. Rachel turned her interests inward, and began unspooling sheaves of adolescent rhyme. She also became a pom-pom girl.

More likely to mention poetry than petty theft when asked her interests, Rachel heard of Lynne almost as soon as she arrived at Redondo High. "She's, like, this goddess of poetry," Rachel was told. "You've definitely got to meet her."

Lynne, to Rachel's surprise, soon learned of her as well. One day in the school cafeteria, Lynne interrupted Rachel's regular meal of milk and a cookie—Rachel rarely bought a full meal, preferring to spend her lunch money on makeup—to discuss poetry. The conversation was brief, and Rachel never mustered the courage to talk to Lynne again in school. Lynne was a senior, her visits to campus were so rare, her life so important . . . who was a sophomore like Rachel to impose on the school's elusive muse?

Now, in the summer of 1966, Rachel found herself in Lynne's company all the time. Along with Joe, and sometimes without him, she would spend hours at the house, which sat on a hill by Prospect Avenue, a few blocks from Redondo High. The goddess of poetry had, in person, some rather un-Olympian habits, chain-smoking and, to Joe's increasing distress, drinking, usually whiskey straight. And though Lynne clearly didn't seek public approval, she also seemed to be tailoring her gestures to those in the room, as if she were performing for an audience. The way she carried herself, her facial expressions, the intonations of her wildly expressive voice—everything, even commonplaces, seemed to be suffused with meaning. Rachel eyed her with not wholly concealed wonderment.

Lynne could be a subtle teacher. At Der Wienerschnitzel, a hot dog franchise on Torrance Boulevard, Rachel ordered a "polish dog"—as in shoe polish.

Lynne nudged the younger girl. "Are you sure that's what you want?"

"Yes . . ." Rachel answered tentatively.

"Are you *sure?*" Lynne repeated.

"Polish dog?" she said, as in Warsaw. "I'll have a Polish dog!" Rachel told the counterman. Lynne was so knowledgeable, Rachel thought. So superior.

It was clear that the two shared many progressive ideas then percolating among the young: a sense of loss over President Kennedy's death, and of betrayal by his war-making successor, Lyndon Johnson; advocacy for civil rights and the movement led by Martin Luther King, Jr.; enthusiasm for the more authentic music being played, and for the folk revival they traced to Woody Guthrie. Lynne pointed Rachel toward writers like Jack Kerouac and Tennessee Williams, writers who were trying to get beyond the surface and into what was "real."

Lynne seemed peculiarly aware of what was real in Redondo, things that other kids seemed to overlook. She pointed out the city's Dow Chemical plant, which she said manufactured insecticides and napalm. "We're fucking up the earth," she would say. Not only was the sentiment unusual, so was the vocabulary. "Fuck" wasn't a word that often sprung from the mouths of Redondo Beach girls in 1966. Rachel was equally impressed with the sophisticated way Lynne dressed: she now was all turtlenecks and black stockings, flats on her feet. Sometimes she wore a flak jacket. The olive drab offset Lynne's red hair nicely, Rachel thought.

The younger girl felt she had little to offer Lynne in return, but did volunteer some tidbits about her own past. In a rare reversal of their roles, Lynne listened raptly as Rachel recounted attending a Byrds concert in Miami Beach and ending up at a party with the band. People were sniffing glue, she recalled, an impressive sight to a fourteen-year-old.

"One of the Byrds tried to seduce me," Rachel volunteered.

"Which one?" Lynne wanted to know. Unfortunately, Rachel didn't remember.

Lynne seemed particularly interested in Rachel's criminal career.

"Once I went into the Maison Blanche department store in New Orleans and put four cotton dresses on under my dress!" Rachel boasted.

"Yeah?" said Lynne.

"And then I sold them to my friends."

Lynne was impressed. Rachel smiled.

More and more, Rachel found herself paying attention to Lynne rather than to Joe. Joe would sit in the house, playing his guitar, folk songs and flamenco, covers of popular tunes, with a virtuosity many thought would land him a professional career. But talented and fun as Joe was, Lynne loomed as a far weightier presence in the Prospect Avenue house. She seemed to have an opinion about everything, yet to have an existence wholly removed from where she was. It was as if she belonged to another time as much as to her own, as if, in a phrase many used to describe Lynne at this point in her life, "she carried the weight of the world." Several worlds, perhaps.

Sometimes, those worlds would intersect in the Prospect Avenue house. One day, Joe and Rachel drove up to find an old, tail-finned car parked in the driveway. Joe was irritated; it meant they would have to park on the street behind the house and come in through the back door. When they did, they discovered Lynne lounging with two men—leather-clad greasers, they looked like—drinking. One of them, the taller, better-looking of the two, was smiling giddily. He seemed awfully intimate with Lynne.

Lynne was not pleased by the sudden arrival of her high school pals, who felt very small in the presence of men who seemed so much older, perhaps as old as twenty-five. After hurried introductions—was that guy's name Jerry? Larry?—the greasers left. Joe and Rachel did not inquire further. It wasn't their business.

Lynne, however, had clear views on Rachel's business.

"Don't you find school boring?" she asked the younger girl. "You're so smart, don't you want to do something else? Maybe get a job? Find a life?"

Many of Lynne's interests surely did not come from school, such as her copy of Erich Fromm's *The Art of Loving*, and the curious old book that Rachel thought contained black magic symbols. Or Lynne's views on dolphins, which sometimes could be spotted frolicking off Redondo's shore.

"They're smarter than people, you know," she observed. "It's not like mankind is the smartest form of life there is. There could be forms of life that we don't even know about." Rachel nodded.

Lynne seemed more inclined to deliver monologues than to engage her friends as equals. But sometimes, she would backtrack, suddenly unsure of what she was saying. "Oh, I'm just all screwed up!" she would proclaim, her vulnerability suddenly showing through the facade. Joe and Rachel would pounce on her. Screwed up? "No, you're not!" they told Lynne. "No, you're not!" The vote of confidence perked Lynne up.

Ike and Tina Turner played at a joint on 190th Street in Torrance that fall of 1966, but the South Bay clearly was too sedate for Lynne. Joe and Rachel knew she hitchhiked up to West Hollywood, some seventeen miles and a world away. West Hollywood was an unincorporated district just outside the Los Angeles city limits, beyond the jurisdiction of the vigilant LAPD. Law enforcement fell to the county sheriff, whose lax oversight led to a proliferation of coffeehouses, speakeasies, and concert dives near the Sunset Strip. It was a place where the fading beatniks and the emerging hippies hung out, where bikers and speed freaks congregated with little interference.

Lynne once brought Joe and Rachel with her to the Troubadour, the Santa Monica Boulevard establishment that housed both a coffeehouse and a concert space. Largely, however, Lynne kept her social circles separate, and rarely spoke of her excursions to her Redondo friends. Nor did she discuss her family, never mentioning her mother or siblings, although Rachel had met Lynne's brother Bill in school. Lynne did let drop that her father kept guns, though, and that he had taught her how to use them. It emerged, ever so vaguely, that Mr. Fromme and Lynette had had conflicts over her taste in music and other seemingly trivial issues.

But Lynne hinted that she hoped to patch things up with her father, eventually: "Someday I'll go back there and it'll be okay." Rachel didn't quite understand the basis of that belief. Several times, she and Joe had collected a hysterical Lynne from her father's apartment, where she had picked up some spare clothes—and apparently a fresh set of bruises.

Once, Rachel went inside. She saw Mr. Fromme.

He was dressed like a middle manager, the man in the gray flannel suit. His long-sleeved white shirt was crisply ironed, his tie carefully knotted, his slacks pressed, and his dress shoes shined. He seemed muscular and tense, like a man in training. He wore a crew cut. He was formal, superior, arrogant, his blue eyes unforgiving. His body language bespoke hostility.

He looked, Rachel thought, like a Nazi.

Around the same time, more details of Lynne's perilous existence began to seep out. Sitting on the porch of the borrowed home, watching the sunset and the occasional carloads of surfers drive by, Lynne recounted a new experience to her friends.

It had happened in May with a guy she was seeing—a teacher, she implied—who had taken her to Long Beach and given her what turned out to be LSD. She had thought it was just speed, which she had been taking for some time. Lynne not so much explained the event as performed it: her voice rising and falling, her hands gesturing to underscore the story, her eyes betraying fear or vulnerability at key moments. Instead of the expected rush, Lynne recounted, she had been devastated, the doors of her perception bolting off their hinges. Long Beach's offshore oil derricks—illuminated at night and decorated to look like tropical islands—were surreal under normal circumstances. Before Lynne, they had metamorphosized into raging demons.

"I was tricked into it. I was tricked, and then I was alone, wandering around Long Beach," she said to her mesmerized friends. "I thought the barges and oil derricks were huge, hulking monsters. I was alone and frightened." Then came the story's moral: "Once again, I had been fucked over."

The nightmare had ended only when she came down off the drug and her companion revealed the true chemical she had ingested. Her narrative not only described the acid trip but ranged through the gamut of topics she favored, touching on Samuel Beckett and human rights, as well as her still-valued Dylan Thomas. Somehow, the acid trip, frightening as it apparently had been, seemed now to have been worth it to Lynne, judging by the spell it allowed her to cast over her audience. Rachel felt queasy. It was as if Lynne had brought her right along on the trip, as if she had taken acid herself.

Owsley Stanley, the Berkeley chemist who popularized lysergic acid diethylamide in California, had been running an LSD laboratory in Los Angeles through the spring of 1966. The drug was then legal, although possession of LSD would become a misdemeanor in October of that year. Word of the mystical substance had entered high school conversations, but neither Rachel nor Joe had known anyone who had taken it, surely not a teacher.

Who was this teacher? Rachel wanted to know. Lynne did not favor simple questions and answers, however, and all her friends could glean was that this man was apparently in his thirties, apparently married, apparently involved in theater in some way. And it appeared to Rachel, sleeping with Lynne. The story seemed rather sinister, even as the upbeat strains of Sonny & Cher and the Beach Boys wafted from passing car radios over the porch on which they sat. No further information was forthcoming.

As the summer of 1966 continued, the relationship between the three in the Prospect Avenue house grew more intense. They listened to blues and comedy records, especially Moms Mobley, the raunchy black comedienne. They looked for clues in the poetic lyrics of the new local favorite, the Doors, and in the songs of everyone's favorite, the Beatles. The evocative, seemingly drug-influenced *Rubber Soul* had been released the previous December; unlike most pop albums, which were forgotten after intense but brief play, it was still in full rotation on Prospect Avenue. *Revolver*, which the Beatles briefly had considered naming *Bubble and Squeak*, came out in August. With its brighter, more aggressive sound and even more intricate, nascently psychedelic lyrics, Lynne and her friends wondered: what were the Beatles telling them?

The three also would put on their own performances, of a sort. They would pore over Lynne's copy of *The Family of Man*, a book of photographic essays showing people of all types—young lovers, dead bodies, the famous and the sad. Lynne would pass out copies of plays and poems and stories she liked, and they would all read aloud. She plaintively recited Dylan Thomas's "Was There a Time."

More confrontational material also was on the bill, with Edward Albee's *Who's Afraid of Virginia Woolf?* a particular favorite of Lynne's. Drink in hand, eyes averted, she asserted that George and Martha, the ruined protagonists, represented marriage in its "purest form." Joe objected; Rachel nodded silently.

When the film version, starring Elizabeth Taylor and Richard Burton, was released, the three piled into Joe's 1957 Ford for a pilgrimage to Hollywood, the only place the picture was playing. Although, to their pleasant surprise, the Ford survived the journey, the group almost didn't get into the theater. Rachel was too young to see a movie reserved for those over seventeen, but Lynne's fast talking got them past the ticket taker.

Oddly, despite Lynne's apparent sophistication, she had trouble dealing with adults. Mannerisms that seemed knowing, or forthright and honest, among her peers became awkward gestures that led adults to pass each other puzzled glances. Slurping her soup seemed cool when the kids were all on their own in the borrowed house; in the company of parents or other grown-ups, it seemed tactless.

Lynne tried her best to avoid encounters with adults. Rachel and Joe had no quarrel with that, and rarely brought her into their families; they did not want to be embarrassed by their friend. She did not seem able to hold jobs long, and ran through a gamut of entry-level positions at places ranging from food stands to a mortgage company.

Yet, on her own terrain, there was no better authority than Lynne. Rachel turned to her for advice, particularly over her romance with Joe.

One evening, as Lynne was cooking rice for dinner—plain rice, a vaguely bohemian kind of dish in a world that favored creamy noodle casseroles—Rachel complained about Joe treating her "unkindly."

"Is this romance going nowhere?" she mused rhetorically.

"You know," Lynne observed, "women don't really need men as much as they think they do."

The response puzzled Rachel, who later mentioned it to her mother, Patricia.

"There's a lot of truth in that," Mrs. Hickerson told her daughter. But this advice didn't help Rachel resolve her own immediate problem: Joe's increasingly pent-up desire. She returned to Lynne.

What, Rachel wanted to know, was sex like?

Lynne, who again was drunk, assured Rachel it was not the hurdle she imagined.

"It's really no big deal," Lynne said. She went on to emphasize how much Joe seemed to love her, how normal and natural it would be. "It's like, you know, I've done it lots of times," said Lynne, proceeding to give Rachel practical, big sisterly advice about the mysterious act. Rachel nodded along, slowly gaining the reassurance she had sought.

"I mean," Lynne continued, sipping whiskey, "I learned all about this, the first time, from my father. My father taught me everything about sex." Rachel decided to change the subject.

The Prospect Avenue sanctuary abruptly closed after the grandmother of Lynne's vacationing friend paid an unexpected visit. The place was a mess. Liquor bottles littered the kitchen and Lynne, entrusted with the property, seemed to be living there with a man: Joe Sandino. The grandmother immediately ordered Lynne and Joe out of the house, and despite Joe's soberly stated explanations, there was to be no bargaining. He returned to his family in Pasadena, after dropping Lynne off at Rachel's home.

Entering the apartment on Beryl Street, Lynne seemed agitated, and in the eyes of Patricia Hickerson, hostile.

"Can Lynne sleep over, Mom?" Rachel asked.

"Of course," Mrs. Hickerson said. "You can sleep down here," she told Lynne, pointing to the convertible sofa, a beige couch decorated with a pattern of lilies.

Lynne muttered her thanks. But later, Rachel told her mother there would be no need to prepare the daybed. Lynne would sleep with Rachel, in Rachel's room. In Rachel's bed.

That night, as they nuzzled together, Lynne wept. She told of her fears—her fears that she had no future at all. When Rachel got up to fetch something, Lynne begged her not to leave the bed. She could not be alone that night.

Rachel, distraught to see her heroine so upset, tried to reassure Lynne.

"You can stay with us as long as you need to," she said. "Things aren't that bad." But, Rachel thought, perhaps they were.

The next morning, Lynne declined the breakfast prepared by Mrs. Hickerson, as well as her maternal interest. Lynne wasn't, she said, going to "mooch."

"I'll get myself together one way or another, no matter what," she told Rachel. One of those ways was to go home again, to the Fromme household in Torrance. When Joe came by later that evening, she asked him to take her home.

Joe and Rachel swallowed their fear of Mr. Fromme, and agreed to the journey. On a rainy September night, they made the ten-minute drive to the apartment complex at the corner of Van Ness Avenue and 182nd Street. Their destination was a maze of modern two-story apartments, landscaped with tropical foliage and illuminated with floodlights. It clearly had been designed to accentuate the reputedly casual lifestyle of the Southern California beach community. But things were far from casual this night. Lynne told her friends she would finally have it out with her father.

Joe and Rachel had been prepared to enter the apartment with Lynne; surely Mr. Fromme would not strike her if they were present. And if he tried—well, Joe could be strong, if he had to. But Lynne, to their surprise, asked that her friends remain in the car. She would confront her father alone. They agreed, trying to conceal the relief and guilt that raced down their backs.

In the pouring rain, Lynne's tiny figure marched up to the apartment complex. Joe and Rachel sat in the car, silently. Would the father yell and start swinging? Would Lynne be able to call for help if she needed it? The few things Lynne possessed were now stored at the Hickersons' apartment. Would Lynne ever return to retrieve them?

Finally, seemingly from nowhere, Lynne materialized, drenched by the still-pouring rain. She was weeping, her arms laden with books, clothing, makeup, and curlers. Joe and Rachel leaped from the car to ease her into the back seat. She cried softly as Joe drove back to Redondo Beach, asking again and again, Why was her father so intolerant?

Joe kept his eyes fixed on the road. Rachel was too fearful to touch Lynne, even as she wanted to. Over and over in her head rang a stanza of "Debut," Lynne's poem about an infant:

You star in traumas,
Yet how soon you forget these things
when some new something you are eyeing.

Lynne was nothing if not resourceful, however, and by the next day she had devised a plan: Get a job, get an apartment, enroll in school—in El Camino Junior College, which Beach Boys Brian Wilson and Al Jardine had once attended. On her own, Lynne obtained a position at Gold's Furniture, located on Hawthorne Boulevard in a sprawling, sterile shopping strip inaptly called the Old Towne Mall. Her job was to help verify the credit of people who wanted to buy sofas on installment.

When she wasn't working, she looked for an apartment. Joe provided the transportation; Rachel sometimes tagged along. The task was frustrating, for Lynne wasn't comfortable in Redondo's poorer districts but could barely afford even the lowest rent. More than that, she had trouble dealing with landlords and apartment managers, the sort of adults whose negative judgment she instinctively tried to avoid.

Finally, she settled on a rooming house by the waterfront, on Catalina Avenue. The rickety structure was just a couple of blocks from the Redondo Beach library, and a few houses down from the Vail Apartments, where Charles Lindbergh and his mother had resided in 1916. Addicts and derelicts now lived on the street. For a monthly rent of about $70, Lynne got a room furnished with a hotplate, a sink, and a bathtub. And a view of the shore. Lynne hated to go to the beach, but she liked to look at the water. She also bought Joe's broken-down old Ford.

Soon, Lynne was comfortable enough to let her old friends know where she was. She dropped in to see Nora Lynn Stevens and her mother in Playa del Rey, and invited her to come by for a visit.

Nora Lynn came down to Redondo with some other girls from the Roncherees, and was a bit taken back by what she saw. To the straitlaced Nora Lynn, the place seemed rather on the edge, as did Lynne, who looked to be heavily into drugs. Lynne was apologetic about the disheveled condition of her flat, and Nora Lynn and she parted on good terms. They saw each other, on occasion, over the next few months.

Things seemed to be looking up. Lynne even called Mrs. Hickerson to thank her for her hospitality. When Rachel stopped by the store on the lunch break, Lynne would detail the business operations, along with her views on how to improve its efficiency.

But her Ford soon died, and Lynne returned to hitchhiking and the public bus. She left the job at the furniture store and dropped out of sight. She rarely was at the rooming house when Rachel came to call, so the younger girl would leave notes in her mailbox. Sometimes it seemed as if Lynne were sharing the rooms with a man, or men. Then it seemed she had moved away entirely. It was a period of bitter disillusionment, Lynne later recalled. "The restaurant fella taught me how to cheat the customer. . . . The pet shop guy was cheating on his income taxes. Every place I went I learned that somehow they were trying to pull the wool over someone's eyes."

One rainy night before Christmas, Lynne suddenly reappeared at the Hickersons' apartment. Wearing a pink and green holiday dress, she bounded into Rachel's room, happier and prettier than she had seemed in weeks. She hadn't been able to enroll in school in the fall, with her job and all, but would attend El Camino College in the spring semester. She had saved enough to get by for the term, and was certain that finally she would straighten things out with her father. The new year—1967—she was sure, would be the turning point in her life.

Rachel was happy to have her friend back, for good, she hoped. They showed one another poems each was working on, and caught up on gossip. Before leaving, Lynne hugged Rachel, thanked her for her friendship, and handed her a present. Without opening it, Rachel ran to her desk and presented a gift to Lynne, a book on spiritualism. The two agreed to read each other's books and discuss their conclusions at their next meeting.

Lynne departed, and Rachel returned to her room to see what gift she had received. It was Lynne's worn copy of *The Family of Man*. Clearly, she had owned this book for many years, for inside its front cover the name "Lynette Fromme" had been written in a big, childish scrawl. The gift touched Rachel. She lay on her bed and cried.

Lynne moved back in with her parents and enrolled at El Camino College. She signed up for French, theater arts, psychology, and modern dance. Jim Van Wagoner, teaching at Redondo High, was happy to hear that Lynne was in college. Keep up her grades, he thought, and she would be able to transfer to the University of California.

But Lynne's reconciliation with her father did not occur. With three weeks left in the spring semester, yet another bitter fight erupted and she was once again out on her own. "We argued over some kind of definition from the dictionary, that's how dumb it was," she later said. "His way or no way. I said, 'yes, but,' and he said, 'yes, but nothing.'"

This time, there were no houses to house-sit, no money for rooms to let. She hitchhiked to Venice, the bohemian district of Los Angeles ten miles north of Redondo Beach. People, she knew, were "living kind of freely" there, and perhaps something would turn up. Besides, now she had no place else to go.

Chapter 2

Charles Manson

Lynne sat on a bench on the Venice Beach boardwalk, staring at the ocean. She hadn't brought much with her—just her mascara, her dictionary, her books. She was eighteen years old.

Then he spoke, in a strange, scratchy, flat, Midwestern male voice that cut through her thoughts like a rusty knife: "What's the problem?"

What she beheld was an unkempt, elflike man in a cap, sporting a two-day beard and a whiff of body odor, or possibly whiskey. He seemed neither old nor young, and carried himself in an elegant, almost formal physical manner. He looked, she thought, like a hobo with a touch of class.

"How did you know—?" she started to say. He smiled brightly at her, his dark brown eyes pushing themselves into her gaze.

"Up in the Haight, I'm called the Gardener," he said by way of explanation. "I tend to all the flower children."

The Gardener. What does a gardener do? A gardener . . . *plants seeds*, she realized, suddenly feeling dangerously exposed. She held her legs together, tightly.

"It's all right," he said, and Lynne felt that it was. But his manner seemed so otherworldly, it almost overwhelmed her. She lowered her head, hoping he would disappear. And when she looked up, the Gardener was gone. She looked right and left, now wishing he was back.

"So your father kicked you out," came the scratchy Midwestern voice. Lynne looked over; the Gardener had reappeared. He sat on the cinderblock wall, looking like a sort of beatnik Rumpelstiltskin. They began to talk, Lynne listing the things about her life she hated, the things in life she craved. She looked at the

Gardener, who seemed to metamorphose even as he smiled at her, one moment a warm father figure, the next a sprightly imp.

"The way out of a room is *not* through the door," he said. "Just *don't want out*, and you're free."

If she didn't want out—or, more precisely, if she didn't think about wanting out—she wouldn't be aware of being in. It did make sense. How come this fancy bum understood so much? How come he could teach her more in a few minutes than she had learned in a whole semester at college?

He explained: Twenty years behind bars had taught him a lot. He told a rambling, disconnected story, with names—Father Flanagan's Boys Town, Ma Barker, Terminal Island—that could have been pulled out of a James Cagney movie. In solitary confinement, the Gardener had been alone with his thoughts, able to think through the walls that held him. When he neared the end of his latest term—seven years for a bad check—the warden said he could get out three weeks early if he put in some work instead of strumming his guitar.

"Get out of where?" the Gardener asked.

"Out of this penitentiary!" yelled the warden.

"What penitentiary? Are you in a penitentiary? I'm not," said the Gardener. Indeed, his years in solitary confinement, the poor man's zen monastery, had taught him a lot. "Am I up from the floor? Or down from the ceiling? Am I right, or left of anything . . . or is it all relative? And if I could conceive a question . . . certainly I could conceive the answer."

He seemed to have conceived many answers. But the fact was, it was time for the Gardener to go. He had stopped in Venice not for any particular reason, but because he felt he had to. Now, however, he was heading up north. Lynne was welcome to come along with him.

No, she said, she had obligations. Three weeks of her freshman semester were left to go. She screwed up her face, and looked at him, thinking hard.

"Well," he said as he started to leave, "I can't make up your mind for you."

"I grabbed my books," Lynne later wrote, "running to catch up with him. I didn't know why—I didn't care—and I never left."

The Gardener, of course, was Charles Manson.

The Making of Charles Manson

Charles Milles Manson was born on November 12, 1934, although he preferred to list his birth date as November 11, Armistice Day. The hospital in Cincinnati, Ohio, registered him as "no name Maddox," because the man who had impregnated sixteen-year-old Kathleen Maddox had not been identified.

Kathleen Maddox briefly married William Manson, and the child received his surname. In 1936, a paternity judgment was entered in Kentucky against a "Colonel Scott," who was ordered to pay the mother of Charles Manson $25, plus $5 per month support. He failed to comply with the order, and Charles Manson later said he never met the man adjudged to be his father.

"My father," Manson would testify, "is the jailhouse."

After his mother was convicted of armed robbery in 1939, Manson was sent to live with his aunt and uncle in West Virginia. Uncle Bill thought young Charles a sissy, and forced him to wear girl's clothes on the first day of school.

Manson returned to his mother's custody when she was paroled in 1942, and followed her as she went through a succession of relationships with men and, on occasion, women. When he was twelve, she sent him off to the Gibault School for Boys in Terre Haute, Indiana, apparently because her lover of the moment considered young Charlie a burden. He fled the institution after ten months, but his mother refused to take him back.

Manson burglarized a grocery store, stole a bicycle, and had enough cash to rent a room for himself. He was arrested after another burglary and sent to juvenile hall in Indianapolis. After escape and recapture, authorities sent him to Father Flanagan's Boys Town, under the mistaken belief he was a Catholic. Four days later, Manson and another ward stole a car and fled to Illinois. Now age thirteen, he committed two armed robberies, of a grocery store and a gambling joint. After several more robberies, Manson was arrested and sent to the Indiana School for Boys in Plainfield, where he was first raped by fellow inmates. It was reported that he burned himself with cigarettes, or ran needles through his flesh, to build his tolerance to pain.

Manson escaped eighteen times from the reform school, and in February 1951 broke out with two other wards. Driving stolen cars, they supported themselves by robbing service stations, before being captured at a police roadblock in Utah. Manson was sent to the National Training School for Boys in Washington, D.C., for having committed a federal offense—transporting a stolen vehicle across state lines. Officials there rated him "average" in intelligence, manual dexterity, and mechanical aptitude. According to records, his favorite subject was music. He was illiterate.

A psychiatrist determined that Manson relied on "certain facile techniques for dealing with people," but ventured that "behind all this lies an extremely sensitive boy who has not yet given up in terms of securing some kind of love and affection from the world." The favorable report allowed Manson to be reassigned to a less regimented facility, the Natural Bridge Honor Camp, that October. Within three months, however, he was transferred to the Federal Reformatory in Petersburg, Virginia: he had sodomized another boy, holding a razor blade against his victim's throat to keep him still. Manson later claimed the encounter was consensual.

Petersburg sent him to the tougher Federal Reformatory in Chillicothe, Ohio, where Manson's behavior apparently improved. He was paroled in May 1954, married a seventeen-year-old girl in January 1955, and worked odd jobs in restaurants, gas stations, and parking lots.

In July, he stole a car and drove with his pregnant wife to California. Apprehended weeks later, he received probation for the crime, on a psychiatrist's hopeful report that married life might encourage the young man to straighten out. When Manson failed to appear at a hearing on another automobile theft charge, his probation was rescinded. Captured in Indianapolis, he was sentenced to three years in Terminal Island, the federal penitentiary off Los Angeles Harbor.

In April 1957, twelve days before a parole hearing, Manson was found outside the prison gates attempting to hot-wire a car; he later said he was trying to get to his wife, who had left him for a truck driver. Manson had five years probation added to his sentence, his wife divorced him, but his behavior again improved. Manson requested—and received—a place in the Dale Carnegie Course, designed by the author of *How to Win Friends and Influence People.*

He also learned pimping from experienced inmates, and after his parole in September 1958, took up this new trade. He lived with a woman whom he also prostituted, and worked Hollywood Boulevard while passing himself off as a "producer." His appearance was that of the quintessential 1950s hoodlum, a smirking young man in grease-slicked hair and denim jacket.

Six months later, Manson stole a government check from a mailbox, forged an endorsement, and tried to cash it in a supermarket. Arrested on two federal charges—forgery and mail theft—he was turned over to the Secret Service. The check disappeared during his questioning. According to a report, the agents felt "certain [that Manson] took it off the table and swallowed it when they momentarily turned their backs." The check had been in the amount of $37.50.

After a nineteen-year-old woman told a federal judge she was pregnant by Manson and that the two were deeply in love, Manson received a ten-year suspended sentence for the check forgery; once again it was hoped domesticity might help the convict adjust to society's rules. The woman, however, had lied about the pregnancy, and Manson was free. His enterprises reportedly included a prostitution ring that operated out of the Hollywood Roosevelt Hotel. In any event, Manson was arrested several times, for grand theft auto, using stolen credit cards, and transporting a woman across state lines for the purpose of prostitution.

The charges were dropped, although a parole officer sought to haul Manson in after an irate parent complained about the ex-convict's behavior toward his daughter. Manson, the father said, had defrauded his daughter, gotten her pregnant, and attempted to turn her to prostitution. Manson also had drugged and raped his daughter's roommate, the father claimed.

The parole officer could not locate Manson. The twenty-five-year-old parolee, who had fathered at least two children while out of confinement, had left California. Manson had brought two of his whores to work a convention in Laredo, Texas. When one of the prostitutes was arrested and implicated Manson, he fled across the border to Mexico, where he said he took hallucinogenic mushrooms with Yaqui Indians. The *federales* picked Manson up at the request of American authorities, and in June 1960 he was returned to U.S. District Court in Los Angeles. His probation revoked, Manson was sent to the penitentiary at McNeil Island, Washington, to serve his ten-year sentence.

There, on the island prison in Puget Sound, Manson encountered much of the alternative thought that was beginning to percolate through society. Mysticism, Eastern philosophy, the occult, hypnotism, and other approaches attracted those unhappy with society's norms, including many convicts. Manson developed a respect for the Black Muslims, observing the way they used their beliefs to give them strength and unity.

At McNeil Island, Manson met Lanier Ramer, a bank robber who tutored him in Scientology, the religion invented by science fiction writer L. Ron Hubbard. Hubbard had mixed psychological theories, Eastern religious ideas, and assertiveness training into his new creed. Ramer taught Manson Scientology's argot, a compendium of philosophical and scientific-sounding terms that seemed to hint at great power. Manson soon was employing phrases such as "cease to exist" and "come to Now," giving him a vaguely spiritual reputation. He also adopted ideas and phrases gleaned from other sources, including the Bible, books on psychology and group therapy, and Robert A. Heinlein's 1961 science fiction novel *Stranger in a Strange Land*.

Heinlein's work concerned a young man, Valentine Michael Smith, born on Mars to human parents, but raised by Martians. Smith lands on an earth ruled by despotic institutions, and introduces a new philosophy based on free love and on a telepathic type of emotional communication called "grokking." The cult eventually turns violent and, it is revealed, stands against the precepts that originally attracted its followers. The jacket copy described *Stranger in a Strange Land* as Heinlein's effort "... to undermine the idea of sexual relations founded on *jealousy*, and to annoy the materialists and the politicians ... [Heinlein aimed] to examine every major axiom of Western culture ... and if possible—to make the antithesis of each axiom appear a possible and perhaps desirable thing— rather than unthinkable." [Italics in the original.]

Years later, Manson would name a son Valentine Michael Manson.

The convict's new enthusiasm carried over into other endeavors. Manson played basketball, softball, and a sport more appropriate for his short stature, croquet. He joined the prison's Self-Improvement Group and its Drama Club. He practiced his guitar regularly, wrote songs, and became a close follower of the Beatles, boasting that he could equal their success, if he had the right connections.

Manson befriended one of the nation's most notorious criminals, Alvin "Creepy" Karpis, who had been transferred to McNeil Island when the government closed its penitentiary at Alcatraz. In the 1930s, J. Edgar Hoover had helped build his reputation on the capture of Karpis, the sole survivor of the Ma Barker gang. Apparently, Manson didn't seek Karpis's advice on criminal techniques; he was interested in learning to play the steel guitar, another of the old gunman's skills. Manson told prison authorities he hoped to work as a musician upon his release.

In the mid 1960s, Manson was transferred back to Terminal, where he met Phil Kaufman, then imprisoned on a marijuana charge. Kaufman had connections to the entertainment industry, and later would become country singer Emmylou Harris's road manager. He was impressed with Manson's musical potential—he sang, Kaufman thought, "like Frankie Laine." Kaufman told Manson to contact his friend Gary Stromberg, a producer who worked in film and music at Universal Studios. Kaufman himself wrote to Stromberg, asking him to lend a hand to a talented musician with interesting ideas.

Manson's release came on March 21, 1967. As the hour of his freedom approached, Manson reflected. "You know what, man, I don't want to leave! I don't have a home out there! Why don't you just take me back inside?" he told the discharge officer.

The officer was amused.

"I'm serious, man! I mean it, I don't want to leave!"

Prison guards replied that they lacked authority to detain Manson further, and out he went.

Manson hitched a ride to Los Angeles with a truck driver, and stayed with him for a few days until the arrangement grew uncomfortable. Rather than track down his old associates from the 1950s, Manson called an ex-convict he knew in San Francisco, and was invited to visit. After telling his parole officer that a "relative" had arranged a job for him in the Bay Area, Manson obtained permission to leave Los Angeles for San Francisco.

Charles Manson had been incarcerated since the Eisenhower administration. The world he encountered upon his release, glimpsed dimly through prison walls, was like nothing he ever had seen. People—young people—up and down California, and especially in such centers of the counterculture as San Francisco and Berkeley, were willing to lend a hand or share their goods with him, based on a nod, a smile, and a pearl of beatific wisdom. He didn't have to steal; he just asked, and he received. "A stranger in a stranger land" is how Manson described his status. He felt right at home.

Manson was old for a youth culture that cautioned against trusting anyone over thirty. But as an ex-convict, he had authentic anti-Establishment credentials, and his facility with fashionable ideas and phrases made it easy for him to acclimate.

In the Haight-Ashbury district, Manson found that marijuana cigarettes and other drugs often were given away. He said he dropped acid for the first time at a Grateful Dead concert at the Avalon Ballroom, and his uninhibited dancing made him a center of attention. He collapsed, and awoke in an unfamiliar room filled with strangers, who nonetheless treated him like one of their own. Later, on a San Francisco street, he shared a sleeping bag, and carnal relations, with a young woman whose name he didn't know, who expected no money or drugs in return. A different world indeed. Manson let his hair grow, and took on a some-time beard.

While strumming his guitar in Berkeley, Manson met a dog, and then the dog's owner: Mary Theresa Brunner, a twenty-three-year-old librarian at the University of California, which had long been a center of youth rebellion. The state superintendent of public instruction, Max Rafferty, liked to say that the curriculum at Berkeley consisted of "sex, drugs, and treason."

Manson invited himself into Mary's apartment, and she let him stay on her couch. When Manson took in a sixteen-year-old lover, Mary became jealous, and brought Manson to her bed. Manson recalled that during sex, the two discussed the taboos with which Mary had been raised, and how they only had inhibited her life. The experience was good for both of them: Mary was grateful for the education and the pleasure she received from her new lover. Manson enjoyed the confidence and power that comes from having a devoted pupil. Authorities would later call Mary Brunner the first member of the "Manson Family."

Manson continued to explore his new world. He picked up tips playing guitar in local clubs. He hitchhiked as far as Sacramento and Reno, and found that the women of the day seemed open to sexual invitation and spiritual discussion in a way he never had imagined.

With a false promise to visit his mother in Washington State, Manson obtained his parole officer's permission to leave California. He and Mary headed up the Pacific Coast Highway to Seattle, to see ex-convict friends from McNeil Island.

He picked up hitchhikers, trading rides for drugs or food or cash or nothing at all. He passed communes and artist colonies, small towns and marijuana farms. When he found his old prison buddies, Manson realized that he now had little in common with them. He returned to Berkeley, left Mary to her job at the university, and headed to Los Angeles. Manson had to show his parole officer a means of support, so he decided to follow up finally on the phone numbers he had been given in the entertainment industry. His contact was out of town, so Manson had to kill time until his return. He visited his old turf in Hollywood, then headed down to Venice, which he had heard was a small sister city of the Haight-Ashbury. There he found a redheaded girl weeping on a bench. She followed him.

Part Two

White

Chapter 3

Princess

in Velvet

Lyn—for that was how she began to spell her name—saw that she was the educational, if not the intellectual, superior of Charlie. She spoke in phrases formed from years of study and struggle with poetry and drama; Charlie seemed to speak more plainly, yet with a wisdom that far transcended that of books. He could hardly read or write, he said, more boast than confession, yet from their different worlds he seemed to understand her fully. So few men understood her at all.

Lyn quickly learned that Charlie was never alone. She met his current companion, a pretty young girl who seemed to look on Charlie as her protector. He explained that he had found the girl in the Haight one day, shaken and scared as some big, mean dude tried to hustle her. The dude had taken her suitcase and wouldn't let her alone. Charlie ran up to the girl and, to her surprise, hugged her like they were old friends.

"Hey man," Charlie told the dude, "get your hands off my sister!" He snatched the suitcase and shepherded the girl away from her tormentor. She was a runaway who had come to the Haight looking to start on her own. Charlie got her some food and warned her that the Haight was filled with creeps who would take advantage of unsuspecting girls. He offered to let her move in with him. Since then, they had been together.

Lyn looked at Charlie and the girl, and started to understand what he was all about. He had said that the young people called him "the Gardener." Well, this gardener truly did "tend the young flowers" sprouting in the Haight, she thought, "while spiders crept in the alleys looking for fresh victims." How nice if the Gardener would show her around that legendary place, protect her as he conjured the magic of the Summer of Love.

For the moment, however, Charlie acted as though the Haight could wait. Charlie not only looked after lost souls, he also seemed to have some business in Hollywood, and was hoping to reach a producer who never seemed to be in. Lyn wasn't happy waiting around, and let the Gardener know she expected him to deliver. She kept asking Charlie when she could see all these wonderful places he was talking about, and after a few days, Charlie decided it was time to return to the Bay Area.

San Francisco overwhelmed Lyn. Unlike Los Angeles, with its deserted sidewalks and private, walled worlds, San Francisco was an endless outdoor carnival. Everywhere she looked, there were young people in the streets, in the parks— relaxed, stretched out, at peace. Everywhere they went, people passed each other flowers and kisses and clothing; and in the Haight, it seemed, everyone seemed to know Charlie. Especially young girls, who would run up to him to report their news. Several joyfully announced that they were at last pregnant. Charlie would smile and give them a friendly pat.

Others came up to the Gardener and said "they had found exactly what they wanted to do and were going off to do it," Lyn observed. No doubt, Charlie had helped these mixed-up kids figure themselves out. Good for them. "People who had lots of things to do never went with Charlie," Lyn noted.

But Lyn had been in enough places to know that the scene wasn't all magic. There were losers and hustlers all around, looking to cash in on all the young love in the street. Charlie said as much. He seemed to have some kind of plan in mind, though, to separate all the good that was going down from the bad that inevitably raced to catch up with it.

When they went to Charlie's place in Berkeley, Lyn met Mary, the bespectacled librarian who lived there with him. Blond and blue-eyed, not especially attractive, Mary had come from Wisconsin, and seemed a little uptight. She was totally into her dog, Lyn thought, and seemed upset that Charlie had been using her toothbrush.

Charlie turned that around on her, and Mary laughed when she realized how silly it was to consider a toothbrush something so personal. "It's your conditioning," Charlie would say, and Mary, and Lyn, too, would nod in understanding.

Charlie was willing to do anything to help free Lyn and Mary from this "conditioning." Once, he called them into the bathroom, where they discovered him on the toilet. He reached out to them, and though they were discomforted, they gave him their hands. Charlie pulled the girls down by his knees, and began to grunt—"loud, exaggerated, devilishly obnoxious grunts," Lyn later described them. "Grunts to twiddle our embarrassment—to the point of being embarrassed about being embarrassed!" The lesson sank in. Another door had opened: the bathroom door.

Mary, Lyn learned, had grown frustrated with her job at the university. She

Jess Bravin

had quit, and wanted to use her last paycheck to underwrite some adventures. The three of them piled into Charlie's 1948 Chevrolet—a man had given it to him, Charlie explained—and headed up to Mendocino County, redwood country. Charlie said he had passed through those parts before, and wanted to explore more deeply the things going on there.

Mendocino County lay along the Pacific Ocean, about one hundred miles north of San Francisco. According to one tradition, its name derived from that of the Spanish viceroy who sent explorer Juan Cabrillo to chart California's coast in 1542. In 1967, the mammoth, sparsely populated expanse of woods and streams was mainly known for *sinsemilla*, the potent strain of marijuana obtained from unpollinated female plants.

They brought more supplies than they would need: Fifty pounds of brown rice and twenty-five of soybeans, a trunkful of clothes, a three-component stereo system. They brought Mary's scruffy dog and her prized toothbrush, and plenty of records: the Beatles, of course, and the Doors and Ravi Shankar, and a favorite of Lyn's: Frank Zappa and the Mothers of Invention, "at their most inventiveness," Lyn later wrote.

They made their way to Caspar, a tiny, nearly deserted hamlet on the coast between the towns of Fort Bragg and Mendocino. The county's isolated settlements had developed their own subcultures over the decades, even their own dialect; in Boonville, about thirty miles inland, old-timers still spoke Boontling, a pidgin English that predated the days of Mark Twain and Ambrose Bierce.

A century back, Mendocino Town and Fort Bragg had been way stations for schooners traveling from California ports to the Pacific Northwest and British Columbia. Most who lived in Mendocino year-round saw themselves as rugged, independent souls. To the more effete denizens of San Francisco, which all Northern Californians called "the City," they were rednecks.

Mendocino County's vast forests and charming settlements had, lately, been attracting a different sort. Veterans of the counterculture who wearied of the intense scene in the Haight or Venice Beach had been moving in, setting up informal communes, reclaiming—or squatting in—rundown old houses, connecting with nature in the woods. Though some of Mendocino's young were intrigued by the newcomers, they were viewed suspiciously by the loggers and farmers, and by the sheriff. Lyn and her friends were three among hundreds of intruders in the county, and attracted no special attention.

They settled into a small cabin in Caspar, a few yards from the ocean, and shared meals and acid with their neighbors. Yet though they were five hundred miles from Redondo Beach, Lyn still carried with her the taboos of long ago.

When she wrote about her sexual initiation with Charles Manson, Lyn was direct.

"Take off your clothes," Charlie said.

They were alone, for the first time in many days. Mary had gone to the store by herself, something that had struck Lyn as unusual. Now she began to understand why.

Charlie took her hand, and ran his fingers up her arm, sliding over each delicate hair. It felt good.

"Well," he said again, "take off your clothes."

She was quiet a long time. Finally, she spoke: "I can't."

"Why can't you?"

"I don't know. I just can't," she said.

"I know better than that. There isn't anything you don't know, Lyn," he said, with a laugh. "Now, take off your clothes. I want to look at you."

Look at her? No one ever had wanted to *look* at her. Men had wanted her, sure. But before they did their business with her, they always turned out the lights. She thought of one boyfriend who went through the motions and then, just like in the movies, lit a cigarette and turned away. She felt she disgusted him. That feeling was nothing new. Dad had been the first to teach her she was ugly, long ago. She would not take off her clothes, even for Charlie.

"Has it been that bad an experience?" he asked. And in asking, he answered, and Lyn felt close to him. She laid her head on his shoulder wanting, all of a sudden, a father to hold her. A father who wouldn't say she was ugly.

His hands began to move up and down her body, touching each inch of her, feeling good, very good—so good, that Lyn grew scared.

She pulled away from him—and instantly, roughly, he pushed her down on the bed. She lay there, shocked, excited—for what she really wanted was for him to pursue her, even as she ran, for him to touch her, even as she withdrew, for him to rape her, even as she clenched her fists. Anything that might feel good, as long as she didn't have to take responsibility. But Charlie wouldn't let her get away with that.

"So you've been hurt and you've locked yourself up—you've got all your love tied up in the past, and associated with bad or sad experiences," he said. "You wanted your daddy to hit you, didn't you."

She had. She had wanted any attention she could get from her father.

"Well, not me," he said. "It's up to you when you want to get unlocked. Come on, Mary's waiting for us."

They found Mary outside, sitting on a log. She was crying.

Standing now between Lyn and Mary, Charlie shrugged. Then he laughed. "If it's not one, it's the other," he seemed to say. "Come here, you crazy ol' things," he beckoned in his Midwestern twang. He took them both in his arms and hugged them, and through their tears, Lyn and Mary began to laugh. They were safe, after all.

Walking through the woods, Charlie explained to Mary the scene that had unfolded within the cabin. "Can you imagine? This girl doesn't like to make love!" Charlie said, with intended irony.

Mary laughed, as if she had been there herself. As if she knew how scary it can seem on the other side of the door.

As the weeks passed, events and faces began to blend together, dropping their artificial divisions and revealing themselves as the *one* Charlie taught of. *When* things happened mattered less than *what* happened, and what happened mattered less than the very fact of happening. Dates on a calendar that once seemed to mean so much, meant nothing at all. There was no Redondo, no Vietnam. All that mattered was here. And Now.

Each day, Lyn became more aware of Charlie, who had seemed from the start so completely aware of her. He had nothing else to do, but to be aware of each tree and each branch and each leaf—and each soul.

"What's happened, see," he would say, "is me *not* adjusting to the 'free world.' I've made up my own world, in other words, I didn't and wouldn't adjust to society and their reality of things, you know, and I've come out, and set down, not getting in their race anymore."

Lyn had left their race long ago, yet only now was she realizing it. But he had gone much further.

"I'm still in solitary confinement, Lyn, and you know, I laugh there. I'm right at home. And brother—sister—when you're at home with yourself, you're at home anywhere."

When Lyn would crawl off to read a book, he would appear, and tell her its essence in a single phrase.

"But I just read that," she would eagerly say, and he would nod as if he had been inside her head, looking through her eyes, always reading a page beyond. And yet, he was practically illiterate. She found herself thinking he had special powers, even supernatural powers—but quickly stopped herself. She couldn't let herself think that. But she gave up reading books, pointless and frozen the moment they were printed—and tried to read Charlie instead.

For one who had spent so many years confined in a cell, he seemed to have an uncanny affinity for nature. He knew every dog and cat in the neighborhood, and often made time to meet with them. "A dog goes to somebody who loves it and takes care of it," Lyn observed. Watching the way Charlie could commune with the dogs, just get down on their level and reflect them, she realized that she never had seen animals as directly as he did. Compared to Charlie, Lyn thought, her experiences were vicarious, from books and words instead of reality. She wanted to experience things first-hand now, the way he did.

He could find lost trails and follow them to the hidden holes where wild animals lived, squirrels and groundhogs and things. Sometimes, instead of following the path, he would go over the branches and through the undertunnels and the thickets, and bring them to places that seemed as though they were waiting for them, all along.

Most of all, Charlie could relate to children. Unlike their parents, he treated the local kids seriously, asking them big questions and listening to their answers as if they knew more than he.

He seemed a man wholly unashamed. When he slipped out of key on his guitar, or stumbled across a chord that would make a trained musician wince, he recovered with a song even more wonderful than the one he had begun. Tripping into a minor key with a flatted melody, he ended up with a song that began, "There's no such thing as a mistake. . . ." And, he was showing her, there wasn't.

He danced wildly, and made funny faces and fell into accents when he felt like it, or for no reason at all. Lyn realized there was no point in trying to classify this man, or figure him out. The trick was to learn to accept him. She began to fall in love, where he already was.

One day, they were driving together when he stopped the car.

"Say *fuck*," he said.

Lyn wouldn't.

"Say *fuck!*" Charlie repeated. He seemed to grow angry. "Well, are you gonna say it or not? Now, say *fuck!*"

She focused her eyes away from him, hoping the torment would end.

"Say it," he repeated. She screwed up her face, defiant.

"Say it!" he yelled, outrageously angry. And now, so was she.

"Well, *fuck you!*" she screamed back.

His anger melted and he smiled at her. "Now, was that really so bad? Listen: *fuck-fuck-fuck-fuck-fuck-suck-suck-suck-fuck*—it's a good sound. It doesn't mean anything but what you want it to mean, Lyn. *Fuck's* a good thing. It's not dirty or bad."

Lyn began to laugh at herself. Her tongue, it seemed, had been freed. Charlie saw that the lesson had been learned, and he pulled the car back onto the road. As they drove, he continued the teaching.

"Say it again, Lyn," he said, and she did. *Fuck* came easily now, a word instead of a hang-up, a sound instead of a meaning.

"That's what the whole thing's about, honey," he explained. Then he added with a mock devilish laugh, "And I am the god of *fuck!*"

But when the time for sex came, Lyn thought, it wasn't just a fuck, like it had been with every other man. She wrote that, for the first time, she made love. Her account was explicit.

His hands covered her body, touching every inch, smoothing and massaging until her fear drained away. Like spiders, his fingers climbed and crawled into each fold and crevice of her body. He slid down between her legs, and licked and kissed, finding his way to an undiscovered part of her anatomy, "a tiny, hard supersensitive thing," she marveled, a part she didn't even know that she had. She knew it was supposed to be wrong. No man ever had gone down on her

Jess Bravin

before, and she never would have dared suggest it. But she always had wondered what it would feel like. Now she knew. She felt, she wrote, like a "princess wrapped in velvet."

Now he was atop her. She looked up at him, at his broad, content smile and his closed, dreamy eyes. She thought she was evaporating and that Charlie had filled himself where she had been. It felt good, she thought, so good, too good— *too good* and she convulsed in fear. He paused, sensing her dread.

"Allow yourself to experience pleasure, Lyn," Charlie counseled. "Allow yourself to let go. To give up. To give up, and love."

Give up. What was she giving up?

"You can go higher and higher if you only give up. What matters is if it feels good—does it?"

It did.

"The fact is," he said, "that if a man loves, he makes a woman feel like the most beautiful creature in the whole world. And if a woman loves, she can accept and feel all of his love, making one love, in one motion, of all feeling at once." She struggled to follow his teaching, torn between wants and fears she did not understand.

She gave up.

The next time, he brought Mary in to watch. Lyn was uncomfortable; she had never had sex before an audience. What would she look like? How would Mary react? Whenever she began to feel good under Charlie's touch, she found herself glancing at Mary. But Mary wasn't horrified or shocked at all. She simply looked back, her blue eyes peaceful, her smile wide.

"It's beautiful," Mary moaned.

Lyn felt at one with her, understanding the wonder of seeing something so exquisite, so amazing, yet hidden behind so many doors. On the floor by the bed, the three hugged, and wept, and laughed. Later, the favor was returned and Lyn got to watch Charlie make love to Mary, and then the two of them watched Charlie have sex with a third girl.

They touched each other, Lyn wrote, and gave up the inhibitions that kept them from loving. She would put flowers in her hair, and decorate Charlie's head with a crown of seashells that looked like horns. In a sheepskin vest, and with a flute he had learned to play, Charlie became Pan, and Lyn and Mary his nymphs. Stripping off their clothes, they would run and Charlie would chase, amid the woods and sometimes by the homes and campers near Caspar, a fairy tale come to life. When the park ranger came to investigate, the trio sneaked back home, laughing all the way. Who was crazy? The ranger thought it was the local housewives, reporting a fantasy.

————

SQUEAKY

With the money left over from Mary's paycheck, they bought an old, round, red trailer, set down right in the sand by the driftwood, beneath spectacular clay bluffs. The beach, Lyn gathered, was caught in a legal dispute over its ownership, and belonged to no one. And everyone. And itself. But for these weeks, it belonged to her.

With the red trailer as their base, Lyn and Mary and Charlie explored the woods and creeks east of the beach, across the Pacific Coast Highway. Even in the farthest reaches of the woods, she found, there were signs: "No Trespassing," "Private Property." Land that wasn't individually owned was held by the state or federal governments, posted and patrolled—or so the signs said. Every square inch was owned by something or someone, except her little private beach, for a little while.

Sometimes they slept in the woods, or in abandoned old houses that, fitting for a place called Caspar, seemed haunted with friendly ghosts. With no cars or tractors or compressors around, Lyn could hear the forest play its own symphony. Every moment was a revelation.

Charlie outstretched his hand, and a squirrel came forth to sniff him. Lyn watched as he stared at the squirrel, seeming to lock eyes, and minds, with him. But then he growled fiercely, and the squirrel fled.

"Why'd you do that, Charlie?" Lyn asked.

"For his own good," he said. "The next human that little feller came to smell might just as soon blow his head off. He was lucky he found me first."

Lyn nodded. She felt lucky, too.

After days of drinking water from a creek, the dulled liquid that spilled from the tap suddenly seemed quite foreign. And when they had meat for dinner, Charlie observed that they might as well be eating his arm as the flesh of a cow or a pig. "We're no different from them or them from us," Charlie said. Lyn quit eating meat.

But not all the folk of Mendocino seemed to appreciate Charlie's lessons. They would laugh at Charlie's stories, and dance to his songs, but behind his back they would grumble about the little man and his strange way. A lot of people, Lyn wrote, don't like themselves, *won't* like themselves. And if you don't like yourself, you can't like Charlie—because, of course, Charlie is the same as you.

The grumbling came because Lyn and Mary and Charlie were more than just a couple, Lyn realized, and folks were scared that some "old lady" might lose her "old man," or vice versa. These phony people would hug and kiss the threesome, say "sorry to see you go," but be happier than anything if they would. They were afraid. They hadn't given up.

One day at the trailer on the beach, the cold winds brought a heavy fog, and Lyn felt it was time to move south. Charlie agreed. They sold the trailer for five dollars—to a young couple that had just dropped out, a teacher and his wife who were living in a tent on the beach with their three kids. Now they had a

J e s s   B r a v i n

good, proper space for their family. Lyn kissed them good-bye, and off they went. Mary now was pregnant with Valentine Michael Manson.

Charlie had been hitchhiking once and was picked up by a fat man with a down attitude. He was dissatisfied with his life, his job, his family. But after he talked to Charlie, Lyn saw, this man had come to understand the meaning of birth, of karma, of death. The fat man was awfully grateful. He seemed to think of Charlie as a teacher, a healer, a Christ. So it was only natural that he brought Lyn and Mary to meet his friend, a former Congregational minister named Dean Morehouse, up in the Mendocino County town of Leggett.

Morehouse lived with a scornful old wife and a beautiful young daughter. Charlie and Morehouse had long talks and didn't quite agree, until after the preacher took LSD.

The days passed into weeks, and Mrs. Morehouse began to grow irritable at the love unfolding in her house, dismissing Lyn and Mary and Charlie as a bunch of long-haired freaks. The wife couldn't stand it, and went off to her sister's place. Lyn was glad to see her go, because she was a bad influence on her daughter, Ruth Ann.

Lyn thought Ruth had a face like a fawn, and long limbs that grew each day. She was only fifteen, but she seemed instinctively to know what mattered, showing Lyn to all the secret pockets of the woods near the house. Ruth thought that the older girls were "supersweet," that Lyn always was "twinkly and happy." They gave Ruth a jewelry box, and a record player and a Donovan album to play on it.

As Lyn told the story, Dean Morehouse seemed to know it was right for his wife to leave. One night, Lyn and Mary sat him down, just to talk, and listened as he explained how free he felt, having given up the lies he had been preaching for so many years, rejuvenated now by love, and by LSD. Now, he said, he was living with God, instead of just talking about him.

But where, Morehouse wanted to know, was his daughter? It was getting late, and Ruth should be home. And where was Charlie? He began to pace the room.

Lyn smiled and assured Morehouse that all was perfect. He must know inside, she thought, that his beautiful daughter was being made love to outdoors, even as he couldn't quite admit it. He must know that it was right for Charlie to do it, for no one could reflect Ruth's innocence as purely as he. Morehouse kissed Lyn and went to sleep.

Ruth went with the group—the family, really—back to Mendocino, where the cops, on orders from the mother, seized her as a runaway. In their grim voices, they told Ruth she had to go with them, back to her mother. Charlie looked at Ruth. "You don't have to go," he said. Charlie was arrested on July 28, 1967, for interfering with police business, and given a thirty-day suspended sentence. He put down his occupation as "minister," and signed his name not as Charles Milles Manson, but Charles Willis Manson, *Charles' Will Is Man's Son.*

They climbed an old Mendo logging road, heading up to the top of a redwood mountain. It was hot, Lyn later wrote, and she no longer wanted to climb. Neither did Mary. They were exhausted, and just didn't want to go on. Charlie stopped and looked back at Lyn, his eyes reflecting her own annoyance, her own emptiness. She didn't like what she saw, and turned away, pouting.

"I don't care," he said. "How many years must I sit down to be miserable with you?"

Lyn didn't know.

"Well," he continued, "when you are ready to give up your misery, all your mother's heavy thoughts, and her pains, and her dissatisfactions, and her judgments of herself—you'll find me."

He continued up the trail. She waited. And then the acid kicked in. Charlie appeared through the trees. He was not climbing the mountain, he *was* the mountain, "the trees, the sod, the leaf beds, the holds and mounds, the prickles and ferns and spiders," she later wrote. "He had become the wide-eyed deer. He looked to Man, and through those eyes, saw the fear. He looked on the city far below . . . a constant rumble of discontent . . . tramping up to the most hidden places to seek him—the animal."

"To feel all at once," Lyn later reflected, "is to experience death. To give up to the feeling is to fall through . . . into birth."

She watched the pictures move in Charlie's mind. A million years of Man, his guilts and burdens and struggles, cascaded through Charlie and into Lyn. She marveled as she saw him confront this knowledge, this presence, by not confronting it at all, by giving up. Lyn sensed that it was a new force that now inhabited Charlie, moving without a sound "like a changing wind, never two motions the same. And it could have no name, but all names, and all faces"— like the Hindu picture she once had seen, of a god going through an infinite number of changes, of evolutions, of incarnations all at once.

Eventually, Charlie bedded down in a pile of leaves. It was night now, and cold, and scary and Lyn and Mary wanted to go, but they would never leave without him. They lay down beside him, and as the shadows fell they started to cry, and he drew them near, and said something funny to make them laugh— something the old "Charlie," the pre-transcendent Charlie might have said. Lyn smiled. And without a word, he agreed to come down off the mountain.

Building the Family

Charlie had traded Dean Morehouse's piano for a 1961 Volkswagen microbus, which Mary had decorated all cozy and freaky and ready for love. They started to travel California, and made an impression wherever they went. People in the Haight, and any place else they stopped long enough to get a reputation, called them "Charlie's Girls."

They visited Santa Barbara, and then went down to Manhattan Beach, just north of Redondo. Lyn knew her way around the South Bay, and helped Charlie find the place where one of his old jail buddies was staying. There, they ran into Katie—or Patricia Krenwinkel, as she was then known.

Katie had gone to Westchester High just a year ahead of Lyn, even had the same English teacher, but the two hadn't known each other in school. Katie had left at the end of her sophomore year and gone to Alabama, where her mother put her in a religious school. That hadn't been Katie's scene, and she returned to Los Angeles, where she stayed with her sister, Charlene, who had dropped out. But Charlene was a heroin addict, and that scene wasn't right for Katie either. So Katie was just hanging out, trying to decide what to do, when Lyn and her friends showed up.

Charlie played his guitar and sang, and Lyn could see that Katie really got into it—she was putting herself out there, despite her fear. Lyn sang, although she knew she couldn't sing as freely as Charlie, and even got Katie to join in a little bit. When they found out how much they had in common, Lyn took Katie for a walk on the beach.

Katie didn't much like herself. In her mind, she was clumsy and not very pretty, and, worst of all, covered with hair in all the wrong places. Calling it an "endocrine problem," as the doctors might, didn't make it any better. Nobody could love Katie because she didn't love herself.

Lyn knew what that was like, and Katie could tell. She could sense the freedom Lyn had found, just living and being, instead of worrying and doing. Lyn's life on the road sure sounded better than Katie's day job—she was a file clerk at an insurance company. By the end of their walk, after they had laughed and composed a poem together, Katie knew what she wanted to do.

"I'm going," she said.

But there were some problems. Katie said her sister wouldn't like it, and it would be hard to make her understand. Lyn knew it wasn't a problem at all. If it was impossible to explain it to Charlene, she told Katie, why try?

Katie understood. When Lyn said, "Well, we will leave the town. We will all just go," Katie knew that Lyn was right. Why try to solve a problem that can't be solved? Instead, just don't have the problem.

Lyn applied the same logic to Katie's other problems, like her job and her parents. No need to give notice, or file a change of address. Just go with what you have, Lyn said. Katie didn't have much with her, just her clothes, her purse, her father's Chevron charge card.

"The more you get caught up tying up loose ends, the more loose ends there are," Lyn said. Charlene put up a fuss, but it didn't matter. Katie was free.

Lyn and Katie and Mary all traveled with Charlie, sleeping four across in the Volkswagen bus, going through changes. Gone were clocks and calendars, the days of the week and the months of the year. At first the girls fought and squabbled like kids on a camping trip, over who would have the blanket, over who would get to drive. They were struggling, without even knowing it, to get over their hang-ups, their ideas, which all came down to the lie that each was supposed to have only one man.

"Charlie is a man," Lyn later testified, "who would be at our feet in his love, but would not let us step on him." Exactly what she needed.

As they drove up and down the state, Charlie would be their teacher and their pupil, their lover and their father.

"Well, now, that guy over there," he would say, "he looks like he is doing this, but you know he is thinking about this." Or, "He is saying that to you, but, you know, check out what he really means."

"We were riding on the wind," she said. Soaring higher and higher.

Visiting some of Charlie's prison chums, going into restaurants or parties, playing music on street corners, people always took note—the small smiling man with his three young women. They would pick up people and let them off, and more and more girls would want to stay with them. They went up to San Francisco, and beyond to Oregon, to Nevada, where Charlie played the casinos and visited a friend at a whorehouse. They went to Seattle—Charlie, among other things, was trying to locate his mother, who had moved to Washington State. It was kind of strange that Charlie was so interested in finding his mom, his mom who found herself pregnant without ever knowing the father. Still, there was a great man who came from the same circumstance, Lyn knew. A man who traveled up and down his land, gathering believers, outcast from the Establishment. A man who fell afoul of the law, and paid the price. A man who taught nothing but love.

They met all kinds of people along the way, including Bruce Davis, a burly twenty-five-year-old from Louisiana who had dropped out and, when he met Charlie, joined them. Bruce knew something about Scientology. He also was an ex-convict and he and Charlie hit it right off. Now there were two men in the van.

When they got to Sacramento, they had outgrown their Volkswagen, and swapped it for a big yellow school bus. Maybe it wasn't an even exchange, but the owner seemed to ease up when Charlie took him aside and showed him how filled with love the girls were. A few extra dollars closed the deal.

The bus meant a lot to Charlie; trading it for the VW, he said, "was like going from a one-room cabin to a mansion." He composed a story about the bus that explained its mystical significance, how the bus contained the souls of children who drowned when it plunged into a river, how the bus could never be owned—and, by signing the certificate of title and stashing it in the glove compartment, how the bus owned itself.

In *The Garbage People*, a 1971 book about the Family, a character who resembles Lyn wrote poems about life on the bus.

> ...The nights reveal the whole universe in motion
>   before your eyes
> The magic of infinite pictures in multicolored
>   dots

The magic of the bus was not always evident to the police, however. They frequently cited it for violating the California Vehicle Code, which held that only buses exclusively used to transport pupils could be yellow. The people in the bus were students, but it was no use to argue; the police wouldn't even come in for coffee and cookies.

To Lyn, the police seemed envious of what Charlie had going. They'd like to do what he's doing, *but* they had their obligations and restrictions. Lyn saw it in their faces. They were so envious. They hated Charlie—and they didn't even know why. "We showed them how good it was *not* to be part of the Establishment," Lyn wrote. They couldn't swallow that.

With the help of some bikers, they painted the bus in splashes of color, but the slogans, like "Fuck the Man," did little to discourage police interference. They decided, then, to paint the bus completely black. Inside, they took out seats to fashion a sleeping area with mattresses and pillows, and started hanging tapestries and painting the walls to make themselves at home, to better reflect themselves, especially when they dropped acid. They kept the inside so dark that the rear of the bus wasn't visible from the front. To Lyn, "the bed rolled off into infinity." Everything became a game, even the most mundane communications grew into florid songs. Lyn turned the phrase "Pass the salt" into an operatic aria. The numbers on the bus grew and grew—and certainly would grow some more, as Mary became ever more pregnant.

The black bus entered Las Vegas one night and immediately was stopped by four patrol cars. As the group lined up to present their IDs to the police, Charlie laughed and said to the lieutenant, "We've only been here two minutes."

"You've been here seven and a half minutes exactly," the lieutenant growled. He informed Charlie that he would have to register as a felon, or leave. They left Las Vegas.

Later, as they drove down a Nevada desert road, Lyn spied in the distance a group of small creatures in red suits. As the bus approached, the red creatures seemed to transform from possible extraterrestrials to a parachute battalion—and then to what they really were, a SWAT team. Bearing high-powered rifles, the police forced the bus to stop by blocking its path with their jeeps. They demanded that the passengers leave the bus, separated them into small groups, and ordered them to keep still with their hands in the air.

"A most unusual search," Lyn observed, "much too frantic to be our usual rousters—the narcotics squad. What in the hell would they want with a bunch of raggedy gypsies in the middle of the desert?"

The police turned the bus inside out, and ran ID checks on all the passengers. As the last officer left the bus, Lyn overheard him say, "No, there's no gun...." The Family was then released to continue on its way. The police gruffly apologized for the inconvenience. They explained that they had mistaken the Family for a band of murderers they were searching for.

The bus returned to California and traveled the coast, "a living advertisement for dropping out, a devilish direct route into the Void," wrote Lyn.

Back in the Bay Area, Lyn saw, the scene was growing uglier. Kids were in the streets, begging for money or food, cut off by their parents, desperate to get out of a life that was beating them down, and into another that would—well, any other life would do. At a big brown house in the Haight, they got loaded and played music and met a girl named Susan Atkins, nineteen years old. She floated in from the kitchen when Charlie sang, as if "The Shadow of Your Smile" had been written just for her. She didn't say much. To Lyn, she was just a whole lot of big eyes.

After she made love with Charlie, Susan—who would become Patty Sue, and then Sadie Mae Glutz—and Lyn got to talking. They had both taken different trips to get to the same place. Sadie's home had fallen apart when she barely was a teenager, after her mother died. She later quit school, left her home in San Jose, and lived on the sly up and down the coast—working as a waitress and in burlesque clubs, traveling with men who were armed robbers and car thieves. Arrested in Oregon while carrying a pistol, she brazenly told the cop she would have shot him if he hadn't drawn first. Her association with the criminals landed her a three-month jail term.

She had made her way down to San Francisco when she got out, and was crashing with dope dealers and working as a topless dancer. San Francisco offered special opportunities. Once, she had played the part of a vampire in a Black Mass staged at a nightclub by Anton LaVey, the occult entrepreneur who ran the Church of Satan. LaVey later served as a technical adviser on Roman Polanski's film, *Rosemary's Baby*.

Sadie lived in the heart of the Haight. Her house stood at the corner of Lyon and Oak streets, by the Panhandle of Golden Gate Park. From the porch, Sadie could hear her neighbor, Janis Joplin, when she sang, and when she partied. Janis partied hard.

Sadie, Lyn quickly saw, was not the introspective type. She was wild, practically out of control. Good. They had a lot to teach each other. But first, they had to pay attention to Charlie.

"The thing we must understand," he explained, "is that the past is over. There is no past. It is dead—severed. In fact, there is no time. Get rid of your watches. You don't need them. There is no time."

Sadie had finally found what she had been looking for. When Charlie said they were going to Los Angeles, Sadie came, too. Her parole officer didn't seem too excited about Sadie's new life, but why would he?

Charlie's parole officer, however, was more understanding. He agreed to transfer parole supervision back to Los Angeles, because Charlie had some encouraging news from Hollywood. Phil Kaufman's producer friend at Universal, Gary Stromberg, wanted to see him. The black bus headed south, stopping in San Jose to visit Ruth Morehouse and to make arrangements for her to join the group after they got down to Los Angeles.

On the bus, on acid, they could watch as Charlie made his lessons manifest. He would unlock the pictures hidden in their minds, and spread them out for everyone to see. "It was like living in Group Therapy *all the time*," as Lyn later described it.

Once, Charlie commanded a biker traveling along with them to die, then restored him to life after he all but decomposed before their eyes. The point was not physical death—something that was just an illusion—but ego death, surrendering the lie that boundaries lay between individuals and their earth, between humans and animals, between Lyn and Charlie. "You must die to self. You must die. You must become one," Charlie instructed. "All is one, all is one, all is one."

Sadie had been such the adventurer, a pretty, pouty girl with a figure that knocked guys out. But Lyn, who used to be so plain but now was radiant, was the favorite. Sadie would have to learn not to be jealous while Lyn and Charlie made love. All the time they were in San Francisco, Charlie only made love to Sadie three times.

As the group grew, Charlie's command of the world seemed to grow as well. He could communicate with anyone, not just girls but cops and old drunks and everybody. They came across a crazy man once who was babbling on and on about the grass, just talking what seemed to be nonsense. "And yesterday I was in Bakersfield in 1941," was the sort of thing he would say. Charlie spoke to him in the exact same terms, just as if it were the most natural thing in the world. The man then opened up, and talked about how lonely he was, about his troubles and his life—and it made sense. It was as if Charlie had cured him.

No, Charlie told Lyn, he hadn't cured the man. Charlie couldn't cure anybody if he didn't want to be cured. He just had helped the man understand that he wanted to be cured. Just as he had helped so many others. And if his music could get out, the numbers of those he could reach would be . . . unquantifiable.

They had been living on the beach under a bridge—"like trolls," Lyn said. Then Charlie met a lady in San Francisco who was into Satanism, and she gave them a place in Los Angeles they could stay. It was a house in Topanga, an area just outside the Los Angeles city limit near Malibu. A lush, untamed canyon, Topanga was filled with seekers and dropouts and a few straights who found the rustic precinct an antidote to work in the city.

It was an old, two-story house that seemed to have slid off its foundation, dominated by a giant twisting stairway. Quickly, they dubbed the place "the Spiral Staircase House." All sorts of folks seemed to crash there, music was always playing, people were tripping, having sex, exploring religious ideas like the occult.

The black bus, filled with about a dozen young women, was instantly welcomed. Sadie could show off her exotic dancing, Charlie always had a chorus around to join in song. They stayed in the bus, or on the adjacent beach, or anywhere nearby.

A guy named Zeb told them that there was good food to be had in the garbage bins kept behind the supermarkets; it was a tip that would feed the Family from then on. At first Lyn would only take the pickings from the top of the bins, but soon, as she saw the promise of buried treasures, she dived in. There were tomatoes between her toes, apples, pears, cucumbers, cheese, eggs—a stew of perishables all over her. "Wow," she thought. "It's like being in a giant salad.... You could feed the world, you really could, with America's garbage."

Not everybody appreciated their salvage work. Lyn watched as an irate produce man stomped over and dumped a box of lettuce over the head of one of her friends. "Why don't you get a job, like the rest of us," he sneered. His irritation, his palpable dissatisfaction, was the answer to his own question, Lyn thought.

One day Lyn, along with Charlie, Bruce, and a few other girls, got in one of the cars to take a ride to the beach. When Charlie saw a hitchhiker along the side of the road, he immediately pulled over.

"Good afternoon," Charlie said, adopting a British accent. "This is Master Bruce, Princess Rooptee-Doo, Countess Diddy-Dad, and, uh, Lady Whatshername. You may call me Charles. I'm the chauffeur. Where did you wish to be taken, sir?"

The hitchhiker said he was just going over the hill. He hopped in the backseat smiling, but as Charlie continued playacting, he grew uncomfortable. Charlie threw away his imaginary chauffeur's cap and dropped the British accent.

"Tell you what," Charlie said, peering at the man in the rearview mirror. "I'll trade you all the money I got in my pocket for all the money you got in yours."

The hitchhiker looked skeptical.

"It could be a very good trade for you," Charlie went on.

The hitchhiker checked his own pocket, felt his cash, and hesitated. "Naw, I don't think so."

"Are you sure, now?" Charlie asked. "You'd better be sure. How do you know I don't have a thousand dollars in my pocket?"

But the hitchhiker had made up his mind. "Naw, I can't do it."

Charlie looked amazed. "You sure?"

"Yeh, I'm sure." The hitchhiker smiled.

"Well, how much you got?" Charlie asked. The hitchhiker pulled out his cash and counted aloud some three dollars and fifty-seven cents.

Charlie laughed. "Oh man, you couldn't give that up?" He pulled out a roll of fifty twenty-dollar bills and raised it up so the hitchhiker could see it.

"A thousand," Charlie said simply. One of the girls had gotten the money from her family earlier in the week and given it to Charlie. He had been carrying it around in his front pocket, Lyn recalled, looking for ways to give it away.

The hitchhiker seemed stunned. "You were really going to give it away?"

"Sure," Charlie said, softening his voice, "if you hadn't been so afraid of losing your change. This stuff's not important. There's no security in it. The security's in you. See, as long as you hang on to that, that's all you got."

Lyn thought about the episode a lot. To people like the hitchhiker, "there's no explaining. They will die clutching their high school rings, with a bank-full of money and yesterday's papers stashed in the garage—still unsatisfied. They will wonder why their life was unfulfilled, and hope to go to heaven, when they could have made heaven right here, would that they feel the pleasure of giving."

They made a lot of interesting friends around this time, like Bobby (Robert Kenneth) Beausoleil, a boyishly handsome actor and musician with a Mephistophelean beard. He was "so good-looking," Charlie would say, "it makes fear come to you." They came to call him Cupid sometimes, after a part he had played in a picture called *Mondo Hollywood.*

Bobby had a lot in common with Charlie. He had studied alternative religions, and had been cast in the title role of *Lucifer Rising,* produced by San Francisco's eccentric filmmaker, Kenneth Anger.

Even more impressive to Lyn, Bobby said he sometimes jammed with Frank Zappa and the Mothers of Invention—though Zappa only let him sing harmony on some of the oldies they did. Charlie, for his part, seemed to respect Bobby because he too had acquired a family of sorts—young women liked Bobby's aura, and traveled with him as he made his way between California's hot spots. Bobby was staying nearby, in the home of a music teacher and UCLA graduate student named Gary Hinman. Perhaps Bobby, who was quite talented, might jam with Charlie.

But there was business to be done, and they couldn't spend all their time crashing in Topanga. When a date was set, Charlie and Lyn headed east on the Ventura Freeway to reach Universal City, the sprawling complex that housed Universal Pictures, MCA Records, and countless other entertainment ventures.

Charlie had trimmed his mustache and dressed up neatly in a sport shirt and jeans for the meeting. Lyn led the girls in scrubbing the bus clean; it was important, they knew, to make a good impression on the people at Universal.

Gary Stromberg and his partner, Corey Allen, occupied a tiny second-story office that overlooked a parking lot. Clearly, they were not the most important people in Universal City, but perhaps they could open some doors. This possibility seemed especially promising when it turned out that Gary, with a background in promotions, produced not only music but movies as well.

Corey also seemed interesting. He had dropped out of the UCLA law school after winning the part of Buzz in *Rebel Without a Cause*—Natalie Wood's boyfriend, best known for driving his car off a cliff after challenging James Dean to a game of chicken. Exactly Charlie's age, thirty-three, Corey somehow seemed older, and had moved from acting to directing.

Neither Gary nor Corey considered himself a writer foremost; nevertheless they had been hired as a writing team to sift potential movies out of what seemed to be thousands of scripts and story ideas. The idea they happened to be pondering when Charlie and Lyn arrived involved the Second Coming of Christ. Specifically, they envisioned Jesus returning as a black man in the American South—a South wrenched by segregation and violence over civil rights.

"What do you think of that?" they asked Charlie.

Charlie, Lyn saw, thought a lot of it. Charlie knew plenty about the problems of blacks, having lived so long in prison. Much of Charlie's speech, Lyn recognized, was derived from black slang picked up from the prison yards. Charlie was raised in the penitentiary; the black man, she would later testify, was Charlie's father.

More than that, in prison and on the road, through acid and peyote as well as hard thought, Charlie had been reflecting on Jesus. He had distilled Jesus' teaching down to one word.

"Submission," Charlie said.

Right there he demonstrated what he meant. "Lyn, come here and kiss my feet," he said. She dropped to her knees and kissed his feet. And then she sat down.

"Now," he said to her, "I will kiss yours."

The Hollywood writers were moved. Gary marveled at how open and trusting Lyn and Charlie were. Corey was even more impressed. He had been developing his own theory of Jesus' teaching, which was remarkably similar to Charlie's— "surrender," he called it, rather than "submission." But the point was the same. True surrender, true submission, Corey and Charlie agreed, wasn't about dominance. If everyone surrenders, if everyone submits, no one can dominate.

To whom, or to what, were they submitting? Charlie and Corey agreed: Love.

Charlie suggested that he might be able to help the writers develop their concept further, and they assented to have him join in their story meetings. Also, Charlie, asked, could he and the girls stay at Corey's house?

Corey ran an acting workshop in an East Hollywood loft, above a grocery story on Western Avenue near Santa Monica Boulevard.

"I guess you could stay there——" Corey offered. Charlie immediately accepted.

"But, Charlie," Corey continued as he handed over the key, "no smoking or funny stuff, that could cost me my business license. Just leave the place the way you found it."

"You got it," Charlie said.

That evening, Corey Allen told his live-in girlfriend, Kim, about the fascinating man he had met. Corey recounted the story of the ex-convict who had come out of Terminal Island so full of love, who sat on the couch with his young female pupils—disciples, really, Corey said—who not only agreed with his thoughts on Jesus but could expand on them in ways Corey hadn't expected.

"It was fun, Kim," Corey said. "You should hear this guy."

Kim was open to the idea. But her attitude changed when she found out Charlie and his Family were staying at Corey's acting studio.

"If he's not out of there tomorrow morning, I'm out of this house," she said.

"Wait a minute, hold on a second," Corey said, startled that Kim would react so poorly to his new friend. "Don't give me ultimatums about somebody you don't even know. You haven't even met this guy!"

"I don't care," said Kim. "It's him or me. Take your pick."

"I don't like being challenged like this," Corey said. But he picked Kim. The next morning, he went to the loft and up the back stairs, finding the key exactly where Charlie said it would be. Neither Charlie nor Lyn nor anyone else was there, and not a thing was missing or out of place. When Charlie and Lyn next came to Universal, Corey explained that he couldn't let them stay at the loft anymore. Charlie accepted the news without a protest. He came by at least a half-dozen more times to help the writers with the project, which had the working title *Black Jesus*.

Charlie later told people about his time at Universal, saying he had parked in Cary Grant's space on the lot, and that he had met Peter Falk and been invited to parties and orgies with various stars and producers.

Gary Stromberg arranged for recording sessions where demo tapes were made of Charlie's songs. Although no agreements were signed for Charlie's music or for his help on *Black Jesus*, things seemed to flow in a natural, almost inevitable way.

Charlie was not interested in a nine-to-five job, however. He had responsibilities, a growing family of children who needed his attention. Though they made their base in Topanga and on the nearby beaches of Malibu, they continued to roam, heading to the Mojave Desert, across the southern United States to Arizona and New Mexico, getting as far as Mississippi and Alabama so Katie could visit her mother.

"We just kept looking, for a place where we could get away from the confusion . . . a spot to lie down," Lyn later reflected.

Charlie continued to educate his children with parables "When I was young," he said, "my window was wide open, and then someone came along and threw a pie in my face, and laughed. Then someone came along and threw another pie, and another, and pretty soon I looked to see them coming, and they all had pies, so I shut my window . . . I just leave my window shut and forget them, just watch them go by with their pies . . . and pretty soon I start thinking . . . 'Well, what's so bad about getting a pie in the face?' It's no fun havin' your window shut, so I open my window . . . and the next time I get a pie in the face, I just groove on the pie . . . and it's good!"

"We got lots of pies in the face—lots of them. But it was always okay," Lyn remembered. On one occasion, the police hauled the entire busload into the station, "to train the rookie cops. We spent all night being processed and reprocessed through sets and sets of paperwork crumpling in the wastebasket. Lots of pies. . . ."

They called their journeys a magical mystery tour, after the Beatles album of that name, which was released in November 1967. Paul McCartney, it was said, had conceived the title after hearing of the Merry Pranksters, the band of psychedelic adventurers who traveled across the country in a converted school bus.

The Pranksters sounded just like Charlie's Family, with a few notable distinctions. Instead of an ex-convict, their leader was Ken Kesey, the author of *One Flew Over the Cuckoo's Nest* and an old friend of Jack Kerouac. Another difference was the way they complied with the school bus color regulations. The Pranksters had painted their vehicle a polychromatic melange, instead of the Family's basic black.

While they were in Los Angeles, Lyn went to visit some of her old friends. Down in Redondo Beach, she paid a call on Randy Hammonds, her high school classmate, who since had married Christy Curtis. With his new responsibilities, and his friends all off at college or in the Army, Randy didn't get to go out much. So when Lyn asked him to give her a lift to visit her grandmother in Seal Beach, he was eager to oblige.

Blasting the radio, driving with the windows down, it was like old times. Except that, perhaps for the first time, Lyn was happy.

She told him she was with a new group, traveling around, having adventures one could never imagine in Redondo. Apart from the frequent hassles from the police, who seemed to take special pleasure in detaining the group—Lyn's most recent arrest was in Redwood City, for vehicle theft—nothing could be better. "It's a beautiful scene, Randy. We have LSD parties all the time," Lyn said. "You've got to come over and try it."

They arrived at Leisure World, a sprawling retirement community in Seal Beach, just over the Orange County line. The complex, its entrance marked by a giant framework globe, was on a street called Golden Rain.

Lyn's scene sounded like a lot of fun, but Randy declined the chance to visit. Working full time as a carpenter, supporting his young wife, helping his father cope with the death of Randy's mother, Mabel, he couldn't start flying off on acid trips. Lyn never called on him again.

She also stopped in to see Nora Lynn Stevens, her old friend from the Lariats. Nora was still living in Playa del Rey, near Westchester. The two women had a lot in common: both had recently gone through changes, and saw their lives unfolding in exciting new directions. Their lifestyles had clearly diverged. Nora, rather against the tide, had grown more conservative over the years, didn't take drugs, and found herself most at home in the conformist environs of USC. Lyn, clearly, was on the cutting edge of the youth culture, eagerly committed to finding what lay beyond conventional morality. But more important than their differences were their years in common; they still could really communicate with each other.

Nora admired the poetic depths she long had seen in her childhood friend. Lyn mentioned that she had attended El Camino Junior College, and hadn't ruled out the possibility of going back. They talked about Thoreau's Walden Pond, about the latest changes in Bob Dylan's music, and about the new group of friends Lyn had found. Their leader—or teacher, really—"was a *man*," Lyn said, stressing the word to set him apart from ordinary adult males. "He really has his act together."

Listening to Lyn talk about her new friends, and the adventures they had experienced, Nora thought to herself, "That sounds great!" Lynny was doing just fine. When all this roaming is over, Nora figured, her old friend will make a marvelously hip college professor.

The most exciting news Nora had was of her new boyfriend, a fellow USC student named Charles.

"What a coincidence!" Lyn exclaimed. "My boyfriend's named Charles, too."

Nora made a mental note to invite Lyn—and Lyn's Charles—to her wedding the following summer.

Most of Lyn's old classmates didn't seem too interested in meeting her new family, but more and more kids were getting on the black bus. In Malibu, it was easy to run into the children of celebrities. Angela Lansbury's daughter, Deirdre, was one of the group that traveled on the bus, and even got a note from her mom the actress saying it was okay.

Didi Lansbury brought Brenda to the family. Hazel-eyed Brenda—who then went by her given name of Nancy Pitman—had a lot in common with Lyn. Brenda's father also was an aeronautical engineer; he designed guidance control systems for missiles. The very same day she met Charlie, Brenda said, her parents had kicked her out.

Had she been having a problem with her parents?

No, Brenda said, they had a problem with her. Now, she had no money, no place to go, just a tiny bag of stuff. The black bus, filled with pillows and candy— or "zuzus," as Charlie called sweets—looked like a good place to be.

"You can stay here if you would like to, you know," Lyn and Katie and the others all said. So Brenda did. She would be the one who first called the group "the Family."

Watching the Family grow, thinking about who was joining, and what they were leaving, Lyn put her thoughts down on paper.

She described the life in which she and the other Family members once led . . . "separate houses with separate doors, in which separate people lived separate lives . . ." Those lives consisted of "listening to the tick of the clock, the latch of lock, the zoom and honk in waves of city . . . and if we were good kids or not and remember to tattle if someone is not, our thoughts pulling and pushing us across our mothers' minds—the struggle, the worry, the negative. We'd had it. We'd had all the money and clothes and TV and canopy beds to match the walls, and artichokes, steaks, wines, social gatherings and get-togethers where nobody touched each other unless they were good and drunk, where everyone talked at once, and the words were the same data like, 'Did you know,' and 'I think.'

"We'd had it, our whole lives . . . success. And yet, not one bit of peace," Lyn concluded. "We knew there must be something else." So, they had "to get away from those doors," Lyn explained "and find something exciting, and do something that felt good . . ."

Valentine Michael Manson, Mary and Charlie's child, was born on April 1, 1968. They also called him Pooh Bear, and Sunstone Hawk, because he was born at dawn, as the sun was just rising, as a hawk flew over the house. They decided they all would raise him together, no one person being mother or father.

The group grew. Sandra Good, a stockbroker's daughter from San Diego, joined the Family. She was twenty-five, a little older than most of the girls, but it wasn't about age, anyway. She had been living in San Francisco, and was visiting Los Angeles when a friend brought her by the Family's encampment. She acted a little haughty at first. With her earrings and makeup Sandra looked out of place among the unadorned women. Slowly, encouraged by the women, Sandra stripped off her makeup and her jewelry, gave away her glasses, and undid the band that tied her hair. After she and Charlie made love, he took her case of birth control pills and crushed them under his foot. She had joined the Family.

Sandra was a sensitive girl, and always would remain a little high-strung, sometimes getting into tantrums or fits. Once, when they were traveling on the bus, Sandy was sitting by herself sulking while the rest of the group all sang. Charlie reached over and pulled her to the center of the circle. He looked her in the eye and said, without a trace of humor, that if she didn't sing, he'd cut

Jess Bravin

off her nose. "She began to sing," Lyn remembered, "with fear—in the most beautiful high vibrato that got stronger by the note."

"Sure," Charlie said, in answer to her unspoken thoughts. "Sure, she been sittin' over there hiding in a corner, holding back." Lyn looked at Sandy: her face was so pretty, all red between the freckles, and she looked so happy. Charlie hugged Sandy, tweaked her nose, and said that she could keep it—for now. At least as long as she kept singing.

Paul Watkins came to the Topanga house looking for a friend who had since moved away. He was greeted at the door by Brenda and Snake.

They were naked. He had a French horn. When Charlie asked, "Won't you stay and make music with us?" Paul—Little Paul, they would call him—knew he had found the right place. Charlie nodded at Lyn. Instantly, she ran to fetch Paul a glass of club soda.

They sang songs, ones Charlie just made up on the spot, and ones that everyone already knew the words to, such as:

Leave your old life far behind you
> You can be what you want to be
> Just don't let your mama find you.

Later on, they all joined hands, and then they made love.

Things were happening very quickly now. Some of the girls met Dennis Wilson, the drummer in the Beach Boys, while hitchhiking. Shortly afterward, the Family moved into his Spanish Colonial Revival mansion on Sunset Boulevard in Pacific Palisades, a house once owned by Will Rogers.

Dennis Wilson was the least known member of the Beach Boys. His older brother, Brian, the group's songwriter, had been a recluse since 1964 but still was more famous. The Beach Boys had popularized the California surf sound in the early 1960s and had been one of the biggest-selling acts on the Capitol label. That was until Capitol added another group, which appeared right behind the Beach Boys in record store bins: the Beatles.

Despite Brian Wilson's efforts to keep up with the times—songs like "Good Vibrations" tried to meld the group's falsetto harmonies with the psychedelic aesthetic—the Beach Boys were sounding dated next to the Doors, Buffalo Springfield, and especially the Beatles. The Beach Boys still sold records, still booked concert halls, but they seemed more and more like a nostalgia act.

Following the Beatles lead, the Beach Boys had traveled to India to visit the Maharishi Mahesh Yogi. The group's front man in Brian's absence, the Wilsons' cousin Mike Love, became a devotee of the Maharishi. Dennis, however, was looking for spiritual guidance closer to home. Having Charlie *in* his home was even better. Dennis said that "Charlie is the most tuned-in dude I ever met." He called him "the Wizard."

"Me and Charlie," Dennis later would say, "we founded the Family."

Dennis took Lyn and some of the other girls with him to a Beach Boys concert in Colorado. Back at his home, Dennis gave the Family his clothes and jewelry, and lent them his Rolls-Royce. Lyn used it to go on garbage runs to supermarket dumpsters.

"If you find an apple that has got a tiny little spot on it, you cut out the spot," Lyn reasoned. It was all part of the magical mystery tour. Lyn would pretend she was rich, and give away things—Dennis's things, like his gold records—to people she'd meet. They would strip the satin sheets from Dennis's bed and make swimsuits and pants out of them. It was like living in one big play.

Dennis seemed so liberated to have met Charlie. He took part in the acid trips and the group love sessions, just like everyone else. Charlie enjoyed helping Dennis, and was glad to have him aboard, but even in a Beach Boy's mansion there was more to be learned from the Beatles. *Pet Sounds* was a good album, but it didn't really speak to you the way even a minor song on *Magical Mystery Tour* did.

Dennis Wilson's house was a great place to watch the currents roll. All kinds of people came through the house, including Dean Martin's daughter, Deana. At one of Dennis's parties, Deana felt that Charlie and the girls were making fun of her date, though, and left. There were old friends, like Dean Morehouse, who had taken to the road to spread the word of LSD. One day, when Dean saw Charlie in Dennis's living room, he crawled up to him on his hands and knees.

"Are you ready to die this instant?" Charlie asked.

"Yes, I am," said Dean.

"Then you can live forever, brother," Charlie said.

Ruth Morehouse, then living in Mendocino County with a boyfriend, was persuaded to come to the Wilson house to visit her father. When Ruth arrived at the house, Charlie ushered her into Dennis's bedroom for a conjugal welcome. Ruth was willing—but felt awkward when Charlie brought Lyn into the bed with them.

Like, no way, thought Ruth. But when Lyn, the big sister, explained to Ruth that this was the way things were done, she relaxed.

Through Dennis, Lyn and Charlie met Gregg Jakobson, a talent scout who was the son-in-law of Lou Costello, the thicker half of Abbott and Costello. Jakobson, too, was impressed with Charlie and the music, and he introduced them to Terry Melcher, a record producer who was Doris Day's son. Melcher took some interest in hearing the Family sing but ultimately decided they had no future in the record business. He lived nearby in Bel-Air, at 10050 Cielo Drive.

But they met plenty more than just celebrities. One guy who joined the Family was Charles Denton Watson, a tall, athletic type with a thick Texas drawl. The Texas accent seemed incongruous because he acted like a mod swinger, and ran a wig shop in Hollywood. He would wear a top hat and nod as if he were an English dandy "Indeed, indeed!" he'd say.

They called him Tex.

Chapter 4

Coming

Down

Fast

Charlie felt that it was bad karma to stay too long in any one place, even a palace like Dennis Wilson's pad. When they weren't crashing there, they now stayed at the Spahn Movie Ranch, in an undeveloped western corner of the San Fernando Valley.

For decades, Hollywood had used the Spahn Ranch as a location for westerns. William S. Hart had once owned the place, Tom Mix and Wallace Beery had played cowboys in Spahn's frontier-town streets. Classic movies, like *Duel in the Sun*, and corny television shows, *The Lone Ranger* among them, had been shot there, as had some Marlboro commercials.

The ranch was owned by George Spahn, a Pennsylvania-born dairyman who had come to California during the Depression. A rugged old guy, it was said he had sired ten children and named each one after a favorite horse.

George had bought the ranch in 1948, when westerns still were popular, and managed it with his ladyfriend, Ruby Pearl. Now he was largely blind, about eighty years old. The ranch was run-down and overgrown, with dust flying and chickens roaming the grounds. Its horses and shacks were tended by ranch hands, some of them out-of-work stuntmen or movie extras, who lived free in exchange for their labor. What little money the ranch made came from renting horses for daytime rides. Westerns had fallen out of favor.

A few hippie types had moved onto the property, among them a friend of Sandy Good's who happened to be a mechanic. Charlie had gone up there to see if Sandy's friend might be able to get the black bus running, and was impressed with what he found. He spoke to George, and the old man seemed willing to let the Family stay there for a few days.

Although some of the ranch hands, like Donald "Shorty" Shea, grumbled about the newcomers, the Family made a good impression. Lyn and the girls set about clearing weeds and cleaning up, and soon were taking care of George himself.

Lyn in particular cared for the old man. She saw him sitting in his old house, with grease and dirt all over, all alone. He was to the point, she saw, where people ignored him, for he was old and blind and couldn't rightly object to anything they might do. So Lyn took over that house, and with the other girls painted it, fixed up the kitchen, kicked out the cowboys with their greasy old stuff, and made George a clean home. Then she sat down to talk to him, and he fell in love with her. He would tell her stories—"stirrys," he called them—from his past, that the milk business was hard work, that Gene Autry was mean and drunk most of the time, so drunk you couldn't get him on a horse, that the singing cowboy was too "high-gafluttin'" to speak to a regular guy. But George didn't have to speak; Lyn could look at his arms, big and muscled, wrinkled and striped with blue veins, and see the stories written on them.

At night, he would call for her. "Hep! Hep! Hep! Somebody come queek!" She'd be there in a flash.

"What is it?"

George told her it was them "cuchamongies" again. "Can't sleep a wink," he said, winking at her.

"Tell me about these 'cuchamongies,'" she said, flopping down right next to the old man on his big, soft feather bed.

"Well, they look a lot like a hand, 'ceptin right here," he said, indicating the palm of his hand. "They got a big eye here so they can see where they're goin'. See, I'll be just layin' here, tryin' to get some sleep, when about eleven or eight of them start divin' off the bedposts, and leapin' up and down, up and down, then they git to the bottom o' the bade, they start nippin' at my toes. How's a man supposed to sleep?"

"Well, where are they?" Lyn said. "I don't see none around."

"You musta scared 'em all away," George said. And he persuaded her to stay for another stirry.

George clearly took more to the young women than to the men who accompanied Charlie. Lyn felt, in fact, that George was jealous of Charlie. "If I could ever let George know, or if he could ever see how much we love him," she wrote, "and that the same love we have for Charlie is for him, too." Deep down, she sensed that George knew that, "but men have been taught crazy competition things." Lyn saw other hang-ups that were the badge of George's generation, like his reluctance to let men touch him. He'd let Charlie take his hand, but with others he said it was "queer"—"a fear of his generation," Lyn thought. "Somethin' that fellas just don't do with each other."

George liked to play around with the sound of words, and soon came up with variations for everyone's name. Ella Bailey became Yeller(stone), Katie was Katydid, Sadie turned into Sadie Mae, Cathy Gillies was Cappy, or Capistrano, Brenda was sometimes Brindle, and Ruth Ann Morehouse became Ouisch—from "wish." Sandy Good, however, was always quiet properly Sandra. Since the old man couldn't see, he had to know them by the sound of their voices, and by the touch of their hands and arms, as well as the way, in George's words, their "ninnies" or "pink marshmallows" felt.

But it was Lyn who became his eyes, and much more than that. She would sit with him for hours, listening to country music on the radio, letting him slide his hand up her skirt. When he pinched her, she would loose a cute little shriek, and George would chuckle. He named her for that sound: "Squeaky."

Living in the fake historical shacks of Spahn Ranch, with the Santa Susana Mountains at their backs and the city seeming far, far away, the Family had found their most comfortable home yet. The setting allowed the magical mystery tour to go to new heights, and Lyn, when she tripped, could be whoever she wanted. She turned into pirates, Greek goddesses, servants, princesses, queens, beggars, court jesters, witches, elves, space creatures, Mad Hatters, minstrels, gypsies, harem girls, angels, and devils. The group would put on cowboy outfits, and turn their world into Abilene, or Dodge City. In the evenings, after the work was done, they'd eat the stews of salvaged vegetables and make love. They'd listen to Donovan, the Moody Blues, the folky pianist Biff Rose, and, of course, the Beatles. And they'd sing their own songs—Charlie's songs. He would sit on a rock, and the girls would gather around in a circle at his feet. The girls who could sing in the higher registers would cluster around one spot, those with lower voices would sit by another.

A few times a week they'd drop acid, and Charlie would use the encounters to bring everybody up to where he was. Other times, he would teach joy simply by the way he did things. He would enter the bathroom to comb his hair, and a whole crowd would come to watch, just because it was so much fun.

"It's a nonsense world, of Alice in Wonderland," Lyn thought, "but it makes a lot of sense. You get what you put out." And she put out a lot.

Charlie had opened Lyn's eyes to what a woman needs to be satisfied. It came from love, and for women love meant pleasing a man. There were so many ways to please a man, not just by making love and being made love to, but through the things man depended on woman for. Cooking and cleaning, sewing and taking care of what needed to be done. Most especially, by carrying man's seed into the world. That's why there were to be no rubbers, or birth control pills, or, above all, abortions. How could woman truly love man if her body denied his call?

They were nearly three dozen, now. Katie took care of the kids. Katie was very much a mother, doing so much washing and cooking and cleaning. Sadie— Sadie was everywhere. She didn't like to do much cleaning, but she loved to cook. And all of the girls, at one time or another, worked on Charlie's vest, onto which they embroidered scenes of the Family's adventures.

Lyn, in addition to taking care of George, soon oversaw the horse-rental business. They were all one, but Charlie knew that skills weren't always distributed evenly. Lyn's cool head and open heart made her the right person to take care of George and his finances. She managed the Family's paperwork, collecting ID cards and charge plates from kids who joined up, making sure everything was in the right place when it was needed. So, though she thought it was great to lie outdoors and just *be*, Lyn really didn't have the time for it, and spent most of the day in George's house. With her complexion, anyway, she would burn if she stayed in the sun naked too long. Though she loved children, and loved to care for them, Lyn just didn't get pregnant. Her attentions were needed elsewhere, perhaps.

With all those people and all those egos together on the ranch, there were moments of discord. Sometimes, Charlie would get so frustrated with Lyn, he'd get all feisty and walk off on his own. Just him being mad made her straighten up. Other times, when her face betrayed guilt, he would bawl her out.

"What am I feeling guilty about?" she then would ask herself, and kick it around till she realized the petty thing that had made her look bad—like eating too much or taking too much from someone else.

But the time when Charlie became most ferocious was when Lyn disrespected a baby. She was sulking, and upset that she didn't have the attention she wanted. When the baby boy came up and started pawing her, she kicked him aside with her foot. Charlie saw that. He let out a big growl and smacked her, hurling her clear across the room. She tumbled head over heels, and jolted up when she landed. It was the most frightful experience she ever had, and she knew something at once—*she had asked for it*. She had kicked the baby for attention, and attention she had gotten, and Charlie had taught her that without saying a word. She loved him more than anything.

While in San Francisco, Lyn and other Family members often visited the Haight-Ashbury Free Clinic to clear up venereal diseases and other health problems. Al Rose, a clinic administrator, was so impressed with the Family that he spent time with them at the Spahn Ranch.

On his return to the clinic, Rose collaborated with Dr. David E. Smith, the clinic director, on a scholarly paper about the Manson Family. It was published in the *Journal of Psychedelic Drugs*.

In their introduction, Smith and Rose said that although much was known about communal living in other lands, "such as Israel where the kibbutz has flourished," little research had been done on the new types of communes that were emerging in "America's 'hippie subculture.'" According to a medical student affiliated with the clinic, there were more than one hundred "cooperative living groups" in Northern California and Oregon alone, involving thousands of people.

Smith and Rose classified several types of communes: "Crash Pad Type, Drug and Non-Drug Family Type, Drug and Non-Drug Marriage Type and Self-Contained Rural Type." Their paper, which identified none of the subjects except the leader (and only by first name) was about another type of living arrangement. It was titled "The Group Marriage Commune: A Case Study."

"Approximately 20 members of this commune [fourteen of whom were women] referred to themselves as a 'family,' but we have chosen the term 'group marriage commune' because of their practice of polygamous sexual relations," the authors stated.

The group was distinguished by its

spiritual leader . . . a "father-figure" [known as] Charlie, a 35-year-old white male with a past history of criminal activity. . . . He was never arrested or convicted of a crime of violence, and, in fact, during the study expressed a philosophy of non-violence. . . . He was an extroverted, persuasive individual who served as absolute ruler of this group marriage commune. . . . Tales of Charlie's sexual prowess were related to all new members . . . Charlie would get up in the morning, make love, eat breakfast, make love and go back to sleep. He would wake up later and make love, have lunch, make love and go back to sleep. Waking up later, he would make love, eat dinner, make love, and go back to sleep—only to wake up in the middle of the night to have intercourse again.

Such stories, although not validated, helped him maintain his leadership role. Charlie had a persuasive mystical philosophy placing great emphasis on the belief that people did not die and that infant consciousness was the ultimate state. . . . Charlie used the words of Jesus, "He who is like the small child shall reap the rewards of heaven," as a guide for the group's child-rearing philosophy. . . . However, Charlie's mysticism often became delusional and he, on occasion, referred to himself as "God" or "God and the Devil." Charlie could probably be diagnosed as an ambulatory schizophrenic. . . .

Charlie set himself up as "initiator of new females" into the commune. He would spend most of their first day making love to them, as he wanted to see if they were just on a "sex trip" (a term used by the group to label someone there only for sexual gratification), or whether they were seriously interested in joining the group. . . . An unwillingness, for example to engage in mutual oral-genital contact was cause for immediate expulsion, for Charlie felt that this was one of the most important indications as to whether the girl would be willing to give up her sexual inhibitions. . . . Charlie felt that getting rid of sexual inhibitions would free people of most of their problems. . . .

The females in the group had as their major role the duty of gratifying the males. This was done by cooking for them and sleeping with them. . . .

Of the fourteen females in the "immediate family," two were pregnant at the time of our observations. Both said that Charlie was the father, although there was no way to verify the claim, as the sexual relations in the group were polygamous. It should be noted that Charlie was held in such high regard by the girls that all of them wanted to carry his child. . . .

The article concluded by asking why this alternative communal lifestyle held "such an attraction for thousands of adolescents and young adults. Why, for example, were these young girls so attracted and captivated by a disturbed mystic such as Charlie?"

The authors did not presume to offer an answer.

When she learned of the article, in 1970, after Dr. Smith talked about it on television and to the *Berkeley Barb* newspaper, Lyn was annoyed.

"We never knew Smith . . . the one who appeared on television talking about us through a transparent black veil, for anonymity," she would complain. "I wondered what he was hiding from. And really, we just figured that the *Barb* must have been hard up for things to write, since I don't recall Dr. Smith ever going to bed with Charlie. As for Al Rose, he tries. We send love. The 'four months' he spent with us amounted to two days at the ranch, and occasional visits with five of the girls that were in jail up north on a possession charge.

"That's okay, though. I don't know what else people who never knew us could write."

Charlie's work at Universal Pictures fizzled out after Corey Allen reported that the higher-ups weren't interested in the Jesus idea. Corey nonetheless was sure that Charlie would have an influence somewhere. "I wouldn't be surprised if he ended up with a multi-picture deal at Warner, someday," Corey said.

But the music continued. Charlie, with the girls sometimes singing back-up, recorded demo tapes at MCA Records, and at Brian Wilson's private studio, thanks to Dennis.

Charlie even wrote a song that the Beach Boys put out, "Cease to Exist." A key verse went:

Give up your world
Come on you can see
I'm your kind, I'm your kind . . .

The song, Lyn felt, explained Charlie's message: it was about giving up the false ego world for the true soul that belongs to everyone. As Charlie said, "It's through death that we come to love."

Brian Wilson and the Beach Boys' management, however, were uncomfortable with the song, particularly with its central concept. The line "Cease to exist" was changed to "Cease to resist." What did that mean? Was it just about sex? Was that all they got out of the song? And the title was switched from "Cease to Exist" to "Never Learn Not to Love." Not exactly catchy.

The song, with C. Manson credited as composer, came out on the B side of the single, "Bluebirds Over the Mountain," and went to number 61 on the charts. Later, the Beach Boys released it on their album *20/20*, best known for the song "I Can Hear Music." They changed the composer's credit, replacing Charlie's name with that of Dennis Wilson. Charlie didn't want a traditional royalty for the song, but was happy when Dennis gave him a motorcycle and a couple of gold records.

At Spahn Ranch, Charlie's message grew increasingly spiritual.

"Hey man, like Jesus, when he rapped about love, wasn't talking about some mealy-mouthed muttering and stuttering," Charlie would say. "He was talking about love with a real spirit . . . love with a dick and balls!"

Moreover, Charlie began to explain the earth's affliction, in ever clearer terms. "It's like the Man, dig . . . programming us with all the garbage on TV: to wear certain clothes and eat certain foods, dig . . . to buy and produce all the rot that pollutes the earth." Through his war machine, the Man was programming eighteen-year-olds "to hate gooks or Japs and to kill them with a bayonet in the name of democracy or the flag or whatever." This frightening reality carried over to the war at home. "It's like the cop in Malibu who pulled me over last week, man," Charlie said. On the officer's helmet, he saw the "the mark of the beast." Why couldn't others?

The grizzly bear on the cop's helmet was the emblem of the state of California. It was everywhere one looked, on the flags outside schools and libraries, over the entrances to city halls and courthouses.

Fortunately, Charlie had a plan for dealing with all this hate. "The idea is to kill off the programs society has stuck us with . . . to get rid of the past shit . . . to submit to the love and come to Now. That's why we sing and make love together and see our fears for what they are." These practices, he said, were merely "steps to a higher consciousness. It's like the man on the cross, dig. He just loved. He just submitted to his love and all his body carried was love; there were no programs inside him. He was clear [a Scientology term, meaning the highest state of consciousness], just a hole in the infinite that love poured out of."

Charlie was interested in the various forms of spirituality, and met with oc-cultists, devil worshippers, and other seekers. Over in Box Canyon, a few miles from the Spahn Ranch, was the site of 1940s religious group called the Fountain of the World.

The Fountain had been founded when a man named Francis Penovic, a former criminal, realized he was Christ and renamed himself Krishna Venta. The bearded holy man's group had met in the natural surroundings of Box Canyon, living in simply built dormitories and engaging in tantric sex to extinguish ego desire. The Fountain's teachings had been too demanding for some, however, and the husband of one of the female adherents couldn't cope with her need for sexual communion with Krishna Venta. In 1958, the husband had come with a case of dynamite and blown up Krishna Venta, along with himself and several other adherents. Charlie carefully considered Krishna Venta's teachings, such as his assignment of colors to various adherents based on their innate selves.

The magical mystery tour reflected a more explicit spiritual focus. They strapped Charlie to a cross when they tripped, and Calvary came to the San Fernando Valley.

The Spahn Ranch was a good base for interior exploration, far from the distractions of the Man's society. But it would have been selfish to keep Charlie's wisdom only for those who found their way there. Besides, it was always possible they might have to leave, and leave in a hurry. So Charlie envisioned branching out to other places. He sent Sadie, Katie, Mary, Pooh Bear, and a few others up to Mendocino, to see about building a base in Northern California.

Lyn loved Mendocino, but Charlie decided she should stay at Spahn Ranch. He depended on her, and couldn't afford to let her get mixed up in business far away. Unfortunately, Sadie and the other girls were unable to keep it cool during their assignment. Staying in a remote cabin near Philo, a tiny settlement in the redwood forest, the girls had begun to spread drugs and sex among the local boys. Soon, they were being called "the Witches of Mendocino."

According to Bob Glover, a Mendocino old timer, the Family girls were somewhat discriminatory and turned away a bunch of older fellows who wanted to share in the love. That, and a bad trip or two among the Mendocino boys, brought the local law down hard—three sheriffs' cars and two from the Highway Patrol—and the girls got busted. Even worse, after the girls were picked up, the guys they had rejected came by and tore up the house they were staying in, stomping on the stereo and smashing their bus. These men then took the girls' clothes and scattered them across the yard, splattering them with orange paint. On the west wall of the house, written in the same orange paint, they left an eerie message: GET OUT OF HERE OR ELSE. Sadie, Katie, and the rest looked at the scrawl and understood.

They called Charlie for help, and he dispatched a rescue party. Throughout the latter part of that year, 1968, they had to shuttle between Los Angeles and Mendocino to get the girls to their court dates.

The trips seemed to be fun for those who went on them, though, and they often ran into folks they knew from before. Once they came across Bobby Beausoleil, who was traveling, as always, with some women. One of them was a girl he had met in the Bay Area, Leslie Van Houten who became Lulu.

Lulu had been through some changes in her life. She had had an abortion when she was fifteen, and had later joined the Self-Realization Fellowship, a spiritualist organization that tried to get people to nirvana through meditation, yoga, and celibacy. That trip had failed.

Bobby brought Lulu down to Spahn Ranch, and she was at home.

But things were getting tougher. In Los Angeles, Dennis Wilson had fallen under some new influences, and moved out of the Sunset Boulevard house. The Family could no longer crash there. There were tensions up at the ranch. Shorty Shea and the other hands were always nosing about, grumbling. Worse, now that the Family wasn't on the road so much and couldn't get pulled over, the cops were coming to them. They would claim they were looking for stolen vehicles and laugh arrogantly when told that people had just "given" their cars to Charlie. They'd come up there looking for kids who were trying hard not to be found by their parents and the society that had done them wrong. Kids, Lyn said, who decided they weren't going back to their parents who had abused them.

Charlie would talk to the police. He was as old as they were and could treat them like his brothers. But still, the harrassment became insufferable. The Family had tried to get away from the city, and now the city was crawling up to the country, coming back to get them. The pressures touched them when they tripped.

On one trip, Lyn clung to Charlie's arm tightly.

"What are you doing?" he asked.

"I'm hanging on to you," she said.

Uncertainty came through his eyes. "No," he said. "I'm hanging on to *you*."

"No, no! I'm hanging on to you!" she wailed, and started thrashing her arms. "No! No, Charlie!" she shouted again. "It's not true. . . . Charlie . . . Charlie! It's not so!"

He said it was. He was hanging on to her, even as he left the room.

She rolled into a woodpile and flailed her arms, kicked her feet, cutting herself on the stacked cords. Her arms and legs, even her face bled before she was pulled away, and talked through her changes, as her body convulsed.

It was time to leave.

The girl they called Capistrano, Cathy Gillies, had a grandmother who owned some property in Inyo County. The place was some ten hours away from Spahn Ranch, practically inaccessible in the desolate outback of California. They drove up the highways to the town of Trona, then down a gravel road that rattled the bus. When the bus could go no farther, they had to hike the rest of the way, a two-and-a-half-hour trek. Sadie and some of the others who marched ahead had trouble with their packs, and sometimes dropped things so they wouldn't have to carry them. Lyn, who took up the rear, was sure to reclaim all the things the others wouldn't carry.

The property—Myers Ranch, and the nearby Barker Ranch—lay in Goler

Wash, which crossed the Panamint Range in the badlands of Death Valley. They were south of the Last Chance Mountains, west of the Funeral Mountains. Charlie liked it. Lyn liked it, too. "I flashed on the reality of Disneyland . . . that it's already here . . . every bit of it!" she recalled.

The county's name, Inyo, was an Indian word meaning "Dwelling place of a great spirit." Out there, among the cactus and the scorpions, was where Charlie wanted to dwell. The rivers that ran down from the mountain ranges flowed underground, feeding the oases where prospectors and hermits built their homes. Charlie explained that the hole that led to this underground world was well known to the native tribes, that the Aztec emperor Montezuma had not perished at the hands of the conquistadors—"cross-peddling Spaniards," he called them—but had left Mexico with a small band of hardy warriors and robust women, and come to the hole in the Valley of Death, Death Valley. It was their cleansing ground of the spirit, and once in the hole you could travel anywhere in the earth. That's how Hopi writings got to the Himalayas, he said. Of course, the hole had remained concealed after Montezuma had descended into it 450 years ago. To find the hole leading to the underground rivers would be really something, Charlie said. Especially since the temperatures in Death Valley could hit 120 degrees in the day, and drop near freezing at night.

The place wasn't much, just two stone houses, a shed, and a small stone-lined pool fed by a trickling stream. The property was adorned with a junk garden made up of rusted car and bicycle parts, and the wreckage of a plane crash. But Charlie was pleased. He gave his framed gold record, awarded for the album *The Beach Boys Today*, to the owner, Arlene Barker.

The Family was so far from the city, they could focus on what was real. And what was real was the music. They had to tighten up the sound, deliver the message better when they went into the studio again. Then they could bring the message to everyone.

For moving to the desert did not bring an end to Charlie's mission. There was still business to conduct all around California, and groups regularly were dispatched to the Bay Area, to Sacramento, and to Los Angeles, for engine parts and drugs and other necessities. Conventional vehicles wouldn't do in Death Valley, so they started to acquire jeeps and dune buggies, fixing them up, hiding them out of the way.

Lyn, accompanied by Sandy and Ouisch, would head into the nearest big city, Las Vegas, and panhandle at colleges and warehouses. They said they were from an Indian tribe in the desert and received donations of ketchup and other foodstuffs for hungry Native Americans. Charlie, meanwhile, went down to Hollywood to connect with his contacts, and brought back word of what was going down.

The country had changed considerably from 1967 to 1968. Shot dead were Bobby Kennedy and Martin Luther King, Jr. The police had rioted at the Democratic National Convention in Chicago, and Jerry Rubin, Abbie Hoffman, Tom Hayden, Bobby Seale, and a bunch of other radicals were being tried as a result.

President Johnson had folded his reelection campaign, and Richard Nixon had defeated Vice President Hubert Humphrey in the November election. The war in Vietnam was growing uglier every day. So was the war at home. The streets of Los Angeles were more violent than ever before. The black man, who had been enslaved and stepped on, sent to war and to prison, wasn't going to take it anymore.

Charlie explained it all in his teachings. "We"—the white man—"came to this country. We ran the Indians out. Then we show them a treaty, and we say 'Peace.' They sign the treaty. They all smoke their pipes and sit around in a circle. And we come in and wipe them out.

"We bring the black people over here to work for us," Charlie continued. "And they are dumb because they have been living in love, they had been living simply. And we show them what to do, and we rape their women, we kill them because they are just nothing, you know. . . . We have, as a race, we have killed anything darker than us, or put it down, or put it away, or we have controlled it."

Now, all that karma was coming right back.

"It's just a matter of time. The shit's gonna come down. . . . It's gonna come down hard."

The Family would be ready.

"What we need to do is program the young love to split . . . when the scene comes down, they're gonna need someplace to go. Well, we got that place. We're here, and we can show the young love where to come. And we can show them with music.

The Family began to sing a new song, "Never Say Never to Always." It was as simple as a nursery rhyme, as stirring as an anthem: "Always is always forever / As one is one is one," it began.

Charlie wasn't the only one making music. It had been three months since the last Beatles single—"Hey Jude," with "Revolution" on the B side—and a year since their last album, *Magical Mystery Tour*. Everyone was excited when the new Beatles record came out in November 1968. It was a double LP set, formally titled *The Beatles* but called the White Album because of its glossy blank cover with the raised letters. Each copy was numbered, as if it were a precious, limited edition.

The track "Glass Onion" was an interpretation of previous Beatles songs, revealing hidden meanings in "Strawberry Fields Forever," "I Am the Walrus," "Fixing a Hole," and others. Clearly, the songs on the White Album had meanings, too. In metaphor and symbol, the songs seemed to underscore all that Charlie had been teaching. Some, like "Revolution 1" and "Happiness Is a Warm Gun," were pretty clear. Others were more subtle. "Blackbird" told the black man it was time to rise. "Piggies" commented on the fate of the pig society, its members blithely consuming "bacon" until they would themselves be consumed by forks and knives. "Helter Skelter" spoke of the revolution, the chaos that would subsume society. And "Revolution 9," not so much a song but a cacophony of painful sound, of war and terror, was pointing the way to what would come next: Revelation 9. It was the final book of the Bible, also called the Apocalypse.

The Good Book prophesied: "And the fifth angel"—there were four Beatles, so who would be the fifth?—"blew his trumpet, and I saw a star fallen from heaven to earth, and he was given the shaft of the bottomless pit, and from the shaft rose smoke like the smoke of a great furnace, and the sun and the air were darkened with the smoke.... Then from the smoke came the locusts"—or beetles? Beatles?—"... and they were given power like ... scorpions"—Charlie was a Scorpio—"they were told not to harm the grass of the earth or any green growth or any tree, but only those of mankind who have not the seal of God upon their foreheads; they were allowed to torture them.... And in those days, men will seek death and will not find it; they will long to die, and death will fly from them." In such a horrifying Apocalypse, Sadie later would observe, death would be the greatest gift one could bestow. "You have to have a real love in your heart to do this for people," she would say, explaining her role in the brutal Tate-LaBianca murders. And, indeed, Revelation 9 concluded: "the rest of mankind, who were not killed by these plagues, did not repent ... of their murders or their sorceries or their immorality or their thefts."

Charlie was determined to find that Bottomless Pit from which the locusts would rise, a pit he sometimes called the "Devil's Hole." The Family would spend many hours in the quest, going through the barren lands of Death Valley.

But for now, Sadie was happy to have found in the White Album a message just for her. Lennon and McCartney had composed a song called "Sexy Sadie," which celebrated the sly trickery of its subject.

Death Valley got awfully cold in the winter, and with all the activity related to the music, there were reasons to start spending more time in Los Angeles. But suddenly, there were problems with George Spahn. He had been acting grumpy, and finally he told Lyn the reason. "Too many guys, too many longhairs and beards, makes a place look bad."

Lyn was upset. Obviously, people had been whispering in George's ear, city slickers or real estate hucksters, playing on his fear of rejection. But how could he take their words so seriously, after all the love they had shared?

George tried to be conciliatory and said that three or four girls could stay at the ranch. But Lyn blew up. How many times had she explained it to George that the Family was all one? George reacted in kind, bawling her out for pressuring him to grow a beard—Charlie had taught that all men should grow beards—for not being in the house at certain times when he wanted phone calls made, for sticking up for the "goddamn guys."

"Well," Lyn yelled, "do you want us to leave?"

He was so mad, he said yes. She slammed the door on her way out. Later, while sitting in the "rabbitory"—George's term for the outhouse the women shared—Lyn calmed down. She saw that it didn't matter how much she did for George, that she should never expect anything back for what she gave. When she was loving George and making him laugh, it had all been for herself.

She led the women back to the old man, and each one kissed him goodbye. Anyway, they had already found another place to stay. Through an ex-con friend, Charlie had found a house in Canoga Park, an old 1920s place with chickens roaming the grounds and a big swing in the backyard. The two-story house, on Gresham Street, was painted lemon yellow, and seemed an apt place to submerge themselves in work on the music. Charlie called the house "the Yellow Submarine," after the Beatles song and animated movie.

Dennis Wilson and Gregg Jakobson visited to check on the progress of the music. They liked Charlie's new songs, like "Look at Your Game, Girl," which described his view of the female ego. Nearly a quarter century later, it would be recorded by Guns N' Roses singer Axl Rose. A sample:

If'n you can't feel and the feelin's not real
Then ya better stop tryin' or you're gonna play cryin'...

Look at your game, girl.

They had some recording sessions, but the engineers and studio people kept trying to tell Charlie what to do, as if they knew his music better than he did. The sound in the studio, with all its equipment and soundproof glass, never came out the way it did when the Family was on its own terrain. Maybe all the artificiality of the studio was corrupting the sound. Things didn't seem to be happening on other fronts, either. Bobby Beausoleil said he had gone to talk to his old friend Frank Zappa about recording the Family, but there just wasn't any interest. It looked like it would be some time until any record came out.

Meanwhile, they had to pay some bills. Charlie helped Sadie and some of the other girls get jobs, as topless dancers, to bring in some money. Lyn went up to speak to George Spahn and persuaded him to take the Family back. They were so close. Maybe, it was thought, George would leave the ranch to Lyn should he pass on somehow.

Charlie started reaching out to more and more people, some of his old friends from the joint, and bikers from gangs like the Jokers Out of Hell, the Satan Slaves, and the Straight Satans. These guys liked to visit the love of the Family, and the girls were happy to sleep with them. They often brought things they had come across, like cars and motorcycles and weapons.

And speed...

Where acid had been the most popular drug in 1967, now amphetamines were taking over. The bikers dealt a lot of speed, because they were less interested in tripping out than in feeling powerful. Speed or crank was helpful in performing magic tricks, and doing other things when you didn't just want to experience new things but control them. It gave you fear. And fear, Charlie taught, was power. With the new drugs, it was easier to focus on the coming travails.

Lyn tried to help the others give up their ego games and get ready, urging: "We have to flow with the love! We have to let the love happen. Charlie is our love and we are Charlie's love. It's all one. It's all happening now . . . so just let it go . . . just drop it . . . let it die . . . die, motherfuckers! Let it die!"

Charlie said that "when it all comes down, we got to be prepared to save the babies. It might mean some sneakin' and peekin' around . . . takin' some chances." They started to practice creepy-crawling, breaking into people's houses just to learn how to do it. Usually they didn't take anything, or not too much, anyway, but it was fun to move the furniture and things around. That would really freak people out, and help them, too. Maybe they would start to question the false world they took for granted, not be so secure in the illusion that was killing them.

At Spahn Ranch, Tex and the bikers worked on the dune buggies and motorcycles. Lyn and the girls stitched clothes from buckskin, things that didn't need much washing and would last in the desert. But whenever they started to get it all together, something would always come stomping down. On April 19, 1969, the Los Angeles County sheriff conducted another raid on the ranch, and Lyn spent three days in custody on suspicion of grand theft, auto. She and the others were released—"insufficient evidence," said the district attorney—but his purpose was accomplished: the endless hassle. So they began to make hiding places, special spots where even the Man with his helicopters couldn't find them. They had a field telephone set up, so when the police came, there would be time to spread the word and hide in the woods. They hung little witchy things in the trees, ornaments made from wires and rocks and branches, to guide them as they moved in the dark. They had one place so remote, hidden between two freeways, it could only be reached by crawling through a sewer pipe. They called it "the In Case Place." It also turned out to be a good place for making love.

For a time, they ran a nightclub out of the ranch's old saloon, painting the walls black and setting up strobe lights, placing murals that foretold, for the tuned in, Helter Skelter. The club was a space where the Valley kids could hang out, where the Family could jam, where Charlie could meet the people he had to connect with. But people on downers would come stumbling in, and bring everybody down with them. Or, once, a bunch of bikers came by, all angry and ready to rape the girls and burn the ranch down. Charlie could always handle it. Depending on the situation, Charlie would make the grandest, fiercest show of emotion, and they would back off. Or he would walk with them, and show them around the ranch. He always knew just exactly what to do.

One time at the club, Charlie broke up a fight between one of their friends, a black belt they called Karate Dave, and a big dude who was hassling the girls. Charlie was small next to the big dude. But he whipped him around and grabbed him between his legs, and escorted him out the door, right into the trash can. He didn't have to hurt the guy; by humiliating him, by leveling his ego, he saved him a lot of trouble.

The cops eventually came down on the club. They followed the San Fernando Valley kids who went there, and cited George Spahn for operating an entertainment establishment without a license. They had to close the club, or get George in trouble. And they didn't want to get George in trouble.

Even when outsiders weren't coming in, Shorty Shea and some of the other ranch hands were around to cause problems, getting high and mighty over all the vehicle parts and equipment that were coming in, acting as if those things were stolen. Lyn would overhear Shorty complain to George about the Family, brag how he could clean up Spahn Ranch if George would only let him. Lyn discussed Shorty's opinions with Charlie. It was another problem that had to be handled. Worse yet, George had made it clear he was hoping to sell the ranch to some developers, folks who would grade the land and build tract homes. That wouldn't be a fitting end for the ranch at all.

It was about this time that Lyn's little brother, Bill, came up to visit. The ranch was a beautiful scene, Lyn had told him, a place where he could really be. Bill didn't like it. He couldn't see the love, and recoiled when he met Charlie, as if Charlie gave him the creeps. Bill kept trying to persuade Lyn to leave. She laughed. He had gotten it all wrong; rather than Lyn leaving, Bill should stay and join the Family. Bill decided to leave.

So much time, so much energy was now being spent on just holding the Family together, safely, as it used to be. What with the bikers, and the speed, and the cops, and all the problems of the city reaching out to them, it would be nice if Helter Skelter finally would come down, if it all would be over with so life could go back to the way it was. Charlie began to carry a sword.

It was almost time to return to Death Valley, he said. "That desert's got everything. Hell, the whole desert ain't nothing but an upside-down river. Water's running under every inch it. . . . It's underground. I haven't explored it yet, but I sat on the edge of the hole and watched the water flowing underground. Man, the possibilities of that place are endless. And we'll find that hole again and build our own city."

Lyn was eager to prepare. She embroidered handsome denim vests for the girls, stitching them in the manner of a varsity jacket: "Devil's Witches—Devil's Hole, Death Valley," they read, complete with a skull and crossbones.

Charlie continued: "Why do you think we been breaking our asses to put together all this equipment?" He listed the goods they were accumulating to build their desert paradise, where there would be "No rent to pay, no laws to obey," and most important, "no cops." They had to move fast, Charlie said. "Look around you, the worm's turning on the white man. Him and his pigs have put the dollar in front of everything. Even his own kids. Blackie's tired of being the doormat for the rich man's pad. So while the white man's locked into his dollars, blackie's balling the blond, blue-eyed daughters and making mixed babies. It's all leading to bad shit."

The Black Muslims and the Black Panthers were highly organized, and had conquered fear. It was only a matter of time until they started striking out against the white pigs at the top of the structure. They'd head into their houses, and put true fear into whitey, Charlie explained.

"Real madness is going to explode soon—everything is going to be Helter Skelter. But that won't affect us, 'cause we'll be in a beautiful land that only we know how to survive in. To be ready, we need equipment and supplies by the tons. If we have to do a little stealing and hustling to get what we need, let's do it."

They bought topographical maps of Death Valley to plan an efficient route for their caravans out of Los Angeles. Lyn and the other girls started wearing knives—Buck knives, only the best.

Even as they were getting ready to clear out of Spahn's, more troubles cropped up. Tex had burned some black dude named Lotsapoppa in a drug deal, and Charlie had to go out to Hollywood to straighten it out. The black dude got killed when Charlie had to shoot him, and the next day they heard in the news that he had been a major Black Panther. Coincidentally, two Black Panthers had been murdered that January, 1969, at UCLA, and their fellows were all riled up. The Panthers weren't the type to sit around and take it if they knew who was to blame. There were witnesses to the Lotsapoppa shooting, and they could tell all about the Family and Spahn Ranch. Blackie, Charlie knew, might be coming up any day to get his revenge. The Family had to be in maximum awareness. Maximum fear. They had to be ready for anything.

Lotsapoppa, whose real name was Bernard Crowe, survived the shooting, and more than a year later would testify against Charlie. There was no connection between the story about the Black Panther and the encounter with Lotsapoppa. But Charlie didn't know that.

Then there was another drug burn.

According to Manson, Bobby Beausoleil had been selling mescaline he got from Gary Hinman, the music teacher in Topanga Canyon. Some bikers who bought the drugs complained that the batch they had gotten was bad and demanded back their money, $2,000. Charlie promised to get it from Gary. But Gary refused, saying the drugs were fine. So Charlie sent Bobby, Sadie, and Mary to work it out with Gary. Even after getting roughed up, though, Gary wouldn't come up with the money. So Charlie went down to handle things. He took his sword, and Gary's ear got sliced off.

Charlie left, and then Gary died after Bobby had to stab him. They had spent three days with Gary in his house, taking care of him after he was hurt, before he finally died. And after all that, they couldn't find the money. They did come across Gary's vehicles, though, a Volkswagen microbus and a Fiat station wagon, along with their purchase slips. They took those, as well as the bagpipes Gary liked to play.

Because they were expecting trouble from the Black Panthers, they had left a message on the living-room wall: POLITICAL PIGGY, written in Gary's blood. Bobby made a paw print—the Panther symbol—with his palm. When the police found it, the story went, they'd go straight to the Panthers. If the Panthers got busted for Gary's murder, it would solve several problems all at once.

But first, Charlie needed to reflect. With all the troubles, the ranch didn't seem a good place for contemplation. Charlie went up to Big Sur, leaving Lyn to keep things moving at the ranch. When he saw Charlie had gone, Bobby also decided he needed to reflect. He headed up the coast, in Gary's Fiat. On August 6, 1969, the Fiat broke down outside San Luis Obispo. Bobby fell asleep in the car, and was rousted by a highway patrolman. When the officer found that the car was wanted in a murder investigation, he busted Bobby and sent him to the Los Angeles County Jail. Bobby called the Spahn Ranch to explain what had happened.

The girls were upset. They would, some of the girls said, do anything for love of brother, and Bobby was a brother and more to them. Different ideas were hashed around. What would make the cops let Bobby out? Nothing, if they thought he was guilty. But if they knew they had the wrong man, they'd have no choice.

Bobby had told the cops he had just gotten the car from a black guy. Made sense, if the evidence at the scene was all about Black Power. If people kept getting murdered in the same way Gary did, the reasoning went, it would be obvious the killer was still at large, that a lot more was going down than just a drug burn. Someone had seen a setup just like that in a movie once.

Charlie returned, finally, on August 8, with a new girl. After depositing her in one of the cabins, Charlie was told about Bobby's arrest.

He got upset. In the autobiographical *Manson in His Own Words*, Charlie said he told his followers "I'm getting my shit together right now, loading it in my truck and getting the fuck out of here. I am not going back to prison because a bunch of kids can't handle their own problems."

Lyn, Charlie recalled, went to him. "No, you can't go, love is one!" she said. "We are one! If one goes, we go together." Sadie and the others all seconded Lyn.

Hearing his own words, Charlie decided to stay and see them through. To improve morale, Charlie told Lyn to give charge cards to Mary and Sandy and send them into town to get some things. Charlie went to Tex, with a plan in mind. He recalled killing the Panther for Tex. Now it was time for Tex to repay the life he owed Charlie. For the love of brother, Tex and some of the girls would have to do something for Bobby.

That evening, Lyn got a phone call from Sandy. She and Mary had been busted for using the credit cards at a Sears store. They were locked up in the Sybil Brand Institute, the women's jail in East Los Angeles.

When Charlie heard the news, he exploded: all these problems coming down, and they were doing nothing to strike back. They would wait no longer. "Now is the time for Helter Skelter," he declared. It was frantic that night, Ouisch remembered, the girls getting the black clothes together, the weapons, "like we were going to get shot if we didn't do it right now."

Charlie gathered them up. Sadie and Katie, and a blond girl named Linda Kasabian—she had joined the Family in July, and, Lyn learned, still had a valid driver's license. It might help to have someone along with a license, just in case. Tex would lead the mission; "Do what Tex says," Charlie told the girls who would go along. Considering who was chosen for the assignment, Ouisch concluded that Charlie "sent out the expendables."

It all happened so fast. "When it got evil," said Ouisch, "it got evil like, boom!"

There was talk the next day of the murders that went down in Bel-Air, of the people who were in the house where Terry Melcher used to live. What "beautiful people," Sadie had thought when she first saw them. Then Tex announced, "I am the Devil and I'm here to do the Devil's business. . . . " The party from Spahn Ranch then shot and stabbed and hanged the victims, killing in brutal and sadistic fashion. Sharon Tate was an actress, twenty-six years old and eight months pregnant. She had appeared in *Valley of the Dolls* and *The Fearless Vampire Killers*, directed by the man she married, Roman Polanski. Abigail Folger, age twenty-five, was a graduate of Radcliffe and an heir to the Folger coffee fortune. Voytek Frykowski, age thirty-two, was Folger's lover and a friend of Polanski. Jay Sebring, age thirty-five, was a celebrity hairstylist. Steven Parent, age eighteen, had no connection to the other victims; he had been visiting his friend, the property's groundskeeper. After the murders, Sadie went to the door and wrote the word PIG in Sharon Tate's blood.

The house where it happened was at 10050 Cielo Drive, Los Angeles. In Spanish, *cielo* means "sky," or "glory," or, rarely, "heaven." "The Soul sure did pick a lulu," Sadie said, pleased. The next night, August 9, Lulu went with them. So did Charlie.

And a similar thing was done in Los Feliz, just east of Hollywood. Charlie led them to a house where he tied up the residents, a grocery store owner and his wife. After Charlie took off, the couple was murdered. In the man's neck they left a knife, and in his stomach a fork. Katie carved the word WAR on his chest, on the wall, she wrote in blood, DEATH TO PIGS and RISE—like the lyric in the Beatles song "Blackbird." On the refrigerator, she left another message in blood: HEALTER SKELTER, it was spelled. One letter away from Helter Skelter. The man's name was Leno LaBianca, forty-four years old. His wife was Rosemary LaBianca, age thirty-eight. They lived across the street from a guy the Family used to know.

No one at Spahn acted particularly upset about the murders, though. Even before "Helter Skelter," even before *Magical Mystery Tour*, hadn't the Beatles explained it, on *Revolver*? "It is not dying . . . it is being," they had sung. Or something like that.

At the ranch, they prepared for their move to the desert, so they'd be safe while Helter Skelter engulfed Los Angeles. The press and the police floated all kinds of theories about the murders, although they did not publicly state that the Hinman, Tate, and LaBianca killings were linked. They barely mentioned Hinman at all, in fact. Perhaps that was because Gary's Topanga house fell under the sheriff's jurisdiction, outside the Los Angeles city limit and the authority of the LAPD.

Nor did the media discuss the role of black militants in the crimes; instead, there was focus on ritual murders, drug deals, and mob connections. The Establishment still refused to see what was right in front of it.

Now, everybody's fear was up. In straight society, word was that people were buying guns, hiring guards, getting aware. At the ranch, the weapons were ready, the dune buggies set to move out. They had all but lost the values of the city, Lyn saw, living in the woods, without any shoes on, even forgetting how to talk. The way civilized people talk, that is.

Then came the raid.

Just before dawn on August 16, one hundred officers or more stormed the Spahn Ranch, with helicopters overhead, black-and-white cars all over the front lot and the street. Slinging automatic weapons, some wearing combat gear, they kicked down the doors—"bam-bam with their big ol' boots," Lyn recalled—and pointed bayonets in the faces of sleeping babies. The fear in their eyes, and the shake in their trigger fingers, Lyn thought, was something to behold.

Nobody fought back, and the cops—sheriff's deputies—had nothing to do but line the girls and the guys up in the street, in a circle. Lyn cried as she was dragged from the house, "What about George? Who's gonna give him his breakfast?"

When they found Charlie, a big hubbub started among the officers, and they said, "So *this* is Manson!" Charlie's name echoed through the throng. He put up no resistance, but three deputies were on him, hauling him in with his hands cuffed behind his back. They marched him before them all, as if to say, What do you think of your leader now?

And then they read him the charges:

Grand theft, auto.

Charlie smiled. On the way to the sheriff's station in Malibu, they sang. When all charges were dropped—the sheriff, it later turned out, had conducted the raid on an expired search warrant—it was clear the Man couldn't touch Charlie.

They hitchhiked back and saw how the cops had destroyed Spahn Ranch. All their things had been taken or smashed, and all their secret hiding places revealed. Charlie believed that Shorty Shea, the ranch hand, had snitched. Snitches had the worst karma. By the end of August, Shorty had disappeared, never to be heard from again.

They had all had it with Los Angeles, and the way it kept stepping on their young love. "Fuck it," said Sandy. Lyn agreed. It was time to return to the desert. She was too busy with preparations to attend the wedding of her childhood friend, Nora Lynn, on August 23.

Once in the desert, with no law to speak of, they could get down to it. Lyn and the other girls cut their hair short, a more practical style for the hard times they saw just around the corner. They carried knives all the time now. They were ready.

It wasn't Mendocino, but it was nice. "Sure gives your eyes a stretch," Lyn thought, looking at the vastness of it all. The stone house they lived in was a spot to get together for singing, a warm place for babies, a watering hole.

But the authorities in Inyo County began harassing them. "Routine Big Brother," thought Lyn. So the Family tried to restrict movements to the night, communicated by radio, even set up dummy camps to throw the cops off the track. They were tired of all the hassles. Some members of the Family couldn't handle the changes. Several drifted off—back to the city, or even to the police. On October 10, there was another raid. The Inyo County sheriff, the California Highway Patrol, and the park rangers all came together, rousting everyone at dawn. Lyn was wearing a big coat to keep warm, and one cop, who thought she had a shotgun inside it, stunned her with a smack across her face. It was only, she knew, because he was so afraid. It took four hands feeling up her clothes to find she had no shotgun.

The police got them all together, on the ground, but none fought back, none resisted. Charlie was nowhere in sight.

"Where's Jesus Christ?" one of the cops barked. "We wanna crucify him!"

"Charlie never calls himself anything," Lyn thought. "Strange that so many recognize him as Christ."

Lyn was booked, yet again, for violating Section 10851 of the California Vehicle Code: theft or taking of a vehicle. Asked her name, she lied, "Elizabeth Elaine Williamson."

They jailed her in the county seat, a town called Independence, 125 miles away. Two days later, Lyn learned, there had been another raid, and the rest of the Family was hauled in. Charlie, who had been in Los Angeles getting supplies when Lyn was arrested, had come back to get the kids out of jail. He arrived just in time for the raid. Police found Charlie in a tiny cabinet, measuring 3 × 1½ × 1½ feet. They booked him as "Manson, Charles M., aka Jesus Christ, God."

Charlie understood that the deputies and the highway patrolmen were supposed to arrest him; that was their role in the play. He was incensed, however, that the park rangers took part in the raid. "How come you guys are hassling me?" he questioned them. "You should be out telling people about the flowers and animals."

The authorities bragged to the press about their skill in apprehending the band of nude and long-haired thieves. They had hauled in twenty-seven men and women, plus eight children, among them two babies they said were suffering from malnutrition. A cache of weapons and six dune buggies police claimed were stolen also were confiscated.

"They gave us a merry chase," said Deputy Sheriff Jerry Hildreth.

Now, with so many of them crowding the Inyo County Jail, the sheriff looked for ways to get rid of them. Since some had been arrested on National Park property, park rangers tried to get them booked on federal charges—and thus taken out of the county sheriff's hands and into those of the federal marshal. They called the newly appointed United States Attorney responsible for Inyo and dozens of California's other inland counties, Dwayne Keyes of Sacramento.

Keyes seemed less than excited about prosecuting barefoot hippies for stealing dune buggies out in the desert, hundreds of miles from his office. He declined to file charges. It would be six years before he had the chance to prosecute Lyn again.

Chapter 5

God

in the

Machine

There wasn't enough evidence to arraign Lyn for stealing cars, and so the charges were dismissed by a justice of the peace. But all kinds of rivalries and ego trips were emerging, and bad things started going down.

Kitty Lutesinger, who was pregnant with Bobby Beausoleil's child, told the police some stories she had heard from Sadie about the death of Gary Hinman. Based on that, detectives from the Los Angeles County sheriff's office came up to talk to Sadie.

She only told them what she thought they already knew. She and Bobby had gone to Gary's house to get some money, and when they didn't get it, Bobby had slashed Gary, and two days later Gary died. They arrested Sadie, and two others whom Kitty had implicated: Katie, and a slender redhead called Mary. The Los Angeles detectives looked over the slender redheads in the Inyo County Jail, and charged Lyn with violating Section 187 of the California Penal Code: murder.

She was transported to Los Angeles and booked on October 17, 1969. They released her the following day, for there was no evidence linking Lyn to any murders. Katie also was released, and went back to Alabama. Sadie, who talked a little too much, wasn't so lucky. She was arraigned on the murder charges and sent to the Sybil Brand Institute to await trial.

Lyn returned to Inyo County to help out, and moved into a motel with Sandy Good and her baby, Ivan. She could visit Charlie, help him tie everything together between the parts of the Family now spread across California. To get by, they lived off welfare, and the checks from Sandy Good's trust fund.

While in jail, Sadie couldn't keep quiet about Charlie's love, and the things he had exposed her to. After she spoke to fellow inmates about what had happened at the Tate and LaBianca houses, Tex, Katie, Lulu, and Linda Kasabian were implicated in some or all of the killings.

To Lyn's surprise, so was Charlie, who apparently hadn't even gone into the Tate house while the people there were alive, and hadn't even so much as touched Mr. or Mrs. LaBianca with a knife or fork. "I don't believe Charlie considered the conspiracy angle," Ruth Morehouse later observed.

As a result, in late November, a prosecutor from Los Angeles came up to Inyo County to poke around. Vincent T. Bugliosi was thirty-five—the same age as Manson—and had worked as a deputy district attorney since his graduation from UCLA law school in 1964. He was intense, and spoke in a clipped, uptight manner that sounded like something from a thirties gangbusters movie.

In his memoir of the Manson case, *Helter Skelter*, Bugliosi recalled his first meeting with Lyn and Sandy. It was a confrontation on the street in Independence.

"Are you Squeaky and Sandy?" he said.

Sure they were. They had nothing to hide.

He wanted them to come down to the Inyo County district attorney's office, for a chat. One o'clock was fine, they told him. If he'd have some candy for them.

Lyn and Sandy came on time. Their message was simple: "Charlie is love." By the incessant questions, however, Bugliosi showed himself to be as dense as anyone Lyn had met.

What is love? he wanted to know, quickly bringing up the question of sex.

"Love is love," they told him. "You can't define it."

Charlie had taught them this, he suggested.

No. Charlie had only helped them see what was right in front of them.

Was Charlie Jesus Christ?

If Bugliosi could have understood the answer, he never would have asked the question. Lyn just smiled.

Did Lyn love George Spahn the way she loved Charlie?

Love is love, she answered. She already had explained that Charlie is love. But George was a beautiful person, and she was in love with George. She told him all about it.

"I'm not that interested in your sex life, Squeaky," he said. "But I am very, very interested in what you know about the Tate, LaBianca, Hinman and other murders."

Lyn wasn't there to talk about ugliness.

He had dates, times, and places he wanted to know about, loose ends to tie up, until he was tied up by them. Was it pointless to talk to him?

Apparently it was, because on December 8, the Los Angeles County grand jury indicted Sadie, Tex, Katie, Leslie, and Linda Kasabian for murder. And Charlie.

The indictment was issued in the name of the People of the State of California. "Looks like the 'People of the State of California' is, collectively, the grand jury, the D.A.'s office, the police departments," Lyn grumbled.

The media focused on Charlie as though he were the Second Coming. Stories on television, in the newspapers and magazines, looked at all of Lyn's friends, portrayed them as deviants and criminals, slaves controlled by a sinister guru. On December 14, the *Los Angeles Times* screamed across its front page, SUSAN ATKINS' STORY OF 2 NIGHTS OF MURDER—a rewrite of things Sadie had told the district attorney and the grand jury.

The reaction came down hard on hippies. On page one, the *San Francisco Chronicle* summed it up in a story from Topanga, a place the Family loved: MANSON ARREST REACTION: THE 'WAR ON THE LONGHAIRS.'

"A housewife sees a long-haired hitchhiker, hesitates, and drives by," the story began. "A bearded man walks into a store and the clerk asks, only half in jest, 'Did you have anything to do with the murders?' "

Esquire later devoted an entire issue to what it called the "New Evil," sending writer Gay Talese to the Spahn Ranch and filling out the magazine with articles on witches in Hollywood, Satanic-themed artwork, and musings on the future of California's latest trend.

And *Life*, describing what it called Manson's "blithe and gory crimes," reported that the prime suspect had "attuned his concepts of villainy to the childish yearnings of his hippie converts, to their weaknesses and catchwords, their fragmentary sense of religion and enchantment with drugs and idleness, and immersed them in his own ego and his idiotic visions of the Apocalypse."

Charlie was unhappy.

"See where it's ending?" he told Lyn and Sandy, when they came to visit him in jail. "I told all of you months ago you had me headed right back to prison. I knew I should have packed my shit and hit the road. But, 'No,' you said, 'please stay, Charlie, we'll take care of everything, we won't let you go back to jail.' Well, here I am, and in deeper trouble than I've ever been in my life. So now what?"

Lyn wept. The charges against Charlie carried a possible death penalty. Death was just another change, but she wasn't ready for him to make that change without her. "Charlie, you weren't in those houses when any of those people were killed. They will have to let you out. We'll tell the whole world about your good, your love. We'll make them see that you're not responsible." Lyn's optimism was not founded in law; under centuries-old legal doctrines, one who instigates a murder can be as culpable as those who carry it out.

While Charlie sat in jail, Lyn would have to keep the love alive outside the prison walls. There was also opportunity within the calamity, for suddenly the whole world knew Charlie's name. They were trying to make him into a monster, the bastard son of a prostitute, or, as *Time* magazine proclaimed "The Demon of Death Valley." But if Lyn tried hard enough, she might be able to get through the lies and let them see the love.

Hundreds of people wrote to Charlie, and he asked Lyn to reply. To a teenage girl in Indiana, Lyn sent a letter decorated with drawings and embellishments, the pictures telling as much as the words.

"The people don't want to find him innocent," she explained. "He is their 'Hippie!' to show the world what they want to do with hippies."

Charlie had already died for them so many times, Lyn wrote. "& they want to crucify him . . . again!" She signed it "getting ready for a new world."

Reporters seemed fascinated by the idea that middle-class, Caucasian females in their teens or early twenties could be cold-blooded killers, that onetime cheerleaders might rip strangers' guts out and be proud of it. How funny, Lyn said, that the opposite was expected of young men—as long as they were put in uniform and shipped off to Vietnam, eight thousand miles away. After all, both boys and girls had been raised on the same curriculum: television shows like *Combat!*, *The Rifleman*, and *The Untouchables*.

Since the murder suspects were in prison and largely unavailable, reporters turned to their sisters on the outside. It was Lyn they turned to most.

"She was the most intelligent, the most cordial and pleasant, the one who could laugh now and then and remember people's names and not always ask for spare change and cigarettes, the one whose presence one most sorely regretted among that hopeless coven," recalled Barry Farrell, who covered the Manson trial for *Life*. "She became the favorite, almost the pet, of the reporters, lawyers and police. Squeaky had a way with older men."

A news photographer described Lyn in less charitable terms. She "had the smarts in the Manson Family. She was the schemer, always thinking." The cameras and microphones focused on Lyn, attracted by her fresh-scrubbed face, her earnest little-girl voice, and her striking red hair. On days she would be on camera, Lyn made sure to wear pretty white blouses. She would stand in the corridors of the Hall of Justice, surrounded by other Family members who nodded approvingly as she spoke.

She read Charlie's statements aloud (after editing them for clarity), complaining that his rights to represent himself were circumscribed in jail—that he was denied access to law books, to phone calls, and to a dictating machine, essential for someone who could hardly read or write.

Impressed with her poise and articulation, the media called Lyn the leader of the Family in Charlie's absence. She warmed to the role. If there was death in the Tate and LaBianca households, if murder befell people at the pinnacle of society, that murder reflected society itself, she claimed. Few who contemplated those horrible crimes reached that conclusion, however.

Instead, the press, with the help of the authorities, grew fixated on Charlie, and the hypnotic, or Satanic, or narco-sexual way he controlled his female slaves. Lyn protested. Rather than dole out the girls' bodies as favors, she insisted, Charlie "was aware of every visitor who wanted a piece of tail. . . . Charlie or one of the guys would have to step up and tell them that we weren't running a whorehouse." The girls, she said with exasperation, weren't exploited at all. Instead, they were treated "like butterflies." The "complete love" Charlie and the Family men displayed "made them kings to us girls—but nobody seems to understand that. They feel that there must be some sort of tyrannical rule to warrant our constant attention. . . ."

The real tyrants were the people paid to stop the love from flowing. "Do you suppose the man behind the badge—the man behind the symbol of the beast— has ever had a brother, or loved another man? 'Together' they stand—in uniform—while they fight to move up in the line of authority, to get each other's jobs." She tried to share what she had seen on her journeys, urging people to look at what man was doing to the trees, the animals, the air—the earth. "There's beer cans and burnt spots in the most hidden places—and all the animals run and hide from us," she said. "The government . . . is shooting for a new planet"—after reaching the moon less than a year before. "But this is the one we've got, and it's a beautiful one. In fact, I was thinking the other day, the guy who sang 'for purple mountains majesty . . .' was standing in the middle of heaven—a clean, new wilderness under an ever-changing sky.

"Now that song is a joke. If everyone were to make this their land—a frightful hard thing to take responsibility for—but if everyone saw it as their own land and took care of it as their own, the place would go through a lot of changes. It's the young that will accept it. . . . If someone would come sit on the porch with us—someone like us, who could slow down enough just to feel us—and be us, then the truth will come out."

Though the cameras lapped up visions of Lyn and her friends, braless in their slight blouses, barefoot and carefree amid the Spahn Ranch sets, the coverage was hardly sympathetic. "It's open journalism," Lyn sighed, and thus the press was free to depict them as "savage cultists, Satan slaves, wild Amazons, sadistic hippies, and, you know, whatever else. Sure wish everyone could see that Svengali is but a reflection of themselves—and that's who they're tryin' to kill."

Since the state was so determined to kill Charlie, Lyn had to devote herself to the practical matters of his defense. Justice, however, cost money. And the Family, despite its fame, didn't have that kind of cash.

"It's okay, though," she said. "See, we've gotten into giving money away whenever we've got it, and we're dumb enough to believe that there are a whole lot of other people who do the same—in fact, we know it. Charlie once gave away $15,000 in a week. A girl came along, met us and drew out all her money. Was she hypnotized? Threatened? I believe I can speak for her and say that she fell in love—terrible thing, you just can't control it, it keeps on going. We all have a heavy case of the above condition. . . .

"So if you want to put out some, we surely accept. We have a box number in Chatsworth. . . . You'll know where to reach us—I know you're out there. The music of Charles Manson speaks truth. It is tuned to a Universe. It SHOWS the gentleness of a man willing to give all—songs like, 'Everyone who is the one, is a-lookin' for the last door . . . ' Songs of the desert, of revelations, of things happening right now, of children old as the moon. . . . He says it all when he sings. He is a hole in the infinite—and infinity has no 'philosophy.' It just Is."

Further, Lyn reckoned, that music might well be the only way to raise enough money to mount Charlie's defense. She had been unable to obtain Charlie's demo tapes from Dennis Wilson—he had told her they had been confiscated by the district attorney—but she was able to link up with Phil Kaufman, Charlie's contact from Terminal Island Penitentiary. Kaufman obtained other tapes of the music and set to work, mastering the records and seeking a distributor.

For the album jacket, they used the most famous picture of Manson: the glowering *Life* magazine cover that was headlined "The Love and Terror Cult." The bold red box that usually spelled LIFE in capital letters was edited to read LIE.

"The idea was that the entire press was lies," Kaufman told reporters. "We tried to find the most offensive of the yellow journalism and present it as it was. But it was also to let you know it was a lie, and that's the idea of the LIE." The back cover included some blank verse Lyn had written, along with an interview with Charlie published in *Tuesday's Child*, an underground newspaper. In its February 9, 1970, issue, *Tuesday's Child* had run the cover story, "Man of the Year: Charles Manson."

RCA, Capitol, Buddha, and every other record company Kaufman approached declined to release the Manson album. Calling it a "moral obligation," Kaufman had the records pressed himself, producing two thousand copies whose sales, at $4.25 each, he said would finance the release of further records, and, ultimately, help pay for Charlie's defense.

The mainstream press all but refused to publicize the album's release, except to note the apparent irony of the song titles: "Cease to Exist," along with "Big Iron Door," "Garbage Dump," "Don't Do Anything Illegal," "Sick City," and "People Say I'm No Good." With Charlie's demonic glare on the jacket—the photo reportedly was taken in Ventura County in 1968 while Manson was on an acid trip—the final song on side B could well have been the title cut. It was called "Eyes of a Dreamer."

Few record stores would carry the album and only a handful were sold, mainly through head shops and by mail order. Even with Charlie's worldwide fame, the music, somehow, would not get out.

Lyn began to realize that Charlie would never be able to match the forces aligned against him. The aggressive prosecutor, Vincent Bugliosi, was almost the least of their problems. Far worse were the judges, who routinely denied Charlie's motions, and the press, whose interest in the case seemed insatiable. As Lyn said in a statement, media reports not only linked Charlie to countless unsolved murders but accused him "of breaking every one of the Ten Commandments," with "headlines implying sadism, cultism, thievery, sexual perversion and racial and social prejudice."

After the judge revoked Charlie's right to represent himself in court, Charlie selected the lawyer he thought the system deserved: Irving Kanarek, a former chemical engineer who was known for his obfuscatory and ponderous courtroom style. Lyn helped arrange for appropriate counsel for the other defendants. Korean-born Daye Shinn, recommended by one of Charlie's former jail buddies, was chosen for Sadie. She had the money to pay him, having sold her account of the murders to a paperback publisher that issued the slim volume titled *The Killing of Sharon Tate*.

Charlie ordered Leslie to dismiss her attorney, Ira Reiner, because he kept trying to distinguish his client from the other defendants. Leslie was implicated only in the two LaBianca murders, not the five at the Tate house, and many observers believed that the case against her was the weakest. In Manson's view Reiner failed to see that the aim of the defense was to demonstrate the Family's unity, not its differences. As Reiner admitted, he had taken the case "for the publicity . . . I figured I'd be in this for two or three months, enhance my reputation, get out and possibly get some big referrals." (Years later, the intense, baritone-voiced Reiner launched a political career that saw him elected district attorney of Los Angeles County. Many expected Reiner to run for governor someday, but his political career derailed after he lost several highly publicized cases, including that of police officers charged with beating a motorist, Rodney King, who fled rather than submit to a traffic stop.)

Reiner was replaced with Ronald Hughes, a rotund, bearded thirty-five-year-old whom the press sometimes called a hippie attorney. Absurdly, Hughes likened the case to the Chicago Seven conspiracy trial, suggesting the prosecution of the Manson Family was an Establishment scheme to discredit the revolutionary youth culture. He often urged reporters to speak to the Family members, not the lawyers, to get a sense of Charlie's views. Moreover, Hughes never before had tried so much as a shoplifting case, much less a capital offense. His lack of courtroom experience made him better suited for the defendants' purposes, they believed. They were not interested in the minutiae of the California Penal Code, but rather the laws of a higher power.

It was deemed useful, however, to have one attorney around who understood both the Family and the law, and for this they selected Paul J. Fitzgerald. For a member of the Establishment, he would become one of Lyn's best friends.

Paul Fitzgerald

The sad-eyed Paul Fitzgerald, whose off-center nose recalled his days as a Golden Gloves state champion, had long nursed an anti-Establishment bent. In the early 1960s, the University of Minnesota graduate was one of many young lawyers who invigorated the lowly regarded specialty of criminal defense, holding that confronting the system on behalf of its outcasts—indigent criminal defendants—was a noble calling. Coming to California at the behest of his wife, who divorced him upon their arrival, Fitzgerald applied to only one employer: the Los Angeles County public defender's office. He quickly rose through the hierarchy, and by 1970 was assistant chief of felony trials, supervising thirty-five attorneys. Practicing in Los Angeles County's stately Hall of Justice, a colonnaded granite block built in 1925, Fitzgerald liked to quote Lenny Bruce: "The only justice in the Hall of Justice is in the hall."

Even more important for his new clients, Fitzgerald had dropped acid, and thus had an inkling of the experiences they had shared. Considering the case, he thought, "This will be remembered as the first of the acid murders . . . we're on the brink of a whole new concept of violence . . . perpetrated against society by people who have reached a different plateau of reality through LSD."

The prospect of finding new law through LSD excited Fitzgerald. Still, his dealings with Lyn and Charlie were not all that smooth. Fitzgerald had been the first lawyer appointed to represent Manson when charges were lodged in December 1969, and had thus been promptly fired. Manson and the other defendants each had gone through several attorneys before the court wearied of the exercise and refused further substitutions. At that time, Fitzgerald had been invited to represent Patricia Krenwinkel. He would continue to represent various members of the Family through 1975.

The assignment cost Fitzgerald his career at the public defender's office; the firm also was representing Bobby Beausoleil in the related Hinman case, and defending a client in the Tate-LaBianca trial posed a conflict of interest. To stay in the Manson case as a pro bono attorney, Fitzgerald had to resign as a public defender and go into private practice. His client, Patricia Krenwinkel, paid him nothing.

Fitzgerald had met Lyn in December 1969, shortly after his appointment to represent Manson. Showing up on his doorstep filled with enthusiasm and energy, Lyn seemed to Fitzgerald far younger than her twenty-one years.

"A very pretty girl," he thought, sizing up the young woman who eschewed makeup, shoes, and brassieres. "A classic American prepubescent beauty." She seemed sincere and decent, the kind of open, trusting person who would look you right in the eye. Fitzgerald soon saw that, despite the Manson Family's notoriety, Lyn charmed almost all she met. Strangers would pick her up hitch-hiking, and drive dozens of miles out of their way to see that she got back to Spahn Ranch safely. Detectives hauling her in for questioning would stop on the way to buy her ice cream.

At the same time, Fitzgerald learned, Lyn was the Family's heartbeat, and its mother hen. Wherever she went, so went the center of the Family; other members came to her to recharge their faith when it ebbed, or to cool down when their tempers flared. Unlike some members of the group, whose seething disaffection or unpredictable quirks made them difficult to deal with, Lyn could move through both the straight world of police and lawyers, and the underground circles where the Family felt most at home. She could drive or sew or take care of any necessary chores, and she knew where to find the best garbage—the Family's regular source of food and goods. Most of all, she felt at home around the babies and little children the Family doted on, even though, oddly, none were her own.

She also seemed quite a world apart from the violence with which so many members of the Family had been charged. Despite all that had happened, Lyn remained obsessed by the message of love, as if the murders were nothing but a contradictory footnote to a much grander story. She attributed them, he thought, "to some part of the emperor [Manson] she did not understand."

Though she sometimes tried to talk tough, she was to Fitzgerald the "petal of a flower, floating around," and his affection for her grew. She liked him, too; with the other girls, she embroidered her hair into one of his jackets. Sometimes, she stayed overnight at his apartment in Los Angeles' Silver Lake district.

Fitzgerald discovered that Lyn "was a sexual little girl. A very loving little girl." She became the lawyer's guide to the Family's world, the interpreter of what Fitzgerald considered the "physio-psychobabble" through which they spoke. He counted on Lyn to locate potential witnesses, to take him to the disparate places the Family had lived, and to reveal the peculiar dynamic that existed between Charlie, Fitzgerald's client Katie, and the other members of the group.

Lyn came across as a "perpetually lost orphan," but Fitzgerald depended on her. And since she was far from dependable, he would have to get after her.

"Godammit, Squeaky, you gotta straighten out, here!" he would say. "You gotta get your shit together. You have to be more, well, *linear*."

She would just shrug her shoulders and roll her twinkling eyes. "Oh, Paul, you know—that's just me," she'd say, and he couldn't resist her. Soon, she was influencing him far more than he affected her.

He would take her to coffee shops like the House of Pies, and watch as she gobbled down ice cream, cake, anything sweet. But her askance looks when Fitzgerald ordered hamburgers or meat loaf got to him; he quit eating meat for the duration of the trial.

By designating Lyn as a "material witness," Fitzgerald was able to bring her with him for jailhouse meetings with Manson, where the two could touch each other unseparated by plexiglass. Fitzgerald brought a lawyerly agenda to discuss—witnesses he wanted to reach, motions he thought should be filed. But Lyn and Charlie had other things on their minds.

"You're doin' well, are ya, Squeaky?" Manson would say.

She would sort of half-kneel, a gesture of love more than obeisance. He then would pepper her with questions, each one less a specific inquiry than a test of her devotion.

"Are you sure the babies are free?" Manson would ask, as if the significance of the question was self-evident. To Lyn it was, and she would excitedly detail the ways in which the babies were, indeed, free.

"Are the children following themselves?" he would inquire, and she would assure him they followed no one else.

"You been talkin' to those people from *Life* magazine?" he might say. "I've seen all those pictures in *Life* magazine. Maybe them people are moving too close, those photographers comin' out to Spahn Ranch."

"Oh, you're right, Charlie, they are," Lyn instantly would reply. "They won't be back, Charlie," she insisted. There was no discussion of what would be done to prevent the photographers from returning.

During one visit, Charlie told Lyn, just off the top of his head, "Wouldn't it be nice if I could see some of God's creatures again?" The comment did not make a big impression on Fitzgerald, who had forgotten it when, one Sunday morning, he brought Lyn and a couple of her friends to visit Charlie. Lyn carried with her a burlap bag, which, mysteriously, deputies didn't bother to search. When Charlie entered the room, Lyn beamed with joy. "Look what we brought you!" she exclaimed. "One of God's little creatures!" Inside the bag was a writhing snake, some four feet long.

Fitzgerald was mortified. "Put that away! Put that away!" he said, whispering at the top of his lungs. He visualized his picture on the front page of the *Los Angeles Times*: LAWYER BRINGS SNAKE TO MANSON.

But Charlie was pleased by the gift. "Oh, that's very nice," he said.

This subtle, empathic form of suggestion was how Charlie issued his instructions. Phrasing commands almost as questions or observations, Manson assigned Lyn hundreds of tasks—people to be contacted, animals to be cared for, children to be watched. Fitzgerald found the meetings unproductive, because so little time, and virtually no interest, remained for the matters on his yellow legal pad.

Excited as she was to see Charlie, the visits to the jail depressed Lyn. She saw the way the guards degraded him and the other prisoners. "Since the procedure's the same, down to the minute, every day, and the only real job of these officers is to tell the inmates what to do, they have to invent things," she said. "They'll say things like, 'Wait over there by that line,' and 'Up against that wall,' while they check with another officer to see if he's really been checked, like he says.

The waiting, and form-filling, and checking was endless—and you could sure see it in the miserable faces of the men."

Outside the jail, Lyn would serve as Manson's courier, bringing messages between the Family members, their affiliates, and their attorneys. Since she had no phone or permanent address, it was impossible for Fitzgerald or the other lawyers to reach Lyn when they needed her. Sooner or later, however, she would show up unannounced, bearing the latest set of nebulous instructions from Manson.

"Charlie wants to see you, Paul," she'd tell Fitzgerald, cornering him outside his house, or at his office. "And he doesn't necessarily think it's wise . . ." she'd continue, her voice trailing off as she lost the substance of the message. "Uh, I'm sorry," she'd say with a giggle. Then, to summarize: "Are you sure what you're doing is right?"

"Yes, Squeaky," Fitzgerald would assure her, and she'd run off, convinced that her vibe had communicated what her words had not.

But Fitzgerald was not at all certain that the case was progressing the way he wanted. Because of the overwhelming degree of pretrial publicity, the defense had sought to move the proceeding to another venue—San Francisco or Oakland, say, whose jury pool might be more sympathetic to hippie defendants.

Judge Malcolm Lucas, a future chief justice of California, denied the motion, concluding that the publicity had been equally pervasive throughout the state's fifty-eight counties. If so, Fitzgerald contended, then it was impossible to obtain a fair trial for the defendants anywhere in California. And if a fair trial was impossible, all charges must be dismissed. The court disagreed; the trial would be held—in Los Angeles. During the voir dire, or jury examination, the court dismissed prospective jurors who opposed the death penalty. The procedure inspired Lyn to write a poem, "Jury." It complained of the absence of "young people," "pretty girls," "men with sideburns," and blacks, Hispanics, Asians, and Native Americans from the jury. It was not among her more subtle works:

If you stand for it, you are a part of it.
If you let them do it, then it shall be done to you also.

Aside from losing key motions, defense lawyers found that Manson and his friends were difficult clients. Having concluded they never would be acquitted through conventional courtroom procedure, the defendants decided to fashion their case as a political show trial, following the example of the Chicago Seven. Manson regularly changed his appearance for court, cutting his hair or shaving his beard, donning different costumes. Katie, Sadie, and Leslie dressed demurely or in mod, satiny dresses or miniskirts, or the pantsuits and cloaks that Lyn and the other women made for them. Smiling, they sang Charlie's songs as they were taken to court: "Always is always forever/As one is one is one . . ." Some reporters theorized that the Family-sewn clothes had been doused with LSD; that way, the defendants could trip in court by sucking on their lapels.

Manson routinely provoked the judges hearing portions of the case: "Go wash your hands. They're dirty," he told Judge William B. Keene after losing the right to act as his own attorney. "It's not me that's on trial here as much as this court is on trial!" According to Lyn, Charlie told her this was "the joke of justice" or, more accurately, "Just Ice . . . cold and indifferent to truth." He said it was part of a grand historical scheme, "from the time it started killing with crosses" through the Crusades, the Inquisitions, the conquest of the New World, and the mechanized horrors of the twentieth century. Charlie's sufferings were on par with the "merciless killing" of the Incas and Mayas, he said, his oppressors "the same as Hitler when he fired up his ovens for the Jews."

Lyn carried on the campaign outside the courtroom. To the Indiana teenager, she wrote,

> Charlie and the girls are starting trial Monday. It's going to be a long summer with a lot of confusion, but if you're strong you'll be able to make it to the desert. If you can get a copy of *Rolling Stone* magazine [which had on its June 25, 1970, cover proclaimed Charlie "the most dangerous man alive"] it has a lot of silly people's intellectual opinions and how they see themselves through us, but if you weed through it you can see that some of our quotes come through.
>
> We loves ya and know we'll all be together, sooner than soon.

She asked the teenager to send a picture they could give to Charlie.

To the general public, Lyn was less intimate. In a statement to reporters, she announced:

"We were met with disillusionment years ago when we first discovered that the court has nothing to do with justice," recalling busts that ranged from marijuana possession and auto theft to trespass and indecent exposure—for which Mary had been cited after breast-feeding in public. Lyn observed that "every set of rules that I've ever seen in the whole system has some sort of clause in it saying, in essence, that they can do whatever they wish."

And so, she announced, "There is no love in that court, no God in the machine—just a lot of big words that swear to God, and stagnate life. . . . rather than administering justice, they make the court into a gladiator ring."

If people could see Charlie, listen to him in court, watch the way the men in suits and uniforms put him down, they would understand, Lyn said.

"So come to the trials—your trials—and see what's going on."

Come they did. Every seat was taken when trial began in Department 104 of the Los Angeles Superior Court.

Jess Bravin

Using a mirror as she might apply makeup, Lyn took a knife to her forehead and carefully ripped her flesh to form the intersecting lines of the letter X. Then, with a blistering-hot needle, she tore open the lacerations, making them large enough to remain visible even after the flesh wound healed.

She had X'ed herself from their world, just as Charlie had. "I stand opposite to what you do and what you have done in the past . . . ," he had said in a news release, given to reporters the day the prosecutor made his opening statement. "I do not accept what you call justice. The lie you live in is falling and I am not a part of it . . . I stand with my X with my love, with my god and by myself. My faith in me is stronger than all your armies, governments, gas chambers or anything you may want to do to me. . . . I am not allowed to speak with words so I have spoken with the mark I will be wearing on my forehead. . . ."

Those who studied the Bible knew that in Revelation 9:4, the locusts, rising from the bottomless pit, "were told not to harm the grass of the earth or any green growth or any tree, but only those of mankind who have not the seal of God upon their foreheads; they were allowed to torture them . . . like the torture of a scorpion." Sadie, Katie, and Leslie X'ed themselves, too, and so did Sandy and Ouisch and Brenda. Because the X frequently had to be refreshed with a razor blade after the scabs healed, Ouisch introduced a new method for making the mark permanent: a soldering iron. "I don't like the sight of blood," she explained.

To her correspondents across the country, Lyn passed word of the changes that were to follow. She wrote to the Indiana teenager, suggesting that she could come as soon as Charlie was sprung.

Do you have a pair of good shoes, a warm coat or cape you could sleep in, a knife and a *small* pack? Are you ready to survive? . . . The time of no time comes soon. . . .

Despite the proximity of Armageddon, there was still time to horse around. On one scorching, 95-degree day, Lyn threw some cold water at Brenda, who responded by tackling Lyn and smearing her face with pumpkin meringue pie. Lyn, her face covered in brown and white pie filling, chased Brenda down the street and into the Hall of Justice, laughing all the way.

Charlie on Trial

"What kind of diabolical, Satanic mind would contemplate or conceive of these mass murders?" asked Vincent Bugliosi in his opening statement to the jury. "We expect the evidence at this trial will show that defendant Charles Manson owned that diabolical mind. Charles Manson, who, the evidence will show, at times has had the infinite humility, if you will, to call himself Jesus Christ."

He called Manson "a vagrant wanderer, a frustrated singer and guitarist, a pseudo-philosopher, but most of all . . . a killer who cleverly masqueraded behind the common image of a hippie, that of being peace-loving."

Bugliosi contended that Manson had ordered the Tate and LaBianca murders to start a race war. The crime scenes were doctored to implicate the Black Panthers, which was to have enraged white society, which would have clamped down further on the blacks, who would have risen up and defeated the whites in a revolution, then found themselves incapable of running society, so therefore would have surrendered the reins of power to Manson and his followers, who had been living in the bottomless pit in the desert, multiplying to the biblically prophesied number of 144,000.

Several journalists were skeptical of this theory. In his account of the trial, *Witness to Evil*, George Bishop wrote that "it was quite possible that Bugliosi believed in Helter Skelter more than did Manson." Bishop suggested that Manson

had fashioned . . . an ersatz philosophy involving his own deification and a twentieth century Armageddon assembled from bits and pieces of vaguely understood extracts from the Bible, the Beatles' songs and whatever other portions of disjointed thoughts he might have assimilated; Manson tested his theory on his Family and on straight people who might help him in his musical career; if his audience went for one section of his demented doctrine the wily ex-con emphasized that point without being capable of the rational thinking process required to put the whole thing together, if, indeed, any such potential entity ever existed.

Vincent Bugliosi supplied that organized, reasoning mind. The temperamental, at times tempestuous young prosecutor possessed just the right qualifications to tie in all of Charles Manson's pseudo-philosophical loose ends.

Former friends and members of the Family testified as to Charlie's pronouncements on race war, on the Beatles' efforts to communicate to him through their songs, and on his insistence that his followers be ready both to die and to kill.

To Lyn, it seemed the prosecution was out to punish any who stayed loyal to Charlie, not just those facing charges. When she and the others tried to enter the courtroom—to sit in one of the four spectator seats reserved for the defense— the district attorney served them with subpoenas. Lyn would have been unlikely to offer any testimony helpful to the prosecution's case, but few believed the district attorney had any intention of calling her to the stand. Instead, the subpoena was issued for its ancillary effect: those served were prohibited from entering the courtroom while witnesses were testifying. The prosecutor did not want his witnesses reminded that most of the Family remained at large. The exclusion of Lyn and the others, Vincent Bugliosi said, "made everyone else breathe a little easier."

Barred from the courtroom, Lyn began a vigil outside. "We have tried to speak, and it doesn't do any good," she told reporters. "So we feel that by standing here, we're saying more than anything. We are putting our love out front. We're letting everyone know what our love is." She added, "We will remain here until all our brothers and sisters are set free."

Starting on September 16, taking turns with other members of the Family, Lyn lived at the northeast corner of Temple Street and Broadway, just outside the Hall of Justice. She watched as, across the street, the nineteenth-century Hall of Records was demolished to make way for a towering new edifice, the Criminal Courts Building. There was just so much crime in Los Angeles, the old Hall of Justice hadn't housed enough courtrooms to run all the trials.

The women made the corner their own, sweeping it and picking up litter, stashing their things out of sight so as not to contribute to the urban clutter. They wore sheathed hunting knives, slept in the bushes, then later in an old van they had acquired—which they religiously moved from 7:00 A.M. to 9:00 A.M., so as not to get a parking ticket. After a while, the police gave up busting them for loitering.

Sewing and singing, handing out occasional statements to the press, the girls on the corner (as they called themselves) became a fixture for tourists and office workers. William C. Melcher, a young deputy district attorney not assigned to the Manson case, had often chatted with Lyn and her friends in the Hall of Justice. At Christmas, Melcher and his wife came by the van to offer the girls a batch of home-baked cookies. Lyn, in turn, had a Christmas present for the Melchers: some beads for their two boys.

Another visitor was Leo Wolinsky, a future city editor of the *Los Angeles Times*. Wolinsky was working his way through college as a messenger for the coroner's office, whose quarters in the Hall of Justice basement required him to pass by Lyn and her friends several times a day. Wolinsky struck up a hopeful friendship with them; the women's attitude toward free love had been widely reported. Once the X's appeared on their foreheads, however, Wolinsky directed his social life elsewhere.

Others, however, were drawn by the women's morbid aura. A groupie named Trudy had pestered the jailed defendants with letters, and haunted the girls on the corner. One night, Trudy came by and propositioned Lyn and the others. They declined. Later, when the girls had retreated to the van and crawled under the covers, they were disturbed by a persistent banging, on the door, the window, even the roof. It was, Lyn saw, "a stumbling-numb Trudy wanting to get in—wanting to talk bla bla bla." They ignored her, until Trudy began to let the air out of the van's tires.

At this, Lyn and her four sleepmates leaped from the van—knives in hand. But instead of frightening Trudy off, Lyn discovered, "she craved this sort of attention and found it sexually satisfying." Rather than flee, the woman reacted lewdly, "wiggling into the point of Sandy's knife while rubbing her peterless crotch. She wouldn't budge. It was then that we once again became aware of the sort of clientele that would be attracted by our wonderful reputations," Lyn reported to the girls in jail. "Well, it wasn't time—no, not quite—for spreading blood on the street . . . tho they do it down on 5th St. every day . . . & in old soggy hotel rooms where people go specifically for those dramas.

"We layed out our wishes for her—told her she'd die soon enough & retired to the truck once again, allowing her a graceful . . . or should I say, *manly* exit."

The women resumed their entertainments in the van, listening to the eight-track tape player.

As the prosecution's case built, as the Family's reaction grew more and more extreme, fewer began to see Manson as a victim of the Establishment. Friendly faces began to stay away. Sandy called the quickly moving passers-by the "grey people."

"Sometimes," she later said, "I just wanted to kill the grey people, because that was the only way they would be able to experience the total Now." She insisted, though, that she hadn't meant the remark literally.

People from Lyn's past kept their distance, too. Phil Hartman, who been participating in peace demonstrations and working as a roadie for a band called Rock and Foo, froze when he saw Lyn on television, reading defenses of Manson. Long hair and acid, which he had seen as emblems of a new era of peace and love, suddenly became symbols of mass murder, and even his old classmate couldn't tell the difference.

"Darkness," Hartman thought, "is descending on the movement."

A Family member named Crystal—Maria Alonzo—was hitchhiking from West Hollywood down to Hawthorne, where she worked in a topless bar. A driver stopped to pick her up; it was Bill Siddons, Lyn's former boyfriend, just leaving his offices at Santa Monica and La Cienega boulevards. Siddons, now manager of the Doors, made it a rule always to pick up hitchhikers.

He quickly noticed the X carved into Crystal's forehead. Siddons had seen Lyn, similarly adorned, on television.

"Do you know Lyn Fromme?" he blurted out. "I used to go to school with her."

Crystal couldn't contain her excitement—any friend of Lyn's, especially any friend with a car, was a friend of hers. She exploded with excitement, telling Siddons all about the changes she and Lyn had undergone, inviting him to come by the corner. Crystal had all the zeal of a convert; not an original member of the Family, she had met Sadie in jail at Sybil Brand, and been seduced by the thought of meeting God himself. It was Sadie who gave Maria Alonzo her new name of Crystal Palace, a moniker that might well spring to the mind of a former stripper.

Siddons reflected on the Manson Family, and thought to himself: "You've fucked up, Bill. Not the kind of people you want to be talking to." He smiled for the rest of the trip to Hawthorne on the way to his home in Manhattan Beach—and resolved to stop picking up hitchhikers. He certainly wouldn't be visiting the corner of Temple and Broadway to visit his high school sweetheart.

The rejections only stiffened Lyn's resolve. To her friend in Indiana, she wrote, ". . . scornful faces—opinions, pities, none of which have any matter & we sing & let the clatter rumble with itself." Yet it was all getting so wearying, she acknowledged, the trial indoors, and life in Los Angeles where the smog sometimes got so thick, motorists had to use their headlights in midafternoon.

"It feels so good to lay down . . . ," she wrote. "It's very funny—that so few people can accept love—& to find someone who can—is to find someone who gives it so much—so much, I laugh and cry all at once."

Then the President of the United States convicted Manson. On August 4, 1970, Richard Nixon commented at a press conference that the media often would "glorify and make heroes out of those engaged in criminal activities." In the case of Manson, Nixon said, "here is a man who was guilty, directly or indirectly, of eight murders without reason. Here is a man who, as far as the coverage was concerned, appeared to be rather a glamorous figure, glamorous to the young people whom he had brought into his operations. . . ."

Nixon's press secretary, Ron Ziegler, later said that the president had inadvertently omitted the word "alleged" from his remarks, and Nixon himself issued a statement saying that "the last thing I would do is prejudice the legal rights of any person, in any circumstances. . . . The defendants should be presumed to be innocent at this stage of the trial." At *this stage* of the trial.

Manson replied in a statement of his own to the press: "Here's a man who is accused of murdering hundreds of thousands in Vietnam who is accusing me of being guilty of eight murders."

The jury had been sequestered at the Ambassador Hotel, the site of Robert Kennedy's assassination, and even the windows of the bus they rode to the Hall of Justice had been obscured to prevent them from reading news headlines on the way to court. Violating the judge's order to keep newspapers from the courtroom, Daye Shinn, Sadie's attorney, had brought a copy of the *Los Angeles Times* on August 5.

When he saw it, Manson grabbed the paper and held it for the jury to read. MANSON GUILTY, NIXON DECLARES, the headline proclaimed. The next day, Sadie, Katie, and Leslie rose and asked the judge, "Your Honor, the President said we are guilty, so why go on with the trial?" Reporters speculated that the prejudicial quality of the president's remark might lead to a mistrial, or a reversal of any conviction.

The judge, Charles H. Older, ruled that Manson had invited the error, and therefore the trial would proceed. For violating his order on newspapers, Older found Shinn in contempt of court and sentenced him to three nights in the county jail. Lyn focused on Nixon's statement. She would never forgive him.

The Honolulu Hamburger

The testimony of Linda Kasabian had heavily damaged the defendants. In exchange for immunity from prosecution, she had described the nights of the Tate and LaBianca murders in detail and with apparent remorse, horror, and sincerity. The witnesses that followed—many of them former members of the Family—corroborated parts of her story, filling in the details of the prosecution's case.

Soon to testify was Barbara Hoyt, an eighteen-year-old who had spent time with the Family from at least April 1969. In Inyo County, Barbara had told police of discussions she had overheard about several murders. She said Charlie remarked that Shorty Shea, the Spahn ranch hand, had been "brought to Now"— and that killing him was difficult, requiring Shorty to be struck on the head, stabbed, beheaded, and dismembered. Barbara also said Sadie had told Ouisch about some of the killings at the Tate house, and later that Ouisch mentioned to Barbara that the Family had murdered ten other people.

Compared to other prosecution witnesses, Barbara was not particularly harmful to the defense. Even so, she seemed unsure about testifying against her old friends. When Ouisch invited her to get together with some Family members, Barbara agreed.

Ouisch herself had almost left the Family fold. After the arrests for auto theft in Inyo County, she had been released on condition that she live with her mother in Minneapolis. Once there, it seemed she might readapt to straight society. The Family was able to reclaim Ouisch, however, by subpoenaing her to testify in Manson's defense. Now she was back at Spahn Ranch, preparing for the end of times that soon would come down fast. She was ready to help Barbara drop out, especially since Lyn explained that the prosecution had pressured Barbara to testify against Charlie.

On September 5, 1970, Lyn and Ouisch met Barbara at a bowling alley in the San Fernando Valley, near Pierce College in Canoga Park. They decided to return to Spahn Ranch, where other members of the Family were happy to see Barbara home.

The way Gypsy—Catherine Share, whose father was Hungarian—remembered it, Barbara was anxious about her upcoming date on the stand. Barbara thought she might skip town instead, perhaps head to New Mexico, where she could get by without much money. They talked about other places Barbara could hide. And when Ouisch suggested going to Hawaii Barbara readily agreed. Ouisch remembered someone else, she wasn't sure who, suggesting a Hawaii trip, and Barbara inviting her to come along.

According to the district attorney's office, the sequence was slightly different. It was Gypsy, authorities said, who asked Barbara if she wanted to go to Hawaii instead of testifying. All accounts agreed that Barbara said yes.

Lyn helped Barbara and Ouisch get some clothes together from the Family's communal wardrobe, and then had Clem—or Steve Grogan, who would later be convicted in the murder of Shorty Shea—drive them all to the North Hollywood home of Dennis Rice, one of their new friends. Born in Cleveland, Rice was a thirty-one-year-old ex-convict whose record consisted mainly of narcotics violations, burglaries, and auto thefts. With Charlie, Tex, Bobby, and other male figures in jail, Lyn and the girls missed having a man around, and took to Dennis Rice. They called him "Fatherman."

They spent the night at Fatherman's place. The next day, Ouisch remembered, he drove the two girls to the Los Angeles airport and gave them $50, a TWA Getaway credit card, and three tabs of acid each. Ouisch bought tickets to Hawaii with the Getaway card; she used the name Amy Riley, while Barbara flew as Jill Morgan.

Once in Honolulu, they rented the fourteenth-story penthouse at the Hilton Hawaiian Village Hotel, Ouisch now as Ruth Rice, Barbara as Mary Kuffan. They planned on finding Barbara a local apartment for the duration of the Manson trial, but for the next three days they just relaxed on the beach. Each day, Ouisch would make a call to a pay phone near Fatherman's house, sometimes talking to Lyn. Afterward, Ouisch would hold deep conversations with Barbara, in which she warned her not to be fooled by the placid environs of Hawaii.

"We all have to go through Helter Skelter," Ouisch explained. "If we don't do it in our heads, we'll have to do it physically. If you don't die in your head, you'll die when it comes down."

After her phone call on the morning of the September 9, Ouisch became even more serious. She would have to return to Los Angeles, to pick up more spending money, but Barbara should stay in Hawaii. They went to the airport, and while waiting for the United Airlines 1:25 P.M. flight, Ouisch offered to buy Barbara a hamburger. Ouisch disappeared, then returned from the airport cafeteria bearing the farewell burger.

Looking at the sandwich, Ouisch remarked, "It would sure be some trip if there was five thousand mikes on that." Five thousand micrograms of LSD would be equivalent to a dose of ten tabs of acid.

"Wow," said Barbara, as she took a bite out of the burger. Ouisch boarded the plane and returned to Los Angeles.

Barbara took a taxi from the airport to a bus stop, boarded a city bus, and suddenly fell ill. She ran off the bus and into a nearby building, found the ladies' restroom, and threw up. Starting to trip, she ran into the street and collapsed outside the Salvation Army building on Iwelei Road, near the Dole pineapple plant.

A passing social worker found her and brought her to an emergency room. When Barbara came to, she mumbled something like, "Call Mr. Bogliogi and tell him I won't be able to testify today in the Sharon Tate trial." She told doctors that her hamburger had been spiked with ten tabs of acid, and received a dose of Valium to help her calm down. Barbara's father came to Honolulu to pick up his daughter, and she returned to Los Angeles.

Years later, Ruth Morehouse insisted that there was no intent to kill Barbara, just to put her out of circulation. Why did the Manson girl, a vegetarian, select a hamburger? "We were not allowed to eat meat," Ruth said, "but we craved it. It was like a treat."

Treat or not, when she got back, Barbara eagerly testified for the prosecution. On the stand, she recalled overhearing Sadie tell Ouisch, "Sharon Tate was the last to go because she had to watch the others die." The defense tried to discredit Barbara, in part by pointing out her severe myopia. But her greatest embarrassment came from a question posed by prosecutor Bugliosi.

On redirect examination, he asked Barbara what Manson had instructed her to do with Juan Flynn, a sometime Family associate and fellow prosecution witness. "That oral watchmacallit," Barbara hesitantly replied. After establishing that she meant "orally copulate," Bugliosi brought out that she only did this while Manson was in the room, and ceased when he left—and thus as evidence of Manson's power to make people do unspeakable things. The press delicately reported that Manson forced Barbara "to perform an unnatural sex act," and left it at that.

Things continued to go poorly for the Family. There was the endless petty harassment. Lyn, in blue jeans and a plain gray T-shirt and gray vest, was leading the daily vigil at Temple and Broadway on Wednesday, September 16, when the police decided to tweak the group. A squad from the LAPD showed up at 8:30 A.M. and busted them all for loitering. Officer Hernandez dutifully logged the suspect's possessions: "Misc. Sewing & Paraphanalia [sic]." Lyn was permitted to retain her cash on hand, forty cents. As that left her considerably short of the $315 bail, she spent four days at Sybil Brand. Lyn eventually pled guilty to the misdemeanor charge, and was sentenced to time served.

On the Saturday following Lyn's release, September 26, the troubles were more serious: Brush fires roared through 100,000 acres of the Simi Hills, consuming the Spahn Ranch in barely an hour. Three of George Spahn's sixty horses died in the blaze, after bolting into the flames. When a reporter suggested to George that some might consider the loss "a God-driven hand of punishment," the old man nodded and said, "They might, I guess." Sources told Bugliosi that the girls at the ranch chanted during the flames: "Helter Skelter is coming down!"

But it did not come down at the Hall of Justice. Instead, the trial progressed, Charlie protested the court's procedures, and Lyn, leading the girls on the corner, continued their demonstrations. On one occasion, she staged a "Crawl for Freedom," nearly fifteen miles along Sunset Boulevard from the beach to downtown Los Angeles. Covered by television cameras, the stunt gave Lyn a chance to make her case to the audience watching at home, as well as the people she met along the way.

"We cried a lot and laughed a lot and got fat blisters on our knees and died of thirst and heat and were always pee-propelled, being as the gas stations were so far apart, and got spat on and hollered at and barked at," Lyn recalled. "When black men in Cadillacs drove up, they looked at us with much understanding, and I felt for the first time that I had no more dues to pay.... Sure took care of a lot of guilt."

When Lyn and the others finally made it to the Hall of Justice, they were "sitting on the sidewalk, unwrapping our bruised, scabbing bloody knees and cleaning our hands with alcohol just" as Bugliosi "in his three-piece tweed suit," greeted them on his way to court.

" 'Hi, girls,' he says ... 'what're you doing?' Brenda looked up and told him we were trying to wake a few people up.

" 'You'll never do it that way,' he said, shaking his head. 'You'd have to put a bomb at their feet.' And with that he was off, said he'd be late—to the prosecution of our friends for mass murder, and though his may sound like the wisest words, being as we thought nine dead bodies would be enough.... It was suicide we wanted by the burial of dead systems of thought."

On October 14, the dead system of thought managed another poke at Lyn: the LAPD arrested her for trespassing on county property. The arrest brought another stay at Sybil Brand, although the charge eventually was dismissed. The arresting officers had failed to read Lyn her *Miranda* warning, to remind her that she had the right to remain silent.

On Thursday, November 19, before calling a single witness, Paul Fitzgerald rose in court and said, "The defense rests." Katie, Sadie, and Leslie immediately stood up and demanded to testify—they were, it was expected, planning to take the stand and accept all responsibility for the murders, exonerating Charles Manson. Charlie's attorney, Irving Kanarek, moved to sever Manson's trial from those of the women, which might permit him to go free if his co-defendants took the blame.

The defense lawyers refused to let the female defendants incriminate themselves; "it would be sort of aiding and abetting a suicide," explained Paul Fitzgerald. If the women were to testify, which was their constitutional right, they would have to be called by the court, thus freeing the defense lawyers from the ethical quandary of contributing to their clients' convictions.

The controversy finally was resolved when Charlie himself took the stand in an extraordinary proceeding. Appearing outside the presence of the jury, he was permitted to testify in a "narrative" form, that is, to speak without answering specific questions from the attorneys. If the novel procedure worked, the judge was prepared to let him repeat his testimony before the jury, subject to questioning by the prosecution.

Manson spoke for more than an hour. He complained that since he had not been allowed to represent himself, he had not been allowed to put on a defense. He belittled the prosecution's evidence and questioned the credibility of its witnesses. He insisted that he was simply a reflection of all those around him.

He also spoke more generally of the phenomenon he was supposed to symbolize. "These children that come at you with knives, they are your children," he said. "You taught them. I didn't teach them, I just tried to help them stand up. Most of the people at the ranch that you call the Family were just people that you did not want, people that went alongside the road, that their parents had kicked them out or they did not want to go to juvenile hall, so I did the best I could and I took them up on my garbage dump and I told them this: that in love there is no wrong. . . .

"These children, they take a lot of narcotics because you tell them not to. . . . You go to the high schools and you show them pills and you show them what not to take. How else would they know what it was unless you tell them? . . .

"I may have implied on several occasions to several different people that I may have been Jesus Christ, but I haven't decided yet what I am or who I am. . . .

"I was working on cleaning up my house, something Nixon should have been doing. He should have been on the side of the road picking up his children. But he wasn't. He was in the White House sending them off to war. . . .

"I haven't got any guilt about anything because I have never been able to say any wrong. I never found any wrong. I looked at wrong, and it is all relative. Wrong is if you haven't got any money. Wrong is if your car payment is overdue. Wrong is if the TV breaks. Wrong is if President Kennedy gets killed. Wrong is, wrong is, wrong is—you keep on, you pile it in your mind. You become belabored with it, and in your confusion. . . .

"Like, Helter Skelter is a nightclub. Helter Skelter means confusion. Literally. It doesn't mean any war with anyone. It doesn't mean that those people are going to kill other people. It only means what it means. Helter Skelter is confusion. Confusion is coming down fast. If you don't see the confusion coming down fast around you, you can call it what you wish. It is not my conspiracy. It is not my music. I hear what it relates. It says, 'Rise!' It says, 'Kill!' Why blame it on me? I didn't write the music. . . .

"You see, you can send me to the penitentiary. It's not a big thing. I've been there all my life, anyway. What about your children? These are just a few, there is many, many more coming right at you. . . .

"Prison's in *your* mind. Can't you see *I'm* free?"

After Charlie spoke, he told the women defendants, "You don't have to testify now." He declined to repeat his performance before the jury, explaining to the judge, "I have already relieved all the pressure I had." His testimony, then, was legally meaningless.

The jury had heard eighty-four prosecution witnesses, none from the defense.

Paul Fitzgerald considered the Honolulu hamburger affair as "kind of a joyous persuasion of a witness." He noted that there is no known fatal dose of LSD, unlike barbiturates and other narcotics that also were readily available. The Family wanted Barbara Hoyt to be temporarily "disoriented," at least for the length of the trial, he said. And by spiking a hamburger, the vegetarian women of the Family were sending Barbara a little message about the price of eating meat.

Vincent Bugliosi was less sanguine about the incident, and ordered an investigation. After a two-and-a-half hour proceeding on December 18, the Los Angeles County grand jury indicted Clem, Fatherman, Gypsy, Ouisch, and Lyn. The indictments held that these five, along with "diverse other persons . . . did wilfully, unlawfully and feloniously conspire, combine, confederate and agree together . . . to pervert and obstruct the due administration of the laws." The charges included conspiracy to prevent and dissuade a witness from attending a trial; conspiracy to bribe a witness; conspiracy to commit assault; assault and attempted murder.

It was not difficult to find most of the suspects. Minutes after the indictment was issued, LAPD Sergeant Phil Sartuche, a LaBianca case detective, walked to the corner of Temple Street and Broadway and found Lyn waiting patiently, in a black dress, a brown sweater, and a red scarf. He arrested her, along with Ouisch and Gypsy, and booked her into the Sybil Brand Institute. Clem already was in custody in connection with the Gary Hinman murder. Fatherman was at large, but surrendered on January 11, 1971. Asked why, he said, "Because there's no place else to go. This is where all the love is."

Bugliosi believed that Lyn and the others had intended Barbara to die, if not directly from the LSD, then from the results of a massive distortion of her reality—on her unanticipated acid trip, the prosecutor thought, she might have run in front of a bus.

But on February 24, 1971, Superior Court Judge Raymond Choate dismissed all charges against the five defendants, except the counts of conspiracy to dissuade a witness and conspiracy to bribe a witness not to attend a trial.

Lyn and her co-defendants repeated the pattern Charlie had established: continuously filing motions, substituting attorneys, protesting their treatment, doing all they could to gum up the justice system. Ouisch, released on her own recognizance because she was pregnant, fled to her sister's house in Nevada. The judge, irritated, denied bail for Lyn and her co-defendants, forcing them to follow the Manson trial from jail.

In his closing argument, Vincent Bugliosi called Charlie "the dictatorial master of a tribe of bootlicking slaves," while Sadie, Katie, and Leslie were "a closely-knit band of mindless robots." He completed his remarks on January 15, 1971, interrupted only, the *Los Angeles Herald Examiner* reported, "when Juli Shapiro, nineteen, a shapely blonde who says she is an apprentice witch, stood up in the courtroom and yelled, 'I have proof that key prosecution witnesses were coerced, bribed and threatened.'" She was removed, and that day the jury began its deliberations.

On January 19, the day Paul McCartney petitioned the High Court of England to dissolve the Beatles' business partnership, the Tate-LaBianca jury asked to have "Helter Skelter" and "Revolution 9" played in their chambers. On January 25, the jury convicted all four defendants on all twenty-seven counts of murder.

Lyn Takes the Stand

While Lyn sat in jail, Sandy Good became the Family spokesman. Sitting on the corner, in sandals and purple slacks, she told reporters, "We've been here five months and we can be here forever, but the city's not going to last that long. He'll be out. All the people will be out—Angela Davis, Bobby Seale. There's a revolution coming. You've all judged yourselves."

The carnival atmosphere of the show trial was gone. Leslie Van Houten's attorney, Ron Hughes, had disappeared before final arguments were made, and later was found dead in a remote section of Ventura County. His death was ruled an accident.

For the defendants, all that remained before the court was the sentence: Life imprisonment, or death.

Paul Fitzgerald, weary and defeated, looked to see what remained in his arsenal, what stratagem he might employ to spare his client the gas chamber. He turned to Lyn. The prosecution had brought out countless details about the Family's life—the group sex, the drug use, the travels—shading them all with a sinister tinge. Fitzgerald wanted to retell these events in a positive light: "to save their lives by explaining the milieu in which the murders occurred," he said. He dreaded putting his own client on the stand; he foresaw Bugliosi asking Katie, "How did it feel when the knife plunged into the lady the first time? What did it feel like the second time? What were you thinking when the blood spurted out? What were you thinking when you put your foot on the body to pull the knife out?" But Lyn, who embodied what Fitzgerald saw as the "wonderful humanity" of the Manson girls, was far more articulate than his client—and would be immune to questions about the murders themselves. Lyn could be Katie, Sadie, and Leslie all rolled into one.

Summoned from the Sybil Brand Institute, Lyn began two days of testimony on Tuesday, February 2, 1971. She knew that now, more than ever before, the lives of the Family depended on her. She was full of joy. Her only regret was that Charlie would be unable to see her; the judge had removed him from the courtroom for striking his attorney.

Smiling, dressed in a purple pantsuit, her red hair falling on her shoulders,

Lyn raised her right hand and solemnly swore "to tell the truth, the whole truth, and nothing but the truth." Vincent Bugliosi was not persuaded; "the parade of perjurers began with little Squeaky," the prosecutor grumbled. Throughout the long months of the Manson case, Bugliosi's efforts to turn Lyn away from Charlie, or at least to glean some insight into the Family's plans, had come to naught. All he had extracted from Lyn were beatific smiles, or ambiguous homilies he understood as threats.

The jury seemed amazed when Lyn took the stand; sequestered for months, their only image of the Family's women had been the giggling, contemptuous trio sitting next to Charlie. Polite, well spoken, and a trifle girlish as she answered Paul Fitzgerald's questions, Lyn laid out her background in Los Angeles suburbia, her first encounter with Charles Manson, and the beginning of their odyssey together.

Fitzgerald brought the Family's story up to the acquisition of their traveling home.

"After you purchased a black bus in Sacramento, what, if anything, did you do?"

"We went back to San Francisco. There were a number of kids who were cut off without any money, begging on the streets, who wanted to go some place, who all they wanted to do was get away from one kind of life that was beating them around and get into another one.

"Now," she instructed the court, her voice rising, "that is our crime and you all know it!"

"Now, wait a minute," Bugliosi objected, "motion to strike that gratuitous remark!"

Judge Older immediately granted the motion. A fighter pilot in World War II, the aptly named Older was the picture of an Establishment judge: graying, authoritarian, wholly uncomprehending of the youth movement. The Family had treated him with everything from mere discourtesy—the women defendants had turned their backs to him in court—to the frightening moment when Manson lunged at the judge from his seat, wielding a sharpened pencil, before he was tackled by the bailiff and removed from court. More than a year into the trial, Older had little patience for the high-strung emotions of the defense camp.

Fitzgerald resumed: "How did you support yourself?"

"People were always giving us things," Lyn answered. "That is, because we gave everything away, and that is something that Charlie learnt in the joint."

"When you say 'in the joint,' what do you mean?"

"In the penitentiary," Lyn explained cheerfully. The audience murmured; how disturbing that such an articulate young woman considered parents criminals, and convicts as exemplars of morality. Lyn continued, describing how Charlie had shown her to look at things anew: "If a person has been locked up for a long time, every little bit of the outside world is like a special treat, like when we ride on the bus to see the freeway or something, after you have been locked up." Now, at the Sybil Brand jail, Lyn was learning this lesson for herself.

Fitzgerald brought out that many traveled on the bus. "Oh yeah," Lyn said, "periodically I mean, you know, a lot of people would come."

"Many would come, but in a sense, few were chosen?" he asked.

"Oh, we did not choose anybody," Lyn said. "They would choose themselves. People would come on the bus and they would want a ride up to Los Angeles"—she said "up" to Los Angeles, a turn of phrase left from her days in Redondo Beach, south of the city. In Northern California, especially in San Francisco, people said they were going "down" to Los Angeles, a connotation extending beyond the geographical. "They would come, they would want a ride somewhere else, or they would want to see what we were doing, or—"

"But," Fitzgerald interrupted, "you stayed for a long time?"

"Forever," Lyn said.

"Now, when you arrived at the Spahn Ranch, was Manson your leader?"

"Manson was never our leader. In the first place," Lyn said, "he would follow us. All he had to do in the whole world after getting out of jail was see what we needed, see what we wanted. He turned us on to that very thing, not by saying it, but because he was doing it with us. All of a sudden, we started seeing that. He really cared about us. He is checking to see. We mention one thing, and he is looking around, and in a little while we have got it. He is asking people. He doesn't mind asking people for anything, because he would give it all away. Boy, sometimes he would give away stuff that I wanted. But at the same time, he couldn't deny anybody."

Judge Older grew weary of Lyn's exposition. In his trademark gesture of annoyance, he would all but flick you out of his eye, Fitzgerald thought.

"Mr. Fitzgerald," the judge said, "let's proceed with questions and answers."

The attorney complied: "Did you have some sort of reveille in the morning, where you all lined up and Charlie gave you orders?"

"We did as women do, what needs to be done," Lyn explained. "At least women should do—women's cleaning that needs to be done. We do the cleaning." As Lyn listed the chores she happily performed—chores that fell to her solely because of her sex—some male observers marveled at Manson's achievement: persuading young women to give up their traditional sexual mores, while embracing domestic duties that had fallen to women for millennia. "And between each other," she said, "this is the one thing that we discovered, that if you are truly, truly selfish, you find out."

The judge interrupted: "Just answer the question, Miss Fromme."

"You find out that the true measure is in giving—" she continued.

"That will be enough," Judge Older said.

"—And helping each other—"

"Answer the question!" the judge commanded.

"This is in answer to the question!" said Lyn.

"No, it isn't," Older corrected. "Listen to the questions that are asked."

Fitzgerald: "Did you love Charlie?"

"Sure."

"Did it appear to you that the other girls at the ranch loved Charlie?"

"Sure. We loved love."

"Did they love him in a traditional fashion the way all of us love one another?"

"Your children are not acting in a traditional fashion, and we are your children," said Lyn. "The traditional fashion is for you to cut your love to one person. We have opened ours up. We have said: I love that one over there. And we have said that is okay, you can love as many as you want, all."

Fitzgerald: "Now, I am going to ask you some questions about—"

Lyn interrupted. "That doesn't mean you have to physically love them. We love Mr. Bugliosi and he is trying to kill us."

Bugliosi shot up. "Motion to strike that, Your Honor!"

"The answer is stricken," Judge Older said. "The jury is admonished to disregard it." He turned to Lyn. "You are not to volunteer any answers," he said sternly. "Just listen to the question and answer the question asked."

Fitzgerald resumed. "Did you love Charles Manson as a father, or as a lover, or as a—"

Lyn jumped in. She was ready to explain a lesson Charlie had taught her: "Every girl loves her father, as all things, but her father doesn't understand that and feels guilty about loving her and watching her grow up. Now, Charlie was a father who knew that it is good to make love, and makes love with love, but not with evil and guilt."

"And did you make love with him from time to time?"

"Yes."

"Was that a guiltless love-making?"

"Uh-huh, yes," Lyn said. "Like being a baby."

"Now, you know Charles Manson well, is that correct?"

"As well as I know myself."

"And I take it you have had probably literally thousands of conversations with him, is that right?"

Thousands? "It is all one big conversation," Lyn said. "See, when we think, we speak to ourselves, and that is the same thing as talking to him. Exactly."

Eventually, Fitzgerald got Lyn to concede that she and Charlie had held conversations over specific topics.

"Now, did Charlie ever mention to you any philosophy of any kind, any philosophy of life, or any political philosophy?"

"No, he didn't," said Lyn. "Coming from the penitentiary, he wasn't allowed to vote and, therefore, he never bothered with politics. . . . We didn't refer to any sort of philosophy. . . ."

"Did it appear to you that Charles Manson had some supernatural or magical powers?"

Lyn hedged. "Many, many miraculous, what people would call miraculous things."

"Did you think, though, that he had some spiritual or magical powers?" If Lyn thought so, Fitzgerald reasoned, then Katie would have thought so. And if she thought she was acting under command of a god, then perhaps her crime would not seem so inhuman as to merit execution.

"It is hard to reflect back upon my own thoughts at another time because I have changed so much," Lyn said.

Fitzgerald pressed: "Did you at any time feel that Charlie was Christ or God or some deity?"

"Well, I have come to look at man in a totally other light, due to coming above my own teaching. I was not taught to be a creature, a woman. I was taught to be a subject of my parents, and of the established way of looking at things, you know what I mean? In fact, I was taught I was ugly." Charlie had taught her she was beautiful.

"What I'm trying to get at," Fitzgerald continued, "is did you personally harbor a belief that Charles Manson was Christ or God or some special deity of some kind?"

"Did I?" How could she say it?

"Did you, yes."

"I believe—well, I don't know what I did—whatever I thought before."

"Did you believe he was a special person, that he was different from the average?"

"He was," Lyn said with understatement, "very, very special to me."

"And as a result of seeing Manson display attributes that were in your opinion not average, did you think he possessed some supernatural powers of some kind?"

"I had those feelings when I met him, when he would say what I was thinking but I would not let myself think that. I denied it to myself." Lyn had said it, without saying it.

"Now," Fitzgerald continued, trying to explore the philosophy Lyn denied they had, "did you hear him talk about blacks and whites more than once?"

"Uh-hum, because we understand what is going to happen," Lyn said. "That is why we are here."

"Did he ever talk about that the white people in this country were going to kill the black people in this country?"

Lyn was incredulous. "*Were* going to? That is all I have to say, you know, we understand what they have been through."

Fitzgerald: "Was he more sympathetic of the black man or was he antagonistic to the black man?"

"No. What I want to say is, that is why we have been out on that corner, because—"

Judge Older had had enough. "Answer the question."

"Okay," said Lyn. She looked up at the judge.

"Listen to the question and just answer the question asked," he said slowly.

Fitzgerald: "Did he say frequently that he loved the black man?"

"He didn't need to. He has said it, I know he has said it, but he has said it in regard to people who would come up to him about this prejudice business," Lyn said. They were not only painting Charlie as a murderer but as a bigot.

"Did it appear to you that in any respect he was racially prejudiced?"

"No."

"Did at any time Manson speak with you about fomenting or starting some race revolution of some kind where the blacks would fight the whites or vice versa?"

"No," said Lyn, annoyed. "He is trying to tell you that you set this time bomb a long time ago!"

Did Manson see a race war coming?

"Yes," said Lyn. "Long before he said anything about it."

Was Manson then a prophet?

"He doesn't call himself a prophet," Lyn said. For he was far more than that.

"Well," said Fitzgerald, "what was his theory about the revolution?"

"His only theory," Lyn shot back, "is your own history, which you have read in your history books." She explained how the white man, throughout the ages, had subjugated any who were of darker hue than himself.

"And this was an integral part of his philosophy," Fitzgerald asked, "the history of the white man versus the colored races?"

"It wasn't 'an integral part of his philosophy,'" Lyn said, exasperated. "His philosophy right now is: *Look what is right in front of you!*" A revolution was not only coming, she said, "actually, it has already started."

"And why was this revolution, according to Charlie, going to occur?"

"Why?" asked Lyn, almost rhetorically.

"Why."

"Why? Yes, why." She paused, as if pondering the question. "That is what all of you should be asking yourselves."

Fitzgerald continued to try to elicit from Lyn Charlie's view of the revolution, to see if she would admit that he felt personally responsible for it. Lyn refused.

"You see what has happened in these courtrooms," she said, to the gallery and those in the press seats. "People fish around—"

"That will be enough, young lady," Judge Older interrupted. "Wait for the question and answer only the question. Do you understand?"

Lyn looked to him, again. Judge Older ruled the court like a father ruled his home. "Whenever I wish to talk to you, could I just talk to you?" she asked the judge.

"No, you may not talk to me," he said. "Just answer the questions that are asked of you."

Fitzgerald: "You said that Manson said that he felt responsible for these historical killings, and he felt it as a man. Could you explain that?"

"Yes. If you were to look at this world from on top of a mountain," Lyn said, remembering the acid trip in Mendocino where it all had come together. "If you were to put yourself up there and look at it—"

The judge silenced her. "There is nothing pending now. Mr. Fitzgerald, would you approach the bench, please, with counsel?"

"There *is* something pending!" Lyn insisted: the moment where everything made sense, the moment she wanted to share with the whole world. But the lawyers, defense and prosecution both, ignored her as they gathered around the judge.

Older told Fitzgerald that, obviously, "this witness is not interested in being responsive to the questions asked her." He urged Fitzgerald to tell Lyn that her testimony, if it continued as it was going, "can only inure to the detriment of these defendants. She is not to use this court as a forum for her philosophies."

Bugliosi chimed in: "I would like to say, if the court is wondering why I am not objecting, I am not objecting because I feel that her testimony is helpful to the prosecution. This is why I am not objecting," he continued. "So, it is a tactful thing on my part, not that I am being slovenly as a prosecutor. I feel that her testimony is helpful, and I wanted the court to know that." Judge Older nodded.

Fitzgerald tried to explain. "I am trying to show this life in the Family, life at the Spahn Ranch, life with Charles Manson, life as one of these girls. In many respects, I think it is bizarre, I think it is incredible, I think it is crazy."

"My comments were not directed to your judgment in calling [her as] a witness—" Older said, charitably.

"Yes," nodded Fitzgerald.

"—regardless of what my own opinion might be on the subject," the judge added.

Fitzgerald resumed the examination. Lyn testified that she was familiar with the term "Helter Skelter"; it meant "confusion, chaos," she explained. "'Helter Skelter' is the Beatle song, you know," she said. "It's come up in this case." It certainly had.

"Did people frequently listen to the Beatle records at the Spahn Ranch?"

"Yes, we loved the Beatles," Lyn said. "I love them, Donovan, the Moody Blues. A lot of people are saying the same thing."

"Were the Beatles more popular with you than the other recording artists you have also mentioned?"

"Well," Lyn said, "as popular as they are with the world." She testified that she had heard the White Album countless times. It was a favorite out at the ranch.

"Did you have some particular affinity with Beatles, and did your group have some particular affinity with the Beatles?" Fitzgerald asked.

"How 'particular affinity'?" asked Lyn.

"Were you particularly close to them in some fashion?" In other words, did Charlie believe they were speaking directly to him?

"Physically, we never met them."

"Did you feel you had some intellectual or mental—"

"They project love," Lyn explained. "They say, 'Dear Prudence, won't you come out and play, come on,' you know. 'This world is for living. This is for having a good time, for loving.'" The song "Dear Prudence," John Lennon later said, had been written about Mia Farrow's sister, who sat in her hut in India too long, meditating. "They sing," Lyn said, "'Love, Love, Love.' And there's many, many people that sing love now. Have you listened to the kids' music?"

Fitzgerald honed in. "They did not then project in your opinion any hate or program anybody to a revolution or a black-white race war or anything?"

Lyn paused. "There is a lot in those albums. There is a lot."

"You did not worship the Beatles as gods or anything, to be absurd?"

"A lot of kids did."

Right. "What about you?" Fitzgerald asked.

"Personally, I did not worship them, no. I love their music, though. In other words, their music brings out the love of your heart, you know what I mean, of your soul. It makes you dance. It makes you freer."

Irving Kanarek, Manson's attorney, was the next to question Lyn.

"Do you remember Mr. Manson discussing any kind of philosophy of life with Mr. [Gregg] Jakobson at Dennis Wilson's?"

"At Dennis Wilson's?" asked Lyn.

"Yes."

"I wish I did."

"Or anywhere," Kanarek said.

"Well, you see," Lyn said, "we are living a philosophy; you can say that. We were always discussing it. Anything we discussed is our philosophy."

"Does Charles Manson have any power?"

"He loves."

"Pardon?"

"He loves, and that is—that is a power. That's the only power that doesn't look like power. It's non-control . . . a release of your love for everything and everybody. It is allowing yourself the pleasure of loving things rather than fighting them, you know. We all, everybody fights with themselves over some things, and we began releasing that fight by saying, 'I love it, I love it, I love it.' For me, because it makes me feel good."

She looked around the courtroom, at the uncomprehending faces of the lawyers and reporters and jurors. She sighed. "I feel so many times that you don't understand what I am saying, but I will say it anyway."

So, Kanarek continued, what did Lyn mean by "power"?

"I believe that God is love, and, just like it says in the Book, and that it is the gentlest thing on this earth and at the same time it makes earthquakes."

(Within a week, the earth would quake again, with an epicenter a few miles from the Spahn Ranch. The Sylmar earthquake was the most devastating to hit Los Angeles in a half century, destroying hospitals and collapsing freeway overpasses. After the temblor, the girls on the corner beamed and told reporters that Charlie had predicted it.)

"Now," Lyn continued, "what man controls an earthquake? What man controls the rain? You know! What man controls wars, even? How long has this earth been fighting with itself? We are giving up the fight. We say, 'Either kill us, but it's okay.' "

"Well," Kanarek resumed, "do you think Charles Manson has any power over other people, any other people?"

"No power against anybody's will, let's say that," Lyn offered. "A power that you speak of would be a control over somebody, is that right?"

"Well, answer as you see fit."

"Yeah, okay. Nothing against anybody's will. Each person has their own will and their individuality, and they do what they wish with it. Milton said it, you know, you make a heaven, you make a hell. You make it." The reference to Book IV of *Paradise Lost* passed over the heads of those in court.

What Milton had written was

Farewell happy Fields
Where Joy for ever dwells: Hail horrors, hail
Infernal world, and thou profoundest Hell
Receive thy new Possessor: One who brings
A mind not to be chang'd by Place or Time.
The mind is its own place, and in itself
Can make a Heav'n of Hell, a Hell of Heav'n.
What matter where, if I be still the same,
And what I should be, all but less than [he]
Whom thunder hath made greater? Here at least
We shall be free; th' Almighty hath not built
Here for his envy, will not drive us hence:
Here we may reign secure, and in my choice
To reign is worth ambition though in Hell:
Better to reign in Hell, than serve in Heav'n.

The speaker was Satan.

"Did you think that Charles Manson was Jesus Christ?"

"I think that Jesus Christ was love," said Lyn. "I think that he went around and that the Christians in the cave and in the woods were a lot of people and a lot of kids, just living and being without guilt, without shame, being able to take off their clothes and lay in the sun and roll around like babies, you know, you see your own kids." Lyn explained it as if she had been there. "That is how I see Christians. And I see Jesus Christ as a man who came from a woman, who did not know who the father of her baby was."

But before this idea could be explored further, Judge Older interrupted.

"We are going to recess at this time, Mr. Kanarek," he said.

Vincent Bugliosi scribbled in pencil: "She's saying Jesus Christ is Manson since Manson supposedly was illegitimate and the son of a prostitute, so Manson's mother probably never knew who Manson's father was."

When court reconvened, Kanarek moved on to another point. He asked Lyn to explain Manson's philosophy.

"... you see," she said, suddenly weary, "we have been using a term, *death*, for an experience of giving up a fight of something. We use that word all the time, *death*. In fact, it is death to be up here. It is a death to be in this case, and there is a part of our mind that you could call the devil, and that part of the mind wants to question you, wants to fight with you and wants to make you worry."

She continued: "You can pick out as many things as you like to worry about. You can worry about walking outside, either that, or you can just do what you do and accept it and be as aware as you can of everything around you. Live and let live. Be, and you reach closer to your subconscious, which is in essence your soul. Your children are at the soul; they move freely, they are not inhibited by what people think. They are fools, and that is what it feels good to be, and we were bringing ourselves down to be fools of a sort, fools enough to laugh at ourselves and to be comfortable with anybody, to feel at home, to be happy with ourselves, because that is the only place anybody can start, is with themselves. All that he was doing was making himself happy, and he allowed us to do something that no man had allowed us girls to do, and that is take care of him ... He allowed us to—"

Again, Judge Older interrupted: "The question was," the exasperated jurist said, 'What do you believe Mr. Manson's philosophy was?' Confine your answer to that question."

"Your Honor," said Lyn, "Mr. Manson's philosophy—"

"Confine your answer to that question, young lady!"

"Mr. Manson's philosophy is *not* confined, not at all!" Lyn insisted. "Mr. Manson's philosophy is whatever one you choose."

Kanarek resumed: "Would you say it is a fair statement that in fact Mr. Manson had no philosophy of life?"

Lyn agreed.

"Now," Kanarek continued, "do you think that Mr. Manson is fit to live?"

Bugliosi objected: "Calls for a conclusion, Your Honor, irrelevant."

"Sustained," said Judge Older.

Kanarek: "Did Mr. Manson ever state that he felt responsible for the killings that were going on in the world?"

Lyn tried to get back to the acid trip in Mendocino, to the epiphany. "He, as I was about to say at one point, he looked down the mountain——"

"You can answer that question yes or no!" thundered Judge Older.

"We are on trial for our lives here!" Lyn shouted back, as if she were shouting at Dad. "You are trying to cut us short!"

"Answer the question, young lady."

"He is a man," said Lyn. "He is responsible for everything man is responsible for, and that is how I see him, and I am responsible for everything woman is responsible for."

Kanarek then sought to get Lyn's recollections of various events at Spahn Ranch, but she couldn't remember all the comings and goings, the conversations between Charlie and the countless people. "In other words," she quipped, "what did you have for lunch yesterday?" Who could remember that?

Then came Vincent Bugliosi's turn. In cross-examination, he quickly established that Lyn was living in jail, and when not in jail, on the corner of Temple and Broadway.

"And you stay there twenty-four hours a day?"

"Yes. . . . We live here. This is our house."

"Why do you want to be there at the corner?"

"Because we want to be together," Lyn said, "and we want to stand out here and not let you people forget about what is going on here."

"Why," Bugliosi asked, "did you put that X on your forehead?"

"We are marked, we are clearly marked. . . . Whoever has an X on the forehead is marked, and that means life."

Paul Fitzgerald rose for his redirect examination.

"What does the X on your forehead symbolize, Miss Fromme, if anything?"

"It is," she explained, "a falling cross. . . . It means that the system as it now stands is falling. Your children don't want it anymore. . . . It is the fact that we are crossed out of the Establishment. We stand by ourselves apart from it. And we realize that you all are employed by this Establishment and, therefore, we are on trial, and it is like everybody is against us. But it is all right."

Irving Kanarek asked the last question.

"Is part of the cross that is on your forehead, is it there because you feel that Mr. Manson is not getting a fair trial?"

"Oh, Your Honor," Bugliosi exploded, "objection!"

"Sustained," said the judge.

"It goes to her state of mind," argued Kanarek.

"I know that," said Lyn. "The jury made the decision with only one side."

"That will be enough," said the judge, admonishing the jury to disregard

Lyn's remark. Kanarek said he had no further questions, and Judge Older turned to Lyn.

"You may step down," he said, coldly.

"Are you mad at me?" Lyn asked, almost hurt.

He ignored her, and recessed the court.

Vincent Bugliosi later paid Lyn the highest compliment he could muster.

"Squeaky," he wrote, "was the least untruthful of the Family members who testified."

Sentenced to Death

Paul Fitzgerald's plan to keep the defendants off the stand failed. They had the right to testify on their own behalf, and the women did so, gleefully confessing to the murders. Asked how she could justify killing a total stranger, Sadie testified: "How could it not be right when it is done with love?. . . I didn't relate to Sharon Tate as being anything but a store mannequin. . . . She kept begging and pleading and pleading and begging, and I got sick of listening to her, so I stabbed her." Did she feel sorry? Sadie was incredulous: "Sorry for doing what was right to me? I have no guilt in me."

Whatever feelings of sympathy Lyn's testimony might have raised in the minds of the jurors quickly evaporated. In his closing statement, Leslie's new attorney, Maxwell Keith, asked for pity. He read what he called "the roll call of the living dead: Leslie, Sadie, Katie, Squeaky, Brenda, Ouisch, Sandy, Cathy, Gypsy, Tex, Clem, Mary, Snake and no doubt many more." Manson had so damaged their lives, Keith said, perhaps "their destruction is beyond repair."

The jury deliberated only ten hours. Summoned to hear the verdict, the defendants entered the courtroom on March 29 with shaved heads. In all cases, the jury recommended death.

"You have just judged yourselves!" Katie yelled, before she and the other defendants were removed for disrupting the proceeding.

When she learned of the verdict, Lyn shaved her head, too.

Across the country, another notorious killer also heard his verdict read. An Army court-martial convicted Lieutenant William L. Calley of the murder of twenty-two Vietnamese civilians, killed in the My Lai massacre. Two days later, he received a life sentence, later commuted.

Prosecutors, faced with several more murder trials involving the Manson Family, were eager to dispose of the relatively weak Barbara Hoyt case. They made a deal with Lyn and her co-defendants: A ninety-day misdemeanor sentence, in exchange for a no-contest plea to a single count of conspiracy to prevent a witness from testifying. All other charges were dismissed, but Lyn would remain in jail for weeks to come.

When it opened in 1961, the Sybil Brand Institute for Women represented the new thinking in correctional sciences. Rehabilitation, rather than retribution, was seen as the enlightened solution to the problems of crime and delinquency. Female criminals in particular were believed to be excellent candidates for reform, as their crimes seemed to spring less from malice than necessity; women most often landed in jail for petty theft, prostitution, and the assorted results of domestic discord. Officials hoped the sparkling new facility in East Los Angeles would turn the lives of wayward women around.

Named after the crusading philanthropist who spearheaded its founding, the Sybil Brand Institute resembled a junior college campus more than a jail, with green landscaping, covered walkways, and low-rise dormitories. The interiors, decorated with cheery pastels and pictures of flowers, were somewhat akin to an elementary school. Probation officers assigned to the women's jail tended to see themselves as counselors more than enforcers. It was hoped that women awaiting trial or serving misdemeanor sentences would benefit from the supportive atmosphere. Inmates called the institution "Sybil's House."

But rather than be reformed by them, Lyn sought to educate her jailers. She tried to explain things to her probation officer, June Ramsay.

Lyn's ebullience contrasted with her X-scarred, shaven head. She spoke about family problems from the age of thirteen, of being on her own at sixteen, of finding Charlie at eighteen. Evidence supported many of Lyn's assertions: not once did her mother or father, her brother or sister come to visit Lyn in jail.

"I grew up on the Spahn Ranch," Lyn told Ramsay. "It was a simple life— like being a pioneer." Her place, she said, was with her "brothers and sisters" on the corner of Temple and Broadway. She said she would return there immediately upon her release.

Rather than have the probation officer speak for her, Lyn wrote her own statement for the judge who would decide her release date. She wrote in pencil on a yellow legal pad, in her formal, librarianlike hand. It was, for Lyn, another opportunity to teach the world what the Family really was all about.

Sir:

I have grown up in the physical circumstances that would enable me to choose and pursue most any vocation and life style. With full knowledge of this, I now stand for what I believe and love. . . .

I once was a child who needed a mother and a father to take care of me, and am now a woman who takes care of others and allows others to take care of me. By isolating ourselves from the established world we have created our own world, a simple one of living to make each other happy. . . . Money and possessions we treat like candy, costumes and trinkets of the kids we liken ourselves to. The cars, the old trucks, even our most treasured instruments we give away and likewise the people of our world give to us, keeping a circulation of toys, food, money.

We have never been in need—for the only thing we really want is to be together.

We have no philosophy, by title, doctrine or rule. . . . We have found our pleasure—our raggedy success—in the hard simplicity of the ancestors we can well imagine crossing this country in constant discovery. . . . I cannot ask you, a man of progress, to understand this movement that is seemingly backward. I only show you a picture of our life style—which has been in itself considered a conspiracy.

She then went over the charges against her, and insisted that it was the women who had planned whatever had happened, while the men involved—Clem, Fatherman—were merely bystanders. But she felt her acts were hardly a crime at all.

It is not unusual for us to help people move out of the established world and we have always been under suspicion for it. I do understand the illegality of doing so in this case. I consider my actions natural since at the time we were re-acting as always with no plan or schedule. . . . I understand that I am not to contact sole prosecution witnesses. I have no desire to contact anyone. My only wish is to be with my bald-headed sisters on the corner. We are becoming increasingly aware of this legal system as we actually *live* in the courts—and I feel steadfastly I belong no other place. . . .

We understand your position. We really do.

With due respect,

Lynette Fromme.

Probation Officer Ramsay found Lyn a puzzling client. "This defendant," Ramsay noted, "was pleasant and cooperative, apparently truthful and frank, and a likable and attractive young person."

But despite being "capable and intelligent, she has chosen over a substantial period of time to alienate herself from society and to become a part of a group following only their own loose rules and inclinations." Lyn, Ramsay felt, was quite similar in her outlook to the other women held in the hamburger affair.

What holds the girls to their present course of action is not understood. They have further accentuated their apartness from accepted mores by the current headshaving and disfiguring scarring. Regardless of the consequences, they are determined to continue their present "lifestyle" and are dedicated to remaining "on the corner" to demonstrate their love and support of the others before the court. Self-support and employment have no place in their pattern, and parasitic living will continue.

As this is an individual and allegedly unalterable choice, then, there could be no benefit from probation which requires more conventional behavior and at least minimal conformance to society's requirements. This defendant has described her plans frankly and unequivocally and is willing to accept the consequences of which she is fully aware. . . .

"In this instance," Ramsay concluded, "probation would be a farce, representing as it does the Establishment from which this defendant claims alienation."

The judge concurred, and Lyn served out the remainder of her sentence at Sybil Brand.

Chapter 6

A Horse

with No

Name

Things were different when Lyn returned to the corner of Temple and Broadway in the late summer of 1971. Charlie was to be sent four hundred miles north, to Death Row at San Quentin. Katie, Leslie, and Sadie, housed at Sybil Brand during their trial, were moved to the California Institution for Women at Frontera. To prevent their escape, police marksmen lined roofs and freeway overpasses along the route to the prison, where a new Death Row was being built just for the Manson "girls." Never before had the state of California confined so many condemned women at the same time.

The news media's interest in the Family had dissipated. Trials continued—Tex Watson for the Tate-LaBianca slayings, Sadie and Charlie for the Gary Hinman murder, and several others—but Manson's image, up for grabs when he was arrested in 1969, had been cemented. He was no impish countercultural trickster, like Abbie Hoffman at the Chicago Seven trial. Nor was he a spiritual revolutionary condemned by a wicked society—akin to one defendant in Jerusalem two millennia before. Instead, Charlie had been defined in Vincent Bugliosi's words: "a vicious, diabolical murderer." Lyn despaired.

Around the country, the hippie movement, in brief bloom through the Woodstock concert of 1969, had degenerated—and the Establishment's hostility had grown more extreme. "If it takes a bloodbath, let's get it over with," was how California Governor Ronald Reagan proposed to deal with antiwar demonstrators. "No more appeasement."

The policy seemed reflected in crackdowns at Berkeley's People's Park, and later at Kent State University in Ohio, where four student protesters were shot dead by National Guardsmen. Stunned, those in the youth movement began to believe, as the Doors' Ray Manzarek later put it, that the Establishment "will kill you if they have to. *They will kill you.*" Thus confronted, many drifted away. Many of those who remained grew more radical, shifting the counterculture from a spiritual insurgency to a political rebellion. Communes were out. Armed struggle, especially in California, was in.

On the corner of Temple and Broadway, the remnants of the Family reviewed their options. The Beach Boys, and whatever other contacts they had made in the entertainment world, would have nothing to do with them. Spahn Ranch, consumed by flames, was gone. Nobody was interested in Charlie's teachings, much less his music.

Paul Fitzgerald encouraged Lyn to find a positive way to continue her struggle. And she did, throwing herself into a new project. Using drawings and stories, Lyn began to assemble a huge, unwieldy book documenting the Family's beautiful journey. The Manson trial had failed to enlighten the world, she realized, but that was a procedure controlled by lawyers and police. By writing a book, Lyn wouldn't have to depend on anyone else's good offices. She could tell the story herself, with all the skill and verve that had always suffused her writings. A book could change minds, explore the mystery and the magic, even perhaps win Charlie a new trial where he could represent himself, and finally reveal the truth. It was the greatest thing Lyn could ever do.

Outside of Lyn's literary endeavors, the Family was finding new friends. While in jail during his trial, Charlie had met the white prison gang known as the Aryan Brotherhood, or the A.B. The gang had emerged in the mid-1960s in reaction to the growing militancy of black and Chicano inmates of the California prisons.

The A.B., whose members wore its initials tattooed on their chests, was less concerned with revolution, or even white supremacy, than with traditional criminal activities: extortion, narcotics trafficking, and murder for hire. Charlie, foreseeing a long future in prison, struck up an arrangement. The A.B. would protect Charlie inside, and Charlie's girls would look after the A.B. guys on the outside. The Aryan Brotherhood may have consisted of hardened career criminals, but they were as happy as any lonely men to have female pen pals.

Shortly after making the deal, Charlie subpoenaed Kenneth Como, an A.B. member from Folsom Prison, to testify in the Gary Hinman–Shorty Shea murder trial. In July 1971, after his transfer to Los Angeles, Como escaped from jail and made his way to the Family. Prisoners were no longer sitting back and taking it; a year before, Jonathan Jackson had burst into the Marin County Courthouse in San Rafael, aiming to break out three convicts being tried for the murder of a prison guard. Although the attempt failed—four died and two were seriously wounded in the shootout—many convicts saw it as an opening skirmish in a coming war against the System. The Manson Family, now allied with the A.B., was angry enough to bring the war right back to the Man.

Charlie would be taken to the Hall of Justice to testify in Clem's trial for the murder of Shorty Shea: a raid could free them both. Of course, an assault on the seat of the county's justice system would require more than the Buck knives Lyn and the other women liked to carry, so Como led several Family members on a crime spree to collect money and firearms. The scheme ran into trouble, however, on August 21, when they tried to rob a military surplus store in Hawthorne, a working-class suburb bordering Redondo Beach. Police captured Como and five others, including Mary Brunner, Gypsy, and Fatherman.

The defendants quickly owned up to their plans, and then some. Not only did they intend to arm themselves in order to free the Family, the Hawthorne Five said in a news release, "We were and are determined to free as many of the victims of this Criminal System as we possibly could and to build and spread this thought to others."

Soon after the failed robbery, members of the Family tried to break Como out of the Hall of Justice jail. With a smuggled hacksaw, the five foot seven, 140-pound prisoner spent several days cutting a 6½ × 15-inch hole in his cell window. At dawn on Wednesday, October 20, he pushed through the gap and into an exercise area between cells. He pried a screen off a thirteenth-story window facing Broadway and used a rope fashioned from mattress covers to lower himself to a ledge on the tenth floor. With a second makeshift rope, he dropped down to the eighth story, which housed the criminal courts. He kicked in a window to Superior Court Department 104—where Manson had been tried, convicted, and condemned—and made his way down the stairwell to the street. There he was pleased to find a red import car with the keys in the ignition; homicide Detective Paul Dorris had mistakenly assumed his vehicle would be safe in the Hall of Justice parking lot.

The sheriff's department later said that Lyn and Brenda were waiting for Como, and that the three of them drove off in Detective Dorris's car. They made their way to a rendezvous point where Sandra Good was parked with the Family van. Lyn and Brenda split up. Como hopped in the van, and he and Sandy headed west on Sunset Boulevard, toward Hollywood.

Unfortunately for getaway purposes, the Family's van had become well known to police during the months it spent parked at Temple and Broadway. One officer, Sheriff's Sergeant Frank Linley, had just heard news of the escape when he spotted the van on Sunset Boulevard. He chased it west on Sunset, following as the van swung right on Curson Avenue, headed north toward the Hollywood Hills, and crashed into a parked car. Como leaped from the driver's side, running around the front of the van and down an alley. Sergeant Linley raced after him, but lost the trail after Como scrambled through a hedge.

Forty officers soon fanned out across the streets of Hollywood, backed by helicopter-borne searchlights in a house-to-house sweep. They finally captured Como at 3:00 A.M., hiding in a toolshed on Gardner Street, two blocks away from the crashed van. Barefoot and still in his blue jail uniform, Como surrendered with no resistance. He received a fifteen years to life sentence.

The police, who now considered Lyn the Manson Family's leader, traced her to a safehouse in Silver Lake, east of Hollywood. She was arrested for conspiracy, but, as usual, prosecutors lacked enough evidence to make the charge stick. Lyn was released the next day, October 21. Brenda was also cleared of any wrong-doing. Sandy received a six-month sentence for aiding and abetting the attempted escape.

As John Lennon's "Power to the People" played on the radio, making Lyn think of People as in *People* vs. *Manson*, she wrote a letter to Charlie reporting the latest news. She described how the Hawthorne robbers were recovering from their wounds ("Gypsy got pellets in her butt & a .38 bullet that put a hole in her shoulder"), passed on girlish gossip, found meaning in "Admiral Halsey," the latest Paul McCartney song. "Hands across the water, water," she wrote. McCartney's lyrics still demonstrated how strong the Family's bond was.

". . . You're coming here soon—I almost said, *home*—but no this ain't it here, no this ain't it at all. But home is where we're somewhat together—all cohorts in one big bag," she wrote, next to a drawing of a bag filled with people. She ended with a plea. "Let us hear from you—maybe Paul [Fitzgerald] could write down a few words for us—ANYTHING!"

October 21, 1971, was an important day for many levels of the justice system. In Washington, D.C., President Nixon nominated William H. Rehnquist to the Supreme Court, while the House Internal Security Committee heard testimony on leftist groups active in California.

More significant to Lyn, it was the day a Los Angeles jury voted to execute Tex Watson, who had been tried separately in the Tate-LaBianca murders. Tex had fled to his home state in 1969, and local officials who were friendly with his family had delayed his extradition until Manson's trial was under way. Unlike the original defendants, Tex had behaved himself in court, attending in jacket and tie, sitting quietly as the attorneys argued the law. Tex's conviction proved Charlie's point: No matter how you acted in court, the result was the same. Might as well go kicking and screaming.

Lyn, meanwhile, had more errands to run. Charlie, now on trial for the murders of Gary Hinman and Shorty Shea, decided that Lyn should visit the judge, Raymond Choate. A year before, Choate had dismissed most of the charges against Lyn in the Barbara Hoyt affair; Charlie concluded that through Lyn, Choate would come to see himself and realize that Charlie should go free.

The judge declined to meet privately with Lyn, but finally granted her a few minutes to air her thoughts. Choate offered Lyn a doughnut from the box his clerk had brought in, but was unpersuaded by her presentation. In court, the judge called Charlie a "whining, complaining delinquent and small-time car thief with an aversion to work," and sentenced him to life imprisonment, on top of the death sentence for the Tate-LaBianca murders.

On November 5, Lyn herself managed to get five days at Sybil Brand, when yet another irritated judge found her in contempt of court in the murder trial of Bruce Davis. After that, Lyn gave up on revolutionary activity, and concentrated on her book.

Steve Bekins

In mid-1971, Lyn had made the acquaintance of Steve Bekins, an Aryan Brotherhood member with a record of burglary, armed robbery, and drug offenses. After years in San Quentin and Folsom, the thirty-three-year-old Bekins had been selected for parole. He was sent to Chino state prison for a rehabilitation program, and received a day pass to get there from downtown Los Angeles.

Bekins had been corresponding with the Manson women, and used his brief liberty to visit the corner of Temple and Broadway. He spent about an hour with Brenda, Sandy, and Lyn, and did not quite connect with the intense trio of Manson adherents. Bekins wanted to know where he could buy some heroin; the shaven-headed women only wanted to preach Charlie's message.

Bekins then headed to Chino, where he had been assigned to a six-month program designed to turn drug-addicted armed robbers into counselors for other inmates. He had long had problems with authority, however, and did not adapt well to the Corrections Department's plans to mold him into an exemplary convict. After a failed attempt to take over the rehab program—and gain access to its federal funds—Bekins spent much of his time at Chino in solitary confinement.

His parole date remained intact. Bekins knew that Governor Reagan was determined to balance the state budget, in part by reducing the prison population. Reagan halted construction of new penitentiaries, and within two years put nearly one-third of California's inmates back on the streets. Bekins was among them. "It was the biggest crime wave California ever had," he later recalled.

Bekins spent his time in solitary catching up on his reading, including the lengthy *Esquire* articles on the Manson Family. Then he received a letter from Brenda, who said that the Manson women had heard about Bekins's upcoming release from Chino. In an enticing tone far different from the strident preachings offered on the corner, Brenda invited the tall, handsome convict to come to the Family's new place in Hollywood as soon as he made parole. She didn't have to ask twice.

Although the Manson women still maintained occasional vigils outside the Hall of Justice, Lyn had moved the group to an apartment at 5244 Melrose Avenue near Wilton Place, in an aged six-story brick building decorated with bas-reliefs of helmeted warriors. Adjacent to Raleigh Studios and across the street from the Paramount Pictures lot, the building stood a few blocks from where her father had lived upon his arrival in Los Angeles thirty years before.

The neighborhood had not improved. It was an increasingly transient area, with poorly kept apartments and landlords who didn't ask many questions. Nearby lived Crystal and a few other Manson followers, along with some men they had picked up. Lyn's apartment, No. 107, was inexpensively, if cheerfully decorated. Those staying there slept communally in the Family fashion, on mattresses shoved together on the floor. Money was always a scramble, and it often took some doing to replenish the stash of drugs. Acid had largely fallen out of favor, with most Family members popping amphetamines, usually whites or mini-bennies. Lyn preferred the more placid buzz of marijuana.

Her most satisfying days were spent in the sun-brightened kitchen, banging out pages of her book on a portable typewriter. It was a slow process; anything but a touch typist, Lyn relied on the hunt-and-peck method to put her words on paper. When her attention drifted, as it so easily did, she would watch the comings and goings of her neighbors and keep tabs on who was up to what in the apartment house. The other tenants came to rely on her, knowing she always kept a watchful eye on the place. Lyn enjoyed playing the den mother.

There were other distractions. She had people to see—attorneys like Paul Fitzgerald, the occasional news reporter, and, of course, many, many friends in prison. Then there was the separation from Sandy, still in jail for her role in the Como escape. Always close, the two had become almost inseparable in the years following Manson's arrest. It seemed that things wouldn't really happen unless Sandy was around to participate.

In the meantime, others who got out of jail often stopped at the house. Various Family associates, A.B. members, and acquaintances would come by the Melrose apartment upon release, using it as a way station before heading out into the world, or, more likely, back toward prison. Steve Bekins showed up early in 1972.

He had hitched a ride from Chino to Hollywood, and was surprised by what he found. With their long, luxuriant hair, round, rosy faces, and warm, easy smiles, the women seemed completely different from the shrill, bald-headed viragoes Bekins had met at Temple and Broadway.

They got high and talked for hours, the women sympathetic to Steve's problems in prison, outraged at the injustice that would lock him—and so many others—up. Steve, in fact, had much in common with the Manson women, the disaffected daughters of the middle class. Like them, Steve had spurned a comfortable birthright for a life of rebellion.

Steve's grandfather had founded the Bekins moving and storage company, and his father, Bruce, ran the Pacific Northwest branch of the business from Portland,

Oregon. Wealth, however, had offered no shield from pain. His mother had died when Steve was nine years old, and shortly afterward his father had married his late wife's nurse. Shattered by the experience, Steve began to fight with his father, who sent him to military and reform schools. Steve was indeed re-formed; he now fully embraced the outlaw's code professed—and enforced—by his fellow wards. Among those he befriended at the MacLaren School for Boys in Woodburn, Oregon, was the future murderer Gary Gilmore, whose own journey to the firing squad in 1977 would inspire Norman Mailer's novel, *The Executioner's Song*.

Steve Bekins was shooting heroin by age seventeen, and a year later was expelled from the Air Force for stealing a car. He soon landed in the Oregon State Penitentiary in Salem for burglary, and years later, at San Quentin for a string of armed robberies. Disinherited by his family, Steve nonetheless retained vestiges of his privileged background; for a strung-out thief, he was usually articulate, even gracious. Women always liked him, it seemed, including his new hosts.

As the evening wore on, and tales of Spahn Ranch were swapped for those of San Quentin, the question that emerged was who Steve would sleep with. The dark-haired Brenda—whom many men would have considered the more attractive—clearly had designs on Steve.

Steve, however, found himself drawn to Lyn, because of her ingenuous manner, her sparkling intelligence, and, especially, her luxuriant red hair. Among other things, Steve considered himself a sucker for redheads. Lyn, however, had no special desire to sleep with Steve. She preferred to let Brenda have him, and Steve, not one to be impolite, obliged.

It was clear that the Family's activities were on hold until Sandy Good got out of jail. Steve Bekins, with nowhere particular to go and happy to share in the drugs and food the women provided, decided to stay. His initial distaste for Brenda, however, increased; she seemed testy and impatient, and despite her good looks, Steve simply did not enjoy her presence.

Lyn, on the other hand, grew ever more attractive to him. She would explain things to him in ways he had never considered, intriguing him with an outlook that was at times bluntly straightforward, at others mystically romantic. Eventually, she let Steve see portions of her book.

The cover was emblazoned with a death's-head, and the first pages contained a roster of the Family members, autographed in blood. Morbid as the decorations were, Lyn's writing was another matter entirely. Not a single word referred to violence or bloodshed. Instead, the story unfolded as a young woman's journey of discovery, courtesy of the gentle sage, Charles Manson.

"It hits you like a sunny day," Steve thought as he turned the pages. "Like you're at a picnic out in the sunshine." The two would spend hours discussing their mutual interests—poetry, music, and Manson. She would reminisce about the days on the ranch, when she used to cook for twenty-five people or more, and about the kind of places the mind can go on acid. She would point out the ways that nature was being destroyed by the Establishment, and Steve would nod, thinking about these issues for the first time.

Still, Steve liked to tweak Lyn. To her annoyance, he would invariably call her Squeaky.

"Oh! Why do you call me that?" Lyn would frown. Steve smiled; he thought she looked especially cute when she was mad, her fair, freckled cheeks all flushed with blood.

Sometimes, Lyn would ask Steve why he didn't make more of a play for Brenda. Aggressive as she was comely, Brenda was not used to being rejected. Steve just shrugged, and smiled at Lyn. According to Steve, soon they were sleeping together, too. To his regret, Steve sensed that Lyn was not fully into the experience, that she was holding back.

But it was different for Sandy, who was released from jail a short while later. Sandy was attracted to Steve, and they were soon sleeping together, usually in the Family van parked outside. According to Steve, then Lyn began to show up when Steve and Sandy made love, and they became a threesome.

They shared everything, all drinking from the same coffee cup, eating vegetarian stews from the same pot, singing in unison Manson's songs with their familiar refrain: *all is one all is one all is one.* Steve began to feel his identity meld into those of Lyn and Sandy, and so he would sometimes slip away, committing robberies and other crimes on the side that he didn't share with the women. Under their influence, he had given up meat, he had given up heroin; Steve needed a sphere of his own, away from the beatific world on Melrose Avenue.

The women, as far as Steve could tell, did not engage in crimes. The only activity he considered morally suspect was their habit of breaking into Salvation Army collection drops and stealing the clothes and broken appliances people had donated to the poor.

Sometimes, in the Family van, its veils and pillows giving the ambience of an Arabian tent, they spoke of fear. A candle flickered and Lyn would explain to the group how to grab hold of fear, how to take it inside, how to use it. Lyn, it seemed, had long ago conquered fear. When others would freak out, she was always there to bring them back. One day, when Steve Bekins had flipped out on a particularly bad dose of acid, Lyn materialized to rescue him from the trip. She took his hand and talked him down, walking him around the block and showing him the trees and flowers that made him know that everything was, after all, all right. He loved her. Once, he tried to kill her.

Steve had returned to the apartment, having filched a handsome leather wallet. After removing the cash and credit cards, he presented it to Lyn as a gift.

Later, she came to him. "Give me my forty dollars back," she demanded. Steve acted like he didn't know what she meant.

Forty dollars, she explained, had been in the wallet's hidden pocket. When last she checked, the money was gone. She wanted it back.

Steve, already loaded, insisted he didn't take the money. But Lyn persisted, and the ex-convict grew angry. He grabbed her hard, wrapped his hands around her slender neck, and squeezed, intent on killing her then and there.

But Lyn didn't flinch. She held herself proud, and stared into Steve's eyes with an intensity he had never encountered, anywhere. Their gazes locked, and he felt his grip loosening, as if it were beyond his control. He thought she commanded a special kind of magic.

Each night, sometimes after taking the mini-bennies, they would discuss the important things: sex, the justice system, politics. Sandy and Brenda, as well as other women who occasionally stopped by, looked to Lyn as their leader, and listened carefully to her explications of rock lyrics and environmental problems. When they received a letter from Charlie, they would gather excitedly as Lyn read it aloud, explaining and annotating the often opaque words scrawled from San Quentin. Sandy might add views of racial issues; she was impressed with the way blacks often addressed each other as "brother" or "sister," as if their race was just one big family. If only the white race behaved the same way, Sandy said. Steve, used to the strict racial divisions among convicts, readily agreed.

The women often spoke of the desert—and of the eerily prescient song by the pop group America, "A Horse with No Name." The lyric, Lyn explained, was suffused with meaning, telling as it did of oceans running beneath the desert surface—the same prophecy, in so many words, that Manson had revealed. After a group acid trip, they felt nostalgic for the times at Death Valley. They decided to take a road trip to the desert.

Barker and Myers ranches seemed a bit too far, however, so they settled on camping at Joshua Tree, in the Mojave Desert east of Los Angeles. They stopped at a friend's house midway to the desert, in a remote section of Riverside County. It seemed to be a commune, with teenagers and young adults all living on their own, in a hippie-decorated house with floor-to-ceiling tropical aquariums that made them feel like they were underwater. They all got high, had sex, then fell asleep. The next day, they headed out to the Mojave for several days of swimming, playing music, looking at animals, dropping acid, and having sex. Life wasn't so bad after all.

Others came by to share in the magic, too. One visitor was Paul Krassner, the comic protégé of Lenny Bruce who had gone on to help concoct the Yippies. Krassner had written to Manson in prison, seeking material for a purported book called *The Parts Left Out of the Manson Case*. "Call Squeaky," Manson had replied. Thoughtfully, Krassner brought to the meeting several 300-microgram tabs of acid, which he, Lyn, Brenda, and Sandy immediately swallowed. Sandy, who had once seen Krassner perform in San Francisco, took the initiative. She asked Krassner, an acquaintance of Yoko Ono, to tell John Lennon to dump his avant-garde Japanese wife. The former Beatle should stay with "his own kind," Sandy instructed.

They walked over to visit Laurence Merrick, a filmmaker who had been assembling a documentary about the Family, largely from footage he shot of Lyn and her friends at Spahn Ranch during the Tate-LaBianca trial. Tripping, Lyn kept telling Merrick that she was afraid of him. On his trip, Krassner decided to explicate the "fascistic implications" of the hit movie, *The French Connection*.

The group returned to a Family crash pad, where they smoked pot and sang along to "A Horse with No Name," as well as to the Moody Blues, one of Lyn's favorite groups. Later, at Lyn's apartment, Sandy proposed that Krassner join the two women in a bath. When Krassner hesitated, Lyn remarked, "You're afraid of me, aren't you?"

"Not really," Krassner insisted. "Should I be?"

"She's *beautiful*, Paul," Sandy interjected. "Just look into her eyes. Isn't she beautiful?" But as Lyn and Krassner sat staring at each other, Sandy filled the tub herself, stripped, and got in. Krassner decided to remain clothed and ogle the bathing Sandra.

Lyn didn't let Krassner leave without showing off the women's handiwork: Charlie's embroidered vest. She invited him to try it on, and Krassner, honored to be involved in a Family ceremony of some sort, complied.

Krassner gave another tab of acid to Brenda, who had asked for it on behalf of Charlie. She pulverized it and affixed the powder to a piece of paper with vegetable dye. "Words fly fast," she inscribed it.

"We really want to have your body, Steve," Lyn and Sandy told Bekins. At first, he was flattered by the continuous sexual attention—they had taken to calling him "Wonder," as in Stevie, a tribute to his physical prowess. Then he began to realize they meant more than just physical desire.

They wanted his body with them, they said, when they went over to the other side. When Armageddon came—or the revolution, or whatever guise Helter Skelter had—and all was destroyed, they hoped that Steve would be with them in the new world to be born. Charlie would join them then. That's why they worked so hard embroidering his vest, so he would have the right thing to wear when he rose.

There were several scenarios the women discussed, including an invasion by a foreign country. But the most common prophecy remained that of a racial uprising, starting in Watts, then engulfing all of Los Angeles, and ultimately the rest of America. Then, just as Charlie had taught them, they would pick everything up and move to the desert. They had kept their skills honed and could live off the land. They were, more than anything, aware.

"Most people, they can't live if they don't have an electric toaster," Lyn observed. "How will they cook their toast?" But the Family, bolstered by strong male recruits like Steve Bekins, could survive anything. The political or racial rebellion would evolve into something else—a day of reckoning. And then they would all go over to the other side—their bodies, their souls. Their love.

Yet the talk of Armageddon didn't seem to dampen anyone's spirits. It was seen as an inevitable event, just around the corner like a change of season, but in the meantime there were things to be done. Chief among them was moving out of Melrose, because the police had discovered the apartment and were paying too much attention to the group's activities, especially the comings and goings of ex-convicts. The group dispersed.

Lyn moved up into the hills, to an apartment house just below the landmark Hollywood sign, with a gaggle of new associates. There was pudgy and plain Heather—Susan Kathryn Murphy—thirty years old. Trained as a nurse, she became known to authorities as an alcoholic and shoplifter. Years later, she would be one of few female inmates robust enough to overpower a federal prison guard and escape custody.

Then there were the Willetts, a strange young couple with an infant daughter and a pregnant cat in tow. Five foot three Lauren Willett, or Reni, was just nineteen years old, with parents living in New England. Her husband James was an ex-Marine from Kentucky, a disoriented twenty-six-year-old who impressed most he met as slightly unstable; the attendant at Hollywood Community Hospital, where the infant Heidi Willett had been born in February, said the mother "seemed like such a nice young girl, but the husband seemed like a kook!" James was somehow mixed up with Lyn's other housemates, a pair of Aryan Brotherhood members called Red Eye and Spider.

Red Eye, born Michael Lee Monfort, was a blond, blue-eyed escapee from the state prison at Susanville, in the remote northeastern corner of California. He was nearly six feet tall, a trim 160 pounds, and a drunk with a weakness for Bacardi rum. On his left breast he bore the Aryan Brotherhood tattoo, a three-leaf clover with the number "6" on each leaf, sprouting between the letters "A.B." Brenda, rejected by Steve Bekins, quickly fell for the twenty-four-year-old felon, and their romance and eventual jailhouse marriage would last for more than two decades.

Red Eye's thirty-three-year-old partner, Spider—James Terrill Craig—was a less impressive specimen. Balding and pot-bellied at five foot eight, the Oklahoma-born Craig was a heroin addict with a criminal record dating from 1957. Also a former Susanville inmate, his nickname derived from the striking tattoo of a spider he bore in the center of his chest. Both Spider and Red Eye favored the bushy sideburns and mustaches of the young outlaw caste.

Like some of the other A.B. members, Red Eye and Spider called themselves "brothers," and made their living through robbery. Never staying too long in one place, they fueled their travels with stolen credit cards, and held up liquor stores and groceries to pay the rent. According to their understanding of the agreement between Charlie and the A.B., Lyn and the other Family women were now the "property" of the Aryan Brotherhood.

Spider, Red Eye, and James Willett often collaborated with Billy Goucher, a twenty-three-year-old ex-convict who was Crystal's main man. Goucher's body was covered with tattoos, mainly self-drawn, picked up in prisons and roughhouse districts across California. Among the more understated markings Goucher bore was a slice of Eastern wisdom, tattooed on his arm in Chinese characters. "Trust No One," it said.

Manson had taught that man was the master of woman, not in a sadistic way but just as the natural order of things. Unfortunately, once Manson had been put away, the Family's women had trouble finding men they felt were worthy of obedience. So they tried to instruct the ones they had.

Lyn, Sandy, and Brenda would spend evenings lecturing Bekins and other male visitors about the superior role of men, and how the uppity followers of women's liberation had so alienated the men of America. American women were trying to wear the pants, they had taken their men's balls and chained them up, to make them their play toys, their little boys, said Sandy in her strident voice, and Lyn would agree. That's why Asian and European women were so popular among American men, Sandy stressed.

The male audience, usually ex-convicts and drifters not accustomed to social critiques of relations between the sexes, listened with amusement or confusion. They certainly enjoyed the physical attention the women would bestow, and several grew to like their thoughtful vegetarian cooking. But the contentious nature of the Family women undercut the philosophy they spouted. It was clear that the only real man they ever had met, by their definition, was Manson himself.

Still, some of the women came to make do with what was available. Not only had Brenda hitched herself to Red Eye, but Sandy had become the consort of Steve Bekins. She began living with him in the Family van—for the first time in years spending most of her nights away from Lyn. Lyn, however, did not find any of the available men particularly appealing. She grew closer, instead, to Heather and Reni Willett. Steve Bekins, though pleased with Sandy's company, was disappointed that Lyn showed so little sexual interest in him.

The group remained close. Sandy and Steve would visit Lyn often, collecting her and other Family members in the van, driving to a secluded spot, swallowing a pile of mini-bennies, and talking until dawn about philosophy, magic, UFOs, and sex. One evening, just after the Willetts' cat had had her kittens, Bekins came by Lyn's apartment to get high. Lyn brought out her stash, and rolled joints until the weed was done. As Bekins was leaving, Lyn gave him one of the kittens to take home. He smiled and put it in his coat pocket, then wandered outside.

Comfortably buzzed as he took in the hillside views, Steve was approached by police officers conducting a neighborhood drug sweep. He managed to ditch his marijuana, so all the police found in his pockets was an expensive, apparently stolen, portable radio, and a tiny, confused kitten.

The officers escorted Steve as he returned to Lyn's apartment to give her back the kitten. He explained that they don't allow pets in jail, and both Steve and Lyn burst out laughing, to the visible annoyance of the police.

Booked into the old county jail near Dodger Stadium, the Lincoln Heights "Glass House," Steve called in a favor from a prison buddy, Eddie Bunker. Bunker was picking up a load of dope when he heard from Lyn and her friends, and had some spare cash to bail Steve out. Since the police hadn't bothered to check Bekins's phony ID, he was on the street within seventy-two hours.

Bunker was no ordinary armed robber. He had been practicing his writing skills in prison, and was on the verge of clinching a publishing deal for his first novel, *No Beast So Fierce*. Bunker and Lyn got to talking, and they agreed to meet later to talk about her book ideas.

The two met at the Holiday Inn near Hollywood Boulevard, where Bunker was staying. Moments after entering the hotel, however, they were swarmed by federal agents who had been waiting for Bunker. "I was shoved into a room and intermittently ignored and ridiculed as agents came in and out," Lyn recalled.

Meanwhile, Steve Bekins, borrowing Bunker's car, had gone to fetch Sandy and Brenda. They walked up to the hotel entrance—and all but collided with some twenty officers escorting a handcuffed Bunker to jail. Bunker instinctively acted like he didn't recognize his visitors, and the three returned the favor, strolling nonchalantly into the lobby.

Once inside the hotel, they scouted for Lyn, fearful that she too had been arrested. No sign of her. They headed back to Bunker's car, only to again encounter the police, who impounded the vehicle and told the scraggly trio of hippies to get lost.

The three made their way back to one of the Family's crash pads, and there found Lyn waiting for them; she had been held for about an hour and released. Eddie Bunker, they learned, had been busted for possession of heroin and cocaine. He would not, it seemed, be able to help Lyn on her book.

Bunker would, however, be able to initiate a project with Bekins, who was getting antsy for action after months with the women. Shortly after making bail, Bunker and Bekins cased the Ahmanson Bank & Trust in Beverly Hills and planned a robbery. Before pulling the job, they stopped by Lyn's place to drop off an extra piece of equipment: a .75 caliber, Czech-made antitank rifle, complete with bipod. It was a bit much to use on the bank job.

In retrospect, the weapon might have come in handy. Police had staked out the bank and captured Bunker during the getaway. Bekins managed to escape with about $1,300, and fled to the East Coast. It was Bunker, however, who would have the brighter future, despite a term in federal prison. *No Beast So Fierce* was published in 1972 and so impressed the actor Dustin Hoffman that he bought the rights and starred in the film adaptation, *Straight Time*. After his release from Terminal Island in 1976, Bunker specialized in writing books and screenplays involving convicts, including the motion picture *Runaway Train* and, in 1996, *Dog Eat Dog*, a novel about criminals facing California's "three strikes and you're out" mandatory sentencing law.

The bank robbery brought the heat down on Lyn and her friends, who once again picked up and moved. Most of the group relocated to the Westlake District, near MacArthur Park. The apartment house at 2308 Fourth Street, by Carondelet Street, was in a declining older area of the city, just west of downtown Los Angeles. Law firms and corporate offices still lined nearby Wilshire Boulevard, but the residential blocks largely were poorly kept tenements from the 1930s, with peeling stucco and chipped Spanish tiles, or cheap, boxy apartments from the 1950s and 1960s.

Lyn lived upstairs, with the Willetts. Sandy and several other women stayed downstairs. Brenda shared another apartment with Red Eye, Spider, and other transient ex-convicts. They were close to their neighbors, and even used one of their cars in some of their crimes.

The group stuck together until June 1972, when Steve Bekins returned from his East Coast hideout and moved in with Sandy. Although they continued to share what they had—Bekins often lent Brenda his gun—it seemed things somehow weren't the same. They discussed their situation frankly. It was accepted that Charlie would someday rise from prison, yet "someday" seemed increasingly far off. Lyn appeared relatively content, occupied with her book, but others in the group were growing discouraged with the string of failures. The communal life so natural at rural Spahn Ranch just didn't seem feasible in urban Los Angeles. The Family van was breaking down so often, it had to be junked. They decided to split up.

Bekins wanted to return to Oregon, and told Sandy of his plans. He preferred the mistier climate of his home state to arid, often smoggy Southern California. He also wanted to avoid getting busted for the bank robbery.

Sandy once had studied art at the University of Oregon in Eugene, and felt at home in the Beaver State. And unlike the more reflective Lyn, Sandy was impatient for action. Bekins seemed to be on a roll, having gotten away with several daring crimes. She wanted to go with him; the moll's life looked like a good way to wait out the Apocalypse.

The plan was set, but for one thing. Sandy wanted Steve to talk to Lyn about it—and get her permission to take her to Oregon.

Nervously, Steve climbed the stairs to Lyn's apartment. He felt like a high school suitor going to ask Sandy's mom for permission to take her to the prom.

Lyn listened carefully to Steve's plans, and then managed a smile. If Sandy wanted to go along with Steve, it was all right with her.

"Steve," Lyn said as he prepared to leave. "Take care of Sandy, willya?"

Steve promised he would.

San Francisco

Lyn left Los Angeles, too. She moved to San Francisco with Heather, who had gotten a nursing job at the French Hospital in the city's largely residential Richmond District. The two women lived a few blocks from the hospital, in a quiet, modern two-story building at 538 Fifth Avenue, Apartment 2. Without the distractions of Los Angeles—and since Heather paid the rent—Lyn hoped she could finally concentrate on her writing.

She liked to keep at least minimal contact with the Establishment, though, particularly with lawyers, who had the privilege of unrestricted contact with inmates. She maintained her correspondence with Paul Fitzgerald, and thanks to an introduction from Steve Bekins, made friends with a Marin County lawyer named George Douglas Vaughn.

The bearded Doug Vaughn wore a cowboy hat and boots, and drove a ¾-ton Ford pickup. Other lawyers in Marin, the upscale, liberal county on the north side of the Golden Gate Bridge, considered him a redneck intruder. But Vaughn, thirty-four years old, was more complicated, or at least contradictory. A registered Republican who had flirted with the idea of running for county supervisor, Vaughn had gotten himself mixed up with the nascent prisoners' rights movement raging at Marin's most famous community, San Quentin.

Convict leader Luis Talamantez, on trial for assaulting another inmate, had lost his first lawyer after the attorney stood up in court and called the trial judge the "chief engineer of the Marin County railroad." The court fished around for someone else to take Talamentez's case. Even though Vaughn never before had tried a felony, the judge asked him to represent Talamantez. As it was bad form, if not foolhardy, for an attorney to turn down a judge's request, Vaughn took the case—even as he suspected he had been chosen as a "lay-down," a giveaway to the prosecution. To everyone's surprise, Vaughn won an acquittal, aided by the testimony of one Steve Bekins, who shared a cell on the same tier as Talamantez and witnessed the alleged assault.

The Talamantez case established Vaughn's credibility to inmates; it also established the inmates' credibility to Vaughn. Whatever they might have done to land themselves in prison, Vaughn saw convicts like Bekins and Talamantez as "stand-up guys"—fearless, loyal men who, unlike his colleagues in the legal system, you could count on in a pinch. If any friend of theirs came calling, Vaughn was ready to open his door and help out however he could.

But while he was used to taking referrals from criminals, he never before had dealt with someone like Lyn. She had first come to see him in the spring of 1972, during one of her visits to San Francisco. Accompanied by the silent, somber Heather, she marched in to Vaughn's San Rafael office, sat herself down, and laid it out. She had this manuscript she'd been working on. She needed some help in getting it to publishers. Was that something he could do?

Vaughn asked to see it, and Lyn, watching him closely, handed it over. It was a 150- to 200-page stack, a mixture of bond, scrap, and binder paper. Some pages were typed, others were written in multicolored pen. There were long stretches of prose and occasional poems. Mixed throughout were drawings, some rather flamboyant. It did not look much like a professional manuscript. But Vaughn was not the judgmental type. His wife taught journalism at a local college, and his brother-in-law worked for a publishing house on the East Coast. He was impressed when Lyn told him she had no interest in profits or royalties from the book, no materialistic aims at all; she just wanted to make a lasting statement about where she was really coming from. He said he'd see what he could do.

Lyn had more to ask, though. With her lifestyle, she was always in danger of having to pick up and move right away. Could Vaughn make a copy of the manuscript and keep it in his office, for safety?

Sure, he said.

Lyn visited Vaughn about a half-dozen times, until she returned in August, accompanied by some of her friends. She had relocated to San Francisco, she said, and was still trying to finish her book. Unfortunately, she lacked an essential tool: a typewriter. Would it be all right if she used his office to work on it?

Vaughn immediately assented. He wanted to encourage Lyn's writing. "It's good to see young people doing positive things," he thought. He looked the Manson women up and down. They were polite, cordial, and deadly serious. "Besides," he told himself, "there are a lot worse things they could be doing."

Lyn, for her part, was pleased with the way things were going. "The book is nearly complete," she enthused in a letter to Katie, "with fine drawings done by convicts."

In Portland, Sandy Good and Steve Bekins moved in with one of Steve's old prison buddies. One night in July 1972, Sandy was in bed when she heard a desperate pounding on the back door. Naked, she ran to open it.

It was Steve. He and a pal had held up a supermarket in East Portland and were being chased by the police. "Listen," he said, "get your stuff right now and let's get out of here!"

Sandy, contentious as always, wanted to talk it out. As they discussed their getaway plans, Steve noticed the police at the next house, talking to neighbors in the backyard. They were combing the neighborhood, and it would be minutes, if not seconds, before they appeared. There was no time to flee.

They went into another room and found a cabinet big enough to hide Steve. Sandy cleared away the knickknacks inside it and stowed her lover within.

Suddenly, the police were pounding on the door. They asked Sandy if she had seen a suspicious character in the vicinity, someone presumed to be armed and dangerous.

"Yeah," she said. "I was just in bed and I heard somebody run through the house and out the front door. But I don't know who it was and I didn't see anything out of place, so I just went back to bed, and now you guys are here. But I didn't get a chance to look at him or anything," she added.

The police didn't believe her. They searched the house, and soon extracted Steve from his hiding place. With Sandy screaming, the police hauled them both off to jail.

Steve wanted to help Sandy get out of the mess he had made, so he called an attorney he knew to have a fondness for young women. "Look, I've got a girl for you. If you can get her out of jail, you can have her," he said. After getting a look at Sandy, the attorney took the case.

Out on bail, she spoke to Steve by telephone. She described the attorney as a "sex maniac," and reported that he had moved on her almost the first instant they were alone.

Steve sensed it was a bad scene and would only get worse. "You oughtta just leave Portland, just go back to San Francisco and be with Squeaky and forget about this," he told her. "Even if they do catch you, they won't give you much trouble on this 'harboring a fugitive' charge." To assuage her disappointment, Bekins promised, "if I get away or something, I'll come find you."

Sandy took Steve's advice. Soon, she was living with Lyn and Heather on San Francisco's Fifth Avenue. Steve did not get away. He was sentenced to twenty years.

Charlie had brought Lyn to San Francisco during the Summer of Love. Now Charlie had brought her back to the city, although his neighborhood was no longer the Haight-Ashbury, but rather the fortress prison across the bay at San Quentin. The Corrections Department considered Lyn a bad influence and refused to let her visit Charlie.

Frustrated, she sought help wherever it might be—particularly from male authority figures. In her usual earnest, girlish manner, she managed to talk her way into the chambers of Judge Charles Renfrew, of the United States District Court in San Francisco.

"My father is in San Quentin," she despairingly told him, "and they won't let me see him. Can't you help me?"

Judge Renfrew didn't recognize the notorious character who sat before him.

Thinking her the daughter of some anonymous convict, he offered Lyn the names of prison lawyers who might be able to help. She shook her head.

"They won't help," she complained. "They only help blacks. I'm white and ignorant and the Family is breaking up."

Renfrew regretted there was not much he could do. Still, Lyn sensed the judge's sympathetic side, and spent several days in his courtroom, hoping he would intervene. But her presence only made Renfrew nervous, and he told his chief clerk to ask Lyn to leave.

As the clerk led Lyn out, he asked, "By the way, did you ever get to see your dad?"

"He's not my 'dad,'" Lyn retorted sharply. "He's my *father*—Charles Manson." She left the Federal Building, exasperated.

At the San Francisco apartment, Lyn worked on the book almost every day, from three in the afternoon until eleven at night. The book was Lyn's conception, but she struggled mightily to make it reflect everyone's experience in the Family. She solicited contributions from all the members she could reach, in towns and prisons across California. The writings of Patricia Krenwinkel, Catherine Share, and the others rarely matched the wordplay Lyn could effect, but she included their anecdotes nonetheless.

Every Friday, she would head to Doug Vaughn's San Rafael office, either taking the bus or, if she were lucky, persuading the attorney to pick her up in his truck. Arriving at 2:00 P.M., she would head to the secretary's room and bang out her writings on an electric typewriter. Often she would have the office to herself, as Vaughn usually had court on Friday afternoons. She emerged at about 4:30, when Vaughn returned. He would drop her off at the bus depot on his way home from work.

In the margins of their relationship, they occasionally chatted over a Coke or a cup of coffee on Vaughn's tab. Lyn would report, in vague terms, the progress of her book, or comment on current affairs, like the hapless campaign of the Democratic presidential nominee, Senator George McGovern.

"They're all just a bunch of liars and crooks," Lyn said of the nation's leaders. "All they're out to do is keep people down and under control." Vaughn nodded assent.

Once, she asked him for two dollars. He gave her a twenty. He couldn't decide whether she reminded him more of his wife or of the daughter he never had. It was, however, a relationship controlled by Lyn. She never gave Vaughn a phone number, so he would have to wait for the eventual collect call from a phone booth somewhere. Whenever possible, he helped her out.

But he could not help publish her book. Vaughn's brother-in-law, the literary editor, had read Lyn's rapturous account of the Manson Family, filled with its stories of communal wonder and spiritual transcendence. He sent an exasperated reply: "Enough of this Love-Love-Love. Where's the Kill-Kill-Kill?"

The Body in the Basement

While Lyn tried to write her book, Spider, Red Eye, and Goucher were traveling California, accompanied by their women. According to police reports, they fueled their cars with pilfered credit cards, packed sawed-off shotguns and .38 caliber revolvers, and hit every corner of the state, from the old Gold Rush hamlets of the Sierra Madre to the Mexican border crossing of San Ysidro. Between July 8 and November 1, the tank of one car was filled 128 times on a single Union Oil charge card, stolen from a law firm. The spree was exciting as it was dangerous; they would spend evenings drinking Bacardi 151 rum—Red Eye's favorite—and smoking hashish, playing with their weapons and snapping provocative photos of the women.

In October 1972, after three months of near-ceaseless travel, the group decided to relocate to Guerneville, a once-fashionable resort in redwood country that lately had become a center for motorcycle gangs and hippies. Four couples composed the group: Brenda and Red Eye, along with Billy Goucher and Crystal. Spider brought his lady, a droopy-eyed former topless dancer named Priscilla Cooper. Now using the nickname Tuffy, Cooper had etched an X on her forehead to fit in with the other women. Then there were James and Reni Willett, with their infant daughter Heidi. The band rented a cabin in the remote former logging town, sixty miles north of San Francisco.

But James Willett, the crazy ex-Marine who had teamed up with the A.B. men for their crime spree, had turned into more trouble than he was worth. Detectives believed Willett had participated in several of the gang's Los Angeles robberies, and even provided the getaway car: his 1965 Ford station wagon, a beige four-door with woody side panels. According to police reports, however, James Willett had told his wife that he was tired of the robbery business, and all but ready to "drop a dime" on the gang. Reni Willett mentioned this to Brenda, who passed it on to the menfolk.

According to police, Red Eye, Spider and Bill Goucher decided to kill Willett. One night, police said, the three A.B. men invited Willett to accompany them to the hills outside of town, on the premise that they needed to find a place to stash their loot. For reasons unclear, Willett wore his blue Marine Corps dress jacket, with its corporal's stripes, brass buttons, and red piping, and joined his pals.

They found a densely wooded area about a half mile out and told Willett to start digging. After he had dug a shallow trench, the others suddenly observed that the spot seemed well suited to test their weapons. One of them blasted a tree with his shotgun, and Willett walked up to inspect the damage. As he did, Red Eye shot him in the back of the head with a .22 caliber pistol. Goucher then came over to the fallen Willett and blasted him with a 12-gauge shotgun, followed by Spider, who twice fired his 20-gauge Champion shotgun into the body.

The three rolled Willett's body into the grave he had dug, beside some rotting logs, and covered it with a thin layer of dirt and leaves.

Authorities speculated that Reni Willett approved of her husband's murder at the hands of their friends. There certainly was no question that she continued to travel with the Aryan Brotherhood/Manson clan of her own free will. On Halloween of 1972, Reni telephoned her mother in Hamden, Connecticut, to ask that she wire some cash right away. She needed the money, Reni told her mother, because her husband had left her.

The group decided to relocate from the rustic beauty of Sonoma County's redwood forest to Stockton, a city of about 200,000 some thirty miles south of Sacramento along Interstate 5. Why Stockton, which San Franciscans considered a decrepit, redneck backwater in the dusty and mercilessly hot San Joaquin Valley?

"Where's the last place you'd think of looking?" Red Eye would later say to reporters.

It fell to Brenda to set up housekeeping. After perusing the Sunday classifieds, she settled on a nondescript house for rent at 720 West Flora Street, in a pleasant residential district north of the city's downtown. Brenda told the manager, Maria Kopes, that she and her husband were artists who had tired of the Bay Area. Brenda had only one question: Was the garbage picked up on time?

"Stockton's garbage collection is very good," Mrs. Kopes said. Indeed it would be, at least on this block; unknown to Brenda, a city councilman lived across the street.

After touring the basement, a crawlspace reachable only through a trapdoor in the bedroom closet, Brenda announced that the place would do. Then she pulled a huge wad of cash from her purse. The rent was $190 per month, plus a $100 cleaning fee. She counted out $290—one twenty, one ten, and the rest in fives—and put the rest away.

"Aren't you afraid to carry so much money around in your purse?" Mrs. Kopes asked.

"No," Brenda replied.

The night after Brenda rented the house, Red Eye and Goucher visited Eden Square Liquors, on Stockton's North El Dorado Street. They lingered in the store long enough to unnerve the clerk, who activated the silent alarm moments before Red Eye and Goucher pulled guns and ordered him to empty the cash register. They forced the clerk to lie on the ground, along with another customer, an off-duty security guard who happened to be in the store. They stole the guard's wallet and his revolver.

"I ought to shoot you for carrying a gun," one of the A.B. men said. They made off with rolls of coins and, for Red Eye, a pint of rum.

But by the time the bandits were ready to leave, the police had arrived—and

arrested the pair as they walked out the door. They booked Goucher under his
true name, but Red Eye had an alias and ID to support it.

"James Lambert Thompson Willett" was how he identified himself.

After talking to Lyn in September, Paul Fitzgerald had begun to grow optimistic
about her future. She reported to him that Sandy had gone off to Oregon, that
Brenda and Capistrano were in parts unknown, that she hadn't heard anything
from Charlie for far too long.

"Girls have finally broken up," Fitzgerald noted in his files. "[Lyn] Sounded
sad. It finally ended. Amen."

Fitzgerald's assessment was premature. In late October 1972, as Lyn put it,
she and Brenda finally "touched up." Lyn shared her frustrations—it had been
cold and rainy in the Northern California fall, and all her efforts to see Charlie
at San Quentin had been rebuffed by the prison. To make things even more
miserable, the Corrections Department had just transferred Manson a hundred
miles away, to Folsom Prison east of Sacramento.

With the arrests of Red Eye and Bill Goucher, however, there wasn't time to
grouse about these problems; the men had to be gotten out of jail as quickly as
possible. Lyn was ready to help.

After his arrest, Goucher had called his mother in Culver City, the Los Angeles
suburb that was home to MGM Studios. Sarah Goucher immediately flew to
Stockton, where she was met by Reni Willett, with baby Heidi in tow, and
Brenda, who introduced herself as Reni's sister, "Elizabeth." They went to the
San Joaquin County Jail, where Mrs. Goucher visited her son. Oddly, however,
Reni Willett didn't insist on seeing the man she said was her husband. In-
stead, it was "Elizabeth" who had a personal visit with her purported brother-
in-law.

Although Mrs. Goucher had come to bail her own son out of jail, Brenda and
Reni persuaded her that "James Willett" needed to get out of jail more than did
Billy; Willett, after all, had a family to look after. Bill Goucher assented—as
long as he would be bailed out next.

Brenda and Reni took Mrs. Goucher to San Francisco, where they spent the
night at Lyn's apartment. Back in Stockton the next day, Reni and Brenda paid
the bail bondsman in quarters, along with the $190 Reni's mother had wired
her. Mrs. Goucher put up her house as a guarantee for the rest of Red Eye's
$10,000 bond.

"James Willett" was released, on condition that he return November 3 for a
court appearance. But Red Eye had other plans.

Still driving the slain Willett's station wagon, the group deposited Mrs.
Goucher at the Stockton airport, and then, after collecting Spider, returned to
San Francisco. Brandishing shotguns, Red Eye and Spider robbed the Safeway

supermarket at 735 Seventh Avenue in San Francisco, just a few blocks from Lyn's apartment.

Red Eye and Brenda then decided on a quick vacation. They flew Delta from San Francisco for a weekend in Jacksonville, Florida, where Red Eye had some connections. In August, one of his Sunshine State friends had tried to mail him an RG-40 snub-nosed pistol, but the package had opened in transit and postal inspectors confiscated the weapon. Red Eye resolved to replenish the arsenal himself.

On November 6, a seventy-one-year-old man hiking in the woods outside Guerneville saw a hand protruding from the ground. Soon thereafter, authorities extracted a headless, rotting body from its grave. The right hand was missing, and the corpse was so badly decomposed that the coroner could not tell whether it had been male or female. He estimated it had been buried for several months, though, in fact, it had only lain there for a few weeks; James Willett had last been seen alive on October 18. Officials later surmised that Willett's body had been partially uncovered by animals, which had torn off and eaten his head, his hand, and much of his insides.

Sonoma County authorities first believed they had found a possible victim of the Hell's Angels motorcycle gang, which had been active around Guerneville. In two days, however, detectives tentatively identified the body as Willett's, and matched the case with the bail jumper in Stockton, more than one hundred miles away. After a fingerprint check revealed Red Eye's true identity, police began to lean on Bill Goucher, still in custody, to tell more about his fellow suspect in the liquor store robbery.

Lyn, meanwhile, had gone to Los Angeles to attend court proceedings for her friends charged in the Hawthorne surplus store shootout. On Thursday, November 9, she telephoned Crystal, then staying at Mrs. Goucher's home in Culver City, and the two resolved to visit Billy in the San Joaquin County Jail. Billy may have been a lover to Crystal, but to Lyn he was something more important: a "brother."

Returning by bus to Northern California, Lyn decided to skip her regular Friday appointment at Doug Vaughn's office and check up on Brenda and the others at their new home in Stockton. Lyn would visit Bill on Saturday; Crystal couldn't wait to see her man, and went on Friday to the jail, located south of Stockton in the rural outpost of French Camp.

Lyn, however, did not know the sorts of things that had been going on with brother Billy. Over the previous several days, detectives had been talking to Goucher about the murder of James Willett, and about his mysterious friend who had used Willett's identification. Bill, sitting in jail while Red Eye roamed free on Mrs. Goucher's bail money, heard rumors that the A.B. had little faith in him and was planning to have him killed. Vacillating between loyalty to the prison gang and the hope of cutting a separate deal with authorities, Goucher had given police the make, model, and license number of Red Eye's car. Detectives decided to see what his girlfriend might have to say as well. They stopped

Crystal as she was leaving the jail, and discovered an illegal switchblade knife in her purse. This gave them grounds to arrest her and begin an evening of conversations.

At 12:47 A.M., Sergeant Richard D. Whiteman extracted the address of 720 West Flora Street; twelve minutes later, Whiteman and two other officers were at the house with weapons ready. There being no sign of the station wagon, however, the team returned to police headquarters and put out a wanted bulletin on Red Eye and his car. Rather than risk alerting their suspect that they were onto him, the police decided not to stake out Flora Street. Instead, patrols periodically checked the suspect's house to see if Red Eye had returned.

Lyn had spent the night with Brenda and friends. The next day she took the bus to French Camp, to see Goucher in jail.

While Lyn was visiting Bill, a Stockton police car spotted the Willett station wagon in the Flora Street driveway. Six officers with shotguns soon surrounded the house, hiding behind cars and shrubs, as Sergeant Whiteman, in plainclothes, knocked on the door.

Brenda popped her head out of an interior door. The exterior door, which she could see through a glass window, remained locked.

"What do you want?" she asked.

"Is Fred home?" said Whiteman.

"Who?"

"Fred."

"Fred don't live here," said Brenda.

"Yes, he does," Whiteman insisted.

"No," she replied. "*We* just moved in."

Whiteman flashed his badge. "Police officer. Could I talk to you?"

Brenda slammed the interior door and vanished.

"Wait a minute," Whiteman shouted, "I want to tell you something." He repeated the message, even louder. Brenda reappeared.

Whiteman said the house was surrounded by armed officers, and that she and her buddies didn't stand a chance.

Brenda slammed the door again.

"Open the door!" Whiteman yelled. He banged on the door and kicked it, shouting repeatedly for the gang to open up. Then he kicked the door open, ripping apart the wooden jamb.

With guns drawn, Whiteman and four other officers charged into the house. They found Brenda, holding the baby Heidi, as well as Tuffy, Spider, and Red Eye. The police quickly lined the group against the wall, palms flat, and questioned them.

Unfortunately for the police, in their rush to apprehend Monfort, they had somehow neglected to look at his booking photograph. As Red Eye and Spider identified themselves as Gordon Foote and Earl Blake—and had the stolen IDs to prove it—the police didn't realize they had the wanted man in custody. They searched the house, hoping to find Monfort hiding in a cabinet or under any of the ubiquitous piles of dirty clothes.

Strewn on the floor of the bedroom closet, Whiteman found the military separation papers of James Willett. Corporal Willett had been granted an honorable discharge.

Police also saw the trapdoor leading to the basement crawlspace. There, officers found a brand-new shovel and a pick, and some freshly turned dirt. No one seemed to be hiding there, however, so they went back upstairs to finish searching the property. There was no sign of Reni Willett.

Lyn had taken the bus from French Camp to Stockton, but the closest stop was a long walk from Brenda's house. She went to a phone booth outside a liquor store and dialed Flora Street.

"Hi, it's me. Are you coming to get me?" she asked.

"Where are you?" asked Sergeant Whiteman.

"Who is this?" asked Lyn.

"Earl," Whiteman said, using Spider's alias.

"B&E Liquors," Lyn said, and hung up. Minutes later, she was arrested by Stockton police. True to their word, they did bring Lyn to the house on Flora Street, before taking the whole group to police headquarters. Several officers remained at the house, in case the elusive Michael Monfort eventually showed up.

Once at the police station in downtown Stockton, Sergeant Whiteman looked through the files and found Red Eye's picture. Confronted, Red Eye admitted who he really was.

"It was the last place I thought you'd look for me," he said.

Armed with a search warrant and accompanied by Deputy District Attorney Steve Demetras, Whiteman and his men returned to Flora Street to look for the weapons that had killed James Willett. They found shotguns, pistols, rifles, and boxes of ammunition, as well as shotgun-cleaning kits. The house was filled with stolen coins, money orders, and a television set, along with Bacardi rum, Coca-Cola, and drug paraphernalia. There also was evidence that, despite the rather pedestrian form of banditry the A.B. men practiced, the women remained focused on their ideals. They found several embroidered vests bearing the legend "Satan's Maidens," and a carefully marked map of the Family's old haunts in Death Valley.

At 4:20 A.M. on Sunday, the police came to the freshly turned earth in the basement, and started digging. "We continued to dig straight down," Whiteman reported, "until we struck something soft."

Wrapped in blood-soaked blankets, Reni Willett had been buried twenty-four inches underground, on her side, her head turned, her legs bent behind so that her feet touched her back. Her body was found barefoot, dressed in blue jeans and a multicolored T-shirt that had been pulled up above her breasts.

On Friday night, while Lyn was en route to Stockton, Red Eye had pointed a .38 caliber Rohn RG revolver at Reni Willett and shot her in the head. The bullet entered just above the right eye and blew her brains out, exiting through the back of the skull.

According to Tuffy, Reni's death had been the unfortunate result of Red Eye's effort to instruct her in firearm safety. Tuffy told police that on Friday she, Brenda, and Reni had been in the dining room, fingering a revolver, when Red Eye came over. Upset at the women's cavalier handling of the weapon, he took it away, sat on the couch, and scolded them for playing with guns. Red Eye then spun the revolver's cylinder and looked down its barrel. He pointed it at Brenda and pulled the trigger, twice. Nothing happened. He looked down the barrel again and pointed the revolver at his head, but didn't pull the trigger. Then he pointed the pistol at some cabinets behind Reni, sitting on a red chair about ten feet away from Red Eye.

Next thing anybody knew, Reni had been shot in the eye. The shot awoke Spider, who ran out of the bedroom and found them huddled around Reni's body.

"How in the fuck did that happen!?" Spider demanded. No one answered, although Red Eye later said he had been drunk, as usual, at the time.

Since Reni still had a faint heartbeat, they hoped to take her to the hospital. But after they had wrapped her in blankets, Red Eye decided it was too late. While Brenda went to comfort the baby, who was crying for her mother, Red Eye and Spider carried Reni's body to the basement, where they decided to bury her, along with all the photographs showing the group together. Later that night, Tuffy told detectives, Lyn arrived and learned about the misfortune that had befallen her friend Reni.

The police had another theory: The killers had come to view Reni as a possible snitch, and wanted her out of the way. If she hadn't known the details of her husband's murder, she could well have found out on November 11, when the identity of the decapitated corpse was released to the press. That news might have spurred Reni to turn on her friends, authorities speculated.

To bolster the theory of premeditated murder, they noted that the gang had purchased their grave-digging tools the very morning Reni died, at the Gemco Department Store on Oxford Street. Clerks there recalled selling items to several members of the group, who, as usual, paid in quarters. The store security guard easily identified Tuffy from the photos police showed him; "he remembers because she did not have on a bra, and has a large bust," investigators reported. "He remembers telling one of the shoe clerks to look as she walked out the door."

Spider conceded that the picks and shovels had been bought to do some digging in the basement. All he had planned to do, however, was bury his guns and scrapbooks in the basement corner. The reason, he said, was that he thought the Flora Street house was "cool."

The suspects followed the usual Family procedure of providing false names, dates of birth, and explanations of their activities. But the police had little trouble identifying such a notorious character as Lyn. When she refused to say a word about what had transpired on Friday night, they booked her for murder.

California, still governed by its nineteenth-century penal code, defined murder as an unlawful killing "with malice aforethought." Malice, the code declared, was implicit "when the circumstances attending the killing show an abandoned and malignant heart."

Lyn called Doug Vaughn.

Jailed

Under the harsh fluorescent light of a jail visiting room, Lyn complained about the turn of events.

"This is really bullshit, Doug," she said, the rare use of profanity indicating her distress. Just as the Family book was beginning to come together, she ends up in the San Joaquin County Jail on a bum murder rap. The arrest, Lyn knew, had consequences beyond her own inconvenience. She was the one maintaining the communication between the different members of the Family in their prison cells and crash pads around the state. People who depended on her grew concerned. "With Squeaky in jail," Paul Fitzgerald glumly reported in a letter to Katie, at the Frontera prison, "the entire communication has broken down."

Lyn told Doug Vaughn that his first order of business was to see Charlie, to explain the situation and receive his guidance. Vaughn dutifully filed requests to visit with Manson, as well as Tex, Steve Grogan, and Bobby Beausoleil. Conveniently, all were then housed at prisons in Northern California.

While waiting to hear if he would receive an audience with Charlie, Vaughn began assembling the more conventional parts of Lyn's defense. The police reports, he was astonished to learn, said nothing about Lyn other than that she called the Flora Street house to ask for a ride. Vaughn concluded there was no case against his client, and confidently told reporters she would be released within days.

The days, however, dragged into weeks, as prosecutors refused to dismiss the murder count. California authorities had long grumbled that no charges ever stuck against the woman they considered the acting leader of the Manson Family. Stockton police, advised by Los Angeles detectives who had worked on the Manson case, held Lyn while awaiting results of handwriting, fingerprint, and chemical analyses they hoped would link her to Reni Willett's slaying.

Lyn, meanwhile, tried to make the best of her incarceration, insisting on vegetarian meals from the jail kitchen and frequently enjoying visits from Sandy Good, who would come with tidings from San Francisco.

Even better, the arrest managed to put Lyn in the spotlight again. Fascinated by what the local press dubbed the "Body-in-Basement" murder, hundreds of spectators packed the San Joaquin County Courthouse for the pretrial hearings.

Lyn's involvement made the Stockton case international news, generating a report in the *New York Times* and media calls from as far away as Denmark and Germany. Journalists, some of whom Lyn knew from Manson's trial, converged on Stockton to interview her, and to take photos of the diminutive defendant as she was led into court with her hands shackled to her waist—an image more symbolic than precautionary, as bailiffs knew that Lyn's wrists were thin enough to slip through the handcuffs. She relished her appearances in court, gesturing theatrically and confusing the judge with references to "waiving motions"—these Vaughn quickly translated as Lyn's insistence that she be granted her right to a speedy trial, which most defendants waive.

In media interviews she stressed her innocence, but was more concerned with conveying Charlie's message. "We foresee a lot of violence in the streets," Lyn told one reporter. "And we only want to survive."

Heidi Willett, an orphan at eight months, also became a momentary celebrity. After the story of her parents' bizarre murders was broadcast nationwide, offers of adoption poured in from all corners of the country. In the end, social workers released Heidi to her maternal grandparents, who took her with them to Connecticut. George and Elvira Olmstead declined to have the media cover the reunion with their granddaughter.

During her stay in the San Joaquin County Jail, Lyn had been visited by a bow tie-wearing lawyer who represented Eddie Bunker. The convict-novelist was finally coming up on the drug charges federal agents busted him for at the Hollywood Holiday Inn, and Lyn was needed as a defense witness.

Now at Sybil Brand, the day of her testimony had arrived. Roused from her cell, Lyn was taken to the federal courthouse in downtown Los Angeles, a stately WPA structure with large, wood-paneled courtrooms. Put on the stand, "I was on exhibit in a short-hem, hand-me-down jail dress, my face dotted with a forgotten dry blob of toothpaste," Lyn recalled in a letter to *Prison Life* magazine.

Lyn was asked what Bunker had worn the day of his arrest. She couldn't recall; "once it was established that I didn't know what Eddie was wearing and didn't recall anything about the day other than it had been gray and probably colder than normal, there was no apparent purpose for my presence."

The key issue, Lyn later learned, was whether Bunker had been wearing long sleeves or short. Agents had claimed that they had merely wanted to talk to Eddie, but noticed fresh needle tracks on his arm; this observation, they asserted, gave them probable cause to arrest him. To this day, Bunker insists he was wearing a long-sleeved shirt.

Because Lyn could not testify to Bunker's wardrobe on the day of the arrest, she later wrote that she "wanted to apologize for not being of any help."

———

Steve Demetras, the deputy district attorney prosecuting the Willett case, finally had to agree with Doug Vaughn. There simply wasn't any evidence linking Lyn to Reni Willett's murder. On December 11, he filed papers reducing the murder charge to being an accessory after the fact. On January 2, 1973, the district attorney moved to dismiss all charges against Lyn and release her that day from the San Joaquin County Jail.

Red Eye pled guilty to the second-degree murder of Reni Willetts. Spider, Tuffy, and Brenda pled guilty to being accessories after the fact. They all went to jail.

Sandy Good would also be unable to welcome Lyn home. On Wednesday, December 20, a policeman had spotted Sandy waiting at a downtown San Francisco bus stop and recognized her as a fugitive. As Sandy had fled Portland rather than face charges of harboring Steve Bekins, she was lodged in the San Francisco City Prison to await extradition to Oregon. Eventually, as Steve Bekins had predicted, she would walk on the charge; a Portland judge sentenced her to three years probation and sent her back to California.

Heather, however, was still free. On January 3, Doug Vaughn picked her up in his truck, and the pair drove to Stockton from San Francisco to welcome Lyn back to freedom. Unfortunately, there were others also waiting at the jail for Lyn's release, and they took priority. As soon as Lyn walked out of the San Joaquin County Jail, she was arrested by Los Angeles police, who charged her with robbing a 7-Eleven store in the San Fernando Valley. Vaughn and Heather traded dumbfounded glances as LAPD Sergeant Robert J. Schebler took Lyn into custody and put her in his van. There was nothing to be done. While Schebler and his prisoner headed down Interstate 5 for the long drive to Los Angeles, Vaughn and Heather dejectedly returned to San Francisco.

The 7-Eleven robbery had stymied the LAPD for weeks. It had happened on Friday, October 13, 1972, when seventeen-year-old Carol Mikoll was working in the 7-Eleven store her family owned at Woodley Avenue and Devonshire Street, in a quiet corner of the San Fernando Valley called Granada Hills.

At about 4:40 P.M., a young woman entered the store, asked Carol about buying some money orders, and left. She returned a few minutes later when the store was empty, this time carrying a paper bag. She pulled a .38 caliber revolver out of it.

"Don't call anybody and don't scream or anything," the young woman commanded. After Carol made up $700 in money orders, a process that took about five minutes, the young woman fled in an aqua blue van with a white stripe across it.

Sergeant Schebler took the robbery report. According to Carol, the suspect was twenty-six to thirty years old, about five foot four, a thin 122 pounds, had strawberry blond hair and blue eyes with brown mascara. She wore blue pants with a white flower-print top. Only four foot eleven herself, Carol had to crane her neck up to see the robber.

"And I noticed that she had a necklace on," Carol added. "It was a heart necklace with a diamond in the middle."

Nearly a month after the robbery, Schebler returned with a half-dozen photos of young women to show Carol. She couldn't identify any of them as the robber. About a week later, he came back with another set of pictures, but Carol didn't recognize any of them, either. He returned the following Friday, November 17, with still more photos. This time, Carol identified the picture of Lynette Fromme, who lately had been in the news for a murder in Northern California.

Sergeant Schebler had immediately notified the San Joaquin County authorities; the LAPD wanted Lyn as soon as Stockton was through with her. Now, in January 1973, Lyn was back at the Sybil Brand Institute, awaiting a preliminary hearing on the robbery charge.

While there, she was visited by her father, William Fromme. Neither said much about the encounter. Probation Officer Henry Watkins, who spoke to the Frommes, summarized the subject tersely in his report to the court: "Relationship with parents fair. Do not want back home."

In documents filed with the jail, Lyn listed three character references, including a Los Angeles police officer and two attorneys, one of them Paul Fitzgerald. Asked her occupation, she put down "self-employed—writer" and told investigators her as-yet-untitled book would be completed within one month. On their forms, the police wrote "unemployed."

With the habitually silent, sullen Heather as his passenger, Doug Vaughn drove down to Los Angeles to attend Lyn's preliminary hearing on January 12. When he got to the courtroom, he immediately expected difficulties; the judge was black and undoubtedly familiar with the more venomous strains of the Manson Family's racial ideology. Vaughn prepared a dramatic defense. Before the hearing began, he took the unusual step of asking that his client be excluded from the proceeding. The judge agreed and Lyn was held outside the courtroom when prosecutor Robert Youngdahl put Carol Mikoll on the stand.

Vaughn, in his cross-examination, brought out that Carol's father paid his relatives under the table, while other employees received regular paychecks.

"So yourself, your mother and younger brother are all paid by cash?" Vaughn asked.

"Uh-huh," Carol testified. The judge, who had been hearing Carol's "uh-huhs" throughout the hearing, grew exasperated. "Would you say *yes* or *no* instead of *uh-huh*," he interjected.

Carol straightened up. "That is correct," she said. "My mother gets food money. She works for nothing, let's put it that way."

"Mothers have that problem," Vaughn said dryly. He continued with his cross-examination, establishing how close the suspect had stood to Carol. Pointing at himself, Vaughn said, "you could see from the crown of her hair down to the forehead of her entire face?" Then, for the record, he added: "I am indicating at least to my eyes from the top of my bald head."

"Uh-huh," Carol testified.

After a recess, Lyn was led into the courtroom. She had been crying before the preliminary hearing, but now her tears were dry, her face emotionless, as she sat at the defense table.

Prosecutor Youngdahl recalled Carol Mikoll to the stand and asked if she could identify the robber.

"Yes," said Carol, indicating Lyn, six feet away. "The girl with the red suit on."

Vaughn resumed his cross-examination. "Do you see anything on her forehead?" he asked.

"Yes, I do," Carol replied.

"What do you see?"

"An X."

"What type of an X?"

"A scar X."

"A scar, isn't it?" Vaughn continued. "Come up here about two feet. Can you still see that X?"

Staring eyeball to eyeball at Lyn, Carol replied, "Yes, I can."

"Did you see that X on that day?" Vaughn asked.

"No I didn't notice."

"Thank you," said Vaughn. "That's all I have." Lyn's X was obviously her most distinguishing feature; few who looked in horror after she first etched it on her head would have imagined the scar would someday exonerate her.

After both Heather and Vaughn himself testified that Lyn had been with them in the San Francisco Bay Area on the day of the robbery—that they specifically remembered joking about it being Friday the 13th—the attorney moved to have the charges dismissed.

"Nobody described the scar on her forehead, she certainly doesn't weigh 130 pounds, she certainly isn't 26 or 30 years old, she certainly doesn't have blond or light hair, she certainly doesn't have blue eyes and she was in my office" on October 13, Vaughn said. Youngdahl looked skeptically at the bearded lawyer from Northern California. He asked Vaughn questions about his relationship with Lyn, and objected to any effort to dismiss the charge.

A few days later, police apprehended a woman who matched the suspect's description—and who had passed one of the stolen money orders the day after the robbery. After she confessed to robbing the 7-Eleven, authorities grudgingly agreed to dismiss the charges against Lyn.

Deputy District Attorney William C. Melcher, who had met Lyn during the Manson trial, signed the documents requesting her release. He said he was glad to help, because there was a good side to the Manson girls that had been overlooked. "I wanted them to know that justice also works on their side of the street," he told the *Los Angeles Times.*

Nevertheless, the LAPD did manage to make one allegation stick against the reputed leader of the Manson Family. Lyn was fined $63 for charges stemming from a violation of Section 21950A of the Vehicle Code, failure to stop for a pedestrian.

After the long series of incarcerations, Lyn had much to do if she were to keep the Family together. Among her first chores was reclaiming the group's possessions from the authorities in Stockton—at least those items that wouldn't be used as evidence in the upcoming murder trials. Lyn didn't have room for everything in the old car she borrowed, so she carefully selected the best among the clothes and pots and pans seized from the Flora Street house. Her former adversaries, Deputy District Attorney Steve Demetras and Sergeant Richard Whiteman, helped her load the car. In common with many men in authority over Lyn, they too had grown to like her.

On Valentine's Day 1973, she sent them a thank-you letter from San Francisco. "I once looked to police as being truthful, then I found myself a fool," she wrote. "I once looked to most cons as truthful, and again I found myself a fool. But I'm still fool enough to believe there's a truth in every one of us (Human Beings). And I'm wise enough now to not trust but a few I know. These few I trust with my life." She typed her signature, "Squeak."

Among "these few" were the Family members in prison—and the five on trial for the Hawthorne shootout, where Gypsy, Fatherman, Mary, and several others had been arrested after trying to steal enough arms to break the rest of the Family out.

By pleading insanity, the Hawthorne robbery defendants were able to turn their trial into a Manson Family reunion. They subpoenaed Bobby Beausoleil, Clem, and even Charlie himself to testify on the origins of their mental state, which, under California law, the defendants would have to prove prevented them from distinguishing between right and wrong.

The chance to see her friends brought Lyn back to Los Angeles. She regularly attended the trial, held opposite the old Hall of Justice in the sterile new Criminal Courts Building. As usual, Family defendants and witnesses treated the trial less as a judicial proceeding than as an exercise in impudent theatrics. Bobby Beausoleil, manacled and in leg chains, made the biggest splash when he testified that "I'm at war with everybody in this courtroom. It's nothing personal, but . . . you better pray I never get out."

Lyn's presence in the courtroom gnawed at Judge Arthur Alarcon. After jurors reported receiving telephoned death threats, Alarcon asked authorities to investigate Lyn's involvement.

No evidence was found to link Lyn to the threats, but Alarcon's patience for her was slim. When she laughed during some of Fatherman's testimony, the judge immediately had her ejected from the courtroom.

"I don't know what he's talking about. I didn't make any threats," Lyn later told a reporter, adding innocently, "I thought someone made up that story."

If the jurors had been threatened, it wasn't to much effect. All of the Hawthorne defendants were convicted and sent to state prison.

Despite Lyn's familiar banter with the news media, the Hawthorne debacle had led the Family into its greatest crisis since the Tate-LaBianca trial. For the first time, central members of the Family were disavowing Charlie—for a new messiah.

Kenneth Como, the A.B. convict who had led the robbery spree in 1971 with the ostensible purpose of freeing Charlie, had instead become a clan leader of his own. The Family members who had followed Como into armed battle with the police now saw him as their supreme leader. Gypsy had declared herself for Como, but even more astonishing to Lyn, so had Mary Brunner—the first to join Charlie back in 1967, the woman with whom Lyn had undergone so many changes, the woman who had borne Charlie's son.

With letters and messages smuggled into prison, Lyn struggled to persuade Mary to put Como aside, to return to the unity they had shared with Charlie. At first Mary ignored the letters, but eventually she felt it necessary to defend her allegiance to Como.

Mary wrote to Lyn. "When I met Charlie, I was looking for a man, and by some roundabout process found more than I ever really hoped I could in [Como], he is my life, my world, my King, you name it, for me, he is it."

Gypsy responded similarly to Lyn's entreaties, appropriating the Family's argot to express her loyalty to Como. "My soul moved me to give my love to one who gives his [Como] all, his life to our dream," Gypsy explained to Lyn.

The dispute between Como and Charlie had led to a breakdown of the pact between the Family and the Aryan Brotherhood. "Something very serious is happening inside the men's prisons," Lyn wrote. ". . . By the very fact that Gypsy and Mary say they are 'Kenny's women'—by the letters that Gypsy has been writing about 'that corner bullshit' we are making Charlie a fool." Not to mention Lyn herself; the "corner bullshit" that Gypsy disparaged was the vigil Lyn had so diligently led at Temple and Broadway.

Lyn, who had always downplayed the racist themes in Charlie's teaching, now felt free to attack the extremism of the Aryan Brotherhood. "A.B. moves much on pure hate, as they want [Charlie] to kill black because black is black. He will not do this and they are against him. . . . I have thought that all would come together but men are playing bullshit games of personality and ego," she despaired.

She flooded Mary and Gypsy with letters trying to reclaim them for the Family. More important than her own missives, of course, were those that came from Charlie. Since he could not communicate directly with his followers in prison, Lyn would painstakingly transcribe his cramped scrawl, typing out letters and inserting parenthetical notes and question marks, and send them through the privileged legal mail of a sympathetic attorney. But Charlie's raps, which had worked so well in the acid-tipped nights of Spahn Ranch, seemed to lose their magic when typed for reading in prison dormitories. Phrases that once seemed knowing and evocative began to look like gibberish.

Como, meanwhile, let Lyn know his opinions as well. According to Lyn, he sent her a greeting card depicting a flower vase, inscribed RED AND BLUE, R.I.P.— Lyn and Sandy's nicknames. Inside, under the saccharine Hallmark copy, Como had added: "In Never Never Land, My skies are always blue. Love ya to death, Jesse"—Como's nickname. "That may not sound like a threat letter to you," Lyn told a friend, "but it is."

The Manson civil war was not merely conducted on paper. Women who had switched their allegiance to Como stayed in touch with Lyn, paying homage to the idea that despite the conflicts, all were still One. During one such visit, a defector sat in Lyn's living room, blithely reporting that Como had been passing along the message that Charlie "was a rat." Despite her skepticism at the claim, the woman added, "But you know, I'm Kenny's woman."

This was too much for Sandy to take. She leaped at the woman and grabbed her by the throat, calling her Como incarnate. They fought, tumbling around the room, until the woman slipped Sandy's grasp and tried to escape. Sandy blocked the door, but the woman let out a fierce scream; since she wouldn't shut up, there was no choice but to let her go. Another humiliation.

Despite Lyn's struggle to reconnect with Mary and Gypsy, the Family continued to unravel around her. Katie, Lyn's most prolific prison correspondent, began to question Lyn's work. If Lyn was so dedicated to the Family, Katie groused, how come she was free while the others sat in prison? "If you do see Squeaky," Katie wrote to a friend, "tell her I said I am surprised she is not a housewife. . . ."

To Brenda, Katie was more direct. "Spahns ranch is *dead*," she wrote.

Chapter 7

Sacramento

Charlie had been transferred from San Quentin, on the San Francisco Bay, to Folsom Prison, one hundred miles inland. Lyn and Sandy, both fresh out of jail, moved to Sacramento, where they would be closer to him—and to the Corrections Department, which they were continually petitioning for permission to visit Charlie.

Sandy scavenged for essentials to set up their household. Riding her bicycle through Sacramento's alleys, she found an old typewriter for Lyn, along with screws, light bulbs, and various other wares. "You wouldn't believe all the junk she brings home," Lyn wrote to friend. "1950 suits for men. Know any 1950 men?"

In years past, however, Lyn had salvaged a lot more. The early garbage runs had yielded a bounty of fruits, vegetables, and assorted goods in decent working order. Now, even though the country seemed more full of trash than ever, the quality of refuse had declined.

"It used to be," Lyn observed, "that you could get some very good things out of the trash, but now people aren't throwing those things away any more. People are tightening up."

Fortunately, it didn't cost much to feed two slim vegetarians, and much of what they ate—tomatoes, string beans, and zucchini—they grew at the community garden. Lyn had helped establish the garden, on state-owned land at Fourteenth and Q streets, and then rented one of the seventy plots there. Busy with her other projects, she turned over much of the work to Sandy.

Soon, there were frictions with the other gardeners. Though the garden's supervisor, Charlene Jacobs, had gotten along with Lyn, Sandra was a different story. After weeks of suspicion, she accused Sandy of stealing other people's vegetables.

Sandy was outraged. She shook her finger and scolded Charlene, "We're doing bigger things than anything you can do in that garden. You're not doing anything, but we are. We're trying to change the world."

"Why don't you start by improving your garden?" Charlene grumbled.

It seemed sometimes like only Lyn could appreciate Sandy. "She walks softly and carries a machine gun," Lyn observed, admiringly. "She don't rampage but when there's a genuine need for it—then cowpokes better watch out!"

Lyn visited as many members and associates of the Family as would see her. Usually, she was able to travel in anonymity; as the seemingly unending sequence of Manson-related trials ground on, the press and the public had begun to tire of the story. There were occasions, though, when Lyn still managed to cause a stir. Authorities in Solano County, an agricultural area midway between San Francisco and Sacramento, took every precaution when they heard the Manson Family's leader was planning to attend the trial of an A.B. member in the local courthouse. Sheriff's deputies, hastily pulled from their beats and ordered into riot gear, were mildly embarrassed when the threat turned out to be the tiny, smiling redhead in a peasant dress.

In June 1973, Lyn and Sandy rented the third-floor garret at 1725 P Street, a once-grand Victorian in downtown Sacramento. The mansion had been built around 1890 for a prominent Sacramento family whose fortune came from making the wooden boxes used for shipping California fruit. The house had been designed to imitate the fanciest East Coast homes, with a downstairs paneled in oak and exquisitely ornamented. The next owner was a doctor who converted the second story into his examination room; in the 1950s, the mansion suffered further degradation when, like many other Victorians in downtown Sacramento, it was divided into small and inexpensive apartments.

Red and white aluminum awnings now marked the structure, along with well-tended front and backyards, and an outbuilding that had been converted from a horse barn into extra apartments. The area wasn't exactly lively—no place in Sacramento was—but it was about as close as could be found to a passable neighborhood in the state capital. Students, old people, and dropouts lived there, people who couldn't afford the more modern housing in the suburbs.

With its grid of alphabet and numbered streets, downtown Sacramento was a transient district where nobody really knew the neighbors too well. The Symbionese Liberation Army, for one, liked the area for those reasons; a few blocks south of Lyn's apartment, on the more dilapidated W Street, they kept a safehouse where they met new recruits and planned bank robberies. Patty Hearst had been staying there earlier in the year, and had gone on jogs around the neighborhood with the SLA's leaders, Bill and Emily Harris.

Lyn, as usual, made a good impression on many of her neighbors. Mona Lynch, the old woman who lived behind the house, doted on Lyn, and had picnics with her and Sandy on the lawn. Decades later, Mrs. Lynch would still carry a snapshot of Lyn, wearing a big, freckly smile, in her wallet. Not everyone, however, was so entranced.

"She talked a lot about death," one neighbor, a twenty-four-year-old woman, recalled. Lyn seemed to crave contact with others, always touching people when she spoke to them, the woman said. "She asked me if I was afraid of dying. A lot of times she didn't make sense." One lady up the street would complain about Lyn's wardrobe, her dress "cut low with her boobies hanging out." Others muttered that Lyn, Sandy, and the other women who came through their flat must have been witches, or lesbians.

Associates of the Family, A.B. members and others, would sometimes stop by, often coming to the P Street apartment right after their release from custody. "They had their own little halfway house for murderers," is how Dwayne Keyes, the United States Attorney in Sacramento, would later describe Lyn's flat.

Ensconced in their new apartment, Lyn and Sandy soon befriended the landlady, Helen White, who lived on the ground floor. Down in Mrs. White's apartment, the three women would do their sewing together, or swap tips on home canning. Lyn occasionally watched television in Mrs. White's living room, catching some of the Watergate hearings as they heated up over the summer. She particularly enjoyed the antics of Martha Mitchell, the alcoholic wife of Attorney General John Mitchell. Martha Mitchell's barbed comments hinted at high crimes and misdemeanors within the Nixon administration, providing plenty of grist for columnists and comedians. Martha Mitchell "really made my day," Lyn wrote to a friend. "Ever caught her act?"

Foremost on Lyn's mind, however, was her book. She would send chapters to other Family members for their critiques, and struggled to incorporate as many points of view as she could.

"I think I mighta got too word-loaded in doing this book," she told a friend, affecting a hillbilly twang. "I get letters that tell me I'm either off in the cosmos, or goin' over heads—I know what I'm saying tho—& that's the trip to me." Always assuming her letters were being read by authorities, Lyn joked that, one day, "I'm gonna take all my letters & sell 'em to the Milton Bradley game company & make these here puzzles for D.A.'s." She was not too far off the mark. After learning of Lyn's presence in town, the head of Sacramento's police intelligence squad, Lieutenant Howard Jernigan, did put the P Street garret under informal surveillance.

At times, the weight of Lyn's mission all but smothered her. "I been crying inside for three days," she wrote on a hot August night. Everything depended on her ability to tell the Family's true history: "The story of how a myth gets rolling. Were this not to be revealed, I wonder why, I wonder why, I wonder what I've been doing."

As she surveyed her manuscript, by now close to six hundred pages' worth, she saw different sides of her personality emerge. The "Freudian freak" was one.

Then there was "me, the old biddy. Me, the sex deviate wild creature lover and I guess, even me, the snotty bitch." She allowed herself a writerly indulgence into self-pity:

> Really, I'm a bit at a standstill. . . . I've read this over twenty thousand times! Talk about tired, Jeez. Wait a sec. Gotta get a cup of coffee. Whatever we got, it's given me the drowsies every day for three weeks now. That's the house wife death. . . .
> I feel like crying right now. I know that's a soggy old story coming from this here Squeak but it's the soft sort that only sez somethin's breaking my heart and a little bit of salt water can soothe the sands.

Lyn struggled. Sandra, however, began to blossom in the Sacramento's muggy clime. Despite the Manson Family's general distaste for institutional learning, she enrolled at Sacramento State University, taking a full undergraduate load and declaring her intention finally to earn her bachelor's degree. Sandra listed her major as ethnobotany, the study of plant lore and customs. School records showed she was a very good student.

During her incarceration at the San Francisco jail in the winter of 1972, Sandra had been visited by Marsha Bradt, a twenty-one-year-old freelance journalist. Bradt, who lived in San Francisco with her boyfriend, Peter Perry, thought the Manson Family women an apt subject for a story. She had unsuccessfully sought to get on the correspondence list of Katie, Lulu, and Sadie at the California Institution for Women in Frontera, but found Sandra eminently accessible in the local jail. Bradt explained that she had every reason to want to help the Manson women; after all, her brother had gone to school with Lulu's brother. It seemed a good enough explanation to Sandy, and the women struck up a friendship that lasted long after Sandra was released from custody.

Often accompanied by Perry and her brother, Peter Bradt, Marsha would visit Lyn and Sandra for good times and talks about philosophy and current affairs, like the resignation of Vice President Spiro Agnew and the report of a UFO sighting in Mississippi. Regardless of any particular day's headlines, however, Lyn and Sandra steadfastly maintained that armed conflagration was right around the corner.

Marsha Bradt and her friends decided it would be interesting to give Lyn and Sandy some exposure to the things they were always talking about. In December 1973, Marsha Bradt, Peter Perry, and Peter Bradt took Lyn and Sandy out to the San Francisco Municipal Rifle Range in Pacifica, just south of the city. There, amid towering pines and croaking frogs, the party unloaded hundreds of rounds from a pair of .22 caliber semi-automatic rifles, and a .22 caliber self-reloading semi-automatic pistol—a dead ringer for the Colt .45 Lyn would later point at President Ford. Marsha took photos of the trip, including one of Lyn carefully aiming her pistol. They had so much fun on Saturday, they returned for another three hours on Sunday.

The experience invigorated Lyn. "Hi goils," she wrote to the incarcerated murderesses at Frontera. "Lost my typewriter; Found my strength." The direct response of the pistol contrasted with the laborious effort to complete the manuscript. "I've been sitting on my ass for so long writing this fairy tale that will be, will be . . . " Lyn reflected. "I'm the one who should do something."

Life assumed a routine for Lyn, as much as it ever had. She continued to travel the state and correspond with the friends she had made over the years, even as their concerns drifted away from the vindication of Manson. Capistrano, who had returned to her family's homestead in Death Valley, complimented Lyn on her writing—"the book is as good as you are good and I love it"—but quickly turned to more pressing matters: the Inyo County Welfare Department, Cappy complained, was planning to cut her $200 monthly check by $50.

In San Francisco, Lyn would occasionally drop in on the satirist Paul Krassner. The two would take walks around the city, discussing various conspiracy theories. Krassner once used a pyramid-shaped seashell to illustrate his model of how secret societies controlled the United States. He gave the shell to Lyn, who grasped it in her palm and rubbed it along her cheek.

"Wow. I can actually *feel* their energy," she said.

Both were convinced that President Kennedy had been assassinated not by a lone gunman but by the CIA. When Krassner tried to expand his conspiracy scenarios to include the Tate-LaBianca murders, however, Lyn vigorously dissented. Could Manson have been the pawn of a mysterious criminal underworld, or perhaps of some devil cult, Krassner postulated, repeating theories that had circulated for years.

"No," Lyn said. Krassner asked if Lyn had seen *Rosemary's Baby*, the Satanic conspiracy movie directed by Roman Polanski in 1968. Lyn insisted that she hadn't.

Krassner wasn't exactly mesmerized by his waifish friend; he found Lyn's occasional racial remarks particularly objectionable. More often, however, he felt sympathy for the young woman whose exuberance and intelligence seemed so woefully misdirected. After listening to one of Lyn's ecology lectures, Krassner challenged her when she lit a cigarette. Women, he told her, had been conditioned to smoke through a sophisticated advertising program mounted by the tobacco companies.

"Okay," Lyn said. She dropped the cigarette and crushed it with her shoe. Although not exactly deferential to Krassner, she treated him with more regard than many she met. After he pointed out a flaw in one of her arguments, she shrugged.

"Well, what do you expect from me?" she said with a laugh. "I'm crazy."

Lyn found one of Sandy's courses at Sacramento State irresistible: a class examining conditions inside prison. She began auditing the course, and struck up a friendship with the instructor, Meredith Taylor. Taylor had come to university teaching through an unconventional route. She had once done time in jail, and collected welfare while raising four children and attending college. She was struck by Lyn's red hair and freckled face, by her exquisite, porcelain complexion. Taylor thought Lyn a beautiful young woman.

Lyn's experiences, however, were another story. Taylor would sit, at once spellbound and repulsed, as Lyn recounted the days at Spahn Ranch—and the nights after the murders when certain Family members would return to the commune and burn the clothes they had worn. Lyn described the events as if she were recounting an especially memorable slumber party, describing who had worn what, and laughing over the zany antics of her friends.

Like others who met Lyn, Taylor was puzzled that she could sometimes be so articulate and at others incomprehensible in her attempts to explain Manson's ideas and justify his actions. As Lyn saw it, the Family was totally nonviolent; if violence came, it was because the victims were asking for it, the victims were invoking a karmic reaction that the Manson Family simply executed. Mentioning Manson, Taylor thought, was like pushing a button on Lyn, instantly converting a charming young woman into a lunatic.

Sandra proved even more mercurial. At a dinner party Taylor held, a faculty member found Sandy attractive, and struck up a conversation that seemed to be going well. Talk inevitably turned to Manson, however, and the instructor made the faux pas of criticizing him. Sandy exploded. The killings were no worse than abortion, she shrieked, no worse than Vietnam or the destruction of the environment. The fellow backed off.

Lyn didn't get out to movies much, but she did manage to catch a documentary on Malcolm X. "Very dynamic," she said of the slain Black Muslim leader. He reminded her of Paul Fitzgerald; like the Beverly Hills attorney, Malcolm X had once been a boxer.

Lyn enrolled for the fall semester at Sacramento City College, which had become something of an educational center for radicals. Not only did the student body vote to name black revolutionary Angela Davis as homecoming queen, but SLA members Bill and Emily Harris, along with Patricia Hearst, attended the community college under assumed names. Lyn received more than educational enrichment by enrolling; she collected $1,100 from a student loan.

Lyn sought some hands-on learning, too. "Having never seen even a flick of a dead body," she wrote to a friend, "I decided I would wedge my way into an autopsy lesson."

As Lyn told the story, she went to the laboratory claiming to be a first-year medical student who wanted to watch a real autopsy. To her surprise, she wasn't invited merely to watch but actually to assist the lone doctor performing the procedure. She had steeled herself for the experience, but the sight of the open corpse affected her nonetheless. Rather than disgust, though, a strange, even spiritual feeling came over her. The dead body was a vacant cage. It meant nothing. It felt empty. The inside of the human body looked, she said, just like steak.

The fear of death she had grown up with, a fear that had haunted her even through her changes with Charlie, seemed to lift as she immersed herself in the technical aspects of the autopsy. Such things had never been shown her in school. The reality of death was kept secret; it was privileged information.

Remaining as quiet as she could, she followed the doctor's cues with her eyes. Groping through the body with her plastic gloves, Lyn tried to act like she knew what she was doing. Above all, she hoped the doctor wouldn't notice that she had put her gown on backwards.

Lyn also pursued her legal education. Vigils and visits to the Corrections Department hadn't gotten her in to see Charlie; the only way, it seemed, was to get a court order. She taught herself to research case law, and began to assemble a petition to see prisoner No. B-33920. So desperate had Lyn become, she even was willing to deal with the hated legal profession. She began to contact attorneys in Los Angeles, San Francisco, and Sacramento, looking for one who might take her case for visiting privileges, pro bono. In one letter, she told a friend she even had called on Melvin Belli, the celebrated San Francisco lawyer who once represented Jack Ruby. Unfortunately, Lyn chose a bad day to drop in: Belli had just learned his Rolls-Royce was missing. "I suppose a wealthy person would really have to be organized to keep track of all his things. I know I have had enough trouble with the little specific stockpiles we have," she mused.

Again, Lyn found herself imposing on Paul Fitzgerald during her visits to Los Angeles. She sensed that her presence was not entirely conducive to the functioning of the law office.

"We shall promise on our honor to conduct ourselves in orderly, ladylike manners," she told Fitzgerald, "to refrain from spilling coffee, cluttering the hallway with baggage, taking off our shoes and anything else we've been known to do that is not professional."

Fitzgerald relented. He couldn't resist an offer like that.

An older couple, Jess and Mary Fain, bought Lyn's building in January 1975 and moved into the ground-floor apartment. The diabetic Mr. Fain, a retired state transportation engineer, maintained good relations with his tenants. He didn't raise the rent, and made no objection to the picture of Manson Lyn kept over her living-room window.

Despite their low expenses and disdain for money, even Lyn and Sandy needed an income boost to get by. The rent was $100 a month, and their only regular support was Sandy's $200 monthly check from her trust fund—an amount that was scheduled to be halved in 1975. Lyn visited the county welfare office, and quickly qualified for $90.90 per month, as well as food stamps. She met the criteria for public assistance, which consisted of being either unemployed or disabled and intending to make Sacramento her home. Over thirteen months, Lyn would receive $1,194.74 from local taxpayers. Sandy also applied for welfare, collecting food stamps and $150.84 cash through August 1974.

Lyn found a more lucrative income source, however, sitting on a park bench. His name was Manny Boro. He was sixty-four, wore his balding hair in a crew cut, dressed in golf caps and polyester sport shirts, and drove a 1963 Cadillac.

Sugar Daddy

He was born Harold Eugene Boro in 1909, but his grandmother had called him Manny, and somehow the name just stuck. Living in Jackson, an old mining town in the foothills of the Sierra Madre, she had raised the boy mostly by herself, after Manny's mother died and his father proved unwilling or unable to care for his son.

The Boros were pioneers in Gold Country. Manny's grandfather had come to Amador County in the late nineteenth century and worked in other men's hard-rock mines before setting up a small mining operation of his own. Although the family did not prosper in the Mother Lode, they did set down long roots there.

During his long, lonely life, Manny himself rarely ventured more than one hundred miles from his birthplace. He had been married once, and produced three children. One child had died, however, and the marriage lasted less than ten years. Manny never remarried. Instead, he worked his civilian job at McClellan Air Force Base, outside Sacramento. He began in 1941, and retired as a draftsman thirty-two years later.

For the last three decades, Manny had largely kept to himself. His outings were limited to weekend visits to Gold Country, where he owned both a forty-acre ranch and the yellow frame house where his son Charles and his family lived. Even in his house in Jackson, at the end of Laughton Lane, Manny would hardly socialize. If he wasn't puttering about the property, he was in the house grumbling, complaining, sometimes acting like an absolute boor.

He would walk into a room where people were watching TV and just change the station, without even asking. He might explode at his grandchildren over the most trifling things; if they finished the half-and-half, he would carry on as if they had stabbed him in the back. He would interrupt a conversation to talk on and on about his health, then leave without showing the slightest interest in the lives of Charles, or his daughter-in-law, Nelda. "Well, I gotta go," Manny would grunt, and that would be it.

Despite his frequent visits, Manny wasn't close to any of his children or grandchildren. If he confided in anyone, it was Nelda, who felt sorry for Manny and tried to excuse his shortcomings. He seemed to have no friends and, as far as Nelda knew, never dated.

One day, Manny appeared at Nelda's door with a surprise guest: Lyn. In her embroidered blouse and bellbottom pants, she looked quite the hippie to Nelda, hardly the sort one expected to be consorting with Manny. At this first meeting, however, he didn't explain their relationship, introducing her to Nelda as just a "friend" from town.

Standing in the large old house, decorated with children's paintings and Gold Country antiques, Lyn clearly was uncomfortable. Nelda tried to make small talk.

"So, Lyn, you live in Sacramento?" Nelda asked.

"Yes," Lyn replied quietly, striving to avoid eye contact. She answered Nelda's questions in monosyllables, and frequently glanced toward the door. After about ten minutes, Manny got the hint.

"Well, we gotta go," Manny grunted, and they drove off in his Cadillac, perhaps to visit the cows that meandered on Manny's ranch.

Later, Manny came to Nelda, more excited than he had been in years. He recounted how he had met Lyn in a park, how she was a "a real friendly girl," just kind of "down and out." Then Manny detailed his sexual relationship with Lyn, how the two of them had taken a trip together to Santa Cruz, how she would stay over at his apartment in Sacramento. He had the pictures to prove it, which he proudly displayed to his daughter-in-law: pictures of Lyn, naked, in his shower. Pictures revealing her breasts, her backside, her everything. Manny, Nelda saw, wanted to prove that a pretty young thing found him attractive.

"My God," Nelda later remarked to her husband, "your father's really going through a change." She told Charles about the female visitor, withholding the more delicate details. Charles, himself a gruff man who worked at the local mill, didn't show much interest. He had as much use for his father as his father had for him.

But Manny was upset when he learned Nelda had told Charles about his girlfriend. He swore Nelda to secrecy, and she never again said a word to anyone about Manny's unusual relationship. Well aware of Manny's social difficulties, Nelda assumed Lyn's interest in him was strictly financial. Lyn might wring a few thousand dollars out of him, Nelda figured, but that's the price someone like Manny would have to pay for company, and the company might do him good.

Still, Nelda had a few misgivings about Manny's new friend. She asked him about the X-shaped scar on Lyn's forehead.

"Oh, did you notice that?" Manny said. He seemed half pleased that the subject came up. Back in the sixties, Manny reported, Lyn had been with Charlie Manson, that hippie murderer from L.A., on a commune in the desert and whatnot. The girl was always talking about it, Manny said, she sort of even worshipped him.

That didn't make Nelda feel any better, but this dalliance with the girl couldn't be much worse than Manny's other hobbies, like betting on sports teams or playing the slots at Lake Tahoe. He didn't have much else to do, Nelda knew, except for puttering around the ranch, and collecting things from World War I, like antique guns.

When Manny learned of Lyn's troubles getting around, he decided to buy her a car. Manny's Cadillac wasn't Lyn's style. She preferred Volkswagens, so when they found a used Beetle advertised in the paper, Manny called the seller, George Blake.

Manny told Blake that he was looking to buy a dependable small car for his "niece." The 1963 VW seemed just about perfect, even down to the color: red. On August 21, 1974, Manny bought the car for $500. Blake transferred the title to Manny, and Lyn immediately registered the car in her name, at her P Street address.

Unfortunately, Lyn found the eleven-year-old Beetle to be a considerable headache, and constantly complained to Manny about it. Manny, in turn, would call Blake, demanding help in keeping the car running. The Blakes quickly grew to view Manny as a nuisance. Finally, Blake's wife Joan told him off: "If you wanted a new car," she said, "why didn't you buy one?"

The VW wasn't in service in October, when Lyn and Sandy decided to take a road trip to see Steve Bekins at the Oregon State Penitentiary. Manny let her use his Cadillac; it was probably safer in an accident, anyway, especially as he had just bought a new set of tires. Driving up to Salem on October 10, Lyn once again managed to run afoul of the law: she collected a speeding ticket.

On the June 9 application to visit the Oregon prison, Lyn, as usual, had listed her occupation as "writer." She received permission to come. Sandy, who admitted on her application that she had been convicted of a misdemeanor, initially was rejected. She persuaded her probation officer to vouch for her, however, and Oregon authorities relented. By now Lyn was intimately familiar with visiting procedures; going to prison was like going home.

The visit was fun. Sandy and Steve groped each other like long-separated lovers, while Lyn smiled approvingly, playing the big sister. They reminisced, and spoke of current events—of Nixon's downfall, and the current adventures of the SLA. At Steve's request, Lyn put another inmate on her list, which got him into the visiting room where Steve could pass him some marijuana.

The visit would be the last between Bekins and the women. Back in the rough and practical prison culture, Bekins had moved on from his more spiritual days as a Family associate. Lyn and Sandy, however, remained obsessed with Manson. The old friends pledged to remain in touch, but it was clear that things had changed since Sandy had left Bekins in Portland in 1972. Her adventure with him had been, in retrospect, her last chance to leave Manson's orbit. And Lyn's, too.

Lyn piloted Manny's Cadillac back toward Sacramento, eschewing the inland Interstate 5 for the scenic U.S. Highway 101, rolling through the verdant, sparsely populated north coast of California. She reached Redwood Valley around 10:00 P.M., and took the turnoff to state Highway 20, cutting eastward toward Sacramento. Chatting animatedly with Sandy as she drove along the dark, two-lane road, Lyn drifted over to the right shoulder. Startled, she overcorrected and lost control of the car, crossing the centerline and crashing into the bank on the far side of the highway.

Lyn and Sandy were unhurt. The same could not be said for Manny's silver four-door Cadillac. After Manny made his way to the bucolic stretch of Lake County where Lyn had been stranded, he was informed that the car was a total loss. The junk dealers gave him back his set of tires, but the wreckage of the uninsured sedan would bring only ten dollars as scrap.

It was hard for Manny to be mad at Lyn, however. She was his closest friend. Lyn, for her part, no longer had anyone else to turn to. George Spahn, her first elderly lover, had died on September 23, 1974, at the age of eighty-five.

Care as she might for Manny, Lyn declined to spend Thanksgiving with him. Rather, she went back to Death Valley, to share the holiday with friends from her Family past.

Sisterhood

Cut off from his women, feuding with the Aryan Brotherhood, Charlie responded by growing ever more mystical. Vaguely aware of current events filtered through the prison walls, he continued to interpret everything outside as a harbinger of the coming revolution: "The SLA fire"—the shootout in Watts with the LAPD—"was our fire and it is locked in the Universe with the Viet Nam monks who burned themselves." Charlie's rambling, cramped letters to Lyn seemed to touch on every topic, from the mistreatment of whales and American Indians to the numerological significance of the telephone number at Spahn Ranch, which, he explained, had foretold the nine murders of which he would be convicted.

For years, Charlie had been referring to the women by color—Lyn was Red; Sandra Blue. Now he codified their chromatic identities in religious terms, which he called the Order of the Rainbow, or the Nanuss, or the Nuness.

The rules were strict: "NO MEAT. NO SMOKING. NO MAKEUP," Charlie empha-sized in a letter to Lyn. On ceremonial occasions, the women were to wear nun's habits sewn in the appropriate color. It wasn't necessary to cover the head in public places, but definitely so "in someone else's home and most of all around people" without beards. Charlie suggested they wear veils.

Adherents were to pray, using beads of alternating colors, picturing a positive thought for each bead in a bracelet. Charlie offered some examples. "You say ten times, 'This is a good day, this day is my day. I give me this day.' This is best said when first up, before anything, while the mind is still open from sleep," he advised.

In contrast to the open love practiced at Spahn Ranch, there was to be, as well, "no fornication or showing your ass, and the morality is the highest on earth. Laws behind the veil as much as it was at the ranch. Outside the veil, we will obey the laws of the land. . . . Oh yeah," he added, "no movies with violence that sets thoughts to death and confusion."

Lyn tried to excite the women at Frontera with Charlie's new religion. "One degree in Nuness can be gotten by sleeping in an open grave," she wrote them. "No violence. Only completion of old Christian fears." But Katie, Sadie, and Lulu were not interested. Neither were the students at Sacramento State, who ignored Lyn's efforts to recruit new followers in the college quads. Instead of coming to Manson, Lyn and Sandy saw to their irritation, young people were drawn to newly imported Eastern religions and gurus. How, they wondered, could so many people fall for such obviously false prophets?

In Washington, meanwhile, one false prophet had been replaced with another. Facing impeachment, President Nixon had resigned. He was replaced by his handpicked vice president, Gerald R. Ford.

About the same time, Charlie was transferred to the California Medical Facility in Vacaville, the prison system's mental hospital near Sacramento. Lyn and Sandy persuaded officials there to let them correspond with Manson, based on the productive lives they were now leading, and the possibility that contact with old friends might bring Charlie out of his "withdrawn" state. Vacaville authorities monitored the correspondence, which to them mainly seemed to involve discussions of philosophy, religion, and ecology, as well as long discourses on gardening.

In November, however, prison officials concluded that Charlie's scrawls amounted to instructions for an escape attempt. When the *Vacaville Reporter* got wind of the alleged plot to free Manson—which authorities said would include both guns and grenades—it splashed the news across the front page and sent it out on the wires. "Silly," was how Lyn described the story.

Soon there was a newsman at Lyn's door asking for a comment. She declined, then turned the interview around. She extracted from the reporter the gist of the confiscated letters, as well as an address so she could reach him for future publicity purposes. Later, Lyn wrote, she had to "steal the newspaper off the porch to keep our mom-like landlady from reading our names. She would either go into shock or ask us to move."

Less silly was another publication released in November 1974: the book *Helter Skelter: The True Story of the Manson Murders*, by Vincent Bugliosi with Curt Gentry. Although several accounts of the Manson Family had been published over the years, the prosecutor's book was by far the most significant. A smash bestseller, it went through seven hardcover printings in four months, putting Manson—and Bugliosi—back in the headlines.

The book was more than a recounting of the trial and the murders. It was a morality play of the highest order, with the crusading prosecutor battling a demonic Manson on one hand and the bumblings of the LAPD on the other. Lyn appeared as a memorable supporting character.

"Although Squeaky was twenty-one and Sandy twenty-five, there was a little-girl quality to them," Bugliosi wrote, "as if they hadn't aged but had been retarded at a certain stage in their childhood. Little girls, playing little-girl games. Including murder? I wondered."

Lyn was furious, particularly at the book's assertion that members of the Family had committed many more murders than the ones they had been convicted of—including that of Ron Hughes, the neophyte defense attorney who disappeared during the trial, only to turn up dead in rural Ventura County. Lyn's mind sped back to the date Hughes's body was found, and how she had been thrown in jail that day for the most trivial of charges, loitering. The bail bondsman, she remembered, told her that he had heard from the D.A.'s office that Hughes had been found with his throat slit. In fact, Hughes's body was too decomposed to tell precisely how he had died, and Lyn now wondered if this had been the beginnings of a possible setup by the D.A.'s office.

Paul Fitzgerald shared Lyn's outrage about Bugliosi's contention that Hughes was murdered. Depicted in less than flattering terms himself, Fitzgerald urged Lyn to take legal action against Bugliosi. Lyn agreed that she had more than ample grounds for a suit, but insisted she could best Bugliosi in the court of public opinion. By finishing her book, Lyn wrote she could "effectively combat the Bugliosi thought syndrome." She complained about Bugliosi's book to virtually everyone she met. When one of the employees of the Corrections Department, whom she was always petitioning for permission to see Charlie, asked Lyn her opinion of *Helter Skelter*, Lyn said that trying to read it had made her sick. It was full of lies. She was writing her own book, which would set the record straight.

But Lyn's book simply was not getting done. By March 1975, she conceded that her literary efforts had reached a standstill and saw no signs of ever reaching fruition. "Bugliosi's [book] has got me so hot, I have to put it down every few minutes and jump around the house," she complained. In a letter to an incarcerated friend, she enclosed a drawing of herself in the cult's new hooded dress, and of a smiling Nero playing the violin as smoke billowed beside him.

She declined, however, to discuss her new projects with the media, even as she had boasted to them about her ill-fated book. After learning of her presence in town, *Sacramento Bee* reporter Don Thornton tried to land an interview. Lyn wanted to ignore him, but the reporter persisted.

"Okay," she finally said, "here's what we want to do. . . . We have many things in mind—but I just cannot trust you with anything. What I'm saying is this, we have something to say. We have something going on between us and the people over there." She pointed toward the state Capitol. Thornton asked Lyn if she meant the legislature or the Corrections Department. Lyn answered evasively, and then concluded, without prompting, "Charles has got the answer."

Vincent Bugliosi was less oblique. Noting that Manson had been returned from Vacaville to Folsom Prison, he commented that Lyn and Sandy were "waiting for their god to be set free, and twenty miles from their god is better than a couple of thousand."

While original members of the Family drifted away, Lyn was collecting a handful of new admirers. One correspondent was a former mental patient named Edward Vandervort. A short, heavyset thirty-four-year-old, Vandervort lived with his mother in York, Pennsylvania. He apparently had read *Helter Skelter* and become enthralled with Lyn. He started sending her whatever dollars he could scrounge, and Lyn responded gently to her new friend. Pleased at the reception, Vandervort sent snapshots of himself as a child in 1962, showing him playing with chipmunks. More recent photos depicted him as he looked in 1975; Vandervort apologized for his appearance.

Lyn sought to boost his self-esteem. "You sure did gain weight, but ten years is a long while for it to creep up on you. As long as you feel good at your present weight, that's good, but if not, it would be a good idea to lose it," she advised.

They corresponded for months, with Vandervort making an effort to enclose items he knew would interest Lyn, such as a knife and an audiotape of Vincent Bugliosi on the Phil Donahue show. According to prosecutors, Lyn concluded from Vandervort's enthusiastic letters that he was unstable enough to kill. And if Vandervort was going to kill someone anyway, Lyn and Sandy decided he should take out someone who deserved it.

"Next I have a project for you and I want you to report to me how you feel about it," Lyn wrote.

In step-by-step instructions, she directed Vandervort to research the names and addresses of top corporate executives and their wives. "If anyone wants to know what you're doing, tell them you're doing a story on wives of executives. You can say you have an economy class or anything you wish," Lyn suggested. Vandervort was then to telephone the targets and, in his "meanest voice," utter the following: " 'Your (product or activity, or you may mention the name of it), is killing, poisoning the world. There is no excuse for it.' Now, say this very slowly: 'If you do not stop killing us, Manson will send for your heart. (If the company pollutes the air, you may say lungs.) Close the shop. Flee the country. Or watch your own blood spell out your crime on the wall. Remember Sharon Tate.' You may vary this. The main thing is to be scary and clear. Practice. Be a thug. You'll be a good one. . . . There is no need to feel guilty about this, because we are not doing anything wrong."

Apparently, Vandervort had good feelings about Lyn. After they exchanged several more letters and telephone calls, she sent him instructions for a more ambitious follow-up. He was to visit the president of "Kaiser Company, makers of more forms of pollution than I can count"; conveniently, the executive lived in Pennsylvania. "Do not threaten him first," the letter instructed. "Kill him. Destroy him." But, "check for kids. We want to avoid hurting any kids." The murder scene was to be an echo of the Tate house, with the bodies painted in pink—the color of Kaiser's machines.

Vandervort was instructed to put an aerosol can in Roesch's mouth, and to leave at the crime scene a copy of the counterculture magazine *New Times*, open to an article on pollution.

"We are making a picture to warn others who pollute," Lyn explained. "Do not write anything about Helter Skelter or any other words you got out of that book. Or anything about Manson. . . . Can you get silencers? Answer this now and throw away. Be good. Be quick. Be love."

Vandervort, however, did not follow through on the plans. When Lyn tried to call him collect, his mother refused to accept the charges.

Lyn continued to grow more extreme as 1975 wore on. "We must show new love—not twisted, spanked, yanked and beat misunderstood love, but RESPECT FIRST," she wrote. "Like the house of Islam, we women are to cover our bodies, wash our faces, put down the cigarettes and leave love making under our own roof in 'our own house,' not to flash bodies on the street for the confused and abused people to desire." With the exception of Manny Boro, Lyn left lovemaking with men altogether. Various acquaintances still drifted by the P Street apartment, but only female visitors could stay inside; male overnight guests slept outside, on the porch.

Dressed in a red robe, Lyn appeared at news bureaus around Sacramento to deliver fearsome press releases attributed to Manson, along with baskets of fresh-baked cookies for the reporters. "We're waiting for our Lord and there's only one thing to do before He comes off the cross and that's clean up the earth," Lyn explained. "We're nuns now. . . . Our red robes are an example of the new morality. . . . They're red with the sacrifice, the blood of the sacrifice."

UPI correspondents Rob Gunnison and Carl Ingram considered Lyn a good cook, although only the *Sacramento Union* published an item on Lyn's warning.

About once a month, Lyn visited Capistrano in Death Valley, where the old friends would get high and discuss their adventures. Occasionally, Lyn would try to reach out to the young people and prospectors who continued to trickle through the region. On several visits, she ran into the owner of the Modoc Mine, Rodney Catsiff, and struck up an acquaintanceship with him; once, he even towed her car to a service station after it ran out of gas. It was a reunion of sorts for Catsiff, as he had been passingly acquainted with the Family when they lived at Spahn Ranch.

Later, Catsiff would tell the FBI about his conversations with Lyn. She had insisted to the mine owner that Shorty Shea had not been murdered by the Family after all, but was alive and well and living in Denver. (This assertion would be proven false in 1979, when Clem led investigators to Shea's body near Spahn Ranch.) She complained about the environmental destruction going on across the country, and criticized the nation's leaders, particularly Secretary of State Henry Kissinger, whom she called a "bureaucratic pig."

Lyn also had personal advice for Catsiff. At one point, she told him to throw away his beer and cigarettes, and eat grass instead. It would be much better for him, she explained.

Other friends, though, began to drift away. Marsha Bradt, who had taken Lyn to the Pacifica firing range, sensed a change in her after the publication of Bugliosi's *Helter Skelter*. Lyn's communications were becoming more violent and more angry, something Bradt ascribed to Sandra Good's influence. Lyn, Bradt later said, was two different people, depending on whether she was around Sandra, whom she considered "more of a catalyst on her than even Charlie." Scared by the new tone, Bradt dropped her friendship with Lyn.

Lyn continued her efforts to visit Manson at Folsom Prison. She regularly petitioned the Corrections Department, and even pressed her case with the lieutenant governor, Mervyn Dymally, whom she buttonholed in a hallway at the state Capitol. Lyn asked Dymally, the only black statewide elected official, for help in getting in to see her incarcerated "husband." Dymally told Lyn to call his office for help. Although a Dymally aide had only positive things to say of Lyn—"she seemed interested in everybody being happy," he recalled—nothing came of the requests.

In May 1975, Lyn called upon yet another lawyer to help her out. Clyde Blackmon was one of Sacramento's rising criminal defense attorneys, and a law partner with a future speaker pro tem of the California state assembly. A bear of a man, he agreed to meet with Lyn, even as his secretary recoiled at the notorious woman in her frightening red robe.

The Berkeley-educated attorney listened carefully to Lyn's request. To Blackmon, visitation rights for prisoners were a matter of principle, regardless of any particular inmate's notoriety. And no inmate could better vindicate the principle than Charles Manson.

Sitting in Blackmon's office, Lyn and Sandra went over their arrest records, and gave him copies of their correspondence with prison officials. Her letters to the Corrections Department "may sound a bit aggressive," Lyn told him, but "only because of the past runaround history." Blackmon saw no legal justification for barring Lyn from visiting Manson. He also was impressed with her polite manners and respectful demeanor. He agreed to take her case, pro bono. A former law school classmate now represented the Department of Corrections, so Blackmon figured he might be able to negotiate an informal compromise over visits. He told Lyn that she probably wouldn't get the full contact visits she wanted, but something might be worked out that could lead to greater privileges in the future.

Lyn, for her part, returned the favor as best she could. She brought Blackmon home-baked cookies, as well as gourmet coffee to replace the undrinkable institutional grind the office served.

Blackmon's interest contrasted with that of a San Francisco legal aid attorney, whom Lyn had been urging to take her case since February 1975. When she began to appear at his home to press her arguments, the lawyer called police. Summoned to the San Francisco Hall of Justice, Lyn was admonished to leave the frazzled attorney alone or face legal action.

Trying to set her personal affairs in order, Lyn wrote to Los Angeles Superior Court Judge Raymond Choate, who had presided over both the Barbara Hoyt case and Manson's convictions for the Gary Hinman and Shorty Shea murders. She confessed to the judge her feelings of guilt for failing to persuade him to set Manson free.

"Instead, I played the father-daughter game with you and took my rebellious child opinion and sent him to prison with it," she wrote. "My own judgment is heavy for this and I realize it more each day. I buried Manson in my own fear."

About a month later, Lyn called Choate at home, to ask him how he felt about "all this killing"—meaning the killing in Vietnam and the "killing of the ecology." She said she planned to do something desperate.

"At first I thought she meant she was going to kill herself," Choate later told a reporter. "But she specifically said she didn't mean suicide."

The International People's Court of Retribution

Lyn had become a Manson nun. In her red robes and daily obeissances, she lived her life in ascetic devotion to the long-gone days of Spahn Ranch and Death Valley. To Lyn, there was no irony. Spahn Ranch may well have been filled with sex, drugs, and wanton irresponsibility—a focus on Now—but in retrospect, it had been about so much more. The Family had lived as a model, and eventually a warning, to the world. A warning, she decided, about the state of the ecology, about the environmental, and thus spiritual, pollution of the earth. That was what the Tate-LaBianca murders must have been about, that must have been the point of Charlie's trials and of Lyn's struggle in the years since. Charlie had taught that "no sense makes sense," and it all made sense to Lyn.

Charlie, Katie, Lulu, Sadie, and Tex had found enough courage to go all the way to the gas chamber. The time had come for Lyn to prove herself worthy of her brothers and sisters: Do something, like the Tate murders years before, that would capture the imagination of the world. In the P Street apartment, Lyn and Sandy launched their plan.

The world had ignored them when trying to get their message out in peaceful fashion. It was easy to ignore a pair of unemployed young women with no leverage beyond Manson's name.

As the Weather Underground and the Symbionese Liberation Army had proved, however, it was a lot harder to ignore a band of terrorists. To seize public attention in the current environment, Lyn and Sandy concluded, they would have to launch a terror campaign of their own—or at least make people think they had. As a counterpoint to the American justice system that had stymied them for so long, they decided their cadre would be called the International People's Court of Retribution. There were so many who deserved retribution.

The International People's Court was not a personal vendetta against those who had wronged Manson. Rather, the targets would be the current enemies of Lyn's world, the corporate executives whose firms chopped down trees, coughed out smog, and clubbed baby seals. It was essential that the International People's Court speak across the country in one loud voice. To accomplish the task, Lyn and Sandy would compile a master list of all the corporate polluters in the nation, and mail them warnings all at once. Stop polluting—or die.

To them, it seemed eminently plausible. If there was one Edward Vandervort ready to execute corporate leaders upon command from Sacramento, there could be thousands of them amid a country of more than 200 million. And so, they assembled the story of the International People's Court of Retribution. It had been founded in the 1950s in the federal penitentiaries at Terminal Island, California, and McNeil Island, Washington—the very prisons where Charles Manson had been incarcerated. It had grown during the Cuban missile crisis, with major expansions in Florida and Mexico, and now consisted of two thousand members throughout the world. After decades underground, the International People's Court of Retribution was ready to strike at the corporate executives who were damaging the environment. Of course, the head of the International People's Court of Retribution was Charles Manson.

Lyn and Sandy would always stress, however, that they themselves were not actually members of the International People's Court, and merely communicated on its behalf when it contacted them. The women did not, they said, even know how to reach the terrorist group on their own initiative.

The head of the FBI's intelligence division, William N. Preusse, would later testify at Sandra Good's trial that the bureau had never heard of the International People's Court of Retribution, despite exhaustive efforts to surveil potential subversives. The International People's Court, the government would contend, existed only in Sandy and Lyn's minds.

In her remarks at trial, Sandy would offer a different explanation for the FBI's ignorance of the terrorist group. Since the days of J. Edgar Hoover, she observed, the bureau had been obsessed with fighting Communists; with such an ideological bias, the FBI could easily have overlooked a non-Marxist, environmentally concerned guerrilla organization like the International People's Court of Retribution.

One night in early July 1975, Lyn and Sandy locked themselves out of their apartment. Frustrated, they banged on their door, and then tried to get in by breaking a window. The noise awoke their downstairs neighbor, Morris Willmarth. Concerned, he bounded up the outdoor staircase to take a look.

In his early twenties and nearly six feet tall, Willmarth was a long-haired, easygoing, hard-drinking type. After his Army service in Korea, he had returned to his family in Sacramento, and later, having rented his own apartment at 1725 P Street, enrolled at Sacramento State University to study chemistry. He was working several jobs over the summer, including one at Fannie Ann's saloon and another at the Libby McNeil factory, where he canned tomato juice. Willmarth had occasionally passed Lyn while coming or leaving his place, but never had been introduced. Now, after an exchange of names, the handy Willmarth helped the women get back into their apartment.

Lyn and Sandy invited their neighbor in. They were impressed by his interest in their predicament. "Not too many people would have bothered to find out what was going on," Lyn said. This led to a conversation about the overall state of society, and Willmarth appeared to have his heart in the right place, even if he was somewhat naive: Willmarth believed for example, that the world could be changed through conventional political activism, and was planning to volunteer for a ballot measure that would restrict nuclear power.

Lyn explained that she and Sandy were full-time ecological activists, and that they were launching a campaign to increase environmental awareness. Mankind, she observed, didn't have many years left if nothing were done to stop pollution. Willmarth readily agreed, and volunteered to help the women in their cause. Moreover, he thought, "Sandra's not half-bad looking." Perhaps he might get a date out of his good works.

Willmarth soon became an almost daily visitor to the women's garret. He would carry their groceries up the stairs for them, and chop carrots and onions for their stews. To help in Willmarth's education, Lyn and Sandra would show him their environmental literature—magazine articles depicting Soviet whaling ships, or the hazards of nuclear waste.

Willmarth noticed a pattern in the women's relationship. While Sandra did most of the talking, Lyn seemed to be in charge. Sandra would get excitable, and sometimes go out on a limb; a glance from Lyn would pull her back. Years later, Willmarth would describe Sandra as "codependent."

It was Sandra who gave Willmarth his first assignment in the ecology campaign: to obtain the address of every newspaper in the United States with a circulation of more than 100,000. They would use the mailing list for environmental awareness press releases, she explained. Willmarth began spending his free hours at the public library, tracking down the addresses.

Lyn did not rely solely on Willmarth to do their research. Using the pseudonym "Lyn White," she sent a request to the Planning and Conservation League, one of California's major environmental organizations. She asked for a list of all the companies, industries, and private individuals responsible for damaging the environment.

"If you do not have such a list, please find the time to compile one for me," she wrote. "My friends and I wish to devote our entire summer to writing hundreds of letters." The envelope was returned to P Street, stamped "Undeliverable as Addressed."

Even before Morris Willmarth finished his mailing list, Lyn and Sandy knew how to reach some news organizations. They had begun their campaign early in July.

Lyn contacted the Associated Press bureau in Sacramento, the *Sacramento Bee,* and KSAN-TV in San Francisco with a news release attributed to Manson. An anonymous female caller (prosecutors later said it was Sandra) telephoned the *San Francisco Chronicle* and read a statement:

> The International People's Court of Retribution is a new justice movement for the balance of the earth. All state, federal and private money interests are now warned: Stop whaling. We consider all wildlife to be part of ourselves and will move viciously to defend our lives. Anyone caught killing wildlife, polluting or cutting down trees will be maimed, poisoned or chopped in a similar manner. A whaler without arms cannot swim.

Their next news release was titled "Manson is Mad at Nixson"—with the parallel spelling intended. It blamed former President Nixon for the conviction of the Tate-LaBianca defendants because of his comment during the trial that Manson was guilty. Along with various other indictments of society, the release pronounced: "If Nixon's reality wearing a Ford face continues to run this country against the law, your homes will be bloodier than the Tate-LaBianca homes and My Lai put together."

Although AP moved the story, the White House was not impressed. The next day, in an address from the Oval Office, Gerald Ford announced his candidacy to win the presidency in his own right.

While they had been pleasant with Morris Willmarth, Lyn and Sandra took a somewhat different tone when discussing their concerns with Lanier Ramer, an ex-convict friend of Charlie who visited the women that same July. The burly and bearded Ramer, now forty-three, had introduced Charlie to Scientology when both were imprisoned at McNeil Island. After his release, Ramer had gone to work for the National Prison Project of the American Civil Liberties Union, and remained in correspondence with Charlie.

Stopping by the Sacramento apartment, Ramer had a long, wide-ranging discussion with Lyn and Sandy. Despite her approval of some of Governor Jerry Brown's proposals, Lyn was distraught at the country's direction. She became emotional as she catalogued the environmental devastation going on. People should be deeply concerned about these problems, and she was committed to doing whatever was necessary to heighten their awareness. She stressed that she would be telephoning and writing letters to various corporate executives and government officials to alert them to her concerns.

But mere words, she realized, would not be enough to stop the strip miners, the forest cutters, and the water polluters. "She told me," Ramer later testified, "that she thought it was quite likely, probably, that some people were going to have to be killed, to set examples."

Could Ramer put her in touch with the Weather Underground, Lyn wanted to know. Could Ramer get her a couple of guns?

Ramer said no, on both accounts. His five convictions—four for unarmed bank robbery, one for auto theft—were all for property crimes, not crimes against persons. He told Lyn that he had strong feelings against physically harming people. Later, Ramer reported the conversation to his probation officer, and to the FBI.

If Lanier Ramer wouldn't provide her with a gun, Lyn knew someone else who would. Manny Boro had once shown her the antique pistol he kept. One July night over at his apartment, Lyn asked to see it again. She explained to him that her life was in danger, and she needed protection. Charlie had a lot of enemies, and now that it was known that she was living in Sacramento, one of those enemies might come to get her.

Manny went to his clothes closet, reached to the top shelf, and took down a box. He brought it to her and removed the contents. It was a Colt .45 semiautomatic pistol, made before World War I. Manny had owned it for five years, but never fired it, never even loaded it with a cartridge.

Now, he showed her how it worked.

"You press this on the back, that's the automatic grip. It won't fire if you press—pull the trigger, it won't fire, you got to pull them both together here."

Manny demonstrated how to drop the clip out, and how to release the safety. He showed her how to disassemble the weapon, and how to rack it, pulling a bullet into the breach. Lyn gazed admiringly at the large, sleek weapon.

But Manny had misgivings about giving the pistol to Lyn. He suggested that perhaps she didn't want this particular gun. It wasn't registered, he explained as he put it back in its holster, and into the box, and then back in the closet. He handed Lyn a gun catalogue, and proposed that she pick out another model. The .45 was a common gun, worth maybe $200. Manny pointed out a pistol in the catalogue. It was much rarer, he said, only 7,800 were made. Wouldn't she prefer something like that?

Lyn leafed through the catalogue and settled on a pistol she wanted. Manny, however, was noncommittal about when he might actually get her the gun. Lyn stood up, walked over to the closet, and removed the .45 he had just put away.

"What are you doing?" Manny asked, as Lyn stuffed the gun, the holster, and twenty-five cartridges into her handbag. She didn't answer, but headed straight for the door. Manny tried to stop her.

The .45 was too heavy, too big, too complicated, too dangerous for Lyn, he said.

Lyn hesitated.

"Get that one in the book," he said. "I'll buy that one for you."

"You will?" she asked.

"Yeah," Manny said.

Lyn thought about it for a few minutes. Then she left, the gun still in her handbag.

Later, Manny told his daughter-in-law, Nelda, that Lyn had taken his gun. "I tried to stop her," he said, "but she just took it and ran out."

"By God, Manny, get out of this situation," Nelda urged. "Why don't you call the authorities?"

Manny said he was afraid to. Scared to death.

But whatever misgivings Manny might have had about Lyn taking his pistol, he seemed more concerned with keeping her happy. When he saw Lyn later that week, he didn't ask for the .45 back. Instead, he brought her more bullets. As he told a neighbor, "My girlfriends keep me busy."

Lyn did not treat her new possession casually. Aware that it was the kind of evidence police would love to find on her, she wrapped the pistol in glassine packaging and buried it in the lawn outside her house, at least ten inches deep. It was also where she kept her stash of marijuana.

Lyn had been communicating with a Denver-based journalist named John Barry, who expressed sympathy with some of her environmental goals. He had suggested that she publish a Manson Family newsletter, as a regular forum for discussing her agenda.

Lyn sent Barry a "Mad at Nixson" news release, and encouraged him to compose an article based on it. "This is the thought we want to push," she told him. "See what you can do with it."

Barry, however, didn't think much could be done with the release, and felt that attacking private citizen Nixon was a bad strategy. His views were seconded by reporters at the *Denver Post* and at the local Associated Press office. The AP bureau chief told Barry he had no interest in running "end-of-the-world-type prophecies."

Though the American press showed little interest in Lyn's latest messages, a German magazine, the racy *Neue Revue*, decided to do a piece on the Manson nuns. The German correspondent, accompanied by a freelance photographer, went to the P Street apartment, where Lyn and Sandy greeted him dressed in red robes. They wore nothing but red these days, they explained, because red symbolized blood.

Sitting on their couch, Lyn displayed some of the photos she had clipped from newspapers and magazines.

"These are people we find very offensive," she said. She held a picture of Nixon, and one of Ford toasting a foreign dignitary. Ford was doing a terrible job, Lyn said, and "he will have to pay for what he's doing. Nixon's karma is getting back at him. Ford is picking up in Nixon's footsteps, and he is just as bad."

Then Lyn showed them a photo of the Pope. He, Lyn said, was responsible for the loose morals of the world.

Next, she pointed to a picture of Gina Lollobrigida, the glamorous Italian actress, wearing a fur coat. Wearing the fur of animals, Lyn explained, was a crime.

Lyn and Sandy complained to the correspondent about the world's fondness for material things, for "hair dryers and makeup." Sex, they declared, was dirty, and few things offended them more than lesbianism.

For the photo shoot, Lyn and Sandy had something special in mind. They put on their wine red cloaks, embroidered with swastikas. They then led their guests to the Sacramento City Cemetery, which had closed for the night. Lyn and Sandy hopped over the fence and wandered among the tombstones. *Neue Revue* published a photo of the hooded women pointing demonstratively at a grave.

This was a very different Lyn from the one who had sung show tunes with the Lariats, who had composed poetry for honors English class. Yet on August 4, she wrote to Jim Van Wagoner, her beloved teacher at Redondo Union High School. The letter came on pastel paper, decorated with whimsical flowers reminiscent of Art Nouveau: "This is Lyn Fromme, former student of yours and occasional pest," it began.

She wanted to know if he would help her in pitching her book to a publisher. She didn't know if she needed an agent; she just wanted someone she could trust. "I thought of you because you could appreciate its literary merit—even if you do not agree with its verbal paintings. I'm assuming that you know me, know where I've been, and know what my book is about—and most importantly that you are the right Mr. Van Wagoner."

Lyn sketched a happy face. The letter concluded: "If not, please return this letter. If so, please reply. I see you well and smiling. Did you quit smoking?"

Years later, Jim Van Wagoner couldn't recall if the letter came in 1974 or 1975. Nevertheless, he certainly did know who Lyn was, and where she had been. Although he still cared for his brilliant former pupil, he was fearful of becoming known to other Manson Family members. He never replied.

In August 1975, Heather Murphy moved into 1725 P Street's basement apartment, paying not only her own rent but that of Lyn and Sandy. Her new residence was not much to speak of, just a simple room with a dresser, a bed, a chair, and a small table. The closet was a cavity in the wall, covered by a curtain.

To Morris Willmarth, Heather seemed mentally troubled. She was slow and shy, parroting whatever Lyn or Sandy said, obeying their instructions without question. They used her, Willmarth thought, like their secretary.

It was Lyn, however, who typed a letter to Charles Rossie, an assignment editor at KNBC-TV in Los Angeles. Rossie had written to Manson requesting an interview, and Manson had forwarded the letter to Lyn for reply. She used the opportunity to comment on various issues bedeviling her, including television's dominance of American culture.

"It was not people the Manson Family was at war with, but a thought. The same thought that sells our children and our more innocent world sex, political ideology, death, theology and toothpaste in one hour," she wrote.

She added a hopeful note. "The media CAN be used to unwind the tangles of a world running circles toward what it fears most"—along those lines, she had recently told an Associated Press reporter that Manson had predicted an earthquake that rattled Northern California on August 1, as a reaction to mankind's abuse of the environment. But, she cautioned Rossie, if Manson was "NOT ALLOWED TO EXPLAIN, THERE WILL BE MANY MORE YOUNG MURDERERS . . ."

The letter made no reference to Rossie's chance of interviewing Manson. But in a postscript, Lyn offered another programming possibility. "Sandra and myself would like to sit next to Bugliosi on one of his talk shows, under the right circumstances. Why don't you give me your thoughts on the best spot for this. I felt that CBS would be the most fair in the editing room," she wrote, perhaps as a dare to the NBC editor.

Lyn mailed the letter from Berkeley on August 13, where she and Sandra had driven to launch another stage of their campaign. While the University of California dominated the eastern half of the city, West Berkeley was home to dozens of small and medium-sized industrial firms. On a Wednesday morning, Lyn piloted her red VW through the industrial district, pulling up at the Berkeley Ready Mix cement factory on Virginia Street.

In their red robes, the women marched into the factory and confronted the manager, Grant Chamberlain. It was time for Berkeley Ready Mix to stop polluting, they explained, or the cement makers would be killed by the International People's Court of Retribution. Chamberlain ordered Lyn and Sandy off the property, and called police.

Lyn and Sandy headed off on a circuit of other industrial firms, receiving a similar reception at each one. After a flurry of complaints, the Berkeley Police Department dispatched Officer J. W. Houpt to investigate. He spotted the red VW on Grayson Street, outside Cutter Laboratories. At the factory, he found Lyn and Sandy inside the restroom, where they had been hiding for ten minutes.

Under questioning, Lyn and Sandy truthfully identified themselves and presented their driver's licenses. They denied, however, that they actually were members of the International People's Court of Retribution; instead, they said they merely were delivering messages on its behalf.

Officer Houpt offered them a choice: They could risk having a complaint filed against them or they could depart Berkeley immediately.

"The suspects," Houpt later reported, "felt that this would probably be a good idea and agreed to leave the city."

While Lyn was not much of a media draw, Charlie remained a source of interest. He finally consented to an interview with KTVV-TV in Oakland, which the station hyped by playing over five consecutive nights in August. Manson's only condition was that a videotape of the interview be sent to Lyn at her Sacramento apartment.

Lyn was excited about Charlie's forthcoming appearance on TV. She told all her friends about it, and sent a floral greeting card to Clyde Blackmon urging him to tune in. Although no fan of Manson, the attorney believed he was making progress for his new client. Blackmon had begun communicating with the Corrections Department, and it seemed he might be able to reach an accommodation with officials so that Lyn could visit Charlie. He told Lyn to contact the Corrections Department to follow up.

Whatever progress Blackmon had been making, however, wasn't evident to Lyn. Her requests to see Manson continued to be denied.

By late August, Morris Willmarth had realized a few things about his upstairs neighbors. He had learned of their devotion to Charles Manson, and of the almost violent extremity of some of their views. More than that, he recognized that his chance of scoring a date with Sandra was quite small; the women insisted that as "nuns of the earth," they were celibate. The news surprised Willmarth, who knew of the Manson Family's reputation for open sexual relationships.

Still, Willmarth enjoyed the two women's company. He found them stimulating, and came to relish the regular arguments he would have with Lyn and Sandy over the propriety of violence, over the justification of the Tate murders and assorted other topics. He liked to get loaded, then head upstairs for an evening of criticism—including his own personal habits. Lyn and Sandy objected to Willmarth's drinking, and regularly encouraged him to grow a beard.

Moreover, Willmarth strongly agreed with the women's ecological agenda. While they might be extreme, he thought, they certainly were committed to getting something done. In the third week of August, he brought a friend into the group, someone who was similarly committed to the environment.

Michael Davies, a college classmate, was visiting Willmarth for dinner when Lyn returned from a trip to San Francisco. Willmarth and Davies helped her carry her things in, and then joined Lyn and Sandy for the evening at their apartment. Sandra explained to Davies about their ecology project, with Lyn occasionally adding details and refinements. They were working to build a better world, where instead of polluting the environment, people would have new jobs planting trees, restoring the ocean, and cleaning up oil slicks. Later, the group was joined by Heather Murphy, who said little before heading over to a small desk where she began to type addresses onto pink envelopes.

Willmarth and Davies returned to the downstairs apartment to check on the stew they were fixing. Willmarth mentioned that Lyn and Sandy were planning to contact the media to raise environmental awareness, and that he was helping by researching newspaper addresses.

"If that's the type of thing they're doing, I'd be willing to do something, too," Davies said. He wasn't too busy over his summer vacation, and shared a concern about the dangers of nuclear power and radioactive waste. The men headed back up the stairs to Lyn's apartment, and Davies volunteered to help the ecology project. He said he was well acquainted with radical activism, having taken part in student demonstrations in Berkeley.

Sandra gave Davies an assignment: Compile a list of every nuclear power plant in America, along with the names and home addresses of their presidents, vice presidents, and boards of directors. The home addresses were needed, she said, because they preferred to contact the executives—or even better, their wives—directly.

Letters sent to company offices usually get screened by a secretary, Sandy explained, and thrown out. "Letters to anyone but the parties themselves and their wives end up in the city dump," she said. "And our survival does not belong in the dump."

Sandy showed Davies a sample letter to a nuclear power executive. The letter stridently outlined the dangers of atomic energy, but seemed to steer clear of any explicit threats. Davies thought it appropriately forceful.

As the evening drew to a close, Davies asked how Lyn and Sandy's environmental views fit with those of Charles Manson. They assured him that Manson had always stood for a pure environment.

But, Davies wondered, would the women be able to discuss their views with people who disagreed?

"Like, if [Vice President] Nelson Rockefeller walked into this room, can you sit down and discuss your point of view with him, you know, just discuss it?" Davies asked.

Sandy, Davies later testified, jumped up lividly. "No," she said. "I'd kill him."

Although Davies found the women's violent streak discomfiting, it wasn't so extreme as to cool his interest in an attractive woman. Later, he invited Sandy to play tennis with him.

Morris Willmarth and Michael Davies regularly visited Lyn's apartment through the summer, where they learned about various ecological problems plaguing the world, and marveled at the women's dedication. Lyn and Sandy's action plan was well under way. They sent a poster to the Alaska Fish and Game Commission opposing the hunting of wolves, and another to the prime minister of Japan, objecting to whaling.

The discussions in the P Street apartment incorporated all manner of current events and philosophical queries. Sandy gave Davies some books by the Austrian psychoanalyst Wilhelm Reich, including one she found especially influential, *The Murder of Christ.*

The women were particularly clear on all the things they disliked. Hollywood, Lyn and Sandy explained, "projected madness in the minds of the world with television and movies . . . Los Angeles sold herself and sold the world as a harlot."

Another problem was spiritual: the country was being invaded by false prophets, like the teenage Maharaj Ji and the self-proclaimed messiah from Korea, the Reverend Sun Myung Moon. The women were outraged that the gurus "were taking advantage of the fact that in this country people don't believe in their Lord anymore, and so they're looking to the east." Lyn showed the men a letter they had written, on Manson's behalf, to the leaders of various Eastern cults they felt were leading Americans astray.

They also criticized feminists, who they said mistakenly were "primarily concerned with bettering themselves economically, and characterizing men as male chauvinist pigs." Women's lib, Sandy insisted, "negated" women's and men's sexuality. She brandished a copy of *Cosmopolitan*, and went into a tirade about the women "who sell their bodies to sell some cosmetics." Then she pulled out a letter the women had written to *Ms.* magazine: "Any woman who cares more about her image, position, paycheck or what she looks like than the earth will be treated like the earth has been treated," the letter said. The editors declined to print the letter.

For his part, Davies mentioned the problems he saw in his Sacramento neighborhood. Developers were destroying the area, filling it with warehouses and apartment complexes. Perhaps developers should also receive a warning letter, Davies suggested.

Lyn and Sandra agreed. But letters weren't enough; "things in the country right now are conducive to a lot of chaotic violence," Sandra observed. "Purposeless violence, in other words, young kids lashing out and committing crimes and they don't even know why." Since the violence was coming, wouldn't it be a good idea to direct it toward beneficial results?

Morris Willmarth mentioned a prank he and his chemistry classmates had pulled. They would mix a mild contact explosive, nitrogen trioxide, place it on the sidewalks outside the chemistry building, and wait for it to dry out. When passers-by stepped on the explosive, it would make loud snaps; people would jump around in fright, unable to see the source of the noise, every step causing another loud *pop.*

Lyn asked Willmarth to fix a batch of nitrogen trioxide for the ecology campaign. If they managed to put some on the doorjambs of corporate offices, they could give those executives a well-deserved shock. Sandy voted for making it a big explosion, but Lyn insisted they weren't aiming to harm anyone—just to scare them.

Willmarth was noncommittal. He said the chemical was unstable after it dried, and he wasn't sure how much it would take to blow off a door, much less how to get it inside a corporate headquarters in the first place. Besides, why would such a trivial act be necessary if all that Lyn and Sandy said about the International People's Court of Retribution was true?

While Willmarth, Davies, and Heather Murphy compiled addresses, Sandy undertook the rest of the International People's Court's business. Because sending thousands of letters would cost a fair amount in postage, Sandy economized by obtaining several boxes of franked envelopes. One set bore the return address of the Church Divinity School of the Pacific, an Episcopal seminary in Berkeley that had ordered the envelopes for a fund-raising campaign. Sandra told Davies that she had taken them from a warehouse. Another stack of postage-paid envelopes came from the California Highway Patrol. Sandy said she found them in a garbage can.

On August 26, Sandy went to the Sierra Copy stationery store and ordered several rubber stamps. One design read: "International People's Court of Retribution," while another featured a "reverse" swastika, a mirror image of the one used by the Nazi Party. Sandy would later claim that the reverse swastika—which she also had embroidered on her robe—stood for the opposite of Nazi beliefs.

Lyn and Sandy soon gave Mike Davies another assignment. The state Department of Fish and Game had authorized an antelope hunt. The women obtained the list of those approved for the hunt, and Davies's job was to persuade the participants not to go. The best way to do that, they decided, was to make the hunters understand that their targets were living, breathing creatures. So Davies was to call the hunters, pretend he was a woodland animal, and make it clear he didn't want them coming into his forest shooting things up.

The day after he was given the list, Davies reported back. "I made a call, and said, like, 'I'm Rocky Raccoon and don't come into my forests.' "

Lyn didn't respond. Sandy kind of laughed.

"No, that's not what you're supposed to do," she said. Lyn looked on as Sandy explained that Davies was to act more *mean* when he called the hunters. Cuddly animals were out; the tone was supposed to be, Davies later testified, "somewhat vicious."

Davies had never made any of the calls. He just didn't have it in him.

Lyn left Sacramento shortly after the Rocky Raccoon incident, on a series of missions around the state. They had not gone well.

Some reports placed her in Hollywood, trying to warn the guitarist Jimmy

Page of an evil portent. She went to the Continental Hyatt House, where, since 1969, the raucous English rock group Led Zeppelin had regularly stayed when visiting Los Angeles—after the Tate-LaBianca murders, the group felt more secure at the modern high-rise than in the secluded bungalows of their original base, the Château Marmont. But peeved desk clerks, experienced in misdirecting celebrity groupies, passed her on to the band's publicist, Danny Goldberg.

Something terrible would befall Page, perhaps even at his next concert, she told Goldberg. She assured him that the last time she had a similar vision, someone had been shot dead before her eyes.

Led Zeppelin, the group that helped create the heavy metal sound, were known for entertaining female callers in their rooms. But Lyn—a frantic, pale creature in beads and a wrinkled dress, at age twenty-six already old for a groupie—did not fit the bill.

Goldberg said that Page was unavailable. He offered to deliver a note to the guitarist on her behalf.

Lyn was frustrated, but didn't want to push the scene any further. She wrote the note—the story went—gave it to Goldberg, and finally left. That night, at Led Zeppelin's Long Beach Arena concert, Page was struck on the head with a roll of toilet paper, but avoided the firecrackers tossed at the stage.

Lyn did not know Page personally, although her old friend Bobby Beausoleil had years before been cast in the title role of a film Page was scoring, *Lucifer Rising*. For various reasons, the underground film, produced by Kenneth Anger, was never completed. Page finished only thirty minutes of music, and Beausoleil, of course, was serving a life sentence for the murder of Gary Hinman.

Lyn had met famous rock stars in her life, but by 1975, it had been years since she traveled in those circles, and perhaps it was not surprising to be blown off by some flack. More disturbing was the cold shoulder she had received from Paul Fitzgerald.

Near the end of August 1975, Lyn, with Sandy and Capistrano in tow, went to visit Fitzgerald in his Beverly Hills office. Dressed in their hand-sewn robes, the women told him about the Order of the Rainbow and its unique liturgy. Lyn's main business, however, was practical, not spiritual. Katie, Sadie, and Lulu, at the Frontera prison, were still refusing her letters, returning them through the mail unopened. Lyn wanted Fitzgerald to intercede.

She repeated to him her troubles in getting in to see Manson, and her difficulty in keeping track of the various Family members and associates. The Family, Lyn seemed to be saying, if not quite admitting to herself, was falling apart.

For years now, Fitzgerald's office had been a principal contact point for the many underground and incarcerated Family members scattered across California. But Fitzgerald, who had worked so hard on the case five years before, proved strangely unhelpful.

"Squeaky, the girls who are in prison want to get paroled," he told her, as if explaining a heretical, even unfathomable idea. And, to Lyn, it was. Previously, the girls, especially Katie, had been haranguing Lyn, needling her for her failure to live up to their example. If Lyn was so committed to the cause, why was she out enjoying the housewife's life while Katie and the others were ready to go all the way to the gas chamber?

Fitzgerald insisted that the women's attitude had changed. "To them, Charlie is poison," he told a disbelieving Lyn. "If they correspond with you, they'll never get out."

Indeed, Sadie Mae Glutz, who now used her given name of Susan Denise Atkins, had proclaimed herself a born-again Christian, and ascribed her time with Charlie to Satanic possession. Katie and Lulu—Patricia Krenwinkel and Leslie Van Houten—had not announced such dramatic religious conversions, but both had professed to apologize for the murders. Just a few years in the joint, with so many ahead, and the girls were repudiating the Family.

Or so Fitzgerald said. Why would they want to return to the corrupt, foul world outside, while Charlie sat within a cage? Of course, Lyn believed, all of them should be out, not one had received a fair trial, none had been recognized for the sacrifice she had made, a sacrifice for the world. Certainly, Lyn would have been willing to make the same sacrifice if she had been called upon to do so.

That she hadn't been called, though, continued to trouble her—not least because she had felt some relief at not having to plunge a knife into a pregnant lady's belly. But her role, perhaps, was outside. She had helped Charlie keep things organized through the early days of the Family, and when it started coming down and Charlie got put in jail, it fell to her to hold it all together and to move everything forward. Compared to the murders, this was easy stuff. It *should* be easy stuff, but things weren't happening. Had she let them all down? Could the girls inside be doubting *her?*

So, there was more work to be done—something, Lyn told Fitzgerald, "drastic." On Wednesday, September 3, she mailed letters to the state assembly's Criminal Justice Committee. The letters were intended as a critique of the justice system.

"In all your schooling, you are blind to the real needs of the country that if not met soon, will unseat you not only from your jobs but from your lives," read part of the three-page epistle.

"... I've told you people over and over—I can release thoughts that will destroy you ... you lawyers, drunk with the blood of dummies like me, are in trouble. You best be thinking on how to save your lives because the other justice is gonna catch up with you ... with points and authorities like you've never imagined."

Lyn typed the name "C. Manson" at the end, along with his prison address, Tamal, California 94964, the site of San Quentin. The return address on the envelopes, though, was Lyn's Sacramento post office box, rented under the pseudonym "Kay Boro." If the committee members refused the letters, she'd know.

Then Lyn returned to the Bay Area, and made yet another unsuccessful application to see Charlie, who had been moved back to San Quentin in the interim. Though she was unsuccessful in gaining access to Charlie under her own name, it would later be reported that "Kay Boro" was on the prison's visitors list. Authorities denied the report, and said that Manson's only visitor had been his attorney, Irving Kanarek.

Meanwhile, Lyn had to put food on the table, and according to one story, she did so by shoplifting. Caught by a grocery manager, Lyn "turned on that flirtatious charm she's noted for," the *San Francisco Chronicle* reported. The manager not only released Lyn before the police arrived, he let her keep the cans of food she had been trying to steal.

That was just getting by. Lyn told a neighbor that she was planning something big, "bigger than the Tate killing and it [would] happen in the next few weeks." She would begin by stopping the antelope hunt, with or without Mike Davies's help. Some of the men authorized to go on the hunt received telephone calls warning them not to participate. Police never established precisely who took part in the telephone project, but Davies later testified that Sandy said she had made some of the calls. Sandy, for her part, told a court that Lyn had gone to Berkeley and stayed up all night with friends—Sandy did not name them—telephoning the hunters.

"Iss zis Allen Salsman?" began one phone call, placed at 2:25 A.M. to Suisun City, in Northern California. The female caller, trying to manage a German accent, spoke intensely.

"No, it isn't—" She cut him off.

"Iss zis—zis is Fred?"

"Yes, it is—"

"Vell, you tell Allen zat he should not go on ze antelope hunt. Accidents happen. And ve are ready to kill. You tell him." The caller hung up.

Fred called Allen. The two discussed the call for about fifteen minutes, and then notified the police. Fred couldn't sleep the rest of the night.

The German-accented voice also awoke Charles Huff, when his phone rang after midnight in his San Mateo home, south of San Francisco. Huff, a supervisor for Caltrans, the state highway department, had been asleep for hours.

"Mr. Huff, you have been chosen for an antelope hunt. If you go, you von't come back. Your brains vill be *schplattered.* Do you understand?" said the caller.

Mr. Huff wasn't yet quite awake.

"Oh, you don't like antelope hunting?" he asked politely. But the caller hung up.

———

In August 1975, California Resources Secretary Claire Dedrick warned that sustained logging in Redwood National Park, some 330 miles north of San Francisco, was threatening a grove of the world's tallest trees. The clear-cutting had caused extensive erosion and silting of Redwood Creek, meaning the trees could be washed out unless the creekbed was strengthened.

Lyn visited a Sacramento TV station to emphasize the story's importance. The news director wasn't available, and neither were any of the reporters or editors. Passed around from employee to employee, she finally got the attention of a cutter, a technician who spliced together film for news segments. He listened impatiently to Lyn's story.

"Not interested," he said, in the curt fashion of news professionals, adding, by way of explanation: "The President's coming to town." That was how Lyn learned of Ford's visit.

Soon Sacramento was agog over the president's impending arrival, with excitement reaching a peak on Thursday, September 4. In the Top Market grocery, at 18th and O streets, Lyn overhead a clerk, Ed Louie, talking about the visit with a neighborhood kid, Tommy Schnoor.

The grocer asked Tommy if he was going to see the president the next morning. Lyn couldn't stand it.

"I hate Ford," she said.

She didn't really hate Gerald Ford, the son of an Omaha wool trader who entered the world in 1913 as Leslie Lynch King, Jr., was renamed after his stepfather when his parents divorced, and rose to prominence through athletic scholarships, a friendly way with people, and lots of luck. What Lyn really hated was what Ford represented. He was a "dead-head," who permitted the destruction of the environment, who presided over a society that seemed oblivious to its mistreatment of the earth.

Ford the man was so much of a nonentity to Lyn that he rarely figured in her mind. She thought of him, when she thought of him at all, as a robot. That all of Sacramento could be so excited about this zero coming to town was offensive to her, even outrageous. Even children, who usually could spot a phony, were now being taken in. She talked to Tommy Schnoor for a while, on topics of more importance than President Ford, like the Northern California motorcycle gang called the Misfits. Lyn, of course, had known many bikers; in high school, she caroused with a crew from the Sunset Strip and later, had done business with the Straight Satans up at Spahn Ranch. Bikers were, in the main, straight-ahead guys. Tommy was impressed.

Lyn made another useless attempt to see Charlie at San Quentin. She returned to Sacramento on a Thursday night, dead tired and despondent. If she had called Clyde Blackmon, the attorney would have told her that he was close to concluding an arrangement for limited visiting privileges with Manson. But Lyn believed there was no hope of getting to see Charlie through normal channels. The only way to move officialdom, it seemed, was through a subpoena. Nursing a cold, she trudged up the stairs to her P Street garret, bringing along the bag she had carried on her recent statewide trip. Sandra was home to greet her, but Lyn was not in a gregarious mood.

A few moments later, while she was unpacking, Michael Davies came by for one of his usual evening visits. He lounged about casually, as if nothing in particular was wrong. Lyn, weary and frustrated with the whole course of recent events, could take it no more. When he got up to use Lyn's telephone, she exploded at him.

"She said something to the effect that my life wasn't worth shit," Davies later testified. He started to defend himself, but Lyn snapped, "Don't talk. We don't have time for your talk."

Lyn left the room, and Sandra took over the critique. She called Davies a "phony" for his claims of being a student radical in Berkeley, for bragging about his experiences burning down buildings and taking part in riots. The argument heated up, with Sandra berating Davies as a "windbag" for always wanting to talk their projects out, wanting to talk them to death.

In Sandra's account, Lyn rejoined the fray. "Don't talk!" she commanded, as Davies tried to explain his position. "We don't have time to listen to your talk." Sandra chimed in: "There's bullshit coming from your mouth."

Davies remembered the phrase differently. He testified that Sandra's words were: "There's blood running from your mouth." Still, the encounter didn't wholly alienate Davies from the women, because Sandra made sure to soften the castigation before he left. She said, Davies testified, "that, you know, basically, I was a nice guy."

Around 10 P.M., Morris Willmarth came by for another talk about environmental projects. Lyn had a nonecological question for him: did he know where she could get a gun? What about that pistol he owned, the .38? How big was it? Lyn said she was concerned about safety in the "isolated" apartment she shared with Sandy.

The gun, Willmarth said, was a five-shooter with a three-inch barrel. But it didn't matter, anyway; he already had sold it.

They turned on the television. Channel 3 was running the pilot of *Medical Story*, starring Jose Ferrer as a crusty senior surgeon and Beau Bridges as the young upstart doctor who challenges him. At 10:45 P.M., however, Channel 3 broke into the program with live coverage of Air Force One's arrival at McClellan Air Force Base, in north Sacramento.

Hundreds of viewers, frustrated that *Medical Story* was interrupted just before the final act, called the station to complain. Lyn, however, watched spellbound as a grinning President Ford emerged from the aircraft and was welcomed with full military honors and the cheers of several hundred Air Force personnel gathered on the tarmac.

Disgusted, Lyn turned to Sandy. Ford was a "dummy, an empty head," she said. The crowds at McClellan were behaving "like sheep. These people are like sheep looking up to this dead-head," she said. "A dead shell with dead thoughts."

They looked at each other and asked, "How long can this go on?" Neither verbalized an answer. But after going over their literature on pollution, on the death of trees, they wept. Then Lyn, feeling ill, fell asleep on the couch.

William Millar Fromme: Lynette's father as he appeared in the 1942 NYU yearbook, shortly before he enlisted in the Army Air Forces. Lynette's childhood friends thought he was "scary." (CREDIT: NEW YORK UNIVERSITY ARCHIVES)

The Eighty-second Street House, Westchester, California: After the war, the bean fields and pig farms near the Los Angeles airport quickly gave way to tract homes and culs-de-sac. Lynette spent her early childhood in this house.
(CREDIT: BEN BRAVIN)

The base of the lamppost (pictured above) where Lynette immortalized her name in wet cement in 1960. (CREDIT: BEN BRAVIN)

The Three Blind Mice: Lynette soon became a star performer in a youth dance troupe, the Westchester Lariats. With two close friends, she formed a tri-color trio of little girls who stole the shows with dances like "The Three Blind Mice." *Front row, left to right:* Brunette Nora Lynn Stevens, redheaded Lynette, blonde Larrine. (CREDIT: COURTESY DR. J. TILLMAN HALL)

On Tour: Lynette, far right, poses at the Seattle World's Fair. Nora Lynn Stevens is second from the left. (CREDIT: COURTESY NORA KANOY)

Garbage Run: The Family's women fed the crew by salvaging vegetables from super-market garbage bins. "It's like being in a giant salad," Lynette wrote. *From left:* Lyn, Sandra Good, Mary Brunner, Ruth "Ouisch" Morehouse. (CREDIT: HERALD EXAMINER COLLECTION/LOS ANGELES PUBLIC LIBRARY)

Spahn Ranch: Lyn is at far right with stick. (CREDIT: HERALD EXAMINER COLLECTION/LOS ANGELES PUBLIC LIBRARY)

Spahn Ranch: The fake historical shacks of the ranch were an apt background for Lyn's magical mystery tour. She wrote that she turned into many things at the ranch, including pirates, Greek goddesses, servants, princesses, queens, beggars, court jesters, witches, elves, space creatures, Mad Hatters, minstrels, gypsies, harem girls, angels, and devils. Lyn is in the foreground; to her right is Catherine "Gypsy" Share, and to her left are Ruth "Ouisch" Morehouse and Sandra Good (in straw hat). Cathy "Capistrano" Gillies is behind and to the left of Lyn. (CREDIT: *HERALD EXAMINER* COLLECTION/LOS ANGELES PUBLIC LIBRARY)

Charles Manson, December 1969: The buckskin-clad Manson shortly after his arrest in Death Valley. (CREDIT: UPI/CORBIS-BETTMANN)

Courtroom Appearance, Independence, California: Even before the Tate-LaBianca murders, the Manson Family had brushes with the law. In the Inyo County Courthouse, Lyn attends a hearing on an auto theft charge against Charles Manson. Sandra Good is at right, holding her son, Ivan. (CREDIT: ARCHIVE PHOTOS)

The Girls on the Corner: Barred from the courtroom, Lyn led her Manson Family "sisters" in a vigil outside the Los Angeles Hall of Justice. They regularly tidied up the corner of Broadway and Temple Street, and moved their van from 7 A.M. to 9 A.M. to avoid getting a parking ticket. *From left:* Catherine "Gypsy" Share, Ruth "Ouisch" Morehouse, Lyn. (CREDIT: AP/WIDE WORLD PHOTOS)

The Honolulu Hamburger Caper: Lyn and Ruth "Ouisch" Morehouse were among those charged in December 1970 with conspiracy to murder Tate prosecution witness Barbara Hoyt. With Lyn's encouragement, Ouisch took Hoyt to Hawaii, where she fed her a hamburger spiked with a heavy dose of LSD. Hoyt survived; in a plea bargain, the charges against Lyn and the others were reduced to a misdemeanor of interfering with a witness. Here, Lyn and the pregnant Ouisch, with X's etched into their foreheads, are returned to jail after a court hearing. (CREDIT: UPI/CORBIS-BETTMANN)

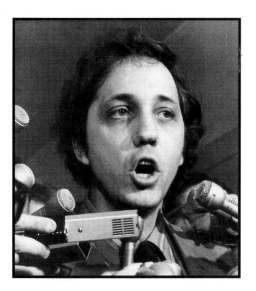

Paul Fitzgerald: The lead attorney for the Tate-LaBianca defendants became a close friend of Lyn. Having dropped acid himself, he was intrigued by a case so heavily shaped by the use of LSD. "This will be remembered as the first of the acid murders," he said, at the time of the trial. "We're on the brink of a whole new concept of violence...perpetrated against society by people who have reached a different plateau of reality through LSD." (CREDIT: REUTERS/CORBIS-BETTMANN)

Death Valley: Lyn foresaw an apocalypse consuming American society, one she planned to wait out with the Manson Family in Death Valley. Here, Lyn (*right*) and friends take a dune buggy trip through their desert home. (CREDIT: STEPHEN G. BEKINS)

RIGHT AND BELOW Red and Blue: From the ribald days of the Spahn Ranch to the ascetic lifestyle they adopted in Sacramento, Lynette ("Red" in Manson's color scheme) and Sandra Good ("Blue") were nearly inseparable. "She walks softly and carries a machine gun," Lyn said admiringly of her friend.
(CREDIT: RIGHT, STEPHEN G. BEKINS; BELOW, UPI/CORBIS-BETTMANN)

Spreading the News: As the years rolled on in Sacramento, Lyn began leading an ascetic life and growing more bitter toward society. When Manson wrote to her about a new religion he had decided to establish, Lyn quickly began to promote its teachings. Wearing hand-sewn robes, she visited college campuses, government offices, and newsrooms. "We're nuns now," she told reporters. "Our red robes are an example of the new morality.... They're red with the sacrifice, the blood of the sacrifice." Here, she delivers a news release to the offices of the *Sacramento Bee*. (CREDIT: *SACRAMENTO BEE*)

The House on P Street: When Manson was moved to Folsom Prison, Lyn relocated to nearby Sacramento, renting the top floor of this house at 1725 P Street. Lyn made a good impression on her neighbors, helping to establish a community garden and having picnics with the elderly lady who lived next door. The landlord testified that Lyn was a "model tenant." U.S. Attorney Dwayne Keyes, on the other hand, noted that ex-convicts frequented the apartment. He called it "a little halfway house for murderers." (CREDIT: JESS BRAVIN)

Sugar Daddy: Lyn met sixty-four-year-old Harold "Manny" Boro in a Sacramento park. Boro soon told his daughter-in-law that he and Lyn were lovers, and showed her nude pictures to prove it. He lent Lyn his Cadillac, bought her a Volkswagen—and gave her a Colt .45 automatic pistol. (Credit: UPI/Corbis-Bettmann)

"Well, are you going to use it?": Lyn strapped this Colt .45 automatic to her leg the morning of September 5, 1975. She maintained that she left her house uncertain what she would do with the weapon, an antique made before World War I. (Credit: U.S. Secret Service)

SACRAMENTO POLICE DEPT
CASE 75-36153
PR # 17090
ITEM(S) 1
TECHN ℳ + ℎ𝓍
DATE 9-5-75

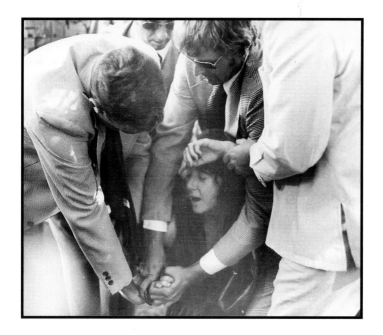

"Easy boys, I'm still!": After pointing a pistol at President Gerald R. Ford in Sacramento's Capitol Park, Lyn is handcuffed by Secret Service agents. Larry Buendorf, the agent who first saw the gun and subdued Lyn, wears sunglasses and stands over the suspect. A few weeks before the pistol incident, Buendorf had confessed to his brother that he did not know if he could really take a bullet to save the president's life. But when the moment came, he proved his courage. (CREDIT: AP/WIDE WORLD PHOTOS)

"It didn't go off!": While agents held her against a magnolia tree, Lyn shouted to the thunderstruck bystanders. Some later told investigators that Lyn made statements like "The damn thing didn't go off," "He is not a public servant," and "Why are you protecting him?" But one witness told a Sacramento police officer that Lyn said "It wasn't loaded anyway." When prosecutors withheld this information from the defense, they risked a mistrial. (CREDIT: DICK SCHMIDT, SACRAMENTO BEE)

After the pistol incident, federal agents entered Lyn's attic apartment at 1725 P Street to seek, in the language of the search warrant, "maps, bullets, weapons, plans, and other instrumentality of attempted murder of the President of the United States." They took this photo during their search.

(CREDIT: U.S. SECRET SERVICE)

Los Angeles Times,
September 5, 1975.

"Mrs. X": Lyn wouldn't give her true name when arrested, but was willing to tell detectives her views on the environment, abortion, and the bad influence of television on children. In an interrogation room shortly after her arrest, Lyn displays her leg holster.

(CREDIT: SACRAMENTO POLICE DEPARTMENT VIA *SACRAMENTO BEE*)

EXTRA

CLOSING N.Y. STOCKS | **Los Angeles Times** | FRIDAY LATE FINAL

MANSON GIRL TRIES TO SHOOT PRESIDENT

Pulls Gun in Crowd at Sacramento

Ungagged: After Judge MacBride lifted a gag order, Lyn immediately called a press conference at the Sacramento County Jail. Separated from reporters by plexiglass, Lyn cradles two phone handsets so she can talk to two people at once. Barred from discussing her case, she instead opined about world events. "How can Kissinger go to the Mideast one week to negotiate peace and the next week go right back there and sell arms?" she asked. "To my simple, childlike mind, I just say No." (CREDIT: SACRAMENTO BEE)

Chief District Judge Thomas J. MacBride: Appointed to the bench by President John F. Kennedy, MacBride had served on the wartime staff of General Douglas MacArthur and practiced law under Earl Warren. In presiding over Lyn's trial, he developed a particular rapport with the defendant. He "treats her like a child who has misbehaved," the *New York Times* reported. "And she treats him like a father who doesn't understand her." (CREDIT: UPI/CORBIS-BETTMANN)

The Lawyers: *From left:* U.S. Attorney Dwayne Keyes, Assistant U.S. Attorney Donald H. Heller, and Federal Public Defender E. Richard Walker leave Judge MacBride's chambers. Lyn did not much care for any of them. She fired Walker, accused Heller of mocking her, and threw an apple at Keyes.
(CREDIT: AP/WIDE WORLD PHOTOS)

"The Most Percipient Witness": Lyn made history by subpoenaing the President of the United States as defense witness. Rather than inconvenience President Ford, Judge MacBride moved his courtroom to Washington, D.C. Ford's testimony was videotaped and later played during the trial. *From left:* MacBride; court reporter Richard Fong; Ford; defense attorney John Virga; U.S. Attorney Dwayne Keyes; Assistant U.S. Attorney Don Heller and Lyn remained in Sacramento. (CREDIT: COURTESY GERALD R. FORD LIBRARY)

"You're gettin' fat, Lynette": When Lyn refused to attend her trial in November, Judge MacBride ordered deputies to carry her to court. Deputy U.S. Marshal Mike Nelson would joke with his prisoner about her weight as he lifted her up. Twenty years later, Nelson, then the chief deputy marshal in Sacramento, believed that Lyn did not intend to kill President Ford. In the background of the top photo U.S. Marshal Arthur Van Court (in shirtsleeves) holds an automatic rifle. (CREDIT, BOTH PHOTOS: AP/WIDE WORLD PHOTOS)

Lynette Fromme, 1988: After hearing a rumor that Charles Manson was dying of cancer, Lyn escaped from the federal women's prison in Alderson, West Virginia, on December 23, 1987. She hoped to find her way to California for a final reunion with "my husband, my brother, my father, my son, the man who's been my friend." But she never made it out of the rugged and soggy highlands near the prison, and was captured on Christmas Day. Here she is escorted by federal marshals to a court hearing in Bluefield, West Virginia.

(CREDIT: AP/WIDE WORLD PHOTOS)

Part Three

Blue

Chapter 8

Ruffles

and

Flourishes

Assassination was in the news. George Wallace, breaking his silence on the shooting that left him paralyzed, said he was convinced that Arthur Bremer had not acted alone but was part of a conspiracy. Civil rights leaders Ralph Abernathy, Dick Gregory, and Jesse Jackson wrote to the White House asking for a new examination of the assassination of Martin Luther King, Jr. In Los Angeles, demands were made to reopen the investigation of Robert Kennedy's murder at the Ambassador Hotel. News reports documented CIA involvement in assassination attempts against Cuba's Fidel Castro and President Salvador Allende of Chile.

As had been the case for years, questions constantly were arising about the findings of the Warren Commission. In Gaithersburg, Maryland, a former CIA official called a press conference to announce that a new lie-detector analysis of Lee Harvey Oswald's voice proved that Oswald was innocent. In Dallas, meanwhile, it was revealed that Oswald had written a letter to the FBI warning agents to stop questioning his wife, the Soviet-born Marina, prior to John Kennedy's visit.

President Ford had both an official and a business interest in the continuing obsession with the Kennedy assassination. Letters challenging the Warren Commission report regularly arrived at the White House, and were politely referred to the Department of Justice for review. Moreover, Ford, who as a congressman had served on the Warren Commission, also had co-written one of the first books about Oswald, *Portrait of the Assassin*, published in 1965. The book, now out of print, never sold enough copies to make back the initial $10,000 advance to the authors. When Ford emerged from obscurity to become the nation's leader, however, publishing interests saw new potential in the property.

The editor who had worked on the book, Peter Schwed of Simon & Schuster, wrote to Ford within days of Nixon's resignation. Schwed enthused over Ford, saying "how thrilled and delighted all of us were" over his accession to the presidency, and recalling the great "privilege" and "honor" of working on *Portrait of the Assassin*. While stressing how "very reluctant" he was to bother the president "at this moment, when you have so many such greater topics on your mind," Schwed inquired about Ford's intentions for the work. And, he added eagerly, "when the perhaps far-off day comes when you will be writing another book about the great events that now fill your life . . . [please] remember us as your past and hopefully future publishers."

Presidential aides believed that reissuing the book would draw unneeded attention to Ford's role on the Warren Commission, and would raise ethical questions about the disposition of royalties. White House counsel Phil Buchen concluded that "it would be inappropriate to have any reprint made" of the book, but thanked Schwed for allowing the rights to revert to the president.

Obsequiousness having failed, Simon & Schuster resorted to hardball. Writing to Ford's literary agent, Owen Laster of the William Morris Agency, Schwed dismissed Buchen's letter as "pleasant enough," but warned that stopping Simon & Schuster from profiting from its rights assuredly was not "as simple as you and Mr. Philip W. Buchen seem to feel it is." The publishing rights "are worth something right now . . . [and] they will continue to be worth something, and possibly considerably more, at some later date. . . . The book is our property," Schwed wrote. He was willing, however, to delay publication until after Ford left office.

Laster reported that the publisher had trumped the president. "I'm very sorry to say that Simon & Schuster has the rights to *Portrait of the Assassin* and will not revert them to the authors," he wrote. Although Simon & Schuster never did reissue the book, Ford managed to repay the firm when he published his memoirs in 1979; *A Time to Heal* bore the imprint of Harper & Row.

In Hollywood, meanwhile, producers had suddenly concluded that of all the works published about the death of President Kennedy, "none is more moving or complete than your book." Indeed, as producer Sheldon Davis of Now Productions wrote Ford, *Portrait of the Assassin* "stands out as the most significant work on the subject." The book would not just make a movie-of-the-week, but could well be "the most significant television event of 1975," Davis assured the president. Not only that, Davis later told a reporter, in Europe, "where the Kennedy legend lingers, people will pay hard money to see it" in movie theaters.

Although Ford had little interest in stirring any of the controversies surrounding the Kennedy assassination, his co-author and longtime friend, John R. Stiles, was eager to exploit the book's renewed potential. A hard-charging former journalist with a stormy personal life, Jack Stiles had remained close to Ford since their fraternity days at the University of Michigan, working on campaigns and holding a White House job where he oversaw construction of the presidential swimming pool.

Stiles pressed Ford for permission to go ahead with the project and eventually won his consent—as long as the movie would not air before the 1976 election. Stiles would earn a generous per diem as consultant to the producers, who were based at MGM and close to signing a deal with CBS-TV. As co-author, the president was entitled to approval of the teleplay and the first rough cut, as well as a 12.5 percent share of the proceeds.

Ford decided to donate his portion to charity. As it happened, however, the film was never made. The project was shelved after a series of misfortunes, including Stiles's death in a Grand Rapids, Michigan, car accident.

Despite his many passing acquaintances with assassination, however, the topic was far from President Ford's mind when he rose at 6:47 A.M. on September 4, 1975. Like most Americans, Ford had never envisioned himself becoming president, or being exposed to the hazards such an office would bring. Instead, Ford's great ambition had been to become Speaker of the House of Representatives, a dream frustrated by the seemingly unbreakable hold the Democrats had on Congress. Ford was perhaps the only politician in American history who accepted the presidency as his second choice.

Anticipating a long day, Ford ate a quick breakfast, then conferred with Secretary of State Henry Kissinger and discussed energy policy with a delegation of congressional leaders. His official business thus dispatched, Ford began his real work at 9:46 A.M., when he left the White House for a Pacific Coast campaign swing.

At Andrews Air Force Base, the president was joined by three westbound Republican politicians: Senator Ted Stevens of Alaska and, from Oregon, Congressman Joel Pritchard and Senator Bob Packwood. Even senators valued rides on *Air Force One.*

The very name of the presidential aircraft, however, was one of many ambiguities in the unelected president's White House. Richard Nixon had optimistically rechristened the jet the *Spirit of '76,* in expectation of leading the nation's bicentennial celebrations at the end of his second term. When Ford prematurely succeeded Nixon in 1974, the new president ordered the name changed back to the familiar *Air Force One.* Ford's instruction, however, was widely disregarded, and White House documents—including the official "Daily Diary of President Gerald R. Ford"—continued to call the plane *Spirit of '76.*

Whatever confusion surrounded the aircraft's name, Ford's West Coast tour promised to be relatively simple. Provincial cities like Seattle, Portland, and Sacramento often were so overjoyed by the prospect of a presidential visit that Ford would be guaranteed lengthy television coverage by uncritical local reporters, massive space in the regional newspapers, and festive welcomes by awestruck officials.

From the outset, however, this trip had problems. The trouble had begun before departure from Washington, when Packwood, the Beaver State's junior senator, complained about being shortchanged on media exposure during the rare presidential visit to Oregon. A White House memorandum reported that Packwood, communicating through his "extremely aggressive press secretary," felt he was being excluded from the prime photo opportunity, the Portland Youth Bicentennial Rally. Noting "some friction or professional jealousy" between Packwood and Oregon's senior senator, fellow Republican Mark Hatfield, the president was cautioned to "be exceedingly careful not to stroke one to the disadvantage of the other."

Ford had to be equally delicate in his communications to the public. The message he sought to deliver was perhaps the least controversial imaginable, one of the country pulling together as it headed into the bicentennial year. But with FBI agents storming Native American protesters holed up at the Oglala Sioux reservation near Pine Ridge, South Dakota, the nation's colonial origins were being questioned nightly on the evening news. The quashing of the disturbance had led thousands to decry federal treatment of American Indians, and everywhere Ford went, demonstrators followed to voice their disapproval.

Arriving at the Seattle Center for a fund-raising luncheon, Ford was met by hundreds of protesters. A contingent of American Indians hammered on the convention center's doors with replica tomahawks, easily stealing media attention from the president's vague message in favor of smaller government.

Inside the exhibition hall, the crowd of eighteen hundred Republican small contributors was friendlier, and party leaders tried to make the most of it. "DY-NO-MITE!" exclaimed an upbeat Washington Governor Dan Evans, standing beside Ford and Packwood on the platform. It was a signal to the few younger people present—and to all of the media within earshot—that the Republican leadership was hip enough to borrow a line from Jimmie Walker, the jive-talking star of television's hit comedy, *Good Times*.

The mood on the floor was more subdued. "He's not super-articulate, but it comes through," said one attendee, trying to sound enthusiastic about Ford. "He's, well, you get the feeling you've known people like him."

After spending most of his time at fund-raisers, the president devoted an hour to the one official part of the Seattle visit, the White House Conference on Domestic and Economic Affairs. Responding to questions, Ford said he would veto a consumer protection bill, declined to comment on the proposed Alaska natural gas pipeline, and affirmed his opposition to a national health care plan. He already had vetoed a $7.5 billion education appropriation; piling on national health insurance would only have "imposed new budget problems," the president said. No sexy headlines, but no gaffes either.

With Senator Packwood continuing to tag along, Ford flew to Portland, where he was greeted by Senator Hatfield and the state's Junior Miss, who presented the president with Portland's symbol, a red rose. Ford's destination, the Sheraton-Portland Hotel, was surrounded by hundreds of protesters. Inside, though, were nearly six hundred people who had bought $100 tickets to the main event, a dinner-dance promoted as the "Hustle with Ford." The president, who had learned to dance when the Charleston was still popular, read in a memorandum that the name referred "to the currently popular dance, 'The Hustle.'"

The "Hustle with Ford" helped haul in $100,000 for the Oregon Republican Party, but the president didn't dally. After finishing a steak dinner, he headed to the Portland Memorial Coliseum, joining twelve thousand Boy Scouts, Girl Scouts, Campfire Girls, and 4-H Club members participating in the bicentennial rally. Senator Packwood at last had been placated with a seat on the platform, where he and other dignitaries could applaud as a Girl Scout presented the president with an ironic souvenir, a blanket made by Oregon Indians. The questions here were the kind that Ford liked.

"What can I as a ten-year-old girl do to help my country?" asked Campfire Girl Rhonda Morrison.

"Rhonda," the president replied, "simply by asking that question and showing an interest in helping your country, you have made a great contribution." The crowd applauded wildly, still more so when Ford joined in a sing-along.

But even this pleasant stopover caused grumbling. "I know it was supposed to be a youth rally," complained Carmelita Emerson, a 4-H Club member, "but there can be too much cuteness." Carmelita had been cut off before finishing her question, which was: How could America afford the joint Apollo-Soyuz space mission with the Soviet Union "when people in this country are starving?"

Outside the Coliseum, the contingent of pro-Indian demonstrators included a local basketball star, Bill Walton of the Portland Trail Blazers, who commanded his own share of media attention. Walton's presence guaranteed that the arrests of two demonstrators and the cries of the others—"Down with the FBI!" and "FBI Out of Pine Ridge!"—would be reported widely.

Even the cops gave Ford a hard time. A Portland police spokesman complained that security for the four-hour visit had cost the city $10,000. Protecting Ford was more than local treasuries could afford, he said; if the president insisted on coming, perhaps the Portland police should send the White House a bill for their services.

Moving on to the last leg of his trip, President Ford arrived at Sacramento's McClellan Air Force Base at 10:45 P.M. As Ford prepared to leave the aircraft, Secret Service Agent Ron Pontius received an ominous warning: an "unknown male" had just called Channel 3 to say that "ten snipers are waiting for the President when he gets off the plane." Ground security found no sign of the assassination squad, however, and the doors to *Air Force One* swung open.

Gerald Ford usually appeared in public with a smile on his face, but now, he was too weary at first to manage a grin for the habitually somber Jerry Brown, who stood on the tarmac in the hot, muggy air. Governor Brown offered boilerplate greetings on behalf of the people of California, and introduced the president to the assorted state officials and businessmen who had come to the airfield. In office for less than a year, the enigmatic Brown was already being mentioned as a possible Democratic presidential contender while many considered Ford's grip on the Republican nomination far from certain.

As Ford finished shaking the hands of the welcoming committee, Brown abruptly dashed over to the crowd of military personnel that had gathered to greet the president, and started grabbing for their outstretched hands.

"Oh— It's Governor Brown," several onlookers said when they unexpectedly found themselves shaking his hand. Ford instinctively followed Brown, and began to work the crowd himself. As the governor pressed ahead, the president put forth a steady stream of "Nice to see you" and "Thanks for coming out." He was met with effusive greetings: "Hiya, Mr. President," "Hello, Chief," and, especially, "Where's Betty?"—referring to the outspoken First Lady, whom several opinion polls rated as more popular than her husband. Betty Ford had remained in Washington for this trip.

After the president kissed a sleeping baby, a blond teenager popped in front of him. "How 'bout a kiss!" she asked the leader of the free world.

"Well, okay!" Ford replied. Although not considered as much of a ladies' man as some occupants of the White House, Ford did enjoy the attention he now received from young women at galas and rallies. Betty, he knew, resented his sometimes flagrant flirting. Ford kissed the teenager on the cheek.

Ahead, meanwhile, Governor Brown had paused to fix a jammed camera brought by one of the spectators. He handed it back before Ford caught up, giving the owner a chance to snap a shot of the president as he made his way along.

"You're one of those mechanical types, huh?" Ford said to Brown, who forged ahead again, seemingly intent on outpoliticianing the president by shaking the hand of everyone present.

The rivalry continued after they arrived at the Senator Hotel in downtown Sacramento. Three hundred onlookers were waiting to welcome Ford as he emerged from his limousine, and the president rushed past Brown to make sure that this time, he got to them first.

It was nearly midnight. Bob Hartmann, Ford's counselor and longtime friend, glanced at his watch, and then over to the re-energized president. "My God, the man isn't human," he muttered, as Ford continued shaking hands, including those of all five members of a mariachi band that had come to play in his honor.

Brown soon caught up with the president, and worked the crowd right behind him. When a spectator yelled "Hi, Jerry!" both Ford and Brown waved back.

The president finally got to his hotel room and fell asleep. Ford had arisen before 7:00 A.M., Eastern time, and been awake and politicking for some twenty hours straight. He would have to be up again the following morning at six-thirty.

The night still was young, however, for Governor Brown, who had the advantage of the three-hour Pacific time differential, as well as almost three decades in age. After depositing the president at his suite, Brown invited a few reporters to join him for a drink across town at the Cosmopolitan Hotel. Invigorated and alert as ever, Brown strolled across Capitol Park, reporters and three gubernatorial aides in tow.

A week before, a plan to kidnap Brown and hold him for $10 million ransom had been found folded inside a lost wallet. The billfold's owner was still at large, but no security checks had been made by any of the half-dozen police agencies involved in the day's planning; this governor's movements were just too hard to predict. Brown's safety fell to a lone highway patrolman tagging along, his assignment to drive the governor home after drinks.

President Ford's security was not so nonchalant. Every stage of his trip had been carefully mapped out by the Secret Service, the agency charged since 1865 with the protection of the president. The service received more than 200,000 tips a year, and conducted at least a cursory investigation of some 15,000 of them. Usually, these resulted in rather one-sided discourses between talkative crackpots and laconic, patient, largely uncomprehending agents.

One such character, Thomas David Elbert, had made the tactical error of calling the Secret Service's Sacramento office on August 16 and saying, "I'm going to kill your boss, President Ford."

In May 1975, the thirty-four-year-old Elbert had been discharged from Terminal Island federal prison—the same institution that Charles Manson left in 1967—after serving five years for threatening President Nixon's life. The call returned Elbert to jail for the duration of Ford's visit. He later pleaded guilty to threatening the president's life.

Down the coast, Santa Barbara police stumbled upon a plot to kill President Ford during his visit to Sacramento. On August 26, they arrested Gary Steven DeSure and Preston Michael Mayo for stealing a television set from a local motel. Once in custody, the pair of drifters, who sported identical mustaches and sideburns, quickly recounted a cross-country odyssey that had been intended to culminate with Ford's assassination.

DeSure, thirty-one, liked to brag that he once had shared a cell with Charles Manson in the Los Angeles County Jail. He reportedly had made an earlier threat on Ford's life and recently had escaped from a mental hospital in Montana. On August 12, 1975, DeSure had teamed up with Mayo, a twenty-four-year-old ex-convict from Virginia, at Montana's Glacier National Park. According to police records, the pair went on the road, financing their travels through robberies and forged checks and stopping on August 19 in Dickson, Tennessee, to draw up the plans for their California trip.

DeSure and Mayo didn't much like the way the way Ford was running the country, or even the man himself. They decided they had to kill him. Writing on a stolen medical prescription pad, they listed their favorite weapons and outlined how to place dynamite for maximum effect. They listed sources for blueprints of the California Capitol and other buildings where Ford might stop. Their plan called for placing explosives in the sewers beneath the city streets. DeSure would detonate the dynamite and act as a lookout. Mayo would fire on the president. The explosion and resulting disruption would make it easy for the pair to escape.

DeSure and Mayo arrived in Los Angeles on August 23. They were driving a rented 1974 Datsun sedan when a California highway patrolman tried to pull them over. Concerned that DeSure's collection of outstanding warrants might impede their plans, the pair sped away, later abandoning the car at the Holly-wood-Burbank airport. They rented another car and headed one hundred miles north to Santa Barbara. But in their haste to desert the Datsun in Burbank, DeSure and Mayo had left behind the outline of the assassination plot.

The burglary charge was enough to hold the pair in lieu of $100,000 bail apiece. When President Ford arrived at McClellan Air Force Base, DeSure and Mayo glumly noted the occasion in the Santa Barbara County Jail.

A few days before the visit, Channel 40 in Sacramento had received a threatening phonecall. "Get your paper and get this," the caller said. "This is the SLA. President Ford is going to die in Sacramento on Thursday." The caller then hung up.

The station reported the call to the Secret Service, but no action was taken. "There were no leads to pursue," agents reported.

The Secret Service

The United States Secret Service, which referred to itself in agency shorthand as "USSS," was the first of what would become an alphabet soup of federal police forces. An arm of the Treasury Department, it had been established under President Abraham Lincoln to fight the counterfeiting of Union currency that grew rampant during the Civil War. After Lincoln's assassination by the actor John Wilkes Booth, the protection of the president was added to the agency's charge. With each successive presidential assassination, the service devoted ever more resources to its prestigious task.

A significant buildup had taken place in 1901, after President William Mc-Kinley was shot dead by anarchist Leon Czolgosz. Czolgosz had been standing in a line of well-wishers; he extended his left hand to shake McKinley's hand, while his right, covered by a handkerchief, aimed a pistol at the president.

An even larger Secret Service expansion came after the 1963 assassination of President John F. Kennedy, which saw the agency harshly criticized by the Warren Commission. In the twelve years since Kennedy's murder in Dallas, the Secret Service budget had grown by 1,600 percent, from $5.8 million to $98 million, and its forces had more than trebled, from 450 agents to 1,830.

Armed with modern surveillance technology and new laws making the assassination of the president or vice president special federal crimes, the Secret Service in the 1960s built a databank of 500,000 people it considered potential assassins. The list grew to include Charles Manson, but not Sirhan Sirhan, who assassinated Senator Robert F. Kennedy in 1968; Arthur Bremer, whose shot had crippled Governor George Wallace in 1972; nor, in fact, any individual who actually shot or attempted to shoot a president or presidential candidate.

Even so, the agency was proud that neither Lyndon Johnson nor Richard Nixon had been shot, despite the unprecedented hostility each aroused among segments of the public. In the early 1970s, however, federal police activities came into question after revelations that agents devoted large efforts to spying on American citizens solely for opposing government policies—especially members of the antiwar and civil rights movements.

Most of the criticism fell on J. Edgar Hoover's FBI, but the Secret Service was embarrassed as well. New York Congresswoman Bella Abzug revealed that the service included among potential assassins the leaders of a Quaker antiwar organization known for its commitment to nonviolence. Professor Arthur R. Miller of Harvard Law School lambasted the Secret Service databank as "just another Enemies List," referring to the Nixon administration's notorious compilation of political opponents targeted for harassment. Senator John Tunney went further. Left unchecked, the California Democrat said, federal surveillance practices represented an unfolding "Orwellian nightmare."

Prodded by Congress, the Secret Service began to reconsider its intelligence operations, and by 1975 reported that it had purged most names from its list of potential assassins. Officials told Congress the "active" file included only 38,947 individuals, 300 of whom were considered extremely dangerous and subject to special surveillance under an operation code-named "Watchbird."

Although agency heads paid some heed to congressional criticism, the Secret Service devoted most of its efforts to pleasing the sitting president. Of all federal agencies, the Secret Service had the most intimate relationship with the nation's leader, staying with him wherever he went and whatever he did, noting when he went to sleep and when he rose, overhearing everything from his most truthful sotto voce observations to the platitudes he routinely uttered over loudspeakers and handshakes.

Not only did Secret Service men strive to keep the president from being assassinated, they also worked to save him from a peril more often on his mind: embarrassment. While some agents were assigned to check onlookers for weapons, others ensured that seating arrangements did not put the president within a photo frame of organized crime figures, scandalized celebrities, or others whose presence might cause controversy or ridicule.

To a degree, the agents' behavior came to reflect that of their client. President Nixon had ordered the uniformed branch of the Secret Service, which guarded the White House, outfitted in resplendent, almost Napoleonic costumes that led observers to dub them "the Palace Guard." The plainclothesmen who accompanied Nixon had used a heavy hand to keep order when the president moved, and were ready to rough up anyone whose looks they figured Nixon wouldn't like. Unfortunately for Ford, personnel rules dictated that the new president inherit Nixon's Secret Service detail, while his "discreet and courteous" vice-presidential squad remained with incoming Vice President Nelson Rockefeller. So, conscious that his style more than his policies would distinguish him from Nixon, Ford had passed word that his security detail loosen up, and not, as he said, "push people around. . . . It was all right if they smiled once in a while."

No one had yet noticed any increase in smiles among the agents, whose trademark look remained sunglasses, earpieces, and a wary equanimity. They were even more uncomfortable with another departure from Nixon, Ford's penchant for diving into any crowd that had assembled to see him. Such embraces built up the president's confidence, and, as Ford and his advisers knew, could generate great wire service and television pictures suggesting the president's popularity.

Ford, at least, had one thing in his favor: he simply wasn't disliked as much as Nixon or Johnson. Agents braced themselves with that thought when they saw Ford, against their repeated advice, pop the top of his bulletproof limousine to wave to spectators, or run up to barricades to grab any hand extended toward him.

On the West Coast trip, Special Agent Ashley "Skip" Williams, a ten-year veteran of the Secret Service, headed a detail of nine plainclothesmen who accompanied the president day and night. Several agents had flown ahead to Sacramento to make sure security was in place for the arrival. Meeting with local authorities, they found a familiar squabble over which police agency would have the privilege of protecting the president during his visit. The California state police, who guarded Capitol Park, insisted that they would accompany the president while he was in their jurisdiction, and that the Sacramento city officers were unnecessary. The Secret Service offered the local police a consolation prize: they could provide security across the street from Capitol Park, at the convention center where Ford would speak and at the Senator Hotel.

As the state's capital city, Sacramento daily played host to political demonstrations. At noon on September 4, while President Ford was still in Seattle, Secret Service men went to Capitol Park to observe the day's measure of free expression. Agents especially were eager to attend the rally jointly sponsored by organizations calling themselves the "Anti-Imperialist Coalition," the "Iranian Students Association," and a group whose name sparked memories of the radical heyday, the "Sacramento SDS." The six protesters who showed up, however, did not seem especially dangerous, and could not manage even one arrest by the Sacramento police. The demonstrators spent ten minutes decrying military spending, unemployment, inflation, and the decontrol of oil prices. Then they left, presumably to make the most of their remaining lunch break.

On the other side of Capitol Park, a larger rally drew more attention from passers-by. About 350 members of a public employees union had come to protest Governor Brown's layoff of several thousand state office workers. The reporting agent noted that "this demonstration was not of interest to USSS and is mentioned only because it occurred at the same time and place as the first demonstration, which was of interest to USSS."

September 5 promised more of interest to USSS. The agent reported that local chapters of the Communist Party and the Progressive Labor Party had announced plans to protest Ford at his 7:30 A.M. stop at the convention center, and later at 9:00 A.M. at the state Capitol. The "CP" and "PLP"—the Secret Service took these groups seriously enough to assign them acronyms—would be watched.

The purpose of President Ford's visit was to deliver the keynote address at the Sacramento Host Breakfast, the annual gathering of business and political leaders sponsored by the chamber of commerce. Traditionally, the governor of California delivered the speech, but when Jerry Brown failed to reply to the Host Committee's repeated invitations, organizers sought to do one better by replacing him with the president. The invitation that arrived at the White House in June 1975 was marked by Ford's schedulers as "extremely doubtful." As the summer progressed, however, and Ronald Reagan seemed an ever greater political threat, the Host Breakfast emerged as a good excuse for a raid into California.

Once it was decided to visit Sacramento, Ford's handlers strived to make the most of it, arranging for the president to address a joint session of the California legislature. As word of the visit spread, Sacramentans of various stripes scrambled to find room on the presidential schedule. Invitations poured into the White House, some piquing the interest of Ford's political operatives, others seeming poignant or perhaps pathetic. The general manager of the Sacramento Regional Transit District sent a telegram to the president, beseeching him to dedicate 103 new buses the city had just acquired.

"A portion of the new fleet could be parked at the site of the breakfast, at the point of your arrival or at any convenient place. We are certain it could be planned so that the bus dedication would not interrupt your schedule or reduce security," the telegram read. The White House sent its regrets. Equally unsuccessful in meeting Ford was Cesar Chavez, founder of the United Farm Workers union, and scourge of the Central Valley agribusinessmen the Ford campaign was counting on. The White House travel office quickly nixed the migrant labor leader's request, misspelling his name "Ceasar Chevez."

Other invitations, however, were taken more seriously. After practically ignoring the White House, the Host Breakfast, and assorted other protocol matters for his first eight months in office, Governor Brown suddenly asked to be placed on the president's Sacramento schedule. The White House grudgingly consented. "Indeed, it would be interpreted as a snub if we refused," an aide concluded, "since the Governor's office is in the same building as the President's address to the Joint Session of the Legislature."

The White House began scrambling to find areas of common ground between the eccentric bachelor governor and the gregarious midwestern Ford. An aide discovered that Brown and actor Steve McQueen had protested a proposed regulation requiring motorcyclists to wear crash helmets. "Frankly, this is the type of issue in which I suspect the President would probably . . . [agree] with McQueen and Brown."

Otherwise, it seemed, there wouldn't much for the two to talk about.

The Host Breakfast was being held at the newly opened Earl Warren Community Convention Center, a sand-colored complex of low-rise buildings intended to lure convention planners seeking an economical alternative to expensive destinations like San Francisco. Conventioneers could visit such nearby attractions as Sutter's Fort, established by Sacramento's Swiss founder, John Sutter, and the State Fair, which was the region's biggest annual event. For nightlife, tourists might venture to Old Sacramento, whose wood-slat sidewalks and Wild West–style buildings had been refurbished to house souvenir stores, restaurants, and bars. The tiny tourist district was all that remained of the city's historic waterfront, which had been bulldozed in the early 1960s to make way for Interstate 5.

Even though the convention center was only three blocks from the Senator Hotel, it had been decided that Ford would motor to his destination, for reasons both of security and propriety; certainly the president did not want to be the only one of a thousand executives to have walked to the Host Breakfast.

Attended by the state's top elected and judicial officers, its San Francisco–based diplomatic corps, and the heads of many of California's largest firms, the Host Breakfast was an occasion for the burghers of Sacramento to assure themselves just how important they were. The first Host Breakfast, held in 1926, was a small, closed-door affair where a handful of businessmen met to discuss the problems wreaked upon California by the immigration of undesirables from elsewhere in the country. The discussions presumably were frank, as reporters were excluded and proceedings kept secret. Beginning in 1933, however, the breakfast began to evolve from a confidential strategy session into a status event for California businessmen. Over the years, the membership grew, the press was invited, and the Host Breakfast assumed its role as a prominent but inconsequential function on the chamber of commerce circuit.

Among the record number of attendees—twelve hundred this year—there were some special guests who sat awaiting President Ford. Governor Brown had decided to attend after all, though as a spectator rather than a speaker. Sherm Chavoor, the Olympic swimming coach who had drilled Debbie Myers and Mark Spitz to gold medals at the 1968 and 1972 Summer Games, brought some athletic glory to the event, despite rumors that he didn't himself know how to swim.

Present, as always, were the three MacBride brothers, members of a distinguished Sacramento family that once had owned the city's largest candy factory.

Frank MacBride, Jr., was president of MacBride Realty and a member of the Host Committee. Kirt MacBride, the family's black sheep, was the gossip columnist of the *Sacramento Union*, his "Kirt's People" an inland echo of Herb Caen's frothy feature in the *San Francisco Chronicle*. And there was Thomas J. MacBride, a former state assemblyman whose work for John Kennedy's presidential campaign had been rewarded with a federal judgeship in 1961.

Now sixty-one years old, Tom MacBride was chief judge of the United States District Court in Sacramento, overseeing federal trials in the thirty-four largely rural counties making up the Eastern District of California. As a naval intelligence officer in World War II, MacBride had served on General Douglas MacArthur's staff. "Stern and determined" is how MacBride remembered his old boss. "A rather pompous and egotistical guy." Educated at Berkeley, MacBride had worked for Attorney General Earl Warren before winning his assembly seat.

Despite a lifetime in high places, MacBride had an easygoing, even folksy manner that belied the arrogant reputation of federal judges. When not in his black robes, the tall, thin-faced man with wire-rimmed spectacles and balding dome could easily have passed for the country store owner as for the region's chief jurist. Unpretentious as he was accomplished, proud of his prowess at fishing and hunting as of his legal acumen, no one better embodied Sacramento's strengths than Judge MacBride.

Perhaps Judge MacBride's opposite in temperament was Don Heller, the federal prosecutor who got into the breakfast when a friend passed him an extra ticket. A brash, excitable New Yorker, Heller had played varsity baseball at Queens College, and paid his way through law school by driving taxicabs at night. His aggressive style grated on the low-key and insular legal community of Sacramento; they had started calling Heller "Mad Dog" after he told a judge in court that he would gladly pull the switch at the defendant's execution. Unfortunately, the drug-dealing charge didn't carry the death penalty.

To the annoyance of many defense attorneys—and some of his California-bred colleagues at the United States Attorney's Office—the short, round-faced Heller had decided to make Sacramento his home. Heller had met his future wife while vacationing in Europe, followed her home to California's Central Valley, and proclaimed it, as he told friends in New York City, "God's country." His presence at the Host Breakfast proved it. Heller may have spent four years as a prosecutor in Manhattan, but it was in Sacramento that he was privileged to dine in the same room as the President of the United States.

Closer to the head table sat Heller's boss, U.S. Attorney Dwayne Keyes. Also a relative newcomer to Sacramento, Keyes came from the often-maligned southern end of the judicial district, Fresno. As an assistant district attorney active in Republican politics, Keyes had applied for the federal prosecutor's position when it opened up in 1970. At the behest of Fresno's business establishment, he had won the endorsement of Senator George Murphy, essential for a patronage appointment such as U.S. Attorney. President Nixon, whose victory in the 1968 election had turned on crossover votes from places like Fresno, rewarded the farming center by naming Keyes the top federal prosecutor for inland California.

With a mop of curly, graying hair, Keyes had a soft-spoken manner that sometimes masked his wry sense of humor. At the Host Breakfast, the prosecutor and his wife, Mary Jo, found themselves seated with a Secret Service man, Larry Buendorf. Agents were instinctually discreet, but by Secret Service standards, Buendorf, a youthful thirty-seven, was positively gregarious.

Wasn't Buendorf's job tough, Keyes asked.

Maybe, the agent replied, but it had its rewards. Buendorf—known as Boon in the agents' abbreviated vocabulary—had joined the Secret Service in 1970, and guarded the 1972 Democratic vice-presidential candidate, Sargent Shriver. The trim and athletic agent, a former Navy pilot, got along well with his protectees. After his marriage in 1973, Boon liked to tell friends, he had received a wistful note from eighteen-year-old Maria Shriver, Sargent's daughter. "Darn it," wrote the future wife of Arnold Schwarzenegger, "you didn't wait."

After the 1972 campaign, Buendorf was promoted to the White House division, where he had guarded Nixon, and—providentially—Ford. A native of rural Wells, Minnesota, Boon happened to be the best skier on the presidential detail, a skill that made him invaluable when the Fords entered the White House.

Buendorf confided to Keyes the significance of this fact. Whenever the president planned a vacation at his retreat in Vail, Colorado, it fell to Boon to make the security arrangements. He would arrive at the ski lodge two weeks before the president, accompany Ford for a week during his vacation, and then take a two-week vacation afterwards. Not bad for government work.

Still, though Buendorf was respected and well liked by his colleagues, he suffered from the doubts that inevitably went with his work. A few weeks before the Sacramento trip, Buendorf had spoken of those doubts with his elder brother, William. Despite the training, despite the ethos of the Secret Service, if the president were threatened, would he really throw himself in front of a bullet? Boon confessed to his brother: he just didn't know.

September 5

At 7:23 A.M., President Ford emerged from the Senator Hotel to ride in his motorcade to the Host Breakfast. Uniformed police stood atop the roofs of the hotel, the convention center, and most of the area's other buildings. They kept watch as a White House aide walked to the grille of Ford's limousine, and, with a quick and practiced motion, unfurled the small American and presidential flags that would wave in the breeze during the three-minute journey.

At the convention center, about fifty protesters waited to greet the president. Their messages ranged from HANDS OFF ANGOLA, the former Portuguese colony now erupting into civil war, to FORD IS A PUPPET OF ITT, the mysterious conglomerate that produced military technology and Wonder Bread. The president, however, didn't even see the demonstrators; his security team had arranged for him to enter the building through the cordoned-off rear entrance.

Once inside, Ford was quickly escorted to the head table as a band, positioned opposite the breakfast fruit selection, broke into "Ruffles and Flourishes" and "Hail to the Chief." After an Episcopal priest read a one-minute invocation, the president settled down for breakfast, and for the scheduled introduction of the guests.

In glancing at the hundreds of pages of material prepared for his trip, Ford had not paid particular attention to a note on one of the documents, observing that "600 guest names will be read off in rapid succession. Custom dictates that when the guest's name is called he stands." When the event chairman began at 7:41 A.M. to introduce the guests, Ford courteously applauded the names of men he had never before heard of. By 8:45 A.M., however, he was doing his best to avoid nodding off as the seemingly endless introductions of beaming agribusiness executives, local judges, and chamber of commerce vice presidents droned into a second hour. Finally, at 9:00 A.M., Ford rose to deliver his twenty-three-minute address, taking his place behind a wood-tone lectern bearing the presidential seal.

Looking out at the sea of well-fed, middle-aged faces, men sitting at tables covered with white linen and decorated with baskets full of California-grown fruit, Ford saw his vision of America's best. Like the businessmen of Grand Rapids, his Michigan hometown, these folks were not glamorous, but they built the wealth that made American great. They had paid nearly $1,000 apiece to come to the breakfast, and they deserved to hear something they'd like.

Reading in his flat, Midwestern timbre, Ford insisted that despite the persistent recession, America's economy was picking up. Citing unnamed economists, he said that by 1980, the country would need 11 million new private-sector jobs, an expansion that would cost some $4 trillion. But, he reassuringly told the executives, the money "won't be raised by the board of directors skipping lunches." Instead, the answer was "getting government out of the way of business."

The enemy, indeed, was the federal government itself, a monstrosity that employed 100,000 regulators "whose principal job is telling you how to do *your* job. It's a bureaucratic's—er, bureaucrat's dream of heaven, but it's a nightmare for those who have to bear the heavy burden," he said, adding the word "heavy" to the prepared text.

"Just to list all of the rules and regulations established last year required 45,000 pages of *very small* print in the *Federal Register*," the president said, squeezing his thumb and forefinger together to emphasize the concept of *very small*. The thought of all those pages moved Ford to add the one reference he would make to the environment while in California.

"I mourn for the trees that were felled in America's forests," the president said, as smiles and laughs broke out among the audience, "to make this exercise in government nagging possible." Applause followed, as it did when he concluded his speech: "Help me . . . help us all to free the—er, free American enterprise system!"

Ford could, at least, take some pride in one area in which the government issued almost no regulations. Under both federal and state law, just about anyone could own virtually any sort of firearm.

After accepting a set of souvenir cufflinks, President Ford returned to his hotel for a twenty-minute break. Looking over his schedule, Ford noted he was to meet later with the chairman of his California reelection effort, state Attorney General Evelle J. Younger.

Younger had been the Los Angeles district attorney during the Tate-LaBianca prosecution, which Manson's lawyer, Irving Kanarek, had contended was politically motivated. In court—where he was immune to a slander suit—Kanarek claimed that Younger and President Nixon had conspired to deprive Manson of a fair trial in order to further their political careers. If true, the ploy succeeded. In November 1970, two months before Manson's conviction on all charges, Younger was elected attorney general of California.

As the state's chief prosecutor, Younger remained professionally interested in the Manson Family. Prior to Younger's 1974 reelection campaign, the attorney general's office issued a report entitled *Terrorism in California*.

"California is confronted by a broad spectrum of terrorism, the ultimate weapon of the new revolutionaries," the report warned. The document included mug shots of twenty-two of the nation's most wanted revolutionaries, all of whom were white and in their twenties or early thirties, mainly university-educated, and middle class. Eight were women, including Katherine Ann Power, who would finally surrender to authorities in 1993, and Bernardine Dohrn, the Weather Underground leader who had exulted when she learned of the Tate-LaBianca murders in 1969.

Younger's report listed several revolutionary organizations as active in California, most of which had emerged from "the student movement of the sixties" and had links to penitentiary inmates, whom the terrorists considered political prisoners. The most dangerous, of course, was the Symbionese Liberation Army, but others included the Black Guerrilla Family, the white supremacist Polar Bear Party, and, on page ten, the "Manson Clan," whose members "continue to cause problems for law enforcement. . . .

"Members of the Manson Clan, because of their past activities and potential for violence, could become involved in a terrorist plot to free Charles Manson or other members of the Manson Clan or Aryan Brotherhood now confined in state prison." Incidentally, the report observed, "Two former members of the Manson Clan are now living in Sacramento."

In preparation for the presidential visit, Ev Younger had sent a good deal of material to his friend Jerry Ford, including his own confidential assessments of the political scene in Sacramento. *Terrorism in California* had not been included, but Younger had recommended the theme of Ford's address to the legislature: crime prevention.

Reviewing his information packet, President Ford could see his next task was simple: "You depart Suite and walk to the California State Capitol."

Ford, had an alternative, however, which might have seemed excessive for anyone other than the President of the United States: the advance team had sketched a motorcade approach, in which Ford would have driven across the street in his armored limousine and entered the Capitol via the legislature's private underground parking garage.

The decision was left to the White House advance man, Frank Ursomarso. Ursomarso also had done the advance work for the president's visit to Salzburg, Austria, the abiding image of which was Ford tripping on the stairs to *Air Force One*. The episode had not been helpful to the fragile presidential image, and Ursomarso was determined to make sure things went smoothly in Sacramento. Well aware of the president's desire to meet the public, Ursomarso waited for the Secret Service assessment of the onlookers in Capitol Park. When agents reported that the crowd was friendly and that no demonstrators were in sight, Ursomarso gave the okay for the walk.

At 10:02 A.M., just three minutes behind schedule, the president emerged from the hotel's L Street entrance and felt the thick, 82-degree Sacramento air. The crowd outside burst into applause, and Ford smiled. This was more like it, the president thought; he had been visibly disappointed earlier in the day, when he saw that only fifty Sacramentans had come to cheer him on his way to the Host Breakfast.

An assistant gave the signal for the president's party to proceed to the state Capitol. With Ford at its vortex, the whirlwind of political advisers, military aides, reporters, plainclothesmen, and uniformed police spun left and swept to the corner of Twelfth and L, then crossed diagonally to the pathway leading to the Capitol.

Meanwhile, White House aide Eric Rosenberger, at thirty-one a veteran of the 1968 and 1972 Nixon campaigns, ran ahead and tried to position the press pools so they could photograph Ford as he came upon the crowd. This, after all, was the reason for the walk. Rosenberger found himself at cross-purposes with Ursomarso, who didn't want his boss lingering too long with the "office workers and secretaries" he figured made up most of the crowd. Ursomarso picked up the pace toward the Capitol, moving so fast that several photographers, who were walking backward to get shots of the president, had trouble keeping their balance. One tripped and fell down, and quickly was righted by Ursomarso and Rosenberger.

Ford, in his blue suit and red, white, and blue tie, marched forward, past a dozen fifty-foot-tall palm trees lining the edge of the park. Surrounded by the undulating bubble of his retinue, the president turned left onto the pathway, a concrete ribbon ten feet wide that curved toward the Capitol's East Wing.

On Ford's left, along the path, stood the cheering crowd, two to four deep. The warmth between them and their president was mutual, and twenty-five feet into the park Ford could no longer resist their agog eyes and smiling faces. He swung over to them, plunging both his hands into the crowd to grab as many people as possible as he moved south toward the Statehouse.

Silently, the Secret Service detail paced alongside, alert in what they called an "uncontrolled environment." Although their fluid motions around the president seemed almost casual in the California sun, the agents were functioning like a crack military unit, each man holding a predetermined position from which his response to any contingency had been drilled in months of training. "You notice kooks and faces and a lot of other things," one agent said of these flesh-pressing regimens, "but hands are most important. You watch for hands—if somebody is going to try to hurt the President, they'll have to use their hands."

To Special Agent Larry Buendorf, in sunglasses, the situation was uncomfortable. Locked to the president's shoulder, he kept working the hands, making sure no one grasped Ford too tightly or for too long, preventing anyone from presenting the president with a gift—or a projectile. As he progressed through the park, Buendorf began to worry that the party was being pushed to the right and could get shoved off the sidewalk—a spatial illusion caused by the walkway's slight curve.

Under the arrangement brokered by the Secret Service, the Sacramento city police officers were to stop at the park's boundary, as state police took over security. But the city patrolmen saw only three members of the state police at their posts; instead of surveying the crowd, thought one aghast Sacramento officer, the starstruck state cops were gaping at the president. Disregarding their agreement with the rival agency, the local police fanned into the park, some, like Officer Gaylen Peterson, continuing behind the presidential party.

The entire assault lasted a split second. Agent Buendorf, assisted by Officer Peterson and a bystander named Jerry Fox, immediately subdued Lyn as she started to point her .45 caliber Colt pistol at the president. Other agents hurried Ford to safety inside the state Capitol, where, after briefly composing himself, he continued on to the governor's office. The meeting was attended only by Governor Brown and his chief of staff, Gray Davis. Secret Service Agent Skip Williams discreetly drew the blinds over the bank of windows facing Capitol Park; he breathed a little easier when another agent informed him the windows were bulletproof.

Neither Brown nor Davis, however, had yet heard about the incident in Capitol Park, and Ford said nothing about it. Brown first learned of the assault more than thirty minutes into the meeting, when White House aide Donald

Rumsfeld appeared with a report for the president. Ford then turned to Brown and described what had happened outside California's Capitol. "In retrospect," Davis later commented, "I'm very impressed with his [Ford's] attentiveness."

Nearly two decades later, Gerald Ford explained his nonchalance toward the encounter with Lynette Fromme: "Once it was over, it was over. We had a schedule to keep. We had a program to do. And there wasn't much point in sitting around and wringing your hands.

"That's my nature," Ford went on. "I've always been very pragmatic about the things that have happened in my life. If they're good, I don't tend to get overjoyed. If they're unhappy or tragic, I don't sit around and mull over it." Ford said he recognized the danger he faced in Capitol Park, "but once it's gone, it's gone."

The president's aides were not so sanguine. Bob Hartmann, the White House counselor, threw up after the incident, and twice more later in the day. Press secretary Ron Nessen told reporters that the incident "scared the shit out of me." Nessen had nightmares upon returning to Washington, dreaming that he had accidentally suffocated his own son.

Mrs. X.

En route to Sacramento police headquarters, Lyn sat in the backseat of the squad car, sandwiched between Secret Service agents Jim Gavin and Tom McCarter. Calm and in control of herself, she complained to the lawmen that her handcuffs were too tight. Asked to identify herself, she gave the name of "Mrs. X."

At police headquarters, Lyn was brought to the second floor and placed in interview room no. 3, a tiny space no larger than six by eight feet in size. Her hands still cuffed behind her back, Lyn was seated in a chair as the Secret Service agents, standing over her, began the interrogation. Moments later, they were joined by a hastily summoned female police officer, Detective Linda Walker, who had no idea who the suspect was or what crime she was charged with.

Lyn was now willing to give the authorities her name and date of birth, but not her address. Told that she was required to reveal her address, Lyn lied and said she lived alone at 1421 G Street, Apartment B. The agents wrote down the address and turned to Detective Walker. They instructed Walker to search Lyn thoroughly, and left the room. Walker verified that Lyn had a holster strapped to her leg with two elastic belts, but found no additional weapons.

Walker would spend five hours with Lyn on September 5, as assorted federal agents, local detectives, and forensic technicians came to shoot photographs or check in on the suspect. Lyn seemed quite comfortable being the center of attention. She noted the many onlookers who paused to gaze at her through the small window in the interview room's door, and said she understood something about how animals felt in the zoo. Of course, Lyn noted, when the apes in the zoo did their tricks, it was the humans they were making fools of.

Soon the two women were having a full-fledged conversation—at least Lyn was, giving her standard assessment of society's ills.

"We are killing our children," Lyn told the detective. "And our children are becoming angry." The country was rich, and yet people couldn't get the things they needed. She said she had to pay fifty cents for a tomato, a tomato she was buying for a houseguest. "That wasn't right," Lyn said.

Even more distressing was the impact of television, which filled people's heads with false ideas, twisting their priorities around. For example, Lyn said, television was selling the "Chicano people" things they don't need—and they were thus unable to buy the things they did. Television should be used to sell health, not things.

Detective Walker commented on the Saturday morning cartoons, filled with commercials that sent children running to their parents, urging them to buy dolls and toys.

"Do your kids do that?" Lyn asked. Walker said she had no children. Did Lyn, the detective asked.

No, Lyn said. But, in a sense, all children were hers. "Children have vivid imaginations. They see colors more vividly and see people more 'animated,' like in cartoons. But as they get older, they are programmed to see things" more rigidly, she explained.

It was her love of children that made her so abhor abortion, Lyn said. That was murder, she said, and dangerous for women, too. She told Walker she had a friend who was a nurse (probably meaning Heather) who had seen doctors make horrible mistakes while performing abortions.

Foremost on Lyn's mind, however, was the dismal state of the environment. She described her recent visit to the offices of the Army Corps of Engineers, and the irony that "they couldn't see the problem, even though it was right outside the window"—that is, the smog brown air that hung over Sacramento every summer.

People needed to take the time to get in touch with the earth, with the woods and trees and flowers and animals, Lyn lectured. She went on to criticize the "money system," describing the virtues of vegetarianism, offering understanding for the predicament of those in law enforcement; according to a friend of hers in prison, Lyn said, "people in law enforcement have too much paperwork. They can't see the problems because of all the paperwork."

After a while, Lyn began to weep. Walker sent an officer to fetch her a box of tissues and a glass of water. Lyn was grateful. Turning to the detective, she offered a compliment.

"You have lots of patience."

Sandra Good had been in bed when the telephone rang at 1725 P Street. It was a *Sacramento Bee* reporter, calling to ask Sandy if she knew where Lyn was.

J E S S   B R A V I N

"She's just gone to the post office," Sandy replied. After turning to Heather for clarification, Sandy continued, "she's just gone up the street."

The reporter asked if Sandy knew that Lyn had been arrested.

"Oh, no, I don't think so," Sandy said. Soon, other reporters were calling for comment, and Sandy was persuaded that Lyn, indeed, had gotten into something big.

Around the city, law enforcement went on the alert, fearful that a Manson-led conspiracy to destroy the nation's leadership might be afoot. But it was not until 11:30 A.M., nearly ninety minutes after the pistol incident, that a Sacramento police squad arrived at the P Street apartment. Heather welcomed the officers into the apartment and introduced them to Sandy. After concluding that no one else was hiding there, the police asked Sandy and Heather to accompany them to headquarters. The women cooperated fully. As they were being escorted downtown, guards were posted in front of the apartment house and by Lyn's Volkswagen, to make sure nothing was tampered with until a search warrant could be executed.

On the way to the police station, Sandy began talking about her friend. "Lyn was upset last night, she was crying and very upset about all the pollution," she told the officers. "If the gun had gone off," she added, "Lyn would have been a true public servant."

At police headquarters, however, Sandra told investigators that Lyn had given no clue of any interest in killing the president. Sandy said that she didn't even know Lyn had a pistol, or where she might have gotten it. In any event, Sandy assured the officers, Lyn was not a "planner" and therefore wouldn't have thought the incident out in advance.

Meanwhile the door to interview room no. 3 was open as technicians continued to take photos of Lyn. Suddenly, a commotion was heard in the hall, and Detective Walker was ordered to shut the door. Locked again inside the tiny room, Lyn walked over to the door and looked through the window. Then she returned to her seat and closed her eyes, wearily resting her chin on her chest.

"Tired?" Walker asked.

Lyn nodded. She said that she hadn't gotten much sleep the night before.

Minutes later, Walker received the instruction to move Lyn to the photo room, a larger space that could be equipped with video equipment to record interrogations. As Lyn was being escorted down the hallway, she passed an open door and saw Sandra and Heather inside interview room no. 4.

"It didn't go off. I'm sorry, Sandy," Lyn called to her friend.

Police Lieutenant Hal Taylor interrupted. "Shut up," he told Lyn. He later testified that Lyn's tone of voice was "apologetic."

"But they didn't know anything about it," Lyn pleaded. The officers hustled her down the hallway. At 11:28 A.M. in the photo room, Agent Gavin read Lyn her rights, and after her handcuffs were removed was ready to start asking questions.

First, however, Lyn had a request: Would they please remove the holster strapped to her leg? Detective Walker did so, and the interrogation began.

Throughout, Gavin later reported, Lyn "was in control of herself and set the pace of the interview." She refused to answer questions about the incident in Capitol Park, and consistently referred to herself in the third person. It would be pointless to try to explain her act to the officers, Lyn said. "The girl's story will come out in court."

Instead, Lyn used the interview to try to educate the investigators. She told the officers that the United States was "going to the dogs" and that "time was running out" to make the needed changes.

"Subject was expressive on one point," the Secret Service report observed: Charles Manson. "According to the subject, if more people followed Manson's work, there would be less world problems." Gavin concluded that Lyn seemed slightly "under the influence of either an intoxicant or a drug," and gave up trying to question her at 12:55 P.M. Minutes later, she was moved to an adjacent room to be examined by Dr. Charles J. Fisher, Jr., of Sacramento Medical Center.

Fisher introduced himself. In a tone that struck the physician as slightly defensive, Lyn asked if he was a psychiatrist.

"No, I'm not," Fisher said. "I'm an internist."

Lyn accepted the information. "I guess you're okay," she said. From that point on, she cooperated with the doctor, who noted a bruise on her left shin. Lyn said that she had bumped into something a few days before, an explanation that seemed reasonable to the doctor. He found her blood pressure to be normal, her mental state to evidence no sign of depression or paranoia or delusional thoughts. "She denied," the doctor later testified, "any suicidal ideation."

Dr. Fisher drew about 30 cc's of blood, and Detective Walker escorted Lyn to the ladies' room to obtain a urine sample. No traces of alcohol or drugs were detected, except for phenylproponalamine, the active ingredient in Contac.

Next, two psychiatrists came to see Lyn. She immediately announced that she would not speak to them. It was nothing personal, Lyn said, but she had her reasons for not wanting to talk to them.

While Lyn sat in a succession of fluorescent-lit interrogation rooms, law enforcement personnel were scrambling to deal with the prosecutorial conundrum she had created for them. Although there had been presidential assassination attempts in American history—by coincidence, the Capitol Park incident had taken place on the eve of the seventy-fourth anniversary of President McKinley's assassination—no one had ever been prosecuted under the special statute enacted after the murder of President Kennedy. Early in the day, it was unclear whether Lyn was to be prosecuted under state law or federal, whether she was to be investigated by the Sacramento police, the Secret Service, or the FBI.

The task of sorting the case out fell to Don Heller, the young federal prosecutor who had applauded President Ford at the Host Breakfast earlier in the
morning. Summoned to police headquarters, Heller found his mind drifting back
to the day President Kennedy was shot, and the chaos that followed in Dallas.
Heller had been a college student then; now, he was the lead attorney in the
middle of the biggest political crime of the 1970s. His immediate concern was
preventing Lyn from asserting what he assumed would be her best defense:
insanity. To that end, he had ordered the blood tests, the psychiatrists, and, more
important, the videotaping of Lyn's behavior.

For procedural reasons, Lyn's state of mind was key to the future of the
prosecution, and perhaps to the career of the prosecutor. Under federal rules, the
government had the burden of proving a defendant's sanity if the accused raised
an insanity defense; under California law, however, the burden fell on the defendant to prove her insanity. The difference in the burden of proof could be
the difference between a conviction or an acquittal. Heller realized that if Lyn
were allowed to claim insanity, state prosecutors could be given the honor of
putting Squeaky Fromme away.

Lyn's calm, sometimes forceful demeanor persuaded Heller that she was, legally anyway, sane. With the suspect in custody, and clearly uncooperative, Heller
turned his attention to the other issues before him. First, he had to check which
law covered the crime of attacking the president. Federal authority derived from
Title 18, Section 1751 of the United States Code, which made it a crime to kill,
kidnap, or attempt to kill the president, the vice president, or their legitimate
successors. Surprisingly, Heller discovered that the statute specified the FBI—
not the Secret Service—as the investigating agency.

The FBI agent who sat in on Lyn's interrogation, Hiram L. Latham, was just
learning the same thing. He telephoned his superiors to report on the less than
illuminating interview, and was told, "By the way, you're in charge of the case."

Latham, who went by his middle name, Lee, had just turned thirty. He had
joined the FBI in 1969, after concluding that law enforcement paid better than
teaching history in East Texas. A tall, burly man, Latham was both a sharp
criminal investigator and a skillful player of the bureaucratic shuffle. To make
sure he ended up on the West Coast, he had listed his preferred assignments as
San Francisco, Seattle, and San Diego. The FBI, he calculated, would reflexively
decline his first choices and send him to Portland, Oregon, or Sacramento.

Now, Latham sat down with Heller to plan the investigation. They sifted
through the materials seized from Lyn's person when she was arrested. She was
carrying an eclectic assortment of things, ranging from a periodic table to a
picture postcard of Pope Paul VI in St. Peter's Square, his face crossed out with
an X. She had on her a driver's license, a Social Security card, $11.76 in cash,
and a twenty-five-cent food-stamp credit slip. A line drawing, perhaps by Lyn,
suggested a critical view of sexual relations: it showed a man making love to a

woman in the missionary position, the man unable to see that the woman rested against a detonator attached to dynamite under the bed. If the man were to press against his lover, the bed presumably would explode.

Of greater interest to the authorities was the collection of photos, correspondence, and notebooks Lyn also carried in her red purse. The lawmen quickly examined them, looking for evidence of a conspiracy. The notebook contained drafts of various Manson news releases, along with mutterings about the "SLA fire," to-do lists, and addresses for reporters and various government officials. Much of the notebook reflected Lyn's thoughts about Charlie's predicament, from questions to pose to the Corrections Department ("Does he [Manson] have to wear handcuffs to the shower?") to a list of the three Supreme Court justices who dissented in the *Faretta* case, concerning a defendant's right to represent himself in court.

Unfortunately, Lyn's discursive letters to Mary Brunner and other Family members made little sense to investigators. One of her dispatches, however, included a clue about her thinking: "I've been living in the happy little world of Squeak . . . [but] if losing my innocence means realizing my responsibility for the whole thing—" she wrote, trailing off. Then she seemed to speculate about her future: ". . . maybe it's in the nut house."

Heller and Latham focused on nailing down the extent of the plot to assassinate the president. They were eager to search Lyn's apartment, and under the doctrine of exigent circumstances, might even be able to do so without a warrant; after the murder of Robert Kennedy, a warrantless search of Sirhan Sirhan's home had been upheld by the California Supreme Court.

Nonetheless, the authorities decided not to risk the chance that a federal judge might exclude evidence taken without a warrant. Since Lyn's apartment had been sealed, and guards were posted at the various approaches to the building, Latham decided the evidence was probably safe. He and his Secret Service counterpart, Jim Gavin, began typing affidavits for a search warrant to present to a federal magistrate.

Elsewhere at police headquarters, Secret Service Agent Tom McCarter was examining Lyn's pistol, trying to determine its model and serial numbers. Fellow agent Tom Grant came by, and noticed that the clip was still inserted into the weapon. He told McCarter to remove the clip, and as he did so, McCarter said he thought there might be a round jammed in the chamber.

Grant took the pistol from McCarter and backed up against the wall. Aiming the weapon toward the opposite side of the room, Grant grabbed the slide and slowly pulled it back, until the chamber was fully exposed. There was no round inside. Later forensic analysis indicated that the weapon, while operational, had not been fired in some time; the bore was filled with dust.

The officers gave Lyn a cup of coffee, and with Detective Walker in the front seat, drove her to the federal courthouse, four blocks away on Capitol Mall. Although Lyn's sedan was unmarked, photographers easily spotted it as the third car in a heavily armed four-car caravan, and close-ups of the defendant in the backseat were flashed around the world.

Arriving at the sterile, 1960s Federal Building, Lyn entered the custody of the stocky, ever-smiling U.S. marshal, Arthur F. Van Court. Federal marshals were patronage appointees of the president, and some who received the post spent their time behind a desk, leaving the field work to the sworn, civil service deputy marshals. Not Art Van Court, who prided himself on never sending a deputy to take a risk he wouldn't face himself. A twenty-year veteran of the Los Angeles Police Department, where he had been a founding member of an elite squad that hunted down violent criminals, Van Court headed security for Barry Goldwater's 1964 Republican presidential campaign, and then served as security chief for Governor Ronald Reagan. Although Van Court was willing to perform politically tinged assignments—among them the investigation of reputed homosexuals in Reagan's administration—he loved the hands-on work of law enforcement. When Richard Nixon won the White House in 1968, Van Court, as solid a Republican as he was a lawman, was the natural choice to head up the federal marshal's office in Sacramento.

After learning he would be taking charge of Lyn, Van Court called his wife at home. Marcia Van Court often assisted her husband in handling female prisoners.

"Don't ask any questions," Van Court said. "Bring the van, and all the red dresses you have." Marcia gathered three red dresses and hurried to the Federal Building.

If there was a conspiracy to assassinate the president, Art Van Court feared that other plotters might try to rescue Lyn Fromme—or kill her, to prevent her from implicating others. With Lyn suddenly notorious for her red robe, Van Court planned to confound potential ambushers by sending three decoy Squeakys on the next leg of Lyn's journey. Marcia Van Court and the female workers in the marshal's office would be the decoys.

"Remember Oswald and Ruby?" Van Court told his wife as he explained his plan.

"Thanks a lot," Marcia grumbled, her thoughts turning to Lee Harvey Oswald's pained expression when shot dead by Jack Ruby. But Marcia determined that her dresses were too dissimilar to Lyn's robes to fool anyone. The red wardrobe would remain on the marshal's doorknob for the rest of the day.

Van Court put extra deputies on patrol in the courthouse hallways, and restricted attendance at the arraignment to reporters whose credentials could be verified. "I don't want any Lee Harvey Oswalds around here," he repeated. A man named James Michael Clair, whom the FBI later said was a boyfriend of Lyn's, tried to enter the courtroom. He was taken away by FBI agents for questioning, and later released without further incident.

Outside the air-conditioned Federal Building, the temperature had climbed to its midday high of 104 degrees. Lyn, beginning to weary in the midst of her busy day, spoke briefly with her new attorney, Federal Public Defender E. Richard Walker. Then, surrounded by more than a dozen officers, the expressionless defendant was brought into the small courtroom of federal magistrate Esther Mix. Representing the government was the U.S. Attorney, Dwayne Keyes, who only hours before had shared a table at the Host Breakfast with Secret Service Agent Larry Buendorf.

After the charges were read, Judge Mix asked Lyn if she had a statement to make before bail was set.

Lyn, now slumped in her chair, uttered a barely audible "No."

Keyes asked that Lyn be held in lieu of $1 million bail, the highest ever sought in the Eastern District of California and four times the amount set for Sirhan Sirhan after his arrest for the murder of Robert Kennedy. Judge Mix immediately granted the government's request. Lyn gasped; some observers saw her tremble.

Then, at Walker's request, the magistrate continued the proceeding until Thursday, September 11. Lyn was quickly ushered from the courtroom to the Sacramento County Jail, which held the contract to house federal prisoners awaiting trial. The harried booking officer, never having logged in a suspect accused of Lyn's crime, consistently misspelled her alleged offense as attempt to "assasinate" the president. With equal confusion, he listed Lyn's AKA as "Sqeky," and ordered that she be kept separate from all other prisoners and be denied telephone calls. The intake form identified Lyn as an escape risk, but the boxes next to "Homosexual," "Emotionally Disturbed," and "Violent" were left blank. Her suicide risk was evaluated as unknown.

Lyn was not wholly uncooperative, and did give some information when requested. The jailer dutifully completed the form: "In Case of Emergency," he wrote, "Call 'Sandy,' 442–5281." Lyn was relieved of her remaining possessions—at this point, five barrettes and a black-stone ring—and forced to trade her red nun's robes for the blue denim uniform of a female inmate. The jailers placed her in a steel-barred cell, under round-the-clock supervision by a woman deputy. At suppertime, Lyn turned down spaghetti with meat sauce, dining instead on coleslaw.

The Search

With little ceremony, Judge Mix had issued the search warrants Lee Latham requested, directing agents to enter Lyn's apartment, Heather's apartment, and the red VW to seize "maps, bullets, weapons, plans, and other instrumentality of the crime of attempted murder of the President of the United States."

It was after six, but the air was still unpleasantly thick and sticky when a fleet of government cars pulled up to 1725 P Street. Dozens of reporters and residents, who had been milling about for hours in anticipation of police action, eagerly turned to watch what *Washington Post* correspondent Jules Witcover would describe as "one of the most open, well-publicized searches for evidence in the annals of American jurisprudence."

Assistant U.S. Attorney Don Heller was present to oversee the multi-agency force that would dissect Lyn's residence. Before allowing the FBI in, Heller himself entered each of the apartments, bringing along a Secret Service agent and a police photographer to record the premises' condition prior to the search. When Heller emerged, FBI agents divided into three teams. In a nod to the rival agencies present, each squad included an officer from the Secret Service and the Sacramento Police Department.

Within minutes of one another, the teams went into action. One group entered Lyn's garret and another Heather's basement apartment, while the third turned its attention to Lyn's Beetle. An agent smashed the car's window and began sorting through inside, discovering, among other items, two tennis racquets, clothes, blankets, and a textbook entitled *Questions and Answers About Criminal Law*. With television cameramen recording his every action, the agent concluded that the materials were not incriminating. He carefully put them back in the car. Agent Latham later recalled receiving a bill from Sandra for the broken window, and paying her $35 for the repair.

A few minutes after the car search, Heather, barefoot and wearing tan corduroy pants, wandered up to the building, bringing a bag of groceries. She chatted amiably with the reporters and neighbors, insisting that neither she nor Sandra had known in advance of Lyn's encounter with President Ford.

What about Manson? someone asked.

"I believe in him. I believe he's honest," she said.

A reporter followed up: "Is he God?"

Heather hesitated. "Yes," she said. "He is." She sat down on the lawn and took a swig from a carton of buttermilk.

Sandra had by now arrived, wearing a red-hooded reverse swastika cassock. Like Heather, Sandy had been released from custody earlier in the day—after President Ford had left Sacramento. In the hours since, Sandy had been pleased to find herself again in the spotlight, as journalists from the world over turned to her to explain her roommate's actions. Sandy seized the moment to extol Lyn's character, as well as to propound the work of the International People's Court of Retribution. She tailored the message to her audience. She warned a Canadian reporter, for example, to "tell your prime minister to stop killing seals and whales or he will be assassinated."

Her house now occupied by FBI agents, Sandra stopped outside to greet her neighbors. Reporters and law officers quickly crowded around her, and once again she became the focus of attention. Clutching a paperback titled *Air and Water Pollution*, Sandy knelt on the lawn and the news cameras rolled.

She said she was "shocked" by events in Capitol Park. The "assassination of Ford won't stop anything," she observed. "We need whole new thoughts."

Don Heller, accompanied by police lieutenant Robbie Waters, began firing questions at Sandy. Was Lyn troubled, unstable, paranoid?

"Lyn is fine. She's concerned about the survival of this planet. She's concerned about the children," Sandra said. "Paranoid? Psychologically, she's fine," the red-hooded roommate assured the crowd. "She's super-sane."

Heller asked Sandy if Lyn had acted strangely the previous night.

Lyn had been "just a little more tired," Sandy said. "A little more aware of the problems." She recalled how the two women had wept about the destruction of the earth. "I guess this morning [Lyn] thought the time for tears was over."

Where did Lyn get the gun?

Sandy said she didn't know, but they had lots of friends who could have guns and know how to use them.

Had Lyn said anything threatening about President Ford?

"No."

Was it wrong to kill?

"I don't believe in killing, myself," Sandy said. "You should take the guns out of the hands—"

"So why did she do it?" Waters interjected.

"You'll have to ask her," said Sandy.

"Does Manson believe in killing?"

"Why don't you talk to him?"

"Do you think killing is a solution?"

"What do you think?" Sandy said. "Are you going to continue to let them pollute the air?... The big, big money people are allowing it to go on. Ford knows it and he's not doing anything about it. We are beyond the point of anger. We have been trying to wake you people up for five years."

Lieutenant Waters received a progress report on the search, and called Sandy aside to question her in private. She voiced her answers loudly enough for the onlookers to hear.

"Did you find anything else interesting?" she said, smiling. "Listen," she added, "why did you break into the car? The keys were right on the table." She then returned to the crowd of reporters, assuring them she would wait outside until investigators finished "ransacking the house."

Was Sandy sorry Lyn hadn't shot the president?

"I'm only sorry if Lynette is sorry," Sandy said.

Had Manson suggested an attack on Ford?

"No, orders didn't come from him," Sandy said. "I read every word he writes. I know he's darn mad at Nixon for what he's done to the people." She repeated the Family's complaint that Charlie sat in jail because Nixon had proclaimed him "guilty" before the trial had ended. Along those lines, she noted with irritation that Nixon, who had received a full pardon from Ford before he was even indicted, remained at large. "Every law was broken to put Manson in prison," Sandy said. "Nixon was freed. The world is falling apart."

Was Manson mad at Ford?

"He never said it. [Ford] is just a robot. An empty-headed robot." Ford was unimportant. What mattered was Lyn and the reasons for her act. And now that Lyn was in jail, Sandy reflected, "all the weight of the world is on my shoulders." She sat down on the lawn next to Heather, and peeled a banana for a snack.

Lee Latham had expected Lyn's home to be a dump, a filthy hippie crash pad. Instead, he found a tidy, even spare little apartment, organized not for tripping but for work. The only obvious indication of the sinister element, Latham noted, was the small portrait of Manson hanging on the wall, along with photos of other Family members.

The women were avid readers, agents soon discovered. There were books like *The Prison Business*, a manuscript entitled "My Experiences with the SLA," and countless articles clipped from both mainstream publications and the underground press—including a *Time* article on the Maharaj Ji and a cover story on the dangers of aerosol propellant from *New Times*. There was a pamphlet from the Environmental Protection Agency, which prominently displayed a quotation: "The nineteen-seventies absolutely must be the years when America pays its debt to the past by reclaiming the purity of its air, its waters and our living environment. It is literally now or never." The speaker was President Richard M. Nixon, quoted on January 1, 1970.

Elsewhere in the apartment, one agent found an embroidered vest, another a doll Manson had made in prison and sent to the women. There were dozens upon dozens of letters from Manson Family members, a letter addressed to the LAPD Homicide Bureau, and a reel-to-reel videotape of a television interview of Manson. Among the huge number of papers, notebooks, and folders containing Lyn's writings were a couple of manuscripts, one called "Inside Out," by Lyn Fromme and Sandra Good, the other "Burning Is the End." The women were found to have $290 cash, kept in a gray knit purse, along with some American Express traveler's checks signed by Sandra.

They also collected knives, most made by the Manson Family's favorite manufacturer, Buck Knives, Inc. And, while Sandra had claimed to know nothing about Lyn's pistol, agents recovered plenty of firearms paraphernalia, including a brown leather cartridge belt, a .38 caliber Smith & Wesson cartridge, a gun registration pamphlet, and a manual, *The Modern Handgun*, which had a chapter on the .45 automatic. In the bathroom, agents found a brown paper bag containing .45 caliber ammunition. The package was partially empty; agents could surmise where four of the cartridges were.

More surprising was the discovery made in Heather's basement single. Agent Bill Carpenter was looking through a carton marked as containing "Feather River Canyon Drinking Water" when he came across a set of pink envelopes. He opened one and read a letter he later recalled as declaring something like "Stop killing the earth or we'll kill you." Nearby, in boxes that originally contained avocados and butane cartridges, Carpenter found hundreds of similar letters, addressed to different corporate executives, filed carefully by state.

A few feet away, Agent Wade Plucker made a similar discovery inside a green canvas bag marked "Starting Point, Inc." The hundreds, perhaps thousands, of letters were organized by the addressee's location in the United States; green nylon bags were marked "Sacto," "S.F.," "North," "South," "Midwest," "East" and "West." Plucker showed Latham what he had found: the letters, most stamped with the reverse swastika and the initials IPC, screamed threats about "steel-toothed dogs of the IPCR" and a mysterious vigilante killer named Crazy Horse Manson, Jr.—"he can make your *bedroom a butcher* shop if you ask him to by killing or destroying any part of my family of air, water, land and wildlife," one letter advised. Latham decided to seize all the letters, along with the women's telephone and personal address directories, their sewing supplies, record albums, prayer beads, and their collection of rubber bands. Agents even took one of Heather's greeting cards, decorated with the popular "Smile" logo.

All in all, the agents hauled thousands of items from the the property of Lyn and her friends. It took two station wagons and a sedan to carry the evidence away. Lee Latham, now conducting the biggest investigation of his career, was, in his own words, "hyper." He couldn't get to sleep that night, and decided to relieve his nerves by taking a four-mile jog around his suburban Sacramento neighborhood in the early morning hours.

Michael Davies had been driving home from school when he heard a report of the Ford incident on the radio. Stopping at the corner grocery store, he came upon a squad of FBI agents asking passers-by if they knew Lynette Fromme. When Davies mentioned his acquaintance with Lyn, agents were immediately interested. They accompanied him home, where they queried him about his relationship with the women of P Street. Davies was forthcoming, except on one point: He said nothing about the letter-writing project he had been helping with.

At about seven-thirty, Davies walked over to P Street and saw Sandy and Heather amid the crowd outside. Sandy smiled and grabbed Davies's arm. "I'm glad you're here," she said, apparently having forgiven him for the failings she had enumerated the night before. Davies, uncomfortable, decided to return home until the crowd dissipated.

Morris Willmarth had been working at the tomato juice cannery when word of the events in Capitol Park began to filter through. He overheard two co-workers speculating on the aftermath of the president's assassination in Sacramento.

Willmarth scoffed. "I don't think anyone's going to try to kill the President here in Sacramento," he said.

"But someone just did," came the reply. It was "a girl"—somehow connected to the Manson Family.

Willmarth immediately knew who it was, and shivered. He had stopped by P Street the night before and caught the drift of the pained, angry conversations. When Willmarth got off work, he immediately cashed his paycheck and had the first of many beers he would down that day. What had Lyn done? The young man was shattered.

At 9:30 P.M., Willmarth, by now in tears, went with Davies to check on their friends. The two were heatedly discussing the day's events as they approached the scene, still "complete chaos" to Willmarth, with police in the basement and reporters hovering everywhere for quotes. Heather would later say that Willmarth was staggering drunk, and that he had to be helped as he walked up the stairs.

Sandy was irritated at what she saw as the men's juvenile behavior. "Fellows," she told them, "you should be brothers. This is no time to be bickering. A woman just gave her life for the balance of this earth." When Willmarth and Davies wouldn't stop, she sternly commanded, "Now cut that out!"

Willmarth turned to Sandy. Why, he asked, had Lyn committed such a "futile, stupid" act? Didn't she realize how far it would set back the cause they all believed in? "She couldn't possibly accomplish as much being incarcerated as she could being out."

"She has been producing constantly to no avail," Sandra retorted. All Lyn's peaceful work, all her efforts at persuasion simply "didn't do any good."

But Willmarth wasn't even listening. He kept crying, muttering to himself, "Why did she do it? Why?"

Sandra grew impatient. "Get ahold of yourself," she told him. "She's my dearest friend and you are reacting 10,000 times more than I am."

As the authorities began to wrap up their search, Sandra decided that the group should take a walk. The evening air still moist, the four headed down P Street to Sixteenth, then over toward the Capitol. Sandra made sure to circle the block, carefully scouting to see if anybody was still watching her house. The group eventually returned to P Street, and Willmarth carried Lyn's belongings from her car—with the window smashed, it wouldn't be safe to leave them there overnight—up to the apartment.

While they were out, they missed a television program that would have fascinated Lyn. According to UPI, CBS News' *The Guns of Autumn* examined the American hunting culture, using "blood-curdling living color" to document "the slaughter of wildlife by men and women who do not so much hunt animals as execute them." Because the news report depicted the killing of black bear, birds, deer, buffalo, and exotic animals, the network advised parental discretion.

At about ten-thirty, Lyn's friends reconvened in the P Street kitchen. Willmarth sat glumly, while Davies examined the inventory list left by the FBI, and

Sandy and Heather inspected the apartment to see what was missing. Heather went downstairs to check her own room, and soon returned carrying a box.

"Look, Blue," she said to Sandra. "They forgot to take these. They didn't take these."

The box was filled with pink envelopes, nearly two hundred of them. Their contents were similar to those seized by the FBI: warnings from the International People's Court of Retribution.

Sandra seemed puzzled. "I wonder why they didn't take these," she said. "Shall I mail them? Shall we mail them, Heather? What should we do with them?"

It would be necessary to mail them, the women decided, because the FBI could return at any moment. If possible, the letters should be sent from somewhere other than Sacramento. Sandra thought it best if they were postmarked in the Bay Area; unfortunately, she said, she now would be too busy to perform the errand herself. Would Davies be willing to drive to San Francisco tomorrow and mail the letters?

Davies agreed. "I've got some friends in Berkeley, I'll go see them," he said. "I could use a vacation."

The women handed Davies two manila envelopes full of the pink letters, along with another envelope containing some of the address lists the FBI had overlooked. Davies was to keep that list in his apartment, in case authorities came back to pick up what they missed. Then Sandy gave Davies five dollars to pay for his gas.

Willmarth went downstairs to his apartment and fell asleep. Davies returned home and looked at the letters. His suspicions about the true purpose of the women's activities had been building for weeks, and Lyn's sensational action in Capitol Park only heightened them. He decided to open one of the letters; after reading it, he resolved to call the FBI.

Aftermath

President Ford had determined to continue with his September 5 schedule as normally as possible. Following his meeting with Governor Brown, the president went on with the planned calls on legislative leaders.

At 11:34 A.M., Governor Brown, standing at the assembly podium before a joint session of the legislature, declared, "It's really a pleasure to introduce the President of the United States." The legislators gave Ford a standing ovation, and the president delivered his speech, sticking exactly to the prepared text. "Peace on Tenth Street in Sacramento is as important to the people who walk and work there as peace in the Sinai Desert," Ford said, his words taking on special meaning in light of the morning's events. "One man or woman or child becomes just as dead from a switchblade slash as from a nuclear missle blast. We must prevent them both."

As the president spoke, an unidentified woman telephoned the UPI bureau in San Francisco to say that a sixty-pound bomb had been placed in the Capitol and would explode at 11:55 A.M.—smack in the middle of Ford's address. Security officers frantically searched the building, but Ford ignored the threat, completing his speech a minute behind schedule at 12:06. No bomb was found. At 12:18, another woman called Sacramento's Channel 10 to say that "this dude is at Sixteenth and J streets, with a shotgun and he's going to make a try at the President. I'm scared to death but at least I tried," she said, and hung up. Secret Service agents rushed to Sixteenth and J, but found no dude with a shotgun.

Meanwhile, a massive law enforcement effort had rolled out to trace the extent of the presidential assassination plot. Outside the Capitol, Sacramento police roped off thirty square yards around the spot where Lyn had been apprehended, and searched in vain for a dropped cartridge. Later, a technician covered the grounds with a metal detector, followed by an officer who used a hand shovel to dig up suspicious items. All he found were lost coins.

Across the country, tipsters deluged law enforcement agencies with reports of encounters with Squeaky Fromme, real and imagined. An Ohio man told investigators he recently had seen Lyn at a Greek restaurant in Cleveland, and overheard her making a threat against President Ford. News agencies scrambled for copies of letters Lyn had sent them, while police departments around the state pulled out their Manson Family files for transmittal to federal agents. Authorities in Sonoma County, where James Willett had been murdered by the A.B. men, announced that Lyn was wanted for skipping a $35 traffic ticket. At the Secret Service, an intelligence officer was assigned to plumb Bugliosi's *Helter Skelter* for clues about the suspect, and quickly drafted a book report for his superiors.

Meanwhile, government agents had determined the legal owner of Lyn's pistol. An FBI car headed out to the Mother Lode, looking for the man intelligence reports identified as Squeaky Fromme's sugar daddy.

Despite the early excitement of his relationship with Lyn, Manny Boro had begun to develop misgivings about his young friend. He muttered to his daughter-in-law, Nelda, that maybe it was time to get away from Lyn, that she was asking for too much money, that sometimes she scared him. Nelda surmised that Lyn was no longer giving Manny sex.

On Friday afternoon, Manny was out at his Gold Country ranch, while his son Charles had just gotten home from work. Charles and Nelda answered a knock at the door, and were greeted by two FBI agents. To Nelda, the well-groomed officers in their tailored suits were striking, handsome men, attractive in a way rarely seen in rugged Amador County.

Charles, however, was unimpressed. When the agents flashed their badges, he sneered, "You can get one of those in any dime store." Charles refused to let the men into the house.

The agents reacted politely, but insisted they really were from the FBI. They asked if the Boros had heard of the day's assassination attempt. Nelda and Charles had.

"Were you aware," an agent continued, "that the gun used belonged to Harold Eugene Boro?"

Charles's eyes widened. He invited the FBI men into the house. In the kitchen, the agents began questioning the Boros about the Sacramento incident, to little result. Minutes later, Manny walked in through the back door. He had spent the day among the cows up on his ranch and had heard nothing.

"Well," said Charles, "here's my dad now."

"Are you Harold Boro?" an agent said.

"Yes," said Manny, somewhat perplexed.

Charles interrupted: "My God, Dad, what the hell is going on with this broad? This broad *used your gun!*"

Nelda tried to moderate. "These are federal agents, Manny. They're here over this thing in Sacramento. They're here to talk to you about Squeaky."

Manny paled in terror. "Oh my God," he whispered, all but passing out. Nelda thought he looked like he was about to die.

The FBI agents took over the proceedings, separating the Boros into different rooms. One agent stayed with Manny in the kitchen.

Nelda told the FBI all she knew about Lyn and Manny, except for the more intimate details of their relationship. To Nelda, the questioning seemed to last an eternity.

After finishing his business at the state Capitol, President Ford returned to the Senator Hotel, traveling this time by armored limousine. At 12:46 P.M., the president made a statement to the press. Although he had been gamely pressing onward through the day, Ford looked drawn and deadly serious under the harsh television lights.

"Let me say very emphatically that I think the Secret Service and the other law enforcement agencies that were on the job were doing a superb job," the president began, his monotone so deliberate as to sound almost robotic.

"I also wish to express to the people of California my gratitude for the warm, very warm welcome that they have given me in the State of California. I would not, under any circumstances, feel that one individual in any way represented the attitude on the part of the people of California. I just thank the Californians for being so friendly and so hospitable.

"Let me end, with great emphasis, this incident, under no circumstances, will prevent me or preclude me from contacting the American people as I travel from one state to another and from one community to another. In my judgment, it is vitally important for a President to see the American people, and I am going to continue to have that personal contact and relationship with the American people. I think it is vital, and I intend to carry it out."

"Mr. President," a reporter asked, "can you tell us what you saw or felt personally at the time?"

"I am not sure that I ought to describe what I saw beyond the fact that I saw a hand coming up behind several others in the front row and, obviously, there was a gun in that hand. I then saw almost instantaneously very quick and very effective action by the Secret Service in taking care of that matter."

"What was your own thought, sir?"

"Well," Ford said, "I was very thankful. I was very thankful to the Secret Service for doing a superb job, but once I saw that they had done it, I thought I better get on with the rest of the day's schedule. Thank you very much."

The president then walked back to his hotel suite, accompanied by aides already evaluating the political impact of the incident. Donald Rumsfeld speculated that Ford's popularity might rise, much as it had with the *Mayaguez* affair earlier in the year, when the president had ordered the military rescue of an American vessel seized by Communist Cambodia. Press secretary Nessen suggested that Ford's apparent brush with death would create a wave of sympathy for the president. Ford listened more than he spoke, but agreed that, politically at least, the encounter with Squeaky Fromme could turn out to be helpful. He then had lunch with a delegation of Republican Party leaders from Nevada.

Meanwhile, across the nation and around the world, news of the incident was striking a nerve.

In Washington, First Lady Betty Ford had been in her second-floor study, a comfortable room with views of the capital city's monuments, when word came. Her telephone conversation was interrupted by Richard Keiser, the head of the White House Secret Service detail, who so resembled President Ford that he was often mistaken for him.

Keiser first assured Mrs. Ford that her husband was safe, then told her what had happened. It was 1:34 P.M., Eastern time, twenty-six minutes after the incident and fourteen minutes after the ABC and CBS television networks had broadcast the news from Sacramento. Another agent went to the third floor of the White House to notify the Fords' two unmarried sons, nineteen-year-old Steve, and Jack, twenty-three. The Ford sons rushed downstairs to comfort their mother, but found her calm and assured.

Mrs. Ford released a statement observing that assassination attempts are "just something you have to live with" when you are the First Family. Vice President Rockefeller, visiting Rochester, New York, was asked by reporters if it was safe for both him and Ford to be away from Washington at the same time. "It's a big country," he said gruffly, "and we're both in the country." Asked his first reaction to the news from Sacramento, Rockefeller said it was "Thank God the President is all right."

The president was indeed all right. By his afternoon return flight to Washington, Ford was joking with his aides about the incident and, as a memento, autographing copies of the advance plan for the walk to the state Capitol. Wearing his blue presidential windbreaker and an open-necked white sport shirt, Ford puffed on his pipe and chatted casually with the reporters on the plane.

The president finally arrived home at 10:50 P.M., Eastern time. The presidential helicopter, *Army One*, landed on the South Lawn of the White House, and Ford emerged to a round of applause from the fifty-odd relatives and officials who had come to greet him—including Attorney General Edward H. Levi, national security assistant Brent Scowcroft, and Alan Greenspan, chairman of the Council of Economic Advisers. Mrs. Ford gave her husband a bear hug, and Steve and Jack, both clad in blue jeans and T-shirts, threw their arms around their father's shoulders. After a second kiss from Betty, the president smiled and said, "Gee, it's good to be home."

Two White House secretaries hoisted hastily lettered cardboard signs—WELL DONE, AGENTS, read one, ESPECIALLY GOOD TO HAVE YOU HOME, read another—and Ford paused to offer appropriate remarks.

"We had a great trip—just a fraction of a second or two kind of distorted things," he said. "Everything else was superb." Ford felt it necessary to assure Californians again that he didn't hold the episode against them. "I wouldn't under any circumstances let one individual's effort undercut the warmth of what we felt in California," he said.

The incident may have lasted only a fraction of a second, but its aftermath would be of longer duration. For many Americans, the sudden prospect of losing Ford crystalized their affection for the nation's leader, even though he had not received a single vote for president. As a newspaper editorial from Salem, Oregon, put it, "in the emotional aftershock . . . comes the full realization of how important President Gerald Ford and his family have become to their countrymen, regardless of political persuasion." The *Baltimore Sun* lamented, "the handgun that failed to shoot President Ford none the less damaged everyone. How much worse if it had gone off." Said Howard K. Smith of ABC News, "No single event of the year has been so chilling as the apparent attempt on the President's life . . ."

Already, the first of thousands of telegrams, letters, greetings cards, gifts, and telephone calls were flooding the White House, expressing concern for the welfare of the president. One of the earliest to arrive was a handwritten note from Ford's predecessor. Richard Nixon, then living at his former western White House, the San Clemente estate known as Casa Pacifica, made no public statement about the events in Sacramento, even as his own security detail was reinforced. To Ford, however, he wrote: "You handled the incident with superb poise and calm courage. And Betty's comments were also right on the mark. Pat joins me in sending our best. R. N."

Shortly after writing his note, Nixon went to play golf on a San Clemente green. As usual, he waved at the attractive young woman whose home overlooked the golf course, and she waved back. Neither Nixon nor his Secret Service squad knew much about the woman; she was the former Nora Lynn Stevens, who had once been Lynette Fromme's best friend.

Foreign leaders and their ambassadors quickly chimed in with their best wishes. Telegrams arrived from the famous and the obscure alike, sent by figures ranging from U.N. Secretary-General Kurt Waldheim to the premier of tiny Antigua, a British colony in the Caribbean.

The Soviet leader, Leonid Brezhnev, sent the Politburo's felicitations. "My colleagues and I feel indignant at the attempt on your life," he wrote. "We are deeply relieved that this criminal act failed and you are unhurt."

Some foreign leaders used the incident as an occasion to remind the president of their own particular interests. The Taiwanese ambassador, still stinging over Nixon's recognition of Communist China, wrote to tell Ford "how happy we feel that you were not hurt in the dastardly attempt on your life by a female fanatic." Ford's composure "was most inspiring and brought great consolation to all the people of the Free World and especially to all Free Chinese," the ambassador added.

Other diplomats went running to their phrase books to find the best word to describe Lynette Fromme and her act. "Dastardly" was the clear favorite, chosen by President Park Chung Hee of South Korea, the Shah of Iran, the president of Liberia, and the Cypriot ambassador, among others. To the ambassador of Honduras, Lyn was "monstrous." Tunisia's president preferred "absurd." "Cowardly," said the ambassador of India. The Italian president favored "deplorable," the Somali ambassador "insane," the Turkish prime minister "treacherous." Emperor Hirohito of Japan condemned Lyn's act as "outrageous," while both the prime minister of Mauritius and the Vatican's apostolic delegate chose "senseless."

The Spanish ambassador, representing Generalissimo Francisco Franco, said behavior like Lyn's "imperils the very foundations of our societies and dampens the sound efforts of mankind toward progress, justice, and better understanding among all men and all nations." The Iranian ambassador had red roses delivered to the White House, and received a thank-you note from Mrs. Ford.

One nation, however, couldn't resist a comment on the behavior of its former colony.

"I hope you will not mind my sending you a personal message to express my heartfelt relief at your escape from the dastardly attempt made on you," wrote British Foreign Minister James Callaghan. "America has been spared yet another self-inflicted wound."

At home, Americans began to sort out the significance of the incident. When the news reached the House of Representatives, Congressman James P. Johnson interrupted a committee meeting chaired by Tom Foley. "Mr. Chairman," the Colorado Republican said, "I think the record should know that for the first time since McKinley, we have a Republican President worth shooting, and I think that's a good sign." Laughter followed.

Friday evening, the Reverend Billy Graham led 35,000 faithful at Lubbock's Texas Tech University in prayer for Ford and his family. The next day, he wrote to remind the president of their last meeting at the White House, where they had discussed Psalm 91:11, "For he shall give his angels charge over thee, to keep thee in all thy ways." In Sacramento, "for a brief moment you stared death in the face," the pastor wrote. "It can happen so quickly. That is why the Scriptures time after time admonish us to live holy and righteous lives, because it is appointed unto man to die—and after that the judgment!"

The Apocalypse aside, Graham offered Ford some reassurance: "I am certain the Lord led President Nixon to nominate you for Vice President. You are exactly the right man in the right place at this moment in American history!"

Prominent citizens were quick to express their concern. Leon Jaworski, the Watergate special prosecutor whose efforts had helped drive Nixon from office, sent his regards to Ford. Petroleum executive Armand Hammer, facing felony charges for making illegal contributions to Nixon's 1972 campaign, told Ford he prayed for him "as you serve America in a time of great difficulty and equally great opportunity." Although Ford sent a "Dear Armand" reply, the president did not intervene in the prosecution, and Hammer entered a guilty plea on October 1.

George Wallace sent a telegram to the president, but neither Wallace nor the White House would reveal its contents; contrary to speculation, it included little that could cause controversy. The Alabamian expressed his relief at Ford's "personal safety" after a "tragic incident," concluding with "God's blessing to you and your family." Ford replied, "I am sure that, better than most, you can understand the depth of my gratitude."

Lyn had finally made an impact on the American psyche. Soldiers stationed around the world wrote Ford to thank him for his inspiring example of grace under fire. Californians apologized to Ford for his unfortunate experience in their state. Clergy of all faiths sent their prayers. Sister Mary Clothilde of San Jose's Holy Family Motherhouse enclosed a list of "astonishing coincidences between Lincoln and Kennedy." Another religious figure, Pat Robertson, showed his concern by booking a purported former Manson Family member on his television program, *The 700 Club*. The woman, identified as the otherwise unknown "Onya Sipe," told Robertson's audience that Lyn was "completely given over to the Devil."

In small towns and large, fraternal lodges, veterans' posts, and sportsmen's organizations all sent the president their best. The Puerto Rican Free Federation of Labor, the West Orange County Board of Realtors, the Consolata Knights Organization of Somerset, New Jersey, the Houston Gulf Freeway Kiwanis Club, and the Women's Aglow Fellowship in Miami wrote of their concern. Sue Benedict of Jackson, Michigan, sent the greetings of her sorority, Beta Sigma Phi; she enclosed "a portion of our closing ritual in hopes that it will give you the strength that it has give to me on many occasions."

Ordinary citizens reached out. Frank Anderson of Chelan, Washington, sent his best, and after describing his German shepherd's health problems, asked for one of the puppies that the Fords' dog, Liberty, was expecting. "P.S.," Anderson wrote, "I want you to know that a dog is more to me than an animal. He is a friend." The president replied that, unfortunately, all the puppies had already been promised. "I know it would be more your friend than just a pet," Ford wrote.

From Ford's hometown, the owner of Grand Rapids Sanitary Supply Company assured the president that "you are always in our prayers" and "that the man in the White House today . . . will go down as the greatest President this country has had to date. . . . Be tough on Communism!" he added.

In Sacramento, V. J. McCambridge sent Ford a greeting card and the Rudyard Kipling poems, "If" and "Recessional." Bret Karr of Martinsville, Illinois, did one better, sending Ford a poem he himself composed in response to Lyn. He titled it, "Don't Shoot Our President." In part, the lengthy elegy read:

You may not like some things he does
And you may feel ignored
But all your troubles won't be solved
By shooting President Ford

But just in case anything should happen to President Ford, several life insurance agents wrote to remind the chief executive of the importance of providing for loved ones. From Shawnee Mission, Kansas, Stephen D. Carrithers and John P. Billingsley conceded that they were "relatively new agents with the Lincoln National Life Insurance Company. . . . We do not profess to be the greatest insurance agents in the industry, but we can offer something no one else can: 100 percent of Pat Billingsley and Steve Carrithers." The president replied that his insurance coverage was adequate.

Nowhere, however, did Lyn's assault have a greater impact than on the elementary schools of America. In classrooms from Media, Pennsylvania, to Mission Hills, California, teachers led discussions with the children over the meaning of the incident in Sacramento. Hundreds then wrote to Ford, although the similarity of many letters suggested they had been copied from a teacher's sample written on the blackboard.

"I'm glad that lady did not shoot you," wrote Tina Evans, a fifth grader from Northport, Alabama. "Our teacher, Mrs. Develle, told us to write this letter. We are all glad you were not shot. Well, that's all I can think of." Few of the children drew conclusions favorable to Lyn. A twelve-year-old from Atlantic City, New Jersey, observed that "it's very disrespectful to try to *kill* a president." And Sue LaFera, age thirteen, of Glen Falls, New York, got right to the point: "I don't think that 'Squeaky' Fromme would at all appreciate it if say Vice President Rockefeller shot or pointed a loaded gun at Charles Manson." Some tried to cheer the president up by sending him gifts. One mailed him a *Peanuts* comic strip, another a dollar bill "to help you get votes." White House staff returned the unsolicited contribution. From Cleveland came a greeting that embodied many of the cultural symbols of the 1970s: the letter was written on a pink sheet of paper with the word "Hello!" splashed across the top in children's script, adorned with a smile sticker and, notably, a string of Pop Rocks, the effervescent candy, taped along the side.

The incident led many Americans to contact the president with concrete suggestions for both government policy and his personal protection. R. M. Stepteau, a public relations consultant in St. Albans, New York, wrote to "Jerry" Ford, feigning friendship with the chief executive "in the hopes that this letter would reach the President personally. . . .

"The office of the President should retain in its services men who closely resemble the President in facial features and other ways, to serve as 'doubles,' so that at least it can be a bit more difficult to ferret out the President as a target. . . . Thus, the game of which is the real Jerry Ford, should serve to amuse, distract and to protect the person of the Chief Executive for his, and the nation's, good."

Most, however, thought the incident underscored the need for gun control. In this they were joined by commentaries in newspapers across the country. The White House announced that the encounter with Lynette Fromme would have no effect on the president's opposition to gun control.

Lyn was on virtually every editorial page in the country, and even around the world. In Moscow, the Communist Party daily *Pravda* opined that "once again, Americans have begun to reconsider the cult of violence ruling the country," while the Soviet youth newspaper *Komsomolskaya Pravda* chided that "each American up to the president continues to live in an atmosphere of uncertainty about his safety. And as before, the most important question remains in the shadows: Where do the Mansons come from?" On the other end of the political spectrum, the conservative *Daily Telegraph* in London condemned Lyn's act and the loose American laws that made guns so widely available—"a blot on the face of the United States," the paper editorialized.

The Fort Worth, Texas, *Star-Telegram* broke tradition and ran a letter to the editor on the front page. "President Ford's courage has sparked fire into my spirit and I see hope for our country in his courage," wrote Ramona Fletcher. "The President has taught me, if just one man can stand and stand strong, then others will follow. This gives me great hope for my country." The editors explained the prominence given to Fletcher's views: "The *Star-Telegram* thought this was such a non-average letter from 'an average American' that it should be moved to Page 1. . . ."

For many pundits, the most disturbing element of the incident was that the apparent victim was as inoffensive a figure as a president could be. Hugh Sidey, *Time*'s White House columnist, was puzzled because Ford was "a really serene man who should not really arouse that kind of passion in anyone." Observed an editorial in the *Boston Globe*, "Gerald Ford cannot be conceived of as a magnet for violence. Affable, open, smiling, relaxed—it is impossible to see him as the target of any sane person's wrath.... That this man could be so seriously threatend is grim comment on the extent to which social values have deteriorated...."

Governor Brown, asked for his comment on the incident, said tersely, "It makes me move a lot faster." In Sacramento, Chief Judge Tom MacBride of the federal district court shrugged, "Well, I suppose that will put Sacramento on the map." And over at San Quentin, Charles Manson had an uncharacteristic reaction. "Oh my God," he said, in a tone prison officials described as "noncommittal and surprised."

Chapter 9

The Gun

Is

Pointed

At the FBI's Sacramento headquarters, Lee Latham set up a command post to oversee the burgeoning investigation, an operation he had code-named (after the principals) "Fromford." As fifteen agents gathered around the office's largest table to go over their assignments, Latham recalled an FBI adage attributed to J. Edgar Hoover: "We not only have to *be* right, we have to *look* right." He assumed the saying actually had been crafted by one of Hoover's image-savvy assistants, but Latham intended to follow it nonetheless. After all, it was nearly fifteen years after Dallas, and people still were second-guessing the JFK investigation. Latham resolved that no clouds of mystery would hang over the Squeaky Fromme case. At the suggestion of one agent, lip-readers were even hired to decode the words Lyn appeared to be mouthing in film shot of her arrest.

Across the country, the investigation rolled forward. Federal agents visited Lyn's parents, now living in Palos Verdes, an upscale suburb south of Redondo Beach. Helen and William Fromme told investigators that Lyn had been under psychiatric care in 1966, but could say little about their daughter since then. Perhaps another visitor to the Fromme condominium, the parish priest, received more frank confessions. Neither he nor the Frommes, however, had anything to say to the public.

Agents interviewed Lyn's sister and brother, while others fanned out to locate members of the Manson Family, in prison and elsewhere. One agent went to Death Valley, and compiled a roster of all Family associates who had passed through in the previous eighteen months. The FBI visited Mary Brunner, Katie, Sadie, and Lulu at the California Institution for Women at Frontera. None seemed to have known in advance of Lyn's action. In Milford, New Hampshire, agents fruitlessly questioned Linda Kasabian, the Tate-LaBianca prosecution's star witness, who now used the name Linda Christian. At San Quentin, the FBI paid a two-hour call on Charles Manson. Manson was willing to discuss his "philosophy," investigators said, but that was all. "This interview was unproductive," an agent tersely reported. Superiors in Washington were advised that, allegedly, "members of the Manson Family use drugs and participated in homosexual and perverted sexual acts."

Meanwhile, reporters pressed jail guards for details of Lyn's behavior behind bars. The suspect, they learned, had turned down the institutional menu of bologna sandwiches and, instead, received peanut butter and jelly, a side of coleslaw, and grape-flavored Kool-Aid. She was spending much of her time watching television, except when she visited the jail's rooftop exercise yard. One guard told a reporter that Lyn was in "good spirits," and had begun to converse casually with her hosts. "Well, you know," a jailer quoted Lyn as saying, "when people around you treat you like a child and pay no attention to the things you say, you have to do something."

Lyn was an obedient prisoner, but she did not intend for her changed circumstances to detract from her work. She wrote a note to the guards, explaining how she differed from the ordinary prisoners in the women's jail.

It is my job to see that the different agencies of our system are aware of what their counterparts are doing, specifically in regard to the preservation of our environment. You may not realize the extent of fact in the saying, 'One hand doesn't know what the other hand is doing' in regard to these agencies—but I have researched the matter & you, yourselves, may be examples of it.

You need a person like me [smiley face] to make sure you are not severed by the thousands of pages of diversified bureaucracy that often completely cover the real issues.

Jail regulations allowed Lyn to send only one page of correspondence per day. She offered to give up that right in exchange for being able to send an unlimited number of postcards. In addition to her "often instantaneous need" to respond to news reports, Lyn said that the matter came down to common courtesy. As one of America's most notorious defendants, she was receiving piles of mail from people who deserved "at least a short reply." Lyn indicated that she would be discreet with her privileges, so that her fellow inmates wouldn't come down with the "'me too' syndrome." Because she had been "pegged to be some sort of revolutionary," Lyn figured the jail might fear her "spreading unhealthy communications." Not so, she insisted. "I do not have blood lust and can see beyond the emotional rebellions" that cause it. More than most, she "understood the terrible consequences of anarchy. . . ."

Besides, Lyn wrote, "unless you can permit me to do my job, I'm going to have to get you to do it, and you don't have the time." She requested "a *small* desk & chair" along with a desk lamp, typewriter and radio. At a minimum, she wanted "a pen or a little pencil sharpener (I don't want to run the officers back and forth sharpening my pencil)."

Despite the thoughtful plea, jail authorities turned her down. When Federal Defender Dick Walker brought the matter before Judge MacBride, something of a compromise was reached. Lyn was granted her pencil sharpener.

At P Street, Sandy Good entertained more visitors from the press. "I don't want Squeaky gone," she told reporters. "I love her.... She's beautiful. She's giving. All she ever does is give.... She does the job none of you have the nerve to do....

"I don't think she ever planned to do Ford," Sandy speculated. "He just happened to be available." Then, under her breath she added: "Fool."

As always, Sandy vigilantly guarded Lyn's reputation. "You newspeople who say she's a drug user," she warned, "you'd better clean that up."

Downstairs, the elderly landlords also vouched for Lyn's character, and Sandy's, too. "They acted like part of the family, almost," Jessie Fain told a reporter. Then, for clarification, he added, "Uh, *our* family, I mean."

Michael Davies had grown less enthusiastic about his dedicated neighbors. On Saturday morning, barely twenty-four hours after Lyn's arrest, he telephoned Leon Brown, an FBI agent he had met outside 1725 P Street the previous afternoon.

"I have something I think the FBI should be aware of," Davies told Brown. At the agent's invitation, Davies drove to the FBI offices on Cottage Way, where he showed Brown two of the pink envelopes franked with the Berkeley seminary's postal permit. Brown, a twenty-five-year FBI veteran, was intrigued. The two went to the parking lot, where Davies fetched from his car a pair of manila envelopes stuffed with the rest of the batch—about 170 pink envelopes altogether.

Law enforcement had never much cared for Sandra Good, and would have been all too happy to file charges against her. Together with Davies's testimony, the threat letters seemed a good basis for a prosecution. Unfortunately, while Davies remembered the iniquitous language used at P Street, he was uncertain which words had been spoken by Lyn, which by Sandy, and which by Heather, and thus his testimony could be taken apart by a defense attorney. Davies volunteered to be a better informant; he would hang around Sandy long enough to report conclusively the unlawful things she was bound to say.

Agent Brown later testified that he tried to discourage Davies from getting "mixed up with people who might be dangerous to him." But Davies was now determined to help put Sandy behind bars, along with Lyn. The P Street women were a danger to society, Davies told Brown. Not only that, they made his friends uncomfortable.

Brown soon concluded that Davies met the FBI's standards for an informant. He asked Davies to keep silent about his visit to the FBI office, to continue his friendship with Sandra Good, and, critically, to keep a detailed diary of her activities over the coming weeks. Davies next saw Sandy and Heather on Sunday, September 7, and acted as if everything was still fine. He told them he had taken the pink letters to Berkeley, and to make it more difficult for the authorities to trace their origin, mailed them from several different locations around the city.

Despite his new role as government informant, Davies had not given the FBI everything he had received from Sandy Good. He kept her mailing lists in his apartment, figuring that sooner or later she'd be at his door demanding them back. Davies was right: Sandy did want them back, with a vengeance. Within days of Lyn's arrest, she dispatched Heather to retrieve the lists, but Davies never seemed to be home when she knocked. The notes Heather left asking for the lists went unanswered. On one occasion, Davies's upstairs neighbor told him that she had heard somebody enter his apartment while he was away and rummage around. Davies never determined the intruder's identity. Finally, Heather managed to catch Davies early one morning as he was rushing out the door to school.

"I want the lists," Heather demanded. Davies told her he was in hurry, but she insisted. Finally, Davies gave in.

When the neighbors mentioned that visits from the friends of Squeaky Fromme disturbed them, Davies made pains to conduct his dealings with Sandy and Heather at their P Street apartment. This made his FBI duties easier, as the women were always at work on the business of the International People's Court of Retribution, clipping articles, writing letters, and updating their files. If Mike Davies came over, they put him to work, too.

"We didn't have time for anybody unless they could be useful to us," Sandy later recalled. "We didn't go out, we didn't party, we didn't have a social life. We made it clear to ... Michael: If you come over, you work."

The visits to P Street gave Davies a chance to further explore the writings of Lyn's friends. He would leaf through the envelopes laying about, taking a particular interest in the cryptic dispatches from Charles Manson. Sandy once snatched a Manson letter from Davies's hands. She eyed him carefully and asked if he were an informer.

"If I was," Davies replied, "I wouldn't be here." Sandy found this answer acceptable.

Morris Willmarth, however, was not so quick as Mike Davies to grasp the implications of the P Street women's project. Although Davies began to confide in Willmarth his misgivings about Lyn and her friends—reading *Helter Skelter* had soured him on the Manson Family—Davies said nothing of his contacts with the FBI. It fell to Sandy to explain to Willmarth the meaning of the International People's Court of Retribution.

"Do you remember the Reign of Terror in France?" she asked Wilmarth, by way of introduction. She continued: "Whenever there is change there often emerges an underground of sophisticated or even not sophisticated"—she paused—"I don't like the word 'sophisticated,'" vanguard to lead the revolution. "We say that their sincerity, their complete sincerity would enable these people to move without mistakes. In other words, their dedication is so strong that there would be no error in their movement. They don't get caught," she explained.

That vanguard was the International People's Court of Retribution. "We say there are people on this earth that are concerned, that do have some soul outside the TV money-minded programming, that they have not been sufficiently brainwashed, that they still have some love for our earth and some concern." These people were "intelligent enough not to be caught blowing up a stupid car or something like that," Sandy told Willmarth. "In other words, when they moved, they moved to kill and they did not make a mistake."

According to Willmarth's testimony, Sandy said the International People's Court of Retribution had one thousand members, every one an assassin dedicated to killing corporate leaders. But this information was hardly top secret; Sandy had been giving press interviews where she identified by name dozens of executives, from such firms as MCA, DuPont, and General Electric, who had been marked for death. When an Associated Press correspondent stopped by P Street, Sandy gave her a list of seventy-nine executives condemned by the International People's Court of Retribution.

By now an expert in dealing with the news media—she had even appeared under "Notable and Quotable" on the *Wall Street Journal*'s editorial page— Sandy made sure to play to local interest. When a New Orleans radio station telephoned for an interview, Sandy focused on victims who lived within the station's broadcast range: six men from Louisiana and East Texas, including an oil man, a candy manufacturer, and the president of a utility company. They would be "terribly, terribly murdered," Sandy warned. Before the executives themselves were killed, she added, their wives would be hacked to death.

To *Detroit Free Press* reporter James Schutze, Sandy played media critic. Apparently confusing Schutze's paper with the *Los Angeles Free Press*, a one-time underground weekly that had devolved into a sex sheet, Sandra asked if the Detroit daily was "like *Screw* magazine or one of those porno papers?"

Schutze insisted that the *Detroit Free Press* was on the up and up. "All right," Sandy continued, not wholly persuaded, "you clean up that paper. I've just been told that it's something of a rag, that you put out those ads for whippings and you know, all that distorted sex...." Then she went on to threaten Michigan corporate executives, including the president of Ford Motor Company, Lee Iacocca. She continued to nurse misgivings about what kind of paper the *Detroit*

Free Press truly was; months later, when Schutze testified in Sandy's conspiracy trial, she cross-examined him about it: "You don't have any ads like the *Berkeley Barb* [which] has an insert where it has ads for a 'Lonely man, 50, wants a gay guy and a woman too'?"

Other correspondents received Sandy's counsel on how to conduct their personal lives. At a news conference she called in the P Street apartment, Sandy lectured the assembled reporters about the coming "wave of assassinations across golf courses and bridge clubs throughout this country. And people in the news media, you better stop lying or you're going to get cut up, too. Your blood is going to be on the walls."

Suddenly, she thrust a wooden crucifix in the face of a young *Newsweek* correspondent, Mary Alice Kellogg.

"You, in your eyeshadow and dyed hair—trying to get your sensational story. Look at this!" Holding the crucifix closer, Sandy continued, "This is you, woman!"

The room was still. Sandy smiled. "I know you're sincere," Sandy said, warmly. "We've all put Charlie on the cross." When Kellogg later covered Lyn's arraignment, the *Sacramento Bee* reported, her face was free of makeup, her blond hair modestly concealed under a plain headscarf.

With behavior like this, many wondered why Sandy was not herself arrested. Prosecutors suggested the problem lay in distinguishing between whether Sandy was threatening people on her own behalf—a criminal act—or merely reporting a threat made by an unrelated third party, which itself would not necessarily be a crime. Pressed for further explanation, Dwayne Keyes demurred. "I don't want to indicate what the problem is because she reads, too," the federal prosecutor said.

The Defense Team

At 9:15 A.M. on Monday, September 8, two investigators from the federal public defender's office signed in to visit Lyn at the Sacramento County Jail. They had come to interview their client, the first step in preparing a defense.

Normally, the big cases would go to the federal defender's chief investigator, Dave Kraft, a former deputy sheriff who still looked, and acted, like a cop. Kraft had met Lyn on the day of her arrest, and the two had not hit it off. Lyn had noted that Kraft's socks were mismatched, and commented unflatteringly on the competence of the federal defender's office. She gave Kraft a nickname that stuck: "Socks."

The federal defender, Dick Walker, decided that things might work better if Kraft did not serve as lead investigator on the Fromme case. Instead, Kraft was assigned to oversee the office's routine matters, while the Fromme case went to a detective hired especially for the job: Philip A. Shelton, who made $100 per day, plus expenses. As Shelton had yet to receive his federal badge, Kraft had to personally escort him into the jail to visit his client.

Phil Shelton was a licensed private investigator, but that was about all he had in common with most detectives. Born in Coeur d'Alene, Idaho, Shelton had come to the Sacramento Valley to study veterinary medicine at the University of California's agricultural campus at Davis. His academic interests shifted, however, and Shelton turned to philosophy, then poetry, zoology, and economics, among other subjects. Now thirty-six, he was still taking courses at UC Davis and Sacramento State University, and teaching part time at Sacramento City College.

Shelton had fallen into detective work as a sideline, and found he had a knack for it. Not only that, he made more money as a private eye than did his friends who were working on graduate fellowships; when Shelton started detective work in 1962, he pulled down an impressive $20 an hour. Shelton reveled in the odd juxtaposition of his interests, highlighting his eccentricities by sporting a Sherlock Holmes pipe, a pocketwatch, and a Vandyke beard. Even his weapons were stylish: a Browning 9 mm and a Walther PP, the longer-barreled cousin of the pistol made famous by James Bond, the PPK.

But Shelton also took into his assignment an unusual sense of purpose. Like most people, he had been stunned by the Ford incident. After getting over the initial horror, however, he felt proud of the tolerance Sacramento had displayed to such an odd-looking creature as Lynette Fromme. While some critics complained that police had been derelict in letting Lyn roam free about the city, Phil Shelton had had the opposite reaction. There she was, he thought, in her Little Red Riding Hood costume, someone clearly out of the mainstream, and yet the legion of police officers in Capitol Park had left her unmolested.

"Law enforcement represents a rather extreme end of our society," the detective later reflected, "and when you see tolerance occurring in that extreme end, you know that quite a bit is happening in society in general. I was kind of proud that she was able to get so close."

When, shortly after the pistol incident, Federal Defender Walker called Shelton onto the case, he felt honored. "I didn't care at the time what the outcome might be," Shelton later said. "I only cared that I had an opportunity to do what I most wanted to do. That is, to make an effort on behalf of someone who was not only powerless but less than powerless and to see if our judicial system was up to it."

Not everyone shared Shelton's view of the nobility of criminal defense, particularly when done on behalf of the Manson Family. Shelton's logic instructor was outraged when he learned his prize pupil was dropping the class in order to help defend Lynette Fromme.

"Why are you muddying your hands with such an evil person?" the instructor demanded. "An obviously guilty person tried to do a despicable act in public," the teacher concluded. That was no reason to hold up one's education.

"Our whole system, the integrity of what we call freedom and justice is tied up in what do we do for the worst among us, not the best," Shelton replied, portentous words that, from him, seemed a beacon of sincerity. Besides, he expected to be done with the case in time to register for the winter quarter.

Whatever high purposes Shelton may have attributed to the defense of Lynette Fromme, the client herself was immediately suspicious of her new advocate. She was suspicious of everyone connected with the criminal justice system, of course, and saw little difference between prosecutors and defense attorneys—particularly public defenders.

She was brought to the jail visiting room, an airless, windowless cubicle with stark fluorescent lights, where prisoners were divided from visitors by a clear plastic separator. Conversation took place through a telephone handset.

Lyn looked exhausted, red-eyed, frightened, when Phil Shelton and Dave Kraft showed up. But she wasn't going to let these strangers take charge of the encounter.

"You're not a detective," she told Shelton. "You're a lawyer, aren't you? In disguise."

"Well," said Shelton, "this is not much of a disguise if I'm a lawyer." He was wearing a dark gray, chalk-striped three-piece suit. "I should have come in dressed as a clown. Then you'd know I was a detective."

Lyn laughed. "Are you a clown?"

"Kind of," said Shelton.

"Well," said Lyn. "I don't like you."

"I think that's to be seen," said Shelton. "You don't know if you like me or not. At the moment, you're stuck with me. I wish it weren't this way, but let's talk for a while and see if we can get anywhere."

"You're not going to understand me," Lyn said. "You will never understand me."

Shelton took up the challenge. He threw questions at her, receiving answers that either were elliptical or polemic, none of which was any use. Then he asked, "If I were a reporter and I had a camera here and I were to ask you, 'Why?' what would you say?"

Lyn answered right away: "For the trees," she said.

Shelton seemed puzzled, so Lyn elaborated. The trees were ancient, she said, many had existed since before Jesus was born. Next to the trees, the human race was insignificant. No other life form was so old.

Shelton disagreed. There was, he believed, a life form as ancient as the redwoods of California: whales. Cetaceans. As Lyn stared, skeptical, Shelton began a discourse on aquatic mammals, explaining how the ancestors of whales probably started in the big ocean bath, emerging from the sea as creodonts, a now-extinct suborder of primitive, flesh-eating mammals, the name derived from the Greek words *kreas*, "flesh," and *odous*, "tooth." "They looked like huge wolves and lived by the edge of the water," Shelton said. But the creodonts found the earth too hard a place to live, and decided to return to the water, eventually evolving into the whales we know today.

"An interesting group of animals," Shelton concluded, "because they *really* chose where they wanted to live."

Shelton's partner, Dave Kraft, was impressed. He didn't even know what a cetacean was, and had hardly expected to learn about them in a jail cell.

Lyn looked interested. But she said nothing. The conversation seemed to have ended. Shelton drew his watch from his vest pocket and checked the time. He stood up.

Lyn stared at the pocketwatch. "May I see that?" she asked.

Shelton held it up for her across the plastic divider. A gift from Shelton's wife, the timepiece with its beautiful pink face could have belonged to Lewis Carroll's March Hare. It seemed to charm Lyn. But after a moment, Shelton snapped the watch shut and thrust it back into his vest pocket. He turned to leave, as if no longer interested in Lyn.

"Wait," Lyn said. "What about the whales?"

Shelton smiled. He sat down.

"Whales," he said. "There are many kinds of whales, huge whales like the blue whale going all the way down to the pilot whale and the mink, but the smallest whales people call dolphins and porpoises."

"Oh, is that right?" said Lyn. "Well, what's the difference between a dolphin and a porpoise?"

"A dolphin has a spade-shaped tooth," Shelton explained. "Like this tooth." He indicated one of his own. "And a porpoise has a cone-shaped tooth, like this tooth. That's the only difference."

"Really?" said Lyn. "So if the whale is related to the dolphin, what is the redwood related to?"

Shelton paused. "The rose," he said.

Lyn's eyes moistened. "I wish I had had your arguments," she said. Had *had* your arguments. She used the past tense.

Shelton continued: "All it takes is a seed, and rain, and the nutrients in the earth to make a redwood, and each redwood looks the same and they are so similar, they are so unerringly similar that they are like timothy."

"Timothy?" said Lyn. "Who's he?"

"No, not a person, the grass. Timothy grass. There's no eight-foot timothy. There is no two-inch timothy. Timothy grows to a certain height unerringly. There is a bell-shaped curve, the bottom of which is the shortest timothy, the middle of which is the average size of timothy, and the top of which is the tallest timothy and the same is true of redwoods and of you and me."

The conversation continued, about the way the earth breathed, about the cycles of oxygenation and the atmosphere's mix of carbon dioxide. Eventually, the time came to end the interview. Shelton said he would return.

"Can we talk about the whales some more?" Lyn asked.

"Sure."

In the afternoon, Dave Kraft returned with a peace offering from the federal defender's office: $50, which could be used to buy sweets in the jail commissary.

Other overtures from the federal defender were less successful. Lyn refused to see two psychiatrists that Walker had sent to examine her, in hopes of preparing an insanity defense.

"I couldn't rely on their opinions when my life is at stake," Lyn explained.

Elsewhere, both sides in the brewing battle between the government and the International People's Court of Retribution continued their quiet preparations. On the government side, FBI agents interviewed Morris Willmarth and began sorting through the boxes of threat letters seized from P Street. Agents continued their effort to track down every person listed in Lyn and Sandy's address books.

Meanwhile, Heather Murphy stopped by the Sierra Copy stationery store to pick up some items ordered a few weeks before: a couple of rubber stamps bearing the name of the International People's Court of Retribution, another shaped like a swastika.

Dick Walker wasn't the only lawyer prepared to defend Lynette Fromme. Daye Shinn, the attorney who represented Sadie at the Tate-LaBianca trial, had flown up from Los Angeles to see if Lyn might require his services. He brought with him a friend and fellow lawyer, Bob Kirste, who in 1970 had met Manson and unsuccessfully sought to represent him. Kirste worked out of the same Crenshaw Boulevard building that Shinn did, and during the Tate trial often found the Manson women floating through his office, casually helping themselves to office supplies and the use of his telephone and photocopier.

Lyn was far more welcoming to Shinn and Kirste than she had been to the federal defender's investigators. She was buoyant and joyful as always, Kirste recalled, "just as though you'd have met her on the street." Of course, Lyn said, she had had no intention of harming the president, but rather of raising the nation's consciousness about the issues that really mattered—like a new trial for Charlie and the other Family members. The authorities' heavy reaction to the pistol incident seemed to surprise her.

"What are they mad about?" Shinn quoted Lyn as saying. "The gun didn't go off."

Lyn also made clear her idea of a proper legal defense. She asked Shinn to prepare papers seeking the right to represent herself in court and, should she be indicted by the grand jury, to seek a change of venue. She would, she said, prefer to be tried in San Francisco.

To Kirste, it seemed that Lyn intended her attorneys to serve less as legal advocates than as errand boys. "That's not," he thought, "why you go to law school."

Authorities did not sense in Lyn the same upbeat demeanor Kirste and Shinn had noticed. In a classification form submitted to the Sacramento County Jail, a federal deputy marshal instructed that Lyn remain separated from other inmates. "Poss. of Attempt Suicide by cutting wrists or any other manner available," the deputy wrote on the form.

After visiting Lyn, Shinn and Kirste paid a call on the P Street apartment. Sandy made them jasmine tea, and they reminisced about old times in Los Angeles, about their mutual friends. Sandy also revisited her usual concerns, outlining the evils of the Establishment and the wrongs being committed by various corporations.

More important, however, were the plans for Lyn's trial. It would be an event many had long awaited, Sandy announced: it would be the reunion of the Manson Family. Shinn and Kirste said nothing as Sandy continued: Lyn planned, she said, to use the court's subpoena power to bring Charlie and every other member of the Family to Sacramento for the trial. This left a critical question to be decided: What color robes did each member of the Family want to wear?

That was where Shinn and Kirste came in, Sandy explained. Could they please find out from the different Family members what colors their robes should be? She needed to know as soon as possible, so the robes could be sewn in time for the trial.

The two lawyers were noncommittal, and bid their farewells.

Shinn, however, was rather outspoken when he talked to reporters about his jailhouse visit with Lyn. Not only did he describe her as being "in fairly good spirits," he revealed what she had told him about plans for her defense, as well as her assertions about lack of intent to kill the president.

Shinn's remarks made front-page news across the country—and incensed Dick Walker. He asked Judge MacBride to issue a gag order preventing comments that could prejudice the jury pool. MacBride complied, posting restrictions perhaps unprecedented in their breadth, not only applying to attorneys and witnesses but also gagging the defendant herself.

Now it was Lyn who objected. Her entire purpose was to reach the world, and a gag order preventing her from talking to the press defeated the whole business. She told Walker to march back into court and get the order lifted. Despite his own concern over what Lyn might say, Walker filed papers contending that the order violated Lyn's "priceless right to speak freely ... only because she happens to be a defendant in a criminal action." Walker knew that judges generally cared less about First Amendment rights than they did the Sixth Amendment guarantee of a fair trial. So, with tongue perhaps in cheek, Walker argued that it was "entirely possible that after hearing the defendant's statements concerning the case ... a member of the public at large might come forward with relevant and meaningful evidence which could be helpful to the defense and promote the interests of justice."

The government disagreed. "To permit Miss Fromme to try her case in the news media would unquestionably result in a serious and imminent threat to the administration of justice and a fair trial," prosecutors argued.

Quickly moving to secure an indictment, U.S. Attorney Dwayne Keyes convened the federal grand jury on Wednesday, September 10. Before the grand jurors could hear the evidence, however, the prosecution's case began to find its way into the press.

Washington columnist Jack Anderson tapped his FBI connections to reveal the source of Lyn's gun. "I reached [Harold] Boro last night at his home in Jackson, California," Anderson reported. "The old man's voice was tired. He said he hadn't been able to sleep since the investigation began. But he refused to discuss the incident with me, saying he'd been instructed by the FBI to say nothing."

In a flash, reporters were swarming through the faded streets of Jackson, surrounding the Boro house on Laughton Lane, knocking on the door, calling on the telephone. Nelda tried to shoo them away, but the press corps was persistent, and soon it seemed that every last soul in town had been interviewed about the elusive "Sugar Daddy." In a typical remark, Manny's Aunt Mildred described him as "a very quiet man who was never interested in women or anything."

Neither Nelda nor Charles Boro would speak to the press, and Lyn had been silenced by court order. It fell to Sandra Good to defend Manny's character.

"That poor guy, they're not showing him any respect at all. He's living his own life, he ought to be left alone," Sandy told the *Sacramento Bee*. "Now he's going to be vamped on by the media. That poor guy." In a rare point of agreement, Dwayne Keyes seconded Sandy's opinion. Manny, he said at a news conference, was just "a nice guy who unwittingly got involved in this thing."

To escape the journalistic siege, Nelda hustled Manny into her car and drove him to an eastern Sacramento County hamlet called Twin Cities. There, she turned the befuddled and embarrassed old man over to FBI agents, who lodged him overnight in a Sacramento hotel. The next morning, they brought Manny to their Cottage Way offices, where they were assembling witnesses subpoenaed to testify before the grand jury. As many as one hundred agents stood guard as the witnesses, each issued a copy of Judge MacBride's gag order, piled into three cars for the six-mile drive to the federal courthouse. Under orders not to discuss the Fromme case, they instead swapped theories about the Kennedy assassination. "We were just kibitzing and someone mentioned Dallas—and that not many of the witnesses there are still alive," recalled Dennis Warren, a neighbor of Lyn who had been summoned to testify.

Once at the courthouse, agents took the witnesses to the judges' private elevators and led them through a maze of offices until they reached the small chamber where the grand jury met behind locked doors. Federal agents had thought of everything, even papering over the jury room's windows so that no prying eyes could intrude. Not only did they guard against troublemakers, the law officers also kept the news media at arm's length, refusing even to confirm that the grand jury had convened. Pursuant to an order of Judge MacBride, cameras and recording equipment were banned in the courtroom, and even in the hallways of the Federal Building. The security measures were the tightest in Sacramento history; according to Keyes, they were imposed at the request of witnesses fearful of being publicly identified.

Federal grand jury proceedings are held in secret, with the public, the press, and even the accused and his or her counsel excluded. The prosecutor chooses what evidence and which witnesses to put forward in support of an indictment, and there is no cross-examination by the defense to challenge the government's version of events. Rarely does a grand jury refuse to return an indictment, but prosecutors weren't taking any chances. Before the testimony began, Keyes and Heller divided the witnesses between them and grilled each one individually before letting them take the stand. The evidence would be carefully choreographed. The nine men and thirteen women of the grand jury convened at 10:00 A.M. on September 10, with a full slate of business. They had to consider indictments in seven routine matters, including interstate auto theft and a narcotics offense, as well as the pistol incident. The press naturally focused on the appearance of the so-called Sugar Daddy. They were less than flattering in their accounts; Manny, reported the *Sacramento Union*, "appeared older than his sixty-five years as he entered the courthouse, walking stoop-shouldered, carrying a soiled golf cap."

There was little dispute over whether a charge against Lyn should issue. Just before 3:00 P.M., the foreman signed the one-count indictment. Reporters and a few members of the public, having been thoroughly searched by federal marshals, were permitted to file into the courtroom to hear the result. As press artists sketched the scene, Judge MacBride read aloud from the bench:

> The Grand Jury charges: THAT LYNETTE ALICE FROMME, defendant herein, on or about September 5, 1975, in the City and County of Sacramento, State and Eastern District of California, did knowingly and wilfully attempt to kill Gerald R. Ford, the President of the United States of America. A TRUE BILL.

Dick Walker was unimpressed. Talking to reporters in the courthouse hallway, the federal defender dismissed the indictment ritual as "just a rubber stamp for the U.S. Attorney." Folksy but determined, Walker seemed a good match for Lyn. Now in his mid-forties, he had left his post as district attorney of rugged Trinity County in northwest California to become public defender for Yolo County, the rural jurisdiction on the west bank of the Sacramento River. Appointed federal defender in 1971, Walker had become known in Sacramento as a vigorous advocate for the rights of defendants. With his Captain Ahab beard and raffish suits, Walker even had the vaguely anti-Establishment look appropriate for a Manson Family attorney.

Behind the scenes, however, there was friction between Walker and Lyn. The two would not discuss the details publicly, but Lyn found it difficult to get her ideas across to the attorney, or to accept what he told her. "I'm not saying Mr. Walker is a liar," Lyn later put it, not wanting to hurt his feelings. "I'm saying that in my experience, I find that attorneys lie." Instead, Lyn warmed to Walker's young assistant, Robert Holley. Age twenty-eight, educated at the state college in bucolic Chico, California, Bob Holley seemed to capture Lyn's attention.

Lyn had already made it clear that she intended to represent herself at trial, and that her court-appointed attorneys would be serving her in a secondary, research-based role. Now she told Walker that she wanted Holley—not Walker— as her co-counsel.

Walker replied that she would have the assistance of "the Federal Defender's Office," including Holley, if appointed. Lyn said that it would have to be Holley, not Walker, who spoke in court.

"We can probably work something out," said Walker, swallowing the insult. Walker had twenty-five years of legal experience; Holley had never tried a felony before a jury. Still suspicious, Lyn agreed to permit the federal defender to continue representing her. On later reflection, Walker told Lyn that he would himself do the speaking in court; because of the magnitude of the case, Judge MacBride had appointed him specifically as counsel, not the federal defender's office as a whole. Lyn steamed.

In Washington, reporters kept pressing for information on the Ford incident and its implications for presidential security. At a news conference, White House press secretary Ron Nessen promised that the Secret Service was conducting an investigation.

"But that is the people in question investigating themselves, isn't it?" a reporter asked.

"Oh, I don't know.... The President has, I think, made clear that he has nothing but praise for the Secret Service.... He has never offered any word of complaint at all about this."

Another question concerned the agent who apprehended Lyn. "Has the President initiated any action to cite Buendorf for his actions in Sacramento?"

"Not that I know of, but I can look into it," Nessen said. "I will look into it." A week later, Buendorf and other members of the Sacramento detail received letters of commendation from Secretary of the Treasury William E. Simon. Perhaps a greater compliment came from the Kremlin. In preparation for the American visit of Foreign Minister Andrei Gromyko, Soviet officials demanded that security be provided not by the State Department guards normally assigned to visiting diplomats, but by the Secret Service.

The Arraignment

Lyn was brought to the courthouse at six-thirty the next morning, September 11, and kept under guard for three hours until the beginning of her arraignment. Surrounded by deputies, she entered the courtroom dressed all in red, from the top of her hooded cape to her matching sneakers.

Under Marshal Van Court's special procedures, those coming to observe were carefully searched and made to sign a register listing their names and affiliations. Sandra Good, dressed almost identically to Lyn, had managed to pass the security gauntlet and taken a seat in the front row. Beside her sat Heather Murphy, who varied the uniform with a red turban and pink slacks. Lyn, at the defense table, glanced around the courtroom, but the phalanx of deputies made it impossible for her to spot her friends. To *San Francisco Chronicle* correspondent Rob Haeseler, the hearing "at times had the air of a Halloween party."

At Judge MacBride's instruction, the court clerk read the charge: "The Grand Jury for this District has returned an indictment charging a violation of Title 18, United States Code, Section 1751(c), attempted assassination of the President of the United States, against Lynette Alice Fromme. Is that your true name?"

"Yes," Lyn said firmly. "It is."

She stood quietly, slowly swaying from side to side, as the judge and attorneys went through the preliminaries of scheduling arguments and hearings. A formal plea was set for September 19. Lyn nodded enthusiastically when MacBride said the trial should begin promptly, seeing as "the defendant is a so-called high-risk defendant."

Walker, however, took exception. "I oppose any characterization of my client as 'high-risk' by this court," he said. "I think that is inappropriate and I think it jeopardizes her in a fair consideration for reasonable bail. And I think—"

MacBride interrupted, promising to consider these questions at a bail hearing set for the following week. Walker also asked for a hearing to reconsider the gag order.

"You are talking about the gag order only as it pertains to the defendant herself?" the judge asked.

"She would like the entire gag order lifted, Your Honor. We intend—"

Now it was Lyn who cut Walker off. "No," she said, "as it pertains to me."

"All right, as it pertains to the defendant," Walker conceded.

The official business was soon completed. "Anything else?" Judge MacBride asked, directing his question to the attorneys. Walker and Keyes said nothing, but Lyn suddenly spoke up. Amplified by the courtroom microphone, her words echoed through the paneled chamber.

"Yes. Your Honor, I would like to speak with you a minute about a problem that is within your jurisdiction. And I want to ask that you have some patience with me in—and some understanding."

"Now, Miss Fromme, before you say anything—"

"Yes."

"—I want you to understand that anything you say in this courtroom, and it's public and it's heard by us, it might very well be held against you. You have been warned of your constitutional rights to remain silent at all times. And from here on out, when you make statements, these statements can be taken down and can very well be held against you. It would be harmful to you. I warn you that the more you talk the more you jeopardize the possibility of you getting a fair trial."

MacBride looked to Walker for support. Lyn continued:

"Well, this is in regard to, as I say, something that's in your jurisdiction. And it's more important to me at this time because I'm the one that's here and I'm the one that sits in the cell and has to worry about—"

"Does it have to do with the conditions of your confinement, Miss Fromme?" the judge asked.

"No, it doesn't. Will you hear me?"

"Have you discussed the matter with your attorney, Mr. Walker?"

"No, I haven't, but I—he has agreed to—" She looked at Walker. "What would you call it?"

Walker spoke. "She discussed with me the fact that she wanted to make a statement to the court."

"Well, Mr. Walker," the judge said, "are you satisfied that she in no way will jeopardize her position by a statement that she's about to make?"

"I am satisfied that she fully understands her rights and is able to deal with that situation, Your Honor. If she makes any statement that could be used against her in any way—"

MacBride interrupted Walker again, turning to the defendant. "And I will tell you this further, Miss Fromme, I don't propose at this time that I would accept any political statement on your part or any statement that might have to do with—"

"This is between—" Lyn began. She and the judge talked over each other.

"—the conditions of the country or anything of that sort," MacBride continued. "We are only concerned in this court in dealing with the question of your guilt or innocence. The purpose of this arraignment is to advise you of the charge that has been placed against you, to determine your identity, to fix a time for your entry of plea, to go into the matter of bail, and deal with matters that are strictly related to the eventual disposition of this case."

"Your Honor, this is in regard to this case. And it's necessary for me to tell you—"

"I will let you get a little start on it," MacBride said, "but I may shut you off and I hope you won't be mad at me if I do but—"

"You know I will!" Lyn seemed already to have established a filial rapport with the judge.

"Oh, you will. All right. I will have to bear up under that. Proceed," he said.

"This is something I want you to know. There are—there is an army of young people and children that want to clean up this earth."

"Miss Fromme. Wait just a minute, Miss Fromme—"

"Now what's involved—" They were talking over each other, again.

"Just a minute, I'm—"

"The redwood trees. That's what I want you to do. I want you to do one of two things, either order the government to buy up the land around the national park—" Lyn was referring to the heavy logging underway in Redwood National Park. She wasn't the only one in Sacramento concerned about the issue; a few blocks away, the State Board of Forestry had convened a hearing to investigate the problem.

"That is enough, Miss Fromme. You've had—"

"—or order the Army Corps of Engineers—"

"Just a minute, Miss Fromme—"

"—in there and have them clean up before we lose them."

MacBride began to lose patience. "I will cause you to be restrained unless you be quiet. It has nothing to do with this case."

"Certainly it does," Lyn insisted. "My intent—"

"No, it has nothing whatever to do with this case and I am sorry I can't permit you to proceed further," he said.

"Will you think about it?" Lyn asked.

"Yes, I'll think about it. I have the first part of the message and I'll think about it, but I can tell you this: It won't have any effect in my decision insofar as the proceedings are concerned or the way this case is going to be tried."

"Well," Lyn said, her voice rising, "that's not important. The important part is the redwood trees. We want to save them. Do you understand this is like cutting down your own arms and legs?"

"All right, Miss Fromme, thank you."

"The gun is pointed, Your Honor," Lyn continued. "The gun is pointed and whether it goes off is up to you all." That phrase, "The gun is pointed," would appear in countless headlines as Squeaky Fromme's latest threat.

MacBride told the bailiff to remove the defendant from the courtroom. A deputy grabbed her arm. Lyn looked at the judge and said cheerfully, "All right, I didn't mean to be rude, but it's necessary."

"You weren't rude and I understand your position," the judge said reassuringly. "But I'm sorry I can't accept your statement today." As the proceedings unfolded through the fall, observers would notice a dynamic in the relationship between Lyn and MacBride, whose own three children, like Lyn, were in their twenties. The judge "treats her like a child who has misbehaved," wrote Lucinda Franks, then a young correspondent for the *New York Times*. "And she treats him like a father who doesn't understand her."

Outside the courtroom, Walker complained that MacBride's characterization of Lyn as a "high-risk" defendant implied that she was "some type of criminal."

Sandy went even further. "This court is stuck in a dead procedure," she said. "The court wants to know *who* did something, instead of *why* something was done."

But some did take note of Lyn's explanation, truncated as it was. In the *Philadelphia Inquirer*, the editorial cartoonist Auth drew a panel depicting a forest of redwoods frowning and wincing as a hooded Lyn strolls by with a placard reading, SAVE A REDWOOD. SHOOT A BUSINESSMAN! Says one redwood to another, "With friends like that, who needs enemies?"

Lyn was not discouraged. Unable to make her full statement in court, she wrote MacBride a letter explaining her concerns with the future of the redwoods, with pollution of the air and the water, with the fate of the nation's children.

United States of America vs. *Lynette Alice Fromme* was not the only legal dispute to arise from the events of September 5, 1975. Another concerned two employees of Channel 13 News, reporter Suzan Kay Harris and cameraman Paul Nyberg.

On the day of Gerald Ford's visit, Nyberg handed Harris a still camera and asked her to snap a photo of him with the president. But when Lyn entered the picture, Harris took a shot of her—one so perfect that *Newsweek* paid $2,000 to use the photo on its cover. Nyberg wanted half the proceeds and possession of the negatives. He had, after all, bought the film. Harris refused, and so the matter entered Sacramento County Superior Court.

Nyberg's attorney likened the parties' relationship to that of songwriters, where a composer and a lyricist split the proceeds of their work. Harris's lawyer, on the other hand, compared his client to an artist and Nyberg to an art supplier, entitled only to the value of the raw materials he provided.

Judge Merle Shreck issued a temporary restraining order barring Harris from spending the money she received from *Newsweek* or from selling any more photos until the matter was resolved. Shreck urged the reporter and cameraman to resolve the dispute on their own. News photos, he observed, were a rather perishable commodity, and the value of Lyn's image would only decrease with each passing day.

Time magazine's cover, a handsome portrait of Lyn against a black background, became embroiled in another kind of controversy. Clare Boothe Luce, widow of *Time* co-founder Henry Luce, protested that "Elizabeth Seton, the first native American to be canonized as a saint, couldn't make the cover of *Time*. But Lynette Fromme made it." Feminists were annoyed at the headline: THE GIRL WHO ALMOST KILLED FORD. Wrote a reader from Central Islip, New York, "If a twenty-seven-year-old male had held the gun, would your headline have been 'THE BOY WHO ALMOST KILLED FORD'?" Many readers accused the magazine of glamorizing terror. One letter came from Beverly Hills. It complained that the cover featuring Lyn "in all her fresh-faced, tender-lipped vulnerability, gazing dreamily into history," was "the epitome of irresponsible journalism. Where she may have failed in her attempt to make violence appealing, your cover certainly has not."

The writer was Roman Polanski.

Judge MacBride took up defense objections to the gag order and the $1 million bail on Tuesday, September 16. With the red-hooded Lyn standing impatiently beside him, Dick Walker implored the judge to let his client speak freely to the press and public. "I suggest to you that it is the defendant's privilege and right . . . particularly in this type of case where it does have, on one hand, the President of the United States making comments which [carry] national coverage."

After Walker concluded his argument, Lyn asked the judge, "May I just speak on my behalf a moment please?"

MacBride looked at the federal defender. "Mr. Walker?"

"We would ask the indulgence of the court, Your Honor," said Walker.

MacBride turned to Lyn. He warned her to keep her remarks limited to the question of the gag order. "Believe me, Miss Fromme," he said, "we're not going to talk about the redwoods."

"All right, Your Honor," Lyn said. "First of all, I feel that—first of all, I make a motion to represent myself in pro per. I'd like you to consider that over the week."

"I will do that."

"Next, I feel that the proceeding was too drawn out. We take too long for things that are very simple, actually. In the U.S. Attorney's points and authorities against the gag order, he states in search of due process the Supreme Court mandated that . . . the trial court must take strong measures to ensure that the balance is never weighted against the accused.

"Your Honor, with the amount of past publicity in the Manson cases of 1969, 1970, with the amount of heavily prejudicial publicity against me, anything that I can say, if I talked all day and all night, could probably not balance what's already been said. And I feel that as long as I don't abuse the privilege, that I should be allowed to express myself. And I have numerous pieces of evidence. *Newsweek* magazine, for one, is so highly prejudicial against me, and this goes into most homes. You can't really expect to find a juror in the whole country that hasn't read some pieces."

The judge seemed unsure how to respond. "The fact there may be a Manson connection or something of that sort . . . apparently you're tied in or you're alleged to have been tied into the Manson matter in some way—and I'm not making a finding in that regard at all—but nevertheless it's true that you, yourself, have made statements in the past which apparently tied you in some way with the Manson affair, the so-called Manson Family."

Lyn tried to interrupt, but MacBride wouldn't let her.

"We are only concerned," the judge continued, "with the fact, did you or did you not attempt to assassinate the President of the United States."

"If we were only concerned with that," Lyn asked, why did the judge impose a gag order preventing her from saying *anything* publicly?

"Miss Fromme," MacBride said, "I haven't yet said—"

"I know," she interjected.

"—what I will do." He promised her a swift decision after both sides had made their arguments.

"All right," she said, "I would like to know then—"

"Don't say I've decided," the judge chided her.

"—if you have read *Newsweek* magazine?" she continued.

Although it was not a legal question, MacBride answered. "I haven't."

"*Time* magazine?"

"I've seen the pictures in *Time* magazine," the judge said, "I'm having trouble with *Time* magazine, I'm having trouble with my subscription with *Time* magazine—"

"It should clear up today," Lyn suggested.

"—they can't seem to get the dates right whether or not my subscription is extended. Anyway, I haven't read the *Time* story. I saw the picture and I had to get on to other matters."

"On this," Lyn said helpfully, "I would suggest that we have a brief recess, maybe later, and I would like to show you the articles. I would like you to see them because I know the circulation of these magazines—and any jury that we bring in here could not help be prejudiced by the kind of lies that were told—and I am not saying by the staff of the magazine. I'm saying that rumors get going and people want something to talk about. And if I'm not allowed to say anything to the contrary of sex fantasies"—the press had eagerly speculated over the Freudian significance of Lyn's encounters with men from Charlie to Manny Boro to President Ford—"things that should not be allowed to, you know, influence people in my trial. All right, that's all."

"Thank you, Miss Fromme," said the judge.

After the prosecution argument, MacBride announced his decision: The gag order on Lyn would be lifted in part, allowing her to speak to the press on any topic other than evidence and trial strategy directly related to the case. "If she wants to talk about the Manson Family, or about the fantasies to which she made earlier reference and so forth, that's her privilege," the judge declared. "I'm not restricting her."

Next was the matter of the $1 million bail. Walker asked that Lyn be released on her own recognizance; she had not, after all, been charged with a capital offense. To support the motion, the defense had assembled a series of witnesses of surprising authority. They would testify over two days.

First to the stand was Clyde Blackmon, the Sacramento attorney who had been helping Lyn in her effort to win prison visitation rights. He testified that Lyn had kept all her appointments and had been "pleasant" and "coherent."

Walker next called Jess Fain, Lyn's landlord. The old man's hands shook as he testified, his voice quavering.

"During the period that you have owned the apartment house, has the rent been paid according to your rental agreement?"

"Absolutely."

"How would you characterize Miss Fromme as a tenant?"

"She was a model tenant in every respect."

"No loud parties?"

"No loud parties."

"Never saw her drunk?"

"I never saw her when she even acted like she might be partly drunk." Fain testified that he had called a meeting of his tenants to discuss the Manson women's future at the apartment house. "We took a vote, secret ballot on who was in favor of leaving the other two girls remain after Miss Fromme was— was arrested and nine out of ten voted to let them stay." They also decided that Lyn, were she released on bail, would be welcome to return home.

Don Heller began the government's cross-examination by urging Jess Fain to relax. "Why don't you sit back in your chair," he suggested. Fain did so.

"In your opinion," Heller asked, "do you think Miss Fromme is a morally responsible person?"

"I think of her as such, yes," Fain said. "Very much so."

"Has she ever expressed any feeling to you in connection with the wrongfulness of killing animals and human beings?"

"She expressed the wrongfulness of killing animals," Fain replied.

William Melcher, the Los Angeles County prosecutor who had befriended Lyn, testified to continuing his correspondence with her even after the pistol incident. He explained why he believed Lyn would make her court appearances if released.

"Sandra and Lynette apparently have a great deal of respect for the court, for Judge MacBride," Melcher said. "They consider him a very fair man. I think they agree and feel they're going to get a fair trial." Then, he added, "this won't carry much weight, but the girl has never lied to me. She has always been very, very truthful. . . . She has stated to me she will attend, and I believe her."

Melcher speculated that rather than fear the coming trial, Lyn would relish the spotlight. "Whether you agree with [her] or not, whether I do or not, is not meaningful," he said. "But I think she would have the ears of the world. . . . I think that pretty well summarizes why I strongly believe that Miss Fromme will make all appearances."

Phil Shelton had been the one to contact Melcher and arrange for his court appearance. Shelton wondered why any prosecutor, particularly one who worked for the same office as Vincent Bugliosi, would want to testify on behalf of the Manson Family's most notorious advocate.

"To be involved in a case where someone is known to much of the world can make you pretty well known, especially if you're trying to get into private practice or move up," Shelton observed. But nothing about Melcher suggested a self-serving motive. "He was like a lot of prosecutors," Shelton recalled. "What may look on the outside like just stiffness is really a clear-minded decision of what they think is right and what they think is wrong. And he thought doing this was right," he said.

It was an uncommon approach. In more than three decades as a detective, Shelton said, Melcher was the only prosecutor he had ever known to testify on behalf of a criminal defendant.

Not all defense witnesses were quite as reputable. Dwayne Keyes got right to the point in cross-examining Sandra Good.

"Is it true that Miss Fromme has not been employed in the last three years since she lived at the P Street address?" he asked.

"She is self-employed," Sandy replied. "We are working for earth in balance." Sandy had demonstrated her own industry that morning, doing some sewing while watching the hearing from the visitors gallery.

Judge MacBride tried to clarify. "I think, Miss Good, what counsel has in mind is to determine whether or not there is any production of money as a result of your work."

Production of money? Sandy seemed surprised by the question. "Oh, no," she said.

Next, Lyn herself took the stand, accentuating each syllable of her name as she was sworn in. Dick Walker asked about her lifestyle. Her needs, she said, were simple: "some air, some water, some land, some sunshine." What about drugs? "I have occasionally smoked marijuana," Lyn said, "but we don't have time for it much anymore. If a person has a purpose, they don't need drugs."

Don Heller stood up for the cross-examination. Lyn noted the prosecutor's youth. "May I ask a question," she said, "I'm just curious how long you've been with the office?"

"That's irrelevant, Miss Fromme," said the judge.

"Oh."

Lyn responded politely as Heller catalogued the varieties of public assistance she had received while in Sacramento. He asked her the exact amount she had received in student loans.

"Good research!" Lyn commented.

"To do research?" asked MacBride.

"No, no," Lyn explained. "I was telling him he was doing good research."

"I'm sorry. I didn't get your answer. You were telling—"

"Your Honor, I was just making a comment to the District Attorney that he had done good research."

"Oh, all right," said the judge.

Heller now moved on to his real objective: demonstrating that Lyn's values were contrary to those of most Americans. He prompted Lyn to detail the kinds of things she salvaged from the trash, things that had been abandoned by others, prompting an exegesis of middle-class material culture. Then he asked: "Do you mean that, as a comment, people have more things than they really need to live by, more clothing than is necessary?"

"Oh, that's obvious," said Lyn.

"Do you think that's wrong?"

"Do I think *what's* wrong?" asked Lyn.

"That people have more things than they really need to live?"

"In other words, am I down on the Establishment?" she said, almost mockingly. "Am I down on materialism?"

"Yes," said Heller.

"No," Lyn replied. "I don't think it's wrong. I think this: that if we don't stop over-consumption, and we don't really take a look at what is essential to our life, that we are all going to over-consume ourselves to death. It's evident in people that are overweight and over-consumption of meat. The doctors are finding out that we are all consuming too much carbohydrates, too many eggs. These are basic things that I have researched myself. And I will tell you this, it's difficult to walk around knowing all this." The question had doubtless pleased Lyn, as these issues—not the trivial events in Capitol Park—were her reasons for coming to court.

"Now," said Heller, "what do you need to live—"

"Wait, Mr. Heller," said Judge MacBride. "That's enough. Get on with something else."

Heller got on with *Helter Skelter*. "And you're mentioned in that book?" he asked.

"That's right," said Lyn. "Slandered, as a matter of fact."

"And you think it was wrong of [Bugliosi] to do that without giving you an opportunity to at least have a section in the book?"

"I'll tell you what's wrong," said Lyn. "A lie is wrong. For somebody to state a fact, that's their privilege. To lie about somebody for one's own benefit is certainly not right to me. I can't do that in good conscience. I can't step on you . . . in front of millions of people, look like a pervert, and feel good about it."

This moralizing answer may not have been what Heller had in mind. He continued:

"Is it fair to say you had no contact with your biological family in the last three years?"

"That's right," said Lyn. "Our family has developed and has been called a family by the news media. It is a family. And I am referring to the people that are in prison over the Manson case, the so-called Manson case. . . . These people gave their word and followed their word all the way through to the gas chamber. . . . Now, I myself gave my word that I would stand on the street corner until Manson and the rest were released. I stood on the street corner for two years, kneeled actually, and crawled twenty-five miles to make a point, and after that time, due to a number of surrounding circumstances, including the removal of Manson, the women and the men from the Los Angeles area, I stepped off the corner and I left my word."

The lawyers did not seem to be fully comprehending Lyn's testimony. She tried to elaborate: "I felt it was important for me to tell you this so that you would believe me again, because I broke my word at that time, and to our family that is a very, very serious thing. It has emotional, mental, physical and spiritual ties that I had never realized before. When you give your word to somebody and specifically to yourself and you break it, very serious things can happen. And I am aware of that now. . . .

"I'm trying to put all of this in terms that I know you can understand," she added.

"No further questions," said Heller.

Dick Walker had one question for redirect examination: Would she keep her word to the court?

Her voice heavy, Lyn leaned into the microphone. "Before the world at this time, my word to myself or to anybody is my life."

Walker moved that Lyn be released on her own recognizance. He observed that in California, the bail for attempted murder cases was about $5,000. For first-degree murder, bail ranged from $13,000 to $50,000, considerably less than the $1 million bond the court had imposed on Lyn.

Walker noted that only a half dozen of his hundreds of clients had jumped bail in nearly five years, and that Lyn did not fit the profile of a bail jumper.

"I believe this defendant will make all appearances. As a matter of fact, I believe she will *insist* on making all appearances," Walker told the judge. "I think she's dedicated to the mission she has in life and that mission at the present also includes this court structure. I think what's important to her is her word and she's given her word under oath to this court that she would make all appearances. . . . She's just the kind of human being that would appear. I don't think there is any question. She's the best client we've had in a long time."

Dwayne Keyes was not persuaded. Noting that Lyn lacked traditional financial or familial ties to Sacramento—factors that weighed heavily in bail guidelines—and the "heinous" nature of the charge, Keyes not only asked that the $1 million bond be retained but that Lyn be required to post it in cash.

Walker objected: "Your Honor, Mr. Keyes said she has no assets to lose. I suggest to the court she has one of the greatest human assets to lose; namely, her word."

Judge MacBride issued his ruling immediately. He ticked off the factors established by the federal bail guidelines; unlike the other judges that Lyn had encountered over the years, MacBride attempted to give some credence to her position. "She does have this 'family' that she speaks of . . . who apparently are tied together in a common cause. They speak of that as their family but I don't think that's the kind of family the Congress of the United States had in mind" in establishing bail criteria.

"Then we get to the question of employment. She has no real employment. This cause that she and Miss Good and Miss Murphy are involved in is certainly a noble cause—the protection of the earth—but nevertheless that is not the kind of employment that Congress had in mind when they set up employment as a criterion to be considered by the court. . . .

"Next is character and mental condition. . . . All I can do is judge her as she appears before me. She's a sincere young lady in her beliefs, such as they are. I can't say I subscribe to all of her beliefs, but nevertheless she demonstrates substantial forthrightness and ability to articulate her views. Looking at that as to her character and her mental condition, I really can't make an adverse finding there. I am neutral on that."

All in all, MacBride found that $1 million was excessive. He lowered Lyn's bail to $350,000.

Lyn entered a plea of not guilty. The judge calendared the trial to begin at 10:00 A.M. on November 4, 1975.

"The sooner the better," said Lyn.

A Fool for a Client

As Sandy and Heather left the courtroom, three plainclothes detectives moved in. They arrested Heather for a probation violation—stemming from her August 1973 conviction for shoplifting $7.03 worth of merchandise from a Sacramento PayLess drugstore.

Probation officers complained that Heather had neglected to keep them updated as to her whereabouts; their records listed her as residing at the Phoenix House drug rehabilitation center, one of at least three halfway houses she had stayed in. "We saw her picture on the front page of the *Union* and realized she had moved," said a probation official.

The detectives brought their suspect before Municipal Judge Rothwell B. Mason, who two years before had sentenced Heather for the theft of a flashlight kit, two batteries, three containers of dye, and a can of spray paint. He ordered Heather released after she promised to get in touch with her probation officer.

Lyn, meanwhile, immediately made use of her new freedom to speak to the press, calling a jailhouse news conference for that evening. She entered the visiting room in her pale blue jail uniform, red and white sandals on her feet, and took her seat on the prisoners' side of the plexiglass. She cradled one telephone handset by each ear, so she could give interviews to reporters two at a time. Dick Walker and Sandra Good, along with three deputies, watched the scene from the side.

As news cameras rolled, Lyn was demonstrably emotional, pacing the floor, shouting, trembling, sometimes coming to the verge of tears. To *Bee* reporter Nancy Skelton, who could watch Lyn through the glass but not hear what she was saying, the theatrical scene was "Marcel Marceauesque."

Those who were on Lyn's interview list heard her views on many issues. Some were predictable, as she urged that "we take our Christ"—Charlie, of course— "off the cross." Others were more topical, even reasonable: "How can Kissinger go to the Mideast one week to negotiate peace and the next week go right back there and sell arms?" she asked. "To my simple, childlike mind, I just say, No."

Then there was the matter of President Ford. Lyn strictly adhered to Judge MacBride's instruction not to discuss her case. But she deplored the president's call for building 145 new nuclear power plants. "Nuclear power is dangerous. Nuclear power kills," said Lyn. And yet, "I saw a very secure, doctorly, fatherly man"—President Ford—"say this is perfectly safe."

As Lyn was led away at the interview's end, Sandy pressed her face to the glass and mouthed a message. Lyn struggled to hear, but couldn't make it out, finally throwing up her hands in frustration. Sandy said it again: "Patty Hearst! Patty Hearst's been busted!"

Lyn had another visitor: Clyde Blackmon. Judge MacBride had asked the attorney to dissuade Lyn from trying to represent herself in court.

He was so confident that Blackmon would persuasively explain to Lyn "the problems, the dangers, the pitfalls" of taking her own case, he didn't even bother to ask Lyn her reaction when the court reconvened. After disposing of routine matters related to the case, MacBride prepared to adjourn before the Friday lunch hour.

"Anything else to come before the court this morning?" MacBride asked.

"She wants to represent herself, Your Honor," Dick Walker reminded the judge. "Could we deal with that?"

"I didn't know," said the judge. "I thought it might have gone away." Laughs echoed through the courtroom.

"No," said Lyn, standing with her arms crossed. She wasn't laughing.

"It hasn't," MacBride acknowledged.

"It has not gone away, Your Honor," said Walker.

"A judge can always hope and pray," MacBride grumbled. He asked Lyn if she understood the charge against her.

"From my understanding," said Lyn, "it is up to the U.S. Attorney to prove that I intentionally went to the State Capitol Building to—with the specific intent of assassinating the President."

"Or attempting to assassinate the President," MacBride corrected.

"Well, that—all right," said Lyn.

"Okay. Now, do you understand what the elements of the crime are? Do you know the two things that have to be proved in order to convict you of this crime?"

"In layman's language, the thought and the overt action is what I understand must be proved."

"Have you ever represented yourself before in any criminal charges or any criminal proceeding of this kind?"

"Just in life," said Lyn.

"Just in life," the judge repeated. "All right." He asked if she understood the local District Court rules or the Federal Rules of Criminal Procedure.

"No, I do not," said Lyn.

"Do you understand the nature of a bill of particulars, do you understand the idea of motions for discovery, do you understand what's involved in a motion for discovery?"

"No, I don't, Your Honor. I know nothing whatsoever about federal law. And very little about state law."

"That's the whole purpose of my questioning you, Miss Fromme," emphasized the judge. "To point out to you that you don't know anything about federal law."

Lyn, however, insisted she had to represent herself, as no attorney could speak in her voice. But MacBride refused to see the trial as an opportunity for self-expression. He kept trying to persuade Lyn that Dick Walker would do a better job in protecting her rights.

"There's no doubt, Your Honor, that from the technical viewpoint Mr. Walker could do it better than I could. At the same time—"

"Well," said the judge, "if he can do it better than you can, why don't you want him to do it?"

"Because the strategy must be mine," she said. "I feel I would have a tendency to be in contempt, Your Honor, if I was not allowed to say the things that I feel would speed up the trial."

"I don't understand your statement that you feel that you would be in contempt."

"If you held me down, if you do not allow me to speak for myself, I feel that I would feel an urgency to speak, and not being able to do it would be very frustrating."

MacBride continued his questions. Did Lyn know how many peremptory challenges she had for potential jurors? No. Did she understand the hearsay rule? No. In fact, Lyn said, "I don't know anything about the law."

MacBride groaned. "Every time you say that, Miss Fromme, that's what worries me. If you don't know anything about the law, why are you trying to be a lawyer?"

"I would rather learn on my way here," Lyn said.

In order to grant Lyn's motion to represent herself, the judge would have to find that she made a "knowing, willing and intelligent waiver" of her right to counsel. And after Lyn's performance Friday morning, MacBride acknowledged that "she makes a very convincing case." But to be sure that Lyn was competent to make that choice—as well as to stand trial—he decided to order a psychiatric examination of the defendant. Lyn was reluctant as ever to talk to a psychiatrist, fearing that her words would be taken out of context. Moreover, as Phil Shelton had explained to Lyn, the consequence of being found unfit to stand trial was worse than conviction. Under federal law, she would be committed to a mental hospital until authorities concluded she was competent—and would then stand trial.

Lyn agreed to the examination. She insisted, however, that there be a witness present—Dick Walker or the deputy federal defender, Bob Holley—and that the interview be taped, just in case the psychiatrist left anything out. Not wanting to destroy his "rapport" with Lyn, MacBride agreed.

After an hour-and-forty-minute interview, Dr. James Richmond concluded that Lyn was mentally competent to stand trial—and to waive her right to counsel. Having set forth a few ground rules, Judge MacBride granted Lyn's request to represent herself in court, and appointed Dick Walker her co-counsel.

Serious as her trial was to Lyn, others were less than overwhelmed. Chicago columnist Mike Royko published an interview with a fictitious conspiracy theorist named "Perry Noyd," who noted that Lyn wore red, that red was the color of rubies, and that Jack Ruby shot Lee Harvey Oswald. "Are you beginning to see the connection?" Perry Noyd asked knowingly.

Syndicated columnist Arthur Hoppe took a different tack, reporting on a fanciful "842-page manuscript" by "Park Lane"—a reference to Kennedy conspiracy theorist Mark Lane—proving conclusively "that Miss Fromme failed to fire not one, but four bullets before she was arrested." After presenting "The Two Miss Frommes Theory," Hoppe reported "eyewitness testimony that, while Miss Fromme was supposedly not firing at the President, somewhere between three and twenty-seven persons on a grassy knoll to the southeast were also not firing at the President."

And in a letter to the *Los Angeles Times*, a reader named Willard Galbraith predicted "the inevitable aftermath of *l'affaire Fromme*. The Secret Service will be accused of police brutality for twisting the arm of Fromme and throwing her to the ground. Agent Larry Buendorf will be sued for having violated Fromme's civil right to protest. It will be alleged that the bail . . . is excessive and was set that high because women are discriminated against. A 'second arm' theory will gain credence because of doubt as to whether there may have been seen another arm between the closely packed spectators. The courthouse will be picketed by persons carry placards reading FREE SQUEAKY. I can hardly wait."

On the other hand, there was evidence that many Americans had yet to grasp what the Fromme case was all about. At the University of Florida, Professor Sanford B. Weinberg had his behavioral studies class survey the local population about the incident in Sacramento. Some 125 residents of Gainesville were queried. While 73.6 percent could identify Lyn, only 26.4 percent could describe her cause. Most respondents believed Lyn had assaulted the president in an effort to free Patty Hearst.

Normally, it would be considered a blessing to be away from Sacramento during the sweltering summer months. For Bruce Babcock, however, it was a misfortune; the senior prosecutor under Dwayne Keyes, Babcock was vacationing in London when he read about the Ford incident. He returned to find Don Heller, for whom he held little personal respect, oozing braggadocio over his place on the prosecution team.

Realizing that the Fromme trial could be a career-making opportunity, Babcock marched over to Keyes. "I'm the best criminal prosecutor in this office," Babcock said, "and I want this case!" Not only did Babcock have the most criminal trial experience, he also knew intimately the court in which they would be arguing; after law school, he had served for two years as Judge MacBride's law clerk, researching legal issues and preparing rulings for the judge's signature. But Keyes had grown comfortable with Heller, and denied Babcock's request.

Babcock would stew throughout the Fromme trial, watching what he thought were missed opportunities and, in one case, a substantial blunder go by. He developed an elaborate theory for the events of September 5, but had no chance to present it to the Fromme jury.

As a consolation prize, Keyes would later assign Babcock to prosecute Sandra Good for her threat letters. The Good trial finally allowed Babcock put his puzzle together before a court. By then, however, the courtroom gallery would be almost empty, and few would learn of Babcock's theory. The enigmatic pixie Lyn was a media star. No one in the press cared much about the fate of an abrasive bit player like Sandra Good.

President Ford had pledged that no pistol in Capitol Park would prevent him from connecting with Californians. Barely two weeks after the encounter with Lyn, Ford's schedulers had routed him for another swing through the Golden State. This time, authorities made sure to keep an eye on the women of P Street. After Judge MacBride adjourned the proceedings on September 19, Sandra Good left the courthouse and immediately noticed an agent following her. She asked him to drive her home. "You're going to be following me anyway," she said, and the two left the building together.

While police staked out P Street, the president played golf at Pebble Beach, dedicated a college athletic building in Malibu, and, at Disneyland, addressed a convention of life insurance agents. Next on the itinerary was San Francisco.

Along the way, the Secret Service had logged the usual number of threats to the president. Early on the morning of September 22, agents outside San Francisco's St. Francis Hotel arrested a Mobile, Alabama, man on suspicion of threatening the president's life. The suspect apparently had tried to deliver an unpleasant letter to Ford, who was scheduled to speak at the hotel later in the day. Unwisely, the man had shown the letter to two hotel employees; they notified security.

Another frustrated individual, Sara Jane Moore, was somewhat more savvy. Often called Sally, the forty-five-year-old Moore had worked as an FBI informant, and become a peripheral figure in Bay Area radical movements. Her contact with the militant left converted her, she later said. Born in West Virginia, divorced, and an accountant by training, Moore resembled a frumpy Middle American mom more than a revolutionary soldier. Indeed, even though she managed to insinuate herself into circles friendly to the Symbionese Liberation Army, her most militant act seemed to be volunteering as a bookkeeper for People in Need, the food-for-the-poor program the SLA had extorted Randolph Hearst into establishing.

Moore seemed to enjoy the attention she received through her contacts with different sides of social tumult—the radicals, the government, and the press. All three groups, however, had grown tired of Moore—a reporter who could be speaking for government agents and Bay Area militants alike called her "flaky"—and her urgent phone calls increasingly went unanswered. On the other hand, one law officer, Inspector Jack O'Shea of the San Francisco Police Department, confiscated a gun from Moore. He warned federal agents that she "could be another Squeaky." Two Secret Service men went to question her, but found no grounds for an arrest. Moore, meanwhile, was not daunted; she bought herself another pistol.

On September 22, Moore took her .38 caliber revolver and mingled amid the crowd outside the St. Francis. Her presence went unnoted by security agents, their gaze instead drawn by protesters hoisting placards with such messages as RELEASE PATTY HEARST, ARREST GERALD FORD! The Secret Service detail persuaded Ford to skip shaking hands with the crowd and instead to head to his limousine.

Sally Moore managed to get a shot off at the president when he emerged from the hotel, but a bystander, Oliver Sipple, deflected her aim. She missed Ford by five feet, with the ricocheting bullet striking a cab driver in the groin. Said Moore upon her arrest: "I'm no Squeaky Fromme." Moore later asserted that, in contrast to herself, Lyn was "insane. . . . She kind of made me mad firing into the air . . . seeking all that attention," Moore told the *Los Angeles Times*.

Like Lyn, Moore at first claimed she had no intention of killing the president. "It was kind of an ultimate protest against the system," she said days after her arrest. "I did not want to kill somebody, but there comes a point when the only way you can make a statement is to pick up a gun." Publicly, Lyn would agree, adding that "there must be a purpose behind the action." Privately, however, Lyn seemed distressed by Moore's act. According to Bob Holley, "she was really upset that someone else tried to do it. She felt she might have started something bad."

After her arrest, Moore insisted that she had a purpose: to unite the Bay Area's radical community, to "forge some kind of unity between the rage that led to the formation of the SLA combined with the theoreticians."

Nearly a year later, after her conviction and life sentence, Moore spoke differently in an interview with *Playboy* magazine. "Since I was arrested, I've been in four different jails. In each of them, people have asked me, 'What were you trying to do when you fired the shot?' I always say, 'I was trying to kill him.' That's good for a minute or two of dead silence, because everybody expects I'm going to be struck dead on the spot. But then—whether the women are black or white, old or young, in for assault and battery, possession of marijuana or whatever—every one of them says, with really intense emotion, 'I wish you *had* killed the motherfucker.' "

Moore seemed particularly angry at one individual for interfering with her goal. Listing all the hitches on her road to assassinate the president, Moore complained that "good old Squeaky Fromme did her thing. If it hadn't been for *that* incident, Ford would probably have crossed the street to shake hands and I would have had a better chance."

Sally Moore's shot failed to unite the radical movement. It did, however, heighten concern in Washington. President Ford called for hiring 150 new Secret Service agents, at a cost of $13.5 million, while Congress launched its first-ever probe of the agency. Treasury Secretary Simon testified that the number of threats against the president had tripled as a consequence of publicity surrounding the California incidents: in the first twenty days of September, authorities had logged 320 threats to Ford.

Secret Service protection was extended to the other major candidates for president, including former Georgia Governor Jimmy Carter, Texas Senator Lloyd Bentsen, Washington Senator Henry Jackson, Indiana Senator Birch Bayh, and Arizona Congressman Morris Udall. Terry Sanford of North Carolina declined the protection, but George Wallace quickly accepted by telegram. Wallace said that three years before, he had ignored Secret Service advice not to enter the shopping mall where he was shot. "I will make one commitment to the future," he said. "I will do my best to follow their advice."

Lyn, however, was unconcerned about the Sally Moore case, even as it tended to distract attention from her own encounter with President Ford. Her focus remained on the Family. On September 22, she wrote to Patricia Krenwinkel's father. She bragged a bit: "I am conducting my trial with as much dignity as possible & I've been commended for it." She enclosed a letter for Mr. Krenwinkel to forward to the incarcerated Kate, Sadie, and Lulu, begging them for support. But no help was to come from the women's prison at Frontera; not even, apparently, an answer.

On the other hand, at least one prisoner tried to contact Lyn. According to Art Van Court, a state prison inmate who knew Lyn told authorities he could communicate with her—and obtain information helpful to the prosecution. The government was willing to give it a try, and had the inmate brought up from the Tehachapi state prison. Van Court then arranged a reunion, taking Lyn to meet the inmate in a marshal's office visiting room. Van Court and his deputies watched through a one-way mirror as Lyn and the inmate embraced with surprising intimacy—a "big love affair scene," in Van Court's words. The marshal barged in to break up the action.

"We're not doing anything!" Lyn protested. "I'm a nun."

"Yeah—and he ain't had none," said Van Court.

The President's Button

Dick Walker had given Phil Shelton a broad mandate. "I want to know 'What's the defense?' " Walker said. Shelton was to interview all witnesses known and unknown, talk to law enforcement personnel who might have had contact with Lyn, and, most of all, "Get to know Squeaky."

Shelton sketched out his investigation plan in typically methodical fashion. He kept two pads of paper listing the tasks to be accomplished, white for within four weeks, yellow for afterwards. He set out to reconstruct Lyn's thoughts and actions in the five days prior to the pistol incident—and, especially, on the morning of September 5.

But despite the high profile of the case and the relatively generous resources that were available to the federal defender as a result, the investigation had not been going well. Shelton received virtually no cooperation from people who ought to have been sympathetic to Lyn; no word from her parents or siblings, not even from other members of the Manson Family. Only Charlie, who sent Shelton a rambling, useless letter, and, of course, Sandy seemed to take interest in Lyn's predicament. On the other hand, one unlikely source did agree to be interviewed: Vincent Bugliosi. Shelton put a trip to Bugliosi's Los Angeles offices on his yellow pad.

A top priority was Manny Boro, but the nervous old man brushed off Shelton's inquiries with curt monosyllables. He would only answer one question definitively: Did Lyn steal his gun? "No," said Manny.

Lyn, who respectfully called him "Mr. Boro," wanted to speak to Manny herself. She told Shelton about wrecking the old man's car. It still seemed to bother her; "like the daughter wrecking her dad's car," Shelton thought. But Manny would not come to the jail to meet with his old friend. Lyn blamed the prosecution and the press for Manny's reticence. They had ruined his reputation in Jackson, calling him her sugar daddy, a "description he doesn't fit at all," she maintained. They were claiming that "we had no concern for him, and we are using him. . . . He might be so insecure that he might believe this. He's a very shy person. He feels intimidated, especially by authority," she said.

Shelton seemed to be gaining Lyn's trust—she nicknamed the imposing detective "the Whale"—but their interviews remained far afield from the events of September 5.

After listening to one of Lyn's diatribes about the consumer culture, Shelton jolted his client by calling her a "materialist." Lyn insisted she was an antimaterialist.

"No," said Shelton. "That's a misunderstanding. Materialists are people who believe in the long-term functionality of minimal items, not the short-term functionality of many items." Shelton, who was teaching a course on Marxism at the community college, began an exegesis of materialism, capitalism, and communism, which Lyn eagerly lapped up.

On another occasion, Shelton tried to move the conversation closer toward the case. He asked why she had the gun.

Lyn said she thought the weapon was "beautiful."

Shelton quickly agreed. The pistol, the pocketwatch—such instruments, the detective said, possessed "the sterile beauty of certain things mechanical."

"I can't imagine you being interested in weapons, or carrying a weapon or doing things with weapons," Lyn said.

"Well, I have this interest in weapons that might be something like yours," Shelton said. "There's something about the precision of them, there's something about the fact that, with just such a little action with my finger, I can do so much. It's the principle of the lever, you know, lift the lever here at *this* end, and at *that* end, while it doesn't move much, it moves great weight. That's the principle of all children's toys."

Lyn considered that concept amusing. The gun as toy.

"Well," Shelton quickly added, "I don't want you to take that—seriously. I don't think a gun is a children's toy. I'm saying, it's an exaggeration of the principle of what makes children happy. A small amount of effort yields a *big* payoff. That's the basic idea behind toys."

Shelton segued into a discussion of one gun in particular: Lyn's Colt .45. How did this "toy" work? How many pieces in it came apart? Lyn explained how to operate the pistol, how to load and remove the magazine, how to place her thumb on the clip release. She said she had been shown how to arm the gun, but lacked the strength to do so—and thus, hadn't. She told him about the precautions she took to keep the weapon safe, such as storing the ammunition separately from the pistol, and keeping the gun buried near her house.

Shelton also inquired, gently, about Lyn's drug use. How often had she taken LSD? About ten times, Lyn replied. Shelton double-checked with Sandy. "Oh, no," Sandy clarified. They had taken acid "thousands" of times.

For the most part, the discussions yielded little of immediate use to Shelton. Talking to Lyn was, Shelton later said, "like having a conversation turned in on itself. It wasn't just a solipsism, because it never made as much sense as a solipsism makes."

Meanwhile, Shelton came to suspect that he was being sandbagged by the feds. Early one morning, when the streets were empty and the mist was streaming from the ground, Shelton emerged from a house where he had been checking on a lead. He got in his car and closed the door; moments later, he heard eight slams in rapid succession. He looked in his mirror and saw eight identical cars with their doors closing. The drivers, Shelton thought, looked like FBI agents, doubtless part of the hundred-man team investigating the Fromme case. He assumed he was being followed and had only spotted his tail because the streets were so vacant.

Years later, Lee Latham would deny that the FBI had put Shelton under surveillance. He was less dismissive of another of Shelton's claims: that government offices had been burglarized during the investigation, and that files related to the Fromme case had gone missing. Although Shelton never was formally accused of doing the job, a member of the prosecution team who was friendly with Shelton told him that he was under suspicion. "We assume it was you because you're clever enough to get away with it. Was it?" the official asked. Shelton denied any involvement.

No mention of the break-in was made to the press, or included among Department of Justice files released under the Freedom of Information Act. But asked if authorities had suspected a break-in, Latham acknowledged, "I think that's safe to say." He then added: "But I wouldn't want to confirm it for you."

For Shelton, the worries kept growing the longer he stayed with the case. He recalled that one afternoon, while driving his Volvo north from Sacramento on Interstate 5, a blue-green Ford Mustang Mark III pulled up alongside him and braked to match his speed. The window was down, and Shelton could see four men in the car. One of them, in his twenties, leveled a snub-nosed revolver at Shelton and fired. Only by slamming on his brakes did Shelton dodge the bullets. The Volvo fishtailed as it screeched to a halt. Shelton then gunned his engine, got his Volvo up to 110 mph, took the first off-ramp, and drove straight to the Highway Patrol.

The incident was obviously unsettling. But despite some immediate suspicions, Shelton grew to doubt that it was related to the Fromme case. "It's no doubt Jungian," he now says. "It just happened."

The defense was not alone in its misgivings about the case. In Washington, top officials of the Ford administration watched nervously as prosecutors they barely knew moved ahead with a case that, if botched, would prove highly embarrassing to the president. The head of the Criminal Division, Assistant Attorney General Richard L. Thornburgh, reminded Dwayne Keyes that "we have followed closely and are keenly interested in the case against Lynette Alice Fromme."

Although the Sacramento prosecutors had managed to keep Lyn in jail prior to trial, their superiors in Washington were not impressed with the way the case was being handled. In a confidential letter to Keyes, Thornburgh, a future attorney general under President George Bush, criticized the first formal act taken in the case: the drafting of the indictment.

Like a law professor grading an exam, Thornburgh wrote that "the wording of the indictment may be subject to a defense objection turning on its failure to include a brief statement of the acts constituting the attempt." Fortunately, he added, the sloppy drafting might not be fatal; a recent Supreme Court decision made it "likely that the Government could successfully resist a motion to dismiss."

Thornburgh had another far more serious concern: that the evidence developed by the government was too weak to guarantee a conviction. "From our review of the initial FBI report . . . it appears that the primary thrust of the defense will be to argue that Ms. Fromme did not intend to shoot the President but rather was simply seeking publicity." The defense, Thornburgh predicted,

> will point to the fact that no round was chambered in Ms. Fromme's pistol and that she allegedly is well trained in the use of weapons of the type involved.
>
> The Government's evidence opposing this contention and establishing the requisite element of intent to kill the President appears to us to be relatively strong. However . . . *it does not appear that the Government possess any one piece of credible evidence which is absolutely conclusive on this issue and which provides virtual certainty of conviction.* Accordingly, if Ms. Fromme's testimony in her own behalf is persuasive and if she can present credible independent evidence of her facility with weapons, it would appear possible that the Government could encounter some difficulty convincing a jury beyond a reasonable doubt of her intent to kill President Ford. [Emphasis added.]

It got worse. Thornburgh's staff had pored over the law books to see if a lesser offense, assault, could be deemed included within the single count against Lyn. Unhappily, Thornburgh wrote, case law in Sacramento's judicial circuit made it "doubtful that the Government could obtain an instruction on assault because of its additional element relating to apprehension of harm by the victim." Thus, if Lyn could persuade the jury she was smart enough to chamber a round in a Colt .45 had she wanted to, the fact that she hadn't could result in total acquittal. Lyn, with her X-scarred forehead and her crimson hood, would walk out the courthouse door free as a bird. The image of the Manson Family besting the Ford administration would hardly build confidence in this particular presidency.

Thornburgh asked Keyes for detailed responses to his legal concerns. If the Sacramento prosecutor didn't face enough pressure, Thornburgh stressed that his office was "prepared to assist you in any way possible in the preparation and prosecution of this case."

Ironically, the defense Thornburgh feared most had similarities to the strategy that Lyn herself was sketching out. Although she planned to stress her frustrations over environmental issues, it was likely that Lyn's intent—as reflected by her failure to chamber a round in the .45—would emerge from her testimony. Lyn told a reporter that her legal approach involved opening "the defendant's mind for scrutiny . . . I'm going to have to say why I did what I did."

The defense team led by Dick Walker, however, was focusing on another approach. Based in part on Phil Shelton's continuing conversations with Lyn, the federal defender's office was preparing a defense turning on diminished mental capacity. "It was based on mental illness," Shelton recalled. "It had everything to do with drug use, drug dependence and, especially, what flashbacks might be caused by marijuana if you've had a long history of acid use." To that end, the defense team had located an expert on drug potentiation—the way use of one drug can intensify the effect of another—based at the University of California, Los Angeles. The defense team was judicious in discussing this approach with Lyn. She was, of course, dead set against any argument that suggested she did not know what she was doing.

Indeed, Lyn now considered herself a formidable participant in the national policy debate. When the Sacramento Union's Washington correspondent, Tom Ochiltree, wrote that President Ford should limit his contact with crowds, Lyn was moved to respond. The Union published her letter on the front page.

"Dear Tom and Union Staff," it began. "First, as to your original thought that the President should be kept at a greater distance, I want to explain something to you which may be so simple you have overlooked the fact. The incumbent President has absolutely no reason to campaign personally. He is already in the position to SHOW his merits. He is already in the position to ENACT what other candidates can only speak and the media is his for the asking."

How, she wanted to know, can "[we] believe any further rhetoric written by one person and spoken by another for the specific purpose of gaining votes. Furthermore, and contrary to your misinformation, I could show you countless discrepancies in executive policy that have jostled the minds of the American public, each situation for which I do have valid alternatives. Unfortunately, through the overall picture painted by the press, you have been left with your opinion that 'Squeaky, a twenty-six-year-old follower of the violent Charles Manson cult, seems to be some sort of kiddie playing radical. She said she threatened Ford because no one was paying any attention to her.' I said nothing of the kind, but I certainly understand where you got this opinion."

As usual, Lyn saw the world situation through a rather personal lens. Once, she wrote, she had shared society's belief in the American system. "I held the same faith until the late Sixties when, like thousands of other young people, I realized the big business of war. . . . Peace that needs to be kept with weapons is not peace. Don't tell me that I don't understand. Explain it.

"There is space and resources enough in this world to provide every person with food, clothing, housing and purpose," she wrote, adding an apparent reference to the Manson Family's own dream: "And to allow every group a place, excluding those whose lifestyle requires dominance over others unless that dominance be by mutual consent."

Phil Shelton was back at the jail for another conversation with Lyn. Once again, they were discussing whales. How did whales speak to each other, Lyn wanted to know.

Shelton explained that whales could communicate with each other through miles and miles of ocean. "The best belief we have at this time is that their communication method is not linear. It's more like sending a television signal— in fact, it's almost the same frequency as a television signal. Whales use many frequencies," he added.

On September 5, before she woke up, Lyn said, she had had a dream about whales. There were these whales in the dark, deep depths of ocean. They couldn't see, they had no way of knowing one another was present, and they were alone and cold and may as well have been dead, until they heard another whale.

Then Lyn saw her father, and she was underwater, and her father was underwater, and she sent out her whale call. And he never answered.

This dream, Lyn told the detective, had been rolling across her mind all through the morning of September 5. A morning that had come after days, weeks, years and years of rejection. No one, not in Los Angeles, not in Sacramento, would hear her message. She recalled what she had been told, in so many ways, so many times: "We're not interested in you and your goddamn trees. President Ford is coming to town." If that's what everybody was interested in, she would be, too. She would do something with President Ford. That would get everybody's attention. The gun was just to get President Ford to notice, Lyn said. Outside the state Capitol, when he came up the path toward her, she didn't want to kill him.

She was sobbing.

Shelton considered Lyn. She had, he thought, the emotional age of a twelve-year-old. That touched him. "She still believes in good," he thought. Collecting himself, he pushed her:

"You had bullets in the gun. You didn't need to take the clip if all you wanted to do was be photographed pointing a gun at the President. You could have done what you wanted to do with a gun with no bullets in it. Why? You tell me when you decided you would not kill Gerald Ford."

Still weeping, Lyn answered, "I left the house not wanting to kill Gerald Ford. By the time I saw him coming, I hated him so much, I then wanted to kill Gerald Ford but didn't know how to arm the gun. Couldn't arm the gun."

"Why?"

"He looked," Lyn said, "like my father." Tears streamed down her face.

Mesmerized, his voice deep with his own emotion, Shelton pressed: *"Why didn't you kill him?"*

"Three steps before I was caught, his button came unbuttoned." She indicated Shelton's waist. The detective looked at her through the plexiglass. He unbuttoned the last button above his belt.

"This one?" he asked.

Nodding, she continued: "On the President of the United States of America. And his belly showed. Just like my father. And I can remember, when I was a little girl, I felt so sorry that my father's button didn't hold, and exposed his tummy. And I couldn't shoot." Lyn cried.

Decades later, Shelton recalled the moment as he closed his button. "I couldn't stand it. I cried hard. And it wasn't because I was somehow in her corner more than I ever would have been before, but it touched me that this great man, this President's button came undone. And it saved his life from what she intended for a moment; had the gun been armed, had she gone there with the intent to kill, had she been as much a killer as she was alleged to have been, had that button not come open we might have had a dead President.

"But there's something even richer about the story knowing that the gun wasn't armed, anyway. She went there like so many people go, trying to do great things unprepared. And we are all so unprepared."

Shelton was now convinced his client was innocent of the charge against her. The defense crystalized in his mind: Lyn's actions in Capitol Park had been instigated by an acid flashback caused by a narcotic potentiation.

"Now," Shelton acknowledged, "you cannot tell a jury this story without invoking some issues having to do with mental state." This idea was abhorrent to the client. "She wouldn't let us. She thought we were trying to prove that she was crazy. She wasn't. I think I wrote in my report, 'she misunderstands what we're trying to do. We're not trying to prove she's crazy.'"

Shelton, the former philosophy student, often thinks of that moment with Lynette Fromme.

"I mean of all the things in America, of all the things that you think of when you think of all the evilness and ugliness of all the stuff you see on television, you never see anything so subtle and simple yet so damning as a button coming open on the President of the United States."

In San Francisco, Federal Circuit Judges Joseph Sneed and Anthony M. Kennedy, a future member of the Supreme Court, denied Lyn's appeal for a reduction of bail. Dick Walker pressed on, filing a petition with Justice William O. Douglas in Washington, D.C.

Appointed by President Franklin Roosevelt, Douglas was an iconoclastic liberal known for his environmentalist philosophy, provocative writings, and controversial private life. In 1970, at the behest of the Nixon Administration, Congressman Gerald Ford had initiated a House inquiry intended to lead to Douglas's impeachment.

The Nixon-Ford attack on Douglas did not go unnoticed by Charles Manson, then on trial in Los Angeles for the murder of Gary Hinman. The day after Congressman Ford demanded that Douglas be investigated, Manson asked to have the justice—"you know, Douglas, that guy who's in trouble in Washington"—appointed as his defense attorney. Superior Court Judge George M. Dell replied that Douglas wasn't available. "He has already got a job as a judge and I hope he keeps it," Dell told Manson.

If Lyn held any particular regard for Justice Douglas, it was not reciprocated. On October 9, 1975, days after receiving her bail petition, Douglas glanced at it and scrawled one word: "Denied." It would be one of his final acts in thirty-six years on the court. On November 12, incapacitated by a stroke, Douglas tendered his resignation to President Gerald Ford.

Two weeks had passed between Lyn's last court appearance and her first day representing herself before Judge MacBride. She had spent the intervening time studying law books, meeting regularly with Dick Walker and Bob Holley, and preparing legal motions. Much as Walker had tried to accommodate his client's wishes, their views of the case diverged sharply. When Lyn and her lawyers entered the courtroom on October 7, strains among the defense team were evident; at one point, she ordered Walker to switch seats with her so she could be closer to the judge.

"Miss Fromme will make the presentation," Walker said.

"All right," said Judge MacBride.

Lyn, standing at the lectern in a red scarf and wraparound dress, read a lengthy list of discovery motions that Walker had written for her. Lyn went through them in an upbeat, even cheerful way. Most were routine. Some, however, were more specific. She asked for the return of personal items—"such as sewing materials"—seized from her house. "I want the court to order the government to return all items that are obviously not necessary for their prosecution before they disappear or show up in a magazine." Indeed, *Time* had published a nude shot of Lyn and Sandy, presumably taken for the entertainment of Charlie's prison friends. Apparently referring to that photo, Lyn complained that "a law enforcement officer of some nature had to get hold of it.... Things have a way of slipping out of these people's hands."

MacBride granted the routine motions, and asked the prosecution to be accommodating to the defense on matters within their discretion. Then Lyn asked that MacBride order the prosecution to turn over to her evidence that would help her be "ex— ex— ex ..."

"Exculpated," the judge supplied.

"That's it," said Lyn.

"That's the word you really want, Miss Fromme," said the judge.

"The only argument I have about that," said Lyn, "is *Brady* vs. *Maryland*. Evidence leading to exculpatory—"

MacBride interrupted. "This is absolutely true, Miss Fromme." The prosecution, he explained, "is under a strict mandate of *Brady* vs. *Maryland* which requires them to furnish to you any and all exculpatory information or witnesses or physical evidence that they may have that could in any way assist in your defense."

Despite the holding of *Brady*, Lyn asked the judge specifically to order the prosecution to turn over exculpatory evidence. MacBride insisted such an order was redundant. If the government failed to turn over such evidence, "they're subject to a reversal, that's what it boils down to. If it turns out they have been in possession of any information that might be exculpatorily helpful to you—"

"Your Honor—" Lyn protested.

"—in the event this in any way comes to light, and the light does leak out, believe it or not, the matter will be brought before the court and I would think that it would not be difficult to obtain a reversal in the event of your conviction," MacBride said. And, "if, for instance an exculpatory statement could come up between now and the time of the trial, or during the trial, the government would still be under the order of *Brady* vs. *Maryland* to reveal that to you."

Lyn relented. "In view of what Senator Frank Church [said], extracting from certain witnesses in his committee proceedings, I think I could make a really good argument," she said. "But I understand your position and I won't."

The judge emphasized that the government would permit Lyn to inspect photos and recordings taken "at the scene of your alleged attempt to assassinate the President of the United States."

"Thank you," said Lyn. "Thank you for the word *alleged*."

Court records do not reflect Don Heller's reaction to the *Brady* exchange.

Later, however, his actions concerning potentially exculpatory evidence would threaten to derail the entire prosecution.

Lyn then presented her legal theory: "The court has stated repeatedly that . . . the defendant will not be permitted to make any political statements or to use the court as a forum for talking about such ecology issues as endangered redwood trees and nuclear power plants. I have talked late into the night with my client— me—affirming my original position in defense. . . . Let [the record] reflect that this defendant is not charged with the murder of the President. That the charge is attempted assassination. That it is this defendant's understanding that the United States Attorney must prove beyond doubt that the defendant intended knowingly and wilfully to murder the President. That intent is very clearly a state of mind, that intent is a thought before and during an action, that the inquiry of such may well open the defendant's mind for scrutiny, and that the defendant's state of mind may be directly concerned with such social matters as the court has deemed unfit for court consumption."

She told the judge she wished to file a motion establishing new procedures that would "include in trials the determination not only of who, what and where, but a most important consideration in stopping the increasing flow of lives who pass through the court. And that consideration is Why? Why crime?

"I ask this court and all future courts in the interests of justice to be duly tolerant of motions heretofore unheard of by the court and to respect one small individual's right to her fair trial by allowing me to move reasonably without precedent. I pray to bring truth into the world. I pray to bring reason into the courtroom as a service to all people, to recognize the laws of cause and effect and to slowly eliminate the cause of the illegal response known as crime."

MacBride did not respond. Lyn continued, announcing now that she had "absolutely no rapport" with Walker—"and a trial in which the attorney and the defendant have no rapport could be anything from a folly to a fist fight."

The judge acknowledged having heard "some rumbling about this," but couldn't quite understand Lyn's problem. He ran down Walker's many accomplishments, and praised his work on Lyn's behalf.

Lyn agreed that "academically, he apparently does fine."

"Boy, that's what you better count on!" said the judge. "That's what you need more than anything else."

Lyn was unpersuaded. She was dismissing Walker. In his place, she wanted Bob Holley.

MacBride said he could not oblige. No attorney as green as Holley could responsibly be appointed for such a serious case.

"I absolutely cannot compromise," said Lyn. "Were I to go on trial in this state of mind, having to struggle with my own co-counsel, Your Honor, I would be absolutely unable to conduct any type of defense at all," she went on, her voice rising angrily. "I might as well just leave."

Said MacBride, glancing around the heavily guarded courtroom, "That might be a little difficult right now, Miss Fromme." The chamber erupted in laughter.

Lyn then offered a compromise: Holley would serve as Lyn's partner, while Walker would become "counsel to both of us."

"Miss Fromme, wait a minute," said the judge. "Mr. Walker brought Holley along as his assistant. Now you want to reverse it and make the Federal Defender the assistant to the assistant."

"Yes," said Lyn. "Just like making the child the parent. I want to reverse it."

"I don't know if—"

"This is part of what I want to say," Lyn insisted. "This is part of what I want to do."

The judge turned to the federal defender. "Wait a minute. Mr. Walker, is this a viable thought at all? Is this possible?"

"I was born humble, Your Honor," said Walker. "It wore off.... As far as I'm concerned, the Federal Defender—we are here to serve. If I could serve by being Mr. Holley's assistant, I could do that."

Judge MacBride put the matter over until the next court session.

Lyn was not mollified. Dutifully, Walker arranged for her to meet with attorneys in private practice who did contract work for the federal defender's office. On Thursday night, after a visit from attorney John Virga, Lyn selected him as her new co-counsel. The next morning, Walker made the necessary motion in court, and turned over the defense to Virga—one of only two lawyers on the federal defender's indigent panel willing to take Lyn's case.

Virga, the brother of a Sacramento County judge, had worked for four years as a deputy district attorney and then spent five years in private practice. In appointing him, MacBride praised Virga as "one of the best attorneys in Sacramento." Lucinda Franks of the *New York Times* was more evocative in describing Virga. With his dark hair and prominent mustache, Lyn's new co-counsel was "a handsome man of thirty-six who resembles Omar Sharif, the actor," she wrote. "He blinks a pair of deep brown eyes like camera shutters, looking wounded, then astonished, and always innocent."

Despite the change in attorneys, Phil Shelton intended to remain on the case; no one on the defense team, after all, had built a relationship with Lyn as complicated or intimate as Shelton. That possibility ended, Shelton said, after Virga showed Shelton's notes to Lyn. Among the detective's remarks to Walker was a statement that read: "If we want to have any kind of shot at a technical defense involving her mental state, we must move now—she's beginning to listen to me."

The comment inflamed Lyn. "When you read that," Shelton later acknowledged, "it looks like, 'Holy shit! This guy wasn't working for me! This guy was actually trying to do something to me!' To a degree, that's true. I wasn't interested in becoming her lifelong friend. I was interested in defending her." Two decades after the Fromme trial, Shelton remained rueful about the turn of events. "It was actually possible for her to walk," he said.

Chapter 10

No More

Duck Hunting

During the Tate-LaBianca trial, a crew of documentary filmmakers had set up shop at the Spahn Ranch. Led by Laurence Merrick and Robert Hendrickson, the crew shot some 10,000 feet of film, capturing the Manson Family at work and at play, singing, dancing, toying with weapons, and, at great length, speaking their minds. Because Charlie, Sadie, Katie, and Lulu were all in jail, the camera focused on Family members still at liberty—and Lyn, her hair cut short in preparation for desert battle, figured prominently. Several segments featured Lyn brandishing knives and firearms—"an urban guerrilla in hot-pants," said one film critic. In one memorable scene, she fondled a rifle and cooed, "You have to make love with it. You have to know every part of it. To know you know it is to know it, so that you could pick it up at any second and shoot!"

The interview segments with Lyn were shot against a black background, perhaps to heighten the intensity of her presence. She continued: "We respond. We respond with our knives. We respond with whatever we have. It feels good. It feels good to be ready to face death and love it. . . . Anybody can kill anyone."

With its sliding split screens and trippy camera tricks, the film's editing aped that of the epochal documentary, *Woodstock*. Instead of performances by the Who, the Grateful Dead, and Jimi Hendrix, however, *Manson* featured the Family singing some of Charlie's songs, as well as musical interludes by a pair who had dropped out of group.

Screened at overseas film festivals in 1972, *Manson* was greeted both with acclaim—it received an Academy Award nomination for best documentary—and contempt. "Clinically expert, horrifyingly brilliant," wrote reviewer William Otterburn-Hall from the Venice Film Festival. The *New York Times's* Vincent

Canby, on the other hand, called *Manson* "one of those rip-off movies that tut-tuts with shock at all the unpleasant details it feels it must give us in the interest of higher sociology and the fast buck."

Audiences would have to wait to judge for themselves. After legal disputes emerged over the film's ownership, it was not released commercially in the United States. Paul Fitzgerald tried to get the producers to screen the picture for him. In April 1973, he wrote to Lyn about his efforts: "Concerning the movie creep, Merrick, I have called him and asked to be allowed to see this great documentary film, *Manson*. He promises he is going to let me see it, but doesn't. I hear from a couple of sources that it is bad, bad, bad."

With Lyn on the front page after the Ford incident, the legal hang-ups vanished and the picture was rushed into theaters. Merrick said that distribution plans had been solidified two months before September 5; whatever the story, the picture soon received a new, more commercial title: *Manson & Squeaky Fromme*. Dick Walker feared that the film could prejudice potential jurors; his last act as Lyn's co-counsel had been to seek an injunction to suppress the picture in the twenty-six counties constituting Sacramento's federal jury pool. The motion, a virtually unprecedented challenge to a First Amendment right, alleged that the film's exhibition would "irreparably harm" Lyn's chances of a fair trial.

Judge MacBride decided to see the eighty-five-minute picture for himself. The grand jury chambers were quickly converted into a screening room, and a small invited audience joined the judge for the show: filmmaker Robert Hendrickson, Don Heller, Bob Holley, John Virga, and the star herself, Lynette Fromme. The film was exhibited on an exotic device that few in 1975 were familiar with: a videocassette player.

After the screening, MacBride remained in his chambers while Lyn returned to the courtroom. Sandy was waiting.

"How was the film?" she asked.

"Oh, it was a lot of dirty blood and sex," said Lyn. "It wasn't Manson's voice. It sounded like an old man."

A deputy marshal warned Lyn to keep silent, and she obediently sat down. After a bit, she stood up again and indicated to Marcia Van Court, serving as the matron, that she wanted to leave the courtroom. As Lyn was escorted out, she turned to her friend. "Sandy," she said, "the problem is they put the whole thing on Manson. They make us out to be innocent children."

Later that day, MacBride issued his order: The film would be banned in his jurisdiction until a verdict was reached or the jury sequestered. The judge had concluded that the filmmakers' First Amendment rights to exhibit their picture were "irreconcilable" with Lyn's Sixth Amendment right to a speedy and fair trial. When such a conflict emerged, the First Amendment "must be subordinated" to the Sixth.

MacBride added that he was making no findings about the film's integrity, authenticity, or whether it had "redeeming social value." He also had a comment for Lyn: Stop making gratuitous remarks in court. "If you make some boneheaded statement," he groused, "that's your problem."

MacBride's order affected an inland region of 2 million people, stretching from the Oregon border to the town of Modesto, southeast of San Francisco. Free speech advocates were outraged. In an editorial, the *Los Angeles Times* condemned MacBride's order as "judicial fanaticism" and "an unprecedented extension of censorship." The American Civil Liberties Union filed suit to lift the ban, listing as plaintiffs three men who wanted to see the film.

Noting that the picture was still playing outside MacBride's jurisdiction, Dick Walker said that the ACLU was "making a mountain out of a molehill." Anyone so desperately interested in the film should buy "a bus ticket and a bag of popcorn and go to San Francisco."

No effort, however, was made to suppress *Helter Skelter*, and sales of the Bugliosi book were going through the roof. Local bookstores quickly sold out, and the waiting list at the Sacramento public library was three months long.

By the time appeals of MacBride's order reached the appellate court, the issue was moot; the jury had been sequestered and the censorship order lifted. When *Manson & Squeaky Fromme* opened in Sacramento, one of the first to see it was Sandra Good. Viewing the film while munching on hot buttered popcorn, Sandy said she was moved by scenes of the beauty and love at Spahn Ranch; she told the *Sacramento Bee* it was like watching home movies. Others, she conceded, would take away a different impression.

"People who view this movie will see what they see. Everybody will see something else, something that they are oriented to seeing. Many people will focus on the blood, the gore, the prosecution witnesses, the cellmates and their personal fantasies that they project on us, you know, the thrill-kill, the thrill-sex-kill trip. That is not us."

Los Angeles Times critic Charles Champlin, for one, did not see the film the way that Sandy did. "The horror of the talk in *Manson*," he wrote, "is that it is the prattling of not very bright children."

The President's Subpoena
On Tuesday, October 7, John Virga asked Judge MacBride to subpoena the President of the United States.

There were few precedents for the request. In 1807, Aaron Burr, on trial for treason, sought a subpoena requiring President Thomas Jefferson to produce certain letters helpful to the defense. Chief Justice John Marshall held that the presidency enjoyed no absolute immunity from judicial process; while a judge could take a president's peculiar obligations into account when ruling on such a motion, authority rested with the court.

Eleven years later, a disgruntled federal appointee subpoenaed President James Monroe to testify in court. Monroe wrote on the back of the subpoena that his official duties required him to remain in Washington, but that he would be willing to sit for a deposition. Monroe answered written interrogatories. Unfortunately for the plaintiff, the case had been dismissed by the time the president's testimony, subject to the vagaries of nineteenth-century transport, arrived in the courtroom.

More recently, the Supreme Court had ruled in a 1974 case that a president had no "executive privilege" permitting him to withhold tape recordings of White House conversations. Seventeen days after the unanimous decision in *United States vs. Nixon*, the president resigned. Nixon, an unindicted co-conspirator in the Watergate inquiry, was spared prosecution only because of President Ford's prophylactic pardon.

In the Fromme case, Virga told Judge MacBride that Ford should be summoned because "he is a percipient witness to this particular ... alleged offense." Specifically, he wanted to ask Ford if he had heard a *click* during his encounter with Lyn—because such a noise spoke to Lyn's intent in pointing her pistol at the president.

Dwayne Keyes objected. "Before this historical precedent is set," he said, some matters should be addressed. "The evidence on trial is going to show that this defendant wanted to kill the President to gain attention regarding her environmental concerns, in regards to Charles Manson's incarceration. No one was listening to this defendant. No one was taking her seriously. Now, on ten days notice, she can get several hours of the President's time. He didn't hear her environmental concerns, but he will have to listen to her legal concerns. She has had in a small way—but perhaps to her in a very large way—a victory." Wouldn't such a victory for Lyn encourage other misfits? "The President is concerned ... that we minimize as best we can that which would excite or encourage the demented mind."

Keyes did not claim that Ford enjoyed an absolute immunity from subpoena, but said the court should not consider the defense request until the prosecution had concluded its case. Keyes noted that the president already had made a statement to the FBI about his recollections of the Capitol Park incident. And since so many witnesses would be testifying about whether or not there was a *click*, the president's testimony might prove to be merely "cumulative."

"There's probably no *click* that's more important than the *click* that wasn't heard by the President, though," said MacBride.

"We're talking about a *click*. That could turn to a *clang* when that cell door slams behind her every night," added Virga, waxing dramatic. "The President of the United States is not above the law, he's not above due process. He should be the epitome of due process and the law. I need not go into Watergate and everything that went on there."

MacBride was ready to make his decision. The president was "the man that was looking right down the barrel of the gun. In this case, he is, in a way— with all due respect to the President, I don't mean to be disrespectful—but he is no different than the poor, little girl who is the teller of a bank who looks down the barrel when somebody holds up a bank. He is the most percipient witness."

There was much the president could contribute, MacBride said. In addition to his account of the alleged *click*, did Ford see Lyn's face? If so, did she wear "an expression of one who might be anticipating the hearing of a loud explosion if she expected the gun to go off. Was it a smile? Was it a look of defiance? Was it a look of hatred?"

Now, MacBride acknowledged, "It's unfortunate that the Chief Executive of the United States has to be put to this burden. At the same time, I don't know what else Congress had in mind when they passed the statute that states it is a federal offense to attempt to take the life of the President of the United States. Certainly, they must have contemplated there would be those circumstances where the President of the United States would have to be a witness whenever such a charge came to trial."

Virga noted that "both myself and Miss Fromme appreciate, you know, that the President has many things to do." Virga proposed that the examination be conducted on videotape, at the president's convenience.

The judge agreed. MacBride extolled the wonders of this new technology, which he had recently seen used in his chambers to screen the *Manson* documentary. The VCR was "a blessing.... It was almost a marvel to see the way they were able to do it. Certainly, with sound movies and the like nowadays, there shouldn't be any difficulty in taking the President's deposition."

Ford would be examined within ten days, at a place of his choosing. One more thing: Lyn would not be coming on the field trip. "Sorry about that, Miss Fromme," said the judge.

Dwayne Keyes would later worry that that decision could be construed as a violation of Lyn's Sixth Amendment rights—and thus be grounds for reversal. Lyn, however, had other concerns. As MacBride was leaving the courtroom for the lunch recess, she chided him, "Your Honor, no more duck hunting. It's shameful that you have to shoot birds out of the sky for recreation." Like many Sacramentans, MacBride was an avid hunter.

Although no mention of it was made in court, an important occasion was coming up for Lyn. On October 22, 1975, she celebrated her twenty-seventh birthday.

White House aides considered appealing MacBride's order, but President Ford settled the matter himself. He would comply with Lyn's subpoena. "I thought it would be an excellent opportunity to show that I wanted justice done," Ford later recollected. "I thought it was my obligation as an eyewitness to go to court." Besides, he said, "if I had not agreed to go, I think it would have looked bad"—especially in the aftermath of the Nixon pardon. "So my willingness to testify was the right thing in more than one way. I felt that at the time, and I still feel it," Ford says now.

And so, a federal marshal appeared at the White House to serve the subpoena. It was directed to "the Honorable Gerald E. Ford, President of the United States." No matter. Gerald R. Ford knew who the court had in mind.

Arrangements had to come into place quickly. Administration aides initially scheduled the deposition for the White House, in the presidential counsel's West Wing office. Dwayne Keyes didn't like the idea. "Let's just find a room somewhere else," he said. "We don't want to dignify this too much, because the more exciting it gets, the more historic it becomes, the worse it might become for other Presidents." On reflection, the Justice Department agreed, and the proceeding was moved across the street to the Old Executive Office Building, former headquarters of the War Department. Another change was made: the date was moved forward one day, from October 31 to November 1. For undisclosed reasons, the government did not want to have Squeaky Fromme's counsel confront the president on Halloween.

"That will satisfy Miss Fromme," said Judge MacBride when he learned of the schedule change. "I won't be able to go duck hunting that day."

Keyes came to the White House on the eve of the deposition to prepare Ford for the proceeding. Arriving at the Oval Office just as Federal Reserve chairman Arthur F. Burns headed out, Keyes was ushered in to meet the president. Ford, though getting over a bad cold, was characteristically friendly to his visitor.

Keyes had to keep his comments limited to the format of the deposition and the general nature of questions Ford might expect; a Justice Department memorandum warned that "anything more definitive ... [might be] construed as an attempt to 'brief' the President on what his testimony *should* be."

At 10:05 A.M. the next morning, Judge MacBride reconvened his court in Room 345 of the Old Executive Office Building. Sitting in were Dick Thornburgh and David Kennerly, the president's personal photographer. Distasteful as the event may have been for the government, it was still history, and a photographic record had to be made. A squad of technicians, drawn from the Navy Department and the White House staff, operated the video equipment. No press or members of the public were admitted. Judge MacBride, who became a solicitous acquaintance of Phil Buchen, made sure to get his picture taken with the president.

Outside the building, reporters speculated about the goings-on inside. CBS News correspondent Fred Graham, later the on-air face of Court TV, told viewers that videotaped testimony had been used only three times before in American criminal trials.

Reporters crowded around Judge MacBride and the Sacramento entourage when they left the Executive Office Building, but got little to enliven their stories. At a White House briefing, correspondents smothered press secretary Ron Nessen with questions about the proceeding's minutiae: What type of videotape was used? How large was the table where the president sat? What was Mr. Ford wearing? To that question, Nessen gave a thorough answer: "A dark blue suit, blue tie with red stripe, shoes, socks, undershirt and underwear."

"Are you sure about the underwear?" asked one reporter, to general laughter.

The entire legal proceeding lasted about forty-five minutes. The president testified for only nineteen minutes; the balance of the hearing was devoted to questions about the videotape's disposition. Three copies of the tape were made. When the fidelity of two tapes had been determined, the third was destroyed. One copy was given to Buchen for safekeeping. MacBride took the other, and locked it overnight in the vault of his hotel. On the return trip, he made special arrangements to clear the tape through airport security, so that it would not be exposed to any possible damage from the X-ray machines.

Back in Sacramento, MacBride had the tape locked in the court safe, awaiting the defense's decision of whether to show the testimony to the jury. If Lyn decided that the president's evidence would not be helpful to her case, the videotape would be destroyed, unseen.

Oblivious to the hoopla in Washington, Lyn stayed in her cell at the Sacramento County Jail. For her, the most exciting event was when someone brought her a flowered nightgown to wear.

While the eyes of the nation focused on the Old Executive Office Building, events of greater significance to Lyn's fate were going on in Sacramento. There, Don Heller, left behind on the Washington trip, placed a telephone call to a less famous witness of September 5's events, James Damir, the government student from Sacramento State.

Damir, a twenty-three-year-old who supported himself as a hospital janitor, had been amid the Capitol Park crowd that had witnessed the pistol incident. Sometime after 4:00 P.M. on September 5, Damir gave an interview to FBI Agent Donald Bolan. In Bolan's report, Damir recalled Lyn yelling, upon her arrest, "It didn't go off anyway, what are you worrying about. He is not really your public servant!"

Hours before speaking to Agent Bolan, however, Damir had been interviewed by Officer Paul Boettin, a fifteen-year veteran of the Sacramento Police Department. Eighty-five minutes after the pistol incident, Damir sat down with Boettin in an office at police headquarters. Boettin took out a legal pad. "Just tell me what happened," he said. "Just tell me what you heard."

She "repeated over and over, 'It's not loaded anyway, it's not loaded anyway,' " according to Boettin's report.

Of the three witnesses Boettin had interviewed, Damir was the only one to recall that particular statement. The officer showed Damir what he had written on his pad. "Are you sure this is what she said?" he asked.

"Yes," said Damir.

Days later, Don Heller reviewed the witness statements while deciding who to call before the grand jury. He read both the Bolan and Boettin reports, and called Damir in. Despite the conflicting statements in the reports, Heller neither mentioned the discrepancy to Dwayne Keyes nor gave a copy of the Boettin report to the defense.

On September 10, Heller summoned Damir to testify before the grand jury. What did Lyn say upon her arrest? Heller asked.

"She was saying things like: 'He's not your public servant.' I heard her say, 'The gun didn't go off anyway,' or something to that effect."

Heller produced Agent Bolan's report. "I show you a statement you made to the FBI. Will you read that?"

Damir read from Bolan's report: " 'It didn't go off anyway, what are you worrying about?' "

"Is that what she said?" Heller asked.

"Yes."

Heller made no reference to the Boettin report, or to the "It's not loaded" remark.

Now some six weeks later, on Sunday, November 2, Damir was back in Heller's office, going over his possible role in the government case. What exactly took place in this meeting never was established definitively, but Heller later would testify that Damir no longer could recall with certainty Lyn's precise remarks upon her arrest.

According to Heller, he showed Damir a transcript of his grand jury testimony, but not the FBI or Sacramento police reports. To further probe Damir's memory, Heller showed frame-by-frame slides of the moments following the incident, taken from news footage. Heller said later that Damir seemed confused about his recollections and nervous about the whole business.

As Damir watched the slides, he visualized himself back in Capitol Park. Suddenly, a phrase popped into his head and out of his mouth: "It's not loaded anyway." Damir would later describe the moment to his mother. "It was so real to him," Rita Damir later testified, "that something just flashed through his mind and he said it."

Either way, this was a detail, that would only complicate the prosecution case. According to Damir, Heller asked him if he was a member of the Manson Family, or if he knew any members of the Manson Family—Damir didn't remember exactly how the question was phrased. Heller said he asked if Damir knew any members of the Manson Family, because Sandra Good had also attended Sacramento State. "And so what I was trying to do, was find out if he knew Sandy Good, maybe that was the reason why he was so nervous." Heller also wanted to know if Damir had read *Helter Skelter*—"to reassure him that he wasn't in danger if he did testify and cooperate in this trial," Heller later said. "I think the point I mentioned was the witnesses in the Manson trial in Los Angeles testified and Manson was sentenced to the gas chamber and none of those witnesses were harmed. He really didn't have anything to worry about. . . . I think he was somewhat reassured that I mentioned the fact that none of the witnesses had been killed in the Manson case."

Whether this information indeed reassured young Damir was not reported. But after he got home, Damir began to doubt whether he really had heard Lyn say, "It's not loaded anyway." He called Heller to report his new lack of clarity.

Heller would maintain that the aim of his dealings with Damir was simply to clear up the testimony. When, weeks later, John Virga learned about the Boettin statement, he had another theory. He would accuse Heller of trying to conceal exculpatory evidence, to frighten Damir by raising the specter of the Manson Family, "to somehow get rid of that statement: 'It's not loaded anyway, it's not loaded anyway.' " Or as Judge MacBride summarized Virga's allegations, Heller was "trying to brainwash the man."

Even as Heller was questioning Damir about his recollections, other leads— or red herrings—were continuing to inundate the authorities. On Monday, November 3, the Secret Service office in Denver received a package containing a toy pistol. It was accompanied by a message that read: "I could have shot Rockefeller when he was in Denver. The gun is now pointed unless you release Lynette Fromme." The note was signed "Michael," but included no other identifying information. Laboratory tests of the package's wrapping and string led nowhere.

Jury of Her Peers

In the view of legal commentators, Judge MacBride was proving himself an assiduous protector of Lyn's Sixth Amendment rights. His rulings had placed her defense over the interest of 2 million Californians in seeing the *Manson* documentary and, even more extraordinary, over the privileges of the President of the United States. MacBride's friends told the *New York Times* that he was determined to avoid any "resemblance to Judge Julius J. Hoffman, who ordered defendants bound and gagged in the Chicago Seven trial."

No one was surprised, then, when MacBride announced that the Fromme jury would be sequestered during its deliberations. He hesitated, however, when asked to sequester the jury for the length of the trial.

Don Heller wanted the jury sequestered from the first day. At a bench conference, he told MacBride that during one of the Manson-related trials in Los Angeles, some jurors had received threatening telephone calls. As a result, the judge there sequestered the entire jury throughout the trial.

"I'm not accusing, you know, any associates of Miss Fromme, but there are nuts on both sides," Heller said. "It could be the kind of nut who calls up a juror and says, 'Hey, this woman attempted to kill the President. If you don't convict her, we'll get you.' "

"That's true," MacBride acknowledged.

This possibility, however, did not worry Lyn, according to John Virga. "Miss

Fromme's position is, Your Honor, that she feels the jury ought to be able to go home at night and stay with their families."

MacBride decided to play it safe. Jurors would be sequestered upon their appointment.

Selection of those jurors was the first act of the Fromme trial, which formally began on November 4, 1975. To prepare for the historic event, federal marshals imposed nearly unprecedented security precautions: six deputies, including two women, were assigned to a barricade outside the courtroom, while another roamed the hallway looking for suspicious activity. Spectators and reporters had to pass through metal detectors and subject their belongings to hand search. Although such security checkpoints would later become routine at courthouses and other public buildings, in 1975 several would-be spectators questioned the government's authority to search them so intrusively. Deputies responded by posting special orders obtained from Judge MacBride.

By 10:00 A.M., the courtroom was packed. "The glamour boys from network television have arrived," noted Rob Haeseler, the no-nonsense correspondent from the *San Francisco Chronicle*. "Sharp suits, custom coiffing." Attention focused on the defendant.

"She is a diminutive person with a small voice that is soft but does not squeak," wrote the *New York Times*'s Lucinda Franks. "With her long wavy red hair, meek mouth and eyes that seem slightly startled, she brings to mind the Alice in Wonderland of the book's noted illustrations by Sir John Tenniel."

According to Haeseler, not all journalists described Lyn in such literary fashion.

"Hey, she's got a nice ass!" said one reporter, as Lyn "bent over the defense table shuffling legal papers."

Judge MacBride called the proceedings to order. Two hundred prospective jurors had been summoned, and now forty-five were led into the courtroom for the voir dire. MacBride began by explaining the rules of sequestration. The jurors would live and dine together for the duration of the trial, which might last as long as four weeks. All visits with family members would take place with deputies present, all telephone calls and mail would be monitored by the marshal, and all books, newspapers, magazines, radio broadcasts, and television programs would be censored to excise any reference to the trial or related events. Jurors would be allowed a maximum of two alcoholic drinks per day, at dinnertime, at their own expense.

Nevertheless, MacBride said, the sacrifice would be worth it. "This case is being watched and heard . . . by a tremendous number of people in the United States and probably throughout the world. It's the first case of its kind that's ever been tried in the history of the United States, and I hope it will be the last." Looking at the men and women gathered from the remote northeastern quarter of California, from towns like Placerville, Yreka, and Yuba City, Mac-

Bride felt confident when he promised, "you will have one of the most interesting experiences you'll have in your life." The judge resumed his discussion of the formalities governing the trial, but Lyn jumped up and strode over to the bench.

"Yes, Miss Fromme?" said MacBride.

"Your Honor, these people cannot judge me," she said. "They can only judge themselves. My Family judges me. That's why I took off my robe today—because my robe belongs to them." Indeed, as Lyn faced the judge, she carried her customary red robe slung over her arm. "Their sacrifice. I feel that it's necessary for me to—" she paused. "I realize that you don't like this."

"Well," said the judge, "I don't know whether I don't like it. You haven't said anything on which I can rule."

"Oh. All right. I find it necessary—"

Don Heller interjected: "Your Honor—"

Lyn: "—to change my plea—"

Heller was urgent: "May we approach the bench outside the hearing of the prospective jurors? I'm afraid Miss Fromme will—"

Lyn: "—to nolo contendere." The functional equivalent of pleading guilty.

The prosecution and defense lawyers, along with the tiny defendant, gathered by the bench. MacBride looked at Lyn. "Now, what is this all about?

"It's about my Family."

"Well, what about your family? We're trying to select a jury."

"I understand that," said Lyn, "and I'm trying to avoid any further delay. And what I've come to in my mind is they didn't get a fair trial. I don't get a trial. I know this. This is the reason I came here. I came to say they didn't get their trial."

"Who is 'they?' " asked the judge.

"Van Houten, Patricia Krenwinkel, and Grogan."

"This has nothing whatever to do with this case, Miss Fromme. You are being tried here for the crime charged against you."

Lyn protested, but the judge cut her off. "I am going to ask you to sit down and remain quiet until I have selected the jury."

"Your Honor, I plead nolo contendere. I give it to you. I would like to tell you what happened."

The judge refused. "Did you know about this, Mr. Virga?" he asked.

"She has discussed it with me and indicated that at various—"

Lyn interrupted: "I am not going to let him argue for me. It's all right, but I have to argue for myself, Your Honor. In other words, he's not my baby-sitter. He's co-counsel and he agreed to let me handle my own case."

"As co-counsel," said Virga, "I feel I should be heard and I feel it would be totally inappropriate for the court to accept a nolo contendere plea."

"Because you want to try the case," Lyn retorted.

"It's not because I want to try the case," Virga protested.

"I'm the one who knows if I'm guilty or not," Lyn insisted.

"Miss Fromme, I'm not going to accept a nolo contendere plea to a charge," said MacBride.

"Are you forcing me to plead guilty?"

"No, I'm not going to force you to plead guilty," said the judge. "I'm ready to try the case."

Lyn looked around at the huddle of male lawyers in their business suits. "All right," she said. "What do I have to do?"

Dwayne Keyes spoke up. "The United States would have to agree and we do not agree."

"I don't have to listen to you," said Lyn.

"You will have to sooner or later," Keyes snapped.

"You'll have to listen to him sooner or later," MacBride agreed. "Even before accepting a plea of nolo contendere, the United States would have to agree and I would have to agree."

"Oh, I didn't know that," said Lyn.

Virga interrupted. "Your Honor, for the record, and for Miss Fromme's benefit, which I am sure she appreciates my sincerity when I say this, I do not feel she is guilty of attempting to assassinate the President. I feel in my own heart, in my own mind, she is not guilty of that. I do not want to see her—"

"That's not me," said Lyn.

"Miss Fromme—" said the judge.

"I'm speaking for myself!"

"Miss Fromme, I'm not going to accept a plea of nolo contendere."

Lyn became petulant. "Then I will have to plead guilty."

"I will not accept a plea of guilty!" said the judge. "I don't think under the circumstances with co-counsel it would be appropriate to accept a plea of guilty."

"I think she has a right to plead guilty," said Don Heller, uncharacteristically defending Lyn's rights.

"Well," Judge MacBride backtracked, "she may have the right to plead guilty, but—"

"That's why we have the Rule 11 procedure, Your Honor," said Keyes.

"Yes," Heller chimed in. "It is a knowing, voluntary plea of guilty. If she admits her guilt, she would have a right."

MacBride looked at the prosecutors. "I know that would be fine with you." He turned to Lyn. "Miss Fromme, do you want to talk with your co-counsel? I will not accept a plea of guilty."

"She has indicated to me without reservations that she feels she did not act with the intent to assassinate the President," said Virga.

"If you did not act with the intent to assassinate the President of the United States," said the judge, "I would not accept a plea from you, Miss Fromme. In other words—"

"Now—" said Lyn.

"Just a minute. I will not allow you to enter a plea of guilty unless I am absolutely satisfied that you are guilty."

"I was thinking," said Lyn.

"What do you mean?" said MacBride. "In connection with what you did?"

"That's right. I thought—"

"Just a minute, Miss Fromme." MacBride looked at Virga. "I think you better have a little talk with your client."

"Judge," said Lyn, "I don't listen to him."

"Will you just be quiet, please," said MacBride. "Because if you are not quiet, I am going to put you back."

"Don't treat me like a child," said Lyn.

"I'll put you in the back and set up a television camera so you can watch this trial and so the trial could go on without you."

"Without me?" gasped Lyn.

"Without you. I'll have to do it. I'm warning you now to just be quiet."

"You're going on without me anyway," said Lyn.

The acrimony continued—until Lyn blurted out the cause of her sudden effort to change her plea.

"Well, Your Honor, I heard you tell the jury that you hoped this would be the last time anything like this ever happened."

"That's right," said MacBride. "I am sincere in that."

"But does this tell the jury that they better lock me up?"

"No," said the judge. "Why don't you wait until we select a jury and until you hear the voir dire questions? Wait until you hear the charge to the jury."

MacBride's patience seemed to be having an impact. With Keyes and Heller still not quite sure what was happening, Lyn changed the subject from her plea to the issuance of witness subpoenas. The judge brought Lyn into his chambers for a private discussion; unknown to the prosecutors, the witnesses Lyn had determined were essential to her defense were Charles Manson and the Family members serving life sentences.

In chambers, Lyn's personality shifted once again. She was all business now, laying out her needs in lawyerly fashion. "Now, what I'll need to do is get an order for two tape recorders, which are very similar to radios," she told MacBride. "They have the same mechanical parts, and consequently a jail or prison would allow them, to do my witness interview. I want to have a witness interview with Manson and the women with Manson first. The witness interview is similar to the videotape, except that I'll need to speak with him more."

MacBride pondered this new development. "What would be the relevance of Mr. Manson's testimony to this case?" he asked.

"That he directly affects me. He's locked up. I want to see him."

"What do you mean, 'He directly affects' you? What do you mean by that?"

"Well," said Lyn, "here's what I suggest, evading the question, it is, the court can hear the tapes, the tapes could go through the court or you could have a copy of them and file them so that there wouldn't be any nonsense going on. It would all be regarding this case and the problems that I'm facing now."

MacBride was still stuck on his first point. "I can't see where Mr. Manson's testimony has any relevance whatsoever to this case."

Lyn considered the judge's question. "Let's see," she said. "What is the legal reason? . . ."

"Mr. Manson is in prison and has been in prison since well before this incident occurred and you haven't stated to me, Miss Fromme, any reason why Mr. Manson should be a witness. . . . And moreover, you're late in your request."

"Yes," said Lyn, "but I cannot get a trial unless I establish contact."

"You what?"

"I cannot go through trial unless I establish contact," Lyn repeated.

"Well," said MacBride, "this is going to go to trial today." Charles Manson, the judge said, was neither "a relevant nor competent witness to this case."

"Your Honor, he's just as competent as Mr. Ford," Lyn insisted. "I think we should have a video, if possible, but I'm satisfied to carry on interviews with him via cassette tape recorders." Written interrogatories wouldn't do, Lyn explained, because Charlie had "a disability in the writing department."

MacBride was not persuaded. "I don't think it's necessary that you have him as a witness on tape recorder, videotape, in person or in any other way."

"That's because you don't understand the dire situation we're in—"

"Miss Fromme—"

"—as a country."

Virga tried to find a way out of the disagreement. "I have spoken with Miss Fromme about having Mr. Manson testify, and I've indicated to her that the only legal basis that I'm able to see where he would be relevant or a material witness would be if he was to testify as to her character for nonviolence and that would be the offer of proof that I would make as to why he would be able to come and testify."

Lyn had another perspective. "Listen," she said, "there are different levels of mind. Things you understand, Your Honor, other people do not understand. The things John understands, Manson would not understand, and the things Manson understands, John surely would not understand."

The judge turned to John Virga, who tried to explain the rationale for bringing Manson in. "From what I know," he said, "there's probably no one who knows Lynette Fromme any better than Charles Manson. . . . During the time that the Family was together, he would have very intimate knowledge of her propensity for nonviolence and it . . . would be relevant." MacBride agreed to consider the request. He asked Virga to prepare a memorandum explaining the legal rationale for calling Charles Manson as a character witness.

MacBride then reconvened the court and dismissed the first jury panel. Lyn's remarks about changing her plea, the judge said, could cause undue prejudice against her. Then, sternly, he warned Lyn against further outbursts. If she was intent on pleading guilty, she had best do so now. "This case is going to either fish or cut bait," MacBride said. "That's putting it to you cold turkey."

Lyn looked him in the eye. "I don't fish," she said.

The argument resumed when the court reconvened after lunch. No more outbursts, MacBride repeated. "I'm not going to dismiss another panel of jurors. That cost us about $850," he said.

"See," said Lyn, "that's what I'm saying. I could buy some redwoods with that."

"All right," said an angered MacBride.

"It's not funny," Lyn insisted. "It's real. I'm trying to clean something up." Now she was ready to plead guilty once more. When MacBride told her to discuss the matter with Virga, she retorted, "He's not being a good parent. But I'm not a child, either."

Once again, MacBride tried to persuade Lyn to proceed with her defense. "Maybe you and your counsel together can work out a defense where you walk out of here," he said.

"Do you really think that's feasible?" Lyn asked. "I was standing there with the gun. Is that assault?" When MacBride wouldn't comment, Lyn said, "I see myself in prison."

"Let's go on with the trial," MacBride pleaded. "Let's go on without your plea of guilty."

"You know, Your Honor," Lyn said, contemplating, "I feel strongly in two directions. I feel to go with you, because I feel I should be able to trust you. At the same time, I feel that there could come a time when we have taken care of all the business at hand and we're ready to start the trial when you might just decide to tuck me away in the back room."

"Oh, come on," said the judge. "The only circumstance under which I am going to tuck you away in the back room is if you insist on disrupting the court . . . I am as anxious to get this trial over with as you are."

"Wait a minute," said Lyn. "You're the one that's anxious. I'm not. I want to see that I understand every bit of it."

"I want to see that justice is done here. Justice means that there's a fair and speedy trial and that all the evidence is adduced and submitted to the jury and the jury makes its decision and that's what justice means in this country," Judge MacBride explained.

"You mean justice could not be a slow and fair trial?"

MacBride allowed that it could. "I suppose justice could be accomplished in that fashion, but it's not my intention to do so. . . . When I say a speedy trial, I mean we'll move along just as promptly as we can do so."

The next step in moving things along, Lyn announced, was the dismissal of Virga as co-counsel. MacBride, as he had in the case of Dick Walker before, urged Lyn not discharge her lawyer. If she insisted, however, MacBride said she would be on her own; there would be no third lawyer in as many months for the Fromme trial. Virga would be reassigned from co-counsel to "standby" counsel—meaning he would sit silently in the court, prepared to take over the defense if the judge had Lyn removed for disrupting the court.

"The way things are going," said Dwayne Keyes, "he won't be standby very long."

At the bench conference, the lawyers began a lengthy discussion of the new particulars of the trial—where, for example, standby counsel Virga would sit, whether he would be allowed to assist Lyn in researching legal motions, what kind of access to materials Lyn would have in her cell.

"Wait, wait, wait," said Lyn, growing tired. "I'll plead guilty. That will solve everything." MacBride said he would accept a guilty plea if indeed she admitted guilt. When Lyn said she would plead guilty only because the court seemed unwilling to let her call Charlie and the Family as witnesses, MacBride shrugged.

"No, I can't take the plea," he said.

"You told me not to lie," Lyn countered.

"All right, I don't want you to lie, but the question is, at the time that you pointed the gun at the President, did you intend to kill him?"

Don Heller knew her answer to that—and feared that if Lyn's guilty plea was accepted under the circumstances, it could lead to a reversal on appeal. "She said the reason she wanted to change her plea is she wanted to make this statement about her Family not getting a fair trial," Heller reminded the judge.

"Well, I won't accept that as a basis for entering a plea," said MacBride.

"No, I am not making a statement," said Lyn. "I'm saying that due to my own conscience and principles it would defeat the very reason I came and I'm giving my life up to a degree. I've got so many years. I would be very disappointed with myself—"

MacBride cut her off. "The reasons you give for entering the plea of guilty are insufficient." The not guilty plea would stand. John Virga, by his own admission "mad" at Lyn for discharging him, moved down to the end of the defense table, hardly speaking a word to his quasi-client. Lyn would be her own attorney, flying solo.

The next panel of jurors was brought in, and MacBride repeated the series of admonitions regarding their duty. He added an inspirational historic footnote. The right to jury trial was "a right our ancestors fought for, not just here in America but all over the world, all the way back to the time of the absolute rule of monarchs when such a thing as being tried by your fellow man was a fantasy.... But now it's a reality, and we have found that this is the fairest system of justice, we hope, on the face of this earth." As MacBride had predicted, about

Jess Bravin

half the panel bowed out of their awesome responsibility. The remainder was ushered into a side room to await the next step in the selection process.

Prior to the voir dire, each side had submitted a list of questions it wanted asked of potential jurors. The prosecution's list was two pages long, with questions about firearms experience and membership in environmental organizations. The defense questions, on the other hand, took up twenty-two pages. They probed what potential jurors had studied in school, what religions they belonged to, and which political activities they had engaged in. Queries ranged from "Do you have any quarrel with the Constitutional right to bear arms?" to "Do you feel any revulsion against the Manson Family?" Several questions dealt with the Tate-LaBianca trials and whether they had caused any prejudice against Lyn, even though she had not been charged in them. Oddly, although many of the prospective jurors were from Stockton, nothing was said about the Willett murder case, in which Lyn had been jailed for two months before being released for lack of evidence.

One by one, members of the jury panel took the stand. First was Hope Abril, a cannery worker from South Stockton. MacBride asked her if she could blank out all the news coverage of the pistol incident, and render a verdict based solely on the evidence presented in court.

Mrs. Abril assured the judge she could. "I didn't read about it," she explained. "I didn't see no pictures or nothing. I work nights."

"How do you feel about so-called long-haired people owning firearms? Do you have any feelings one way or the other?"

"No."

After Abril answered the remaining battery of questions, MacBride asked if either side had anything to add. Lyn did. She passed a note to the judge asking if Abril had a happy domestic life.

MacBride scowled. "This question is not relevant to the issues that are before us," he said.

"Your Honor," Lyn protested, "if the person is having problems with their own personal life, they have a tendency to reflect on whoever they're judging. This is natural. Now if a person does not love another person or is unhappily married, if there's going to be a divorce or separation, then this would be taken out on me inadvertently."

MacBride stood firm, and neither Lyn nor the government objected to Abril. She was appointed to the jury.

Next up was Ronald Anderson, a forest ranger from tiny Mount Shasta, a New Age mecca in the northern woods of California. Anderson rang several alarms for the prosecution; not only did he wear a beard and serve as president of an Audubon Society chapter, he also was intimately familiar with the .45 automatic, having used one in the service. "Government would thank and excuse Mr. Ronald Anderson," said Dwayne Keyes.

Questioning Annie Banks of Sacramento, MacBride asked, "Now is there anything physically wrong with you that would prevent you from being in this trial for three or four weeks?"

"I have gas sometimes when I sit so long because when I eat I have to watch what I eat," she replied.

When the time came to exercise challenges, Lyn said, sympathetically, "Mrs. Banks, I'm going to dismiss you so you don't—"

The judge interrupted: "All right, Mrs. Banks, thank you for coming."

Edward Hoagland, a civilian electronics repairman at McClellan Air Force Base, told MacBride he wanted to serve because "it's history being made...I'd like to have a ringside seat."

"Do you have any feeling of revulsion against the Manson Family because of their lifestyle?" asked the judge.

"No, if they want to live that way, that's their business," Hoagland said. "But I don't think they should go around killing people." He was appointed to the jury.

MacBride conducted the voir dire in his usual, easygoing way. At times, though, Lyn had the impression he wasn't taking the matter seriously enough. In trying to give jurors an idea of how to approach their deliberations, MacBride said to think of the consideration they gave to job offers, retirement plans, and automobile purchases—"contrasted with the simple, day-to-day decisions that you make."

"Don't you think my life is worth more than a new car?" Lyn asked.

"I'm sure it is, Miss Fromme, but frankly I've been asking that question for fourteen years, and I don't propose to stop now."

But when MacBride addressed a new panel, he modified his analogy. Potential jurors should think of the verdict like such important decisions as "whether you're going to get married, whether you're going to get divorced, whether you're going to change your employment, whether you're going to start a business, whether you're going to buy a home, whether you're going to buy a Rolls-Royce—" The judge turned to Lyn. "That's for you, Miss Fromme, the Rolls-Royce."

Over the passing days, John Virga had reconciled with Lyn, even giving her occasional courtroom tips. When he saw her nodding off during one session, he jabbed her with his elbow. "Hey, lawyers don't go to sleep in the courtroom," Virga advised.

Lyn, for her part, had asked Virga to prepare a motion for her. This rankled MacBride, who called a bench conference. Now that he was standby counsel, it would not be appropriate for Virga to actually draft legal memoranda for Lyn.

"Well, Your Honor, unless you want to transport me to a law library or give me some kind of access, I have no way of being able to prepare a motion," Lyn said. "And I understand you're telling me I should have thought of that before I fired Mr. Virga, but I found it was necessary for another reason."

"What reason?" pleaded the judge. "I wish you would state the reason why you did fire Mr. Virga."

"Because, number one, you have a tendency toward depending on Mr. Virga, and I have a tendency to listen to whoever I am consulting, anyway, and I would rather conduct this for myself."

"In other words, have you lost rapport with Mr. Virga?"

"No," said Lyn. "Not at all."

"Do you think Mr. Virga is acting against your interests?"

"No, I don't," said Lyn. The problem, she explained, was that if Virga were allowed to speak in court, everyone would pay attention to him—and not to her. She would be pleased if Virga would do the legal research for her case.

MacBride decided that while Lyn would present the case in the courtroom, Virga could continue to do research and offer advice to the defendant.

Virga asked for clarification. "I am at the point right now where I am wondering whether I am a fish or fowl."

"You're just a fish," said Lyn.

"I think it's great," said cannery worker Leroy Lee, when asked his feelings about young people "wanting to change things more quickly than people of your own age group." Nevertheless, Lyn challenged Lee; he had said he hunted deer, and that was unacceptable. Dwayne Keyes declined to argue the point, and so MacBride asked Lyn to elaborate.

Lyn said her defense would involve her concern for animals, "particularly the deer," and might amount to a challenge to Lee's lifestyle. "He would be deliberating about himself," Lyn said, and thus could not judge her fairly.

"All right," said MacBride. "I will accept your challenge."

Keyes's mouth dropped open. "Your Honor?"

"Yes?" said the judge.

"Are hunters going to be automatically—"

"If you wanted to argue it, why didn't you say something?"

"I thought the court would require a *legal* cause," said Keyes. "That's not a legal cause."

"The legal cause is she states Mr. Lee might be prejudiced against her because she's going to argue, obviously, against hunters and those who she thinks are destroying the environment."

"After her argument, there may be a lot of people who may be prejudiced against her," said Keyes. He insisted that Lyn's views on hunters were not a legitimate reason to screen jurors for bias. "Cause has to exist in that man's mind and not in her personal feelings about that prospective juror," he said.

MacBride turned to Lyn.

"Your Honor, it's not a matter of me saying I don't like hunters. It's not a matter of personality. It's a matter that the case that I intend to present should be much stronger than 'I don't like hunters.' It would cause the jury to do some soul-searching and determine whether they, themselves, would have to give this [hunting] up. And I don't—I think that is a hard thing for jurors to do, especially when we can pinpoint it right now and avoid the problem."

The judge looked at Lee. "Like yourself, I happen to be a hunter," MacBride said. "Would this prejudice you against this defendant by reason of the fact that she is critical of people who hunt and fish?"

"Well," said Lee, "there's a lot of things in the environmental [movement] that I agree with." He was certain he could be a fair juror. When MacBride decided to keep Lee on the panel, Lyn used one of her ten peremptory challenges to excuse him.

"All right," said the increasingly weary judge. "Anything else, Miss Fromme?"

"Yes, *Frum-me,*" she said, correcting him. For the first time in years, she had begun to insist on the way her parents always pronounced the surname. She had even sent MacBride a note with a phonetic spelling of her two-syllable name.

"Frum-me?" said the judge.

"Right."

"Have you always gone by that pronunciation?"

"Well, You're Honor, I've acquiesced."

MacBride had been having trouble getting her name right throughout, even calling her "Miss Manson" on occasion. He made an effort to be accommodating.

"*Frahm? Froo-me? Frah-me?*" he asked

"No," she said, giggling. "*Frum-me.*"

MacBride offered a slight grin. "From me to you?" he said.

Voir dire continued.

A school bus driver, Larry Barrie, asked to be excused. He was afraid he'd be asked too many questions by "the little kids and the upper graders" who rode his bus.

"Hey," said Lyn, "we could use them for a jury! That's who I want."

MacBride ignored the remark. "Mr. Barrie, you see, they won't be asking questions; you're going to be sequestered."

"Yeah," said the bus driver, "I know it and I'm nervous also." MacBride excused him.

Gregory Delarosa gave his occupation as "scaler of ingredients" for the Campbell Soup factory in Sacramento. Like most of the prospective jurors, he said he rarely followed the news, had barely any knowledge of the Capitol Park incident or the Tate-LaBianca case and held no negative impression of the Manson Family. His reticence in answering these questions bothered Lyn.

"Your Honor, I feel that some of the jurors might be hesitant to be honest about what they've heard because they might feel that it would offend either me or their standing as a juror," she said. "To me, logic and reason dictate that some of the answers that he gave were not valid."

Delarosa responded directly to Lyn, saying he didn't follow the Manson case in the newspaper. "Besides," he said, "what happened over there has nothing to do with your case. See, I'm going by what's going to happen here."

Lyn used a peremptory challenge to excuse him. She elaborated to MacBride: "It's hard for me to believe that when it's reported that the President of the United States was assaulted, or somebody attempted to assassinate him, that all these people had nothing to say. Isn't that unusual to you? . . . It's not an everyday occurrence, I mean."

"No, it really isn't. You're right, there," MacBride conceded. But this comment gave the judge no legal matter on which to rule.

Lyn continued her critique after Otis Dosher, a retired railroad car inspector from Roseville, said he held no hostility toward Manson or his followers, even though he knew of the murder convictions.

"Mr. Dosher," Lyn said, "you can be completely honest with me . . . I want to know if you're telling me that you had no feeling about nine murders."

"Well, if he was convicted, if he committed the crime, he will have to pay the penalty, that's all," Dosher said.

Lyn turned to the judge. "I feel that there were many questions the juror was evading . . . particularly in regard to what he's heard about the Manson case. I note the grimace on certain jurors' faces. If they would just be honest, I would hold nothing against them. Everybody's been exposed to this publicity. The only way that we can clean it up is to be honest about it. That's all."

"All right, thank you," said the judge. "Mr. Keyes, is there anything you want to say?"

"I'm not sure if that was an objection, Your Honor."

"Well, it really isn't an objection. Her point is she feels that the prospective jurors are being evasive. I don't see it."

When Frank Duncan, a Yuba City carpenter, took the stand, Lyn finally got someone she respected. Duncan said he had seen news footage of Lyn being seized by police, and couldn't block it out. That was enough for MacBride to excuse him, but Lyn wanted to ask if Duncan could set aside the television images.

"Well, I've been trying that all day and I can't get it out of the back of my mind," Duncan said. "And it was reported that you said, 'It didn't fire,' or something in that order. 'It didn't go off,' or something."

"Anything else?" Lyn asked.

"Just a minute," MacBride interrupted, "this witness—this juror has already said—"

"This juror is honest," said Lyn.

"This juror is honest, but he says he can't get it out of his mind," said the judge. Duncan had admitted he had a legal "prejudice" against Lyn, and therefore his service on the jury would "just be a travesty."

Lyn turned to the juror. "Mr. Duncan, do you believe everything you hear or see?"

"Miss Fromme, will you please sit down?" said MacBride.

"This is a valuable juror," Lyn said. "He's honest."

"I'm sure he's an honest man, and that's why he shouldn't be on your jury."

Lyn stared at the judge. He reflected for a moment, then continued: "That wasn't artfully stated—that's for sure—but he's so honest [about] what he has in mind against [you] that he shouldn't be on the jury." MacBride then sought to say something reassuring. "I'm going to try my best to get all honest men and women on your jury, Miss Fromme, believe me."

Eloise Kosta was a mother of five from the Sacramento Valley town of Lodi. When MacBride asked her initial impressions of Lyn's guilt, Kosta drew from her own experience. "I found this out being a mother, there's always times when a child can be in a spot where they're almost exactly guilty, but yet things can happen to make you change you opinion." Asked to elaborate, she said that "sometimes people will do something abnormal or extreme to gain attention. A child lays on the floor and kicks his feet. An adult can't do things like that, so they will develop something as flamboyant or noticeable."

Mrs. Kosta was the first person the prosecution excused with a peremptory challenge.

Larry Nelson, a civil engineer with the state Department of Fish and Game, came to the jury box with several indirect connections to the Fromme case. One of Nelson's fellow Fish and Game engineers lived next door to Lyn in Sacramento. More important, perhaps, was that three of Nelson's co-workers were named on a list seized from Lyn's apartment—a document MacBride described as "the so-called death list."

Nelson said that this fact would not prejudice him against Lyn. "I don't think it was any direct threat," he said.

The judge asked if Nelson was "critical of young people who sort of want to clean up the earth a little quicker than maybe the Department of Fish and Game does?"

"No, no," said Nelson.

Lyn was not satisfied that Nelson, a recreational hunter who had used firearms since the age of twelve, would be an impartial juror. She asked what kind of list Nelson thought had been found in her apartment.

Nelson acknowledged he had heard the document described "as supposedly a death list," but insisted that his friends "felt no concern" that they were included on it.

"It's hard for me to accept that you wouldn't be prejudiced," Lyn said. "It's really hard for me to accept that, that your friends took it casually. Would you be satisfied to have twelve people of your state of mind sit in judgment on you if you were similarly charged?"

"Yes," said Nelson.

"In regard to cleaning up the earth a little faster than the Department of Fish and Game, are you prepared to get your ass in gear?"

"All right, Miss Fromme," said the judge.

But Nelson answered her question. "If we get enough money," he said.

"Money!" Lyn exclaimed. She asked MacBride to dismiss Nelson. After Mac-Bride declined, Lyn excused Nelson with a peremptory challenge.

Next up was Kenneth Partlow, a logger from the Siskiyou County town of Fort Jones, near the Oregon border. MacBride asked his reaction upon hearing news of the pistol incident.

"Nothing much," Partlow said. "I figured it was another incident that happened down south."

"I don't understand," said MacBride.

"Well, we don't hold a high opinion of Southern California up north."

"You mean you're putting Sacramento in the same class as Southern California?" MacBride asked incredulously.

"Yeah, when you're up that far north," said Partlow.

Not only was Sacramento four hundred miles north of Los Angeles, it occupied a higher latitude than even the quintessential Northern California city, San Francisco. On the other hand, Fort Jones was more than two hundred miles north of Sacramento.

MacBride asked if the logger had discussed the case with anyone.

"Not really, because up north we've got more worries about than—"

"Than we have down here?" MacBride interrupted, still a bit miffed about having his hometown—center of a region the *Sacramento Bee* referred to as "Superior California"—lumped in with the Southern California megalopolis. But the judge decided there was no cause to dismiss Partlow, and neither Lyn nor the prosecution challenged him.

After having reviewed forty-six people for jury selection, the last prospective juror was James Pruitt, a naval machinist from the historic town of Benicia, which had served briefly as the state capital in 1853.

MacBride wanted to know if, in light of the case's notoriety, Pruitt might be embarrassed if he voted to acquit Lyn. If somebody asked " 'How the Sam Hill could you do that?' it wouldn't bother you in the least?"

Pruitt asserted it would not. He was appointed to the jury.

The next morning, the judge conducted the final phase of jury selection. The jury wheel was spun and names chosen. Lyn used all of her ten challenges for the jurors; prosecutors exercised four of their six. The resulting jury was equally divided between men and women, most of whom were older than fifty years; there were no blacks among them. Moments later, after one juror reported having the flu, he was replaced with the first alternate, the wife of a Sacramento letter carrier. Later, another juror would be replaced, leaving the panel with eight women and four men.

Judge MacBride addressed the jury box. "The reason why we have twelve of you is . . . each of you may see and view something different from the standpoint of your own experiences in life. . . . And in this way, the twelve of you will sort of act as a polishing stone in a gem machine where you work off the rough spots by the twelve of you using, say, the abrasiveness of your own intelligence . . . and you will finally come up with what we hope is a just solution to the problem with which you will be confronted, namely, the question of whether or not this defendant is guilty or innocent."

Pundits were less than impressed with the jury. The *San Francisco Examiner* published a story detailing how little each member knew about its charge, seemingly amazed at "a jury by its own admission so ignorant of the case." The *San Francisco Chronicle* observed that the parties made sure the jury would have no independent basis to consider a key issue, firearms. Lyn had excused all the hunters she could, while the prosecution had taken pains to remove those familiar with the operation of the .45 automatic.

Propensity for Violence

With John Virga's help, Lyn had prepared the motion seeking a subpoena for Charles Manson. It explained that if called, Charlie would testify "to my reputation and propensity for violence."

MacBride called a meeting in his chambers to discuss the motion. Because Lyn had not spoken to Charlie for six years and had only been able to correspond with him over the past year, the judge wanted to know what, exactly, Manson could offer to Lyn's defense.

Lyn's explanation, which she insisted be placed in the record, was less a legal argument than a witness to Charlie's greatness—and his sacrifice. She read from notes, speaking of his musical ability, of the fact that "Mr. Manson is a dancer of exceptional, and awesome, capability . . .

"In case the judge has not read of the so-called Manson case, I inform you that there is something [to] repulse everybody. Manson has been reported as a white racist nigger-loving devil Christ with Hitlerian Marxist philosophy. Nobody knows him. But maybe the court knows that Charles Manson is the only human being who knows me well and could, if so decided, give testimony as to my character leading to my intent. Charles Manson is the only one who can save me the hell he has been through his entire life and, I add, the only one who can in truth save my physical life."

MacBride sat silent as Lyn continued: "Mr. Manson has a third-grade education and his mind works much faster than his pencil can equal. Physically in repose, his mind is clear. He has no trouble communicating the spoken word. I have attempted to communicate with him in letters and find this much too difficult. I came to this court via the alleged crime specifically to offer my only chance to fix our world and to save my own life. I do not have the answers, and it is a great offense for me as a woman to ride over and sit on the truth as I have done for over a thousand years."

As the judge contemplated this, Lyn swung back to a more legalistic approach, citing three cases. "Admittedly," she said, "these cases to my untrained mind are not to the point or not on point. But I am attaching them anyway." She tried to apply at least some of Virga's reasoning. She cited her rights under the First, Fifth, Sixth, Eighth, and Fourteenth Amendments and stressed that she didn't intend for MacBride to make significant new law by granting her motion.

She described the conditions of Manson's imprisonment, noting that he did not receive special privileges from the Corrections Department. In fact, she said, he was kept in solitary confinement "not because he is a violent, unruly or unreasonable inmate but because of the notoriety of his case. For four years Manson has been asking for a guitar. He has nothing to do but sit. He has repeatedly been—"

MacBride finally spoke up. "Miss Fromme, really, that has nothing—"

"It has to do with my state of mind," said Lyn.

"Well, I'm sorry. But I'm telling you the fact Manson doesn't have a guitar has nothing whatever to do with the issue that is before us in this motion."

"Well, it leads to my intent."

The judge looked at the papers in front of her. "How much do you have there, a couple more pages?" he asked.

"Yes."

"I'll hear it out. Go ahead. Put it on the record."

Lyn resumed her speech: "He has repeatedly been denied a guitar because the administration has stated they would need to supply all other prisoners housed in his unit with musical instruments. Most prisoners in the isolation units are there because of disciplinary problems. Mr. Manson should, to alleviate a terrible and cruel punishment, in the spectrum of legal rule, be allowed a guitar. The denial of same has directly affected the state of mind and therefore leads to intent in this case. With that in mind, I also would subpoena one or two guards or administrators from the prison with whom I have had numerous conversations. Mr. Manson has been in a four-by-eight cell for four years with nothing to do. He has been outside very few times since this incarceration. I pray that Your Honor take a few moments in reflection of this punishment in view of my insistence that Charles Manson was and is not guilty as charged and was unjustly convicted. It is now and has been my feeling that my life is in great danger. I declare and believe this to be true. I declare and believe that this witness, Charles Manson, is the only person who could save my life. Personalities aside, no one can speak for me but him. All the witnesses may testify to my character as they know it, but I have known Mr. Manson for nine years and no one knows me better. I have put my life up here to clean up a mess that each person in this world has contributed to directly or indirectly. In order to put on this case for which I came, I must be permitted the presence of witnesses necessary to an adequate defense which entirely hinges on intent."

"Does that complete your statement?" asked the judge.

"That's all," said Lyn.

"May I make a statement?" asked Virga. "The affidavit indicates 'character for violence.' It should be 'character for *non-violence.*' "

MacBride looked at the document. "It states, 'The witness will testify to my reputation and propensity for violence.' "

"It should be non-violence."

"It should be non-violence," repeated the judge. "I'll correct that." He then addressed the substance of Lyn's motion.

"Miss Fromme, I cannot issue this subpoena. You have not seen Mr. Manson for six years. . . . He would be in no position to testify with any degree of validity whatever concerning your propensity for non-violence for the reason in that six-year period changes could have come over you that he would not know about." Under these circumstances, MacBride said, bringing in Manson would be "folly."

"Your Honor," said Lyn, "what I am arguing is that I came to the court specifically to give him a voice."

"Well, that doesn't have anything to do with it," said the judge. "You might have had this in mind, but I cannot take that into consideration in deciding whether or not he should be brought here."

"Your Honor, it's going to get bloody. That's what I'm trying to tell you."

"What I am trying to tell *you* is that you have stated no legal justification for my issuing the subpoena."

"What about the fact that's why I came?"

"Miss Fromme, maybe that's what's in your mind—"

"That's my whole defense."

"You say you have to have him here," said MacBride. "What is the purpose of your doing this?"

"To give him a voice," Lyn explained. "To allow us to communicate and communicate to many children who need a new thought to live in."

"I am sorry, Miss Fromme, but I must deny your request."

"You're denying my defense," she said.

"I don't know what your defense is, but I can tell you this, that the defense that you—"

"Your Honor," said Lyn, "I'm the whole country."

"Maybe you're the whole country, but in this particular case you're the defendant in *United States* vs. *Fromme* and you're charged with having attempted to kill the President of the United States. We are only concerned here with whether or not you did intend to kill the President of the United States."

Lyn struggled to make the judge understand her. "I'm trying to save some lives," she said. "That's all. If nothing else, I'll have to shut up."

"Well, I'm sorry, but there is no basis for the issuance of this subpoena."

"What about if I beg you?" Lyn pleaded.

"Beg me? Miss Fromme, I can only respond to what is a legal request."

"I understand."

"I cannot respond to a beg."

"Is there any—"

"It's pretty hard for a judge to be nice," MacBride continued. "I just have to be legal and stick—"

"I know," Lyn said.

"—with what is brought before me and under this circumstance there is just insufficient reason for the issuance of a subpoena."

MacBride then moved on to an administrative matter. Virga's legal staff was unwilling to take direction from Lyn herself, so Virga wanted permission to supervise their work on the Fromme case. This question was all but irrelevant to Lyn, however, who persisted in seeking a subpoena for Charlie. "He can testify why kids are coming up with guns and knives," she said, echoing Manson's soliloquy at the Tate-LaBianca trial.

"Miss Fromme, will you please stick to the issue presently before us? I have already decided that question."

"I didn't shoot him and I didn't conscientiously shoot him and I didn't want to shoot him." At last, exasperated, she had acknowledged the incident that brought her into federal custody. It was as if by so doing, she could dispose of the matter and return to the real point of the whole business: Manson's message. And yet, Judge MacBride seemed determined to shut his eyes.

"I have no intelligence into that," he said.

"The point is people are getting violent," Lyn said. "They are going to get really violent if they"—the Family—"don't explain it. There were nine murders in Los Angeles and people didn't even find out why, and it was their own kids." It was another recitation of the Family credo, the insistence that a mystical, world-changing purpose lay beneath the mass murders of 1969, a purpose suppressed by the justice system in Los Angeles, a purpose that ultimately would be revealed if only society—in this case, embodied by District Judge Thomas J. MacBride—agreed to hear. And yet again, like an episode in early Christian martyrdom, society was refusing to listen.

"Well, can we get back to the issue of the attorney?" asked the judge.

"Your Honor, I'm sorry," said Lyn. And she fell silent.

Had he been called to testify, Manson's comments on Lyn's "propensity for non-violence" would have been legally irrelevant to the charge against her. But Manson might instead have answered another question that puzzled many over the years, Lyn included: In August 1969, why had Lyn not been chosen for the cataclysmic, bloody murder spree that defined the Manson Family for all time to come?

Chapter 11

The Government's

Case

Judge MacBride reconvened the court. "The jurors are all present, defendant is present with counsel." He turned to Dwayne Keyes. "You may proceed."

The prosecutor began his opening argument. "Your Honor, counsel, ladies and gentlemen of the jury—"

Ignoring Keyes, Lyn stood up and strode to the lectern. "Wait a minute, excuse me just one minute," she said, her voice rising. "Your Honor, Manson and that Family is my own heartbeat and if they're not allowed to put on a fair trial, lives will be lost all over the country."

"Miss—" said the judge.

"I cannot go to trial—"

"I am going to ask you—"

"—unless they get a fair trial."

MacBride turned to Art Van Court. "Mr. Marshal, will you take the—"

"That's why I came here," Lyn proclaimed.

"Take her in hand now!" the judge ordered.

"I'm changing my plea—"

"Just a minute!" said the judge.

"—to guilty."

"Remove the defendant!" MacBride commanded.

"Your Honor, it's going to get bloody if they're not allowed to speak," said Lyn. Deputies led her from the courtroom; as they did, she shouted over her shoulder, "You can't have a trial without me!" But the judge seemed more than ready to do so.

MacBride had the jury escorted out, then told the marshal to bring Lyn back to the courtroom.

She was defiant upon her return. "Will you explain to me, please, what's going on?" she said.

MacBride had a lecture ready for her: "This is the second time you disrupted the trial. The first time, of course, was on the day you announced you could not be tried by any jury except your own Family. And at the same time you announced to the court that you were firing Mr. Virga. Also, you made a statement in open court which necessitated my sending home a jury panel that was all set up to go. I considered that a disruption of the trial, a delay in the orderly process of the trial and a detriment to the trial itself. Now, your action today constitutes the same thing. I've tried to accommodate you in every possible way I can. I have gone along with you when you didn't want Mr. Walker. I gave you another attorney, whom I considered a competent attorney. He has done a great job, I think, in preparing the case for you.

"On the very day the trial commenced, you fired him and insisted upon taking over yourself. Now, today, you, again, have caused another disruption. We're going to have to change the whole setup."

Through his wire-rimmed spectacles, the judge focused on Lyn. "I will give you one more chance," he said. If she disrupted the trial again, she would be confined in a cell. There, she could watch on closed-circuit television as Virga conducted the defense. "Now," said the judge, "what's it going to be?"

"Your Honor, I want to go to trial."

"Well, then, if you want to go to trial, why don't you comport yourself in a manner that will permit us to go on with the trial?"

"It goes against the whole purpose of why I came here and that's to get them a fair trial, my Family a fair trial."

Once again, said MacBride, "that matter has nothing to do with this case. I'm merely asking you if you're ready to go to trial on the issues of this case and that is, did you attempt to kill the President of the United States? That is the only issue before us. Did you attempt to kill the President of the United States?"

"No," said Lyn.

"All right," said the judge. "Why don't you sit down and let's go on with the trial. The alternative, he repeated, was having Virga take over.

"Mr. Virga can't possibly put on my defense," said Lyn. "I'm the only one who knows what happened that day and what my specific intent is."

"I'm not going to debate it with you now," said MacBride. "I'm telling you the way I'm going to run this case and that's all there is to it. If I am wrong in the way I run it, then the Ninth Circuit will tell me so, in the event you're convicted. And, if you don't like what they do, in the event they affirm me, you can take it up to the Supreme Court. But I'm going to run this case in the manner that I think a case of this nature should be conducted. And, believe me, I have nothing in mind except to give you a fair and impartial trial, a good trial, with a good attorney, and to be sure that all the rules of evidence are observed and all the rules of this court are observed, all to the end that when this trial is over, justice will be done, however it comes out. . . . I don't know whether you're going to be convicted or whether you're going to be acquitted; but when it's over, I will assure you, as far as I'm concerned, I will be satisfied that justice has been done insofar as my conduct of this trial is concerned. Now, that's my obligation."

"Your Honor, how can I have a fair trial if I can't put on my defense?"

"Well, Mr. Virga and you've been preparing this defense for three weeks."

"But I'm the initial character in this defense. I'm the whole defense."

"Well, all right, you're going to be here. You can take the witness stand."

"But my witnesses are Manson and the women, all my whole Family are my witnesses. Furthermore, I came here specifically for that purpose, that is my intent. If I—"

MacBride cut her off again. "One time I accused you of making bonehead statements in court and that you ought to stop doing that. And you're starting to do it again. You make statements that can only be considered prejudicial to you, and each time you make these statements, you're hurting yourself further. And I'm sure that when you make these statements, Mr. Virga must tremble in his boots over there, because he knows that he possibly might have to take over in this trial."

"I have advised Mr. Virga not to take over in this case," said Lyn.

"Well, Mr. Virga is going to take over in this case, believe me."

"I also advise you, Your Honor, that were you to set up the television cameras and so forth, I would not watch them."

"That's up to you," said the judge.

"Furthermore, I would, despite the fact that I don't wish to be difficult, I would not come to the courtroom."

"That's up to you, Miss Fromme. The courtroom is here and the trial is scheduled to go."

"In other words," she said, "they're going to have to carry me out of the jailhouse."

"If they have to, that's it," said MacBride. "Frankly, I'm not concerned with that."

"Your Honor, how hard should I fight for the lives of the people in this country?"

"I would suggest right now you're fighting for, not your life, but you're fighting for your future, that's for sure, and I would suggest that—"

"Well, I put my life on the Family and their abilities to straighten out the country and the world. That's why I can't go to trial."

MacBride had had enough. "I am putting it to you cold turkey: Are you going to sit down and be quiet, or do we evict you from the courtroom and let the trial go on? Now, make up your mind."

"Manson is the only one that can speak for me."

"Are you going to sit down and be quiet?" said the judge, like a father addressing an unruly a child.

"Manson is the only one that can speak for me," she repeated.

The judge tried once more: "Does that mean that you will not be quiet?"

"I will be quiet in my cell," said Lyn.

"Then go to your cell!" commanded the judge. After deputies took Lyn away, spectators heard a haunting cry from beyond the courtroom: "I WANT TO CHANGE MY PLEA TO GUILTY!" MacBride ignored it. "Mr. Virga, you're appointed as counsel in this case," he said.

Following arrangements he had made for just such an occurrence, Art Van Court prepared the closed-circuit monitors in a back room of the marshal's office. He then went to Lyn's courthouse cell and asked if she would accompany him to watch the proceedings on television. Lyn refused.

"If I listen to that," she said, "it will drive me crazy." Van Court shrugged and told his deputies to escort Lyn to the television room if she should change her mind.

MacBride brought the jury back into the courtroom and explained the changes. The cameras now facing the attorneys' lectern and the witness stand would transmit the proceedings to the defendant. John Virga would conduct the entire defense, in consultation with Lyn, who would be permitted to return to the courtroom if she agreed to comport herself as a normal defendant.

"Now, ladies and gentlemen of the jury, this defendant is being difficult, to say the least," the judge said. "But I don't want you to allow that to influence you in your deliberations in this case. . . . You've got to decide on the basis of the evidence that's produced in this courtroom and that's all. The fact that she may conduct herself in this fashion is not to influence you in any way."

Dwayne Keyes finally had the chance to deliver his opening statement. He spent twenty-two minutes sketching in his soft, flat voice his theory of the case: Lyn was frustrated because the press no longer considered her hysterical communiqués to be news. She had determined to get them some hard news, namely, the assassination of the president. After MacBride agreed to take judicial notice that "on September 5 Gerald R. Ford was the President of the United States" (one of three elements of the crime charged), Keyes then called the first government witness, Larry Buendorf.

Keyes got right to the point. Using Heller as Lyn and Buendorf as Ford, he staged for the jury a reenactment of the Capitol Park incident, replete with the actual gun she had carried. After Buendorf demonstrated how he grabbed the pistol, Keyes had the lights dimmed, and presented a slide show of the events in Capitol Park, taken from news footage.

Buendorf described Lyn shouting, " 'It didn't go off! It didn't go off!' and saying it in disbelief."

Virga objected. Buendorf, he said, was not qualified to speculate on the meaning contained in Lyn's tone of voice.

"This will be the first in a series of objections, I'm sure," said Keyes, who was planning to question other witnesses about what Lyn seemed to be expressing. Once again, MacBride excused the jury so the attorneys could argue the issue.

Heller spoke up, citing both the Federal Rules of Evidence and comments by Learned Hand, the legendary New York judge. Tone of voice was essential, Heller said. "People have occasion to say 'No' in a negative way to mean yes. I'll use an example of my mother: It's after dinner, and she's offered dessert. She says, 'Oh, no,' and goes right on to eat it," he said.

The judge ruled. "It is possible for a person in the position of Mr. Buendorf to hear a statement made and use his ability to form an opinion as to the manner in which the words were spoken." Witnesses would be able to tell the jury their impression of the degree of disbelief in which Lyn was shouting.

Still, Virga may have gotten the best of Buendorf's testimony. Following Keyes's example, he too had Buendorf take part in a reenactment of Lyn's apprehension. A defense investigator held the pistol; when Buendorf grabbed it, the gun made a small, mechanical *clank.*

"Did you feel a vibration through the weapon?" Virga asked.

"Yes, a moving in her hand," said Buendorf.

Virga then pulled the trigger: *Click!* The sound echoed through the courtroom. "Like that?" Virga asked.

"No, sir," replied Buendorf. "I don't recall hearing anything like that."

MacBride adjourned court early on Friday. Lyn, he said, would be permitted to attend her trial "if she's a good girl."

November 9

On Monday morning, Deputy Marshal Mike Nelson came to the jail to bring Lyn to court.

"I'm not going," said Lyn. She wore a red bandanna as a blindfold, explaining to Nelson, "justice is blind, so I might as well be blind." But there was no anger in her voice. During her months of incarceration, she had spent countless hours with Marshal Van Court and his deputies, developing an easy rapport with them. She respected the job they had to do, and they came to admire her intelligence and wit. Some even did business with her; Deputy Marshal Warren Steeves paid Lyn $20 for one of her Buck knives.

"Come on, Lynette," said Nelson, "you gotta go to court. You gotta be in court."

"I don't want to go to court," she repeated. Nelson, however, insisted. "I'll go," she relented, "but you're gonna have to carry me."

"Okay, come on, Lynette," said the beefy deputy. He picked her up, carried her out, and put her in the marshal's van. With news photographers staking out the jail, shots of the tiny, blindfolded defendant held by stone-faced officers were flashed around the world. Lyn persisted in refusing to walk for several weeks, and carrying her to court became a routine duty for members of the marshal's office. The deputies tried to maintain a light touch.

"You're gettin' too heavy, Lynette," Nelson teased her. "You're gettin' fat."

MacBride had decided that before each trial session began, Lyn would be given an opportunity to return to the courtroom. She removed her blindfold when she was brought before the judge.

"I want you to know," she said, "that this is not a frivolous disruption, that I had considered this some time ago and was waiting for your decision on the [Manson] motion. I committed myself and it's a matter of principle."

"Well, Miss Fromme, really, I can't go into your reasons at this time," said the judge. His only interest was whether she would conduct herself as a proper defendant, and let her attorney present the case.

"No, Your Honor, he can't put it on for me." She told him she would not sit quietly or watch the trial.

"You say you have to stay out of the courtroom?" MacBride asked.

Lyn shook her head affirmatively.

"Very well, you may do so. One other thing, Miss Fromme, before you go." MacBride had decided to settle once and for all the pronunciation of the defendant's name. "I want to call your attention to the proceedings that took place in this courtroom on September the 11th at 9:30. This is the time when you were arraigned and the clerk read the following: *United States* vs. *Lynette Alice Fromme*." The judge addressed the court reporter, Dick Fong. "I would assume, Mr. Reporter, that you would put on your dictaphone different symbols for pronunciations of Fromme than you would for the pronunciation for *Fro-may* or *Frum-me* or anything of that sort, is that correct, Mr. Reporter?"

"Yes," said Fong.

"I remember consenting to him calling me *Froam*," Lyn acknowledged.

"Very well," said MacBride, "that will be the name, that's the pronunciation under which you'll be tried from here on out." In court, as in the popular memory, she would remain Squeaky Froam.

In addition to an unpredictable client, Virga had to contend with the Federal Rules of Discovery which, compared to state court procedure, gave an advantage to the government. Prosecutors were not required to turn over investigatory reports to the defense until after each witness had testified, meaning that Virga would have only a few minutes, if that, to prepare for his cross-examination.

"It's as though Heller said, 'Let's play a game and call it war—I'll start by throwing hand grenades and you have to see which way they're coming from,'" Virga told *New York Times* reporter Lucinda Franks. Considering the tension and troubling implications of the crime charged, Franks wrote that the trial "seemed at times less like a courtroom proceeding than a Roman circus," with Virga and Heller sparring "like the Christian and the lion."

From an oddsmaker's point of view, what had seemed like a simple case for the government now looked even simpler. Although on trial for her conduct in Capitol Park, not her courtroom behavior, Lyn's emotional outbursts and ultimate eviction from the chamber obviously made an impression on the jury. Whether or not she truly was a would-be assassin, she surely acted like one. The U.S. Attorney need only connect the dots to assure a conviction.

But even as Lyn seemed bent on sabotaging her case, the government began to stumble on the second day of testimony. After hearing from Secret Service agents Buendorf and Gerald Kluber, Dwayne Keyes tried to call Lanier Ramer, Manson's former prison buddy who had visited Lyn in Sacramento. Ramer, however, refused to testify—and sent two high-powered lawyers to keep him off the stand. The former bank robber was now a valued worker at the ACLU's National Prison Project, and the organization was ready to help him out.

The ACLU lawyers, led by Alvin Bronstein of Washington, D.C., argued that forcing Ramer to testify would place his life in danger—and make him useless in their work with convicts.

"The reason we hired Mr. Ramer...was because we needed people who could analyze what the prisoners say and recognize what is true and not true," Bronstein told the court. "If he were to testify and be labeled an informer, as he surely would, he would have no value in my office thereafter"—or at the New York State Corrections Commission, where Ramer was scheduled to start work. Forcing Ramer to testify, Bronstein said, would ruin his ability to do "the one thing he can do constructively after having spent many, many years in custody."

Keyes, however, maintained that Ramer's testimony was essential. The ex-convict was the only witness the government found who had sat in Lyn's apartment, conversing with her about her environmental views, her efforts to reach radical underground groups, and her desire to obtain firearms. Keyes tried to be conciliatory toward Ramer. "I appreciate his position," he said. "I certainly would not subpoena him unless I felt we had to."

Don Heller, on the other hand, evinced little sympathy. "Each question is a separate contempt," he told the judge, "and I think you can give him six months on each question."

MacBride reluctantly denied Ramer's motion to quash the subpoena, and the bearded ex-convict took the stand. Heller began firing questions at him, but Ramer, courteous throughout, declined to answer.

The judge said he had no choice but to find Ramer in contempt of court. "My heart goes out to the poor guy, it's a tough deal," he said. "But I cannot rule from the heart. I have to rule from the mind in a situation like this." Rather than jail the witness, however, he granted Bronstein's request that Ramer remain free for the day while deciding whether to appeal. The prosecutors could not believe such lenient treatment.

"What's your problem?" MacBride asked Keyes and Heller. "Your heads look like they're going to wag off."

Heller showed why they called him Mad Dog. "The purpose of the contempt statute is to punish summarily and remand summarily someone who is refusing to obey the lawful order of the court. The teeth of the statute would be lost if Mr. Ramer is permitted to spend the evening in the comfort of his motel room rather than in the comfort of the Sacramento County Jail."

"Mr. Heller," said the judge, "knowing the circumstances of Mr. Ramer, I really don't think that is going to make a lot of difference."

"It may, Judge. He's been there before and it may refresh his recollection."

MacBride was unpersuaded, and Ramer walked out of the courtroom.

The prosecution ran into more trouble when it tried to examine Edward Vandervort, the former mental patient from Pennsylvania who corresponded with Lyn over much of 1975. Brought into the state by federal agents, Vandervort was treated like a star witness, kept under "protective custody" by Marshal Van Court. Through Vandervort's testimony, the government planned to demonstrate Lyn's longstanding commitment to terrorism, as evidenced by the very specific instructions Vandervort received concerning the execution of corporate executives.

But before Vandervort could take the stand, Virga lodged a strenuous objection. Far from proving Lyn's propensity for violence, Virga said, the government had not even shown that their witness had even communicated with Lyn. Indeed, prosecutors had offered only questionable evidence about the identity of Vandervort's telephone pal: Heller had played for Vandervort a tape of Lyn's police interrogation, and asked whether the voice resembled the one he had heard over a long-distance phone call. Virga complained that such an identification technique invited error. As he would say in another context, "the test of time has shown that it's extremely easy for the police to suggest"—by manipulating lineups or photos—that a witness identify a particular person as a suspect. MacBride agreed, forcing Keyes to withdraw Vandervort until prosecutors could provide an adequate foundation for his testimony.

Instead of showing Lyn's longstanding interest in harming somebody big, the prosecution retreated to the day of the incident, calling a witness from Capitol Park, the Reverend James Porter. With his long hair and gold-rimmed spectacles, the youthful Porter may have seemed more a contemporary of Lyn than an Episcopal priest. On September 5, he had been visiting from Gridley, about ninety miles north in rural Butte County.

What, Heller wanted to know, was Lyn's tone of voice when she said, "It didn't go off?"

"Extreme disappointment," said Porter.

Virga objected; Porter, he said, was not an expert on vocal inflection.

Objection overruled. As a priest, MacBride said, Porter was familiar with the tones of people's voices. "If it goes up, it means one thing, if it goes down, it means another," said the judge.

And Lyn's tone of voice when she said, "He's not serving the people?"

"It was as though she was trying . . . to convince the people that she was talking to that she was attempting to do them a favor."

Again, Virga objected. MacBride asked the priest to elaborate. "Can you reconstruct in your mind and then tell us how she stated it so that you reach one conclusion and opinion that she was greatly disappointed, and the other, that she was in fact trying to tell the people that she was doing them a favor?"

"Do I talk now?" asked Porter.

"It's your turn," said the judge. "You must have a well-ordered church."

"Not well enough," joked the priest. He said Lyn's tone just indicated that she meant, "Can't you see I was trying to do you a favor? It didn't work. Don't be mad at me."

During his cross-examination, Virga posed different interpretations of Lyn's remarks. "Can you consider the interpretation, 'He's not the servant of the people,' as meaning that he does not serve the people, in reality the people serve him? Did you consider that?"

No, said Porter.

"All right. You're in the ministry?"

"Yes, sir."

"Do you serve Christ or does he serve you?"

"I serve Christ."

"So, Christ is not the servant of the people?"

"No. He's a servant, too."

"So he is a servant of the people, isn't he?"

"Christ or the President?" asked the priest.

"Christ."

"Yes."

"If in fact he did not serve the people, then you would state he is not a servant of the people, isn't that correct?"

"I would, but I don't believe that."

"What if you did believe it?" asked Virga.

"Then I wouldn't be a Christian."

This line of questioning ground to a halt. Virga refocused on Lyn's tone of voice. Almost badgering Porter, he wanted to know exactly how one might express by voice varied states of mind. "What is bewildered? What is calm? What is frightened? What is complacent? What is gloomy? What is sullen? What is quarrelsome? What is pleasant?" The judge was unenthusiastic about this question but, after considerable argument, permitted Virga to ask what "yardstick" Porter used when interpreting Lyn's tone of voice.

The priest was ready: If a group of actors was brought before him to read the sentences in different ways, he said, "they might not be able to convince me, but I would know that they were acting. But I don't think this woman was acting that day. I think my perception was, is, that the way she responded, the way she talked, the way she physically moved her body, the whole demeanor that she expressed was—it was genuine, it was pure, it was frustration and it was disappointment."

This was not the answer Virga had hoped for. "You could hear a pin drop in the courtroom," Heller later recalled, with a chuckle. So harmful was the testimony to the defense that Heller used it for years in his lectures on trial practice. It became his favorite example of the hazards of asking "one question too many."

The government called Morris Willmarth to relate Lyn's effort to borrow his .38. Virga cross-examined him: Regarding Lyn and Sandy's environmental views, "you did not think they were full of baloney, did you?"

"No, not at all," said Willmarth.

Then Manny Boro took the stand. The prosecution and the defense both limited their questions to the day Lyn obtained Manny's .45. Not a word was said about the relationship that made that day possible.

Lanier Ramer didn't know what he should do. In the evening after court adjourned, he called a reporter to discuss his predicament. Now on parole, he was looking forward to his work as a consultant for the New York State Corrections Commission. But, he said, complying with the subpoena would "destroy my credibility and trust" with convicts. Being known as an informer, he said, also created a "real and significant threat to my family."

On the other hand, failing to testify meant not only jail for contempt of court but also a parole violation. "It makes it quite possible that I'll be sent back to prison for six or seven years," Ramer said.

It was Lyn herself who solved Ramer's dilemma. On the morning of November 11—Charlie's asserted birthday—she asked to meet with Ramer's attorney, Alvin Bronstein. With Virga present, she told him that Ramer should testify against her rather than return to jail. Bronstein explained that Ramer's testimony could well be harmful to her. Nonetheless, the lawyer said, "she in the strongest possible language urged me to urge Mr. Ramer to testify." Ramer agreed.

Before the proceedings began, however, MacBride had Lyn brought to the courtroom. Ramer waved at her, and the judge asked if she was ready to behave in court. If so, he said, "you are as welcome as the flowers in May."

"Your Honor," she said, "my defense is the defense of the world. And without Manson I am dead." She was escorted back to her cell, and Ramer took the stand.

Under Heller's questioning, Ramer related Lyn's interest in meeting up with the Weather Underground and procuring weapons. Red-faced, frequently sighing, the witness's unease was palpable.

Did Lyn indicate that anything might happen to corporate executives who failed to mend their ways?

"Yes, she told me that, I don't recall her exact words," Ramer said, trailing off. He looked up. Finally, he finished the statement. "She told me that she thought it was quite likely, probable, that some people were going to have to be killed to set examples toward getting that kind of thing stopped."

"You're not very comfortable up there, are you?" asked Heller.

"Not at all," Ramer said.

Virga wanted to know about Ramer's criminal past. "Were you captured immediately after each of the bank robberies?"

"Unfortunately," Ramer said. "The FBI liked what I did for their statistics. . . . I was a very dumb bank robber."

The prosecution decided to switch emphasis, putting on a series of witnesses who had observed the events of September 5. Ranging from local college students to Secret Service agents, the witnesses were asked to place themselves in photographs of the incident, and to describe what they saw and heard of Lyn's actions. Virga's cross-examination focused on ambiguities in the testimony; no one, after all, had heard her declare her intention to kill the president, or her frustration that he had survived their encounter. When Secret Service Agent Tom McCarter took the stand, Virga tried to use the agency's trademark against him.

Looking at a slide of the agent helping to apprehend Lyn, Virga asked, "What's that thing in your ear?"

It was an earpiece for the remote radio transmitter Secret Service agents routinely wore. McCarter said the earpiece did not interfere with his ability to hear sounds around him, but after Virga made him laboriously explain how the apparatus operated, the point came through: Maybe static had obscured the ability of agents like McCarter to hear Lyn's exact remarks.

Vandervort

The government was still determined to put Edward Vandervort on the witness stand. John Virga was equally resolved to keep him off. MacBride ordered a hearing on Vandervort outside the jury's presence.

On the afternoon of Wednesday, November 11, the jurors left the courtroom and Vandervort, brought in under heavy security, took the stand. In response to Dwayne Keyes's questions, Vandervort said he had exchanged nearly a dozen letters with Lyn. He identified photographs of Lyn that she had sent him, and reported his various small efforts on her behalf, Keyes read back to him the letters Lyn had sent, laying out instructions on murdering corporate executives, and Vandervort confirmed that he had received them. The presentation seemed certain to ensure the admissibility of Vandervort's testimony, a perfect device for the government to demonstrate Lyn's murderous intentions.

"Cross-examine," MacBride told Virga.

Referring to an alleged June 21, 1975, telephone conversation with Lyn, Virga asked, "Have you ever told anyone...that you lied about that and there was really no telephone conversation?"

"There was a telephone conversation," Vandervort insisted.

"Okay. But did you ever tell anyone that you lied about the telephone conversation?"

"Yes."

"Who did you tell that to?"

"The FBI," Vandervort said.

"In fact, you've told them on at least three occasions that you lied about that?"

"Yes."

Virga brought out that Vandervort had had a long relationship with the FBI, making various and contradictory claims about his dealings with Lyn. "In fact," Virga continued, "in one document that you sent to the director of the FBI, Mr. [Clarence] Kelley, you told him you loved Lynette Fromme, didn't you?"

"Yes," Vandervort said. The love was unconsummated, however, as Vandervort had never even seen Lyn in person.

Virga then brought out Vandervort's four-month stay in a mental hospital. Vandervort said that he had suffered a nervous breakdown.

Virga continued: "When you were relating to the FBI this information that you had about Lynette Fromme...you also told them that you had information, documents also, and pictures of Patty Hearst and also the SLA, is that right?"

"Yes," Vandervort admitted.

"How about documents with regard to the AIM, the American Indian Movement?"

"Yes."

"Are they destroyed?"

"No."

"But you told the FBI they were, is that right?"

"Yes."

"And you indicated that all documents with regard to other political groups are destroyed, is that right?"

"Yes."

"But you weren't telling the truth, is that right?"

"No."

"And to this day you still refuse to tell the FBI where they are, is that right?"

"Yes."

"Is that because they don't exist?"

"They exist."

"In your mind or in fact?" asked Virga.

"In fact," Vandervort insisted.

Nevertheless, under Virga's questioning, Vandervort said that he had told the FBI he knew where the fugitive Patty Hearst was hiding and that he had information about the killing of federal agents at Pine Ridge. Things looked even shakier after Vandervort explained how he came to testify at the Fromme trial. Investigators had tracked him to York after finding his name in Lyn's apartment. They asked him flat out if Lyn had ever threatened the president's life—and Vandervort had said yes.

"And you knew at that time when you were sitting there that they wanted information about Lynette Fromme, is that right?" asked Virga. "If you don't give them information, you feel you're going to be prosecuted, is that right?"

"I felt that way, yes," said Vandervort. He said he believed he was being granted immunity in exchange for his testimony—a delusion, apparently, since Heller vigorously denied the contention.

"Mr. Vandervort, it is correct to say, is it not, that the only reason you are here is because you've been granted immunity?"

"That's what I believe, yes."

"And it is also correct, is it not, to state that you would like to save your own hide?"

Vandervort had said earlier that he feared for his life, and government sources had said they were holding him in "protective custody." Nonetheless, Vandervort answered the question, "No."

Virga asked that Vandervort's mental health records be obtained from Pennsylvania. MacBride agreed—and thought there might be a fast way to get them. During the trial, he had seen a remarkable new technology used to transmit documents. He addressed FBI Agent Lee Latham, who sat by the prosecution table.

"Is there a possibility that the FBI could put them on—whatever it is they put them on? You got something just yesterday. You got it in a matter of hours. What is it?"

"A facsimile," said Latham.

"A facsimile," MacBride repeated. Fax machines were still a decade away from common use, and MacBride had never seen one.

But the machine turned out to be unnecessary. After Virga's withering cross-examination, prosecutors dropped their effort to put Vandervort on the stand. "He was one piece of work," Heller said years later. "A real nut."

Judge MacBride had ordered that a television monitor depicting the trial always be available to Lyn, a matter that caused Marshal Van Court some consternation. Having grown familiar with Lyn's mercurial personality, he was concerned that in a fit of rage, she might try to destroy the TV set. Van Court tried various approaches to minimize this danger, from placing the monitor outside the bars of Lyn's cell to bringing her to a marshal's office conference room, where Marcia Van Court could sit with her—and where the monitor was set high out of reach. Despite Lyn's determination not to watch the proceedings, deputies on occasion caught her stealing a glance. She at least listened sporadically, and wrote notes to Virga concerning the conduct of the defense.

Lyn was now spending almost all her time in the company of the marshals, and in particular with Marcia Van Court. Required, in the parlance of the Marshals Service, to "manage" inmates, Marcia became familiar with Lyn's moods and mannerisms. As a vegetarian, Lyn had little interest in the jail menu, which relied heavily on processed meats. Marcia would bring Lyn fruits and vegetables from home, and occasionally make her special treats. Marcia had a penchant for peanut butter and pickle sandwiches, and offered to make one for Lyn.

"I'll try it," said Lyn, and Marcia made sure to prepare it with whole-grain bread. Lyn liked the unusual sandwich, and so peanut butter and pickle became a staple in her jailhouse diet.

There were times, Marcia said, when Lyn would fall silent, close her eyes, and begin to rock back and forth. "I knew she was going off on an LSD trance," Marcia recalled. "That's when she became difficult and you couldn't reason with her."

Lyn always seemed to be probing her captors—not for lapses in security, but rather the state of their minds. One morning when Marcia arrived at the jail to escort Lyn to the courthouse, Lyn handed her a matchbox.

"I've caught a fly," said Lyn. "Would you release it outside?"

"Yes, Lynette." (Out of respect, Marcia always referred to her prisoner as "Lynette," even though the marshals preferred to call her "Squeaky.") When Marcia opened the box outdoors, she found it empty. Puzzled, she went to Lyn's cell.

"There was no fly in that box," Marcia told Lyn.

Lyn offered an enigmatic smile. Marcia suspected that she had just passed another test: Lyn knew that she actually had tried to release the fly instead of tossing the box and lying about it.

The seventh day of the trial, November 13, began with the usual ritual: Lyn entering the courtroom so Judge MacBride could ask if she was ready to behave.

"No," said Lyn.

"Very well, thank you," said the judge.

"And I never said I hated Ford, and I don't even blame Ford," Lyn added.

She seemed to be responding to the testimony of grocer Ed Louie, who told the court that prior to the pistol incident, he had overheard Lyn say that she did, indeed, hate Ford. "Ford," Lyn continued, "is Nixon in reality bumping his head against the wall."

Deputies escorted her out. Once back in her cell, she resumed her personal legal struggle. With a felt pen and a yellow legal pad, she wrote a letter to attorney Clyde Blackmon, whom she still felt was committed to helping her gain visiting privileges with Charlie.

Lyn reported that her efforts had not been successful and that she wanted Blackmon to do the legal research regarding a tape-recorded interview with Charlie. If he did, Lyn would herself draft a new motion to present to MacBride.

"Whether you agree or disagree, understand or not, I am telling you that my very life depends upon these tape-recorded conversations," she wrote, insisting that they would not be "for personal purposes of chit-chat or love talk."

The response was another disappointment. "Since you are now represented by Mr. John Virga," Blackmon wrote, "it would be inappropriate for me to become involved and I suggest that you discuss your request with him."

In the courtroom, the government called a number of witnesses who had received the "Manson Is Mad at Nixson" new release. John Barry, the Colorado freelance writer who had corresponded with Lyn and proposed that she start a Manson Family newsletter, said he was impressed with Lyn's passion about the environment.

"Her language is very strong and rather threatening, but so is Pontius and so is D. H. Lawrence and so are many other writers in Western civilization," said Barry, according to the court transcript (which may have mangled the names of the writers he cited).

MacBride's interest was piqued when prosecutors put their weapons expert, FBI Agent James B. Bolenbach, on the stand. A former gunsmith and firearms instructor, Bolenbach had analyzed Lyn's pistol at the FBI Laboratory in Washington, D.C. As Dwayne Keyes led him through his direct examination, Bolenbach demonstrated the operation and features of the .45.

"Is it possible to pull the slide back, fully cock the weapon and yet not have a shell go into the chamber?" asked Keyes. The implication was significant: If so, then Lyn could have tried to arm the weapon even though no bullet was found in the chamber.

"Yes, it is," said Bolenbach. "You insert the loaded magazine and the slide need only be pulled about halfway back to cock . . . the hammer like that. . . . But that is not sufficiently far back . . . to chamber the first round." He demonstrated the action for the jury.

Keyes then asked Bolenbach to explain the operation of the .38 five-shot revolver, the weapon Lyn had wanted to borrow from Morris Willmarth. Its design was sufficiently different, Keyes implied, that Lyn may have failed to fire the .45 by trying to operate it as a .38.

Virga, on the other hand, emphasized that the gun itself provided no indication that Lyn had tried to fire it. Bolenbach had shot the pistol himself and found that it operated perfectly. Moreover, none of the bullets had been struck by the firing pin.

MacBride, who knew a bit about guns himself, started asking his own questions of the witness. Was it possible that a fifth cartridge had previously been fired, leaving four in the magazine without chambering a new round?

"I suppose anything is possible," Bolenbach replied, but such an outcome was virtually unknown.

"I see," said the judge. "I used to have a Browning automatic and there was a little lever I could push back and I could fire a shell in the chamber and yet the other two wouldn't come up. . . . Is there any such device on this gun?"

No, said Bolenbach.

Stephen Crane was a dictation machine salesman whose clients included the U.S. Attorney's Office in Sacramento. Crane had gone to see President Ford in Capitol Park on September 5, and found a prime spot along the walkway to the Statehouse. When Ford came up the path, Crane extended his right hand, and awkwardly juggling a camera in his left hand, planned to snap a picture. When the moment arrived, however, Crane was too awestruck to get off the shot. Hoping at least to get a picture of the president as he moved away, Crane turned—and witnessed the pistol incident. The event was deeply troubling to Crane, who tried to unburden himself by writing about his feelings to President Ford.

Handwritten on notebook paper, the missive evoked the emotional ambiguity that characterized the 1970s. "I'm not sure why I'm writing this letter to you," Crane began. "It's something I wanted to [on] Friday after the happening that day. You see, I was about five feet away from you when the attempt on your life occurred. The terror and fear I felt at the time lingers with me and probably always will."

Had he seen the letter, Ford might have told Crane to get over it; the president himself had quickly put the incident behind him. As it was, Crane's name did not register with White House staffers who screened incoming mail for letters from VIPs. As a result, Crane was consigned to the "General" file, meaning he was answered with a form reply signed by an autograph machine.

Dwayne Keyes and Don Heller, however, were more interested in Crane's experiences: the salesman had told detectives he had heard the pivotal noise in the prosecution case, the *click*. Indeed, Crane had mentioned the sound in his letter to Ford. Called to the stand on November 13, he related his impressions to the jury.

"When you first heard this *click*," Virga asked in cross-examination, "you did not know what it was, did you?"

"I wasn't sure, no sir," said Crane. "I didn't associate it with the gun."

"In fact, when you first heard it you thought it was a click of a camera, didn't you?"

It was only when he saw the pistol that he concluded the sound had probably come from the gun.

"So had you not seen the weapon, your feeling would have been that it was the click of a camera. That's correct isn't it?"

"Right," said Crane.

Don Heller planned to score a major blow on the last day of the government case. Heading to the courtroom on November 13, he whispered to a reporter, "This next witness is going to blast your socks off!"

Heller was planning to call Sacramento Lieutenant Hal Taylor, who on September 5 had been escorting Lyn through the police station when she saw Sandra Good and exclaimed, "But it didn't go off. I'm sorry, Sandy."

Heller believed the statement would show Lyn's disappointment at Ford surviving the pistol incident. But John Virga objected; Lyn had made the comment before being read her constitutional rights, including the right to remain silent. Don Heller told the judge that the remark was a "spontaneous statement" of the defendant, a statement she made without any prompting by a police officer, and therefore not subject to the famous *Miranda* rule.

Virga suggested a more sinister circumstance. Unable to get Lyn to answer their questions, detectives intentionally confronted her with Sandy hoping that the sight of her intimate friend would spark just such an incriminating remark. Together with the statement police took from Lyn shortly afterwards—a videotaped interview made with such disregard for Lyn's rights that prosecutors dared not introduce it in court—Virga suggested that the "I'm sorry, Sandy" remark was inadmissible "fruit of the poison tree." The "totality" was so egregious, Virga insisted, that it should be presented "in every police class in the United States on how not to take a statement and oppressive police work."

Heller disagreed intensely. The government took the statement not to develop evidence against Lyn in the criminal case, but simply to demonstrate that she was rational, coherent, and in full charge of her mental faculties. "Far too often we see in these courtrooms phony insanity defenses presented," Heller said. The videotaped statement would be a hedge against such a defense and authorities "should be commended for what they did and not abused."

Virga shot back: "I want the record to reflect they should be commended for violating every constitutional right that Miss Fromme had."

MacBride did not take sides in the spat between Virga and Heller. Instead, he focused on the issue presented. Even if Lyn's police interrogation statement was inadmissible, the "I'm sorry, Sandy" episode preceded it in time. "You can't poison a statement made up earlier in the stream, so to speak, before the poison is put in the stream," said the judge.

Prosecutors introduced the "I'm sorry, Sandy" statement. After a couple of inconsequential witnesses who testified to the authenticity of certain photographs or other evidence, the government rested its case. MacBride recessed the court for the lunch break.

Chapter 12

The Defense

The previous afternoon, deputies had wheeled four special 24-inch television monitors into the courtroom. Jurors may have puzzled over their presence until court reconvened, and MacBride told the defense to begin its case.

"Mr. Virga, are you ready to call your first witness?"

"Yes, Your Honor. I'd like to call as my first witness the President of the United States, Gerald R. Ford."

A hush fell over the courtroom, packed with spectators eager to watch legal history being made. Nearly forty reporters—and ten sketch artists—were present, as were eleven deputy marshals. At MacBride's direction, a technician turned on the videocassette player. The four screens hummed to life, depicting a head and shoulder shot of the chief executive, sitting behind two microphones and in front of a blue curtain. MacBride's voice could be heard as he swore Ford in as a witness and then directed Virga to begin his examination. The camera remained fixed on Ford during the entire 25-minute, 35-second tape.

Virga: Where was Lynette Fromme when you first observed her, if you recall?

Ford: Approximately halfway between L Street and the state Capitol, I noticed a person in the second or third row in a brightly colored dress who appeared to want to either shake hands or speak or at least wanted to get closer to me. I stopped because I was gradually moving toward the state Capitol, and that was my first impression of a person who had a dress on. I, of course, didn't know who it was—of that bright color I should say.

Virga: When you first observed the woman who you've described, can you tell me what her demeanor was? By that, I mean she was calm, nervous, or just in your own words how would you describe her behavior when you first observed her?

Ford: My first impression was that she wanted to come closer and extend—I thought at the time—a hand to shake, or to say something to me. But I can't recollect anything beyond that.

Virga: Do you recall anything about the condition of her face when you first observed her? Was it flushed, pale, weathered—I know you used the term "weathered" before. Is that your recollection?

Ford: It looked weathered but there were many faces, but the brightness of the dress attracted my attention and in the process of noticing the dress I thought her face did appear to be somewhat weathered.

Virga asked about the pistol. "Could you tell if her finger was on the trigger?"

"I could not."

"And I would assume also that you could not tell from your observations whether or not she pulled the trigger?"

"I could not."

Then came the key question: "Did you ever hear the gun click?"

"I have no recollection of it clicking or not clicking," said the president.

Virga was done.

"Is there any examination by the United States Attorney?" asked the judge.

"No, Your Honor," said Dwayne Keyes.

"Very well, then that concludes the hearing. Thank you very much, Mr. President, and you're released from the subpoena."

"Thank you very much, Your Honor," said the president.

As cameras were not permitted in MacBride's courtroom, artists sketched the scene of judge, lawyers, and jury gazing intently at Ford's unsmiling face peering out of the video monitors. Reporters fished for a telling detail to convey the event. The *New York Times* noted that the president "appeared tense," while the *Los Angeles Times* recorded that he was "businesslike and did not smile. He occasionally gestured with his hands as he testified."

John Virga, besieged by reporters after the court session, was asked if he had been "nervous" while questioning the president.

"Yeah, I was nervous," said Virga. "So was he."

''It's Not Loaded Anyway''

Following the conclusion of the government case on Friday, November 14, prosecutors, as required by federal rules, readied a 150-page stack of witness interviews for release to the defense. John Virga picked up the materials on Saturday, around noon. He did not recognize most of the fifty-odd witnesses because they had never testified in court. Among them was the one-page interview Officer

Paul Boettin had conducted with Jim Damir—where Damir said Lyn had screamed, "It's not loaded anyway."

When Virga saw that document, he nearly went through the roof. To Virga, the remark helped prove that Lyn had not intended to kill the president, that she had known all along that her pistol was not operational—and the government's concealment of the statement was nothing less than an obstruction of justice. As the judge had reminded prosecutors at the earliest proceedings, they had a legal duty under the *Brady* doctrine to give the defense exculpatory statements.

To confirm his understanding of events, Virga and his investigators spent the weekend interviewing Damir and Boettin, and researching the relevant legal issues. To Virga, Damir now seemed so confused about what he had heard and what he had said, what prosecutors had told him and what he had told investigators, he didn't "know whether he's on foot or horseback."

When court reconvened on Monday, November 17, Virga was expected to present his opening statement. Instead, he asked for a mistrial, and that the charges against Lyn be dismissed because of the government's "wilful suppression of evidence." If the motion were granted, Lyn would go free.

The courtroom buzzed at the stunning turn of events. MacBride shook his head, disbelieving, as Virga listed other ways he said prosecutors had impeded his defense. "You know what they have done," he told the judge. "They have flooded me with material at the end so I cannot prepare a defense. This is as obvious as the nose on your face." Virga asked MacBride to imagine that "I represented your son or daughter. Would you not feel that the only way I would be effective counsel for one of your loved ones would be to adequately prepare the case?"

Don Heller reacted angrily, accusing Virga of "misrepresentations." He told the judge that, in the totality of the situation, he had been convinced that Damir had merely misspoken when he told Boettin about the "It's not loaded anyway" remark. Besides, Heller said, "the evidence in this case was the gun was loaded, everyone knew that right from the start—"

MacBride, visibly irritated, interrupted. That, he said, was the entire issue in the case. While Lyn's gun might have been loaded under law enforcement definitions, "the lay person could have an entirely different interpretation of what is the meaning of the expression, 'It wasn't loaded anyway.' . . . That's going to be one of the main issues when the argument is made to the jury, and that is, if there was not a shell in the chamber because she did not intend to have a shell in the chamber, or because she thought the shell was in the chamber when she put the clip in the gun." The judge's own anger was rising. "That's what this case is all about and I just can't understand how you could decide that you will make this determination as to whether or not that was, in fact, an exculpatory statement when I had explicitly ordered you at the outset of the trial . . . [to] immediately provide all exculpatory statements in evidence. . . . You said that you would, that you understood the law and that you would. That's the problem with which we're faced, unhappily."

Heller again started to explain, saying that Damir had "repudiated" his statement and that no other witness had reported hearing those words. The Boettin statement was of "rather nebulous" value to the defense, he insisted.

MacBride disagreed. If Virga had known about the statement, his questions to the government witnesses would have been different. "He would also have said, Is there a possibility that you might have also heard, 'It wasn't loaded anyway, it wasn't loaded anyway,' and then they heard, 'It didn't go off, it didn't go off.'"

"Well," said Heller, "we could make available—"

"Or, the other way around," MacBride continued, ignoring Heller, " 'It didn't go off, it didn't go off because it wasn't loaded anyway, it wasn't loaded anyway.'"

Heller offered to make the witnesses available if Virga wanted to question them further along those lines. He tried then to change the subject. "I just spoke with Jim Damir outside in the hallway prior to court convening," Heller said. "Now, Mr. Damir told me he got the distinct impression from the way Mr. Virga questioned him that Virga wanted him to claim that we coerced him into changing his mind, which is not the case. Now, I find that to be—"

"Oh, well," said the judge, shrugging off its importance.

"—of some degree of seriousness."

MacBride was not impressed. "I think this other thing is more serious than that. Of course, he's going to do that and you might try to do the same thing. I'm not concerned with that. I am concerned with the fact that you were ordered to deliver to the defendant all exculpatory evidence that the government might have pursuant to the *Brady* case and I'm not—I'm not going to say right now that you haven't. But I'll tell you this: I'm plenty worried. I'm plenty worried right now," the judge repeated, "I'm quite concerned. I'm very concerned because certainly in this case, a statement such as that must certainly be looked upon as an exculpatory statement."

Then he addressed the lawyers: "I want both of you to submit points and authorities immediately on the motion to dismiss and/or for mistrial, and I want you to get to work right away." So that there would be no distractions, MacBride ordered a two-day continuance of the trial, and excused the jury until November 19.

Heller, however, was still steaming over Virga's accusation. To prove his "good faith," he wanted immediately to call Boettin and Damir to the stand. Virga was derisive, and began reading from the Supreme Court's 1963 *Brady* opinion: "Suppression by prosecution of evidence favorable to an accused upon request violates due process where evidence is material either to guilt or to punishment, irrespective of the good faith or bad faith of the prosecution." That being the case, Virga said, "what is the purpose of this hearing?... Their motive is the only thing they want to have you explore and their motive is not relevant."

MacBride said the motive may indeed be relevant—that intentional suppression of evidence could tip the balance in a tainted case from mistrial (which could lead to another trial), to dismissal, meaning the charges would vanish forever. But leaving that aside, did the government have any response to the motion for mistrial?

Heller insisted that the damage to the defense case, if there was any, could easily be repaired. "We could make available the Secret Service agents who testified as to statements. And we could have them back here in a day—all the civilian witnesses."

"Would you or Mr. Keyes pay their fare?" scowled the judge. "I don't mean to jest. You say it so lightly that all we have to do is make a phone call and have these people from Washington come back out here. You express the idea so flippantly and so easily, as if, 'All right, now we should have turned it over to them now that they discovered that we should have.' "

"I didn't mean it flippantly, Judge," said Heller. "You know, I've been deeply concerned about this. I've been doing this for six and a half years and I've never been accused of anything of this nature," he added, defensively.

The hearing went forward. Jim Damir, wearing a tennis sweater over his shirt and tie, took the stand to recount the events regarding his statement, as best he could remember. Unfortunately, Damir could not remember very well. When Virga asked what he now remembered Lyn saying, Damir said, "It didn't go off" and, "He's not your public servant."

"But you're not clear that she said, 'It's not loaded anyway?' " Virga asked.

"No, I'm not."

"But you think she might have said that, don't you?"

Damir hesitated. "I— No, I don't. I can't place it. I've read the statement and things, so, I guess I have doubts about it."

In an unusual maneuver, Dwayne Keyes called Don Heller to the stand. Under Keyes's gentle questioning, Heller related his version of his dealings with Jim Damir. Then it was Virga's turn to cross-examine.

"I waited two months for this, Your Honor," said Virga. "I'm so excited I don't know what to do."

"Do you want to sit down for a minute?" asked the judge.

"Maybe I better. May I have a glass of water?"

Then Virga launched the interrogation of his courtroom adversary. Heller had shown Damir the statement he gave to FBI Agent Bolan, but not the Boettin statement, right?

"Yes," said Heller. "But the reason for that—"

"Just a minute," said Virga, savoring the moment. "I didn't ask you for the reason."

"Okay," said Heller, resigned. As a witness, he could only answer the questions Virga chose to ask him. Did he think "It's not loaded anyway" was exculpatory?

Not at all, said Heller. In his mind, it was similar to saying, "I goofed," after forgetting to load film in a camera. The prosecutor had not bothered to ask Officer Boettin for any clarification of what Damir had meant—and had not, of course, told the grand jury considering Lyn's indictment about the statement.

Virga sliced into him: "You did not feel, then, it was your duty and responsibility to help the grand jurors fairly and impartially weigh this without being bound by your locked-in thinking on the matter, is that right?"

"I thought it was my duty to present the evidence fairly to both the United States and to Lynette Fromme, and that's what I did to the best of my ability."

"How long have you been a prosecutor?"

"Six and one-half years."

"How many cases have you prosecuted?"

"Thousands—"

Keyes objected. "Your Honor, this is irrelevant."

"Heller," Virga countered, "is no greenhorn. He has been through this many, many times in different cases. He has to weigh and evaluate *Brady* and what's exculpatory and what isn't."

"The objection is overruled," said MacBride.

Virga honed in on Heller's talks with Damir. "When you met him on November 2 . . . did you tell him he was going to be testifying again and he would have to tell the truth?"

"I told him he may be testifying. I wasn't sure whether we would use him. And I reiterated that the only thing we are interested in is the truth."

"As *you* see it? The truth as you see it?"

"The truth as he saw it."

"Objection, Your Honor," said Keyes.

"It is argumentative," the judge agreed.

Virga focused on Heller's effort to tell Damir about *Helter Skelter*, assertedly to "reassure" him that he was safe since none of the Tate-LaBianca witnesses were known to have been murdered.

"Did he tell you he was worried about any members of the Manson Family, or did you ask him if he was?"

"I asked him because he was very nervous," said Heller.

"Well, when you asked him the question about the Manson Family in *Helter Skelter*, his nervousness probably went up a heck of a lot, is that right?"

"No, it kind of remained the same," said Heller. "He was nervous when he got there and he was nervous when he left."

"So nervous," Virga said, "that if he was to testify and state under oath that she stated 'It wasn't loaded anyway, it wasn't loaded anyway,' that she might walk and Lord knows what might happen after that, is that right, Mr. Heller?"

"That's argumentative," Keyes objected. Objection sustained.

When the blistering cross-examination ended, MacBride had a question of his own. "Let me just ask you this question, Mr. Heller: If you were in Mr. Virga's shoes, would you like to have that statement before trial?"

"Yes," Heller admitted.

In the argument over the alleged bad faith of the prosecution, Virga restated the sequence of events that he said showed the wilfulness of concealing Damir's statement. He returned to the curious fact that Heller brought up *Helter Skelter* just as Damir was puzzling over what precisely he heard Lyn say. "I read that book," said Virga, "and it scared me. Anyone who reads that book, it would have to scare them. People know about the Manson Family. Anyone who tells me they are not scared when they read about or hear about some of those things, they are fools. What is the subtlety of that? What's the residue of talking about that? Why talk about it?

"Then [Damir] calls and says, 'You know, I'm now convinced I didn't hear that.' So now you have a situation when Mr. Heller knows that a witness, when he gave his first statement when the events were very fresh in his mind, 11:25 A.M., made a statement that if this jury believed it would totally exonerate her from the charge of attempting to assassinate the President. And I say to you, whether you call it overzealousness rather than intentional misconduct, it amounts to the same thing. . . . If that occurred, then the case has to be dismissed."

MacBride invited Keyes to argue his side. The prosecutor asked for time to brief the issue.

The Damir controversy stunned trial observers. The defense, wrote the *Sacramento Bee*, "drove a technical stake perilously close to the heart of the prosecution." Heller, asked by reporters why he had not turned over the Damir statement earlier, said only that "I really don't know. It was such an innocuous thing."

For his part, a pleased Virga said, "I've got them where it hurts, and I'm not going to let go."

Although it was Heller's conduct at issue, Dwayne Keyes offered the government's reply. He conceded, for the purpose of argument, that Damir's remarks were a *Brady* statement. But that being so, Keyes insisted that federal courts were divided on when exculpatory material had to be given to the defense, and thus prosecutors had been reasonable in holding on to Damir's statement until they rested their case. "We were not trying to be cute legally, we felt we had a solid position," Keyes said.

With the benefit of hindsight, however, Keyes said perhaps the government could have provided the substance of the statement to Virga without Damir's name, thus preserving the confidentiality of the grand jury process. At this point, he conceded, it was "obviously regrettable" that prosecutors had not done so, "but we were not trying to hide anything."

Keyes seemed to distinguish between the government's standing obligations under *Brady* and an explicit order from the trial judge to turn over exculpatory material. This infuriated MacBride. He now felt the prosecutors were playing games. "I could guarantee from here on out, regardless of what happens in this case, I am no longer going to rely on the statement of the United States Attorney that says, 'Don't worry, Judge, we know the *Brady* law and we will comply with the *Brady* law.' I can tell you from here on out—you can count on it—I'm going to order the *Brady* material turned over, and if you don't want to do it, we will go from there and see what happens. Let's go on."

"All right, Your Honor," said Keyes, hoping for a respite from the judge's tongue-lashing.

"Because I can tell you this, that's what I intend to do," MacBride continued, sputtering over his outrage. "When the motion was made—it's water over the dam now, but when you fellows said—and you have always said it every time a defense attorney comes in and asks for *Brady* material, you have always said it and—"

"We have," said the sheepish Keyes.

"—all of you have always said, 'We know the *Brady* rule. We know that we have to turn over *Brady* material. And I have said, 'All right,' and I have repeatedly said, 'There's no need for my making this order because I know they will comply.' But no more. From here on out, I'm going to order you to turn over the *Brady* material."

Left unmentioned was the author of the original motion instructing the government to comply with *Brady:* Lynette Fromme. Always correcting her understanding of the law, MacBride had assured Lyn that her motion was unnecessary because prosecutors already knew their duty under the law.

MacBride was determined to find out the story behind the Damir situation. He wanted to know Dwayne Keyes's involvement in withholding the statement, but the prosecutor seemed to obfuscate over when, precisely, he had learned about the "It's not loaded anyway" remark. Exasperated, the judge demanded, "I would just ask you again, Mr. Keyes, you're an officer of the court, I'm going to have to rely on your integrity, did you know of the Damir statement—"

"No," said the prosecutor.

"Let me finish my question," the judge said. "Did you know of the existence of the Damir statement on October the 7th?"

"No."

"You mean Mr. Heller hadn't told you in connection with the grand jury proceeding on September the 10th that this Damir statement existed, that the Damir statement where he said the gun wasn't loaded, where she said the gun wasn't loaded—"

"Not to my knowledge, Your Honor."

The judge swiveled in his chair and looked right at Keyes. "This is incredible," he said. "You mean to tell me, you're the captain of the ship, you're running the show over there and that with this statement in your office, this statement of Damir to Boettin, in your office that you knew absolutely nothing about that statement at the time the matter was presented to the grand jury on September the 10th and nor did you know anything about the statement on October the 7th when the request was made that all *Brady* material be delivered to me; you didn't even know the existence of the statement?"

"That is correct, Your Honor." Keyes tried to explain how complicated it had been to keep track of the witnesses. MacBride was not impressed.

"You don't have to explain it, Mr. Keyes. You've made a statement, you've told me, as an officer of the court, that you knew absolutely nothing about the existence of the Damir statement prior to the presentation to the grand jury on September the 10th, nor even after the presentation and up to the time that Mr. Virga made his motion for disclosure and even after that you didn't learn of the existence of this statement in your office, or otherwise until—" The judge paused in his excoriation. "When was the first time that you, as the United States Attorney for this District and the person that's prosecuting this case, learned of the existence of that statement?"

Once again, Keyes said that, "to my best recollection," it was on November 2.

MacBride gave Virga fifteen minutes to respond to the halting, quasi-coherent argument by the prosecution. Again, he laid out the conspiracy he saw in the government's conduct: Not only had Jim Damir been frightened and turned around by Heller's blandishments, but the procedural device of listing Damir as a potential witness had given the prosecution cover to withhold his name from the defense until the government rested its case.

"Isn't that the perfect subterfuge?" Virga asked. "Take them to the grand jury so I don't get it. Put him under subpoena so I don't get it? Keep him away totally?"

The prosecution's actions had so tainted Damir's evidence, so polluted Lyn's constitutional rights, Virga said, that "now, what [prosecutors] are asking you to do is drink sewer water. It's bad, Your Honor. It's very bad. They have contaminated Lynette Fromme's chance to have a fair trial."

MacBride was still ruminating on Virga's *Helter Skelter* argument. "You are suggesting that Heller was threatening [him] with retribution on the part of members of the Manson Family if he testified to the truth? . . . Why would Heller want to threaten them with Manson Family reprisals if he came in with the statement which in effect was exculpatory, which would exonerate her? Why would he want to threaten Damir with that action on the part of Manson if he testified favorably to Miss Fromme? So I don't get your argument."

"I'm not necessarily saying threatening him with reprisal with the Manson Family," said Virga. "I'm saying these are dangerous people. 'If you testify to this, she could go free. And we don't want dangerous people to go free. She's a bad person.' The ends of justice fit the means."

"All right," said MacBride. "I have your argument."

Virga concluded by citing a case from the federal Court of Appeals for the Ninth Circuit, which governed the Sacramento judicial district. "If the prosecutorial conduct was censurable," Virga read from *United States* vs. *Garrison*, "we might reverse a conviction in the interest of keeping the administration of justice beyond the suspicion of reproach or perhaps as a prophylactic against wilful prosecutorial misconduct." Given that the victim of the alleged offense was the President of the United States, nothing could send a stronger message to prosecutors than to quash the indictment and dismiss all charges against Lynette Alice Fromme.

Lyn's fate was not the only one that hung in the balance as Judge MacBride considered the motion to dismiss. Next to her, the person with the most to lose was Don Heller; blowing the Fromme case would be the death knell of his career as a prosecutor. Dwayne Keyes, already viewed by some observers as the junior partner on the government team despite his higher rank, would see his hopes of advancement end as well; the U.S. Attorney had decided to try the case personally because of its importance, and its dismissal under such humiliating circumstances would erase any chance of higher office in the Ford administration.

John Virga, on the other hand, might well catapult to the top ranks of the defense bar. Observers would be quick to contrast the performance of the unknown Virga in a supposedly open and shut case with that of F. Lee Bailey, the legendary attorney defending Patricia Hearst in San Francisco. With many more resources at his disposal, a far more sympathetic client, and a weaker prosecution case, Bailey nonetheless lost; it was only a presidential pardon that eventually freed Patty.

Judge Tom MacBride, suddenly a nationally known figure after fourteen years on the bench, would enter history as the man who set Squeaky Fromme free. The Kennedy appointee would become a darling of civil libertarians who cherished constitutional freedoms, and a symbol to others of a federal judiciary run amok, with unaccountable, life-tenured judges elevating criminals' rights over the protection of society. Alternatively, if MacBride were to rule for the government and subsequently be reversed by the Court of Appeals, he would be viewed by many as too weak to stand up for due process when it was needed most, by a defendant as unpopular as could be imagined.

In either event, such notoriety was likely to end whatever small chance MacBride had of elevation to a higher court. Already in his sixties and a Democrat, MacBride was unlikely to appeal to a Republican president considering judicial appointments. Nonetheless, despite his liberal reputation during his years as a state assemblyman, MacBride had been studiously nonpartisan since his appointment to the bench, and noticeably friendly to President Ford's close friend, White House counsel Phil Buchen, after meeting him in the course of the Fromme trial.

Beyond the individuals who sat in the Sacramento courthouse were implications for the entire country. Already in the midst of deep self-examination after the Vietnam War and the Nixon administration scandals, American society had been jolted by the incident in Capitol Park—an assault that garnered far more attention, and provoked far more discussion, than the occasional threats or attacks on presidents who would follow Gerald Ford into office. Americans in the mid-1970s were questioning if their country could do anything right, from elect an honest man to build cars as good as those from Japan. The government's inability to convict as wretched an opponent as Squeaky Fromme would doubtless fuel what President Jimmy Carter later called the national "malaise."

So, even though John Virga had called upon the judge to "not consider who the victim of this offense is," everyone knew that the victim—and the defendant—made all the difference in the world.

The Point of Uncertainty

In delivering his opinion to the tense courtroom, Judge MacBride proceeded deliberately through the legal issues raised. "In this case, there's no doubt in my mind that the conduct of Mr. Heller in presenting the matter before the grand jury and, frankly, in some areas in the case is not a model of prosecutorial conduct," he said. Nonetheless, the indictment would stand. The grand jury's only function was to determine if enough evidence existed to bring a defendant to trial. Even had the grand jurors known of the "It wasn't loaded anyway" statement, as they should have, the government still had presented enough evidence to warrant an indictment.

MacBride then addressed the defense's stronger legal claims, for dismissal of charges, or at least a mistrial. Conceding that he might be "wrong," MacBride said that Damir was not the crucial witness Virga had maintained him to be. Because Damir had changed his story so many times, whatever he might have to say simply would not be that persuasive. Moreover, poor as the government's conduct had been in regard to Damir, the judge was not willing to ascribe an impure motive to prosecutors. "I don't think really that I can impugn their integrity to that extent," he said. Thus, under "the totality of circumstances and facts, and the law in this case, I must deny the motion to dismiss, or to grant a new trial."

After recessing court, Judge MacBride took the unusual step of explaining his decision to a journalist. Don Heller, he said, had acted "with stupidity," but apparently not in bad faith, "although," he added reservedly, "I could be overturned by the appeals court."

The once-cocksure Heller had been visibly humbled. Ashen-faced, on the verge of tears, he poured himself out to reporters waiting by the courtroom. "For a while, the judge held my life in his hands," he said. "I haven't eaten in days. Maybe now, I can hold some food down."

Despite the reprieve, Heller now was damaged goods in the Fromme trial. While he had been the dominant courtroom presence during the prosecution case, he now would sit silently while Dwayne Keyes questioned witnesses and delivered the closing argument.

The next day, Thursday, November 20, began with a bomb threat, telephoned in to the jurors' motel, the Ponderosa Motor Inn, by an anonymous caller. Deputies hustled eleven of the jurors out, without explaining the reason for the early departure. Dorothy Markel, however, was a late sleeper who just didn't want to leave; to rouse her, deputies were forced to tell her the reason. They swore her to secrecy, but rumors quickly circulated among the jurors. By the time they got to the courthouse, everyone seemed to believe it was a bomb.

While the jurors waited in their assembly room, proceedings got under way before MacBride. In the wake of the Damir affair, the judge and prosecutors now seemed to bend over backwards to placate John Virga. Virtually all government records Virga requested would be handed over without objection, even though prosecutors could well have argued otherwise. And when MacBride turned to whether Keyes or Heller would be forced to take the stand before the jury, Lyn, listening to the hearing from her cell, just had to see for herself. She had a marshal escort her to the courtroom—her first appearance at her trial in nine days.

Snapping her fingers as she walked in, Lyn turned to Keyes. "I couldn't resist it," she told him. But when she wandered over to talk to Heller, the judge cut her off. "Would you please, frankly, remain quiet?"

Lyn tried to hold her peace, and was rewarded when the judge ruled that Virga could require Heller to testify about the alleged suppression of Damir's statement. "I realize he is going to make an attempt to try Mr. Heller instead of trying Miss Fromme," MacBride said, "but I think under the circumstances . . . that he is entitled to do it." At least Heller could take solace in the fact that Lyn, removed as her own counsel, could not conduct the direct examination herself.

Still locked in their assembly room, jurors had continued to speculate over the reason for their hurried evacuation from the motel. With Lyn still present in court, MacBride asked the lawyers to help him decide what, if anything, the jury should be told about the incident.

Virga tried to hash the problem out. "My gut reaction," he said, "is obviously the jurors would appreciate this bomb threat did not come [from] anyone connected with the government. They are going to discount that right away. The only one it could come from would be someone connected with Lynette Fromme. The next point that I arrive at in the process of mental gymnastics is . . . what do you do? Let them go on with a lingering doubt and wonder whether there was one or wasn't one? Can you be in a position where you would tell them, you know?"

Lyn spoke up: "Yeah. Tell them the truth."

"Tell them," Virga repeated. "Okay. I think you're right. Tell them there was in fact a bomb threat and get it out in the open rather than having it be a smoldering type of prejudice."

"I think so," MacBride agreed. "I think you're wise."

"Wait a minute, Your Honor, please," said Lyn. "I'm leaving."

"You're leaving?"

"Yes."

"Adios," said the judge. The trial seemed to be wearing on him. He had the jury brought in, and told them about the bomb threat. And he apologized for the bad food they had at a restaurant chosen by the marshals.

The following morning, Friday, November 21, the defense case finally began. Lyn declined to attend, and Virga waived his right to make an opening statement. He would rely instead on the testimony of his witnesses. They, he said, "will speak much more frankly than anything I can state." In fact, Virga's reluctance to deliver the statement had to do with the uncertainty of one particular witness, Lyn. She had been vacillating on whether to take the stand in her own defense. Without knowing whether such a sensational witness would be the centerpiece of his case, Virga decided to start with caution.

The case unfolded simply. First, Virga tried to demonstrate that Lyn had not behaved as one might expect a frustrated, failed assassin to act, and that her statement to Sandy in the police hallway did not have the significance prosecutors implied. He recalled Detective Linda Walker to the stand, and quizzed her about Lyn's conduct while in custody on September 5. Walker recounted the subjects of their discussions that day: children, ecology, television.

What impression did Walker get of her captive?

"I got the impression that she was tired," the detective said.

Virga next sought to show that Lyn knew enough about firearms to kill a president, had she wanted to. He called Peter Perry, the auto mechanic who, with his girlfriend, Marsha Bradt, and her brother, Peter Bradt, had taken Lyn target-shooting outside San Francisco. He testified that he had seen Lyn operate the .22 caliber High Standard semi-automatic pistol. She had inserted the clip and pulled back the slide, arming it. And she had fired it.

Virga introduced into evidence photos Marsha Bradt had taken of Lyn firing the weapon, several of which had been published in *Time* magazine. How many rounds had Lyn fired with the .22 pistol? Virga asked.

"I'd say somewhere between 100 and 150," said Perry.

"Mr. Perry, you're not a member of the Manson Family, are you?" The twenty-four-year-old Perry, with his long hair, mustache, and aviator glasses, might well look like a Manson Family member to the matrons and retirees on Lyn's jury.

"No, I'm not," Perry said.

"Never have been?"

"No, I have never."

"What was the purpose in going out to shoot the guns?"

"Well, we all thought it might be interesting to give them some exposure to all these things they've been talking about. They talked about using force in certain instances, this sort of thing, we thought if they'd see what firearms actually were and how difficult it is to use them, they'd perhaps think a little better [about something] as foolish as that."

"Was there any other purpose?"

"Not that I can recall," Perry said.

Keyes launched his cross-examination. His tone of voice, if not mocking, displayed at least incredulity. "Now, are you stating that there was a benevolent effort to try to dissuade the defendant from doing something by going to the firing range?"

"Yes."

"What was it that you were concerned about?"

"Well, they had appeared to have advocated, since they were associated with the Manson Family, all sorts of things that have been alluded to in newspapers or whatever," said Perry.

"Well, I don't want you to talk about what has been 'alluded to.' I want you to talk about what you know," Keyes said. "What did the defendant say to you that caused you to take her to the firing range?"

"Well, I don't think there was anything specifically said to me, no," Perry said.

"And then what was your purpose to dissuade her?" Keyes asked.

Perry had trouble explaining. "Because, as I say—tried to say before, it appeared that it was—trying to be said that the Family had a violent nature, whatever, and they tried to force people to do things or whatever and I—in my talks with Lynette, I didn't see that she had been involved in any of that."

"So you took her to the firing range to teach her how to fire a weapon, is that right?"

"Well, to show her what it was like to do that, give her that experience."

"Did she enjoy it?" Keyes asked.

Virga objected; MacBride sustained. "Irrelevant," said the judge.

Keyes resumed. "When you stated previously that you wanted to dissuade her from a certain course of conduct, would you please explain to us what you meant by that?"

"Well," said Perry, "if you could perhaps allow me to say in my own words, I was hoping if she perhaps saw it wasn't as easy as portrayed in television and movies to be accurate with a weapon or be able to use a weapon without a great deal of practice and ability, then she wouldn't try and do it."

"In other words, she couldn't use it accurately without a lot of practice?"

"That's what I was trying to show her. It wasn't something you picked up and did. You had to practice and be good at it."

"But you took her out there two successive days for her to practice, isn't that right?"

"Yes, I did," said Perry.

"Did you personally instruct her?" Keyes asked.

"I don't think that's the correct word, 'instruct,'" said Perry, increasingly defensive. "I think I showed her things, you know, specific methods of operations. But I don't— I didn't instruct her. I didn't start out and give a lecture in the beginning and say how you do it. I didn't do that at all, no."

Keyes moved to wrap things up. Did Lyn ask for advice on using the firearms? Perry said she had.

"Did she indicate to you that she didn't know how?"

"Well, she tried on her own, and then when she couldn't do it, then she asked me what needed to be done," said Perry.

Virga next called the day's star witness: James Damir. He hemmed and hawed through his testimony and, as predicted, could no longer say anything about the "It's not loaded anyway" remark. "I have no recollection of making that statement," he testified.

"As you sit here right now, and correct me if I'm wrong," Virga said, "you're confused now about what happened that day, aren't you?"

"Concerning that one statement, yes."

Virga then laid the foundation for his coming attack on Don Heller. "So as you sit there now, what you're saying is that you did not hear Lynette Fromme say in the park on that date, September the 5th, 'It's not loaded anyway, it's not loaded anyway,' over, over, over and over again, is that right?"

"I don't recall her saying that, yes."

"Do you have any possible explanation to this jury as to why those words would pop in your mind while watching the slides?"

"I thought about it a lot and I cannot explain it, no sir," said Damir.

"It certainly is unusual that all of a sudden you speak those words while watching those slides and then find out it's actually in a police report, isn't it?" asked Virga.

"Yes, it is," Damir agreed.

"Call Mr. Heller," said John Virga. The defense's most reluctant witness, the Assistant U.S. Attorney, took the stand.

Virga's questioning was hardly gentle. But in the midst of the barrage, Heller had a chance to explain himself. The words poured out: "Of course I was interested in the statement to the police officer, 'It wasn't loaded anyway, [sic] It wasn't loaded anyway.' Because if that was correct, if that was his recollection, he was very significant, I agree, he would have been an exculpatory witness and would have made us re-evaluate our case as to how far away he was from her when he heard this statement, if that's what she said, it would have been evidence to me, in my mind, that maybe she didn't intend to kill the President and was something to look into because on September 10, I had a tentative conclusion in my mind as to what she intended to do in the park, but I'm always open—my mind is always open to change and I've had cases in the middle of trial where I've learned something and threw the cases out. So, I wasn't fixed—it wasn't my feeling that I don't care what the evidence is, I'm going to prosecute Lynette Fromme for the attempted murder—or the attempted assassination of the President, my mind was not closed, but after speaking to Damir, I was convinced that the statement in the police report, either Boettin inaccurately took it down or Damir, when he said it to Boettin was confused because he was very convincing in my mind at the grand jury and at the—and at my pre-grand jury interview with him."

"All right," said Virga. "The normal way to clear up inconsistencies is to let a witness look at the reports and study them, isn't that right?"

Heller said there were many ways to deal with inconsistencies.

"He's trying to make the jurors think he is Simon Pure in there," Virga grumbled to the judge. Nonetheless, he told MacBride he was on the verge of resting his case. Only one question remained: Would Lyn testify?

Like all criminal defendants, Lyn could not be forced to testify. Taking the stand would give her the chance to reveal her state of mind, in her own words, to the entire world. If she chose to testify, however, she would be subject to cross-examination by the government. For this reason, in most cases, defense attorneys advise their clients not to testify. "She's got me between a rock and a hard place," Virga later told reporters. Lyn's testimony could well be helpful but, "obviously, there are areas she can get hurt in. And hurt bad."

The choice was Lyn's. If she did decide to take the stand, Virga had prepared several other witnesses to mitigate whatever damage the prosecution might cause in its cross-examination. If not, Virga said, he would rest his case then and there.

Virga had been discussing this question with his client for some time. Lyn had been vacillating; when last asked, however, she had said she did not wish to testify. For the record, Judge MacBride decided to query her in open court, outside the jury's presence.

"Your Honor, I can't answer that question right now," Lyn said, standing before the robed judge in a shapeless aquamarine pantsuit.

"Well, when will you be able to answer that question? This is an ongoing trial. We have a jury that's here and we're ready to try you now."

"I will answer—" Lyn began.

The judge continued over her: "I believe we've been at this now since November the 4th."

"I will answer it on Monday," Lyn announced. The judge agreed.

MacBride then had the jury brought in. "Now, ladies and gentlemen of the jury, there's been an unexpected development in this case. There is a possibility that we may conclude this case sooner than we expected. On the other hand, it may go longer than we expected. Right now, we're at the point, shall we say, of complete uncertainty."

Over the weekend, Lyn discussed the case with Virga, and ruminated about what role she should take as the trial wound down. She had intended to prepare a script for Virga to read as his argument, but Virga refused. So she decided to stand on principle. Not only would she decline to testify, or even attend, her trial; she wanted the judge to know that she disapproved of Virga's plans to downplay the violent communiqués she and Sandy had issued over the previous year.

On Monday, November 24, Lyn again was brought before the court. She made it clear how unhappy she was with the argument Virga planned to offer.

The judge assured her that as an officer of the court, "I'm expecting him to argue your defense in the manner that he deems most appropriate—"

"To lie?" Lyn asked.

"I don't expect him to lie," said the judge. "I expect him to present a defense which will be most effective insofar as you're concerned, that is, in his opinion. I don't think we can go any further than that."

Lyn dropped the point and moved on. "In regard to testimony," she said, "all I'm saying is, Don't make us shoot. Don't make us be violent."

The judge was stern now. He lectured her, but carefully: "The administration of justice requires an orderly proceeding. We cannot have this court go up and down on a yo-yo at the whim and caprice of either the defendant or the prosecution or even the court, for that matter. . . . I have extended to you every possible courtesy that I know of that has ever been extended to any person in this court in the fourteen years that I have been on the bench."

"Your Honor, I believe you have," said Lyn.

"Thank you," MacBride said.

"Here's what I want to know," Lyn continued. "I thought the whole object was to come in here and present the truth."

MacBride ignored the question. Instead, he asked her again if she would attend the trial, or testify for her defense.

To the first question, she answered, "It's not my trial." To the second, "If it's not my trial, how could I take the stand in my own behalf?" And she left the courtroom.

John Virga, speaking "for the record," told MacBride that he had, in the end, asked Lyn to testify, and that she refused. "If she wanted to testify she can indicate whatever it is she wants to indicate, but then I cannot be in the position where I can stand up here and represent to the jury what she has to say without her saying it. . . . I told her that . . . the case could only be argued in a manner that would correspond with the evidence and that that was her choice."

The judge acknowledged Virga's plight. "I think we have dealt with the subject sufficiently," he said. The defense formally rested its case, and the government declined to put on a rebuttal.

Chapter 13

The Verdict

"It is now time to hear the arguments," Judge MacBride told the jurors. "The government has the laboring oar in this case and, therefore, they will make the opening statement."

Dwayne Keyes stood. He opened his argument dramatically, dimming the lights and showing the television footage of the pistol incident. "You will be instructed," he said, speaking in his quiet monotone, "that you may consider the defendant's intent from all the surrounding circumstances of this case. Statements made and acts done by the defendant. It is ordinarily reasonable to infer that a person intends the natural and probable consequences of acts knowingly done. You will further be instructed that a semiautomatic pistol is a loaded pistol within the meaning of the law if the magazine contains a loaded cartridge or bullet which may be instantly transferred into the firing chamber by pulling the slide back and allowing it to move forward.

"Now, let's look at some of the circumstances of this case. What do we know about this defendant, about her actions and about her thoughts about the President of the United States prior to the morning of September the 5th?"

He mentioned a few of Lyn's actions: she had gone to get a gun from Manny Boro and she had delivered the "Manson Is Mad at Nixson," the "Ford face" statement to reporters. "So we know," Keyes said, "that in early July this defendant was thinking about President Ford." She had told Lanier Ramer that " 'some people are going to have to be killed' " if the earth wasn't cleaned up, and she had written to TV news editor Rossie that " 'if Nixon's reality wearing a Ford face continues to run this country against the law ... your homes will be bloodier than the Tate-LaBianca houses and My Lai put together. ... Manson can explain it. If not allowed to explain, there will be many more young murderers, beginning with the person typing this letter.'

"A grisly prophecy," Keyes said. "Who even fantasizing would write those words on a piece of paper? Perhaps someone who advocated death as a means to the end."

The judge interrupted: "Can everyone hear all right?" He looked at Keyes. "You speak rather softly."

Keyes tried to be louder. "Can the jury hear me?" They nodded, and the prosecutor resumed.

He turned to the night of September 4, when Lyn was discussing ecology and things in general with Morris Willmarth. "The defendant asked him at that time if she could borrow his .38 caliber revolver, the one that only had a three-inch barrel. She said she wanted it for protection. Do you believe that?

"And so we come to the midmorning of September the 5th, and we know these things about the defendant. When the defendant left her apartment that morning, she was wearing a long red robe. Concealed under that robe and strapped to her left leg was a holster. And you have seen that—the holster strapped to her leg. Not everyday wearing apparel. She was armed with a .45 automatic, and that .45 automatic had a magazine in it and that magazine had four live rounds in it.

"You heard Mr. Boro testify that he never put any bullets in that clip the whole time he owned the weapon. Who put the bullets in the clip? Who put the clip in the weapon? Who took the weapon to Capitol Park? We know the defendant said she hated Ford.

"I submit to you that reason and logic would indicate that one of those four bullets was meant for the President of the United States. We know she found the President that morning," Keyes said. Several Secret Service agents and bystanders had heard a "metallic *click*." Keyes displayed Lyn's pistol, now known as Exhibit 9-B, and pulled the trigger. *Click!*

"That indicates something was going on with that weapon at that moment," he said.

"What about her statements? Has anyone testified that they heard the defendant say: 'It was a joke?' Did anyone hear her say: 'I didn't intend to kill the President?' " Keyes then listed the various witnesses who had characterized Lyn's tone of voice upon her arrest as "exasperated," "surprised," "angry," "disappointed," "disbelief," or "irritation."

"Are all of these people wrong?" Keyes asked. "Did they not perceive anything that morning? I think, ladies and gentlemen, that the evidence is substantial of why the defendant was there, what her purpose was. Reason and logic lend themselves to that conclusion. Who straps the holster on their leg? Who takes a .45 with four live rounds in the magazine, and the magazine in the weapon, for any other reason than to kill? What's the purpose of that weapon? It isn't a weapon for sport hunting. It's a weapon for killing and not killing animals but killing people.

"The United States asks, ladies and gentlemen, you return a verdict of guilty as charged. Thank you." And Dwayne Keyes sat down.

After a ten-minute recess, John Virga rose to present his argument for the acquittal of Lynette Fromme. To convict, he said, the jurors must reach "an abiding conviction" of her guilt.

"What is an abiding conviction?" Virga asked. "It's a lasting conviction, not just today or tomorrow, or the next day, but next year, five years from now, ten years from now, someone comes up to you and says, Mr. Pruitt, Mrs. Kubillus, Mr. Conboy, Mrs. Abril, any one of you, 'Was Lynette Fromme guilty of the charge that you found her guilty of?' You should unhesitatingly say, 'Yes.' It's a lasting conviction. A conviction in your mind that must last with you as long as it lasts with her, not one that you just forget about when you walk out of here."

Virga then turned to his single objective: Persuading the jurors not to acquit Lyn of attempted murder, but to convict her of the lesser included offense of assault on the president. Now it was the defense, not the government, that looked to an assault conviction as the last, best hope to salvage victory from the Fromme trial. "Any conduct which manifests a wilful attempt or inflicts injury upon the person or presents an apparent ability to do so constitutes an assault. An assault can be committed without actually touching or striking or doing bodily harm. . . . So if you have the apparent ability and you point a gun at someone, you're guilty of . . . assault. And really, in this particular case, the final decision that you're going to have to make is: Did she act with the intent to kill the President or did she assault him. Both are serious felonies. I am telling you now . . . that you should return a verdict of guilty of assaulting the President. Because that's what she did. But she did not act with the intent to kill the President."

That predicate established, Virga turned to his most challenging task: To bring the twelve middle-aged Middle Americans of the jury into the mind of Lynette Fromme.

"Mr. Keyes spoke with you about some of the letters that Lynette Fromme had written. And I want to read the Rossie letter to you because I think [it] really sums up what she has to say. And it is evidence and it was offered by the prosecution, so this letter is just as if she were here testifying. . . .

"You know that Lynette Fromme is an admitted member of the Manson Family. . . . You know that she believes in Charles Manson. The reason she is not present in court is because she wants Manson here to relate his thoughts and his feelings to you. He is not permitted to be here," Virga said, beginning to echo his client.

But just "because someone believes in another person that you don't approve of, it does not mean that the person who believes this . . . is a bad person. . . . Many people believed in Hitler and they were not all bad people. Many of the greatest generals in the world fought with him. Rommel, the Desert Fox. They made a movie about him, but he was not a bad person. She says in here: *I am certain that you could find in history men with as strange and mystical, individual and yet all-encompassing qualities as Manson, if one could only think to compare.*

"Now, you might not agree with what she has to say but at least think to compare. We can think of Christ, we can think of Einstein, we can think of Freud, we can think of many artists, many writers, many men in [the] history of our country. *A braver (real) man would take a good long look at a phenomenon to see not what others think or fear about it, but WHAT IS.*"

Virga, sounding more like a preacher conducting a biblical exegesis than a lawyer arguing his client's innocence, paused over each line as if it were fraught with meaning.

"Isn't that the truth?" he asked. "When you look at something, you have to consider what is, not what others think or feel about it, but what is. What is true? Sometimes we want to close our eyes to that. Well, that's what you have to do in this trial. You cannot be motivated by passion, prejudice, public opinion, public feeling. . . . The letter goes on to say: *This is difficult for the schooled mind to see, and you are to be respected for trying, not by me or anyone, but yourself.*

"And you know, sometimes it is difficult for a schooled mind to think. I think we could all appreciate . . . [that] sometimes people who just have booklearning really don't know what life is all about. And there is an old saying, 'If you haven't walked a mile in my moccasins, you don't really understand me.' And you know, when I finished law school there was a pamphlet they put out. It was called, 'How to Find the Courthouse.' It's a sad commentary but that's the way it was. I had all the booklearning that I need and really no practical experience. I did not have that understanding that I talked about before. . . . How many people have you met in your lifetime that you could say, with all of the training that that particular person has, he or she cannot see the forest through the trees?"

Virga returned to the Rossie letter: *"Through the images set out for us by the leaders with enough financial backing to take a step forward/whip-lashing suddenly at that certain point in time when fashion swung to the revolution—the American mind is left blocked by dozens of already tried solutions, to the OVER-ALL problems, that have fizzled. Nevertheless, the thoughts are still moving."*

Then he focused on the politicians that Lyn, and most Americans, viewed with such low regard. "What images have they set out—honesty, to cut spending, stop wars, 'I'm going to this,' 'I'm going to do that'? And the reality is that when they are elected, how many of them really stick by their promises? Don't we just change the face? And I know that happens all too often. And what happens when that occurs? The young people lose faith because—not only the young people, but all people should believe in the dignity of man. When we are told certain things and we are led to believe certain things and those things don't materialize, you are very likely to have a revolution on your hands.

"Look what happened in the 1960s," Virga went on. "The civil rights movements, People's Park in [Berkeley]. The problem at the Induction Center, the Berrigan brothers. Two Jesuits with the priest pouring blood on the draft records. There was a time of great revolution in this country because people were stuck in an old thought.

"You know ... this country will be celebrating its 200th birthday in 1976. The reason the Revolution came about is because people wanted a new thought. . . . People wanted equality, freedom of speech, freedom of religion, a jury trial, the right to be tried by your peers and to be judged by them, not a star chamber proceeding, a fair and open hearing. Then there was a burden of proof into that, beyond all reasonable doubt and to a moral certainty . . .

"Think further about the 'images that are set out' and the 'problems that have fizzled' as she set forth in this letter to Mr. Rossie. In 1954, there was a landmark decision, *Brown* vs. *Board of Education*. It was a Supreme Court decision. Up until that time in our educational system, the supreme law of this land was that if educational opportunities were equal, separate but equal, then everything was all right. Black children in the South went to all-black schools. They couldn't eat in restaurants, they had to use different bathrooms, yet they could go and fight wars and lose their lives to protect those liberties. And the question is, Why? Who is the real enemy? Who is suppressed? Who keeps you down? Without equality and justice, we have nothing.

"She says: Even though the problems have 'fizzled,' nevertheless, 'the thoughts are still moving.' And that's right. Even though the problems have fizzled, the thoughts have to keep moving. The thoughts are going to move one way or another, hopefully forward and not backwards. But if they remain in a status quo, they deteriorate.

"She says: *It was not people that the Manson Family was at war with, but a thought. The same thought that sells our children and our more innocent world sex, political ideology, death, theology and toothpaste in one hour.* Think about that. Isn't that a fact? Your children watch television and, on the commercials, that's what they get. Look at the violence that's portrayed on television, a very antiseptic violence. You know that your children go out and you know that their minds are many times the reflection of the television set and your apathy towards them. People do things because they need to do things. Nothing happens in a vacuum. What about selling our children these things? How do you people feel about that? Is this language that you don't understand? . . .

"You know, since I've become involved in this case and evaluated all the materials and this letter in particular, I have asked myself: 'What have you done?' And I probably came up with the same answer that most of you have: I haven't really done too much, if anything. So, I'm not telling you that I am some superhuman being. We all have the same frailties. Our appetites and instincts have a very keen way of prevailing over our logic and reasoning sometimes. But what about our children? What about 'our more innocent world' and the things that we put out to them? What about the way they sell theology? Think about that. What is Christmas? Is it Santa Claus? Is it all the presents? How many children really understand what Christmas is, because of the money and the big business involved with it? How many children understand what Easter is? Is it the Easter Bunny? How did these things come about? Because of the monetary gain involved; that's how they came about. You can sell things at this point in time—I'm not saying that I don't enjoy the Christmas season and the exchanging of gifts—"

Judge MacBride finally lost his patience. "Mr. Virga, I've allowed you quite a bit of latitude on this and, by all means, you're entitled to go into her letter, but I really feel you're going on a little bit afield here. As I will later instruct the jury, motive and intent are not to become confused—and motive is not a defense to a crime of this kind. . . . We haven't even come to Thanksgiving yet, and you're at Christmas!"

Virga protested: "I think that Mr. Keyes has attempted to, so to speak, give a history of Lynette Fromme to put her in a proper perspective and that's all I'm trying to do. . . . It's like going to the doctor. He needs a history first, before he can really analyze and diagnose what's wrong with you."

"But you're giving the history of the world," MacBride countered. "You're not just giving the history of Lynette Fromme. I'm sorry, Mr. Virga, I'm going to have to cut you down."

Virga resumed his deconstruction of the Rossie letter. "She says: *We will not, for the sake of drama, and an old school of thought where the misery needs company and the subtleties of emotions and treasures of a writer's hard work, accept Tennessee Williams for lifestyle.*

"Well, what is Tennessee Williams? What's she referring to there? Tennessee Williams is really, I guess you could say, 'nothing is worth living for.' Maybe another way to put it is, his writings reflect a theater of despair." Virga paused, as if the jurors might not know who Tennessee Williams was. "Some of his writings are *The Glass Menagerie, Cat on a Hot Tin Roof, A Streetcar Named Desire.* He's a playwright," Virga added.

"*To perpetuate what is dead is killing the rest. To perpetuate the whole thought is killing the new one. There is—around the corner of evolution—a new experience, awareness, and perception beyond anything we have yet experienced—and this itself is so feared that it has been locked up. The death of an old thought is the completion of a long line of grandmother's ways, and hard for most to let go of.*

"That's true. You know that's a fact. The old thoughts are hard to let go of.

"*The media* CAN *be used to unwind the tangles of a world running in circles toward what it fears most.* Death or truth, or both. And isn't that a correct statement? The media can be used to unwind those tangles if it's used properly. She says: *Manson can explain the self-destructive thought. He can explain the Christ thought.* I think the most basic concept of the Christ thought is, Love thy neighbor, do unto others as you would have them do unto you, and by not doing that, you have all been through the self-destructive thoughts because you care for no one but yourself. *Without personal meanness, I say to you that* YOU ARE RESPONSIBLE FOR OUR CHILDREN AND THE MIND OF THE WORLD *into which you pass* THOUGHTS. *The leaders who have held the people down in order to control them have fallen off the top and as the people are waking to the lie, in anger, they will tear the world apart with no new purpose to live.*

"That ties in with what I said before, people don't want to be lied to and told certain things that they have certain rights and not have those rights be manifested.

"*With the media, each home can learn a garden* [sic], *and woman can be shown not as a whore or a neuter computer, but as a mother who* WANTS TO *live and is doing everything under the sun to* INSURE *the survival of her world.* What about the 'neuter computer?' Is that an unemotional thing? It doesn't have any emotion. What do you remember of your children's needs? Don't they need emotional nutrition? Is our society's lack of emotion creating emotional cripples? . . . *You must understand the Christ thought first. I cannot explain it, but it would fascinate you! Love in truth is worship—and begins with worship of the earth we walk on, the air we breathe, the water we drink and so on.*

"There's not one of you that disagrees with that. *The country has the resources and the young and old energy alike to clean it up and provide new purpose for living, new thoughts that send a mind spiraling upward and outward, not into the drug stores, booze bottles, and morgues.* I am certain you all agree with that. *But will the Tate-LaBianca murders need to be repeated to tell the truth of the thoughts we have been raised into? Or will the people finally see that they are being killed by big money and the thoughts that perpetuate it and pay attention to the new young government of the world? Will there be blood in the faces of our working people, or will 20 million mother bears arise to protect their cubs?*

"What were the thoughts that we were raised into that caused the Tate-LaBianca murders? Do we close our eyes to that and not want to know? . . . What happened to these people involved in the Tate-LaBianca situation, [these] middle-class American children? Do you want to know?

"*Woman will need to sit down with her men and understand them as parts of herself. To compete with each other is to create conflict in the kids and leave the real problems of no place to play, no trees, bad air, water and cancer-causing foods—on the sidewalks with the twelve- and thirteen-year-olds who learned in their dope-prevention classes how not to shoot dope and are laughing about it with needles in their arms. We have to take care of our own children.*" Virga's interpretation: "The family unit has to be restored."

He recited Ogden Nash's poem called "The Song of the Open Road," which states that the poet will "never see / A billboard lovely as a tree."

"How many of our kids went to the nut houses across the country just because they saw the concrete billboard cancer reality killing the world and they could not cope. Would you or I give our lives to stop the world from burning? What happens when it's burned? Think about it.

"Charles Manson, Bruce Davis, Steve Grogan, Robert Beausoleil, Charles Watson, Patricia Krenwinkle, [sic] Leslie Van Houten and Susan Atkins did. Put Nixon and the Pope in a courtroom with Manson and Family and we will see what has been running our ignorances, what truth has been in closets, and who are the real servants of the people and earth.

"What has she been talking about in this case? 'He's not a public servant.'

"The truth is as bad as it is good. Manson can explain it. If not allowed to explain, there will be many more young murderers, beginning with the person typing this letter. You do not realize all the thoughts that are moving within the minds of not only this country, but the world. Manson has been thinking through the world for five years in that closet. He has been under the sun three times in the last four years. For those of us outside to imagine this would be hard. What man could lay in a cell with nothing to do and all the negative thoughts of the world on his back, with every reach of competition trying with sharp nails to pick his brain, and down him, so that they, him, her, Ms., it can be him—what man of clear awareness and perception of thoughts beyond most men's minds, past or present, could know what people are really thinking, accept them without judgment, yet reflect their own judgments of themselves in truth for their own balance and sight, often to his own detriment?

"I will just summarize that. It takes a man of courage to tell people what they don't want to hear and be able to reflect themselves back on them again, because when you do that it's to your own detriment. People don't like you then.

"She says: *It is an exceptional man who tells the truth that others do not want to hear. Those of us not exceptional, caught up in foolish formalities signifying nothing, may learn to face ourselves through him—but only while he lives. If he dies, the truth along with him dies. There are many children with knives who love the earth and put their very lives on his name, pledging not to allow this.*

"Making reference to his ideas. What he's been through and what he now knows. *The always nice face will not give you the meanness that may raise your strength and help you to survive. The gift of the mean, hard truth can save lives if we but accept it as a part of the thoughts that are moving. If not, it is bloody bedrooms and screams in the night, unanswered.* What does this mean? That means we don't understand the truth, are these things going to happen again? Will there be other children and this will come up and possibly these things will happen?"

Virga, who had been following the text of the Rossie letter closely, skipped the next passage. In it, Lyn had called for someone to "get" multimillionaire Robert Abplanalp, the secretive intimate of Richard Nixon who also happened to be the inventor of the first mass-production aerosol spray valve. Virga resumed:

"If Nixon can steal the country and sell it out the back door while the CIA tracks blood all over the world and the Pope shakes hands on the deal—what is Joe Gonzales doing in jail for stealing bread? Why is George Brown going to prison for dope? Why did Sylvia kill her mother? Why did Pat Krenwinkle, Leslie Van Houten, Susan Atkins, Charles Watson, Robert Beausoleil, Stephen Grogan, and Bruce Davis kill nine people? Why did Charles Manson get life in prison for telling the truth? Manson can explain it. In a courtroom with Nixon, and the Pope—the world would know why.

"Why did Joe Gonzales go to prison for stealing bread and other people go to prison for doing things while Nixon walks free? Is it selective justice in this country?

"All right, the other letters are basically the same thing, so I'm not going to read those to you. . . . The last letter says that in a new courtroom Manson can explain the thought that all of you have overlooked and stop this killing—not precipitate it but *stop* it. That's the concluding remark in each and every one of these letters. So you cannot just isolate out certain factors. You have to consider the whole thing. . . .

"Lynette Fromme had a cause. She wanted people to know about these things in her letter. You might not agree with [everything] that is there but there is an awful lot of it, if you are being honest with yourselves, that you do have to agree with. She has been successful in capturing the media throughout the nation by going to the park that day, but did she go there with the intent to kill the President? I submit to you that the answer to that is No. . . .

"Certainly, there is a certain amount of what I would call fear tactics in her writings. But that's nothing new to mankind. Just look at religion itself. There's a lot of fear in there that motivates people to do things—the fear of going to Hell. You tell your children you'll spank them if they do something and that's a form of fear. Fear can be a very motivating thing. . . .

"She wanted a forum. She wanted people to listen to her. She felt that these problems were urgent and that someone should look at them, that we should look at them. Maybe, to sum up her message, it is: Wake up, America. I remember seeing a special about three or four years ago about Lake Erie . . . with all the manufacturing, the residue from manufacturing, the pollution that went into the waters. . . . It described it as a cesspool.

"Now, we do have to wake up and I ask you this: If she had killed President Ford, who possibly was going to listen to her? She knew that no one would listen. Why? Because if there was anything she learned from what the other members of the Manson Family did, it is that when you actually murder, people will not listen." On the other hand, Virga asserted that it would be equally useless for Lyn to approach the president with an unloaded weapon. "If she went into that park with an empty gun with no bullets in the clip at all, the only forum she would have had would be a psychiatrist. She had two psychiatrists come down to the jail as it was. That wasn't the forum she wanted."

Now, Virga insisted, "the last thing I'm trying to tell you is she had any mental distress or defect." He cited the report of Dr. Charles Fisher, who examined Lyn upon her arrest. " 'Her thoughts were well organized. . . . I saw no instances of nor did she give any indications of having any delusions or bizarre ideations or paranoid feelings.' He eliminates all that and that's what I'm trying to tell you. When she went out there, she went out there for a purpose. She wasn't under the influence of anything, she wasn't under the influence of any drug or narcotic so that she would not know fully and completely what she was doing. She had a cause that she wanted you to listen to." Lyn, he reminded the jury, had started her day by taking a decongestant capsule. "She remembers and tells the doctor about a Contac she took and yet you are to believe that she forgot to put a shell in the chamber of that weapon, or that somehow it didn't get in there." On the contrary, Virga said, "she never intended to put one in there.

"Let's go to the evidence in the park. . . . Now, if Lynette Fromme went out to the park to kill the President, then she [alone] knew she was going to do it. . . . If I know what I'm going to do and you don't know what I'm going to do, then there's the element of surprise involved and I can act very rapidly. . . . It's going to be extremely difficult for you to stop me if I'm really bent on killing the President.

"There has been talk about this .38 that she'd asked for from Mr. Willmarth. . . . I think what the prosecution was trying to tell you is, the reason she wanted a revolver is that she didn't know how to use an automatic. . . . Now, you know that she has had experience with an automatic weapon and there's a picture of it: there she is with a weapon in her hand. . . .

"All right, she's in the park. She's in a crowd. Everyone is looking at the President. No one is really paying that much attention to her. She can have that weapon in any position she wants it to be in. She has this long robe on and she pulls [the pistol] up and brings it out and lets it fire. . . . That's not what happened. Do you know what the President said about the look on her face? He said, 'It's like someone who wanted to shake my hand, someone who wanted to talk to me.' Obviously she had a look of concern and he . . . hesitated. That's the word he used. He didn't see a look of violence in her face or a look of anger in her eyes.

"Agent Buendorf was walking along and he was moving his hands, right? She knows there are a lot of Secret Service agents around the President. Everyone knows that. . . . She could have jumped out in front of the President and just shot. That is not what she did. She brings the weapon up and there's Buendorf coming along with his hands.

"I submit to you that she moved that weapon at a point in time when she knew the Secret Service agent was there, when she knows the weapon is going to be taken away from her and she doesn't want to have anyone get hurt. If she had jumped out in front of the President and shot him, then she would know that he would be shot and then there would be no message."

Virga contrasted the situation to the Kennedy assassination in Dallas, 1963. "It's not like you're up on a building and you snipe someone and then they have to find out which building that person is [in] and so forth. She's right there. She knows she's going to be apprehended. There's no question about that. And she was apprehended because she pointed that weapon at the President. By doing that, she committed a crime of assaulting the President.

"I believe in Lynette Fromme's mind that weapon was a symbol of what can happen when that gun is pointed. It can go off. It can, if we don't listen. We will be destroying ourselves. Really, the weapon is pointed at all of us because we are destroying our earth and when we do we will destroy ourselves."

Virga observed that there was no evidence that Lyn's hand, or her trigger finger, was injured or bruised. "The President says he never saw her finger on the trigger. Buendorf says he doesn't recall seeing her finger on the trigger. None of them even said she had a grip on the gun that would lead you circumstantially to believe she had her finger on the trigger."

Because of this, Virga asserted, the government had to fish around for other evidence of Lyn's intent, and settled on using witness interpretations of her tone of voice. But, the defense counsel said, "Buendorf didn't have anything in his original report about any tone of voice ... and neither did Kluber or McCarter." Virga said the government had "obviously" assumed that Lyn would use an insanity defense, and thus her intent would not be at issue. When prosecutors realized that Lyn would present a straight not guilty plea, "they had to go back and reconstruct. Now, how do [her] words gain meaning? If the things are that significant at the time, why aren't they included? Because, without some significance to those words, some reflection on that tone of voice, then it's an assault, plain and simple."

Most witnesses could not see Lyn's face when she uttered the incriminating words, Virga said. He told the jurors to "experiment" when they began their deliberations. "Have someone stand behind a door so you can't see them, so you can't see their face and have them say the words." Without telling the listeners, the speaker would try to express "surprise," "frustration," "disappointment," and "disbelief" by tone of voice. Could the listeners then accurately identify the speaker's intent? "There's not one of you that's going to get it right, not one of you. There will be as many different answers as there are jurors, because tone of voice is such a nebulous thing."

MacBride finally interrupted. "We'll take our noon recess at this time."

Before lunch, Virga had argued that the government contorted the evidence to attach criminal significance to Lyn's remarks upon her arrest. When court reconvened, he let the other shoe drop: while exaggerating incriminating evidence, prosecutors—or, more specifically, Assistant U.S. Attorney Heller—had suppressed evidence showing Lyn's innocence. And that was the Jim Damir statement taken by Officer Paul Boettin.

" 'It's not loaded anyway,' " Virga said, "obviously would indicate that she knew that the weapon wasn't loaded and what she meant by that is that there was not a bullet in the chamber." Technically, the gun may have been loaded, "but in her mind, with an automatic, it can't fire until you put one in the chamber."

Dwayne Keyes objected. "We have no evidence of that," he said.

Overruled. "He's merely arguing what he believes was in her mind," the judge said. "That's what it's all about."

Virga resumed. He acknowledged that Damir had changed his story, but "considering the totality of the circumstances that led to his final statement, are you convinced that he didn't hear this out there? Are you really? Are you convinced beyond all reasonable doubt and to a moral certainty that he did not hear that out there?"

And if Don Heller thought the Boettin report was so obviously insupportable, why did he work so hard to prevent anyone else from seeing it? "Why not show the grand jury?" More telling, "Why didn't Mr. Heller show Mr. Keyes that report? Give me one reason why. One valid reason why. Mr. Keyes is the United States Attorney for this district"—and he didn't see the Boettin report until November 2. The implication: The pugnacious Heller, whose volatility was so evident the courtroom, had feared that the more seasoned, measured Keyes might have thrown the case out.

Virga then pulled back. "You know we have talked about the environment, ecology, this and that and other things. I want to read you one passage:

" 'Violence against our environment is another form of destruction that implicates our very survival, and it may well be a manifestation of deep subconscious forces. Our real alma mater is the earth, without whom we are lost. Yet man's most devastating drives are acts of aggression against her.' "

The writer of that passage, Virga said, went on to deal "with environmental issues, water, radiation, pesticides . . . the problems of the children, the restriction of the family. You know who wrote this?" The answer was not Lynette Fromme; it was Justice William O. Douglas, in his book, *The Three Hundred Year War: A Chronicle of Ecological Disaster* (1972). "No man has served longer on the court than this man," Virga said, without mentioning that one of Douglas's final acts was denying Lyn's bail petition.

"So these are very, very real problems. I think this"—apparently, the Capitol Park incident—"is just Lynette Fromme coming off the wall with something she wants people to pay attention to. Have your eyes not been opened about these things? In all of the letters it says: 'The killing must stop.' It doesn't say, 'go on.' " Virga looked at the jurors, simple working-class folk, churchgoers and retirees and people who didn't read newspapers.

"I am certain that many of you are aware of the story I'm about to tell you," he said. "I'm going to conclude with this. You remember the story of the Apostles being out on the water and Christ appeared and he said, 'Peter, come to me.' And Peter starts to walk on the water and he looked down and he started to sink because he lost his faith. You"—the jurors, holders of a sacred duty— "cannot look down because you have to have faith in your judicial system. This is what the new thought that we fought so hard for twenty years ago [was]," he said, possibly meaning to say "two hundred" years ago, even as he used the Mansonian term, "new thought."

"You have to have that faith and you have to evaluate the evidence by the rules of law and the facts. And if you don't know what to believe, then you are in a position of reasonable doubt."

Virga wrapped up: "You have been a very attentive jury and I thank you."

Lyn, listening in her cell, had been attentive, too. She was pleased. "Mr. Virga," she said later, "did not lie in his final arguments, as I had hoped that he wouldn't."

Dwayne Keyes got the last word, with the government rebuttal. "Mr. Virga read to you from Justice Douglas's book on the environment. I don't think anyone would ever suggest to you that Justice Douglas or anybody else would ever have written the Rossie letter. . . .

"Do you think the defendant went to the park with a loaded .45 just to point it at the President? You have to forget about all the evidence, everything you know about the defendant prior to the time she walked into that park. You have to forget all the correspondence, the statements she made, her conversation with Ed Louie the day before, that she hated the President."

Keyes ridiculed the assertion that Lyn had no choice but to point a gun at Gerald Ford. "There are many ways to get attention when you're in proximity to the President of the United States. You can slap at him. You can yell an obscenity. You can use an imitation weapon and that will get you arrested and that will get you a trial. That will get you a forum." Indeed, although Keyes did not mention it, such an event had occurred only three days before, in Miami. During a campaign stop, a twenty-year-old man named Michael Carvin had pointed a toy pistol at presidential candidate Ronald Reagan. Carvin's weapon was a replica of the .45 automatic.

"But use your reason and logic," Keyes continued. "Why do you strap and conceal a holster on your leg and put a loaded .45 in that holster and walk into the park? Consider the workings of the .45 automatic and [those of] the .22 automatic, which is the only weapon that we know that she ever fired, and there is one single significant difference. There is a hammer on this weapon. . . . What would happen if, in the excitement of the moment—and don't think that wasn't a moment for her, she was going to get her attention—she forgot the slide? Is that unusual? Have hunters ever forgotten to do one act and point the weapon and pull the trigger and realize they'd forgotten to do something and it didn't go off in the excitement of the moment? . . .

"We all have to live with what we are, we are what we are because of our time living here and this applies to the defendant, Lynette Fromme. She had been caught up in a cause and it wasn't going anywhere. Charles Manson wasn't getting out of prison and nobody was listening to her. Nobody was going to print her information, they wanted hard news. Was she willing to go to that park with a loaded .45 and kill the President of the United States? Her own words were, 'Would you or I give our lives to stop the world from burning? Think about it.' Her friends did, Manson, Davis, Grogan, et cetera. 'The truth is as bad as it is good. Manson can explain it. If not allowed to explain, there will be many more young murderers, beginning with the person typing this letter.'

"Ladies and gentlemen of the jury, I think you're entitled to take her at her word," said Keyes. "I ask that you return a verdict of guilty as charged."

The Deliberation

Judge MacBride instructed the jurors on their task. "The law forbids you to be governed by suspicion, speculation or conjecture; by sentiment, pity or sympathy for a defendant or by passion, prejudice, public opinion or public feeling against her," he told them, before launching into boilerplate instructions regarding the credibility of witnesses, the burden of proof, the distinction between direct and circumstantial evidence, the meaning of "reasonable doubt," and other judicial touchstones the jury was to employ during its deliberations. MacBride noticed some of the jurors starting to nod off.

"I think we will all stand," he said. "I want to be sure you are all awake and alert to what I am saying."

The jurors rose. "All right, thank you very much. Let's be seated."

He continued: "To constitute the crime charged in the indictment there must be the joint operation of two essential elements, an act forbidden by law and the intent to do the act. . . ." Judge MacBride went on to distinguish between the attempted assassination charge and that of assault on the president, which he had determined was, by necessity, a lesser included offense.

MacBride then turned to the calendar: it was Monday, November 24, three days from Thanksgiving. The judge had assured the jury that, if they didn't reach a verdict by then, the marshals would provide a turkey dinner. It would be up to the jurors whether they wanted to deliberate on the holiday.

Lyn's jury had been enjoying a simple if monotonous and heavily regulated life since their sequestration. To house the group, Marshal Van Court had rented a second-floor wing at the Ponderosa Motor Inn in downtown Sacramento, a few blocks from the courthouse. The jurors each had a room on a corridor separated by closed doors from the rest of the motel, and a private entrance and dining hall. The deputies had removed the television sets and telephones before the jurors arrived; they were only allowed to see broadcasts or talk to their families under supervision.

Marshals accompanied jurors everywhere and took care of all their needs. In the morning, they brought doughnuts. Lunch and dinner came from McDonald's, Kentucky Fried Chicken, and Bob's Big Boy. For variety, jurors got Mexican and Chinese food, or were escorted for heartier fare to Sam's Stage Inn or the Marina Inn Wheel House. When they traveled, whether to the courthouse or for a dinner in town, the jurors boarded the Marshals Service school bus, an old International model affectionately dubbed "the Blue Goose." Just as with the Tate-LaBianca jury, deputies covered the windows so that jurors wouldn't inadvertently see a newspaper headline as they drove through town.

Van Court took pains to keep the jurors entertained. A 16-mm projector was borrowed from the Air Force base, along with some of the films that were airmen's favorites: a documentary about Jesse Owens in Berlin, another about the C-5 Galaxy aircraft, a morale builder called *Old Glory*, and all three reels of Bob Hope's 1967 variety show for the Armed Forces. One weekend, jurors had a special treat: Deputies loaded them into two station wagons for a drive to Pollock Pines, a camping area some eighty miles east in the Eldorado National Forest.

There had, of course, been problems. The bomb threat had rattled everyone's nerves and the burdens of sequestration were taking a toll on the jurors' personal lives. One juror's husband repeatedly bawled her out over the telephone for abandoning him, forcing him to cook his own meals, and clean house himself. When he threatened her with violence, sending the juror into tears, Deputy Marshal Warren Steeves intervened. "You can't be threatening your wife over the phone," he told the husband. "We have to keep these jurors happy." After the trial, Steeves said, the juror got a divorce.

But these facts of sequestered life were now almost behind them. At last, the jury's work truly began. At 4:50 P.M. on November 24, after receiving Judge MacBride's instructions, they retired to the jury room to begin their deliberations. Told to elect a "foreman or a forelady," they chose Helen LeRoy. An elderly hotel clerk, LeRoy had said during voir dire that she didn't see any news of the events of September 5. "The day it happened, my television set went out of order," she explained.

At 7:35, the jury returned to the courtroom asking to have crucial testimony read back: That of Capitol Park witnesses Sue Folsom and Jim Damir. Both had heard Lyn say things upon her arrest that suggested she knew her gun was unarmed, thus raising questions about her intent to kill: Damir's famous and flawed "It's not loaded anyway" report, and Folsom's uncertainty over whether Lyn said, "it wouldn't go off" or "it *couldn't* go off."

It took one hour and eighteen minutes to read the testimony back, after which the jurors resumed their work. At 10:00 P.M., MacBride asked his clerk to see if the jury wanted to continue deliberations.

"They said they're pretty well pooped out," the clerk reported. MacBride told the jurors to call it quits till the following morning.

By the next day, it was clear that the jury could not quite understand how they were to approach the "lesser included offense" concept. MacBride had instructed jurors that they could only consider the assault charge if they first acquitted Lyn of attempted assassination. If they deadlocked on the primary charge, then they were not to consider the lesser offense.

The questions coming from the jury room, however, indicated that jurors could not reach consensus on Lyn's intent to kill—and that they thus wanted to know what they had to do to get to the assault charge. MacBride, after conferring with the attorneys, concluded that the law on this point was ambiguous. He revised his instructions: If jurors hung up on the principal charge, they could then move on to assault.

Courtroom observers predicted an assault conviction—and a hung jury on attempted assassination—coming down. Reporters readied stories describing the complicated verdict they expected, with instructions for editors to hold for color from the courtroom when the decision was announced.

The U.S. Attorney's Office also prepared for an assault verdict. Dwayne Keyes said that if Lyn were convicted under those circumstances, prosecutors would not seek to retry her for attempted assassination. The decision had significance for Lyn: The maximum penalty for assault on the president was ten years. The maximum for attempted assassination was life.

The experience was intense for the jurors. As they settled down for supper at a Chinese restaurant, Marcia Van Court stood and said: "Have you all made your decisions?"

The jurors looked at Marcia aghast, and she realized that they thought she was asking for the verdict. "I mean, have you decided what you're going to eat?" The tension vanished and the jurors shared a laugh with Marcia and the deputies.

Marcia said she thought one juror had particular trouble contemplating a guilty verdict. An observant Catholic with a gravely ill daughter, the juror feared that if she convicted Lyn, God would let her own daughter die. Jurors are neither told potential sentences nor are they to consider them when reaching a verdict; nonetheless, the woman believed Lyn's offense carried the death penalty, and a guilty verdict would send Lyn to the electric chair.

The jury continued deliberating on Wednesday; as the hour crept closer to Thanksgiving, deputies completed preparations for the holiday dinner. Judge Mac-Bride visited the jury room during the afternoon to check on progress toward a verdict—and to subtly push jurors to reach a conclusion. The judge seemed pleased that, after days of deliberations, things finally were coming along. At 5:00 P.M., he told reporters about his impressions.

"I just got the feeling they're bound and determined to get the job done. . . . There's no feeling of anybody about being browbeaten or discouraged."

The Verdict

At 8:28 P.M., word came: after nineteen and a half hours of deliberations over three days, the jury had reached a verdict. Within half an hour, MacBride had reconvened court and summoned Lyn from her cell. She wore her green corduroy pantsuit and, as she had since she first left the trial, carried her red robe over her arm.

It had been a tough week for Lyn. She looked haggard and small, her eyes underscored with dark circles. But she was not the only one whose nerves were showing. Judge MacBride, when he first spoke to Lyn, addressed her as "Miss Verdict." Would she attend the proceeding or stay in her cell?

"Well, you understand why I won't be here," Lyn said, her voice fragile. "But I do want to place into the record that I didn't—"

"Miss Fromme, there is just nothing else," said the judge. If she were convicted, she could make a statement before he imposed sentence.

"I will be listening," Lyn said as she was led away. "I told you before I wouldn't watch it."

MacBride then announced to the press gallery that the jurors would not grant interviews after the verdict was announced. And, apparently speaking to Sandra Good, still keeping vigil in the courtroom, he said that no outbursts would be tolerated. "I'm warning anyone present who might be so inclined to restrain themselves in an orderly fashion."

At 9:03 P.M., the jury returned to the courtroom. Following the age-old trial ritual, MacBride asked Forelady LeRoy if a verdict had been reached. "Yes," she said.

"Will you hand it to the marshal, please." The one-page form passed through the appropriate judicial hands. "All right, Mr. Clerk, will you read the verdict, please."

"Yes, Your Honor," said the clerk. "Ladies and gentlemen of the jury, harken to your verdict as it shall stand recorded:

" 'We, the jury in the above entitled case, find the defendant Lynette Alice Fromme guilty of the attempted assassination of the President of the United States of America, Gerald R. Ford."

After days during which the jury seemed ready to let Lyn off the hook, the conviction stunned the courtroom. MacBride dismissed the jury, and reporters rushed to file their stories.

Lyn was returned to the courtroom, where MacBride told her she would be sentenced on December 17. Lyn, however, already was fretting about the pre-sentencing report that a probation officer would prepare for the judge.

"I feel that it's an unreasonable burden and unfair to place yourself in a position where one's entire future rests on the . . . opinions and interpretations of one individual," she said.

The judge interrupted. Probation reports were compiled to help the authorities do "what we think is best for you," he said. "One [purpose] is possible punish-ment, one is possible rehabilitation and one is . . . deterrence of any others who might be inclined to commit the same crime of which you now have been convicted."

"In regard to this probation report," Lyn said, "I want a tape recorder and a witness there or else I can't submit to it."

"That is up to you, Miss Fromme," said the judge. "I'm not going to order a witness or tape recorder to be present. Miss Fromme, you have to realize there is nothing special about you as a defendant. Now let's get that straight."

"Your Honor, I think it's important that every single defendant, every single person that goes through these courts and must go to prison not be subjected to the opinions of one individual that goes—"

"All right, take her out," the judge ordered the marshal. "Remove her."

Four deputies grabbed Lyn, but she wriggled away. "All right, take it easy! Let me walk myself. I think that should set a precedent. Don't push me," she said as she was led back to jail.

Outside the courtroom, the attorneys and other trial characters gathered before reporters. "I think the verdict reflects a lot of thought," said the quiet Dwayne Keyes. Privately, he grumbled that "the jury took a little longer than they should have." John Virga announced that the verdict "definitely would be appealed." He said that if the trial had been held in state court, the outcome would probably have been different "because the rules of discovery [there] allow the defense to be given all the evidence and statements of prosecution witnesses"—a claim to which Don Heller retorted, "Nonsense." Still, Virga said that the jury "acted in good faith" and that he wouldn't "yell sour grapes" about the verdict.

Sandra Good was less restrained. "Once again you have judged a reflection of yourselves," she said, echoing the remarks she made after the Tate-LaBianca convictions. "Los Angeles will burn to the ground. Your children will rise up and kill you."

At San Quentin, Charles Manson had no comment. Neither did the White House. But by coincidence, the day Lyn was convicted of attempting to assassi-nate him, President Ford announced that the United States would forswear con-ducting any assassinations of its own. At a news conference, the president said he had "issued specific instructions to U.S. intelligence agencies that under no circumstances shall any agencies participate or plan any assassination of foreign leaders."

Apparently, however, it remained open season on Ford. That evening, a young man scaled a White House fence and crept some fifty yards into the grounds before tripping an alarm. He then crossed the tennis courts, crawled to a drive-way, and approached the president's daughter, Susan, who was unloading camera equipment from a car. A guard spotted the intruder and grabbed him. Like Lyn, the man's motive was to seek attention for a loved one he felt had been unjustly convicted: a relative was serving a sentence for drug smuggling. Unlike Lyn, the man was charged with unlawful entry and released.

None of the jurors would speak to the press, or even be photographed leaving the courthouse. Authorities said that they feared reprisals from the Manson Fam-ily. "If you had been a member of a jury in this type of situation, wouldn't you be worried about your security?" asked Marshal Van Court. He urged reporters not to make much of the jurors' fears. "The more it's played up, it might get weirdos thinking about it."

And so, as the jurors rushed home to prepare for Thanksgiving, speculation raged over their verdict. Commentators suggested that despite MacBride's instruc-tions, the jury first had found Lyn guilty of assault, and then moved on to the attempted murder charge. Juror Robert Conboy, a Teamster by trade, later said that until the final hours, the jury was stuck on the absence of a bullet in the firing chamber. "A lot of people believed that with no cartridge in the chamber, the gun wasn't a weapon," he said. Marcia Van Court thought the jury would have preferred to continue deliberating. "It was only Thanksgiving that made them stop," she said.

The holiday was nothing special for Lyn. She received the same meal all inmates got: turkey, cranberries, string beans, nuts and candy. "All she ate was the nuts and candy," said a jail spokesman. "I guess she wasn't too hungry."

The verdict did little to dissipate tension among trial participants. Days after the jury's decision, Judge MacBride's car, a 1961 Ford Falcon, was stolen from outside his home. When it was found, abandoned, in a Sacramento neighborhood, dep-uties cordoned off the area and sent a bomb squad to check for explosives—a "precautionary measure," said a sheriff's spokesman. No bomb was found, and the incident was classified as "a routine auto theft."

The Sentence

December 17 arrived, and Lyn, again in her green corduroy pantsuit, her robe over her arm, returned to the courthouse. She seemed upbeat, talking casually with the marshals, who let her walk unrestrained into the building. Prior to the hearing, she met briefly with Judge MacBride, to discuss the 128 handwritten pages of notes she had sent him for consideration during sentencing.

Before the sentencing could take place, the court had to dispose of a number of motions. Virga, angling for a reversal on appeal, brought up another prosecutorial indiscretion: the government had failed to turn over to him until December 11 (after Lyn's conviction) a report FBI Agent Larry Ott had written on his interview with the Reverend James Porter.

Lyn, impatient to make her statement to the court, jumped up. "If you don't want to hear what I have to say—what does Ott have to do with any of this?"

"Miss Virga—" said the judge, clearly on edge.

"From-me," she corrected him. "F-R-O-M-M-E."

"Miss Fromme, Mr. Virga is making an argument on your behalf and I would—"

"He is no longer my counsel," said Lyn.

"Sit down and be quiet, please. Will you please sit down and be quiet and let Mr. Virga make his argument for you."

"For you," said Lyn, "yes."

"Thank you. Thank you, Miss Fromme." He turned to Virga: "Now proceed."

As it turned out, the U.S. Attorney's Office did not get the Ott report until after the trial ended, either. And the report, the judge concluded, contained nothing of substantial benefit to the defense. So, MacBride said, although the Ott report should have been given to the defense during the trial, that failure was but harmless error. Motions for dismissal and a new trial were denied.

MacBride then considered Virga's final motion, that the judge personally examine the prosecution's files to see if any more exculpatory evidence was hidden within. MacBride said he was satisfied that the government had turned everything over. If he found out that wasn't so, "most likely ... I would just simply dismiss as a means of demonstrating to the government that prosecutorial misconduct will not be countenanced by the court."

"How will you know that there is nothing unless you look at the file?" asked Virga.

"I am relying on their common sense," said the judge, as Heller and Keyes sat silently. "I hope I have their attention. As the saying goes, sometimes you have to hit the mule over the head with a two-by-four to get their attention." Motion denied.

"At this time," the judge announced, "I am prepared to pronounce sentence."

Virga and Lyn rose. As Lyn approached the bench, a Rome Beauty apple, big and red, dropped from her robe and rolled across the floor. A deputy picked it up and handed it back to her.

"Who's the apple for?" asked the judge, amused.

"You," said Lyn, quietly. "Is there any particular place you want me to stand?"

"You can stand right there, that's fine," said the judge. He asked Dwayne Keyes, waiting four feet away from Lyn, to speak for the government.

In his familiar monotone, the prosecutor read from prepared remarks: "The two factors involved in sentencing are punishment and rehabilitation. When possible, the punishment should fit the crime. And this is, if not the most, one of the most serious federal crimes. I think that the punishment should be severe for two reasons, for the first reason of punishment and for the second reason of deterrence to others. In addition to punishment, there is also the concept of rehabilitation. Now, the defendant has shown herself, through evidence that has been adduced at trial, to be a person who does have and is filled with feelings of hatred toward others. She has shown herself to be a person who would not hesitate to use violence to achieve any particular end she deemed appropriate at any particular time—"

Splat! Lyn had stepped back, swung her right arm up, and hurled the apple at Keyes's head.

"Hatred?" she screamed.

Soft and ripe, the apple exploded just above the prosecutor's temple, knocking his glasses to the ground. Bits of the fruit covered Keyes's hair, and some hit the judge. Spectators went pale, and the courtroom fell into a stunned silence. Two deputies and a matron grabbed Lyn, while Don Heller moved aside so that courtroom artists could capture the scene.

"Now Miss Fromme—" said MacBride.

"That was just a response," said Lyn.

"It was quite obvious it was a response. What are you going to do, Miss Fromme? Are you going to act up during the rest of this proceeding?"

"No, no," said Lyn. "I'll be very still."

"You will either be still or—" the judge paused. "I want you here. I am going to require you to be here during the sentencing. . . . If there are further outbursts from you of any kind, I am going to cause you to be confined to a wheelchair with your mouth taped and your hands strapped."

"He just spurred the inspiration in me, you know?" Lyn said, her voice rising to a shout. "I mean, he's the one that's talking about hate. I never said anything about hate."

"Do you have any more apples in your bag?" MacBride asked, sternly.

"No, I didn't bring any more apples today," said Lyn, calming a bit. "That one was for you."

"That's what I was afraid of," said the judge. "Proceed, Mr. Keyes."

Keyes, who had wiped his face with a white handkerchief, continued his statement: "She has reached a point where, perhaps, Your Honor, rehabilitation may be out of reach for her."

"Could be," Lyn agreed.

"She may not be capable of change at this particular time or any future time and this, I think, is a factor that should be taken into consideration," Keyes went on. "The length of sentence should be such that if rehabilitation does not take place, society will be protected. Imposing a sentence upon a defendant is . . .

perhaps the most difficult task a judge has to perform. However, considering all the factors in this case, the United States asks this court to impose the sentence of life on this defendant."

Now it was John Virga's turn. "The only thing I have to say, Your Honor, is that I feel that had Miss Fromme wanted to kill the President, he would be dead. And that she did want to draw attention to her ecological issues."

Lyn interrupted. "You don't know how—"

"Let me finish!" Virga cried. "I would ask that you not consider a life sentence. She's young. Certainly, her conduct that day was very foolish and potentially very dangerous. I would ask that you consider a sentence that leaves the path to rehabilitation open to her. With a life sentence, it will mean she's not eligible for parole for fifteen years."

Last of the speakers would be Lyn herself. "I assume that we're taking this very seriously?" she asked the judge.

"I hope you are—" said MacBride.

"I am."

"—'cause I sure am."

"I am."

"Very well," said the judge.

Lyn began: "I wrote you 120 pages of my heart and my mind. The D.A. talks about offending common sense. All of us are offending common sense when we destroy the earth like we're doing now." She recalled MacBride's remarks about the prosecutors' conduct. "You said the only way to get their attention is to do something drastic. That's what you told me. All of you lawyers throw words around. From what I've seen, if I lay my heart out to you it's like throwing it away. You are—lawyers to me from my experience are machines that work or may not work when you put in your quarter.

"I want Manson out. I want my world at peace. I know that none of you can bring it. We have ten years of air and water. That's not very long. You would rather die than notice yourself killing. I have tried to hold you up so we could let it down gently. And I've stood with a gun and said, 'Don't make me shoot.' And you keep saying, 'Do it, do it, do it.' You keep asking for it. I feel that I've done all I can, save killing you. I cannot be rehabilitated because I haven't done anything wrong. As soon as you let that Family together speak in a trial, then I'm free. Otherwise—"

"Otherwise what?" said the judge.

"Otherwise my freedom will be in seeing the International People's Court of Retribution give you what you deserve."

"Now, Miss Fromme," said MacBride, "are you talking about me individually or are you talking about society in general?"

"Your Honor, I consider you as the public opinion. I feel that's all you are, as a judge."

"Does that complete your statement?"

"That's right," said Lyn.

MacBride looked at his notes. He had drafted a statement of his own.

"I am not unaware of the rather awesome responsibility I have in pronouncing sentence in this particular case. I have no guidelines to assist me.... It's the first time anyone has ever been sentenced for the attempted assassination of the President of the United States, so the sentence that I pronounce is based entirely on what I've observed in the trial, what I've read...and then my overall experience in this entire matter.

"Now, Miss Fromme...you send me this statement...I want you to know that I spent hours reading that statement and pondering it.... Some parts I read over and over again to see if I could glean from that statement some understanding of you and possibly something that I could find in this that would assist me in mitigating any sentence that I might otherwise impose upon you. I searched in vain. I searched in vain in that statement for anything that would lead me to mitigate sentence. Ninety-five percent of the statement was devoted to your condemnation of society in general. Your—"

"Condemnation?" Lyn interrupted.

"Yes, that's the way I read it."

"Of people themselves?"

"Of what people are doing," said the judge.

"What are they doing?" asked Lyn.

But MacBride was not interested in a Socratic dialogue with Lyn. "You have had your turn and I'm going to have my turn now," he said. "You keep referring to this rotten mess and that society generally is to be condemned and that's—"

"Did I call it a 'rotten mess,' or did I tell you there's chemicals in the water?" Lyn said.

"There's no sense in your interrupting me because I'm going to say what I'm going to say."

Lyn continued her lesson: "Did I call it names or did I ask you to get it out of the water?"

"I'm telling you, Miss Fromme, I'm going to complete this statement and you're going to stand there either taped or not. Now, can we do this peacefully, please? I gave you an opportunity to make whatever statement you wanted."

"You fool," said Lyn. "I'm trying to save your life."

"Well, I also read that in the statement and I took it seriously. I really did, the statement you made in your letter to me. But I repeat that your statement was almost entirely [about], let's put it this way, your philosophy toward society, your attitude, your feelings concerning our environment and finally your defense of Charles Manson and other members of the Manson Family who are presently imprisoned and your justification for the Tate-LaBianca murders."

"Excuse me, Your Honor, I didn't 'justify' the Tate-LaBianca murders," Lyn said. "I asked that they be allowed to explain those murders."

"Well, anyway," the judge continued, "the remainder of your statement was devoted to your view of what happened on the days leading up to September 5th and September 5th itself." In the letter, Lyn had written that before leaving her apartment, she had put a cartridge into the Colt .45's firing chamber and then ejected it, leaving the chamber empty. "I ejected that one and saw it fall to the floor," the letter said. She wrote that she had no intention of killing the president.

"Now, unfortunately, your version of what happened on that day comes too late," said the judge. "Unfortunately, having been afforded the opportunity to testify and having refused it, your explanation of the incident, even if it's to be believed . . . is now wasted. It is of no help whatsoever for any legal purpose insofar as this case is concerned. Now, your discussion of the environmental problems disturbs me, and it disturbs me not because I disagree with you that our environment can stand all the help that it can get, but rather because of the violent extremes to which you have committed yourself to correct what you believed to be our environmental problems and, incidentally, to help Manson and your Manson Family—"

"He's the only one that can save us," Lyn insisted, pounding the lectern.

"You said that repeatedly in your statement. 'Manson is the only one that can lead us out of this mess.' I recall that being stated a number of times in your statement. Now, the evidence in this case and your written statement to me, together with the letters that you wrote to Charles Rossie of NBC and to Edward Vandervort, have convinced me that you would murder or that you would cause others to commit murder in what I consider to be your false and distorted belief that only terror and violence can save our environment and our natural resources. Now, I want to suggest to you that the most precious natural resource in the world is a human life."

"*You* are suggesting that to *me*?" Lyn was incredulous. For that had been the entire point of her act, of her whole life, perhaps. And the judge, after their months together, after their moments of empathy, seemed not to have understood a thing.

"I'm suggesting it to you," MacBride said. "I'm suggesting it to anyone that will listen and those who might hear of this trial that the most precious natural resource in the world is a human life. To casually and coldly and without conscience take a human life solely for the purpose of calling attention to a cause is to me the most reprehensible and despicable of crimes."

"What if *they* are taking thousands of lives? Thousands of lives and slowly, very slowly?" Lyn shouted.

"And moreover," the judge continued, "a murder such as the one that you attempted in this case would impoverish the nation and, frankly, it would have done absolutely nothing to further the cause that you espouse."

"Well, I saw that," said Lyn.

"If John Kennedy, Robert Kennedy or Martin Luther King had been allowed to live out their lives rather than having fallen at the hands of a person like yourself, they could have accomplished more for your environment and for all mankind than all the terrorists in the history of the world—you and Charles Manson included."

"We are not terrorists!" Lyn screamed.

"In this case," the judge said, "I am satisfied that you deserve a punishment equal to the harshness of the deed you attempted to commit. Now, by your own admission . . . you cannot be rehabilitated."

"That's true," said Lyn. "I didn't do anything wrong. You noticed I didn't kill him. Are you telling me I should have?"

"Now I accept your statement that you cannot be rehabilitated. I am convinced that you are so committed to violence as a means of getting your way—"

"That's why I've been killing all this time," Lyn said sarcastically.

"—in accomplishing your ill-conceived—"

"That's why I came to you to beg on my knees. That's why I kneeled on the street corner for two years. That's why I crawled twenty-five miles—because I'm *so* committed to violence," she continued, mocking the judge.

"All right," said MacBride. "Shall I try again? Frankly, I don't think that any amount of rehabilitative effort will change you and I think you agreed to this yourself. So this leads to the matter of deterrence and I believe the only way to deter you from further violence or the encouragement of violence on the part of others . . . is to separate you from the society with which you cannot agree and the society from which you've already crossed yourself out by your own admission, by the X on your forehead, and, accordingly, being unable to find any reason or justification for imposing a sentence of less severity than the maximum provided by Congress for the commission of the crime with which you've been convicted, it is the sentence of this court that you be imprisoned for the term of your natural life in the custody of the Attorney General of the United States."

It was the first life sentence MacBride had ever imposed. It also was Lyn's first felony conviction.

Emotionless at the sentence, Lyn told the judge that she was dismissing Virga and that she would handle her own appeal.

MacBride said that was none of his business. "The defendant is remanded to the custody of the marshal to carry out the sentence."

"Your Honor, I'd also—"

Deputies, prepared for the moment, grabbed Lyn and began to take her away.

"Wait a minute! Just hang on a second—Hey!"

MacBride stopped them. "What is it you want?"

"First of all I'd like my property. I'd like my robe."

"That will be brought down to you," said the judge.

"All right. I would like to make a motion for return of property."

"You may make that at a different time."

"At a different time? Will you call me back?"

MacBride said she would be held at the county jail while her prison assignment was being considered. She could make her motions from there.

"You're just using words, aren't you? Are you being serious?" Lyn shouted.

That was it. "I am remanding you to the custody of the marshal right now to take you out," said Judge MacBride.

As deputies moved to grab her, Lyn threw herself to the floor. The marshals picked her up by her arms and legs, and as she flailed and howled, rushed her like a battering ram through the courtroom doors.

"Quit pushing me," she yelled.

"You animals!" shouted Sandra Good.

From the courtroom hallway, spectators heard Lyn's last utterance—a blood-curdling scream.

Epilogue

V a c a n t

At 2:00 A.M. on Saturday, December 20, Deputy Marshals Warren Steeves and Mike Nelson roused Lyn from her cell. It was time to move her to the federal prison system, starting with a temporary confinement at the Metropolitan Correctional Center in San Diego. Lyn was surprised; she was planning to file an appeal and didn't realize that she would enter the custody of the Bureau of Prisons so quickly.

"Can't I wait here?" she asked. The answer was no. The deputies brought her to a waiting van. The early hour had been chosen for law enforcement's convenience; with the streets empty, it would be easier for the marshals to detect anyone trying to tail them. They drove to State Highway 99 outside Sacramento, where, under the direction of Marshal Art Van Court, a convoy assembled for the six-hundred-mile journey to San Diego. Two chase cars, ready to intercept any breakout attempts, accompanied the prisoner van. Lyn sat quietly or slept for most of the trip through California's agricultural Central Valley. With thick tule fog hanging over the highway and cutting visibility to a few yards, the convoy rarely went over twenty-five miles per hour.

At the San Diego prison, Lyn bid a gracious farewell to her Sacramento jailers. She thanked each marshal, especially Steeves. "Warren, I thank you for being a gentleman and taking care of me." Steeves nodded; he had tried to treat her like a lady and was glad Lyn had seen that. Despite the circumstances, Steeves and Nelson had grown fond of their captive. Years later, Nelson maintained that she had been unjustly convicted of the attempted murder charge.

"I don't think she really had an intent" to kill the president, said Nelson, who had been promoted to chief deputy federal marshal in Sacramento. "Her cause was just," he said. "But her method was suspect."

Steeves, for his part, thought that Lyn had pulled the .45's trigger. Nonetheless, he was pleased when he received letters from her, alerting the deputy to the destruction of rain forests in Brazil.

Steeves and Nelson remained with the Sacramento marshal's office for their civil service careers. Marshal Art Van Court held his post whenever there was a Republican in the White House; except for the years of 1977 through 1981 when Democrat Jimmy Carter was president, Van Court served continuously until 1993, when another Democrat, Bill Clinton, removed him. The Republican governor of California, Pete Wilson, then appointed Van Court to the state parole board.

Art and Marcia Van Court also heard occasionally from their former prisoners. Lyn wrote to Marcia Van Court, which did little to squelch the rumors that she had been the one who innocently gave Lyn an apple on the day of her sentencing. Art Van Court, for his part, received a gift from Edward Vandervort, the Pennsylvania man who never got to testify before the jury. Vandervort sent the marshal a nineteenth-century biography of General George Custer, a rare first edition.

Lyn was not the last Manson Family member to pass under Marshal Van Court's custody. On December 22, 1975, five days after Lyn was sentenced, federal agents arrested Sandra Good and Susan "Heather" Murphy for conspiracy to send threatening letters through the mail. Lyn was identified as an unindicted co-conspirator, but as she already was serving a life term, prosecutors declined to charge her as a matter of judicial economy.

Once again, Judge MacBride presided over the trial. And Sandy, repeating the pattern set by Lyn, obtained permission to represent herself. Unlike Dick Walker and John Virga, who attempted to mount vigorous defenses for Lyn, Sandy's court-appointed co-counsel did not quarrel with his client's legal strategy. Like Lyn, Sandy saw the courtroom less as a chance to avoid prison than as a platform to express her views. Bill Shubb, a former federal prosecutor, took the appointment reluctantly. But Sandy appreciated Shubb's forthrightness, and the two developed a rapport.

At Sandy's request, Shubb met with Charles Manson, filed the papers necessary to summon Lyn as a defense witness, and even smuggled carrots and celery sticks for Sandy to snack on in her cell. Shubb later was appointed a federal judge by President George Bush and decorated his chambers with artist sketches of the Good trial.

Sandy subpoenaed Lyn and shared a cell with her for part of the trial. In court, Sandy cross-examined the witnesses against her—including her neighbors Michael Davies and Morris Willmarth—in a conversational, occasionally confrontational manner. When the day of Lyn's testimony arrived, however, the defense came to an end. Lyn, wearing a black robe and headdress that resembled that of a nun, made the sign of the cross when she took the stand. Then she announced: "I cannot testify until my Family gets a trial."

Sandy then stood and walked over to the witness box, beside her friend. "I want to go with Lyn," she said. "I want to leave . . . I want to go with her to prison right now."

Lyn elaborated: "Your Honor, we are two churches. I am a Catholic church and she is the Protestant church." When Lyn then rose to address the gallery, MacBride cut off her microphone and ordered deputies to return her to prison. She was carried shrieking from the courtroom, a sight that caused some spectators to laugh.

Sandy turned to the gallery. "That was very funny, wasn't it, lady in green?" Sandy scowled. "Sharon Tate, woman, is your reality."

MacBride interrupted. "Look, Miss Good, I share your feelings. There was nothing funny about that incident at all." He addressed the courtroom: "This young lady that was just taken out of the courtroom has been sentenced to life in prison."

"I want life in prison, too," said Sandy. "My faith is stronger than all your prisons and gas chambers put together."

Sandy's wish was not granted; although she was convicted on all five counts against her, each carried only a five-year term. With two sentences running concurrently and credit for good behavior, she served only ten years, many of those at the same prison with Lyn. In 1985, she followed the example Manson set in 1967 by asking to remain in prison. "I have too much anger inside me" to function in society, she told a reporter. "It's actually a rage." Federal prison authorities, she said, were "really stupid" to set her free. Sandy received a supervised release in Vermont; when she was relieved of all federal supervision, she moved to the central California town of Hanford, a few miles from Manson's cell at Corcoran State Prison. Still denied permission to see Manson, she filed a lawsuit against the State of California seeking visitation rights.

Heather Murphy managed to create a few moments of havoc during her trial with Sandra Good. On one day, Heather came to court dressed in a Catholic nun's habit. "I'm a sister in Manson's church," she announced. Judge MacBride warned her that not only was such attire prejudicial, it might violate a state law prohibiting the impersonation of a nun. Heather undertook an even more provocative act before the trial's conclusion. Free on bail, she obtained copies of the threat letters introduced as evidence against her and Sandy. Before the trial's conclusion, she mailed them to their recipients. Shortly afterward, Heather was convicted of one count of conspiracy to send threats through the mail and sentenced to five years.

Unlike Lyn and Sandra, who often spoke of violence but rarely seemed to act violently themselves, Heather in prison displayed an aggressive side. In August 1976, Heather and another female inmate clubbed a woman prison guard and escaped from Terminal Island. Lyn apparently was not pleased with Heather's action. From prison, she telephoned the Associated Press with a message for the fugitive: "You are not Manson Family but you carry that name. I wish you well, but you'd best realize your life is on the line, and not because of the FBI. This Family is for earth balance, not money, dope or power plays." Thirteen days after her escape, Heather was captured in Portland, Oregon. She received an additional ten-year sentence for the jailbreak.

Like Marshal Van Court, Dwayne Keyes lost his political appointment as United States Attorney after President Ford's defeat in the 1976 election. A Republican governor later appointed Keyes to the Superior Court in Fresno, and he rose to become the county's presiding judge.

Don Heller left government service for private practice and became one of Sacramento's most prominent criminal defense attorneys. The prosecutor who once offered to personally pull the switch on the electric chair changed his views on criminal justice and became an opponent of the death penalty. Heller's clients included lobbyists accused of corruption, as well as murder suspects.

Tom MacBride retired as an active judge in 1979, on his sixty-fifth birthday. He remained on the bench as a senior judge, which allowed him to hear a number of cases per year. His order requiring President Ford to testify via videotape became precedent for the rare occasions when presidents were subpoenaed as witnesses in criminal cases. In later years, Ronald Reagan, George Bush, and Bill Clinton would follow Ford's example in testifying before a video camera. More than twenty years after Lyn's conviction, MacBride's courthouse became the setting for the trial of another extremist charged with ecologically motivated terrorist acts: that of Theodore J. Kaczynski, the alleged Unabomber.

After Lyn's conviction, John Virga told reporters that, like Don Heller, he occasionally had carried a gun during the trial. He did not fear Lyn or Sandy, he said, but "in a case like this, you can't help but wonder who will come out of the woodwork." Virga planned to conduct Lyn's appeal, but his client dropped the case.

Phil Shelton never returned to complete his degree in philosophy. His joined the public defender's office in Santa Barbara and rose to become its chief investigator. He lives just a few miles from Lyn's retired English teacher, Jim Van Wagoner.

Dick Walker, the federal defender in Sacramento, continued to head up the office for another decade, after which he retired to Washington State.

Paul Fitzgerald remained in private practice, specializing in criminal defense. He had so many clients in prison, he liked to joke, they named a wing after him at San Quentin.

Steve Bekins bounced in and out of jail for years, until a conviction for a 1990 robbery landed him a twenty-seven year sentence in federal prison. While admitting to other crimes, Bekins denies having committed the offense that brought him, in effect, a life sentence. Continuing to have disciplinary problems with prison officials, Bekins resolved to follow the path of his onetime associate, Edward Bunker, and become a jailhouse writer. His first project was a children's story.

Many of Lyn's childhood friends continued to nurse fond memories of her, even after her conviction. From the Lariats, Chuck Lynch grew up to become a public school administrator, while Nora Lynn Stevens raised a family in Orange County, California. Tillman and Louise Hall remained fixtures in Westchester, California, continuing to live just a couple of blocks away from the house where Lyn spent her early childhood.

Rachel Hickerson, who shared a tumultuous teenage summer with Lyn, became a freelance writer and, briefly, the fiancée of satirist Paul Krassner. Hickerson later took up work as a free-speech activist in New York City.

Craig South became a graphic designer, and composed a commemorative T-shirt for the twenty-fifth reunion of the Redondo Union High School Class of 1966. It featured a yearbook photo of Lyn, in a page-boy haircut with a bow in her hair, above the caption, "Most Likely To . . ."

Susan Atkins, Patricia Krenwinkel, and Leslie Van Houten are serving life sentences at the California Institution for Women at Frontera. Charles "Tex" Watson and Bobby Beausoleil are serving their life sentences at the California Men's Colony at San Luis Obispo. Charles Manson is imprisoned at the California State Prison at Corcoran. All of those convicted in the Manson killings are entitled to regular parole hearings because the murder statutes in effect at the time of their conviction did not offer the option of life without parole.

Harold Boro resumed his inconspicuous life after the Fromme trial and died in 1990. He was eighty-one years old.

William Millar Fromme, Lyn's father, suffered a fatal heart attack in 1989, at age sixty-nine. Lyn's mother, Helen Fromme, continues to live quietly in Southern California. In 1992, she wrote to the author about Lynette. "My relationship with her is good and I would like to keep it that way," Mrs. Fromme said in her letter. She complained that the news media had it out for her daughter, always editing Lyn's interviews "to show her in the worst possible light."

Within a month of her sentencing, Lynette Fromme used privileged attorney-client mail to send a letter from prison to the administrator of the federal Environmental Protection Agency, Russell Train. The letter accused Train of being a "weak mealy mouth" whose failure to clean up the environment rendered him "useless." Train, Lyn wrote, deserved to have his "face shoved in the pollution which you allow to go on and on and on." Prison officials did not press charges against Lyn, but did suspend her right to use privileged mail.

In April 1976, CBS broadcast a two-part television version of *Helter Skelter*. The special was a ratings success, giving the network first place over ABC for the first time in three months and winning a bigger audience than the Academy Awards. One viewer was particularly disappointed; "The portrayal of Manson was ludicrous," Lyn said in a telephone call to a news reporter. "It made a genius look like a contemptuous idiot."

As she grew accustomed to the routines of prison, Lyn gave up on the hope of vindication through the justice system. In September 1976, she dropped the appeal of her conviction, seemingly accepting her projected release date of 2005. She instead focused on more modest goals: obtaining her red robe from the evidence lockup at the Sacramento Federal Building. The following July, after the federal government opened its first maximum-security lockup for women, Lyn was transferred to the Federal Correctional Institution at Alderson, West Virginia. Located in the Allegheny Mountains, the institution was modeled after the campus of Bucknell University in Pennsylvania. Alderson, which opened in the 1920s, was the only federal prison devoted exclusively to women and once held such famous inmates as Tokyo Rose and the singer Billie Holiday. Lyn said she liked her new surroundings, especially since Sandra Good soon joined her at Alderson. "Manson's from West Virginia, you know. He radiates some of the color," Lyn told a reporter. "I like people in West Virginia."

Nevertheless, when the government converted a Pleasanton, California, facility from a youth camp to an all-female prison, Lyn and Sandy requested a transfer. An hour east of San Francisco, Pleasanton was in the same state as Charles Manson. As authorities had found the women to be model prisoners, the request was granted. There they joined another notorious inmate, Patricia Hearst. Lyn and Sandy, Hearst recalled, "were as crazy as ever," free again to dress in their flowing robes and answering only to the names Red and Blue. Lyn's rapid acclimation to confinement, however, came to an end in March 1979. While working in a prison garden, Lyn attacked fellow inmate Julienne Busic with the claw end of a hammer. According to witnesses, Lyn shouted that Busic was "a white, middle-class, rich bitch and doesn't deserve to live." Imprisoned in connection with a 1976 airline hijacking, Busic, a Croatian nationalist, recovered. According to a letter Lyn sent to the Associated Press, Busic was "a rat, was Patricia Hearst's best friend and [was] very disrespectful to me." As punishment, Lyn was returned to the maximum-security unit at Alderson. Sandra soon followed.

In 1984, a *People* magazine correspondent visited Lyn. He was impressed by her knowledge of environmental issues and the nonplussed attitude she brought to life in prison. Only the occasional, non-sequitur references to Charles Manson disturbed him about his subject. "In a frightening way," he reported to his editors, spending time with Lyn was comparable to the "wide-ranging, wonderfully intelligent conversations" he'd had with his children as they grew up. "Incidentally," the correspondent concluded, "if Lynette Fromme ever gets out or into a rehabilitation program for the 'outside,' I suggest she'd make a dandy researcher for *People* magazine."

Lyn became eligible to apply for parole in 1985, but never sought a release hearing. Soon thereafter, Lyn did get out—but on terms unlikely to bring her employment at *People*. At 9:30 P.M. on December 23, 1987, she was reported missing from the Alderson prison. A national alert went out and security was tightened for former President Ford and the principals in the Fromme prosecution. Within hours, more than one hundred federal, state, and local officers, some with bloodhounds, began combing the cold, rainy West Virginia highlands. They could find no sign of the fugitive or clues to how she managed to escape. Despite sightings of Lyn being reported from as far away as Minnesota, the jailbreak came to an anticlimactic end just two miles south of the penitentiary fence. On Christmas Day, a pair of prison employees driving down rural Creamery Road spotted Lyn walking out of the woods near a fishing camp. They pulled over and Lyn, soaking wet from the rain, got in the car. She was dressed in two pairs of pants, a green overcoat, and a crocheted hat. Given the conditions—the nighttime temperature fell below 20 degrees—she was found to be in good shape. On *The MacNeil/Lehrer NewsHour*, anchorman Jim Lehrer summed up the day's big stories: "The celebration of Christmas by Christians around the world and the recapture of Lynette 'Squeaky' Fromme."

Lyn's escape, which required her to scale an eight-foot-tall barbed wire fence, apparently was motivated by the wish to see Manson one last time. Charlie had told a sympathizer that he was dying of testicular cancer. The sympathizer mentioned this to Lyn in a telephone call on December 23. "It seems I broke the news to her. And she was shocked," the sympathizer said. Ninety minutes later, Lyn left the prison compound.

Lyn attempted to plead no contest to escape charges, urging that fees to pay her attorney instead be given to a 4-H club or the West Virginia Soil Conservation Service for a tree planting program. "Legally, I am guilty," Lyn told the federal court in Beckley, West Virginia. "Morally and spiritually, I am not guilty."

Prosecutors, however, refused to agree to the no-contest plea, insisting instead on a full conviction or an unambiguous guilty plea. And while Judge Elizabeth

Hallanan granted Lyn's request to represent herself, she refused to redistribute defense attorney fees, requiring instead that Lyn have a standby counsel, just as in Judge MacBride's courtroom.

The trial was brief. Lyn called herself as the sole defense witness. "I got word that [Manson] had cancer. He needs a relative, somebody to check on him," she told the jury. Manson, she said, was "my husband, my brother, my father, my son, the man who's been my friend." She had no choice but to escape, she testified, because "my access to him is so limited. I've been feeling helpless for years."

Lyn studiously followed the judge's instructions to testify via questions and answers. Seeming to enjoy playing the role of questioner as well as witness, she said, "Miss Fromme, you talk too much" and, "Wait a minute, you're getting ahead of yourself." In summing up the case, though, Lyn was direct in addressing the jury. "You don't have any choice," she said. "I'm guilty as charged, legally, and without remorse, morally, so that's that." The jurors took ten minutes to convict her.

At sentencing, prosecutor Kirk Brandfass urged a stiff punishment. "This defendant is not some kind of earth mother, traipsing through the woods with bluebirds on her shoulder," he said. "She is a twisted follower of the twisted demonic murderer, Charles Manson."

Lyn objected: "Mr. Manson is not on trial here," she said.

As evidence of Lyn's bad character, Brandfass contended that she planned her escape on Christmas Eve, so that hundreds of law officers would have to spend the holiday searching for her. Lyn denied the charge. "I was on the road wondering how to preserve the land, water, air, and wildlife," she said. "It was so fulfilling that I truly did not know so many people were looking for me."

Judge Hallanan asked if Lyn might try to escape again. "Well, yes," she said. "It floats through my mind now and then. I wouldn't ever say that I wouldn't try again." Nevertheless, Hallanan imposed considerably less than the maximum sentence of five years and a $250,000 fine. Instead, the judge added fifteen months onto Lyn's life term and assessed a $400 fine.

Lyn was transferred to a tougher prison in Lexington, Kentucky, and then to a new institution opening in the Florida panhandle town of Marianna, where she remains to this day.

After Lyn's conviction on the Ford charge, the *Sacramento Bee* editorialized that "there is a degree of damage which does not allow salvage. The brooding life of Lynette Fromme ... has surely reached that point." The trial "was a nightmare of tension and apprehension, punctuated by the hysterical outbursts of a rebellious defendant and pervaded by the potential to attract violence."

On the other hand, some thought Lyn's life sentence was hypocritical. In a letter to the *New York Times*, a John Illo of Shippensburg, Pennsylvania, cited the United States government's efforts to assassinate foreign leaders. "In a nation of official crime and legal corruption, a life sentence seems excessive for what was rather a momentary aberration than a premeditated malice."

Clare Boothe Luce, in an essay titled "The Significance of Squeaky Fromme," concluded that Lynette Fromme was the grotesque result of a society that had abandoned religious values for "Existentialism" and its attendant moral relativism. Lyn had grown up in a country where values were turned on their head.

The students who rioted at Berkeley for the right to use themselves the four-letter words used in the novels they were given to read in their English Lit. classes, were being seen as defenders of the First Amendment. The students who cut classes that bored them were only demanding a "relevant" education. The lads who burned their draft cards and destroyed ROTC buildings were enlightened patriots. The lads and lassies who shacked up together in the dormitories against rules were discarding the obsolete taboos of puritanism, and the last vestiges of Victorian sexual hypocrisy. Altogether, the youth rebels were creating a "New Morality" and a "New Politics." . . . In the words of my first boss, Condé Nast, who published *Vogue*, "Style percolates down." So do ideas. In the course of this century, atheistic liberalism, or as the intellectuals prefer to call it, "Humanism," has become the dominant philosophy of our educators. Its dregs are the ideas of the counterculture.

After the piece appeared in the *Wall Street Journal*, reaction was intense. One reader complained that blaming "the mad acts of Squeaky Fromme . . . on Sartre and Camus is like blaming Christ for the atrocities of the Crusades." Another reader, however, called Luce's essay probably "the most incisive, enlightened and instructive article I have ever seen."

Despite Luce's effort to establish Lyn as an icon in the intellectual debate over social morals, she became a symbol of another sort. Several fringe characters took up Lyn's cause, threatening acts of terrorism if she were not released. In October 1976, a man in his twenties was arrested on the West Coast after he sent letters threatening to kill President Ford, Governor Brown, and members of the Women's Parole Board if Lyn, Sandy, and Heather were not released. Four years later, a fifty-one-year-old Pennsylvania man tried to hijack an Atlanta-bound airliner, demanding a flight to Cuba, a $3.4 million ransom, and the release of Lynette Fromme and Sara Jane Moore. He was arrested by the FBI and ordered to undergo psychiatric examination.

In the broader popular culture, Squeaky Fromme secured a place as troubling footnote. Songwriters from Loudon Wainwright III to the Indigo Girls' Amy Ray wrote lyrics in which Squeaky symbolized an ambiguous kind of rebellion, if not outright evil. In the 1990s, she became a character in John Moran's modern opera, *The Manson Family*, commissioned by Lincoln Center and produced with the help of Philip Glass. Stephen Sondheim gave his Squeaky the signature duet in his 1991 musical, *Assassins,* where she joins John Hinckley, who shot Ronald Reagan, to sing "Unworthy of Your Love." Since 1975, she has been mentioned thousands of times in books, newspapers, magazines, films, and television programs. In most instances, the name Squeaky Fromme is used as shorthand for a violence-prone kook.

In 1994, Rachel Hickerson wrote to Lynette Fromme at the Marianna prison. Hickerson had not communicated with Lyn since 1967 and made it clear in her letter that her interest had been sparked by the interviews she gave for this book. Lyn responded and the two began an intermittent correspondence that dealt with many issues, from their high school friends to the conditions of prison life; back in 1967, Lyn wrote, she would have expected both Rachel and herself to be "mommies by now." Lyn remained an adamant defender of her actions and generally those of the Manson Family, but did not dwell on the subject when talking to Rachel. She sent Rachel photos of herself in the jail and a *National Geographic* article about the ecological role played by bats. At Lyn's request, Rachel sent her a copy of Paul Krassner's autobiography, *Confessions of a Raving, Unconfined Nut.* She also asked for a book by Christopher Cerf on politically correct phrases.

Different as Lyn's experience might have been from that of the average American, she admitted she shared the national obsession of the moment: the O. J. Simpson saga. Lyn told Rachel that she watched the trial proceedings religiously, and had quickly sized up the main players. She was disdainful of the Los Angeles district attorney, Gil Garcetti ("you already have sympathy for the victim," Lyn said, but Garcetti was a "phony" who "makes you want him to lose."). On the other hand, she was impressed by the first leader of the Simpson defense team, Robert Shapiro, who she called "the best lawyer I've seen in a long time."

The Simpson case was mesmerizing, Lyn said, because it touched on so many issues, both personal and social. On the other hand, she reflected, it was just another trial. "I found myself getting interested in this and I thought, 'Is my life that vacant?' And partly," Lyn said, "it is."

Acknowledgments

Space does not allow me to thank all who extended courtesies or aid to this project, but I would like to recognize at least some who contributed. Of course, all mistakes and indelicacies are my responsibility alone.

First, I thank President Gerald R. Ford, who not only consented to speak about one of the most horrifying events of his life but who also volunteered his good offices to assist me. The Gerald R. Ford Foundation awarded me a research grant, allowing for study at the Ford Presidential Library at the University of Michigan. The library's staff enthusiastically greeted a project outside the familiar bounds of presidential library research. In particular, I thank library director Frank Mackaman, supervisory archivist David Horrocks, and archivists Helmi Raaska and Ken Hafeli.

Researching this book brought the author into contact with many unusual people. A couple of them bear special note: Rachel Hickerson, dauntless champion of free expression, became a confidante whose countless hours of thought and work helped make this story as complete and fair as possible. Paul Fitzgerald, indefatigable defender of the accused, gave exuberantly of his recollections and connections to escort me through the mysteries of the case.

Many people granted interviews or were helpful in other ways. I am grateful to Corey Allen, Tamara Ambroson, Bruce Babcock, Steve Bekins, Clyde Blackmon, Vincent Bugliosi, Edward Bunker, Dick Cable, Rod Catsiff, Penny Circle, Noam Cohen, Tony Curto, Nelda Evans, Lisa Fancher, Nathan Fong, Richard J. Fong, Jim Furumasu, Curt Gentry, Bob and Ava Glover, Danny Goldberg, Sandra Good, Andrew Gross, Sandy Guegel, Tillman and Louise Hall, Randy Hammonds, Phil Hartman, Donald Heller, Patricia Hickerson, Leo Janos, Lonn Johnston, Nora Kanoy, Dwayne Keyes, Bob Kirste, David Kraft, Paul Krassner, Christy Lau, Lee Latham, Randy Lewis, Clara Livsey, Gary Luke, Chuck Lynch, Thomas J. MacBride, Sylvia McAfee, Ruth Morehouse, John Moulds, Jeanine Gardner Nichols, Marjorie Noble, Bob Orben, Robert Peters, Edna Rappaport, Edward B. Rasch, Saul Rosenthal, Joe Sandino, Philip A. Shelton, William B. Shubb, Bill Siddons, Helen Sinsabaugh, Karen Skelton, David E. Smith, Craig South, James

Van Wagoner, Doug Vaughn, Dermot Walker, E. Richard Walker, David Wall, Marshall R. Williams, Cheryl Willmarth, Morris Willmarth, Jennifer Wyss-Jones, and Richard Zoglin. Sources who asked for anonymity carry my gratitude in private.

Fellow journalists helped me extensively, belying the profession's competitive reputation. At the Los Angeles Times, Sacramento bureau chief George Skelton let me set up shop in his office while reporters Carl Ingram and Larry Stammer and metropolitan editor Leo C. Wolinsky shared their recollections. At the San Francisco Chronicle, Rob Gunnison recounted anecdotes and helped with research, while Rob Haeseler, who covered the Fromme trial in 1975, made available his exhaustive notes on the case. Dan Weintraub, now of the Orange County Register, and Janice Selby were good friends who accommodated me in Sacramento on short notice. Gregory Favre of the Sacramento Bee, Betty Liddick of the Stockton Record, Mike Parman of Santa Rosa's Press Democrat, and Richard Rico and Teri Gilmore of the Vacaville Reporter opened their newspaper archives to me. At KCRA-TV Channel 3 in Sacramento, general manager John Serrao and the news staff made available both broadcast tapes and raw footage of the Fromme case.

A number of law enforcement agencies assisted in ways beyond the minimal requirements of the public records statutes. I appreciate the cooperation of the United States Secret Service and the considered attention of Deputy Director Guy P. Caputo. At the U.S. Department of Justice, I thank the Criminal Division, the Executive Office for U.S. Attorneys, and the Sacramento branch of the U.S. Marshals Service, home to Marshal Arthur Van Court, Marcia Van Court, Chief Deputy Marshal Mike Nelson, and Supervisor Warren Steeves. Appreciation also to Lieutenant Andrew Jackson of the Stockton Police Department, Stephen R. Kay of the Los Angeles County District Attorney's Office, and Donna Hopkins of the California Department of Justice, as well as to the Los Angeles Police Department, the Los Angeles County Sheriff's Department, and the Sacramento County Sheriff's Department.

Readers of the manuscript brought different perspectives and offered thoughtful critiques that improved the finished product. They included David Coleman, Tom Goldstein, Jan Herman, Heather McCabe, Abigail McGanney-Nolan, Joe Menn, and Peter Sagal. The faculty and administration of Boalt Hall, the law school of the University of California at Berkeley, made many accommodations so I could complete this project while maintaining my obligations to the school.

Thank you to Chandler Crawford and Colin Crawford for introducing me to the world of publishing. My literary agent, Sandra Dijkstra, was the greatest advocate an author could hope for—steadfast, tireless, and encouraging even in difficult times. I appreciate the work of the people at the Sandra Dijkstra Literary Agency, in particular Rita Holm and Rebecca Lowen; Nina Weiner of Buzz Books; Dana Albarella, Jamie Brickhouse, Regan Good, John Murphy, Tara

Schimming, and Nelson Taylor of St. Martin's Press; and Eric J. Weisberg, prudent and thorough legal counselor.

Truth be told, the godfather of this book is James Fitzgerald, executive editor of St. Martin's Press. It was Jim who first suggested that the life of Lynette Fromme merited a serious and contextual treatment. He remained an active observer and welcome contributor to its progress. At precisely the right moment, Jim stepped in to rescue this book and see it to completion, wrestling an unruly manuscript into a work infinitely more cogent and telling.

I am grateful to my parents and my brother Nick for their unflagging support of my various adventures, and offer a special thanks to my best gal, the irresistible Morgana Sofia Rasch. Over a long journey, from the first day to the last page, Morgana helped guide this book and its author in innumerable ways, tangible and transcendent.

—J.B.

Notes

Key

GRF Library: Gerald R. Ford Library

LAFP: *Los Angeles Free Press*

LAHX: *Los Angeles Herald Examiner*

LAT: *Los Angeles Times*

LF: Lynette Fromme

LFMT: Lynette Fromme's testimony in *People of the State of California* vs. *Charles M. Manson et al.*, Feb. 2–3, 1971.

LFUP: Unpublished papers of Lynette Fromme

NYT: *New York Times*

SB: *Sacramento Bee*

SFC: *San Francisco Chronicle*

SFX: *San Francisco Examiner*

USLF: Transcript of *United States of America* vs. *Lynette Alice Fromme* (1975)

USSG: Transcript of *United States of America* vs. *Sandra Collins Good and Susan Kathryn Murphy* (1976)

USSS: United States Secret Service

Prologue

The account of the September 5 incident was based on published and unpublished newspaper and magazine reports; television broadcasts; investigations conducted by the U.S. Secret Service, the Federal Bureau of Investigation, and the Sacramento Police Department; and interviews conducted by the author.

4: "are you going to use it?": Wayne Wilson interview, *SB*, September 7, 1980.

7: "Oh, what a beautiful day": Karen Skelton, interview with the author.

10: shots might be fired: Ron Nessen, *It Sure Looks Different from the Inside* (Chicago: Playboy Press, 1978), 179.

10: ENTER AT YOUR OWN RISK: White House Sacramento briefing memorandum, GRF Library.

10: "...next to that woman...": Karen Skelton, interview with the author.

11: "We've got an assassination attempt...": *SB*, September 10, 1975.

Chapter 1: Houses with Doors

15: "...houses with doors": LFUP.

18: "...Look at those eyes!": Nora Stevens Kanoy, interview with the author.

18: "...aaa-nee-mules!": Nora Stevens Kanoy, interview with the author.

19: "...avoiding juvenile delinquency": "41 Lariat Dancers, 8 Parents Will Leave on Cross-Nation Tour Today," *LAT*, August 1959; Tillman Hall, interview with the author.

20: The Fromme house: Nora Stevens Kanoy and Chuck Lynch, interviews with the author.

21: a Caspar Milquetoast: Louise Hall, interview with the author.

22: "The Three Blind Mice": Nora Stevens Kanoy and Chuck Lynch, interviews with the author.

22–23: Disney's ranch...Ray Bolger: Louise Hall, interview with the author.

24: "...such a dear...": Francelle Buckminster to Mr. and Mrs. Stevens, September 3, 1959. Nora Stevens Kanoy recalls that a similar letter was sent to Mr. and Mrs. Fromme.

24: a staff engineer: William Fromme's work recalled by Milt Kuska, former Northrop executive, in interview with the author.

25: confiscate the car keys...scrub neighbors' floors...odometer readings: Louise Hall, interview with the author.

25: William Fromme was "disappointed"..."not a happy one.": Clara Livsey, *The Manson Women* (New York: Richard Marek, 1980), 195. Livsey, whom the author interviewed, said that much of her information regarding Lynette Fromme's childhood came from her interviews with Helen Fromme.

25: "My dad won't speak to me....": *Newsweek*, September 22, 1975, 30.

25: "...you want to adopt...": Tillman Hall, interview with the author.

26: "Very sweet..." Phil Hartman, interview with the author.

27: "I don't want it to be like this....": Chuck Lynch, interview with the author.

29: John Birch Society: Rachel Hickerson, interview with the author.

29: "in competition with me": LF to Los Angeles County Superior Court, April 5, 1971.

29: "I wanted my mother...": Livsey, 190.

30: "I want you to have this": Christy Curtis Lau, interview with the author.

31: She had had a fight with her father: Bill Siddons, interview with the author. Siddons remembers Fromme saying the fight took place when she was eleven or twelve. However, a 1971 Los Angeles County Probation Department report states that Fromme said "she had conflicts with her family from the age of 13, and was put out at the age of 16." I have used the Probation Department dates.

31: directed by a young Robert Altman: Patrick McGilligan, *Robert Altman: Jumping Off the Cliff* (New York: St. Martin's Press, 1989), 179.

32: "...wild, man, wild": James Van Wagoner, interview with the author.

33: "...almost *too* brilliant": Tamara Simon Ambroson, interview with the author.

33: "...always pissed off...": Jeanine Gardner Nichols, interview with the author.

33: "...chin tilted down...": Maurya Simon, interview with the author.

34: In the middle of the night: James Van Wagoner, interview with the author.

34: barbiturates...slit her wrists: Livsey, 196.

34: Randy Hammonds: Randy Hammonds, interview with the author.

35: "She was thoughtful...": Craig South, interview with the author.

36: Mark's idol: Mark Hammonds, interview with the author.

37: under psychiatric care: USSS memorandum, September 6, 1975.

37: "What's wrong, Lynne?": Marjorie Arnold Noble, interview with the author.

38: Lynne eventually did find a place: Rachel Hickerson, Joe Sandino, interviews with the author. Hickerson also wrote about her experiences in the summer of 1966 in "American Graffiti in Redondo Beach: Growing Up with Squeaky Fromme," *City of San Francisco* magazine, September 23, 1975.

41–42: Owsley Stanley...drug was then legal: Charles Perry, *The Haight-Ashbury: A History* (New York: Vintage, 1985), 80, 95.

42: *Bubble and Squeak*: William J. Dowlding, *Beatlesongs* (New York: Fireside, 1989), 132.

43: "...I've done it lots of times": Rachel Hickerson, interview with the author.

45: Nora Lynn came down: Nora Stevens Kanoy, interview with the author.

46: "The restaurant fella...": Wayne Wilson interview, *SB*, September 7, 1980.

46: "We argued over...": Wayne Wilson interview, *SB*, September 7, 1980.

46: "...kind of freely": LFMT.

Chapter 2: Charles Manson

47: Lynne sat on a bench: LFUP.

48: Charles Miles Manson: Manson's background compiled principally from newspaper and magazine accounts and the following books: Vincent Bugliosi with Curt Gentry, *Helter Skelter* (New York: Norton, 1974; New York: Bantam, 1975), 184–199; Charles Manson as told to Nuel Emmons, *Manson in His Own Words* (New York, Grove Press, 1986), 21–108; Ed Sanders, *The Family*, 1st ed. (New York: Dutton, 1971), 21–39.

49: "My father...is the jailhouse.": Bugliosi, 526.

49: burned himself with cigarettes: John Gilmore and Ron Kenner, *The Garbage People* (Los Angeles: Omega Press, 1971), 23.

50: The check had been...$37.50: Another account says it was $34.50. Sanders, *The Family*, 1st ed., 23.

52: "like Frankie Laine": *LAT*, December 12, 1993.

53: "sex, drugs, and treason": *SFC*, October 27, 1969.

Chapter 3: Princess in Velvet

Unless otherwise noted, principal episodes and quotations in this chapter are cited LFUP.

57: girl in the Haight: LFUP; Emmons, 87.

60: Dad had been the first: LFUP; LFMT.

61: "But I just read that": LFUP; LFMT.

61: She couldn't let herself: LFMT.

61: "A dog goes . . .": "The Story of Squeaky," *Newsweek*, September 15, 1975, 18.

61: He could find lost trails: LFMT.

65: a former Congregational minister: LFUP; Ruth Morehouse, interview with the author.

65: Charlie was arrested: Bugliosi, 316.

67: Lyn took Katie: LFUP; LFMT.

68: Chevron charge card: Ed Sanders, *The Family*, 1989 ed. (New York: Signet, 1989), 26.

68: loose ends: LF testimony, *People* vs. *Manson*, Feb. 2, 1971.

68: "Charlie is a man": LFMT.

68: ". . . riding on the wind": LFMT.

68: They went to Seattle: Emmons, 116.

68: The bus meant a lot: A "novella" about the bus attributed to Manson appears in Nikolas Schreck, ed., *The Manson File* (New York: Amok Press, 1988), 95.

68: ". . . like going from a one-room cabin . . .": Emmons, 117.

69: ". . . The nights reveal . . .": Gilmore, 55.

69: "We showed them . . .": *LAFP*, Feb. 6, 1970.

70: She floated in: Lawrence Schiller, *The Killing of Sharon Tate* (New York: Signet, 1970), 81.

70: a three-month jail term: Bugliosi, 253.

70: the part of a vampire: Bugliosi, 639; Schreck, 132.

71: "The thing we must understand . . .": Susan Atkins as told to Bob Slosser, *Child of Satan, Child of God* (Logos International, 1977), excerpted in *SFC*, August 29, 1977.

71: "You must die . . .": Atkins, *Child of Satan, Child of God*, excerpted in *SFC*.

71: Sadie would have to learn . . . three times: Schiller, 87.

71: They came across a crazy man: LFMT.

73: He was "so good-looking": Sy Wizinski, *Charles Manson: Love Letters to a Secret Disciple: A Psychoanalytical Search* (Terre Haute, Ind.: Moonmad Press, 1976), 71.

73: *Mondo Hollywood*: Sanders, *The Family*, 1989 ed., 294.

73: *Lucifer Rising*: Bugliosi, 639.

73: jammed with Frank Zappa: Ed Sanders, *LAFP*, November 6, 1970.

73: Charlie had trimmed: Emmons, 131.

74: a tiny second-story office: This episode from Corey Allen, interview with the author, supplemented by published accounts, e.g., Emmons, 131.

74: the black man ... was Charlie's father: LFMT.

75: his time at Universal: *See,* e.g., "Manson's Letter to the *Hollywood Star,*" in Schreck, 171.

76: a magical mystery tour: LFMT.

76: most recent arrest: According to Los Angeles County Probation Department records, Fromme was detained by police on February 23, 1968. Fromme said the car was borrowed, and no charges were brought.

76: "It's a beautiful scene ...": Randy Hammonds, interview with the author.

77: Their leader ... "was a *man*": Nora Stevens Kanoy, interview with the author.

77: Angela Lansbury's daughter: Nancy Pitman testimony, *People* vs. *Manson,* February 3, 1971; Sanders, *The Family,* 1st ed., 51.

78: they had a problem with her: Nancy Pitman testimony, *People* vs. *Manson,* February 3, 1971.

78: called the group "the Family": Nancy Pitman testimony, *People* vs. *Manson,* February 3, 1971.

78: Sunstone Hawk: LFMT. Another source reports that Sunstone is Sandra Good's child. Bugliosi, 170.

78: Sandra Good, a stockbroker's daughter: LFUP; Emmons, 138.

78: tantrums or fits: Paul Watkins with Guillermo Soledad, *My Life with Charles Manson* (New York: Bantam, 1979), 50.

79: He had a French horn: Watkins, 12.

80: "... the most tuned-in dude ...": Watkins, 38.

80: "we founded the Family": Joel Selvin, *SFX,* September 8, 1984.

80: concert in Colorado: Sanders, *The Family,* 1989 ed., 49.

80: "If you find an apple" ... give away things: LFMT.

80: strip the satin sheets: Ruth Morehouse, interview with the author.

80: Dean Martin's daughter: *Los Angeles Herald Examiner,* August 21, 1971.

80: "Are you ready to die ...": Watkins, 59.

80: When Ruth arrived ...: Ruth Morehouse, interview with the author.

81: "Indeed, indeed!": LFMT.

Chapter 4: Coming Down Fast

Unless otherwise noted, principal episodes and quotations in this chapter are cited to LFUP.

83: the Spahn Movie Ranch: For a portrait of the Spahn Ranch, see Gay Talese, "Charlie Manson's Home on the Range," *Esquire,* March 1970.

83: a friend of Sandy Good's: Emmons, 140.

84: grease and dirt: LFMT.

84: Gene Autry was mean and drunk: Autry later wrote that he overcame his drinking problem. Gene Autry with Mickey Herskowitz, *Back In the Saddle Again* (Garden City, N.Y.: Doubleday, 1978).

85: He named her... "Squeaky": LFUP; Watkins, 40.

85: "It's a nonsense world...": LFMT.

86: She managed the Family's paperwork: Sanders, *The Family*, 1989 ed., 176; Emmons, 195.

86: "What am I feeling guilty about?": LFMT.

86: Lyn disrespected a baby: LFMT.

86: the Haight-Ashbury Free Clinic: Dr. David E. Smith, interview with the author.

87: "The Group Marriage Commune: A Case Study": *Journal of Psychedelic Drugs*, September 1970.

88: "We never knew Smith...": *LAFP*, February 6, 1970.

88: "...a multi-picture deal...": Corey Allen, interview with the author.

88: "It's through death...": Watkins, 61.

89: "Never Learn Not to Love"... number 61 on the charts: John Naughton, "The Devil's Music," *Q* magazine [England], August 1994.

89: "...mealy-mouthed muttering...": Watkins, 47.

89: "It's like the Man, dig...": Watkins, 65.

89: "...a hole in the infinite...": Watkins, 64.

90: strapped Charlie to a cross: Leslie Van Houten, "Turning Point," ABC-TV, March 10, 1994.

90: GET OUT OF HERE: Bob Glover, interview with the author.

90: Lulu had been through some changes: Livsey, 225.

91: cops were coming to them... parents who had abused them: LFMT.

91: "I'm hanging on to *you*": Watkins, 106.

91: Lyn... took up the rear: Emmons, 155.

92: his framed gold record: Bugliosi, 173.

92. They said they were from an Indian tribe: Ruth Morehouse, interview with the author.

93: "...We ran the Indians out...": LFMT.

93: "...just a matter of time... program the young love...": Watkins, 132.

94: "...a real love in your heart...": Bugliosi, 115.

95: recorded by... Axl Rose: Another 1990s pop group, the Lemonheads, recorded Manson's "Your Home is Where You're Happy."

95: his old friend Frank Zappa: Ed Sanders, *LAFP*, November 6, 1970.

95: topless dancers: Watkins, 144.

95–96: bikers.... And fear: Dr. David E. Smith, interview with the author. Smith, an expert in toxicology, remains director of the Haight-Ashbury Free Clinic and is an associate clinical professor at the University of California, San Francisco. Based on personal observations and later discussions with Susan Atkins, he believes that the turn from psychedelics to amphetamines was critical in changing the nature of the Family's activities. "High doses of amphetamines really do create a paranoid delusional system," Smith said, adding that such megalomaniacs as Hitler and Jim Jones also favored this drug.

96: "We have to flow with the love! . . .": Watkins, 151.

96: "when it all comes down . . .": Watkins, 151.

96: On April 19, 1969: Los Angeles County Sheriff's Department records.

97: a nightclub . . . Helter Skelter: LF testimony, *People* vs. *Manson,* Feb. 2, 1971; Ed Sanders, *The Family,* 1989 ed., 144; Watkins, 154.

96–97: a bunch of bikers. . . . Karate Dave: LFMT.

97: Lyn would overhear Shorty: Bugliosi, 143.

97: Lyn's little brother, Bill: Rachel Hickerson, interview with the author. Hickerson reports that Bill Fromme told her this story in 1970.

98: "That desert's got everything": Emmons, 172.

98: "No rent to pay . . .": Emmons, 172.

99: The girls were upset: This is the explanation of the events prior to the Tate-LaBianca murders, given by Manson and members of the Family.

99: "I'm getting my shit together . . .": Emmons, 194.

100: "Now is the time for Helter Skelter": Linda Kasabian testimony, quoted in George Bishop, *Witness to Evil* (Los Angeles: Nash Publishing, 1971), 143.

100: It was frantic: Ruth Morehouse, interview with the author.

100: a valid driver's license: Ed Sanders, *The Family,* 1989 ed., 231.

100: Charlie "sent out the expendables. . . . When it got evil": Ruth Morehouse, interview with the author.

100: "beautiful people": Bugliosi, 243.

100: "I am the Devil . . .": Bugliosi, 237.

100: "The Soul sure did pick a lulu": Bugliosi, 244; Gilmore, 127.

101: One letter away from Helter Skelter: Presumably, the misspelling was not intentional.

101: lost the values of the city: LFMT.

101: "bam-bam with their big ol' boots": *LAFP,* February 6, 1970.

102: "Fuck it": *LAFP,* February 6, 1970.

102: ". . . gives your eyes a stretch": *LAFP,* February 6, 1970.

102: "Routine Big Brother": *LAFP,* February 6, 1970.

102: four hands feeling up her clothes: *LAFP,* February 6, 1970.

102: "Where's Jesus Christ?": *LAFP,* February 6, 1970.

103: ". . . telling people about the flowers . . .": Bob Murphy, *Desert Shadows* (Billings, Mont.: Falcon Press, 1986), 94. This is an account by one of the officers who pursued Manson in Inyo County.

103: "They gave us a merry chase": "The Desert's Nude Thieves," *SFC,* October 10, 1969.

Chapter 5: God in the Machine

Unless otherwise noted, principal episodes and quotations in this chapter are cited to LFUP.

106: "...the conspiracy angle": Ruth Morehouse, interview with the author.

106: his first meeting with Lyn: Bugliosi, 176.

107: "Looks like the 'People of the State of California'...": *LAFP*, February 6, 1970.

107: "See where it's ending?": Emmons, 222.

108: "The people don't want...": Wizinski, n.p. All future references to the Indiana teenager letters are similarly cited.

109: "...every visitor who wanted a piece of tail...": *LAFP*, February 27, 1970.

109: "...beer cans and burnt spots...": *LAFP*, February 6, 1970.

110: "...the entire press was lies": Dave Mason, *LAFP*, March 13, 1970.

111: "of breaking every one of the Ten Commandments": *LAFP*, March 27, 1970.

111: *The Killing of Sharon Tate*: The freelance writer who helped finesse Sadie's words into a publishable manuscript was Laurence Schiller, who a quarter-century later performed the same function for O.J. Simpson's jailhouse story, *I Want to Tell You*. Shinn, however, would not enjoy so prosperous a future, being disbarred in 1992 for defrauding a client.

111: "for the publicity...": Bishop, 87.

112: "...the first of the acid murders...": Bishop, 8.

112: "A very pretty girl": Paul Fitzgerald, interview with the author.

114: "You're doin' well, are ya, Squeaky?": Paul Fitzgerald, interview with the author.

114: "...the procedure's the same...": *LAFP*, February 6, 1970.

116: doused with LSD: Bishop, 190.

116: "Go wash your hands....": Bugliosi, 359.

116: "We were met with disillusionment...": *LAFP*, February 6, 1970.

116: "...come to the trials—your trials...": *LAFP*, February 27, 1970.

117: a soldering iron: Ruth Morehouse, interview with the author.

118: "...possible that Bugliosi believed...more than did Manson": Bishop, 351.

118: "...breathe a little easier": Bugliosi, 420.

119: a Christmas present for the Melchers: Melcher testimony, USLF.

119: Another visitor was Leo Wolinsky: Wolinsky, interview with the author.

120: "...I just wanted to kill...": Paul Krassner, *Confessions of a Raving, Unconfined Nut* (New York: Simon & Schuster, 1993), 205.

120: "Darkness...descending on the movement": Phil Hartman, interview with the author.

120: "Do you know Lyn Fromme?": Bill Siddons, interview with the author.

122: Barbara Hoyt...spent time with the Family: Bugliosi, 220.

123: The way Gypsy...remembered: Catherine Share statement to Los Angeles County Probation Department.

123: "We all have to go through Helter Skelter": Bugliosi, 474.

123: "Call Mr. Bogliogi . . .": Bugliosi, 475.

124: "We were not allowed to eat meat": Ruth Morehouse, interview with the author.

124: "That oral watchmacallit": Bishop, 331.

124: "a God-driven hand of punishment": *SFC,* September 28, 1970.

125: ". . . unwrapping our bruised, scabbing bloody knees . . .": LF letter, n.d., Schreck, 153.

127: ". . . joyous persuasion . . .": Paul Fitzgerald, interview with the author.

127: ". . . there's no place else to go . . .": *LAT,* January 12, 1971.

128: ". . . You've all judged yourselves": *LAT,* January 26, 1971.

129: "the parade of perjurers . . .": Bugliosi, 567.

139: "Squeaky . . . was the least untruthful . . .": Bugliosi, 568.

Chapter 6: A Horse with No Name

Unless otherwise noted, principal episodes and quotations in this chapter are cited to LFUP.

143: "If it takes a bloodbath . . .": Todd Gitlin, *The Sixties: Years of Hope, Days of Rage* (New York: Bantam, 1987), 415.

144: the Establishment "will kill you . . .": Jess Bravin, "Fans Not Ready to Close the Doors," *LAT,* July 30, 1991.

144: extortion, narcotics trafficking: *Terrorism in California* (Sacramento: California Department of Justice, 1974).

145: ". . . the victims of this Criminal System . . .": Bill Cardoso, "Keepers of the Manson Faith," October 7, 1972.

145: to break Como out of the Hall of Justice: *LAHX,* October 20, 1971.

147: ". . . the biggest crime wave . . .": Brian T. Meehan, *Oregonian* (Portland), March 16, 1992.

149: Steve . . . found himself drawn to Lyn: Steve Bekins, interview with the author.

151: One visitor was Paul Krassner: Krassner, interview with the author; Krassner, *Confessions of a Raving, Unconfined Nut,* 204.

153: ". . . if they don't have an electric toaster": Steve Bekins, interview with the author.

153: ". . . the husband seemed like a kook!": Stockton, Calif., Police Department records.

155: a favor from a prison buddy: Steve Bekins, Edward Bunker, interviews with the author.

155: "I was shoved into a room . . .": LF to *Prison Life* magazine, January 1996.

157: "chief engineer of the Marin County railroad": Doug Vaughn, interview with the author.

158: Vaughn won an acquittal: Talamantez would go on to greater notoriety as one of the San Quentin Six charged in the brutal Adjustment Center escape attempt that left three inmates, including prison revolutionary George Jackson, and three guards dead. Talamantez was one of three defendants acquitted of all ninety-seven felony counts in the sensational 1971 crime.

159: she managed to talk her way into the chambers: Herb Caen, *SFC*, September 17, 1975.

161: The Body in the Basement: This episode compiled principally from police reports and newspaper accounts.

161: a droopy-eyed former topless dancer: *SFC*, November 15, 1972.

162: The three rolled Willett's body into the grave: Monfort and Goucher later pled guilty to the second-degree murder of Willett. Craig pled guilty to being an accessory after the fact. All three served time for their involvement in the homicide.

162: "... the last place you'd think of looking?": *Stockton Record*, November 19, 1972.

162: Was the garbage picked up on time?: Stockton Police Department records.

167: "How in the fuck ...": Stockton Police Department records.

167: said he had been drunk: *Stockton Record*, May 1, 1973.

169: slip through the handcuffs: *Stockton Record*, September 14, 1975.

169: "We foresee a lot of violence ...": *Stockton Record*, November 19, 1972.

169: "... a forgotten blob of toothpaste": LF to *Prison Life* magazine, January 1996.

173: "... justice also works on their side ...": Bugliosi, 661.

173: "I once looked to police ...": *Stockton Record*, September 14, 1975.

173: "I'm at war with everybody ...": *LAT*, February 24, 1973.

174: "... I didn't make any threats": *LAT*, February 24, 1973.

Chapter 7: Sacramento

Unless otherwise noted, principal episodes and quotations in this chapter are cited to LFUP.

177: "... some very good things out of the trash ...": USLF.

178: "... We're trying to change the world": *SFC*, September 6, 1975.

178: built around 1890: Jeff and Jan Gilster, residents of 1725 P Street, interview with the author.

179: "... if I was afraid of dying ...": *LAT*, September 6, 1975.

179: "... her boobies hanging out": *SFC*, September 6, 1975.

179: "... halfway house for murderers": Dwayne Keyes, interview with the author.

181: the satirist Paul Krassner: Paul Krassner, interview with the author and material provided by Krassner, later published in *Confessions of a Raving, Unconfined Nut*.

182: the instructor, Meredith Taylor: Doug Underwood, "Lansing Woman 'Close to' Fromme, Good," Lansing, Mich., newspaper, November 1975.

182: an educational center for radicals: Sam Samdusky, Sacramento City College admissions director, interview with the author.

185: "So, Lyn, you live in Sacramento?": Nelda Evans, interview with the author.

186: "... why didn't you buy one?": Rob Haeseler, unpublished notes.

186: The visit was fun: Steve Bekins, interview with the author.

186: Lyn piloted Manny's Cadillac: Haeseler, unpublished notes.

189: "... Little girls, playing little girl games ...": Bugliosi, 178.

189: "... many things in mind ...": *SB*, February 7, 1975.

190: "waiting for their god ...": *SB*, February 7, 1975.

190: Edward Vandervort: USLF.

190: "... I have a project for you ...": USLF.

190: "Kill him. Destroy him": USLF.

191: male overnight guests: Morris Willmarth, interview with the author.

191: the owner of the Modoc mine: FBI reports; Rodney Catsiff, interview with the author.

192: "more of a catalyst ... than even Charlie": *LAHX*, September 16, 1975.

192: "she seemed interested in everybody being happy": *SB*, September 5, 1975.

192: The Berkeley-educated attorney: Clyde Blackmon, interview with the author.

193: "... I played the father-daughter game ...": *LAT*, September 10, 1975.

194: the story of the International People's Court of Retribution: USSG.

194: One night in early July: Morris Willmarth, interview with the author.

197: Manny went to his clothes closet: Harold Boro testimony, USLF.

198: "I tried to stop her": Nelda Evans, interview with the author.

198: she wrapped the pistol in glassine: Philip Shelton, interview with the author.

198: "... the thought we want to push": John Barry testimony, USLF.

203: "... Los Angeles sold herself.... people don't believe in their Lord ...": USSG.

204–205: the guitarist Jimmy Page: Richard Cole with Richard Trubo, *Stairway to Heaven: Led Zeppelin Uncensored* (New York: HarperCollins, 1992); Stephen Davis, *Hammer of the Gods* (New York: Ballantine, 1985), 248. Davis reports the note was burned, unread. Danny Goldberg suggests that the Davis version probably is more accurate because "I think he was in the hotel room when the girl came to the door." Goldberg to Bravin, March 16, 1994.

205: a film Page was scoring, *Lucifer Rising*: Davis, 154; 227; Cole, 265.

207: "... that flirtatious charm ...": *SFC*, September 14, 1975.

207: "bigger than the Tate killing ...": *SB*, September 6, 1975.

208: "Not interested," he said: Philip Shelton, interview with the author.

208: "I hate Ford": Ed Louie testimony, USLF.

210: a "dummy, an empty head": *LAT*, September 6, 1975.

Chapter 8: Ruffles and Flourishes

Unless otherwise noted, principal episodes and quotations in this chapter are cited to LFUP.

214: "how thrilled and delighted...": Schwed to Ford, August 15, 1974. GRF Library.

214: "it would be inappropriate...": Buchen to Schwed, September 4, 1974. GRF Library.

214: "...the rights to *Portrait of the Assassin*...": Laster to Buchen, September 30, 1974. GRF Library.

214: "none is more moving or complete...": Davis to Ford, December 6, 1974. GRF Library.

219: more than 200,000 tips: *Washington Post,* September 9, 1975.

219: "I'm going to kill your boss...": *NYT,* September 13, 1975.

219: DeSure...liked to brag: *Santa Barbara News Press,* September 5, 1975.

221: "just another Enemies List": *NYT,* September 10, 1975.

221: "Orwellian nightmare": *NYT,* September 10, 1975.

222: "discreet and courteous": Robert L. Hartmann, *Palace Politics: An Inside Account of the Ford Years* (New York: McGraw-Hill, 1980), 41.

222: "push people around....": Gerald R. Ford, *A Time to Heal* (New York: Harper & Row, 1979), 127.

225: "Stern and determined": *Boalt Hall Transcript,* School of Law, University of California, Berkeley, Spring 1995.

226: Buendorf had spoken of those doubts: *Washington Post,* September 6, 1975.

229: "office workers and secretaries": Ursomarso statement to the FBI.

230: Under the arrangement brokered by the Secret Service: John Berthelsen and Steve Gibson, "Security Snafu in Ford Assassination Try," *SB,* September 6, 1975. The department head responsible for the state police, Leonard M. Grimes, disputed the story.

231: "Once it was over, it was over...": Gerald R. Ford, interview with the author.

231: Hartmann...threw up: Nessen, 183.

231: "scared the shit out of me": Unpublished press pool report, September 5, 1975.

231: Nessen had nightmares: Nessen, 183.

232: "We are killing our children": Linda Walker's police report and testimony.

237: "Remember Oswald and Ruby?": Arthur Van Court, interview with the author.

237: "Thanks a lot": Marcia Van Court, interview with the author.

245: "in any dime store": Nelda Evans, interview with the author.

247: Ford's popularity might rise: Gerald R. Ford, interview with the author.

248: "in the emotional aftershock...": "Misfired Pistol Shows Impact of Jerry Ford," *Oregon Statesman* (Salem), September 6, 1975.

249: "...superb poise and calm courage..." Nixon to Ford, September 5, 1975. GRF Library.

Chapter 9: The Gun Is Pointed

Unless otherwise noted, principal episodes and quotations in this chapter are cited to USLF and USSG.

255: code-named . . . "Fromford": Hiram L. Latham, interview with the author.

256: "when people around you treat you like a child . . .": *Washington Post*, September 8, 1975.

256: "It is my job to see . . .": U.S. Marshal Service files.

257: ". . . something the FBI should be aware of": Informant episode from Michael Davies, Leon Brown testimony and Sandra Good statements, USSG.

259: ". . . the Reign of Terror in France?": Sandra Good statements, USSG.

260: she thrust a wooden crucifix: *SB*, September 14, 1975.

260: Kraft's socks were mismatched: David Kraft, interview with the author.

261: ". . . someone who was not only powerless . . .": Philip Shelton, interview with the author.

262: "You're not a detective": Philip Shelton, David Kraft, interviews with the author.

264: "just as though you'd have met her in the street": Robert Landon Kirste, interview with the author.

264: "What are they mad about?": *SFC*, September 10, 1975.

272: Nyberg handed Harris a still camera: *SB*, October 9, 1975.

272: "Elizabeth Seton, the first native American . . .": Clare Boothe Luce, "The Significance of Squeaky Fromme," *Wall Street Journal*, September 24, 1975.

284: "could be another Squeaky": *Time*, October 6, 1975.

285: ". . . kind of an ultimate protest . . .": *LAT*, September 25, 1975.

285: "there must be a purpose . . . ": *LAT*, September 27, 1975.

285: "she was really upset . . .": Robert Holley, interview with the author.

285: "I will make one commitment . . .": NBC News report, October 1, 1975.

286: a "big love affair scene": Arthur Van Court, interview with the author.

288: "I think that's safe to say": Hiram L. Latham, interview with the author.

289: "we have closely followed and are keenly interested . . . ' ": Richard L. Thornburgh to Dwayne Keyes, September 30, 1975.

290: opening "the defendant's mind for scrutiny . . .": *LAT*, September 27, 1975.

291: they were discussing whales: Philip Shelton, interview with the author.

293: ". . . Douglas, that guy who's in trouble in Washington": *LAHX*, April 4, 1970.

Chapter 10: No More Duck Hunting

Unless otherwise noted, principal episodes and quotations in this chapter are cited to USLF and USSG.

299: some 10,000 feet of film: Vernon Scott, United Press International, November 11, 1985.

299: "an urban guerrilla in hot-pants": Charles Champlin, *LAT,* September 24, 1975.

299: "Clinically expert, horrifyingly brilliant": William Otterburn-Hall, *SFC,* October 15, 1972.

300: "...one of those rip-off movies...": Vincent Canby, *NYT,* January 31, 1976.

300: "...a lot of dirty blood and sex.... They make us out to be innocent children": *SB,* October 17, 1975.

301: "judicial fanaticism": "A Judge Looks Down on a Jury," editorial, *LAT,* October 20, 1975.

301: "...the prattling of not very bright children": Charles Champlin, *LAT,* September 24, 1975.

303: Dwayne Keyes would later worry: Keyes, interview with the author.

303: "...an excellent opportunity to show that I wanted justice done": Gerald R. Ford, interview with the author.

304: "Let's just find a room somewhere else": Dwayne Keyes, interview with the author.

322: "a jury by its own admission so ignorant...": *SFX,* November 11, 1975.

Chapter 11: The Government's Case

336: "You could hear a pin drop...": Donald H. Heller, interview with the author.

336: "destroy my credibility and trust": *NYT,* November 12, 1975.

339: "...one piece of work": Donald H. Heller, interview with the author.

340: "...she was going off on an LSD trance": Marcia Van Court, interview with the author.

342: "I'm not sure why I'm writing this letter...": Stephen Crane to Gerald R. Ford, September 6, 1975. GRF Library.

Chapter 12: The Defense

355: acted "with stupidity": *NYT,* November 20, 1975.

Chapter 13: The Verdict

378: "Have you all made your decisions?": Marcia Van Court, interview with the author.

380: "the jury took a little longer...": Dwayne Keyes, interview with the author.

381: "...with no cartridge in the chamber...": *Newsweek,* December 8, 1975.

381: "...only Thanksgiving made them stop": Marcia Van Court, interview with the author.

386: "I ejected that one and saw it fall...": *SFX,* December 19, 1975.

Epilogue

389: "Warren, I thank you for being a gentleman . . .": Warren Steeves, interview with the author.

389: "I don't think she really had an intent": Michael R. Nelson, interview with the author.

391: "I have too much anger inside me": *LAT*, March 2, 1985.

394: "were as crazy as ever": Patricia Campbell Hearst with Alvin Moscow, *Every Secret Thing* (New York: Pinnacle, 1982), 474.

394: "a white, middle-class, rich bitch . . .": *LAT*, March 14, 1979.

395: "It seems I broke the news to her . . .": Schreck, 163.

397: "The Significance of Squeaky Fromme": Clare Booth Luce, *Wall Street Journal*, September 24, 1975.

397: lyrics in which Squeaky symbolized: Loudon Wainwright III, "California Prison Blues"; Amy Ray, "The Ballad of Squeaky Fromme."

Index

Dedrick, Claire, 208
Delarosa, Gregory, 318–19
Dell, George M., 293
Demetras, Steve, 166, 170, 173
Democratic National Convention, 1968, 92
Denver Post, 198
Department of Fish and Game, 204
DeSure, Gary Steven, 219–20
Detroit Free Press, 259–60
Diminished mental capacity, defense of, 290
Disney, Walt, 22
Dog Eat Dog, 156
Dohrn, Bernadine, 228
Donovan, 85
"Don't Shoot Our President," 251
Doors, the, 31, 79, 120, 144
Dorris, Paul, 145
Dosher, Otis, 319
Douglas, William O., 293, 374, 375
Douglas Aircraft, 17
Downs, Alice, 18
"Dream Riders," 31–32
Duncan, Frank, 319–20
"Dylan," 33–34, 36
Dylan, Bob, 32, 77
Dymally, Mervyn, 192

Eastern religions, 188
Elbert, Thomas David, 219
El Camino Junior College, 45, 46, 77
Emerson, Carmelita, 217
Environmental issues, Lyn's concern for, 39, 151, 181, 191–97, 198–208, 232, 333, 337, 341, 394
    letters to corporate America, 202, 204, 241–42, 244, 257, 258, 264, 338, 361
    statements at her trial, 271, 272, 386
Environmental Protection Agency, 241, 394
Esquire, 107, 147
Evans, Dan, 216
Evans, Tina, 251
Executioner's Song, The (Mailer), 149

Fain, Jess, 275
Falk, Peter, 75
Family of Man, The, 42, 46
Faretta case, 236
Farrell, Barry, 108
Father Flanagan's Boys Town, 49

Federal Bureau of Investigation (FBI), 191, 194, 197, 213, 216, 221, 266, 289, 338–39
    investigation of assassination attempt, 11, 234, 235–36, 239–44, 255–57, 264, 302
    burglarizing of government offices and, 288
Federal Correctional Institution at Alderson, West Virginia, 394, 395
Federal Reformatory, Chillicothe, 49
Federal Reformatory, Petersburg, 49
Federal Rules of Discovery, 333–34, 380
Feminism, 203, 272
Fisher, Dr. Charles J., Jr., 234, 372
Fitzgerald, Paul J., 148, 157, 163, 168, 183, 189, 205–206, 300, 392
    Tate-LaBianca murder trial and, 111–15, 125, 127
    penalty phase, 128–35, 138
Flynn, Juan, 124
Foley, Tom, 249
Folger, Abigail, 100
Folsom, Sue, 6, 7, 377
Folsom Prison, Manson in, 163, 177, 190
Fong, Dick, 332
Ford, Betty, 218, 247, 248
Ford, Gerald R., 196, 380–81
    becomes president, 188
    books authored by, 213–15
    William O. Douglas and, 293
    foreign assassinations and, 380
    Fromme's attempted assassination of, *see* Assassination attempt by Lyn on Ford
    Lyn's views on policies of, 199, 208, 210, 280
    Moore's assassination attempt on, 284–86
    pardoning of Nixon, 302
    return to California and Moore's assassination attempt, 283–86
    Sacramento trip, *see* Sacramento, California, Ford's trip to
    subpoena and videotaped deposition, 301–305, 345–46, 392
    on Warren Commission, 213
Ford, Jack, 247, 248
Ford, Steve, 247, 248
Ford, Susan, 381
Fort Worth Star-Telegram, 252
Fountain of the World, 89
Fox, Jerry, 8, 230
Franks, Lucinda, 271, 308, 333
Freedom of Information Act, 288